The Illustrated Horse Doctor, Being an Accurate and Detailed Account of the Various Diseases to Which the Equine Race Are Subjected

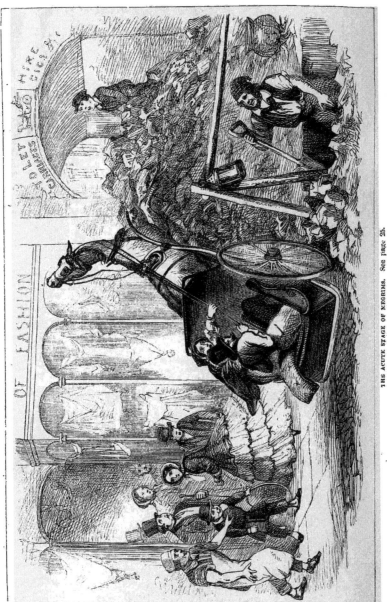

THE ACUTE STAGE OF NEGRIMS. See page 25.

THE

ILLUSTRATED

HORSE DOCTOR

BEING

AN ACCURATE AND DETAILED ACCOUNT OF THE VARIOUS DISEASES
TO WHICH THE EQUINE RACE ARE SUBJECTED

TOGETHER

WITH THE LATEST MODE OF TREATMENT, AND
ALL THE REQUISITE PRESCRIPTIONS.

WRITTEN IN PLAIN ENGLISH.

ACCOMPANIED BY

More than Four Hundred Pictorial Representations.

BY

EDWARD MAYHEW, M.R.C.V.S.

AUTHOR OF "THE HORSE'S MOUTH," "DOGS. THEIR MANAGEMENT," EDITOR OF "BLAIN'S VETERINARY
ART," ETC. ETC

PHILADELPHIA:
J. B LIPPINCOTT & CO.
1862.

TO

Sir Benjamin Brodie, Baronet,

AS A

TESTIMONY OF THE BENEVOLENCE AND SKILL

WHICH

RESCUED THE AUTHOR FROM IMPENDING DEATH,

This Book is Dedicated,

BY

HIS MOST HUMBLE SERVANT,

EDWARD MAYHEW.

ADVERTISEMENT.

THE publishers of the present work have long been impressed with the idea that a new book upon the Diseases of the Horse, written in simple language, and specially designed as a guide for non-professional readers, had grown to be a public necessity. While waiting for an opportunity to carry this notion into effect, they were fortunate enough to become acquainted with a gentleman whose proficiency in veterinary science is undisputed. To that individual the present work was intrusted; and it was nearly completed when the publishers heard with surprise that Mr. Mayhew employed the pencil in a manner only secondary to his use of the pen.

Acting on this information, the publishers were induced to persuade the author to illustrate his text by drawings descriptive of the various stages and aspects of disease. The addition of above four hundred wood engravings has, of course, materially increased the expense of publication. A heavy outlay has been incurred, while, at the same time, the spirit of the age is decidedly against paying a large sum for any work of general information. These circumstances render the present volume doubly hazardous. However, it is confidently hoped that, when the accuracy of the illustrations and the perspicuity of the letter-press are appreciated, a large sale will more than recompense any amount of outlay.

PREFACE.

WHEN laying the present volume before the public, the author cannot but feel he addresses two very opposite parties: one, and by far the larger portion of society, views the subject of which this book pretends to treat simply as a working machine, and regards all those who speak of the creature as endowed with intelligence or possessed of sensibility as fanciful sentimentalists checked by no limit to assertion. The other class—a small, but a highly-educated and an influential section of the public—sees the matter in a very contrary light. In their ideas, the equine race, though endowed with voice, is not entirely without reason, but possessed of the keenest feelings and capable of the tenderest emotions.

The last party, however, expect so little from living writers that probably they will be pleased with opinions which they may hail as an advance toward the truth. The first order of readers, however, the author cannot think to propitiate. Before the opening article is perused, one of these gentlemen will probably fling the volume aside with a sneer, and exclaim—

"Why, what would this fellow have? Does he desire we should build hospitals for horses?"

To the uninformed mind such a question will suggest a preposterous image. But, when calmly considered, a hospital is perceived to be nothing more than a place where disease in the aggregate is cheaply treated, and the trouble or the expense of individual remedies thereby is prevented. A hospital for horses, sanctioned by government, and honored with the highest patronage, does even now exist in the Royal Veterinary College of Camden Town. Such a

(9)

foundation, therefore, would prove no positive novelty; but were such institutions more general, a necesssity now universally felt would be supplied, while the duty incumbent on mankind to conserve the lives of beings intrusted to their care would, in such structures, be gracefully acknowledged and openly enforced.

No man possessing a horse is willing the animal should perish. His interest clearly is in the prolongation of its life; and he would gladly part with some money rather than be reduced to the ownership of a carcass. That, however, which he wishes to have accomplished he desires should be performed cheaply. Hospitals—supposing such places existed, and were of different grades or of different scales of charges—would afford the best prospect of relief at the smallest remunerative cost. Still, any application to such establishments must of necessity prove a tax, the only known preventive against the visitation of which would be the exercise of a little humanity.

A very slight expenditure of the last-named quality would save the equine race from a long list of ills which now are consequent upon mortal ignorance or upon human brutality. It is painful to reflect how many of those affections spoken of as equine disorders might be cheaply eradicated by the more reasonable treatment of the animal which man proverbially esteems to be his most hazardous property.

Cruelty is a very extravagant indulgence. There are now living persons who merely treat their horses according to the dictates of reason, and whose stables are graced by working lives of an extreme age. When he last walked through the Royal Mews, the author was much gratified to behold several fine animals, in the full enjoyment of strength and of vigor, which had more than attained their twentieth year

It might prove nationally remunerative if all of her Britannic Majesty's subjects would permit the creatures over which they exercise legal ownership to live and to labor for their natural terms of existence However, during the glorious days of post chaises, the horses for these vehicles generally cost £30, while, as an average, they existed upon the road only two years

What a sacrifice of life and of money! Each horse cost the postmaster £15 yearly; while the animals working for the queen, and drawing carriages not conspicuous for lightness, if bought originally for a like sum, would not cost more than £1 per annum. The contrast is certainly startling. But to perfect it, there remain to picture the sorry jade which was formerly harnessed to the public chaise, and the stately creature which, in all the delight of beauty, accompanies Royalty to the Parliament House.

But there are other items to be considered before the opposite accounts can be fairly placed one against the other. A post-house generally was a pest-house. The miserable inhabitants of such a building did not suddenly die off, but, like other things, horses rocked to and fro before they fell. The closing scene of life was heralded by many fits of sickness, each of which was of varying duration. Were we to reckon the money which loss of services abstracted, the extra cost of those attentions which are imperative when health is failing, and the hard cash paid for veterinary assistance, very probably a far wider distance than at first glance is apparent would divide the Royal Mews from the sheds which used to form a part of every large roadside hotel.

In the writer's conviction, humanity toward animals should be more commonly practiced—if not from any higher motive, because it is certainly the truest economy. To make this fact plain is the intention of the present publication To prove that horses are gifted with something beyond the mere sensation which is common to all moving things is the object of the present work. To convince the public, by appealing to the eye and to the understanding through the means of engravings and of letter-press, that the equine race inherit higher feelings than the vast majority of mankind are prepared to admit, is the purpose of the book now in the hands of the reader. To demonstrate how closely nature has associated man and horse in their liabilities and in their diseases—to induce men, by informing their sympathies, to treat more tenderly the timid life which is disposed to serve and is also willing to love them—is the highest reward the author of the following pages can picture to himself.

When making the foregoing acknowledgments, the author does not affect to disdain that recompense which is the due of every person who labors in any arduous pursuit. This, of course, he accepts. Though it did not enter into his thoughts when contemplating the composition of the present book, it nevertheless may have stimulated his exertions to perfect it. But, in addition to any weight that can be attached to such a motive, he desired to compose a work which should render the gentleman who had consulted it independent of his groom's dictation; which should enable any person who had read it capable of talking to a veterinary surgeon without displaying either total ignorance or pitiable prejudice; which, in cases of emergency, might direct the uninitiated in the primary measures necessary to arrest the progress of disease; and which, when professional assistance could not be obtained, might even instruct the novice how to treat equine disorders in such a manner as would afford a reasonable prospect of success.

When the regular diet and simple lives of most horses are regarded, the latter expectations certainly do not seem beyond the reach of human ambition. Cleanly and simple remedies alone are required; and these gentlemen of the highest rank may, without fear of taint or of ridicule, condescend to prescribe. To secure such an end, the present book has been written in plain language. The author has endeavored to eschew hieroglyphics and to avoid technicalities. The meaning has shaped the terms employed, and all the graces of style have been intentionally discarded.

In conclusion, the author has to thank the publishers for the very handsome shape in which they have been pleased to embody his efforts; likewise he has to acknowledge an obligation to the skill and the ability with which the Messrs. Dalziel have seconded his endeavors.

CONTENTS.

CHAPTER I.

The Brain and Nervous System—Their Accidents and their Diseases.

CHAPTER II.

The Eyes—Their Accidents and their Diseases.

CHAPTER III.

The Mouth—Its Accidents and its Diseases.

CHAPTER IV.

The Nostrils—Their Accidents and their Diseases.

CHAPTER V.

The Throat—Its Accidents and its Diseases.

(13)

CHAPTER VI.

The Chest and its Contents—Their Accidents and their Diseases.

CHAPTER VII.

The Stomach, Liver, etc.—Their Accidents and their Diseases.

CHAPTER VIII

The Abdomen—Its Accidents and its Diseases.

CHAPTER IX.

The Urinary Organs—Their Accidents and their Diseases.

CHAPTER X.

The Skin—Its Accidents and its Diseases.

CHAPTER XI.

Specific Diseases—Their Varieties and their Treatment.

CHAPTER XII.

Limbs—Their Accidents and their Diseases.

CHAPTER XIII.

The Feet—Their Accidents and their Diseases.

CHAPTER XIV.

Injuries—Their Nature and their Treatment.

CHAPTER XV.

Operations.

THE

ILLUSTRATED HORSE DOCTOR.

CHAPTER I.

THE BRAIN AND NERVOUS SYSTEM—THEIR ACCIDENTS AND THEIR DISEASES.

PHRENITIS.

Phrenitis implies inflammation of the brain. Madness and extreme violence are the consequences. The animal, in this condition, disregards all recognitions, and, apparently, loses all timidity. It suffers the

A HORSE MAD, OR WITH INFLAMMATION OF THE BRAIN.

greatest agony, and no terror can appal it. It would rejoice, could it anticipate the effects, if the mouth of a loaded cannon were pointed

toward itself, and would look for relief when the portfire descended
upon the touch-hole.   Every movement seems designed to end its own
existence ; but the furor has no malice in it.   The creature strives only
to injure himself.   It may in its efforts shatter and demolish the structures which surround it; but it does so without intention.   That is
merely the result of its being carried away beyond the things of this
world by a mighty anguish.   It desires harm to no one; but it cannot
remain quiescent, and endure the torment which rages within its skull.

When this stage of the malady appears, the best thing is to anticipate the evident wish of the animal.   The teaching of schools, which
instructs young men to meddle with the strength of an infuriated horse,
is mere prattle.   However, if the disease, as it seldom happens, is perceived approaching, something may be attempted.   Before the violence
commences, the horse is generally dull.   It does not obey the rein or
answer to the lash.   It is heavy beyond man's control.   It snores as it
breathes.   The lids drop; the head sinks ; the body is cold ; the membrane of the nose is leaden in color; and, from being the obedient,
watchful, and willing slave, its entire nature appears to have changed.
It does not attend to the goad, and the voice of the driver may bawl in
the harshest key, but the sound which used to excite seems unheard and
is unheeded.

The remedy for the earlier stage is copious blood-letting   Open
both jugulars and allow the current to flow till the countenance bright-
ens or the animal sinks.   Bleed again and again, if necessary.   Give
purgatives of double strength, and repeat them every three hours, till
the bowels are copiously relieved or the pulse changes, or the general
appearance indicates improvement.   Afterward, administer sedatives,
always as infusions   A scruple of tobacco, half a drachm of aconite
root, or a drachm of digitalis should have a pint of hot water poured
upon it.   When the liquid is nearly cold, it should be strained, and the
dose may be repeated every half hour, until its operation is witnessed
in the more quiet behavior of the animal.

In the generality of cases, however, no opportunity for such treatment is presented.   The disease is most common in the agricultural districts, and is usually seen where carters indulge their passion in the
butt-end of the whip employed upon the horse's head.   The cause is,
however, carefully concealed, and, after the violent stage has set in, the
original wound is generally mistaken for some self-inflicted injury.
Thus, the horse, even in the most horrid of deaths, with a generosity
characteristic of its nature, contrives to shield the being whom it served
and loved, from the consequences of his inhumanity

Should the animal, by such means, recover, treat it gently ; do not excite it; for phrenitis is apt to return. Even recovery is not always to be wished for. The depletion, imperative for the cure, too often engenders the weakness which no care can eradicate; and the animal survives only to change from the willing servant into a troublesome valetudinarian.

ABSCESS WITHIN THE BRAIN.

This sad affection is invariably produced by external injury. A horse runs away and comes in contact with some hard substance. The blow is of sufficient violence to fracture the strong cranium of the quadruped and to smash all that remains harnessed to the animal. Here we have a reason why man should establish more than a brutal mastery over the

A HORSE DYING FROM ABSCESS WITHIN THE BRAIN.

animal he possesses. The horse is the most timid of creatures. It, however, quickly learns to recognize the voice of its owner. In its vast affection, it soon trusts with confidence to the person who is kind to it. An occasional word thrown to a patient and willing servant, spoken softly to the animal which is putting forth all its strength for our pleasure, would not be cast away. When dread overpowers the horse and it begins to run at its topmost speed, do not pull the reins: the first check should be given by the voice. Speak cheerfully to a timid creature. If the first word produces no effect, repeat it. Watch the ears. If these are turned backward to catch the accents, talk encouragingly to the horse. The voice of one it loves will restore its confidence. The pace will slacken. Talk on, but always in a tone calculated to soothe distress. Then gently touch the reins. The first gentle movement may not be responded to, but the second or the third will be; and the animal, released from terror, is once more under your control.

This is much better than tugging and flogging, which obviously are thrown away upon a body that horror has deprived of sensation. The noise and the resistance but feed the wildness of the fear, and, in the end, the driver is carried to a hospital, the horse being laid prostrate among the ruins it has made

When led back to the stable, a wound is discovered on the animal's forehead It is so small it is deemed of no consequence A little water oozes from it—that is all—it does not send forth matter, or it might deserve attention. However, in a short time the horse becomes dull It will not eat. Soon it falls down and commences dashing its head upon the pavement. There it lies, and, day and night, continues its dreadful occupation. One side of the face is terribly excoriated, and must be acutely painful; but the horrid labor still goes on, each stroke shaking the solid earth, which it indents At last death ends the misery, and a small abscess, containing about half a drachm of healthy pus, is discovered in the superficial substance of the brain.

Physic or operation is of no use here. The cranium of the horse is covered by the thick temporalis muscles. This alone would prevent the trephine being resorted to. Blood would follow the removal of any portion of the skull. Besides, what or who is to keep the head still during the operation? and, were the operation possible, who would own an animal with a hole in its skull? The only means of cure would be to afford exit to the matter; and to do that is beyond human ingenuity.

STAGGERS—SLEEPY STAGGERS AND MAD STAGGERS.

Staggers means no more than a staggering or unsteady gait; an incapacity in the limbs to support the body. It therefore, by itself, represents only that want of control over voluntary motion which generally accompanies injuries to the brain. **Mad** and **sleepy staggers** represent only different symptoms or stages of cerebral affection. **Sleepy staggers** implies the dull stage, which indicates that the brain is oppressed **Mad staggers** denotes the furious stage, when the brain has become acutely inflamed.

There is but one origin-known for staggers, and that is over-feeding. Carters take the team out and forget the nose-bags The omission is not discovered till far on the road No thought is entertained of turning back The poor drudges, consequently, have to journey far, to pull hard and long upon empty stomachs.

When home is at length reached, the driver thinks to make amends for neglect; the rack and manger are loaded. Such animals as are not too tired to feed, eat ravenously. The stomach is soon crammed; but fatigue has weakened the natural instincts, and domestication has taught the horse to depend entirely on man. The creature continues to feed, till a distended stomach produces an oppressed brain. An uneasy sleep interrupts the gormandizing. The eye closes and the head droops. Suddenly the horse awakens with a start. It looks around, becomes assured and takes another mouthful. However, before mastication can be completed, sleep intervenes, and the morsel falls from the mouth or continues retained between the jaws

This state may continue for days. The horse may perish without recovering its sensibility; or mad staggers may at any period succeed, and the animal exhibit the extreme of violence.

Mad staggers equally results from carelessness in the horsekeeper. The animal which gives itself up entirely to the custody of man, too often experiences a fearful return in recompense for its trustfulness. Any neglect with regard to the feeding of a horse, may entail the worst; and a most cruel death upon the inhabitant of the stable is too often its reward. The groom, perhaps, may slight his work, lock the stable door and hurry to his beer-shop, leaving the lid of the corn-bin unclosed. The horse in his stall, with his exquisite sense of smell, scents the provender and becomes restless. His desire is to escape from the halter. With fatal ingenuity the object is accomplished, and the next moment the animal stands with its nose among the coveted oats. It eats and eats as only that being can whose highest pleasures are limited to animal enjoyments. After a time it becomes lethargic; but from that state it is soon aroused by a burning thirst. The corn has absorbed all the moisture of the stomach, the viscus being dry and distended. Pain must be felt, but thirst is the predominant feeling Water is sought for None is to be found; and the sufferer takes his station near the door, to await the appearance of his attendant.

No sooner is the entrance opened, than the quadruped dashes out. With all speed it makes for the nearest pond. There it drinks the long and the sweet draught few in this life can taste; but to know which, is to die a terrible death. The corn swells more with the liquid imbibed. The stomach is now stretched to the uttermost. Continued tension causes inflammation. The brain sympathizes, and the horse speedily becomes acutely phrenitic.

There is, however, a strange symptom, in which the two disorders appear mingled The sleepy fit is not entirely removed, nor are the violent symptoms fully developed. The horse, in this condition, will press its head against a wall. In doing this, it only displays an impulse common to most animals in the sleepy stage; but the peculiarity is, that the eye may be half unclosed and the limbs vigorously employed, as though a trotting match were going forward. The breath will quicken and the creature be coated with perspiration. This attitude and motion may subside, and recovery may ensue; but commonly the quadruped drops, moves the limbs as it lies upon the ground, and is only quieted by death. In a few instances horses have left the wall to exhibit the utmost violence, and to sink at last.

When corn has been gorged during the night, the animal must be rigidly kept from drinking. A quart of any oil should be immediately administered. A pint of oil is the ordinary dose; but here there exists more than an ordinary disease. Besides, much of the fluid will sink between the grains, and, probably, not half of it will reach the membrane of the stomach.

Oil is preferable to the solution of aloes, which is generally given, inasmuch as it will not act upon or swell the corn so readily as any medicine dissolved in water. Should no amendment be detected, in six hours repeat the dose. In another six hours, give another dose with twenty drops of croton oil in it. When another period has elapsed, should no improvement be noted, give thirty drops of croton in another quart of oil. Should none of these drinks have taken effect, the round must once more be gone over. However, at the slightest mitigation of the symptoms or even suspicion of amendment, stop all medicine at once. The altered aspect of the horse is the earliest symptom that the distention is relieved.

In **sleepy staggers**, the head hangs pendulous or is pressed firmly

SLEEPY STAGGERS, FROM OVER-GORGING.

against some prominence. The pulse throbs heavily—the breathing is laborious, and the animal snores at each inspiration. The eye is closed; the skin cold and the coat staring. The nasal membrane leaden. The mouth clammy; the ears motionless; the tail without movement, and the breathing alone testifies that it is a living animal we look upon.

The signs that announce the advent of mad staggers, from whichever cause the disease may arise, are always alike. The lid is raised, and the eye assumes an unnatural brightness. The nasal membrane reddens; the surface becomes as hot as it was previously deficient in warmth; the movements are quick and jerking. The breath is no longer laborious— it is rapid, sharp, and drawn with a kind of panting action. The whole appearance is altered. The characteristics of approaching frenzy can hardly be mistaken.

Then comes the most painful duty of ownership over life. The proprietor has, then, to make a speedy choice, whether his dumb servant is to take a desperate chance and undergo a torture for which the concentrated pleasure of many lives could not atone, or be deprived of the fatal power to injure others and itself. Humanity would unhesitatingly pronounce for death, and, in this case, there is need of haste. The symptoms are so rapidly matured, that, in ten minutes, the poor horse may be sadly hurt and bleeding, panting and rearing, in the center of a

THE HORSE DURING THE MAD STAGE OF STAGGERS.

desolated stable. A mad horse is a terrible object! Its strength is so vast that ordinary fastenings yield before it; but the animal, even when deprived of reason, wins our respect. Suffering will find expression in energetic action. Man, when a tooth is about to be extracted, generally clinches something; but what were a hundred teeth to the agony which causes every fiber in the huge framework to quiver? The perspiration rolls off the creature's body   The eye glares with anguish, not with malice; the body is strangely contorted, but there is no desire to injure.   Who, contemplating such a picture, could forbear speaking the word which should grant peace to the sufferer, although the order necessitate some violence to the feelings of him who is invested with power to command?

MEGRIMS

So little sympathy exists between man and horse, so little are the ailments of the animal really studied, that the likeness between certain diseases affecting the master and the servant have not been observed. **Megrims,** evidently, is a form of epilepsy; yet, to speak of an epileptic horse would, probably, induce laughter in any society.   Notwithstanding which, man is not isolated in this world: he is associated with the creatures of the earth not only by a common habitation, but by similar wants and like diseases.   He is united by nature to every life that breathes.   His heart should feel for, and his charity embrace, every animal which serves him.   He has his duty toward, and is bound by obligations to, every creature placed under his control.   None are so subject to his will as is the horse; none have such powerful claims to his kindness and forbearance.   The noble animal is begotten by man's permission; its course in life depends upon his word: for his service it surrenders everything—freedom, companions, and paternity—it relinquishes all   Its owner's pleasure becomes its delight; its master's profit is its recreation.   It is the perfect type of an abandoned slave; body and soul, it devotes itself to captivity   It is sad to think how bitter is its recompense, when an obvious similarity, even in affliction, has not to this hour been recognized.

Megrims, like epilepsy in man, will in certain subjects appear only during some kind of exertion.   In others, it will be present only during particular states of rest   It is uncertain in its attacks.   It is not understood; and of the many theories which have been advanced, none explain it.

All horses may show megrims; some when at work, and some only while in the stable; others in the glare of day, and a few during the darkness of night; but of all, draught horses are the most liable to the malady.   This may be because harness horses are subjected to the most laborious and most continuous species of toil.   A horse fettered to a vehicle obviously must strain to propel as much or as long as the person intrusted with the whip thinks the animal should draw   Men's consciences, where their own convenience and another's exertions are the stake, generally possess an elastic property. It takes a great deal to stretch them to the utmost. An Arabian proverb says, "it is the last feather which breaks the camel's back;" but the English driver knows the entire pull is upon the collar, and he is moved by no considerations about the back. If the whip cannot flog the poor flesh onward, a shout and a heavy kick under the belly may excite the spasm, which, in its severity, shall put the load in motion.

Age does not influence the liability to megrims. The colt, which has done no work, may exhibit the disease, and the old stager may not be subject to its attacks. One horse may die in the field from exertion and never display the malady; another shall be led through the streets and exemplify megrims in all its severity. One shall be merely dull—the disorder shall never get to the acute stage, though the fits may be repeated. This last, to the surprise of its master, shall every now and then stop, stare about, and proceed as though nothing were the matter. A second, when mounted, will be seized by a sudden impulse and run into shop doors; while a third, being between the shafts, will be possessed with an irrepressible desire to inspect the driver's boots.

The horse often becomes suddenly stubborn. The reins are jagged and the whip plied to no purpose. The animal will only go its own way, which is commonly beset with danger. Perhaps, it may persist upon galloping, head foremost, down an open sewer; probably, it will rush up the steps leading to some mansion, and beat the door in with tremendous knocking.

Then come convulsions, followed by insensibility. If such a scene occur in a city, of course a crowd collects. Opinions are noisy and various; but a majority incline toward bleeding from the mouth. It is only to cut the palate, and a dozen knives, already opened, are proffered for the purpose. However, let the person in charge attend to no street suggestion. Let him at once seat himself upon the horse's head, and remain there till consciousness returns; then speak kindly to the sufferer, loosen the harness, and take care that the animal is perfectly recovered before it is permitted to rise.

THE EXPRESSION CHARACTERISTIC OF REPEATED ATTACKS OF MEGRIMS.

Dealers pretend that a horse subject to megrims is to be readily told. A horse, after repeated fits, is easily singled out; but the animal which has experienced only a single attack,

no man could challenge. One attack, however severe may be its character, will not necessarily leave its impress upon the countenance. But
the creature subject to such visitations soon assumes a heavy, flaccid,
and stupid expression. The disease distorts no feature, but it leaves its
mark behind, and any man, acquainted with the subject, would have
no difficulty in picking from a drove the horse which has endured repeated fits of this disorder.

Another class of knowing ones pretend they can drive a megrimed
horse any distance, by simply keeping a wet cloth over the brain. This
last experiment is, however, not inviting; and the author has yet to be
assured by science that a wet rag over the brain would repose upon
the primary seat of the disease.

When a horse has the first fit of megrims, at once throw the animal
up. Do not strive to sell the diseased creature, as such a sale is illegal.
The law presumes everything sold to be fit for its uses Thus, a person
buying rotten eggs can recover at law, because eggs are sold for human
food, and no man can eat a tainted egg. So a megrimed horse is unfit
for employment. Recovery in this disease is always doubtful A chance
is best secured by throwing the horse up on the first attack. Do not
turn a sick animal out to grass. Keep in a loose box, covered with
plenty of straw. Feed liberally, and with the best food Have the
body regularly dressed, and the animal led to, not ridden to, exercise
Allow a quart of stout every morning and half a pint of oil every night.
Above all things, attend to the stabling. Let the box be large and well
ventilated. Food is eaten but occasionally during the day. Air is as
essential as more substantial nutriment to life, and is consumed night
and day Food has to undergo a complicated change, and to travel far,
before it joins the blood Air is no sooner inhaled than it is immediately absorbed by the blood After such a statement, it is left to the
reader's reason to decide upon the importance of pure air toward sustaining health Probably, were stables erected with a little less regard
to the proprietor's expense and the builder's convenience, probably, were
they made in some degree proportioned to the magnitude of their future
inhabitants, and were the comfort of the captive a very little considered
in their construction,—the health of a horse might not be so very telling
a proverb; while megrims, under a better treatment, if it did not disappear, might not be so very common.

HYDROPHOBIA.

This is always the fruit of contagion, received from some stable-pet, in the shape of a dog or cat. It is essentially a nervous disorder. From the first, it influences the brain to a degree which no other malady seems capable of exercising. The animal constantly licks some portion of the body. The place appears to itch violently, and the tongue is applied with an energy and a perseverance highly characteristic of an over-wrought nervous distemper. The appetite always is affected; sometimes it is ravenous. The rack is not only emptied with unusual speed, but the bed, however soiled, is also consumed with more than apparent relish. Generally, however, the desire for provender is destroyed. Sometimes, the longing for fluids is morbidly increased. The horse plunges his head to the bottom of the pail, will bite at the groom who endeavors to interrupt the draught, or seize the wood between its teeth and crush it with a powerful gripe. More frequently, water will cause spasm, and be avoided with horror. The animal's likings may be morbidly changed: it will occasionally devour its own excrement, and lick up its emissions.

The nervous system is always highly developed. The horse starts at the smallest sound, trembles violently without a cause, flies backward, hangs upon the halter, stares wildly, and bursts into a copious sweat without any apparent reason being detected. Its voice is also changed, and the expression of the countenance invariably altered. The neigh is squeaking, and the face is at the commencement characterized by immense anxiety, which is soon changed for a peculiar aspect of cunning, mixed with a grinning ferocity.

THE COUNTENANCE OF A HORSE WITH HYDROPHOBIA.

Rarely, however, all the foregoing symptoms are absent. The horse is harnessed and taken to work. Suddenly it stops, appears stupid, and threatens to fall. In a short time it recovers, and the labor is proceeded with. The fits occur again and again. At length they end in violent shivering. When the tremor ceases, the recognition is not perfectly recovered. The breathing is quick and sharp; the eye bright and wild. The animal is turned homeward, but seldom reaches the stable before the furious stage begins.

Hydrophobia is commonly matured before the expiration of the sixth week. A fortnight is the earliest period of its appearance; but writers have asserted that the imbibed virus will remain dormant for twelve months. The author has no experience which justifies the last opinion.

Whenever a suspicion of this incurable and horrible disorder is entertained, place the horse by itself in a building with bare walls, but capa-

THE DESTRUCTIVE IMPULSE OF HYDROPHOBIA.

ble of being looked into through a window. Put food and water in the house, and, if the door be not strong, have it barricaded. Let no one enter for at least three days, as, during this disease, the horse is both mischievous and dangerous. The pain is such that it seeks relief in destruction. All breathing and moving creatures first attract its rage; but, wanting these, its frenzy is expended in breaking, rending, and scattering inanimate objects. Its ability to destroy is only limited by the duration of the disorder.

Let as few people as possible be near the hydrophobic horse. The quadruped's nerves are then alive to every impression. The presence will be detected, though the person be assiduously concealed. The sound of breathing even adds to the torture. Keep all people away but one; and that one should be the best shot in the neighborhood. Let him approach, aim steadily, and pull the trigger; for a bullet well placed is the only remedy the author knows which can stay this fearful disorder.

TETANUS.

Tetanus is defined to be spasm of the muscles of voluntary motion. That definition is right, as far as it goes. The disease, however, is the same in man and horse. The human being complains of the breathing being much oppressed, and of pain at the pit of the stomach. Such complaints show the diaphragm to be involved, while the large doses of strong medicine which can be swallowed with impunity prove the abdominal contents have not .escaped. Therefore, the author regards tetanus as spasm of the entire muscular system.

A horse of any age may exhibit tetanus Colts, newly dropped, have displayed the disorder, and all animals are liable to its attacks; but the very aged are least subject to this malady. Animals of a highly nervous temperament are most inclined toward it.

It is said to be of two kinds; but, in truth, it only has two origins. Traumatic tetanus is when it springs from a wound; idiopathic tetanus is when it appears without there being any known lesion to account for its presence. It may display its symptoms immediately or within a month of the injury. From the sixth to the fourteenth day is the most likely period for the advent of the disorder.

Cold, rain, draughts of air, and too much light, are all likely to originate it. Their potency, perhaps, ranges in the order they are placed. A .gentleman is apt to dismount at some hospitable house and to leave the animal, which has quickly borne him thither, shivering in the night air. The master enjoys himself, probably, more than is good for his health. The patient steed waits and waits, more quietly than the most faithful of human slaves. It shivers in the night air; its limbs become cramped with the cold The wind gets up, as the owner, before a cheerful fire, mixes another glass and takes another cigar. Still the horse remains almost in the spot where it was placed. The perspiration which covered the body dries in the darkness; evaporation quickly chills the blood which violent exercise had heated. The pulse sinks; spasms creep over the frame, but there is none near to note them. In solitude and discomfort the most painful of maladies is imbibed: in due time it breaks forth to the astonishment of the proprietor.

Another man rides far and fast through a heavy shower. He reaches a distant house and flings himself from the saddle, fastening the horse to the door-post. Cordials are ready for the man, and business is discussed over a glass No one thinks seriously of the poor life fastened to the door-post. "The horse is wet and can take no harm" "The gallop home will warm it," and so forth Therefore, the animal remains, to be drenched by the rain and to creep as near to the house as it may for partial shelter; the posterior part of the body, however, projects, and the drops fall, heavy and cold as lead, upon the loins of the patient beast The blood loses its warmth and the limbs their elasticity. When the owner again crosses the saddle he may be jolly; but it needs both spur and whip to cause the dripping and frozen animal to move.

When tetanus originates in some wound, the horse is generally nerv-ous from the first. It fidgets in the stall; it lacks the repose which usually sits so beautifully upon the sick horse's frame. It is excited at the approach of any person, and, commonly, very obstinate when given physic. The wound may, nevertheless, be healthy. Sometimes, as the outbreak draws near, the wound may rapidly close, become morbidly dry, or, instead of pus, send forth only a foul and scanty serum. Instances are narrated of tetanus supervening upon mortification; but such re-ported cases are, in the horse, very rare. Commonly, the wound pre-sents no appearance by which any man, however profound his knowledge, could guess the consequence to which it had given rise.

Tetanus is announced by an appearance of excitement. The tail is erect; the ears pointed forward; the head elevated; the legs stiffened

and stretched out. This aspect of excitement is not temporary. The groom passes through the stable and the attitude is main-tained. He wonders "what ails the horse?" It seems all alive; yet, though the groom shout out "come over," the order is obeyed with difficulty. The food is not eaten. It is picked and strewed about, but not devoured. When master returns home, the groom

THE TEST FOR TETANUS, WHEN NOT FULLY DEVELOPED.

wishes he would "*just look*" at the horse. It is very strange indeed! Why, the tail is quivering and the body feels quite hard—not like flesh. Hopes are expressed and the "veterinary" sent for. He proceeds at once to the manger, observing the animal as he approaches. With one hand he raises the horse's head. The haw is projected over the eye, and a case of tetanus is recognized.

Most persons know what bellyache and cramp are. Well, these are but spasms affecting different parts of the body: tetanus is spasm affect-ing every part of the body at the same time. The spasm is always pres-ent; but it admits of aggravation. Any painful operation, any sudden fright, or the slightest sound, will produce a paroxysm, during which the horse's body is fearfully contorted; and the animal writhes as it falls to the ground. Left alone, however, the horse may rise after some time; for nothing causes the quadruped so much dread as an inability to stand. It may totter or fall about, but it refuses to lie down, even though rest must be greatly needed and would act as the best of medicine. It stands day after day in the same spot. It does not move, as any motion may bring on one of those terrible paroxysms. The matter is rendered worse by the brain, during the entire period, being sensible. Every pain is felt, and the wretched animal has leisure to appreciate its agony. This is bad enough; but the torture is aggravated by the appetite of the animal not being dormant. Hunger still exists, and a sense of starvation augments the suffering. The jaw is closely locked. The creature cannot feed; but the presence of hunger is no supposition, for if a mash be held to the mouth, with a look of piteous gratitude the liquid portion is often drawn through the closed teeth. Hunger frequently impels the horse to make a desperate effort. The jaws are forced a little way asunder; a morsel is seized between the incisors; mastication commences, but cannot be perfected. The agony attendant upon motion forces the famishing creature to desist; and the poor horse is often found with a mouthful of hay firmly clenched and hanging from the mouth.

The animal may have been conspicuous for its beauty. The harmony of form may, in it, have been united to agility of limb. The creature

SHOWING HOW FAR AN ANIMAL WITH THE DISEASE IS CAPABLE OF MOTION.

may have been the pride of its proprietor; but a few days of this disease will work a mighty change. The limbs are moved with difficulty; the body has lost all its undulating grace; and the flesh has parted with its elasticity. The master in vain seeks for the object of his admiration in the painful sight which he then looks upon.

One peculiarity of tetanus is too marked not to be noticed. Persons have complained of the wooden appearance of the body; but, in severe cases, the height of the animal seems diminished and the length shortened. This appearance is more than the result of mere imagination. Many of the bones are divided by a fibro-cartilaginous substance: this substance force can compress. For that reason, a man is shorter when he retires at night than when he rises in the morning. No weight, however, can act with the energy of excited contractibility, and of that tetanus is composed: all the muscles are violently in action or energetically contracting A single muscle, when excited, shortens to that degree, which moves some portion of the body; but, when the entire mass of muscles simultaneously contract, they compress the frame, as in a vice. The grace of the animal is lost; the height is diminished, and the length is lessened, under so powerful and general an action.

All kinds of treatment have been tried for tetanus, and it is said that each has resulted in success. The majority of these popular methods, however, are sheer barbarities; and if they were successful, they were so against probability. The plan at present adopted is much more humane: the animal's shoes are removed, that no sound may follow the tread, and a solitary shed is strewn with refuse tan. Food, in the form of an ample malt mash and a pail of thin gruel, is placed within easy reach. The shed must be approached but once daily—then by the man most accustomed to the horse; and he speaks soothingly as he nears the building to change the provender.

This species of treatment, when preceded by a large dose of purgative medicine, is usually successful. Mix four drachms of aloes or six drachms of aloetic mass, and four drachms of extract of gentian, with one scruple of croton ferina. This tremendous purgative may be confidently given, as everything during this disease depends upon the maintenance of quiet, and upon getting the bowels open.

As all people, however, may not live where solitude can be commanded; then, give the purgative, render the room dark, and allow as few curious visitors as the pleading of sincerity cannot prevent intruding upon the sick and disabled quadruped. Pulling the animal about to administer medicine seems to do more harm than the most powerful drugs can counteract. Permit no blisters; sanction no firing: counter-irritants, however beneficial in other cases, are positive irritants, when applied to a body nervously excited to the highest degree. Grant permission for no operation to be performed, as any person of ordinary imagination may picture the effect of bustle, followed by sharp pain, upon a creature which cannot endure even the slightest sound.

Should, however, the case last so long as to warrant fear of the life sinking through starvation, food may be given even in quantities. Blood-warm linseed gruel should be procured—a gallon will be sufficient.

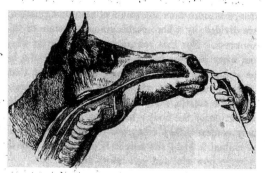

THE MODE OF FEEDING A HORSE WITH CHRONIC TETANUS.

The horse could swallow more; but after a prolonged fast there is danger in loading the stomach. Fix the horse catheter to the stomach-pump; then place the free end of the catheter in the nostril of the quadruped and push it forward, having previously slightly bent the end of the tube downward. Should the insertion provoke coughing, withdraw the catheter and commence afresh. Two feet of the instrument having disappeared, and no alarming symptom being present, begin to pump; do this as fast as possible, till the gallon of linseed gruel has been exhausted: such a resort is, however, better adapted to tetanus of the chronic description.

When applied to the acute form of the disorder, it is too apt to induce violent spasm. The acute disease, however, speedily terminates, and positive starvation is all but impossible during its brief continuance.

STRINGHALT.

Stringhalt is the imperfect development of that form of disease which, in man and in dogs, is called chorea, or St. Vitus's dance. In dogs it jerks the whole body, even to the face. The lower jaw will continue moving and the eye twitching, while the animal is prostrate and asleep. In the horse, however, it is seen only in the hind extremities. In the dog it will continue during progression, sometimes shaking the creature from its balance, and it often terminates in death. In the horse it is never fatal; and, save when about to start, is seldom to be detected. Then it causes the hind limbs to be quickly raised in succession. The movement is rapid, full of energy, and entirely involuntary. These

3

motions over, the horse proceeds, nor is the symptom usually witnessed again till the animal has once more to start; although a few exceptional cases are on record where stringhalt was perceptible at every step.

A HORSE HAVING STRINGHALT MUST MAKE SEVERAL INVOLUNTARY MOVEMENTS WITH THE HIND LEGS
BEFORE IT CAN PROGRESS.

Guilford, the racer, exhibited the disease in its worst form. In that animal, stringhalt was present in such severity as prevented the signal being obeyed before the several eccentric movements had been performed. The horse was esteemed good for its purposes; but the ground lost at starting gave away its chances, and it was consequently sold. From the pampered stable of the race-horse, it descended rapidly through various grades until the creature came to be harnessed to a London omnibus. While in that position, the disease was so aggravated that the pastern used to hit violently against the belly, till the hair of both was partially removed by the repeated blows. The Society for the Prevention of Cruelty then purchased the miserable carcass for three pounds, and had the life and the suffering extinguished.

The body was given to the Royal Veterinary College for dissection. Professor Spooner relates that he found blood effused on the sheath of the sacro-sciatic nerve. This, however, must have been an accident produced by the death struggle: that nerve moves the flexor muscles. Stringhalt is the disease of the extensor muscles only; therefore, the condition of the nerve alluded to by Professor Spooner could in no way influence the motions of the limb. Messrs. Percivall and Goodwin both appeal to instances, where, in animals affected with stringhalt, pressure existed upon the posterior portion of the spinal column. The last observation accords much more with the writer's notions of cause and effect

Nevertheless, the inexperienced reader may ask, how can the posterior portion of the horse's spinal column become affected ? Of all the vertebræ, those of the lumbar region are endowed with the greatest motion, and consequently are the most exposed to injury. The uses to which man puts the animal are not so very gentle but a delicate structure, however deeply seated, might be hurt. However, grant all these are harmless, which is indeed to allow a great deal to pass, the stables are enough to provoke stringhalt in half the horses now resident in London. Has the intelligent reader visited these places ? He knows the holes in which poor humanity is obliged to stive. Well, any place not good enough for a man to live in is esteemed luxurious lodging for a horse. Many of the places are undrained ; frequently have light or air admitted only by the doorway, and the stalls are seldom more than four feet wide. The wretched captives cannot turn their bodies round in the allotted space. A horse being in, when wanted abroad, must be backed into the gangway, and thus made to "face about " It is not creditable to human nature when we perceive its most valuable and willing servant is begrudged the space in which its useful body rests. The labor of the day should at least earn for the horse a sufficient bed.

The exhaustion of the toil—for man has nicely calculated the work a horse can perform, and generally exacts the quotum to the full—has merited the night's repose, which shall fit for the morrow's fatigue ; but man is most particular in all that concerns the quadruped. He has reckoned up the food it may eat, the water it may drink, the space it may occupy ; the keep, the keeper, the lodging, and the very harness that fastens it to the load,—all are precisely calculated. There is no law to interpose between man and horse, even should the estimate be run "too fine." Against sore shoulders there is some enactment, which is only enforced through a constable specially retained by a private association. No clause teaches man his duty toward his inferiors. The lower animals have no protection against the exhausting labor and inadequate provision that maims a body or wastes a life.

The servant, observing the master to be without feeling, apes his better. A bad example always finds plenty of imitators. The horse may be wanted in a hurry ; the groom commands it to "come round." It is too much trouble to back the animal as usual ; the master is in

haste and the servant has no time to lose.   The poor animal endeavors
to obey; it squeezes and twists its body: the head is seized, a blow is
given, and the difficulty is vanquished.   But at what a cost!   One bone
of the spine has been injured.   Bone is slow in its developments.   No
immediate consequence results; but months afterward, the injured place
throws out a spicula of bone, no larger than a needle's point, perhaps,
but it presses upon the spinal marrow, and lasting stringhalt is the
effect.

Of course no drug can reach the part affected; no cunning preparation can remove even a needle's point from the interior of the spinal
canal.   The stinghalt, once exhibited, is beyond cure, and never disappears but with the life.   However, it mostly affects high-spirited, nervous horses, and not being generally observable during progression, some
of the quadrupeds thus diseased sell for large sums.

PARTIAL PARALYSIS.

Paralysis, in the horse, save when it appears toward the termination
of violent disorders, is never more than partial.   It locates itself in the

THE UNSTEADY WALK OF A HORSE WHEN SUFFERING UNDER PARTIAL PARALYSIS OF THE HIND LEGS.

hind limbs, and, though it does not destroy all motion, yet it destroys all
strength or utility.   The power to move with speed is entirely lost, nor
is the ability to progress at a slower pace by any means assured.   One

hind foot is perpetually getting in the way of the other, and constantly threatening to throw the animal down, whose walk already is rolling or unsteady.

This affection is the property of matured animals; so rarely as to be exceptional is it to be seen attacking colts. Fast trotters, omnibus horses, hunters, and creatures subjected to extreme exertion, are most liable to it. It creeps on insidiously. At first the pace is as fast as ever, but something is suspected wrong in the manner of going. After a time the creature is brought to a veterinary surgeon as a lame horse. The suspicions are then destroyed and the real malady is announced

The decay of the more showy powers seems to bring forward the gentler qualities of the horse's nature. The animal, which once was dangerous, loses all its dreaded attributes: with paralysis, it becomes meek or tame, as though the big life felt its great affliction and sought to compensate, by amiability, for the trouble it necessarily gave, or, in other words, that the animal was mildly pleading for existence. No doubt much of such a sentiment, if not all, resides in the mind of the spectator, the animal only being subdued by sickness. Still, it is very sad to contemplate the horse, which once could outstrip the sparrow in its flight, reduced to a pace which the tortoise might leave behind; to behold the beast, once powerful and proud of its strength, humbled to a feebleness which the push of any child might overthrow. It is more sorrowful, when we think its hurt was received from him to whom its welfare was intrusted; that its injury was the consequence of an over-anxiety to please and to obey. It may be well doubted whether, when man was given dominion over the beasts of the field, he was invested with an absolute authority over God's creatures, which had no moral duties nor obligations attached to it. At all events, it would be difficult to find an object more suggestive of pity, or better calculated to excite our inward reflections, than a horse suffering under partial paralysis.

Paralysis is generally past all cure; occasionally, however, it admits of relief. It is an eccentric disorder, and it is difficult to say, positively, what medicine will be of use. The horse, however, during paralysis, should enjoy absolute rest. In its disabled state, a little walk is as great an exertion as once was a breathing gallop; and it was over-exercise which induced the disorder. The animal should receive only strengthening physic and the most nourishing of food. The following ball should be administered, night and morning:—

Strychnia, half a grain, gradually, or in six weeks to be worked up to a grain and a half; iodide of iron, one grain; quassia powder and treacle, a sufficiency: to be given night and morning.

The grooming should be persevered with, the animal being carefully dressed twice each day, and the process ending by brushing the quarters thoroughly with a new birch broom. The bed should be ample; the box should be padded and a warm cloth always kept over the loins. A piece of wet flannel, covered with a rug, placed over the lumbar region, has on occasions induced a return of warmth. The bowels should be regulated, if possible, with mashes and green meat; but, when costiveness exists, a pint of oil is to be preferred to even three drachms of aloes The one exhausts, the other nurtures as well as relaxes the body.

The hope of amendment must, however, be indulged with caution The disease is of chronic growth, and therefore will be of long duration At all events, it is not one horse in four which recovers from an attack of partial paralysis; and not one in twenty that is afterward fit for its former uses

GUTTA SERENA

Gutta serena is fixed dilatation of the pupillary opening, owing to paralysis of the optic nerve; the affection is, consequently, accompanied by permanent blindness

The causes of this malady are blows upon the head, quick driving, excessive hemorrhage, stomach staggers, unwholesome stables, poor food, exhausting labor, or anything which may decidedly undermine the constitution.

The majority of these causes are inflicted by man, the remainder are within his control Any person has but to reflect how very precious eyesight is to mankind. Having settled that point, he has only to conjecture how much more dear it must be to a creature forbid to enjoy the pleasures of conversation To take away sight, is to deprive the animal of a faculty with which it is endowed to perfection, in some measure to compensate for the absence of reason and the deficiency of speech A horse can see farther than its master. The human eye is, frequently, dormant, when the thought is active: the healthy, equine eye never rests The creature sleeps so lightly that very seldom is it caught napping We may imagine, therefore, the gratification bestowed by an organ so constantly employed. To blind a horse, is to deprive a breathing body of half its life's pleasure. It is more, when we consider the natural disposition of the quadruped: it is to deprive timidity of its watchfulness, fear of its protection. It is even yet more, when we think upon the habits of the horse—its spirits, its pleasure, its joy—all are expressed by means of a gallop But what speed can the horse indulge in, when cruelty has taken away the power to guide with rapidity? To destroy the horse's sight, is to condemn a creature to live on, but to take from life the gayety of existence.

The eye recently afflicted with gutta serena, or rather the eyes, (for this deprivation, commonly affects both orbs,) is, to the uninformed inspection, perfect. The internal structures are in their proper places, and the pupil is beautifully dilated. A very little instruction, however, enables the spectator to distinguish between fixedness and dilatation. A trifle more tuition will point out that the pupil is not so dark as in the organ of the healthy animal: that it has an opaque milky cast, accompanied very frequently with a bright light-green shining through it, as though a piece of tinsel were within the posterior chamber. After gaining such information, probably the notion before expressed about beauty may be

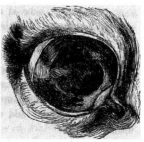

AN EYE AFFECTED WITH GUTTA SERENA.

changed. Most things are most beautiful as nature formed them; and no little expression resides in the ever-changing dimension of the pupillary opening.

THE MODE IN WHICH A HORSE, WHEN QUITE BLIND, PROGRESSES.

The symptoms of blindness are equally pathetic and characteristic. The nostrils are constantly at work and the ears perpetually in motion—life is endeavoring, by exercising other senses, to compensate for the one lost. Then, the movements are peculiar. A blind man commonly

shuffles along, endeavoring "to feel" his way. The horny hoof lacks
the human faculty, but the horse endeavors to surmount objects by stepping high. A blind man turns the sightless face heavenward; the
animal, likewise, raises its head, as it were, to expose its sightless orbs
to its Creator. There is another strange peculiarity also, exemplified
by the blind horse. The sightless quadruped, contrary to the majority
of its species, generally carries a rough coat in summer and a blooming
coat in winter.

Now, a high stepper, a well-carried head, a lively ear, and a blooming
coat, are great points in a horse, especially about London, and with
gentlemen of little information. To prevent imposition, always place
the horse in a full light. Should the pupils continue large, have the
horse put into a dark house. A quarter of an hour afterward, take a
candle, and by its light regard the eye. If the pupil is still dilated,
hold the candle near to the eye. The iris will not contract quickly upon
artificial light, but in five minutes it ought to move. However, suppose
you imagine it to remain stationary; then,
placing yourself by the head, have the
horse led out into sunshine. If it exhibit
no change to mark the passage from darkness to daylight you may certainly conclude the optic nerve is paralyzed.

There are other tests, but these are not
satisfactory; such as covering the eye with
the hand or a hat. The hand is semi-
transparent, and so can only induce partial darkness; the hat does not fit the
inequalities of the horse's countenance,
therefore it is useless. Of the same nature
is aiming pretended blows at, or moving
the hand before, the suspected eye. The
other senses, by constant exercise, become
so very acute during loss of sight, that
winking is no proof of vision: the lid may
move, and, nevertheless, the horse be stone
blind.

THE BASE OF THE BRAIN.

a. The point of junction between the
right and left optic nerves.
b b. The healthy optic nerve of a white
color, originating on the left side and proceeding to the left eye.
c c. The paralyzed or unhealthy optic
nerve, diminished in size and darker in
color. It ran to the right eye; but its
diseased condition can be clearly traced to
originate from the left side of the brain.

Nothing can be done for paralysis of
the optic nerve. The injury once established, its effects are lasting. Butchers
and other people, who foolishly pride
themselves upon their fast trotting steeds, and whose natures are not
unpleasantly susceptible, often induce the affection. It lessens the value

of the horse, dooms it to a lower class of proprietors, and takes from the creature's life much of the pleasure which otherwise might lighten the animal's existence.

After death, an anatomical peculiarity is observed. The optic nerves, subsequent to leaving the brain, unite and exchange fibers Neither nerve pursues an absolute course; yet, consequent on decease, if the right eye were blind from gutta serena, the left nerve, or the nerve originating from the left side of the brain, alone is affected: the disease seems confined to that part. The opposite nerve is perfectly white and healthy; but the one affected with paralysis is of a yellowish color, softer nature, and sensibly diminished in bulk. So, if blindness afflict both eyes, both optic nerves are then of diminished size and of a yellowish hue.

CHAPTER II.

SIMPLE OPHTHALMIA.

THE following engraving illustrates some of the accidents which attend upon injured sight in the horse. The eyes are probably more important to the safety and pleasure of the master than any other portion of the quadruped's frame. Let the smallest impediment exist, and

SOME OF THE RESULTS OF IMPERFECT VISION.

there is no telling in what way it may operate. Certain horses are most affected by near objects; others exhibit alarm only when bodies are approaching them; another class of creatures will look upon most forward sights with indifference, but will invariably be horror-struck whenever the view is extensive; while a fourth group will shy violently without mortal vision being able to recognize any cause for terror. In every case, the dread excited overmasters all other feelings. The presence of extreme fear releases the horse from the dominion of its proprietor; its movements are sudden, jerking, and eccentric; the animal has lost all self-control, and there is no saying in what direction it may move or what it may attempt to do. It is regardless of its own life, therefore

(42)

it is careless about the welfare of others, and he is very fortunate who possesses such a servant and escapes without accident.

There is no cure for a disposition depending upon a change of structure; but there may be a preventive. Would all horse-owners preserve their tempers and forbear from slashing a horse over the head, they would be vast gainers in a pecuniary sense, and would certainly escape very many of those ills now commonly attendant upon equestrian exercises

Whoever has a shying horse had better discard the creature from all private uses. Send the animal to some work in which the habit will be accompanied with less danger, or never allow the quadruped to quit the stable without having the sight securely blinded. Such things are necessary; but the feeling man, when he considers how much the exercise of the senses sweeten mere animal existence, will sigh over the order which compels him to deprive a horse of that which the common sense of the English has denominated "precious sight."

Simple ophthalmia is inflammation of the fine membrane which covers the horse's eye; it reaches no deeper, it does not affect the internal structures of the organ, and it is not so much to be dreaded in its immediate as in its after consequences. It is caused by accident and by the violence of man.

As the reader has walked the streets, he surely must have seen men indulge their temper by cutting a horse over the head with the whip. The animal capers about and shakes the ears, endeavoring to avoid the chastisement; the man becomes more enraged; the reins are pulled tight, while the master stands up in the gig, and for minutes continues chastising a creature that is bound to the shafts and comparatively at his mercy. Were the horse, thus tortured, to run away, the person who abused his authority would have provoked a severe retribution; but the animal has no such intention. The fault may be far more imaginary than real. The timidity of the horse prevents it from willfully inviting the dreaded lash; possibly the offense resides more with the individual invested with trust over life than with the creature that patiently submits to most unworthy control. At all events, the thong curls about the face; now it cuts the lips, in which the sense of touch resides; the pain is maddening; the horse capers and shakes its head, striving to avoid a repetition of the torture. The next slash, however, turns sharply round the blinkers and lights upon the eye; the horse is held tight, the man feels happy, he has discovered a tender place; the whip is plied again and again, always falling true. It hits the mark. When the animal reaches home, the lid of one eye is closed, and many tears have wetted the cheek, while scars remain after the immediate consequences have passed; the vision is interfered with, and timidity becomes an inveterate shyer.

Also, from the manner in which the rack is placed, a hay-seed frequently falls into the eye   The hay is always kept in the loft above the stables, and a narrow trap-door opens into the rack.   This is very convenient for the groom; how could any architect be so very "maudlin" as to design a stable with the slightest consideration for a horse?   At every mouthful the head has to be raised and the provender pulled out; probably, human ingenuity could not invent a machine more likely to be attended with injury.   The head uplifted, the eye open to direct the bite, the dry grass shaken to pull out the morsel, of course the loose particles are dislodged, and what wonder if one of the hay-seeds should fall into the open eye?   This body is small, dry, harsh, and sharp; moved about by the motion of the lid it commits fearful ravages upon the tender organ to which it has found admittance, and simple ophthalmia is the consequence

Man is too proud to learn from nature, or he might observe horses always depress their heads when in the field.   The common parent, with care for all her children's comfort, makes the animal stoop to crop the herbage; man causes the creature to upraise and outstretch the neck to reach its sustenance.   However, the horse is not always free from accidents when it quits the stall.   Carters often amuse the weary way by striking what they term a "stubborn and foolish horse" over the head with the butt end of the whip   This action, though most irritating to witness, is generally less important in its results than any of the injuries previously remarked upon   The lid shields the eye; consequently, a largely swollen covering and a slightly injured membrane are the consequences.

Many brutal drivers have "a happy nack" of kicking at the head of a fallen animal to make it rise.   This act may extinguish vision or provoke simple ophthalmia; but, it is hoped, all such are exceptional cases, therefore these are willingly not remarked upon.

Frequently horses try to while away the long hours of confinement by playing with one another; one horse will lean its head over the division to the stalls and for hours together lick its fellow prisoner's neck. Sometimes a day's rest begets high spirits, and the animals indulge in a more boisterous amusement; they bite and snap at one another's heads. Domestication has, however, disabled the creature to nicely measure distances; standing all day long with the nose close to a glaring white wall has probably impaired the vision.   One horse projects its teeth too far; they simply graze the eye; but a small flap of membrane is the consequence.   The bite of an enraged horse is fearful; and were not the animal gently inclined, more than a minute portion of fine skin would testify its intention. Simple ophthalmia, accompanied with a small abscess upon the cornea, is the result.

The treatment of simple ophthalmia is somewhat homely. Put on a bridle, or a leather head-stall; or a halter will answer the purpose; fasten a cord loosely to either side, so that it may cross the forehead; on this line suspend a cloth several times doubled; but, mind it is large enough to cover both eyes, for the visual organs are so sympathetic, that when one is inflamed the other is very likely to exhibit disease. Keep the cloth continually dripping with the following lotion.

Fill a two-quart saucepan with poppy heads, cover these with water; boil, till the poppy heads are quite soft; pour off the liquor, strain, filter, and, adding thereto

A READY MODE OF BLINDING A HORSE, AND OF APPLYING A LOTION TO THE EYES IN SIMPLE OPHTHALMIA.

one ounce of tincture of arnica, the preparation, when cold, is fit for use.

On the first morning, an inspection should be gently attempted; for the eye is generally so very tender, and the animal so resistful, that no examination at that time is generally satisfactory. On the following day, however, the lotion will have reduced the swelling, mitigated the agony, and have enabled the horse to be more obedient; then make another and a thorough examination. The skin upon the eye will be white and opaque, the lining of the lid inflamed, while numerous tears will pour down the cheek according to the severity of the injury. Remove any substance found underneath the eyelid. If the hay-seed or sharp particle shaken from the provender stick firmly into the outer covering of the eye, grasp it tightly with a pair of forceps, and endeavor to pull it out. Should it be fixed too deeply for any ordinary force to move it, do not exert all your power, but take a sharp-pointed knife, which is better than a lancet, because more under command, and placing its tip below the obstacle, with a motion, of the wrist oblige it

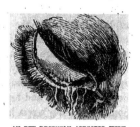

AN EYE RECENTLY AFFECTED WITH SIMPLE OPHTHALMIA.

to quit its situation or to come forth between the ends of the forceps.

Should a flap of the cornea be left by a bite, probably pus will be secreted beneath it; the place must be watched till the local inflammation has subsided, and a spot of yellow, opaque matter can be detected under the transparent membrane. With a slight incision the pus must be released and the eye bathed with a lotion composed of water and chloride of zinc, one grain to the ounce.

Other cases will rather be known by the variety of marks left behind than by any difference in their necessary treatment. A lotion is generally everything required; however, should the inflammation become excessive, it may be necessary to open the eye-vein or the vessel which, journeying toward its larger trunk, runs directly beneath and from the eye. When this prominent and visible vein is pierced, it frequently, although distended, will not bleed. Then place some favorite food upon the ground,—the bending of the head and the movement of the jaw will cause the current to flow forth freely.

It is among the most beautiful attributes of the horse, that though so very timid, it never suspects nor can it understand actual injury. Thus, the flowing of its own blood does not affect it; it is otherwise with other animals not more intelligent. If a dog or cat be hurt, no delicacy can tempt the creature to feed. The horse, when in battle deprived of its limb, is so accustomed to restraint and so unsuspicious of harm, that it has been found, after the strife was ended, maimed, and yet cropping the herbage about it. The generous beast, when domesticated, retains its gentle disposition, and soon forgets to recognize danger; it becomes attached to its superior, and though its treatment be coarse and its usage brutal, it can pardon all.

The consequences of simple ophthalmia are little, white, opaque spots upon the membrane. Streaks of the same sort are occasionally left upon

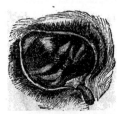

the organ by the abuse of the whip; the amount of blemish, of course, will be decided by the original injury. Never purchase an animal thus disfigured; better buy a blind horse. The opaque places prevent many rays of light from reaching the optic nerve; the sight is irreparably impaired; the horse sees imperfectly; it may behold the head of a man, while the opaque scar conceals the body. Timidity takes alarm at the apparently spectral object. It has no reason to explain, and it wants intelligence to understand. The poor abused quadruped becomes a dangerous shyer.

HORSE'S EYE INJURED BY THE LASH.

SPECIFIC OPHTHALMIA.

Before we touch upon the subject which forms the heading to this article, we wish to establish one proposition, because it will smooth the way to an understanding between author and reader.

Man cannot make a property of life; he has no power over its continuance; it may cease to-morrow without his permission and against his wishes; it is removed from and independent of his control. Man can have nothing like a property in that which is altogether above his sway. He then, obviously, has no right to enslave any living creature, and take no care of the existence which he has deprived of liberty to provide for itself. When he captures a wild animal and retains it in captivity, he entails upon himself the duty of providing for its wants, and becomes answerable for its welfare. He violently usurps nature's province—obviously, he adopts nature's obligations; if he rebel against such a moral contract and persist in viewing dominion as absolute authority, as something which invests him with power to feed or starve at his pleasure, house or turn into the air according to his will, nature opposes such arrogance, and, releasing the life by death, takes the oppressed creature from the tyranny of the oppressor.

Under some such compact the horse is given to man. The implied, not written obligation, may not be acknowledged or understood; but, nevertheless, it exists, and the terms of the bond are rigidly exacted. Let us regard this matter in relation to specific ophthalmia. A gentleman possesses five horses; he builds a stable twenty feet long, twelve feet wide, and nine feet high; into this place he crams the five huge lives. We will suppose the place to be good of its kind, to be paved with Dutch clinkers and to be perfectly drained; still each horse stands in a stall four feet wide; in this it has to remain all night and the major portion of the day. In this space it has to relieve its body; the liquid, to be sure, may run off by the drain, but it has to fall upon straw, which imbibes some, and to flow over bricks, which absorb more; the solid excrement is during the day removed by the groom as it falls, but it remains in an open basket to taint the air of the place. We will suppose the horses and their attendants, occasionally, are the sole inhabitants, and the building contains none of those things, living and otherwise, which ladies are pleased to order should "be carried into the stable."

THE SPECIES OF EYE WHICH IS GENERALLY SUPPOSED TO BE MOST LIABLE TO OPHTHALMIA.

Will the sane reader assert that the space is large enough for its purposes? The stable never can be sufficiently ventilated: it will smell of impurity—of hay, straw, oats, ammonia, and of various other things. The air feels hot. Can it be wondered at? Ten large lungs have been breathing it for weeks and years, during twenty out of every twenty-four hours. Five huge creatures have been cabined there, living by day, sleeping by night, feeding and performing all the other offices of nature. Is it astonishing that the air feels and smells close? Ought we not rather to wonder that animal life can exist in such an atmosphere? The chief contamination is ammonia; ammonia will not support vitality. The reader has inhaled smelling salts; those are purified carbonate of ammonia; have these not made the eyes water? The ammonia of the stable affects the eye of the horse; it also undermines the constitution; but, by constantly entering upon the lungs and stimulating the eyes, it causes the constitutional disease to first affect the visual organs; in short, specific ophthalmia is generated.

Now, to prove the case here stated. In the south of Ireland, where poverty prevails, humanity is obliged to shelter itself in strange places, and any hole is there esteemed good lodging for a horse. In that part of the kingdom ophthalmia affects the majority of animals; it not only preys on horses, but it seizes upon mankind; for the author, a few years ago, was much struck by the quantity of blind beggars to be encountered in the streets of Cork. Here we have the conclusion of the argument; its moral exemplified and enforced. If animals are foully housed and poorly kept, they generate disorders, which at length extend to the human race; therefore he who contends for a better treatment of the horse, also indirectly pleads for the immunity of mankind from certain diseases. Man cannot hold life as a property, or abuse life without his ill deeds by the ordinances of nature recoiling on himself.

Specific ophthalmia is a constitutional disease affecting the eyes; it has been submitted to all kinds of rude treatment; no cruelty but has been experimented with; no barbarity but has been resorted to. It has been traced to various sources; its origin has been frequently detected; but the real cause of the disease, to this day, has not been recognized. The veterinary surgeon is often sent for to just look at a horse which

"has got a hay-seed in its eye." This mistake is very common, as ophthalmia generally breaks forth during the long night hours, while the stable is made secure and the confined air is foulest. The groom sees an animal with a pendant, swollen lid, and with a cheek bedewed by copious tears; he can imagine only an accident; but the medical examiner must obey the summons with an unprejudiced mind, because simple ophthalmia is a mere misfortune, specific ophthalmia is a constitutional disorder.

THE FIRST APPEARANCE OF SPECIFIC OPHTHALMIA.

The veterinary surgeon, firstly, in the groom's convictions, makes a grievous mistake. He goes up to the horse on the opposite side to the affection; being there, he takes the pulse, remarks the breathing, observes the coat, feels the feet, examines the mouth, and looks at the nasal membrane. If simple ophthalmia be present, some of these may be altered from long-endured pain; but if specific ophthalmia exist, the general disturbance denotes a constitutional disorder. The pulse is hard, the breathing sharp, the coat staring, the feet cold, the mouth clammy, and the nasal membrane inflamed or leaden-colored.

The horse is next ordered round to the stable window, with the diseased eye toward the light. A pretense is then made of forcing the lid open; if simple ophthalmia be present, the resistance is energetic, but not violent. Should specific ophthalmia be the affection, the horse struggles against the intimation with the wildness of timidity, striving to escape a terrible torture. The animal is, thereupon, brought into some shady corner; its fears are allayed, and it permits the lid to

RAISING THE UPPER LID OF AN EYE AFFECTED WITH SPECIFIC OPHTHALMIA.

be raised with little difficulty. Should the eye have been injured by an accident, the most prominent part of the ball is likely to be hurt. The internal structures are unaffected; the pupil generally is larger than usual, and the iris is unchanged. The haw may be or may not be projected; but the color, form, and aspect of the iris is unaltered. During the commencement of specific ophthalmia, the center of the cornea may be transparent, but the circumference of the ball is violently inflamed; the reason being that a constitutional disorder always first attacks the more vascular structures, and, therefore, commences in the

DIAGRAM OF THE EYE IN SIMPLE OPHTHALMIA. THE DARK LINE INDICATES THE EXTENT TO WHICH HAW MAY PROTRUDE.

DIAGRAM OF THE HORSE'S EYE WHEN SUFFERING FROM SPECIFIC OPHTHALMIA.

loose conjunctiva, covering the white of the globe. In specific ophthalmia, the color of the eye has changed to a lighter hue, and the pupillary opening is firmly closed, to prevent the entrance of the dreaded light.

Weakness increases as specific ophthalmia progresses. The attack, however, is seldom stationary; the eye first involved may suddenly become clear and healthy, and the opposite organ may exhibit the ravage of the disease; thus, the affection keeps rapidly moving about; when it suddenly quits both eyes, the inflammation commonly fixes upon some distant part of the body, as the lungs or feet. No one can predicate how short will be its stay or how long the attack may last; it has disappeared in a week, it has continued two months. It seldom reaches its climax during the first assault. It will occur again and again; generally it ends in the destruction of one or both eyes; but never, so far as the author's knowledge extends, causes gutta serena. Like scrofulous affections in the human being, which it greatly resembles, it generally is the inheritance of youth; after maturity or after the eighth year has been attained, it is rarely witnessed.

When this terrible affliction visits a stable, let the proprietor firmly oppose all active measures. A shed ought to be procured, cool or shady, and screened on every side, excepting on the north. Every hole, however minute, should be-stopped, because light shines through a small opening with a force proportioned to its diminutiveness. The stars and candles in the once popular London Diorama were only small holes cut in the canvas.

The eye-vein is then to be opened, and the lid, if much enlarged, punctured in several places; when the bleeding has ceased, a cloth, saturated in cold water, is to be put over both eyes. As to other remedies, they must be regulated by the condition of the animal. Should it be poor, oats and beans, ground and scalded; cut green meat; gruel made of hay-tea, etc., should be given. No dry fodder must be allowed; all the provender must be so soft that mastication may be dispensed with. The movement of the jaw, sending blood to the head, is highly injurious during an attack of specific ophthalmia.

Let the following ball be given twice, daily:—

Powdered colchicum	Two drachms.
Iodide of iron	One drachm.
Calomel	One scruple.

Make into a ball with extract of gentian.

Observe the teeth while this physic is being taken. The author has taken twenty-five grains of calomel daily, for a month, with impunity; lately, he was slightly salivated by two grains, when not expecting any effect. Mercury, therefore, operates in accordance with the system; it is strong or weak as the body is sickly or robust.

Should the animal be fat, do not therefore conclude that it is strong;

obesity is always accompanied with debility. But if the horse be a hunter or a racer, in training condition, still give the medicine prescribed, with soft food, not quite so stimulating, and the ball twice daily. However, as soon as the medicine begins to take effect, which it will do soonest upon the weakly, change it for :—

> Liquor arsenicalis . . . . Three ounces
> Muriated tincture of iron . . . . . Five ounces.

Mix, and give half an ounce in a tumbler of water twice daily.

Do not bother about the bowels; endeavor to regulate them by mashes and with green meat; if they should not respond, do not resort to more active measures. Should the pulse be increased, a scruple of tincture of aconite root may be administered every hour, in a wineglass of water; should the pain appear to be excessive, the like amount of extract of belladonna may be rubbed down in a similar quantity of water, and be given at the periods already stated; only always be content with doing one thing at a time. Thus reduce the pulse, for, with the lowering of the vascular action, the agony may become less intense; however, so long as the beats of the artery are not more in a minute than sixty-five, and not very thin or hard, the aconite should be withheld, for during an acutely painful disorder the heart must be in some degree excited.

The grand measure, however, remains to be told. Remove every horse from the stable in which the attack occurred; then elevate the roof, widen the gangway, and enlarge the stalls; improve the ventilation, overlook the drains, lay down new pavement—in fact, reconstruct the edifice. It is felt that, in giving these directions, a proposal is offered to demolish a building. The author is fully alive to the expense of such a transaction; but one valuable horse will pay for a great deal of bricks and mortar. Experience has decided that the most humane way is, in the long run, the cheapest method of proceeding. Ophthalmia is a teasing and a vexatious disorder. If the owner has no feeling with the inhabitants of his homestead, still let him study his own comfort, for it is astonishing how very much good stabling adds to the appearance and to the happiness of a mansion.

Specific ophthalmia does not terminate in death; it usually leaves the victim blind in one or both eyes. In England, however, it is mostly satisfied with the destruction of one organ; the strength of the other becoming, after its departure, considerably improved. At the same time, having caused the lids to swell, it leaves them in a wrinkled or a puckered state; the remaining eye is likewise somewhat sensitive to light. To gain in some measure the shadow of the brow, and to escape the full glare of day, the eye is retracted; all the muscles are employed to gain this end, but the power of the levator of the upper lid causes the eye to assume somewhat of a three-cornered aspect.

It is always desirable to recognize the animal which may be or may

AN EYE DISPLAYING THE RAVAGES OF SPECIFIC OPHTHALMIA.

have been liable to so fearful an affection. One symptom of having experienced an attack is discovered on the margin of the transparent cornea. The inflammation extends from the circumference to the center. The margin of the transparent ball is generally the last place it quits; here it frequently leaves an irregular line of opacity altogether different to and distinct from the evenly-clouded indication of the cornea's junction with the sclerotic, which last is natural development.

Nevertheless, the internal structure best display the ravages of specific ophthalmia; it is upon these the terrible scourge exhausts its strength. The eye becomes cloudy; loses its liquid appearance; the black bodies attached to the edges of the pupillary opening either fall or seem about to leave their natural situation. The pupil becomes turbid, then white; the iris grows light in color, and at last remains stationary, having previously been morbidly active. The whiteness of the pupil grows more and more confirmed, and every part grows opaque; by this circumstance,

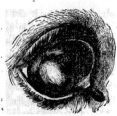

TERMINATION TO SPECIFIC OPH-THALMIA.

the total cataract, arising from specific ophthalmia, is frequently to be challenged. The lens, moreover, is often driven, by the force of the disease, from its position; it lodges against the inner surface of the globe. Very common is a torn or ragged state of the pupil witnessed, as was stated, during the intensity of the attack, for the iris contracts to exclude the light; remaining thus for any period, it becomes attached to the capsule of the lens; when the

disease mitigates, it often rends its own structure by its efforts to expand. Should those efforts prove unavailing, the pupillary opening, as sometimes happens, is lost forever.

In the previous description of disorder, no mention has been made of the cartilago nictitans, or haw, or third eyelid, as it has been called. This thin body is very active, and resides at the inner corner of the eye; of course, in a disease under which the eye is pained by light, the haw is protruded to the utmost. In ophthalmia, however, it is covered by an inflamed membrane, and though in health its movements are so rapid that it may easily escape notice, yet in this disease it lies before the eye, red and swollen; this substance it was once common for farriers to excise, under a foolish notion of removing the cause of the disorder.

The use of the cartilago nictitans in the healthy eye will now be explained Let the reader inspect any of the illustrations to this article; he will find the outer corner represented as being much higher than the inner corner of the eye, where the active little body resides. Under the upper lid, near to the outer corner, is situated the lachrymal gland, which secretes the water or tears of the eye.

Suppose any substance "gets into the eye;" being between two layers of conjunctiva, it creates much anguish, it provokes constant motion of the lid, which in its turn causes the lachrymal gland to pour forth its secretion. Liquid flowing over a smooth globe of course gravitates; the substance "in the eye" is thus partly washed and partly pushed toward the inner corner.

Now, the base of the cartilago nictitans rests upon the fat at the back of the eye Pain causes the globe to be retracted by spasmodic jerks; adipose matter cannot be compressed, and it is therefore driven forward every time the muscles act. The fat carries with it the cartilago nictitans, and the edge of the body being very fine and lying close to the globe, shovels up any foreign substance that may be within its reach, to place it upon the rounded development at the inner corner of the eye. Still may the reader inquire, if the cartilago nictitans is covered with conjunctival membrane, and the inner corner of the eye is enveloped in the same, does not the foreign substance occasion pain to these as it did to the globe of the eye? No; it was just hinted that conjunctiva is not sensitive except two layers of the membrane are together, as the ball and the inner surface of the eyelid The haw, therefore, has no sensation upon its external surface, neither has the inner corner of the eye, whence all foreign bodies are quickly washed by the overflow of tears.

Farriers, however, are not an extinct race; many of the fraternity still exist, still practice, and are, it is to be feared, very little improved. Should one of these gentlemen offer to cure specific ophthalmia, it is hoped the owner, after the foregoing explanation, will not allow the "haw" to be excised.

Let every man treat the animals over which he is given authority with kindness, as temporary visitors with himself upon earth, and fellow-inhabitants of a striving world. Let him look around him; behold the owner of a coveted and highly-prized racer to-day, in a week reduced to the possessor of a blind and wretched jade; then ask himself what kind of property that is to boast of, which may be deteriorated or taken from him without his sanction? Having answered that question, let him inquire whether it is better to propitiate the higher being by showing tenderness toward his creatures, or to defy the power which can in an instant snatch away his possessions.

CATARACT.

Cataract is a white spot within the pupillary opening. The spot may be indistinct or conspicuous,—soft, undefined or determined; it may be

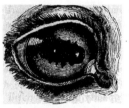

as small as the point of a needle, or so big as to fill the entire space: in short, any indication of whiteness or opacity upon the pupil is regarded as a cataract.

Cataracts are designated according to the parts on which they reside. The lens of the eye is contained within a capsule, as an egg is within its shell. Any whiteness upon this capsule is termed a **capsular cataract.** The lens floats in a liquor which surrounds it, as

PARTIAL CATARACTS, OR SMALL WHITE
SPECK WITHIN THE PUPIL OF THE EYE.

the white does the yolk of an egg. Any turbidness in this fluid is termed a **milky cataract;** any speck upon the lens is a **lenticular cataract;** and any little glistening appearance behind the capsule is spoken of as a **spurious cataract.**

Moreover, there are the **osseous,** the **cartilaginous,** and the **opaque cataracts;** but those distinctions rather concern the anatomist than the pathologist, as they may be guessed at, yet are not to be distinguished with certainty one from another, during life.

That which more concerns the reader is, to learn the manner, if possible, of preventing cataract from disfiguring his horse's eyes. Then will the gentleman be kind enough to hold a sheet of white paper close to his nose, so that the eyes may see nothing else, for a single half hour. Let us suppose the trial has been made. With many people the head has become dizzy and the sight indistinct. In some persons singing noises are heard and a sensation of sickness has been created. Let the author strive to explain this fact. Travelers, passing over the Alps, wear green veils, to prevent the strain or excitement which looking upon a mass of white snow occasions the visual organs. Any excitement is prejudicial to the eye. Workers at trades dealing in minute objects, often go blind, and the use of the miscroscope has frequently to be discontinued. But to look continuously upon a white mass is the most harmful of all other causes.

This fact must be considered as established. And what does the horse proprietor have done to his stable? He orders the interior to be whitewashed. It looks so clean, he delights to see it; but do the horses—does nature equally enjoy to look upon those walls of "spotless purity?" Before those walls, with its head tied to the manger, stands the animal through the hours of the day. Close to its nose shines the painful whiteness which the master so enjoys. Is it, then, surprising (seeing how nature for its own wise purposes has connected all life) that the equine eye, doomed to perpetual excitement, sometimes shows disease?

A horse with imperfect vision is a dangerous animal. A small speck upon the lens confuses' the sight as much as a comparatively large mark upon the cornea. To render this clear, let the reader hold a pen close to the eye; it prevents more vision than yonder huge post obstructs. So impediments are important, as they near the optic nerve. The lens is nearer than the cornea, and therefore any opacity upon the first structure is more to be dreaded.

However, let it be imagined a horse, with an opacity upon the pupil, and the sight confused by staring at a white flat mass spread out before it, is led forth for its master's use. By the aid of the groom and its own recollections, it manages to tread the gangway, and even to reach the well-known house door in safety. The owner, an aged gentleman, of the highest respectability, comes forth in riding costume. He mounts, and throwing the reins upon the neck of the animal, sets his nag into walking motion, while he, erect and stately, looks about him and proceeds to pull on his gloves. The horse, however, has not gone many steps before the cataract and the confused vision, acting conjointly, produce alarm. The steed shies and the gentleman loses his seat, being very nearly off. The passengers laugh, the proprietor suffers in his temper, but the whip is used, and the equestrian is soon out of sight.

The man and horse proceed some distance; the gentleman becomes much more calm, and the horse recovers sufficient composure to try and look around it. The pace now is rather brisk, when the horse thinks, or its disabled vision causes it to imagine, it sees some frightful object in the distance. The timid animal suddenly wheels round. The rider is not prepared for the eccentric motion: he is shot out of the saddle. He falls upon his head; he is picked up and carried home; but afterward he avoids the saddle.

Never buy the horse with imperfect vision; never have the interior of your stable whitewashed. Then what color is to be employed? Probably blue would absorb too many of the rays of light; at all events, it seems preferable to copy nature. Green is the livery of the fields. In these the eyes take no injury, although the horse's head be bent toward the grass for the greater number of the hours. Consequently, the writer recommends that green wash, which is cheap enough, should be employed, instead of the obnoxious white, for the interior of stables.

For complete cataract nothing can be done. In man, operation or couching may be performed with success; but the horse can retract the

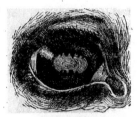

COMPLETE CATARACT.

eye and protrude the cartilago nictitans. Thereby difficulties are created; but these may be overcome. However, when an opening through the cornea is perfected, the spasmodic contraction of the muscles of the eye, acting upon the fibrous covering of the globe, is apt to drive forth the liquid contents of the organ in a jet: this is irreparable, of course. When so fearful a catastrophe does not ensue, still the capsule

of the lens is always difficult to divide, and the lens itself cannot easily be broken down. The lens, therefore, must be abstracted; but that necessitates a large incision, which the previously named probability forbids. Displacement is the only resort left; but the lens, when forced from its situation into the posterior or dark cavity, is, by the contraction of the muscles, forced up again. The uncertainty of the result, even when the operation is successfully performed, is peculiarly disheartening. Half lose their eyes in consequence of the attempt; half the remainder are in no way benefited; to the rest, as these cannot wear spectacles to supply the place of the absent lens, of course the pain endured becomes useless torture.

Where partial cataract is feared but cannot be detected, then arti-

DIAGRAM ILLUSTRATING THE ACTION OF BELLADONNA.

The inner space represents the natural pupil, on which no cataract is to be observed. The second space represents the pupillary opening as it may be enlarged by the application of belladonna, whereon two partial cataracts are to be remarked. The other space merely represents the dilated pupil.

ficially dilate the pupil. Rub down two drachms of the extract of belladonna in one ounce of water. Have this applied, with friction, to the exterior of the lids and about the eye; mind none gets into the eye. The belladonna, acted upon by the secretions, turns to grit; inflammation is the consequence, and the clearness of the cornea is impaired. When the belladonna is properly used, it dilates the iris and exposes the margin of the lens, thus enabling the practitioner to inspect the eye in a full light.

To tell a spurious cataract, which defect is never permanent, first observe the spot. Note if it present any metallic appearance, and try whether, as the horse's head is moved, it alters in shape, catching irregular lights. Then inspect the exterior of the eye; see if it retain any signs of recent injury. Subsequently endeavor, so far as may be possible, to ascertain the exact position occupied by the defect: upon all this evidence put together, make up your opinion.

To distinguish between the different kinds of cataract, apply the belladonna. Next place the horse near a window or under a door. Should the sun shine, have the animal led into the full glare of day. Look steadily into the eye from different points of view. Then have the horse's head moved about, all the time keeping your sight fixed upon the part you are desirous of inspecting.

Should one spot continue in every position, of one bulk, and of one aspect, never becoming very narrow and always occupying one place throughout the examination,—it is a lenticular cataract that is beheld.

If the whiteness changes appearances, in some positions seeming very thin or perceptibly less bulky, it is assuredly a capsular cataract which is inspected.

DIAGRAM ILLUSTRATING THE DIFFERENT KINDS OF CATARACT.

1. A capsular cataract or an opacity, situated on the envelope of the lens.
2. A lenticular cataract or an opacity, within the substance of the lens.
3. A spurious cataract, or a particle of lymph adhering to the inner surface of the lenticular capsule.

Most cataracts may either be partial or complete; but a spurious cataract is always partial, never permanent, and invariably caused by violence.

For spurious cataract, treat the injury to the exterior of the eye. For other cataracts, do nothing: there is no known medicine of any beneficial effect. However, it is well to add, the author's and the general opinion favors the absorption of cataract; or that these opacities may appear and after a time go away without the aid of medicine. Nevertheless, to hasten such a process, have the interior of the stable colored. However much in favor a clean white wall may be with grooms or with the lower order, exercise an informed judgment; have the wall shaded of the tint most pleasant to the inhabitants' sight, and the prospect of recovery will by so trivial an outlay be materially facilitated.

FUNGOID TUMORS WITHIN THE SUBSTANCE OF THE EYE.

These, fortunately, are rare affections. We know of no immediate cause for their production. No man can prophesy their appearance. The horse, to human judgment, may enjoy the top of health; may be in flesh and full of spirit—altogether blooming. Nevertheless, the action of the legs may perceptibly grow higher, and the ears become more active. The animal will wait to be urged or guided, when the road is

clear. Also, it may run into obstacles, when the rider does not touch
the rein. Should anything be left in the gangway of the stable, it is

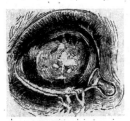

certain to be upset, by what the groom terms
"that clumsy horse." Sometimes it will
stand for hours together neglecting its food,
with the head held piteously on one side.
Occasionally, when at grass, it may be found
separated from its companions, alone and
dejected, with the head as before, held on
one side, while the waters of the eye copiously bedew the cheek.

FUNGUS HÆMATOIDES, OR CANCEROUS
GROWTHS WITHIN THE SUBSTANCE
OF THE EYE.

At last the eyes are examined. The eyeball may be clear, but some brilliant yellow
substance may be discerned shooting from the base of the interior, and
the horse is declared contaminated by a cancerous disease.

All is now explained : the sight is lost ; the horse is blind. There
are three terrible decisions now left to the master. Is the life to be
shortened? The thought shudders at taking existence, when misery
pleads for consolation. Is the animal to live on and nurture to maturity
the seeds of a cancerous disease? The mind shrinks from subjecting any
creature to the terrible depression and hopeless agony attendant upon
such disorders. Is an operation to be performed? Shall the surgeon
extirpate the eye? This last proposal seems the worst of all ; nor does
inquiry improve the prospect. The cancer does not entirely reside within
the eye ; it is not limited to that part. The taint is in the constitution,
and the operation can do no more than retard its effect. The eye removed, the cancerous growth will soon fill the vacant orbit. After two
or several months of dreadful suspense, the life at last will be exacted,
and the animal, worn out with suffering, will expire.

Under such circumstances, the writer recommends death, before the
full violence of the disease is endured. Should, however, the reader
think differently, and prefer the extirpation of the eyeball, the operation
will here be described. First, mind the operator has two knives not
generally kept by veterinary surgeons : one of small size and slightly
bent to one side ; the other larger, and curved to one side till it has
nearly reached a semicircle. Mind the operator has everything ready
before he begin : a sharp scalpel, two straight triangular-pointed needles,
each armed with strong twine ; one curved needle, similarly provided ;
sponge, water, injecting tube, bellows, lint,—and all things at hand. It
is necessary the proprietor should see to this, as some men will commence
an operation upon a mere horse and be obliged to stop in the middle, not
having brought all the instruments which they may require.

Cast the horse. Impale both eyelids, each with one of the straight needles, and leave the assistant to tie the thread into loops. Through these loops the assistant places the fore-finger of each hand, and then looks toward his superior. The sign being given, the man pulls the eyelid asunder, while the surgeon rapidly grasps the straight knife and describes a circle round the globe, thereby sundering the conjunctival membrane. The knife is then changed, the small curved blade being taken. The assistant again makes traction, and the knife, being passed through the divided conjunctiva, is carried round the eyeball, close to the bone; the levator and depressor muscles are detached by this movement. The assistant again relaxes his hold; the operator relinquishing the knife, selects the curved needle.

With this the cornea is transfixed. The thread is drawn through and is then looped. Into this loop the surgeon puts the fore-finger of his left hand, and giving the sign once more to his assistant, takes hold of the large bladed knife. Traction is made on all the loops. The curved knife is inserted into the orbit, and, with a sawing motion, is passed round the organ. The posterior structures are thereby divided, and the eye is drawn forth.

The operation ought to be over in less time than five minutes; but speed depends on previous prepara-

EXTIRPATION OF THE EYE.

tion. The assistant, during the operation, should rest his hand upon the horse's jaw and face; sad accidents by that means are prevented; but, above all things, he should be cool, doing just what is sufficient and no more.

Some hemorrhage follows the removal of the orb; to stop it, inject cold water into the empty socket; should that have no effect, drive a current of air from the bellows upon the divided parts; if this be of no avail, softly plug the cavity with lint, bandage the wound to keep in the dressing, and leave the issue to nature.

Such is the undisguised operation for extirpating the horse's eye. The reader is confidently asked, whether a few months of miserable existence, with the certainty of a fearful death, are not dearly purchased at so great a suffering?

LACERATED EYELID.

Horses frequently endeavor to amuse the weary hours by a playful game with one another; if accident results, it is not wholly the fault of the guileless animals; they are tied to the mangers; they cannot exert their activity; otherwise their principal enjoyment resides in the freedom of their heels. And looking at a blank mass of monotonous white for many hours may have disabled the sight or have confused the judgment.

The groom being absent, advantage is taken of the event to have a romp. The animals snap at one another over the divisions to their stalls; often the amusement extends, and four or five heads may be beheld united in the sport. Generally, however, the game is confined to two players; but, either way, no injury is meant; the teeth rattle, but they are intended to close upon empty space. However, man has to bear the consequences which his errors provoke. That species of confinement to which horses are subjected renders the judgment uncertain and the sight untrue. The animal pretends to snap, but, either from one head not being removed quick enough or from the other head being protruded too far, the teeth catch the eyelid and divide it through the center. The injury is not very serious, for had malice impelled the assault, much more than an eyelid would have been grasped between the jaws.

In other cases, the groom has driven nails into the wall of the gang-way; grooms are fond of seeing the stable decorated with pendant objects of various kinds. So long as the nails are occupied, little danger ensues; but they are apt to be left vacant, and horses are constantly passing along the gangway. To leave room for the servant obliges the animal, very often, to keep close to the wall; the projecting nail catches the lid of the eye, and a long rent, commencing upon the outer side, usually results.

EYELID TORN BY A NAIL.

Such an injury creates great alarm, but it is less serious than it appears to be. Let the wound, from whatever cause it springs, be well bathed with a soft sponge and cold water; this should be done till the bleeding ceases. Afterward, the wound should be let alone for two or three hours, that the edges may become partially sticky; then let there be procured a long piece of strong thread, having a needle at each end; the needles should be new, very sharp, and of the stronger sort employed by glovers. Let all the punctures be made from within outward, to avoid injuring the eyeball, and a separate needle be employed for each divided surface. The thread being brought through, cut off the needles, and loop, but do not tie the thread. Proceed with another suture, and do not tie that; then with another, observing the same directions, and thus, till the eyelid has a sufficient number of sutures. Then proceed to draw all to an even tightness—none should be absolutely tight. The parts ought only to be approximated, not tied firmly together; well, all the sutures being of equal size, they are fastened, and the operation is concluded.

But as the wound begins to heal it is apt to itch, and the horse will often rub the eye violently to ease the irritation. To prevent this, fasten the animal to the pillar-reins of its stall, and let it remain there till the wound has healed; the injury will in a short time close, but the sutures should be watched. When the holes begin to enlarge, the thread can be snipped. If the punctures be dry, let the divided sutures remain till nature shall remove them. If they are moist, and the wound appears united, you may try each thread with a pair of forceps; should any appear loose, then withdraw it, for after division it can be of no use, and may provoke irritation; however, should it be retained, employ no force; have patience, and it will come forth without man's interference.

Feed liberally, regulate the bowels by mashes and green meat; smear the wound with oil of tar to dispel the flies; for should the accident happen during the warmer months, these pests biting and blowing upon so delicate a part as the eye may occasion more harm than our best efforts can rectify. When the lid is bitten through, the operation is precisely similar; the divided edges are to be brought to-

THE LID, WHEN DIVIDED BY THE TEETH, BROUGHT TOGETHER BY MEANS OF SUTURES.

gether by sutures. To prevent needless repetition, an engraving of the bitten lid, after the operation has been performed, is here presented.

IMPEDIMENT IN THE LACHRYMAL DUCT.

The **lachrymal duct** in the horse is a small canal leading from the eye to the nostril; it commences by two very minute openings near the terminations of the upper and lower lids, at the inner corner of the eye; it emerges upon the dark skin which lines the commencement of the horse's nostril, being on the inner side of the internal membrane.

Its use is to carry off the superflux of tears; hence, with human beings, who have a like structure, "much weeping at the theaters provokes loud blowing of noses."

The channel being so minute, any substance getting into it soon be-

comes swollen with the moisture and closes the passage. The tears cannot escape, and being secreted, flow upon the cheek. The perpetual stream pouring over a part not designed for such uses, causes the hair to fall off, and thus forms gutters, along which the fluid continues to run. The flesh at length excoriates, and numerous sores are established; the lids swell and become raw at the margins; the conjunctiva reddens, and the transparency of the cornea is greatly lessened by the spread of inflammation.

A HORSE'S HEAD, DISPLAYING OB-
STRUCTION OF THE LACHRYMAL
GLAND.

The wretched animal in this condition presents a very sentimental appearance to a person ignorant of the facts of the case. The swollen lid, because of its weight, is permitted to close over the eye, while the tears, flowing fast upon the cheek, with the general dejection, gives the creature an aspect of weeping over some heavy affliction.

Like the late William Percivall, whose works on veterinary subjects remain a monument to his memory, the author has encountered but a single case of this description; it was in a matured but not a very aged animal. The report was, that a year ago it had been attacked by influenza; the lid then enlarged, and the near cheek had been wet ever since.

Referring to the pages of Percivall's "Hippopathology," the author procured a thin, elastic probe, about twelve inches long; the horse being cast, and an assistant holding the upper lid, the probe was introduced at the inner corner of the eye, by the lower opening to the duct; the entrance was easy enough, but the passage was soon obstructed; then the probe was inserted at the opening of the duct within the nostril. The way in this direction was longer, but the end came at last, without any good being effected. Next, a syringe being charged, the fine point was introduced up the nasal termination of the duct, the power of the jet effectually removing every impediment; the water streamed through the upper openings, and the horse was sent home cured.

The writer saw the animal six months subsequent to the operation; it was apparently in excellent health, and obviously in amended condition. The owner said the horse soon got well after it reached home; but, being pressed to say how great a duration "soon" represented, he re-joined "*about* six weeks, *perhaps.*"

Three months afterward, however, the horse was once more brought with "watery eye," and again operation was successful. The proprie-tor then received back and soon sold the creature, which being past the age when horses are most valuable, seemed likely to become an expen-sive retainer.

CHAPTER III.

EXCORIATED ANGLES OF THE MOUTH

LET no man punish a horse for want of obedience; the sole use of the creature and its only delight is to obey. Let no person abuse it for having a hard mouth, or for not answering to the rein Man had the formation of the mouth, and its condition can be no fault in the possessor; the horse's pleasure is the gratification of its master. Observe the antics of the nag thoroughly trained and perfectly up to the rider's point of jockeyship Does not every fiber seem to quiver with excess of happiness? There is a tacit understanding between man and horse; the pretty arts and graceful prancings of the animal tell how joyful it is made by the conviction that it is sharing man's amusement But let the equestrian dismount, and another, above or below the horse's educational point, assume the saddle, that understanding no longer exists. The harmony is destroyed; there is no intelligence between horse and man. All the playfulness disappears; the entire aspect of the animal is changed, and it sinks to a commonplace "ugly brute "

The majority of drivers are very particular about the horse's mouth; yet they all abuse the animal as though it was their desire to destroy that which each professes to admire. Every supposed error is punished with the lash, but the whip can convey no idea, the lash does not instruct the animal; beat a horse all day, and it will only be stupid at sunset. All the horse can comprehend from the smart is a desire that the pace should be quickened; that wish it endeavors to comply with The person who guides the vehicle generally becomes fanatic at such perversity; he begins "jagging" and "sawing" the reins. The iron is violently pulled against the angles of the mouth, or rapidly passes from one side to the other Would the owner or driver take the trouble to instruct his dumb servant in his wishes, the poor drudge would rejoice to exhibit its accomplishments But no information is communicated by first urging and then checking; the timidity is increased by the one, the angles of the mouth are excoriated by the other.

Ladies' horses invariably have admirable mouths; ladies generally are very poor equestrians, yet they encounter few accidents Men, who ride better, are oftener thrown and hurt The gentleness of the woman, or the sympathy existing between two gentle beings, produces this effect

(64)

The horse is never dangerous when not alarmed; the feminine hand pats the neck of the steed; the feminine voice assures the timidity; the whip never slashes; the reins are never converted into instruments of torture; the weight is light and the pace is easy. A perfect under-

VARIOUS MODES OF FORMING THAT WHICH ALL MEN SPEAK OF WITH ADMIRATION, AS A "GOOD MOUTH."

standing is soon established between the two, and the rider, notwithstanding her weakness, her indifferent jockeyship, and her flapping dress, sits the saddle in safety, while the animal increases in value under her care.

Man certainly does not gain by the contrast; the male treatment does not improve the animal. The horse's memory, like that of most dumb creatures, is very tenacious; the quadruped is not made more steady by ill usage; the sore corners of the mouth oblige the animal to be laid up "for a time," and the expense of medical treatment increases the sacrifice consequent upon loss of services.

Trouble attends the circumstance, at which the favorite groom is sure to grumble, even if the master does not receive "notice." The food must be prepared; a few oats thrown into the manger, and a little hay forked into the rack will not now suffice; all the provender must be carefully prepared. At first, good thick gruel and hay tea must be the only support. In a few days, boiled and mashed roots may be introduced; these may be followed by cut roots boiled, but not mashed, the whole being succeeded by scalded hay with bruised and mashed oats. When all is done however,

EXCORIATED ANGLES OF THE MOUTH.

5

the horse's temper is not improved, and its mouth is decidedly injured. Such results will vex the temper of any good groom, and very many it will anger to the throwing up of their situations. They "will not get a horse into beautiful condition for master only to spoil."

When the horse is thus injured, ignore all filthy ointments; such things consist of verdigris, carbonate of zinc, horse turpentine, blue, green or white vitriol, mixed up with dirty tallow or rank lard. Now, to grease a horse's teeth is not much worse than to tallow its lips; if the former prevent it from feeding, the latter is not calculated to improve the appetite.

Discarding all unguents, have the following lotion prepared:—

Chloride of zinc.	Two scruples.
Water	Two pints.
Essence of aniseed	A sufficiency.

Pour some of this into a saucer, and, with anything soft, apply the lotion to the sore places; do not rub or scrub; do your ministering gently; so the parts are wet, no further good can be accomplished; use this wash after every feeding or watering. In a little while amendment is generally perceptible; where violence has been used, it is impossible to foretell the extent of the injury. A superficial slough may be cast off; this process is attended with fetor; that the lotion will correct, and thus add to the comfort of the horse. The cure, however, will possibly leave the horse of a lessened value; where the skin has been destroyed it is never reproduced; the wound will, therefore, probably blemish, and may lead a future purchaser to suspect "all sorts of things." The horse is certainly deteriorated; with the skin the natural sensibility of the part is lost.

PERMANENT BLEMISH AND DESTRUCTION OF THE NICE SENSIBILITY OF THE MOUTH.

A cicatrix, consisting only of condensed cellular tissue, must form upon the spot; this structure is very feebly, if at all, nervous, and when compared to the smooth and soft covering of the lips, may be said to be without feeling, and is very liable to ulceration.

PARROT-MOUTH.

This, strictly speaking, is not a disease; it is a malformation; the upper incisors, from those of the lower jaw not being sufficiently developed, meet with no opposing members; they consequently grow very long, and from their form are likened to the bill of a parrot.

This formation is not unsoundness, but it cannot be a recommendation; the horse can only gather up its corn imperfectly; much falls from the mouth during mastication. The animal which requires four feeds and a half daily to support the condition another maintains upon four feeds, must be the more expensive retainer of the two. Moreover, it is a virtue in a horse to thoroughly clear out the manger; a healthy animal not only licks out corners to catch stray grains, but hunts among the straw for any corns that may have fallen. This duty the parrot-mouth disables a horse from performing; the good feeder alone is equal to the work.

COPIED FROM THE AU- THOR'S WORK, EN- TITLED "THE HORSE'S MOUTH," PUBLISHED BY MESSRS. FORES, PICCADILLY.

Besides, a rider is always pleased, when sauntering down the green lanes during the spring of the year, to see the horse's neck stretched out to catch a twig of the shooting hedge; this can do no harm; but it is hard alike upon horse and man to always have a tight hold of the rein when the fresh scent of the budding thorn tempts the mouth to its enjoyment. And yet, in the majority of instances, it would be cruelty to yield and permit the parrot-mouth to bite; the under teeth very often rest against the palate. No more need be said to caution owners pos- sessed of an animal thus afflicted, against a natural indulgence. The parrot-jaw is a deformity for the perpetuation of which man is respon- sible; dispositions and formations are hereditary. Would the owners of stock only exercise some judgment in their selections, this misfortune might speedily be eradicated.

LAMPAS.

The horse's lot is, indeed, a hard one; it is not only chastised by the master, but it also has to submit to the fancies of the groom. "Lam- pas" is an imaginary disease, but it is a vast favorite among stable attendants. Whenever an animal is "off its feed," the servant looks into the mouth, and to his

THE LAMPAS IRON.

own conviction discovers the "lampas." That affection is supposed to consist of inflammation, which enlarges the bars of the palate and forces them to the level of or a little below the biting edges of the upper incisor teeth.

Would the groom take the trouble to examine the mouths of other young horses which "eat all before them," the "lampas" would be ascertained to be a natural development; but the ignorant always act upon faith, and never proceed on inquiry. Young horses alone are sup- posed to be subject to "lampas;" young horses have not finished teething till the fifth year. Horses are "broken" during colthood; they are always placed in stables and forced to masticate dry, artificial food before all their teeth are cut; shedding the primary molars is especially painful; of course, during such a process, the animal endeavors to feed as little as possible. A refusal to eat is the groom's strongest proof that lampas is present. But, putting the teeth on one side, would it be surprising if a change of food and a total change of habit in a young creature were occasionally attended with temporary loss of appetite? Is "lampas" necessary to account for so very probable a consequence? The writer has often tried to explain this to stable servants; but the very ignorant are generally the very prejudiced. While the author has been talking, the groom has been smiling; looking most provokingly knowing, and every now and then shaking his head, as much as to say, "ah, my lad, you can't gammon me!"

Young horses are taken from the field to the stable, from juicy grass to dry fodder, from natural exercise to constrained stagnation. Is it so very astonishing if, under such a total change of life, the digestion becomes sometimes deranged before the system is altogether adapted to its new situation? Is it matter for alarm should the appetite occasionally fail? But grooms, like most of their class, regard eating as the only proof of health. They have no confidence in abstinence; they cannot comprehend any loss of appetite; they love to see the "beards wagging," and reckon the state of body by the amount of provision consumed.

The prejudices of ignorance are subjects for pity; the slothfulness of

BURNING FOR LAMPAS.

the better educated merits reprobation. The groom always gets the master's sanction before he takes a horse to be cruelly tortured for an imaginary disease. Into the hands of the proprietor has a Higher Power intrusted the life of His creature; and surely there shall be demanded a strict account of the stewardship. It can be no excuse for permitting the living sensation to be abused, that a groom asked and the master willingly left his duties to another. Man has no business to collect breathing life about him and then to neglect it. Every human being who has a servant, a beast or a bird about his homestead, has no right to rest content with the assertions of his dependents. For every benefit he is bound to confer some kindness. His liberality should testify to his superiority; but he obviously betrays his trust and abuses the blessings of Providence when he permits the welfare of the creatures, dependent on him, to be controlled by any judgment but his own.

The author will not describe the mode of firing for lampas. It is sufficient here to inform the reader that the operation consists in burning away the groom's imaginary prominences upon the palate The living and feeling substance within a sensitive and timid animal's mouth is actually consumed by fire. He, however, who plays with such tools as red-hot irons cannot say, "thus far shalt thou go." He loses all command when the fearful instrument touches the living flesh: the palate has been burnt away, and the admirable service performed by the bars, that of retaining the food during mastication, destroyed. The bone beneath the palate has been injured; much time and much money have been wasted to remedy the consequence of a needless barbarity, and, after all, the horse has been left a confirmed "wheezer." The animal's sense being confused, and its brain agitated by the agony, the lower jaw has closed spasmodically upon the red-hot iron; and the teeth have seized with the tenacity of madness upon the heated metal

When the lampas is reported to you, refuse to sanction so terrible a remedy; order the horse a little rest, and cooling or soft food. In short, only pursue those measures which the employment of the farrier's cure would have rendered imperative, and, in far less time than the groom's proposition would have occupied, the horse will be quite well and once more fit for service.

INJURIES TO THE JAW.

Save when needless severity urges timidity to madness, the horse is naturally obedient. This is the instinct of the race. The strong quadruped delights to labor under the command of the weaker biped. Its movements are regulated by him who sits above or behind it. It often waits for hours with its head pulled backward, its mouth pained, and its eyes blinded. All its learning is attention to the sounds of the human voice. It is guided by touches. It submits to the whip when it might easily destroy the whipper It eats, it drinks, it rests only by man's permission. Yet there are such words as "vice" and "spite" connected with the horse; but there remains to be spoken the word which shall fitly characterize the self-sacrificing life of the noble animal.

Man could not endure such tyranny, nor does the horse, notwithstanding its submissive instinct, live under it very long. The majority perish before they are eight years old. They are worked to an early grave—often they are distorted before the body's growth is completed. Is there any other life so serviceable? Is there any other life which reads so sad a moral? For the time it is allowed to breathe and labor, the horse patiently obeys its tyrant It aids his vanity; it conforms to his pleasure; it devotes strength, will, and life to man's service.

Let every owner of a horse treat his slave with gentleness. Above all things, let no individual employ the reins as instruments of torture. The horse will neither be wiser nor better for such a mode of punishment. Besides, the man may deteriorate his own or another's property. With the bit a jaw has been broken; and with the snaffle the bone has been injured. An animal with a good neck carries the chin near to the chest. The iron of the snaffle, therefore, cannot pull against the angles of the mouth. It rests upon the gums, and because this point is by some disputed, the following illustration of the fact is inserted.

THE SNAFFLE BEARING UPON THE LOWER JAW.

The cruel bit is, however, in general use with carriage horses. Fashion delights in a vehicle stopped smartly at a door. The greatest noise possible then announces the new arrival. The wheels grate— the horses struggle. The coachman pulls hard—the vehicle sways to and fro. The footman jumps down and pulls at the bell as though life and death depended on a speedy answer to his summons.

All this is, doubtless, very pleasant, but how does it operate upon the poor horses? These, to be pulled up suddenly, must be thrown upon their haunches by the unscrupulous use of the bit. The pressure often wounds more than the gums; frequently the bone of the lower jaw is bruised. The gum then must slough, and a portion of bone must be cast off. The exfoliation of bone is a tedious process accompanied with an abominable stench. The surgeon must be constantly in attendance; otherwise the gum might close over the exfoliating bone and numerous sinuses might be established within the mouth. The exfoliated substance must come away. The abscess, which would announce its retention, would be more painful than the open wound, and ultimately would turn to a foul and ragged ulcer. Such an injury may occur wherever the bit rests, before or behind the tush, and a similar injury, though not to the same extent, will result from an unscrupulous use of the snaffle.

THE EFFECTS PRODUCED ON THE LOWER JAW BY THE ENERGETIC USE OF THE SNAFFLE OR BIT.

The most forward and smaller mark indicates the injury usually done by pulling at the snaffle. The more backward dark place indicates the spot where tugging at the bit bruises the bone of the lower jaw.

Supposing a case of this description is submitted to your notice upon the day succeeding its occurrence. No change is anticipated, such as would denote a bruise to other structures. The covering to the gums is thick and hard, and it will conceal much that may be taking place beneath it. If any spot be darker, redder, or whiter in color,—if any place be more sensitive than the adjacent parts, the knife is there inserted till it grate upon the bone. The extent of the necessary incision is decided by the efforts made in resistance. A thin fluid may issue from the orifice; but when the knife grates upon the bone, then the animal's struggles announce the extent of the bruise. Sound bone may be cut, scraped, or even burnt with impunity; but when bruised or otherwise diseased, the structure is most acutely sensitive.

When the wound emits its characteristic odor, a lotion composed of chloride of zinc, one scruple; water, one pint; ess. of aniseeed a sufficiency, should be syringed into the openings, several times during the day. The lotion, also, has a tendency to heal the sores, which must be counteracted by the employment of the knife. Occasionally, however wide the incision, it may be too small for the cast off bone to escape from. The knife again must enlarge the orifice, and the forceps be inserted to grasp the exfoliated substance. That taken away, the lotion is continued and the injury left to heal at Nature's pleasure.

INJURY SOMETIMES ACCOMPLISHED WITH THE PORT OF THE BIT.

The late W. Percivall, in his excellent work, entitled "Hippopathology," describes horses as sometimes injured under the tongue by the port of the bit. An engraving, representing such an injury, is given; but it is hoped no gentleman of the present day would employ the severe invention by which alone such a hurt could be produced. The consequences may be lasting. The terminations of the sublingual ducts are included in the blackness. Were these bruised and inflamed, their delicate mouths might be obliterated and hopeless fistula be established.

The bit must be sharply and strongly tugged at before it can harm the roof the mouth. Any one who has seen horses pulled up before a fashionable mansion must have observed them open wide their mouths. They do this to escape the wound of the bit. The animals extend their jaws to prevent it striking the roof of the mouth. Notwithstanding the existing age is more civilized than those which preceded it, the bits used at the present time can, without any vast display of genius, be made to injure the obedient animal, for whose mouth

THE UPPER JAW INJURED BY THE BARBAROUS USE OF THE BIT.

such ferocious checks are forged. An injury thus inflicted is sufficiently serious. The bony roof not only supports the bars, but also forms the solid floor of the nostrils. As it is not very thick, the greater is the danger when it is injured. The wound, because of the unyielding substance on which it is inflicted, is more painful than that of the lower jaw. It is also for the same reason more severe.

The last injury demands the same treatment as has already been described, only the remedies are far more difficult to apply. Should the entire portion of bone exfoliate and a hole be left behind, the consequence is not of fatal import. Bone can reproduce itself, though it is somewhat eccentric in its growth. So after the opening is closed, the surface toward the nostrils may be uneven, and the horse be rendered an inveterate wheezer.

When the animal is once injured, never, for your own safety, afterward employ a bit. If it be ridden or driven, always use a snaffle, and use even that most tenderly. The horse has vivid recollections, and man is naturally forgetful. When power is entrusted to the oblivious, danger is apt to be close at hand.

The inferior margin of the jaw-bone is liable to harm from the curb chain, and some men *will* have the curb chain tight. Such people are commonly very imperious. They shout, and slash, and tug when they want obedience from an animal whose delight is to be allowed to please. Their meaning is seldom comprehended, and therefore their orders are rarely obeyed; whereas, they would be humbly propitiated, were their commands only given as though the animal had no interest to rebel.

The result of such violence is, from the curb chain being ruthlessly

TUMOR PROVOKED BY THE ABUSE OF THE CURB CHAIN.

jerked, the jaw-bone soon enlarges. A portion of the bone having been bruised, has to exfoliate; a foul abscess forms; tumor speedily succeeds to tumor; osseous structure is thrown out and a swelling is matured, before the enlargement heals.

The treatment of such a case is similar to that already directed. Keep the wound freely open, to permit the unimpeded exit of exfoliated bone. Use the lotion, previously directed, liberally and constantly. The healing process may then take place without deformity being left behind.

APHTHA.

Nothing proves the sympathy which binds nature more strongly than the sameness or similarity of the diseases that affect man and animals. Tetanus, pneumonia, enteritis, etc. are so alike as to be the same in the human being and in the horse. From the cow was derived the safe-guard from the ravages of the small-pox, and the medical profession has, by its want of feeling, more than recognized a likeness, linking humanity to the dog; in the motive which alone could prompt abuse of a most affectionate animal.

It is a sad proof of the stubbornness of pride, that a unity, thus enforced by suffering, should be ignored, as though it were an insult to the superior. No compact, founded by nature, can be dependent upon man's liking. The terms may be laughed at, scorned or denied, but these exist. Man is declared in affliction to be the companion of other life. When will this truth be acknowledged, and the entire family of nature live in one brotherhood?

Aphtha is a human disorder as well as an equine disease. It generally appears in spring and autumn, being produced by heat of body. May not a slight attack of aphtha sometimes explain that which the groom intends by lampas? At all events, aphtha is accompanied by dullness and a refusal to feed. Both lips commonly swell as the lethargy increases; the tongue tumefies, becomes decidedly red, and generally hangs out of the mouth, partly for the sake of coolness, partly to accommodate its enlarged size. Around the mouth little lumps break forth, which at first are stony hard, and others, though of a larger size, may be felt upon the tongue. Vesicles are soon developed

APHTHA.

from these spots, and each contains a small quantity of clear gelatinous fluid. The bladders burst; crusts form; and by the time these fall off, the complaint has disappeared.

Some good thick gruel and a few boiled roots, which should be repeatedly changed, must constitute the nourishment while the disease lasts, or during the period that the mouth is sore. No medicine; a little kindness is now worth a ship load of drugs. When the pimples are about to burst, the following may be prepared:—

Borax	Five ounces.
Boiling water	One gallon.
Honey or treacle	Two pints.

When the mixture has cooled, hold up the horse's head and pour half a pint into the mouth　Half a minute afterward remove the hand; allow the head to fall and the fluid to run out of the lips　This mixture should be used several times during the day.　Beyond this nothing is needed, excepting a cool, loose box, a good bed, body and head clothing, with flannel bandages, not too tight, about the legs.　Work should on no account be sanctioned until the last vestige of the disorder has vanished, and its attendant weakness has entirely disappeared.

LACERATED TONGUE.

Men who become proprietors of animal life undertake a larger responsibility than the generality of horse owners are willing to admit. They are answerable for their own conduct toward the dumb existence over which they are legally invested with the right of property; they are also morally accountable for the conduct of those to whose charge they entrust their living possessions.　The appearance of those men who congregate about the stable doors of the rich is not very prepossessing. Their looks express cunning far more than goodness　Their long narrow heads denote none of that wisdom which alone can comprehend and practice kindness for its own sake　Their eyes and actions have a quickness at sad variance with the affected repose of their manners. Their dress declares a vanity, that is much opposed to the humility in which a wise man loves to confide.

There is nothing about horses which should degrade men; yet it cannot be denied, that the vast majority of stable men are rogues.　How can this be accounted for?　Is it difficult to understand, when we see the unlimited trust put into a groom's hands, and the common abuse of confidence by the man who enjoys it?　No slave proprietor possesses the power with which the groom is invested.　It is true, the slave owner can lash the flesh he terms his property.　However, there is in humanity a voice which puts some limit to the ill usage of the negro.　The groom can beat and beat again, at any time or in any place.　No voice can be raised in appeal to nature.　The groom's charge lives beneath him, and day or night is exposed to his tyranny.　He may chastise the body and steal the food, still, so no human eye detect, the horse will quietly look upon the wronger it never can accuse.

A good man would seek far, before he would repose so large a trust in another person.　The *gentleman* generally engages the groom after a trivial questioning　His desire is to have a servant entirely corrupt; one who asserts a knowledge how to *trick* animals into health　No examination is made into the real character of the applicant　A vast confidence is off-hand reposed in an individual who may be without a single moral attribute: Who deserves blame for such an abuse of responsibility? He who has been educated into knowingness, and, having become thoroughly degraded, esteems himself fully qualified for the situation he demands to fill, or he who, having the benefit of education, and being blessed with leisure for self-inquiry, shirks his duty and transfers his authority to unworthy hands?

Every groom fancies he knows how to compound something he calls a condition ball,—that is, a certain mixture of drugs, which shall bring a living body suddenly into "tip-top" health. A bevy of companions are invited to see "Jim give a ball." They duly arrive, and part of the horse's tongue is speedily made to protrude from the mouth, this portion being firmly held by "Jim's" free hand. The condition ball is in "Jim's"

STICKING TO A HORSE.

other hand, and the exhibition consists in the marvelous adroitness with which the ball can be introduced between the animal's jaws. The horse soon sympathizes with the excitement that surrounds it. Jim, "quick as lightning," makes a thrust with the ball, whereupon the startled animal raises the head and retreats. "Stick to him, Jim!" "stick to him!" shout the visitors. Jim does stick to him until his hand is covered with blood, or, without quitting its gripe, suddenly loses the resistance, which constituted its hold. Should it be the former, the frœnum of the tongue is ruptured, and a wetted sponge soon clears the hand of the groom as well as the mouth of the horse. A general curse and a kick under the belly of the rebellious steed end the amusements for one day. Should it be the latter, Jim finds the larger portion of the quadruped's tongue left in his hand. This is an awful accident. The blood is wiped off, and the groom next morning goes to his master with, "Please, sir, see what 'Fugleman' has done in his sleep!"

A farmer engages a pretty-looking stable boy. The young scamp is sufficiently a groom to glory in nothing so much as deception. The farmer, however, takes this pretty boy to the fair, where an additional horse is purchased. With the new "dobbin" the boy is entrusted, being cautioned to lead it gently home With numerous protestations boy and horse depart, but have barely reached the suburbs before the knowing youngster stops "dobbin," and, twisting the halter in " a chaw," leads the animal to the nearest gate, where the lad climbs upon its back.

"A chaw" is the slang short phrase for something to chew. This is made by twisting the halter into the animal's mouth so as to encircle the jaw. In this position the rope is thought by some knowing people to answer the purposes of a bridle To this rope the boy hangs, rolling to either side; now, nearly off—and now, jerked from his seat, as "dobbin," after repeated urgings, starts off into the lazy pretense at a trot

Anything inserted into a horse's mouth provokes the curiosity of the animal It is felt and poked about with the tongue, till at last the lingual organ is, by the exercise of much ingenuity, inserted beneath the obstacle. In this state of affairs, "dobbin" and the pretty boy finish the latter half of the journey. The youngster laughing, as the rough action of the horse bumps him up and down, he all the time dragging at the halter. Before home is reached, night has set in; the boy dismounts, and with all the simplicity his face can assume leads "dobbin" to the homestead.

The boy is protesting about being so very tired after his long walk, when the horse's mouth is discovered to be stained with blood The youthful expression of surprise exceeds that of the elder's. Next the halter is found to be rich with the same fluid. The horse's mouth is then opened, it is full of blood, and the tongue nearly cut through. Accusations are made against the lad; at first they are replied to with defiance; at last they are propitiated with tears, drawn forth by the idea of honesty being suspected. Youthful knowing, however, is not in the long run a match for the self-interest of age; and perseverance is rewarded by a full confession.

"The chaw" is an artifice recognized in every stable. Grooms have their tastes. It is very unpleasant to these gentry when they behold some unmannerly horse hang back in the halter. Stalls are drained into a main channel, situated at the edge of the gangway. The pavement on which the animal stands consequently slants from the manger to the footpath. This nice arrangement obliges the horse always to stand with the toes in the air and throws the weight of the body upon the back sinews. To ease its aching limbs the animal is apt to go to the extent of its rope, so as to place the hind feet upon the gangway, and even occasionally to give the toe an opposite direction by allowing it to sink into the open drain. Such presumption horrifies the groom's sense of propriety. The ignorant mind's idea of beauty is "everything to match." He thinks all is so nice when the animals dress to a line, like soldiers on parade. To have this line preserved, even in his absence, he puts "a chaw" into the refractory "brute's" mouth. This chaw is to be preserved night and day. The tongue soon gets under the rope. Timidity is rendered yet more fearful

ABUSE OF THE HALTER.

by persecution. The voice of the groom has become a terror to the quadruped. It hangs back for ease, and is surprised by the vehement exclamation of the tormentor. Back goes the neck and up goes the head. The animal runs to its manger, but something has fallen upon the floor! The horse was luxuriating in hanging back to the full extent when surprised. The sudden start jerked the halter rein, and the result is the free portion of the tongue falls from the mouth, severed by the rope.

These are lamentable instances of the general behavior of grooms to the creatures entrusted to their care. Nothing is so corruptive as misplaced authority. A little mind knows no difference between the possession of power and the indulgence of tyranny. The use and the abuse are synonyms to the ignorant; and the sins committed principally reside with him who places the life Heaven has entrusted to his care in such unworthy custody.

When a tongue is partially divided, do not insert sutures of any kind. Metallic sutures wound the fleshy palate, and silk sutures soon slough out. Neither, therefore, does good, and each serves to confine the food which enters the division. Foreign matter irritates a wound and retards its healing. Consequently, do nothing to the tongue when partially divided. Feed the patient on gruel until the healing is complete, and wash out the mouth thrice daily, with some chloride of zinc lotion, one scruple of the salt to a pint of water, after the manner described in the preceding article.

THE TONGUE HEALED AFTER HAVING BEEN DEEPLY CUT BUT NOT SUNDERED.

The jaw has been divided to show the injured tongue, as it would appear in the mouth.

a. The indentation at the seat of injury, and which will remain so long as life shall continue.

Should the tongue be separated to that extent which divides the vessels, then, with a knife remove the lacerated part, which otherwise being deprived of support, must slough off. Still do nothing to the tongue afterward. Feed on thick gruel and wash out the mouth with the lotion. A horse with half a tongue will manage to eat and drink, but some food is spilt and some left in the manger. Constant dribbling of saliva is the chief consequence of such an injury. This is unpleasant, and arises from deglutition being injured. A horse which has had the tongue lacerated only, but not divided, forever retains the evidence of the injury; and as the food is apt to accumulate at the point of union, the animal ever after demands attention subsequent to every meal.

TEETH.

No fact is more discreditable to humanity than the small attention it has wasted upon the beautiful lives entrusted to its charge. Mortal pride asserts these creatures are given man for his use. Yes. But is the full use obtained? Are not the lives sacrificed? The horse has been the partner of mankind from the earliest period. For centuries at least the animal has been watched throughout the day; yet, even at this time, equine disorders are only beginning to be understood. Does this fact denote that care which such a charge demanded?

Cutting the permanent teeth seems, in the horse, to be effected at some expense to the system; it was a favorite custom with the farriers of the last century to trace numerous affections to the teething of the animal. Further inquiries have proved our grandfathers knew positively nothing about those growths, concerning which they assumed so much. The late W. Percivall traced sickness in the horse to irritation, arising from cutting of the tushes; there, however, our knowledge ends. Veterinarians have not, as a rule, either leisure or the necessary power to observe those animals it is their province to treat; they generally are but passing visitors to the stables into which they are called. Those who have studs of horses nominally placed under their charge feel they are retained not to watch, but to physic the animals to which the groom directs their attention.

The tushes of the upper jaw may, however, be fully up, and yet not have appeared in the mouth; this fact is easily explained. The advent of the tushes provoked acute inflammation of the membrane covering the jaw. The horse was cured of the attendant constitutional symptoms, but the cause of the disorder was mistaken. The acute inflammation changed into chronic irritation. The membrane, which in the first instance should have been lanced, thickened and imprisoned the tush beneath it; an incision is even now the only remedy, and should instantly be made.

Neither tushes nor incisors are known to be exposed to other accidents; it is, however, different with the molar teeth. These teeth consist of three components; bone or ivory constitutes the chief bulk of the organ, and over that is spread a thin covering of inorganic enamel, the whole being invested with a fibrous coating of crusta petrosa. The enamel is the material on which the tooth depends for its cutting properties; the manner in which the edge is preserved deserves attention, for the brick-layer's trowel appears to have been suggested by it. A thin coat of hard but brittle enamel is held between the two other bulky and tough substances, just as a thin layer of steel is protected by coatings of yielding iron in the house-builder's instrument.

The highly organized crusta petrosa is often injured; to understand this, we must first comprehend the vast power which urges the jaw of the horse. The motion resides entirely in the lower portion of the skull, which is moved by strong, very strong muscles, going direct from their attachments to their insertions. No force is lost by the arrangement, and no less a motor power was required to comminute the hays and oats on which the horse subsists. The machinery seems to be admirably adapted to its purposes; and to be so strongly framed as to defy all chance of injury. Man, however, has a mighty talent for evil; it does not always suit the convenience of the groom to sift the pebbles from the grain; corn and stones are hastily cast into the manger, and the poor horse, having no hands to select with, must masticate all alike. The reader can imagine the wrench which will ensue, when a flint suddenly checks the movement of the molar teeth. The crusta

A HORSE WITH TOOTHACHE.

petrosa is bruised upon the large fang of the tooth. Disease is established, and sad toothache has soon to be endured.

Then there are the effects of the powerful acids in much favor with most grooms and too many veterinary surgeons; moreover, there are the sulphates, which in every possible form enter into veterinary medicine; the nitrates, likewise, are much esteemed, and are given in enormous doses. All of these much affect the crystalline enamel of the molar tooth; a small hole is first

A HORSE QUIDDING, OR ALLOWING THE FOOD TO FALL FROM ITS MOUTH SUBSEQUENT TO MASTICATION.

formed; into this the food enters and there putrifies; caries and toothache are the result.

A horse with toothache upon certain days sweats and labors at its work; saliva hangs in long bands from the under lip; the countenance is utterly dejected; the head is carried on one side or pressed against some solid substance, as a wall. The food is "quidded"—that is, it is partially masticated, when, from acute agony, the jaws relax, the teeth separate, the lips part, and the morsel falls from the mouth, more or less resembling what is termed "a quid of tobacco."

Upon other days the animal is bounding with life and spirits; the movements are light, and the motions are expressive of perfect happiness. The head is carried jauntily; the lips are compressed; the saliva ceases to exude; the food is devoured with an evident relish, and the general health appears to be better than it was before the strange disease. The continuance of such bliss is, however, very doubtful; the different stages will often succeed one another with vexatious rapidity.

If nothing be done, the horse alternates between anguish and happiness for an unascertained period, when all acute symptoms apparently cease. The lips, though no longer actually wet, are not positively dry; the food is often eaten; but as time progresses a sort of gloom hangs about the animal, and deepens every day. The horse seems never free from some unaccountable torture; more time is now occupied in clearing the manger; then the hay may be consumed, but the oats remain untouched. These last are found soaked in apparent water; the fluid turns out to be saliva; the symptoms by degrees become more severe; a strangely unpleasant odor characterizes the breath; the flesh wastes, and the animal ultimately exhibits hide-bound.

This stage being attained, and the proprietor becoming much perplexed, he is one morning informed by the groom, who displays many nods and winks, of a certain mysterious receipt for a wonderful ball that never fails, but always cures. The potent bolus is sent for to the chemist,

A MOLAR TOOTH HAS BECOME VERY LONG FROM THE WANT OF ATTRITION IN THE OPPOSING JAW.

and, after sundry explanations, is compounded. The groom, stiff with pride, takes the magic morsel; it is pushed rapidly into the horse's mouth; an exclamation from the man follows the disappearance of the hand, which is retracted bathed in blood.

To afford time for the writer to explain this incident, the reader must vouchsafe some patience. The horse's molar teeth are miniature grindstones. To supply the wear and tear of so violent a service, the molar teeth, originally, have enormous fangs, and, as the eating surface is worn away, the fangs are thrust into the mouth by the contraction of the jaw-bones.

Caries at first pains, but at last destroys all feeling or life in the tooth; the dead organ ceases to possess any vital quality; it loses all power of self-preservation, and is a mere piece of dead matter opposed to a living agent. In consequence, it breaks away, while the opposing molar projects more forward from the absence of attrition. The healthy tooth at last bears against the unprotected gum, upon which it presses severely, and provokes the greatest agony. The animal endeavors to prevent the prominent tooth from paining the jaw by masticating entirely upon the sound side. Hunger is slowly, and perhaps

THE MOLAR TEETH HAVE BEEN GROUND SLANT-ING, AND HAVE SHARP EDGES, FROM THE HORSE MASTICATING ONLY UPON ONE SIDE.

never, satisfied by such imperfect comminution; the outside of the upper molars and the inside of the lower molars become slanting; the first being almost as sharp as razors, wound the membrane of the mouth and lay open the hand which is thrust into the cavity.

If the disease be still neglected and permitted to increase, the stench grows more formidable; nasal gleet appears; the discharge is copious, accompanied by a putrid odor; osseous tumors commence; the bones of the face are distorted; the eye is imprisoned, and ultimately obliterated within the socket by actual pressure; eating becomes more and more painful, until starvation wastes the body and reduces the horse to a hide-bound skeleton.

If such a case be taken early, its cure is easy and certain; the dead tooth must be extracted, and the prominent molar shortened, by means of the adjusting forceps and the guarded chisel, invented by Mr. T. W. Gowing, veterinary surgeon, of Camden Town. Then the sharp edges must be lowered by the tooth-file, and if these things appear to occupy time, it is better done at two or even three operations, than unduly prolong the agony of a sick animal. This being accomplished, all is not ended; the horse's mouth must, from time to time, be again and again operated upon; nor will the creature offer much opposition to the proceeding, if only proper gentleness be observed.

Aged horses, from the contraction of the lower jaw, (which change is natural to increase of years in the equine race,) frequently have their upper molars ground to a knife-like sharpness. They wound the inside of the cheeks, cause a disinclination to eat, and provoke a dribbling of saliva. The cure is the tooth-file, which should be applied until the

6

natural level is attained.   This should be followed by the frequent use
of the wash recommended for *aphtha,* or by the chloride of zinc lotion.

It may probably provoke a laugh among gentlemen and horsemen to
read of toothache in the horse.   Few, very few grooms may have witnessed or have noticed such a disease, but the fact exists; it is, indeed,
a cruel reality to the animal which experiences it.   The ignorance of
stable men can establish nothing, for they are, as a class, equally pre-
sumptuous and ignorant; they have seen the horse for years, and yet are
acquainted with neither the natural ailments nor the proper treatment of
the animal.   The toothache is to the creature a most agonizing disorder.   We have only to look at the healthy horse, to observe how
exquisitely it is clothed, how finely it is framed, to imagine how sensitive must be the body.   The horse seems capable of a fear the most
cowardly of mankind never conceived.   So its face, though not made for
expression, can denote an anguish which the human mind fortunately has
no capacity to picture.   The eye is often painful in its speaking.   It
embodies a desperation, a weariness of the world, and a prayer for
death, such as few people comprehend; or the cry would rise, from the
length and breadth of the land, demanding, as with one voice, the more
Christian treatment of man's fellow-creature

SCALD MOUTH.

This is an accident which occasionally occurs where grooms are too
ignorant, or too thoughtless to read the direction labeled upon every
bottle sent into the stable.   Potent fluids are sometimes transmitted
pure, in small bottles, though the custom is highly reprehensible; nor is the
practice bettered because the label orders the contents to be mixed with
water before the medicine is administered to the horse.   Grooms are
generally careless, and proverbially in a hurry; one of them enters the
stable to give the drench, sees the bottle, seizes it in haste, calls the helper
nearest the stable door, and, with such assistance, pours the liquid fire
down the animal's throat.

The mouth is by the potent drug deprived of its lining membrane, and
the stomach is lastingly injured; even if the dose be too small to occasion death, the interior of the mouth is rendered raw   Fortunate is the
man who can be certain the evil there begins and extends no farther;
but who can calculate the effect upon delicate, internal organs?   The
mouth may be healed, but who can ascertain the state of the deeper injury?   Animals are treated as though their sensibilities were not affected
by any medium pain; something must be visible before the groom sanctions the right in his charge to be restless   All signs and motions

denoting a gnawing agony, but not expressive of overpowering anguish, are visited with chastisement.

The groom is not entirely to blame. The fault resides with his superiors, whom the servant apes. The sin rests with those who (unable to keep a stud-groom) think their duty is discharged by a daily scamper through the stable before they go to business; with those who by their manners corrupt the groom's simplicity, while by a strange costume they induce the ignorant fellow to regard the badge of his disgrace as the upholder of his pride. To the upper classes, the shortcomings of stable men cling; with the superiors, whose example should instruct, rests the real blame of the servant. With educated men abide the errors of the ignorant.

After a scalding drench, an unusual redness declares the state of the mouth; a quantity of saliva flows from the restless lips, which are constantly in motion; they are being moved perpetually up and down, and are always parting with a smack. The food, for a time, is rejected, but good gruel, if cold, is generally taken freely. Boiled roots should constitute the nourishment for two months afterward, the mouth being all the while washed with the application recommended for aphtha.

SCALD MOUTH.

No immediate danger is to be apprehended from scald mouth. The stomach is more disposed to assume chronic than acute disease. Probably the temporary services of the animal might well be dispensed with, and much might be gained by an extra months' continuance of the prepared food. At all events, the experiment would be intended to ward off a possible evil; and, if we are to believe at all the motive, being based on goodness, the act would not be without its reward.

CHAPTER IV.

THE NOSTRILS—THEIR ACCIDENTS AND THEIR DISEASES.

COLD.

It should not excite surprise if the horse, though generally strong, and exposed to every abuse, is occasionally subject to the disease which, in man, is almost the property of the delicately nurtured. The

SELLING "A CAPTAIN," AS ANY HORSE WITH A NASAL DISCHARGE IS CALLED BY THE LOW DEALERS.

animal exists in a stable commonly kept at a high temperature by means of contaminated air; it is taken thence into a wintry atmosphere to stand for an uncertain period before the master's door. There it has to remain inactive, shivering in the blast, until it suits the proprietor's convenience to come forth; next, it is pushed along till the perspiration bedews the sides. Then it has to remain, generally unprotected, in the cold until some business is transacted, when it is flurried home again, and often has to wait afterward till it suits the groom's leisure to dry the reeking frame.

Can it create astonishment if an animal so treated exhibit that nasal affection denominated "cold?" The case is similar with hunters. They leave hot stables to join the distant meet. Game may be soon started, or "the find" may occupy hours; at last, men, horses, and hounds scamper off; the fences are cleared; the fields, though they be swampy or plowed, are crossed at the longest stride. The pace is killing while it lasts; at length, comes a check. That saves many a steed, whose breathing ability was well nigh exhausted; but every animal has to shiver till the "view holloa!" again summons the assembly to motion.

How often does my lady's "carriage stop the way?" And how long have the horses to stand in the rain before it does go? How frequently does the gig or brougham linger near the curb, while another glass to good fellowship is drained? Then, we have to reflect upon the breathing forms harnessed to hired carriages; how the street cab rests in storms! How, day or night, the horses must be exposed to all the varied seasons! Unsheltered from the sun; with no protection from the frost! Let the reader reflect upon this and say, not if it be wonderful that a few horses exhibit the affection denominated cold; but whether it is not a legitimate matter for surprise every second horse is not thus affected?

A mild cold, with care, is readily alleviated. A few mashes, a little green meat, an extra rug and a day or two of rest, commonly end the business. When the attack is more severe, the horse is dull; the coat is rough; the body is of unequal temperatures, hot in parts, in places icy cold. The membrane of the nose at first is dry and pale or leaden colored; the facial sinuses are clogged; the head aches; the appetite has fled; often tears trickle from the eyes, simple ophthalmia being no rare accompaniment to severe cold; till at length a

A HORSE'S HEAD, EXHIBITING A COLD.

copious defluxion falls from the nostrils without immediately improving the general appearance of the animal.

The treatment is plain. When mucous membrane is involved, all depletion must be avoided; the invalid should be comfortably and warmly housed; should have an ample bed, and the body should be plentifully clothed. Then a hair bag, half as long and half as wide again as the ordinary nose-bag, should be buckled by a broad strap on to the sick horse's head; into the bag should be previously inserted one gallon of yellow deal saw-dust; upon the saw-dust, through an opening guarded with a flap upon the side of the bag, should be emptied a kettle of boiling water, the superfluity of which may run or drain through the hair composing the bag.

The boiling water ought to be renewed every twenty minutes, as the bag should be retained upon the head for an hour each time. Should not yellow deal saw-dust be obtainable, procure some of common deal,

STEAMING THE NOSE OF A HORSE WITH COLD.

upon which last pour one ounce of spirits of turpentine. Mix well and thoroughly before you apply the bag to the head; but should not a proper apparatus be in the stable, then it is better to forego the steaming, as the common nose-bag is far too short and too tight for safety. The cloth moreover is apt to swell and not to allow the free passage of the water. Sad accidents have ensued upon the incautious employment of the ordinary nose-bag for steaming purposes.

If the horse appear to be weak, and there is the slightest suspicion that the weight of the appliance for the time directed may tax the strength, let some substance, as a stool, a form or chair, be placed beneath the bag. The animal will require no teaching to understand the use of the intended resting-place. As the weight begins to drag, the head will be lowered, and after a very brief space the steaming apparatus will be found reposing upon its intended support.

While the membrane is dry, use the steaming-bag six times daily. When a copious stream of pus flows from the nose, its application thrice daily will be sufficient. At the same time let the food consist of grass with mashes, to regulate the bowels and subdue the attendant fever. Give no medicine; but the discharge being established, three daily feeds of crushed and scalded oats, with a few broken beans added to them, will do no harm. Likewise, should the weakness be great, a couple of pots of stout, one pot at night and the other at morning, will be beneficial. Good nursing, a loose box, fresh air, warmth, and not even exercise till the disorder abates, are also to be commended. Afterward take to full work with caution, as much debility is apt to ensue upon severe cold. It will also sometimes lead to other diseases, as those of the larynx, air-passages, and lungs. Should the symptoms deepen, the treatment must be changed; the lesser affection (cold) being swallowed up by the greater disorder, which is superadded; consequently, disregard the original ailment, taking those measures requisite to relieve the new and more important affliction.

Animals with **chronic cold,** or with a constant running from the nose, soon exhibit excessive weakness. Nothing taxes the strength so much as the prolonged disorder of any mucous surface.

All that ignorant people know of glanders is, that the disease is accompanied with a nasal defluxion. The more cunning in horse flesh, likewise, are aware that glanders causes the lymphatic gland within the jaw to swell, or that a glandered horse is always, as such people assert, jugged.

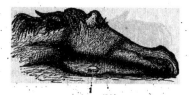

HEAD OF A HORSE WITH "A JUG," OR WITH ONE OF THE LYMPHATIC GLANDS OF THE THROAT SWOLLEN.

1. The enlarged lymphatic within the jaw.

Now, both the discharge and the enlargement are generally present during inveterate cold. Animals of this kind are sold to the unwary as sound horses. The vendors believe the quadruped to be glandered, or to be affected with the most terrible of equine diseases; and the purchaser wants knowledge to perceive the contrary.

Let, therefore, no man who buys "a captain," (which is the slang for a horse with nasal discharge,) become alarmed, and to some member of the gang from whom it was bought, resell his bargain for a few shillings. Large sums are often made by thus disposing of a diseased animal for a high price; then, directly afterward, frightening the purchaser with a view to buying back at a cheap rate the supposed glandered horse. Always take the animal to the nearest veterinary surgeon. Have the quadruped examined; and, if really glandered, order it to be immediately destroyed. Listen to no offer; but have the order obeyed.

A gentleman once attending a sale, bought for a large price a fine black horse. No sooner had the money been paid, than a man came up and informed the purchaser of the real character of his recent acquisition, offering to take the bargain off the new owner's hands for fewer shillings than pounds had just been given. The proposal was indignantly refused. Others came, but all encountered the same answer. The terms were gradually heightened, till double the money expended was tendered. The horse, however, was destroyed; thus a gang of swindlers were deprived of a property which, they owned, had for the last year earned them an easy thousand pounds.

Every man, however, must not anticipate so favorable a proposal. The animals mostly are worthless, and would only be rebought for a very trifle; the swindlers, generally, being perfectly indifferent whether their eyes ever again behold a creature which can be easily replaced.

NASAL POLYPUS.

A **polypus**, when not otherwise distinguished, represents a pear-shaped body, which has little sensation, but great vascularity. It is not malignant, and its growth is generally rapid. By the increase of its weight,

the polypus ultimately hangs from the spot where it grew, and becomes pendant by a sort of stalk, formed principally by the blood-vessels enveloped in the membrane which coats the tumor. Such growths are peculiar to mucous tissues, or to all the cavities of the body which communicate with the external air. With regard to the horse, polypus is mostly met with in the nostrils.

It is a disputed point how these growths are occasioned.

A POLYPUS.

However, no compliment is paid to the veterinary science, when it is asserted that, even to this day, no recognized plan of treatment for polypus has been laid down. Such tumors are allowed to be removed with the knife, by ligature, by traction, and by tortion; in short, as you please. The first has generally been employed after a most butcherly fashion, slicing a piece off one day, and taking a morsel the next, till by slow degrees the whole was extirpated. So barbarous an operation is only worthy of ancient farriery; the blood lost must be enormous, and the subsequent weakness of the animal must more than counterbalance any benefit which the operation could have promised. Mr. Varnell, assistant professor at the Royal Veterinary College, lately removed a growth of this kind in a much more surgical fashion. That gentleman had a knife made with an angular blade; by employing this instrument, he was enabled to excise the tumor with a single cut, inflicting little pain, but affording immediate and lasting benefit to the creature. Where it can be employed, Mr. Varnell's angular knife is to be

recommended, as the quickest and most efficient means of eradication which the public possess.

Tortion is more repulsive in appearance than in reality. A pair of scissors having sharp curved claws, at the expanded ends of blunt blades, are employed. The tumor is seized by the claws, a little pressure is made, and, at the same time, the scissors are drawn slightly forward. By that means the points are driven into the substance, and a firm hold is obtained.

POLYPUS FORCEPS OR SCISSORS.

The handles of the scissors are next fastened together with wire, or not, at the pleasure of the operator. The scissors are afterward made to revolve several times, and with each revolution they oblige the polypus to turn upon its pedicle, which motion first twists and ultimately ruptures it. The growth is thus removed; as the polypus is not very sensitive, and the operation should be soon over, small suffering is inflicted, when compared with the permanent ease which the proceeding insures.

Of the operation by traction or dragging away, no notice will be taken; it is a vulgar and a cruel affair. Ligature, however, where it can be used, is generally preferred; because the employment of it is not so sudden, and, consequently, not apparently so violent; because no blood generally follows the removal, and therefore there is no visible evidence of pain. The writer is not certain it is the least painful of the methods proposed; the relief is delayed, although the appearance and the appetite of the animal are assurances that nothing approaching to agony is inflicted.

For ligature procure a fine, hollow tube, having at one end a cover made to screw on and off; the opposite extremity must be open, and should have a cross bar attached externally, one inch from the termination. Upon the cover two holes must be bored, each large enough to admit a fine wire; to arm this instrument, which should be about eighteen inches long, procure a piece of zinc wire one yard and a half long; push this through one of the

DIAGRAM OF A TUBE FOR THE REMOVAL OF NASAL POLYPUS.

holes on the unscrewed cover and down the tube; screw on the cover; fasten the projecting end of the wire to the cross bar; return the wire through the other hole, and, passing it down the tube, leave it hanging free. Form of the wire a loop, large enough to surround the polypus; pass it gently over the head of the growth; by means of the tube, work the loop upward, tightening the wire as the size of the polypus diminishes. When the wire is round the pedicle, fix it by winding it also over the cross bar; then slowly make turns with the tube, observing the growth while so doing. When the tumor changes color or the animal exhibits pain, discontinue all further movements; release the wires from the cross bar and withdraw the tube, leaving the ends of the ligature protruding from the nostril and turned up on one side of the face.

Order the horse to be fastened to the pillar-reins that night, and to be watched while feeding. The next day, if the tumor do not feel sensibly cold and has not evidently lost the living hue, reinsert the wires into the tube, fix them again on the cross bar, and give another turn or two. If small alteration be subsequently observed, the same evening the proceeding may be repeated; but, when death appears confirmed in the tumor, twist the tube till the pedicle gives way.

The advantages possessed by this invention is, firstly, the ability of twisting a ligature tight when the growth is partly removed from view. Also, in the adoption of wire which will retain the form it is placed in, and remain unaffected by the moisture natural to the nostrils. Moreover, the tube can be made without the screwing head-piece, and answers quite as well, or even better, when solid. If made without the screwing head-piece, it can assume a flattened form, and it is somewhat easier to introduce; but the wire, in that case, must have both ends pushed through the holes down the tube.

The **bleeding polypus** is not met with in the horse. For that polypus which sprouts from the nasal membrane and extends to the fauces, impeding respiration and deglutition, appearing like a disease of the structure, to which it is attached by a broad base, nothing can be done. It grows fast, and in a short time renders longer life a larger misery.

The polypus which admits of removal is a smooth, moist, glistening and vascular body. It greatly impedes the breathing. These growths have been known to push out the cartilaginous division of the nostrils until the once free passage was all but obliterated. They provoke a

A TENACULUM.

constant discharge of pure mucus, and, on that account, the horse, thus affected, has been condemned as glandered. However, the truth may be at once recognized by closing the nostrils alternately. It is then easy to discover which cavity is affected, as a resistance is provoked by stopping the free channel, which bears no resemblance to glanders. To bring down the polypus, cough the horse, by making gentle pressure upon the topmost part of the windpipe; for, during the stages of glanders, any appearance at all resembling polypus is never present. It was usual, the instant the growth was visible, to transfer it with a tenaculum. This, however, like other barbarities, only did harm. The substance of a polypus is easily rent, and it bleeds freely. The bleeding concealed much, which, after proceedings rendered necessary, should be plainly seen. It is better, when sufficient room is not left for operation or inspection, to proceed with greater boldness, so as to ascertain the advantages likely to result from further measures. Then throw the horse, and with a probe-pointed, straight bistoury, slit up the nostril upon the outer side. That done, release the animal till all bleeding has ceased, when the endeavors may be renewed with a better prospect of success. Afterward, close the incision with a double set of sutures, (one set to the true nostril and another for the false nostril.) Apply to the wound the chloride of zinc wash, and in a short time all will be healed.

Nasal polypus, nevertheless, is an affection often requiring the performance of tracheotomy, before any examination can be attempted. For this necessity, the operator must be prepared; but, as tracheotomy is required only to relieve the breathing during examination, the temporary tube invented

NASAL POLYPUS.

by Mr. Gowing is, in that instance, decidedly to be recommended.

NASAL GLEET.

This terrible affliction is suppuration of the mucous membrane, lining the facial sinuses. It rarely occurs in the stable; but when it does, the cause mostly is to be traced to the projection of some molar tooth, and the disease is then generally hopeless. The pressure of the tooth has provoked irritation of the bone. The sinuses are no longer hollow spaces, but have been converted into cavities crowded with bony network. To cleanse them in that condition is impossible, and death is the only resort left to a humane proprietor.

Horses, when allowed a run at grass, are often taken up with the bones of the face swollen and soft. Percussion draws forth the same response as would be elicited by rapping upon a pumpkin. The animal, suddenly released from toil, has been playing in the field with its new associates. The simple creature could not comprehend the feet were fettered. The equine race always display joy with their heels, and the hoof, which unshod might lightly touch the neighbor's skull and no injury result, being armed with iron carries additional weight with the blow, and leaves behind a deadly bruise upon the facial bones. The following engraving, representing an extreme case of this kind, is a warning never to turn your animal into a field where others are grazing; but if you are obliged to starve a horse on grass, at all events choose a spot where it can be alone.

NASAL GLEET.

Besides the distortion, the next prominent symptom attending nasal gleet is fetor. Discharge is not always present. It is irregular in its appearance, but can generally be made to flow, by a brisk trot or by some tempting food

being placed upon the ground. Stench and discharge, often coming
only from one nostril, but occasionally from two, are likewise symptomatic of the same disorder.

Pus is, naturally, the blandest secretion of the body; but being confined, it corrupts, and then smells abominably. The blow, which started
up the secretion, injured the bones forming facial sinuses. Those cavities
open to the nostril on either side by two comparatively small flaps, slits,
or valves. These are their only means of communication with the external atmosphere; and through these valves all the pus must flow. Is
it surprising if such structures occasionally become clogged, till the
accumulated secretion, or the increased breathing, or the position of the
head, obliges the passage to give way?

The chances likely to result upon treatment are about equal, but the
process is generally slow. The trephine has to be employed upon the
facial sinus, and circular portions of bone have to be removed. Into
the openings thus made is to be injected, by means of a pint pewter
syringe, half a gallon of tepid water, or water heated to ninety-six degrees, in which half a drachm of chloride of zinc is dissolved. The
chloride of zinc not only destroys the fetor, but also disposes the membrane to take on a new action.

The injection, however, only cleanses the sinuses, and the nose also
becomes involved by the disease. It is usual to describe the turbinated
bones, or the fragile bones situated within the nostrils, as thin osseous

THE TREPHINE, BY MEANS OF
WHICH A CIRCULAR PIECE OF
BONE MAY BE REMOVED.

INJECTING THE HEAD OF A HORSE FOR NASAL GLEET.
Copied from a work by La Fosse.

structures, making numerous convolutions upon themselves. They favor
such an opinion when viewed *in situ;* but, being removed, are found to
consist of ample sacs or bags, which the external layer concealed from
view. These hidden spaces soon fill with pus; here it remains; the

position of the head even cannot entirely dislodge it, as the head is seldom carried perpendicularly. Here the pus hardens or concretes, until by degrees the cavities are filled with a foul and solid matter.

THE TURBINATED BONE WITHIN THE NOSTRIL OF A HORSE AFFECTED WITH NASAL GLEET; PARTLY ABSORBED BY PRESSURE AND PARTLY DISTENDED BY AN ACCUMULATION OF CON-CRETE PUS.

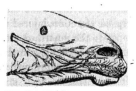

PART OF A HORSE'S HEAD WHICH HAS THE BONE TREPHINED SO AS TO EN-ABLE THE SURGEON TO EMPTY THE TURBINATED BONE. THE COURSE OF THE NERVES IS SHOWN.

Such a store-house of disease may thus be opened and cleansed. Mark with chalk or charcoal the spot in a line with the infra-orbital foramen, and a little anterior to the third molar tooth; the positions of both may be clearly ascertained by feeling externally upon the head of the living horse. At that place cut through the skin, but no deeper. Make a **T** incision, only reverse the letter **⊥**. Withdraw the two flaps of skin; remove by means of blunt hooks any structures that conceal the bone, upon which last, when clear, employ the trephine.

The side of the face being opened, insert through the opening a steel probe. Thrust it through the concrete pus, and strive to discover the most depending portion of the sac. To this spot, if possible, apply a hollow metallic tube, about twelve inches long. This instrument has a horn-shaped mouth at the blunt extremity, and a fine sharp steel saw at the other. The saw being fixed upon the spot indicated by the probe, and a few revolutions being given to the horn-shaped end, between the

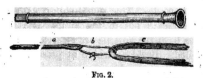

FIG. 2.

Fig. 1. The hollow metallic tube, having at one extremity a horn-shaped mouth for the convenience of inserting a gum-elastic probe, and at the other end a fine saw for cutting through the turbinated bone.

Fig. 2. *a.* A gum-elastic probe to be threaded through the metallic tube, and so forced out of the nostril. *b.* A portion of string passed through the eye of the probe and forming a loop. *c.* The tape which constitutes the seton passed through the looped string.

palms of the hands, a circular portion of the bony net-work which characterizes the turbinated structures is removed.

Now, so soon as this is accomplished, force through the hollow instrument last employed an elastic probe armed with a piece of linen tape. The probe, being about eighteen inches long, will, by the application of very gentle force, soon glide through the opening last made, and out of the nostril. The tape is, by traction, made to follow, and the ends being tied, a seton is established. By the daily movement of this last contrivance, the concrete matter may effectually be displaced.

This being finished, the syringe is to be daily employed; and the cure may be often expedited by the following ball, which should be given once every twenty-four hours:—

Balsam of copaiba	. . . . . Half an ounce.
Cantharides (in powder) .	. . . Four grains.
Cubebs	. . . A sufficiency.—*Mix.*

Should this appear to affect the urinary system, immediately discontinue it. In its place, half a drachm of belladonna should be rubbed down in one ounce of water, and administered every hour, till all appetite is destroyed, and the drug should be discontinued after this effect is gained. The belladonna, however, should be exhibited only every fourth day.

The lymphatic glands under the horse's jaw occasionally enlarge; but as the affection is destroyed the swelling will disappear. However, the cure may be expedited by commodious lodging and liberal food. It evidently is folly to stint the provender and expect a starved nature to vanquish disease.

HIGHBLOWING AND WHEEZING.

These peculiarities admit of no pictorial illustration. Obviously, it is impossible to picture a sound. Both affections are known by the noises to which they give rise.

Highblowing is complained of only in saddle horses. It consists of forcing the respiration violently through the nostrils, whereby a bur-r-r-ing kind of noise is made. This sound children are fond of imitating, when they play "horses;" but in the animal it is unpleasant to the equestrian, because by it the nostrils are cleared, and the trousers of the rider are often soiled. Besides, fashion at present favors a quiet steed. For this habit there is no remedy, except throwing up the horse for harness purposes, in which employment the habit is not generally regarded as objectionable.

Wheezing is a thin, whistling noise, heard only during inspiration. It is provoked by some impediment to the breathing, and the cause always resides in the nasal chambers. It is astonishing how small an obstacle engenders this affection. This, like the former peculiarity, is equally incurable. It is easy to stop each nostril, and thus to tell from which the noise proceeds; yet, for its removal, the affection demands a purely experimental destruction of parts, so ample, that even veterinary science shrinks from the attempt.

However, to such chances the life of a horse is exposed. The indulgence of a habit which adds to the animal's beauty in the eyes of the foot passenger, is regarded as objectionable in one position, while it is admired in another situation; the advent of the smallest excrescence in a large cavity can deteriorate the value of a life. A loss of value entails loss of caste. The life descends to harder work and lessened care The first step taken, the others rapidly succeed, for it cannot be asserted that, as a general rule, the lower classes appear to advantage, when the custody of a beautiful animal is morally considered.

CHAPTER V.

SORE THROAT.

There is, among horse owners, much dispute as to the proper mode of harnessing a horse. Gentility has no feeling either for itself or with any of the many lives by which it is surrounded; this vice of modern time delights in labored imposture, and is always best pleased when it

WITH AND WITHOUT THE BEARING-REIN.

is mistaken for something that it is not. Gentility favors the use of a bearing-rein in the horse's harness. The object is to keep up the head, and to give to an animal with a ewe neck the aspect of one having a lofty crest. The artifice is very transparent; it should deceive nobody save him who is foolish enough to adopt it; but it deprives the poor horse of no little of its natural power. Gentlemen's coachmen complain of the work when their horses are driven ten miles daily, although the distance may be repeatedly broken by visits and by shopping. The cabs of London can only employ the horses which gentlemen have discarded; with these last vehicles, however, no bearing-reins are adopted. The cast-off animal that previously fagged over ten miles, when reduced to the rank, has to pull loads which no genteel carriage would carry, and

(96)

to travel a sufficient distance to pay horse, driver, conveyance, and proprietor. In the possibility of such a contrast is, perhaps, best exemplified the cruelty of the bearing-rein.

When the fine structure of the horse's body is regarded, and we reflect that a creature of so beautiful a frame is by man's will taken from the fields, where every bite of grass is of a different flavor—now hot and pungent by an admixture of the buttercup, then cool and bland by the marsh-mallow mingling with the morsel—where, unknown as yet to toil, such sustenance is sufficient for growth and idleness; when we consider that an animal is suddenly snatched from such a diet, every mouthful of which was endowed not only with a varied taste, but with a change of perfume; when we feebly conjecture how grateful this ever-varying savor must have rendered herbage to any being possessed of the admirable sense of smell with which the equine species are gifted, it can create but small surprise that, when taken into stables, put to exhausting labor, and day after day made to eat a stinted allowance of dry food, the sameness of the diet and the change in habit should occasionally derange the digestion. **Sore throat** is, however, frequently a sign of some graver disorder; the affection should, therefore, be cautiously treated as a local malady.

When it is present, the symptoms are a constant deglutition of saliva, a want of appetite, accompanied by an inability to swallow liquids. The pail being presented, the act of drinking is accomplished with evident effort; the drops are forced down by a series of jerks, which are often made more emphatic by an audible accompaniment. Notwithstanding this labor, only a portion of the fluid enters the gullet, the greater part returning by the nostrils.

So soon as this is observed, throw the horse up, for sore throat is always attended with weakness. Clothe fully, bandage the legs, place in a well-ventilated and amply littered loose box; feed upon green meat for a couple of days, at the same time always having present a pail of thick, well-made gruel, which should be regularly changed, thrice daily. Morning, noon, and night, a pottle of bruised oats, with a handful of old beans

A HORSE WITH SORE THROAT ENDEAVORING TO DRINK.

distributed among them, should be scalded, and, when blood-warm, placed in the manger.

Frequently, this is all that is required, and the disorder is well cured, which yields without medicine. Should the bowels prove obstinate, and after the second day continue constipated, a mild dose of solution of aloes should be administered.

> Solution of aloes . . . . Four ounces
> Essence of aniseseed . . . . Half an ounce.
> Water . . . . One pint.

Mix, and give.

This, with the diet previously recommended, is rarely required, as the food alone, so far as the author's experience can justify an opinion, never fails in relaxing the body. However, should the sore throat remain, dissolve half an ounce of extract of belladonna in one gallon of water. Hold up the head of the animal and put half a pint of this liquid into the mouth; allow the fluid to be retained for thirty seconds, then take away the support, and the medicine will run from the lips. Repeat this frequently, or from six to eight times during the day.

If the soreness of the throat should appear indisposed to heal, but, on the contrary, should seem inclined to spread, lose no time in resorting to the next preparation Permanganate of potash, (prepared by Squires, chemist, of Oxford Street,) half a pint; distilled water, one gallon; half a pint to be used to cleanse the horse's mouth, in the manner just directed for diluted belladonna, six times daily, or—

> Chloride of zinc . . . . Three drachms.
> Extract of belladonna . . . . Half an ounce.
> Tincture of capsicums . . . . Two drachms.
> Water . . . . One gallon.

Mix, and use as directed for the previous recipe.

Occasionally the disease does not spread, but, spite of our best endeavors, it will remain stationary. Then try the brewers' stout. Give one quart morning and evening. However, see that the animal has the beer, for men are partial to that fluid, even more than horses Should no change be remarked in forty-eight hours, blister the throat. Do this with one part of powdered cantharides soaked for a month in seven parts of olive oil, adding to the whole one part by weight of camphor. Rub this oil, when filtered through blotting paper, into the throat for ten minutes in summer, and a quarter of an hour in winter.

All the endeavors may be useless Then cast the horse. Have ready some nitrate of silver, dissolved in distilled water—five grains of the active salt to one ounce of the fluid Saturate in the solution a sponge four inches wide, tied on to the end of a stick eighteen inches long. Have the sponge made as dry as possible without squeezing it. Put a balling iron into the mouth. Insert the sponge through the iron, and having pushed it down to the back of the tongue, rapidly press it against the side of the cavity. Be prepared for what you are about to do, and do it quickly. The operation stops the breathing, and calls forth the resistance which is natural to impending suffocation.

The horse being released, give the following ball. in addition to the stout, twice each day:—

Powdered oak bark and treacle, a sufficiency of each to form a mass.

If none of these measures are successful, the sore throat must be the symptom only of some greater disorder, and all local remedies, in that case, must be ingulfed in the general treatment. However, it is not every measure which will cure every sore throat. In young horses, when first taken from the pure air into the contaminated atmosphere of most stables, such affections are common, but in old animals they are generally most severe. It is a usual plan to turn a horse out to grass when afflicted with obstinate sore throat: this is cruel. The animal, whose labor we enjoyed during its health, has a positive claim on us for kindness and for care when overtaken by disease. Moreover, those who laugh at the above may become serious, when they are informed that animals turned to grass for sore throat are not unfrequently taken up virulently glandered. So closely are moral duty and self-interest associated, when the operation of both is rightly considered.

COUGH.

Cough is too often caused by unhealthy lodging. Few stables are perfectly drained and ventilated; the very great majority are close with impurity. No surprise, then, need be exhibited, if the entrance to the air-passages should display disease, when an animal, so naturally cleanly, is imprisoned in the space man is too thoughtless to keep uncontaminated

The larynx is the seat of cough, when the affection exists by itself, although the annoyance is often a symptom of some other derangement, and may then spring from laryngeal sympathy with some comparatively remote organ It may arise from a very trivial cause, as teething; or it may be a sign attendant on the worst of disorders, as farcy and glanders. Broken wind, roaring, laryngitis, bronchitis, chronic diseases of the lungs, stomach, bowels, worms, etc. etc.; all are attended by cough, which is more frequently present as a symptom than as a disease Hot stables, coarse and dusty provender, rank bedding, and irregular work, are the general provocatives of cough, as a distinct affection.

The name is evidently derived from the noise which constitutes the chief symptom of the disorder. Cough consists in spasm of all the muscles of expiration. The air is violently expelled, and an explosive sound is the consequence. During this spasm, the soft palate is raised, and the breath is allowed to pass through the mouth as well as through the nostrils. The horse, as a rule, being able only to respire through the nostrils.

The characteristic noise is generally annoying to the master. Warmth, however, is popularly esteemed the cure for cold. The horse proprietor, therefore, thrusts his animal into an abode heated by impurity, only to find the annoyance aggravated. This fact is soon explained. Stables are not heated by fire or by water; their warmth is entirely derived from the fermentation of excrement. Were they well ventilated, efficiently built and cleanly kept, these places, having no artificial heat, must be cold; but the owner loves warmth; it feels so comfortable; it is so nice! He does not inquire if it is derived from the right source; he

THE ACT OF COUGHING.

hates the bother of investigating Nothing can be proper if you are to consult medical men! They talk and discuss, but no good comes of their verbosity! And by such sayings, the horse proprietor blinds his judgment, permitting to continue the evil which ignorance institutes. **Chronic cough** cannot, when thus treated, amend. It continues till the membrane covering the larynx be thickened and morbidly sensitive; then the cough is an appendage to the life, and roaring is its companion.

For the cure of chronic cough, scald and crush the oats, damp the hay, and give thin gruel or linseed tea for drink. At the same time see that the air is pure: the human nose is a sufficiently good test of atmosphere—that of the stable should not smell of horses, or of any taint whatever. If the ventilation is good, the drainage clear, and the bedding clean, the interior of a stable should be as odorless as any lady's apartment.

Cough, or the noise which accompanies stages of different disorders, will be described as the various affections of which it is a symptom are passed before the reader. Chronic cough, or the sound that follows a draught of cold water, and is heard when the horse quits the stable for the open air, is most distressing. It is a constant accompaniment during the commencement of a journey, and requires that the food and lodging should be looked to. Clothe warmly, and give half a pint of the following, in a tumbler of cold water, thrice daily :—

Extract of belladonna (rubbed down in a pint
   of cold water) . . . . One drachm.
Tincture of squills . . . . Ten ounces.
Tincture of ipecacuanha . . . . Eight ounces.
   Mix.

If no beneficial change be witnessed, try the subjoined :—

Barbadoes tar (or common tar if none other
   be at hand) . . . . Half an ounce.
Calomel . . . . Five grains.
Linseed meal . . . . A sufficiency.
   Mix, and give as one ball, night and morning.

Should no improvement result, the next may be substituted :—

Powdered aloes . . . . One drachm.
Balsam of copaiba . . . . Three drachms.
Cantharides . . . . Three grains.
Common mass . . . . A sufficiency.
   Mix, and give first thing in the morning.

A bundle of cut grass, every day, has done much good in the spring; so, also, has a lump of rock salt placed in the manger, during any season of the year. The horse, however, should be observed. If it eat the litter, no straw, during the daytime, should cover the stall; and, at night, a muzzle should be fixed upon the animal. The cough must be more than of a simple character which does not vanish before the proposed measures are exhausted. Cut roots, also, are beneficial during this disease. The hay should not be abundant, and should always be moistened. But, above all things, attend to the drainage and ventilation of the stable.

LARYNGITIS.

The common cause of this disorder is foul stables. When we see the animal associated with the nobleman in his pride, and linked as the willing slave of the merchant for his profit, it does seem strange that a creature, thus connected, should be subject to disease from scant and tainted lodging. When we consider the subject from another point of view, and regard the eautiful frame-work, animated by the affectionate disposition of the horse, it sounds more than cruel, to say the most valuable and amiable assistant man has on earth dies neglected in age, and, during the vigor of its prime, encounters disease from the niggard provision made for its welfare. The devotion of a life ought to entitle the laborer to breathing space, after the labor of the day has ended. But noblemen, professional men, merchants, tradesmen, mechanics, all sin in this respect alike. The horse, when not toiling, is pushed away into the narrowest possible limits. The prisoner is permitted only to breathe a limited quantity of the air which nature has supplied in so great abundance and in such purity. That quantity must, from the time of close confinement, be frequently respired during the night; and, when the air of the place has become hot and heavy, the quadruped, at the command of its attendant, quits its abode for the cold atmosphere without the walls.

The pure air which circulates about our globe is certainly much to be preferred to the close interior of the stable. Yet, to the larynx, in some measure accustomed to the last, a sudden draught of the first is the almost certain source of disease. It acts as a stimulant upon a part rendered delicate by abiding in a morbid medium. It operates violently upon a structure which had almost become familiarized with impurity. Inflammation is the result, and laryngitis is established.

The symptoms are broadly marked and prominently characterized. Dullness is present. There is a slight enlargement, which may be observed externally, and over the region of the larynx. The most distant attempt to handle the throat produces energetic resistance. The head is carried awkwardly, as though the neck were "stiff." A short cough is frequently to be heard almost at every inspiration. At the same time, there is often to be detected a hoarse sound, which becomes a sort of grunt, when the ear is placed against the trachea. The breath is hurried and catching; the pulse is full and throbbing; while the nasal membrane approaches to a scarlet hue.

THE STEAMING-BAG.
For a full description see p. 85.

The pulse requires the first attention. It must be rendered less frequent and more soft, by drachm doses of tincture of aconite root in wineglasses of water, which should be repeated every half hour. This is better than blood-letting, as laryngitis is to be most dreaded because of its tendency to assume the chronic form. This tendency venesection favors; therefore, save under professional advice, refrain from bleeding.

After the pulse, the breathing next demands our care. Warmth and moisture are curative and pleasant to an inflamed surface. Procure the steaming-bag, and keep it almost constantly applied. The steaming-bag in laryngitis is of the first importance. A day's delay in its use may so aggravate the disorder as to oblige the resort to tracheotomy.

Should the steaming apparatus appear to distress the animal, it must be used only for a limited period, and be reapplied after its effect has subsided. To aid its operation, some soft hay must be obtained. Soak this in boiling water and fix it upon the throat, by means of an eight-tailed bandage, a representation of which is given below.

EIGHT-TAILED BANDAGE.

A piece of stout canvas or flannel, one yard and a quarter long, and nine inches wide, is procured. Three slits are to be made at either end; each should be a quarter of a yard deep. This is placed round the throat and the ends are tied, four in front of, and four behind, the ears.

So soon as the animal appears capable of enduring interference, the appended drink should be given thrice daily. While administering it, watch the horse with the utmost attention. If the slightest inclination to cough be exhibited, immediately lower the head, or the liquid may, during the spasm, be drawn down the windpipe. It is far better to lose much physic than to kill one animal. It will, generally, be more readily swallowed, if made blood warm: on no account should the twitch be used or the jaws be forced widely asunder. The neck of the bottle should be inserted into the corner of the mouth, and the quadruped should be permitted to use its discretion as to the time occupied before each gulp is swallowed.

Infusion of squills	Two ounces.
Infusion of ipecacuanha	Two ounces.
Infusion of aconite	Half an ounce.
Extract of belladonna	One drachm, rubbed down with a pint of warm water.

Mix, and give thrice daily.

The lodging should be a cool, well-aired and thickly-littered loose box. The legs ought to be bandaged and the body fully clothed. The food, during the violence of the disorder, must consist only of well-made gruel. It may be untouched; but, nevertheless, it must be changed, thrice daily, for no one can tell when the appetite may return.

The signs of the disease becoming worse are, increased noise in the breathing; the respiration and pulse quicken; the cough is suppressed; the nasal membrane changes to a leaden hue; the standing becomes unsteady; the horse moves about; partial sweats break forth, etc.

The symptoms of improvement are, the membrane becoming paler, or more natural in color; the cough growing freer or louder; a white, thick discharge flowing from the nostrils; the breathing, also, is easier and less noisy; together with the general demonstrations of health.

Then a little moist and succulent food may be allowed, but nothing harsh or fibrous should be presented. When the amendment is confirmed, a seton, or, in other words, a piece of tape, may be put between the skin and flesh, in the place indicated by one of the next engravings.

The seton should be moved daily, and ought to be kept in so long only as is necessary for the secretion of healthy pus. That object being obtained, cut off one of the knots, and by pulling at the other, withdraw the agent. Some slight alteration is next made in the solidity or dryness of the food; and then the neck or throat is blistered, the size and extent of the blister being indicated in a subjoined illustration.

A SETON IN THE THROAT OF A HORSE.

A HORSE WITH THE THROAT BLISTERED.

The action of the vesicatory having subsided, the natural food may be returned to, only with certain cautions. The hay must be shaken out, to remove dust, and it should also be picked, to take away any harsh substances, pieces of stick, or thistle leaves. Then, the fodder being perfectly clean, should be sprinkled with water and allowed to remain soaking, at least six hours prior to its being placed before the animal. The oats, likewise, should be twice sifted and once examined thoroughly by the hand. Afterward, warm water ought to be freely poured upon them, and the grain be permitted to soak six hours before being put into the manger.

The popular opinion declares sore throat to be always present during laryngitis. That notion springs from the horse always quidding, or rejecting the pellet it has masticated, while suffering under an attack of the last-mentioned disease. The two disorders, however, are distinct; likewise the remedies for each are separate. The **quidding,** during lar-yngitis, springs from the act of de-glutition, obliging the sore and in-flamed larnyx to rise and press the pellet against the roof of the fauces. That act occasions much pain; hence the aversion to swallow solid sub-stances. Sore throat is, however, by no means the necessary accompani-

A HORSE IN THE ACT OF QUIDDING.

ment of laryngitis. Neither are the bowels invariably confined during the disease. It has been known that the purgation existed in such energy as to require remedies. Consequently, no absolute plan of treat-ment can be laid down. However, depletion should be avoided to every extent which may be possible. The chronic form of the malady, conse-quent upon debility, is to be much dreaded. Effusion into the mem-brane, covering the rim of the larynx and its attendant roaring, is too frequently the result of that weakness which is produced by active measures. Among the lesser evils are cough, which not unfrequently proves but the precursor of more potent ills. Therefore, while laryngitis lasts, rather check the fever by gentle measures than resort to antimonials, niter, or the host of lowering agents.

So soon as the case is observed, change the stable: the horse will do far better in the open air than in the foul atmosphere which originated and must aggravate the disorder. Rain, snow, or frost are more whole-some than the polluted warmth man's most humble slave is too often doomed to inhale. The roofs of many stables are terribly low; in no building of this kind is the covering too high. The welfare of the horse seems always sacrified to the imaginary interests of its master. Thus, above the stable is built a loft for the hay and a residence for the groom. To save expense, the building is raised as small a distance from the ground as possible. The height of modern buildings would be by no means extravagant, were an entire stable of ordinary dimensions left free for a single quadruped to breathe in. A puerile parsimony, however, denies the huge lungs of the animal the only food life cannot do without, for even a short space. Disease and death consequently soon waste treble the money ample accommodation would not have consumed. Ignorance is the most expensive quality a proprietor of horse-flesh can indulge; for nature invariably refuses to be made subject to man's convenience.

ROARING.

A horse is said to roar when, during progression, he emits any unnatural sound. The noise is not exactly of the same intensity in any two animals. Some creatures roar so loud as to attract attention from the foot passengers; others have so trivial a defect in this particular, that it can only be detected after a breathing gallop. In all, however, it materially lessens the value.

It is usual to cough horses suspected of being **roarers**; this, however, is wrong. The constant pinching of the larynx may induce the affection. The cough of a confirmed roarer, however, is peculiar. It consist of a double effort; a spasmodic expulsion of the air, followed by a deep and audible inspiration.

The best mode of detecting a roarer, where exercise is forbidden or impossible, is to get a stick and to quietly approach the suspected animal. Having reached the head, take a short hold of the halter, and all at once display the weapon, at the same time making a pretense as though about to use it violently upon the abdomen The horse in alarm will run toward the manger, and, if a roarer, the action will be accompanied by an audible grunt. This proof, taken with the refusal to allow the horse to be tried, is generally conclusive; though by itself the test is by no means satisfactory. Many horses that are not roarers will sometimes grunt under the emotion of fear.

Of **roaring** there are two kinds, acute and chronic. **Acute roaring** is that which is merely symptomatic of a disease. It may be produced by the tumor of strangles compressing the larynx; by the impediment, in choking, being situated so high up as to interfere with the breathing; and by many other causes. In these cases remove the excitant, and the effect will immediately cease. Acute roaring is, therefore, a very trivial affair, excepting so far as it indicates the severity of the complaint, which generates the affection

Chronic roaring is a very different business. This mostly results from the abuse to which a generous animal is subject, during the early period of its domestication. A carriage horse may be serviceable, and even dashing, when the twentieth year has passed; but the vast majority of these animals perish before maturity is reached. A handsome pair of Cleveland bays pull some fashionable lady round the park, before their bones are formed or the teeth perfected The animals have also to take their mistress the circle of morning calls, and to be smartly stopped short at the door of every house she visits, while their sinews are still soft and yielding. They have to "go faster," when their mistress is in a hurry, and have to wait her pleasure when she is disposed to linger. They have to do all this, while their bodies are distorted by the bearing-rein; the balance of their frames being violently made to conform to the capricious notions of modern fashion. For the illustration of this subject, an animal, with a head rather well put on, has been chosen. The engraving represents a horse undergoing the torture of the bearing-rein. The next illustration exhibits the horse carrying its head as it would, were it free to exercise a choice. The reader is not asked which delineation looks the best. Any appeal to his taste is forborne, because the generality of eyes are perverted by the dictates of custom.

A HORSE'S HEAD PULLED UP BY THE BEARING-REIN.   A HORSE'S HEAD WITHOUT THE BEARING-REIN.

But he is asked to inspect the representations. Let him look well and long at them; then declare which appears most at ease. Let his heart instruct his eyes, and, to its teaching, let him subject his liking; for there can be no beauty where constraint is perceptible. In the most vigorous of the ancient statuary repose may be absent, the muscles may be strained and the attitude violent; still all the parts balance. "Yes," it may be replied, "but in the Elgin marbles the horses' heads are thrown back." So they are; but not fixed back. The horses are ridden without bridles. The elevation of the head, therefore, denotes spirit, and represents no more than the action of a moment. The modern carriage horse, whether galloping, trotting, or standing still, always has the head in one attitude, save when the muzzle is thrown into the air to ease, for an instant, the pained angles of the mouth, inhumanly tugged at by the bearing-rein.

Which of the foregoing engravings looks most at ease? Does not the fashionable horse appear suffering constraint and torture? The face is disguised and concealed by the harness; but enough is left visible to suggest the agony compulsion inflicts. "Pride," says the proverb, "has no feeling." Therefore, no expectation is formed of any appeal to the fashionable circles; but by the ignorance of the public is this barbarity

licensed. Were the mass properly informed, the hooting of the popu-
lace would soon drive fashion into a more humane usage.

THE HEALTHY LARYNX.

1. The thyro-hyordeus muscle.
2. The crico-thyroideus muscle.
3. The arytenoideus muscle.
4. The crico-arytenoideus posticus muscle.
a. a. The thyroid bone.
A. The epiglottis (a cartilage.)
B. The arytenoid cartilages.
C. The thyroid cartilage.
D. The cricoid cartilage.
E. E. E. The commencement of the trachea.

THE EFFECT PRODUCED BY THE BEARING-REIN.

a. The healthy arytenoideus muscle.
b. The healthy crico-artenoideus posticus muscle.
A. The arytenoideus muscle paralyzed and partially absorbed by the constant use of the
bearing-rein.
B. The crico-arytenoideus posticus muscle rendered pallid, and deprived of power by the
use of the bearing rein.

The left engraving represents the larynx in a state of health. The
larynx is the most sensitive organ in the body. If a crumb of bread, a
particle of salt, or a drop of water "go the wrong way," or enter the
larynx, everybody has felt the convulsive coughing that immediately
ensues. Yet this larynx, so exquisitively sensitive, and so resentful of
the lightest touch, is forced out of place and shape by the adoption of
the bearing-rein. The whole weight of the head is made to press against
the larynx; the action of the part is stopped; certain muscles are thrown
out of use. Now, doom a part to constant rest, and paralysis soon
results. This is exactly what follows the often long stoppage of that
freedom which is necessary to the health of any structure. Certain of
the muscles are absorbed; they lose their bulk and part with their color;
their function is destroyed: the consequence is, the horse becomes a
confirmed and an incurable roarer.

So fearful a result, as a life of anguish to any creature, might be
thought sufficient to amend a triviality like the whim of fashion. Still,
sad as that consequence is, it is not all which this folly engenders.

The larynx, sensitive and delicately constructed, is formed upon different pieces of cartilage. This substance is slowly organized and very
yielding. The structures of the youthful horse's frame are not con-

firmed. All are soft, especially a substance naturally semi-elastic. The bearing-rein forces the head upon the neck; the larynx thereby is compressed. It assumes strange forms, when it is forced from its natural position. As maturity arrives, the various structures harden. Then distortion of the larynx becomes fixed. This organ has been taken from the bodies of old animals, of the shape here depicted. The morbid specimen, from which the following was copied, is, unfortunately, too common, as the late Professor Sewell clearly demonstrated. But, what a price is this to pay for fashion—to sit for hours behind a noble creature, whose exertions are adding to our pleasure, and at the same time to be entailing deformity upon the animal! Physical soundness is of far more importance to the horse than to the human being. The value of the quadruped, its man-

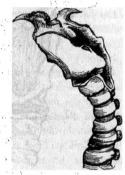

THE TRACHEA AND LARYNX DISTORTED THROUGH THE CONSTANT USE OF THE BEARING-REIN.

ner of life, its kind of treatment, the sufficiency of its food, and the comparative comfort of its lodging,—all are regulated by the soundness of its body.

There are those who assert roaring is no injury to the powers of a horse. Certain animals, to be sure, can hunt and keep a good pace, although thus afflicted; but Nimrod (as the well-known, late sporting writer called himself) soon found out to his cost that all roarers were not fit to ride across country. The writer has seen a sailor, deprived of one leg, dance a hornpipe with wonderful agility; but it would be folly, therefore, to say sailors were not injured as dancers by the loss of a limb. That which impedes the free passage of air to the lungs must be a rather serious detriment to exertion. The cab proprietors of London, who cannot afford to purchase very sound animals, and then to let them out at so much per day to strange drivers, have discovered a way to prevent the noise generally made by roarers. This end is attained by placing a pad under a portion of the harness. In the following engraving this pad is indicated by a white mark; though in reality it is so colored as to blend with the coat of the horse. It

THE CABMAN'S REMEDY FOR ROARING.

presses upon the nostrils near to their openings, and by thus limiting the extent of their expansion, by controlling the space through which the air has to pass, it also commands the quantity of atmosphere which is inspired. Thus the bulk of air is regulated to the diminution of the respiratory organs. The horse breathes freer, and no noise is made during the act Yet, although such a contrivance may do very well for a London cab, the pace of which is regulated by Act of Parliament, it evidently is unsuited to the field, where everything depends on the capacity of the lungs, and nothing upon the sound made during inspiration.

Other causes are mentioned by different writers as provocatives of roaring, besides tight reining Some of these, like thickening and ulceration of the membrane lining the larynx, are the after consequences of acute disease, and, as such, are to be prevented only by judicious treatment during the existence of the primary disorder. Among other causes, bands of coagulable lymph in the trachea, and congenital deformity, are too rare to deserve the attention they have received.

There is one consolation, however, connected with the subject which breeders may accept with confidence. Roaring is not necessarily hereditary. There is, moreover, a caution, which, associated with roaring, may be given to purchasers When trying a horse at the top of its speed, never hold in the reins tightly. By so doing, you draw the head upon the neck, compress the larynx, and may make almost any animal, however sound, "roar like a bull." Rather wait till the animal has stopped. Then dismount, place your ear against the windpipe, and, if the horse is a roarer, the deep inspirations necessary to tranquilize the system will inform you plainly enough of the fact.

CHOKING.

Gentlemen have something to answer for, when they employ the knowing and the ignorant as grooms about their stables The writer wishes women would undertake to tend on horses. The animal requires no service that the female strength would not be equal to, while the female mind would soon comprehend and appreciate the gentleness of the quadruped. The timidity of the equine race would meet with womanly sympathy; and no one can have observed the attachments which spring up between the female and domesticated creatures, but must in heart have confessed that the care of the stable was, as much as the watching of the sick-room, especially woman's province.

The foolish fellows, now congregated about a mews, are constantly longing for something which shall magically do their work for them. They have a firm belief in charms and an utter hatred of labor They sigh for some spell which shall marvelously improve the appearance of their master's property without exertion on their parts. Their pride centers in the blooming coats of their charges. They have a large confidence in all sorts of condition balls. Such secrets constitute the mystery of their craft. As a general rule, the faith is proportioned to the strength of the ingredient. Arsenic is, by the lower order of stable keepers, contemplated with positive love. Vitriol, in the uneducated groom, engenders the warmth of passion Niter breeds delight; and confidence is, by the better sort of horse attendants, bestowed on any filth or trash. Raw tobacco has some repute; but the ashes of the weed, collected and wrapped in several papers, are much more esteemed in the generality of stables. Half a pint of human urine, forced down the cleanly throat of the horse, is not an unfrequent benefit bestowed upon the animal; but, happily, this specific is recognized only by the more learned of the class. Of all things, however, to amend condition, perhaps, a raw egg driven into the horse's œsophagus, before any food has been consumed, may be honored by the most universal regard.

Nevertheless, be the condition-worker what it may, the groom generally keeps his own counsel. Arsenic and vitriol are commonly favorites with agricultural carters, who poison their horses with the intention of over-much kindness. Tobacco ashes and eggs are popular with the more refined of the order Both classes, however, are too self-confident and too ignorant to have any fear of consequences. With the groom, the egg is thrust into the fasting gullet. Its size excites the contractibility of the muscular fiber; the substance is soon grasped by the living tube with spasmodic tenacity. There it is retained. The symptoms consequent upon **choking** are soon exhibited; but the groom looks on unmoved. At first, he thinks the evidence of agony is proof in favor of his charm; subsequently he resolves, with the cunning of ignorance, "not to split upon hisself."

Now, in a case of this description, never depend upon any report you may have received. Recollect choking may spring from two opposite causes The symptoms may result from disease, as strangles; or they may arise from any tumor pressing against the respiratory channel. In that instance, however, remove the cause, and the effect will cease. Of genuine choking, during health, there remain two sorts: the high and the low choke. Thus, if the substance has become fixed in the pharynx, or has only passed six inches down the œsophagus, the symptoms are urgent The remedy must be at hand, else the life is quickly lost.

In the **high choke** the head is raised; saliva bedews the lips; a discharge soils the nostrils; the eyes are inflamed and watery; the countenance is haggard; the breathing audible; the muscles of the neck are tetanic; the flanks heave; the body is in constant motion; the fore legs paw and stamp; the hind legs crouch and dance; perspiration breaks forth; every movement expresses agony: wherefore, if relief be not quickly afforded, the horse falls and dies of suffocation.

THE HIGH CHOKE.

The veterinary surgeon should attend such a case, prepared to perform tracheotomy, which sometimes is absolutely necessary, before anything intended to remove the obstruction can be attempted. The operation, in this case, is designed to be no more than temporary; therefore, the use of **Mr. Gowing's** tracheotomy tube is here decidedly in its proper place. It can be inserted; a few moments after it can be removed, and leave behind no loss of substance to be supplied or to retard recovery.

The balling-iron, after tracheotomy is accomplished, should be fixed in the mouth and the hand then introduced. Sometimes the impacted substance can be felt, but cannot be grasped. In this last case, a rough

AN EXTEMPORIZED HOOK TO RELIEVE HIGH CHOKING.

hook is to be extemporized out of any wire which may be at hand. It should be of the shape indicated in the preceding engraving, and of sufficient length to reach behind the obstruction. The hook is to be gently worked into its situation, and, with a sudden jerk, the foreign body is to be removed from the œsophagus.

Occasionally, the substance is so firmly embraced as not to permit any instrument to pass beside it. Sulphuric ether must then be inhaled, in the hope of thus overcoming the spasm. The ether, however, does not in every instance prove successful; and, as an egg, probably, alone could be of sufficient size to resist all the measures adopted for its removal, a large darning-needle must then be procured. That, being first armed with a piece of strong twine, must be driven through the skin and made to enter the globular impactment. There is no danger of injuring nerves or arteries while doing this; all vessels are pushed on one side by the enlargement, caused by the choking substance. The integrity of the shell being destroyed, the egg may easily be broken by external pressure. Another plan proposed, is to insert a fine trocar, and draw off the contents of the egg. Either method would answer, but it is always well to wound the lining membrane of the œsophagus as little as may be possible.

The employment of the cow probang has been advocated; the egg to be broken, if this recommendation is adopted, by the employment of the whalebone stilet. The œsophagus of the cow and horse, however, are of such different construction, that he must be a very bold or a very ignorant person who dare employ an instrument made for the first, to remove an obstruction within the gullet of the last.

THE COW PROBANG, USED TO BREAK AN EGG.

An old and hardened ball may provoke this accident; but then the impactment is not complete, because such substances are seldom of a perfect round. The sides are opened, and the obstruction is, therefore, more easily removed. Horses are not like the bovine race, so greedy as to swallow potatoes or small turnips, without mastication. Besides, man's favorite is more under domestication, and, therefore, less exposed to such accidents.

When the choking occurs low down, or within the thoracic portion of the œsophagus, the symptoms are less urgent. The animal ceases to feed. If water is attempted to be swallowed, it returns by the nostrils. The countenance expresses anguish; but the head is not held erect, neither are the muscles of the neck spasmodically contracted. Saliva flows from the mouth, and a copious discharge runs from the nose. The breathing is labored; but it is seldom noisy. The back is roached, the flanks tucked up, and the horse often stands as if desirous of elevating the quarters.

After two or three days, (for the **low choke** may continue such a period,) the accumulation of wind within the abdomen becomes excessive;

the breathing quickens; the pulse fails, and the animal (if not relieved) perishes from suffocation, induced by tympanitis.

For low choke more time than nature allows, when the impediment is situated near the mouth, may be occupied. No hurry nor any speedy remedy is required. Give oil, by the quarter of a pint, every hour. In the intermediate half hours give strong antispasmodics, using the horse probang after every dose of the latter. Sulphuric ether, two ounces; laudanum, two ounces; water, half a pint, will constitute the proper drench. Should the whole be returned, chloroform must be administered, by inhalation, till total insensibility results. Then, the head being extended, the probang should be introduced, and gentle but steady pressure made to force the obstruction onward. If success comes early, it is easily welcomed; but it is well not to expect success before the expiration of twenty minutes. When movement is felt, do not increase the force.

THE LOW CHOKE.

Maintain a steady pressure, never relaxing and never augmenting the power exerted. Drive the substance slowly before you, but do not, by sudden energy, risk either the provocation of spasmodic action or a rupture of the œsophagus.

Before using the probang, always calculate the length of the whalebone, so as to judge when the end has nearly entered the stomach. It is always well, if possible, to avoid forcing the end of the probang through the cardiac opening, as the termination of the œsophagus is called. The muscular fibers here are strongly developed, and are formed to resist the passage of any substance out of the stomach. To be sure, the animal is under the influence of chloroform; but that powerful agent seems more particularly to exert its action upon the voluntary muscles; whereas, the cardiac orifice is guarded by white, involuntary muscular fiber.

A few days subsequent to the removal of the obstruction, no matter where it may have been situated, feed on soft-boiled food—not bran mashes; and in case of roots not being at hand, sustain the life with smoothly-made gruel.   Let the animal be observed, when watered Should the liquid be returned by the nostrils, injury to the lining membrane of the œsophagus is indicated ; stricture may then be anticipated. Though it be not probable that any medicine will now be beneficial, nevertheless, as an experiment, administer, thrice daily, four ounces of water in which four grains of chloride of zinc have been dissolved.

Such is a true and brief history of the terrible mishaps that result from the mingled knowingness and ignorance which characterize the majority of grooms.   A good or simple lad would be sadly out of place in a modern stable, though the writer should recommend the employment of such to become more general.   The tricks and arts of professed grooms are all worthless or injurious   To such men, however, is the timid horse intrusted ; and so much are our minds enslaved by custom, that the hint only of employing women in the stable will, no doubt, be received with general indignation.   Let us, however, endeavor to view the matter without prejudice.   Women work in the fields ; women fill the situations of men as domestic servants ; women carry heavy loads ; women, on the continent, perform the duties of men ; women commonly tend an animal of inferior intelligence, the cow, women are subordinate to men only where strength is concerned.   In the stable no strength is required. Courage, even, is out of place there   Gentleness is the only quality imperative, and gentleness so habitual that it never will alarm timidity. This attribute seems to reside in the feminine mind, and, however opposed it may be to habit, the author cannot but lament the barrier which prevents the horse from becoming known to its natural attendant.

RUPTURE AND STRICTURE OF THE ŒSOPHAGUS.

The gullet or œsophagus of the horse is, perhaps, the most compact and delicate structure in a beautiful body.   Its mucous lining membrane is thrown into minute folds, thereby announcing to the studious anatomist the degree of extension the tube was designed to endure.   Its exterior is enveloped by a large mass of cellular tissue, by which means the independence of its motion is secured ; it will permit of less violence than almost any other part.   Small as its channel and delicate as its lining membrane are, the tube is amply large and strong enough for a creature which masticates long before it deglutates once, and which is by nature forbidden to regurgitate.

However, stable-men seek not to understand but love to master the quadruped intrusted to their charge. The butt-end of a carter's whip is a favorite resort with these people, whether serving some farmer or acting as grooms to some lord. When any mighty specific happens to stick in its passage to the stomach, the butt-end of the whip is employed to drive the obstinate charm onward. Should the obstruction be situated low down, the whip is neither small enough nor pliable enough to touch the offending matter. Should the choking mass be lodged high up, by compelling it beyond the reach of human hand, positive injury is done; and ultimate relief is rendered very problematical indeed; however, ignorance is not often to be deterred by difficulties. As the passage narrows, greater violence is resorted to; the men push and strive till at last the whip moves onward, and the stable-men congratulate each other upon "all being right at last."

When the whip seemed to yield, something more than the obstruction gave way; the walls of the canal were ruptured; an almost inevitable death then awaits the unfortunate animal. The food is rejected; drink is refused; the creature stands motionless, the picture of horror; it seems to comprehend and to await its approaching fate. The neck begins to swell; the swelling creeps on till it invests the entire body. Gas has found entrance into the cellular tissue, through the divided gullet. Death at last ensues, because the inflation impedes the vital functions, and, being corruptive, is incompatible with the preservation of living organism.

More often, however, the whip only tears the internal membrane; the obstruction has been dislodged and removed, but a worse evil has been

The dilated œsophagus or sac superior to the stricture.

The Stricture.

The tube of its natural size.
STRICTURE OF THE ŒSOPHAGUS.

created. The horse for a time refuses food, and the anxious master wonders "what can be the matter!" At last the pain may cease, the appetite return, for nature may strive to repair the damage. The whip usually tears a flap of membrane, which, obedient to the laws of gravity, hangs pendant within the œsophagus. Our common parent, however, does not, after the human pattern, repair the evil which man induces. She has no mortal hand wherewith to restore the rent membrane to its place. The sides of the wound, however, strive to unite, and by the date when this junction is accomplished, the mucous membrane being inelastic, the magnitude of the canal is seriously diminished. Nature seems to feel that the chief strain of deglutition will be upon this lessened spot, which, therefore, she endeavors to support and strengthen.

Lymph is deposited about the place, till ultimately a firm and solid stricture is formed.

This, however, though bad enough, is not the worst. Lymph, after a time, has a tendency to contract. With the diminution of the external ring, of course the internal canal decreases; it is strained at every meal; but straining only provokes its contractive power, till at length hardly the best comminuted morsel could pass the opening. Such, however, rarely enters the strictured œsophagus; the difficulty of deglutition renders it impossible for the appetite to be appeased. No sooner is the food placed before the animal than, because of hunger, induced by prolonged starvation, it is bolted, almost unprepared by mastication and insalivation. Nourishment in that state cannot pass the stricture; it lodges above the contraction; still, hunger impels the horse to eat on. It does so till the œsophagus becomes distended. Gullets have been taken from animals, stretched till they are thinner than the paper upon which this book is printed, and so much enlarged as to admit a boy's clenched fist.

After the affection reaches this stage, the swollen œsophagus, when loaded, presses upon the trachea and larynx so severely as materially to impede the breathing, and it is at this period that instinct develops a strange artifice. The horse has no power to vomit; the fibers of the healthy œsophagus impel but in one direction; still, no sooner has the gullet become distended than the impaired breathing creates a desire to remove the obstruction. The chin is lowered; the crest is thus curved to the utmost, when the muscles of the neck are brought into violent action, and the impacted provender is shot back through the mouth and nostrils.

THE HORSE ENDEAVORING TO CAST UP THE PROVENDER WITH WHICH THE SAC OF A STRICTURED ŒSOPHAGUS IS LOADED.

This description reads bad enough, but regard for veracity obliges the statement that is not yet complete. Hunger, when excessive, causes the stomach to pour forth its acid secretion; this effect is produced by the sight of provender; but the gastric juice not being given food to act upon, passes into the intestines; there it provokes the most intense spasm; so that it is common to see the hind legs raised to violently strike the aching belly, while the labored breathing announces that abstinence from any kind of exertion has become a primary necessity of life.

The only palliative for so pitiable a condition is carefully-prepared food—gruel and such substances given in small quantities at a time. The horse, however, when it requires such support, generally has been so much lowered by disease as not to be worth its ordinary keep. No one cares merely to prolong the equine life; the animal is only permitted to live because of the profit man can make out of its labor; yet, for the full meanness of the last motive, let the horse proprietor seek a better class of servants for his grooms. Let him abolish the stunted, long-faced, narrow-headed compounds of mischief and of treachery which are now the common inhabitants of every mews. Before doing so, however, he must amend himself; he must be prepared to teach by example; the present groom only fulfills the wishes and panders to the pride of the master. Were a higher order of stable-men desired, the longing could easily be supplied; but fashion pronounces in favor of the present, natty affectations, and men with more solid qualities naturally refuse to compete in an arena so unworthily occupied.

Before quitting this subject, a caution must be given against all pro-bangs as at present made. The cow probang is evidently unsuited to the equine gullet. The horse instrument has the bell of the cow probang attached to a piece of whalebone; when a narrow channel is to be entered, the bulk of the leading substance is of all importance. That which goes in front, not that which lies behind, has then to be considered; so, in spite of the whalebone, the present horse probang is nothing more than the cow instrument in disguise.

The probang intended for the horse should be formed like that employed upon the human subject. It should consist of a long slip of fine whalebone, having a sponge fixed to one end; when required, the sponge should be thoroughly saturated in water or in oil, (according to the circumstances,) then squeezed dry and forced down the œsophagus. The

The horse probang as at the present made.

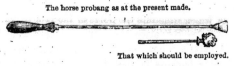

That which should be employed.

THE HORSE PROBANG, AS IT IS AND AS IT OUGHT TO BE.

material would adapt itself to every cavity, would fill the largest, but could not harm the smallest; would as effectually remove every obstruction, but would not be so difficult to retract, if the head should by accident pass the cardiac orifice.

BRONCHOCELE.

This disease, which entails much suffering upon the human species, under the name of "goitre," is, in the horse, a very trivial affair. The cause of its orign has not yet been made plain. It is, however, a sign that nature suffers in some essential particular. In the sunless depths of the valleys about the Alps, it is, with man, a frightful deformity. May not the dark and close stables, in which horses too often are confined, have something to do with its production in these animals?

It is an enlargement of a substance anatomically called the thyroid gland. This body resides upon the larynx, immediately under the jaw. It is occasionally as large as a hen's egg, but seldom is of greater magnitude. Its natural size is-that of half a chestnut. The enlargement appears to occasion no inconvenience, and is only objected to because horsemen consider it unsightly. Purchasers, moreover, are fastidious about buying an animal which exhibits any unusual development.

It, however, generally yields to treatment, and the animal need not be taken from gentle work during the time occupied by the cure. Let the following drink be given night and morning :—

Iodide of potassium	Half a drachm.
Liquor potassæ	One drachm.
Distilled water	Halt a pint

At the periods stated for giving the medicine, rub into the enlargement a portion of the annexed ointment. Remember, any of the unguent being left upon the hair is proof positive that sufficient friction has not been employed. The ointment can in no way benefit the external covering. The object of friction is to get the ointment absorbed. This it effects by promoting warmth, and thereby inducing dryness, both of which stimulate the pores of the skin to take up outward moisture.

When this is being accomplished, there is no necessity for extraordinary care or excessive attention The tumor, which constitutes **bronchocele**, is certainly not endowed with morbid sensibility. Sufficient force for the purpose in view, therefore, may be safely exerted; but, at the same time, it is always well, where horses are concerned, to discard anything approaching to violence. Consequently, exercise a proper discretion when employing the following ointment :—

Iodide of lead	One drachm.
Simple cerate	One ounce.

Supposing the tumor to be present only upon one side, a piece of the ointment as large as a hazelnut will be sufficient, if well rubbed in each time. Twice the quantity will be necessary when the swelling

A HORSE WITH BRONCHOCELE.

is to be seen upon both sides of the neck; and should the part become sore, of course all application must be stopped for the time necessarily occupied by the healing process.

CHAPTER VI.

CONGESTION IN THE FIELD.

It is a dangerous thing to trust a dumb animal to the guidance of an ignorant man; such a person is dangerous because he does not understand that certain preparation adapts vitality to particular usages. A racer may be a mysterious creature, about which he dares to think nothing,

A HORSE PROSTRATE FROM BEING OVERRIDDEN.

excepting that it is a horse, very beautiful and very fleet; a hunter, in his notion, is any horse running after hounds; he takes the stable favorite out for a morning canter, crosses the hunt, and immediately, with no thought of harm, joins the field. For the first few acres a very ungentlemanly person may, in a very gruff voice, request him to "hold hard and not to ride over the dogs;" but the first three fields passed, there is no need of such a caution. The horse, with that perfect abandonment of self which makes its will its master's choice, and converts the rider's pleasure into its delight, strains every nerve; its head is protruded and its legs outstretched; it struggles hard, but can make no way. 'Voice, whip, and spur by turns urge the animal onward, but it has been taken suddenly from its uses; the horse thinks not of that, it only seeks to gratify the being who for a time has become its ruler. To his amusement it devotes itself, and obedient to this idea, it runs, or endeavors to run, till its limbs are with difficulty lifted from the ground; it reels, it falls, and the would-be huntsman stands over a prostrate steed.

The horse has **congestion of the lungs.** Yes; but what caused it? Over-exertion, accompanied by a consequent absence of nervous energy. The sensibility of the larynx, feeling the exhaustion before the body appreciated it, inclined inward; they prevented the atmosphere from oxygenating the blood. Deficient oxygen causes the frame, spite of violent exertion, to feel clammy cold. The brain being supplied with impure blood, produces temporary insensibility. Vitality seems to be contesting with death.

Now, were a fleam, and some one who understood how to use it, at hand, venesection might do good; neither are to be found; the animal after some time rises, and with difficulty is led to shelter. Country opinions always incline to stimulants; gin and pepper is, in all rural districts, a potent horse physic   A dose is administered; the horse seems to amend; another and another jorum is poured down the animal's throat. After the third potion it is clear to all the horse is becoming worse. Bloody water, is soon blown from the nostrils; partial sweats break forth; the eye assumes a gray appearance; all at once the departing life appears to rally; the animal seems to walk with a firmer step; but just as this fact has been observed, it falls, and almost without a struggle expires.

Such is a lamentable instance of the general ignorance which prevails concerning horses. Firmly as nature may have united man and horse, gentility would dissever them; it is not polite in society to speak of man's most patient companion and most faithful slave. Gentility condescends to use animals, but loves to prate only of frivolity. The education of the young, which should be directed by the conversation of the matured, is thus neglected; boys, London boys especially, regard the stable as a place to be avoided; they view horses, not as the gentlest of created beings, but as creatures it were a breach of good manners to speak of "before ladies." They learn to consider these animals and all that concerns them, as subjects to be forgotten the instant "*society* is entered." From the ignorance thus fostered, and from the fashion which prefers to talk about trifles to conversing of those matters which constitute the facts of reality and involve the instruction of the youthful, springs that mishap which has been described as congestion of the lungs.

A noble animal is thus, by prejudice, denied the benefit which would otherwise result from social opinion. Woman, whose gentleness fits her for the companionship of the timid horse, is, as by design, kept in perfect ignorance of her lawful possession. The creature is separated even from those benefits which would result from the expression of feminine sentiment. A being that seeks protection, that with a submission amounting to a perfect denial of self, entreats for shelter and begs to serve, is handed over to the harshest order of the human race. Much more than this, it is transferred to the custody of the ignorant, who view its nature as requiring to be subdued, and think they display spirit when they treat the most fearful of living creatures as though it were a carnivorous brute bent upon ravening and destroying.

When a horse sinks in the field, bleed if possible; should the necessary means not be at hand, a vein may be punctured with a knife, and every vein in the body is then turgid with congestion. There is no difficulty of seeing where to puncture, and a pint taken at this time does more good than a gallon abstracted one hour subsequently. Then cover the body; pull off your own coat of there be any want of clothing; you caused the mischief and should not heed personal nicety when reparation is possible. Lead quickly but gently to the nearest stable; there heap hot rugs upon the body; the desire is to relieve the lungs by determining the blood to the surface; bandage the legs and cover the neck; warm the stable either with fire or by means of tubs full of boiling water. This being done, if a chemist lives in the neighborhood, procure one ounce of ether and half an ounce of laudanum, which dose, in rather more than half a pint of water, should be given, without any noise or bustle, every half hour. Should no chemist be near, take two tablespoonfuls of turpentine, which beat up with the yolk of an egg, and give in half a pint of water. Place a pailful of cold gruel within easy reach of the horse, and see that there is an ample bed under it   These things being done, do not leave the place before the fate of the horse is determined, which it invariably is before thirty hours have expired; for the proprietor's presence is the only surety that orders are obeyed, where horses and the uninstructed are concerned.

CONGESTION IN THE STABLE

This affection mostly attacks debilitated or fat horses These creatures are driven far in a four-wheeled carriage, heavily laden. One animal, of small size, has to drag an entire family. Else, the quadruped has to journey fast to avoid a shower of rain The horse is flogged onward. A horse, whose motions are quickened by the lash, is not likely to be very closely observed. It is much more probable the speed will be blamed as laziness, than the laboring life be pitied for exhaustion. Yet, when **congestion** follows, it is proof positive that the powers of nature were overtaxed.

The wretched slave, after the distance is accomplished, is taken from the shafts and led into the stable; it is hardly tied to the manger before a sickening sensation seizes on the body. The head hangs down; the furnished rack and manger are not glanced at. This alarms the groom's prejudices. At length the man imagines it must be thirst which prevents his charge from eating. The attendant hastens for water, but on his return he finds the horse blowing; that is, panting or breathing quickly.

CONGESTION IN THE STABLE.

This symptom, which only denotes exhaustion, used to be regarded as the forerunner of inflammation of the lungs. Doubtless, it would terminate thus seriously, were nothing done to arrest the progress of the affection. The change from extreme labor to perfect rest produces a revulsion of the system. The capillaries contract and soon become in a congested condition. Not only does this state affect the lungs, but it is present all over the body. Should the pulse be now taken, the artery will be round and gorged. The beat may be either quicker or slower than most books fix the number at; but it will be very feeble and will convey no idea of vital activity. It hardly stirs, suggesting the surging of a tranquil summer sea upon a sandy shore. Partial perspirations may break forth, and the body may become wet with a fluid of no higher temperature than the skin from which it exudes. The feet are cold; the eye is fixed; the living type of obedience moves not, when commanded; hearing is lost; all natural functions appear to be arrested, except the breathing; and that being involuntary, nevertheless is evidently disordered.

If this condition be immediately attended to, it will disappear almost as quickly as it was exhibited. Take two ounces each of sulphuric ether and of laudanum; cold water, one pint. Give this drink with caution, as the animal to which it is administered is not conscious. Have patience with sickness, and the whole will be swallowed; or the fumes will be inhaled and do almost as much good as the imbibition of the fluid.

The drink being given, do not leave the stable. Wait by the side of the horse, watching the effect of the draught. If in ten minutes the horse has not perfectly recovered, or be but partially restored, let another similar portion be poured into the body. More will seldom be required; but, notwithstanding, watch for twenty minutes after the last drink, as such fits occasionally vanish and reappear.

The rack and the manger must be emptied. Gruel is all we dare at present trust within reach of an exhausted frame. Though the animal would eat, solid food must be withheld The body should be lightly, but well clothed; and a pail of gruel should be suspended from the manger, so that a heavy head need not be raised high to partake of it.

The next day the creature, thus treated, may return to its customary food and be as well as ever; but when the animal reached home, should the groom have been in a hurry, if company should have been waiting for dinner, and the horse should be hastily turned into the stall by the only servant kept by gentility; then the congestion is unseen, and any disease may follow it This condition used to be, as fainting in the human being once was, treated by the abstraction of blood. But to bleed a debilitated horse, is to increase the cause of the affection, which it should be the province of physic to destroy. By the stimulant, which leaves behind no inflammatory tendency; by the subtle distillation, which speedily traverses the frame, we revive the system and awaken lagging nature once more to vital activity.

When congestion is not noticed in the first instance, and has time to become confirmed, the original disorder is invariably swallowed up in some greater evil. Pneumonia and pleurisy are the favorite shapes which it assumes; but it has terminated in fatal enteritis.

BRONCHITIS, OR INFLAMMATION OF THE AIR-PASSAGES.

This serious affection is, mostly, the consequence of man's neglect. The master rides far and fast. He dismounts at some pleasant threshold and remains long under the roof. During that time the horse stands outside, either shivering in the cold or pelted by the storm The general treatment seems to say, that life and machinery, being equally subservient to man's will, are, in fact, the same things in man's regard.

Even the wheels and bars of polished iron, however, require care or they
soon become useless; the thews and sinews of a living body cannot be
abused with impunity. So plain a truth should be acknowledged by
something more than words   Life and functions connect men and animals. Their habits may be dissimilar and their food not alike; ·but,
when we consider the wants of each, their liabilities and their diseases,
the approach to actual sameness becomes almost startling. The man
who can enjoy himself, without bestowing a serious thought upon the
unfortunate steed which has carried him hither and will bear him hence,
deserves to lose the life of which he is so culpably careless. Change the
places of the two existences. Let the horse be rendered comfortable
and the man be stationed outside. The result would be the same: the
man would in that case probably suffer from bronchitis. Does intelligence
require a more startling evidence of the link which binds master and
servant while sojourners upon this earth ?

Bronchitis is indeed a painful malady. Originally situated upon and
confined to the membrane lining the air tubes, it has an aptitude to involve the entire contents of the thorax   Being the ailment of mucous
membranes, it requires cautious treatment. A small blood-letting may
induce the prostration no tonics can remove; a slight dose of aloes often
starts up the purgation no astringents will check. It is agile at metas--
tisis   It too often leaves behind the evidence of its visitation. Add to
all this, that though so much to be feared, it does not announce its advent
with a thundering double knock. It creeps on insidiously, and comes in
so gradual a form, as if it intended to deceive the groom. The appetite,
during the primary stage, is often unaffected, nay, is sometimes increased.
Stable-men have a strong prejudice where feeding is concerned. The
most educated of the class can imagine nothing more than a slight
cold, while the corn is only partially consumed. Thus the disease, in
consequence of delay, mounts into fury, before its presence is fully recognized.

Very rarely is the groom's attention excited during the approach of
the disorder, or while a short cough simply bespeaks irritation; while
the breathing is merely excited; while the legs are warm; while the
mouth is moist, and the nasal membrane only a little deeper in hue than
is positively consonant with perfect health. No ! The stable-man is
content while any desire for food remains. Let appetite be quite gone ;
let the horse be averse to move ; the cough sore, but evidently suppressed
and painful; the breathing quick and audible; the nasal membrane
violently scarlet; the mouth hot, dry, and clammy; the legs and body
of uneven temperatures—here, cold as ice—there, of a dusty heat.
When danger cannot be mistaken, and hope has almost fled, then the

stable-man creeps to the parlor, with "Please, sir, I wish you would step and look at the horse."

In a case of such a description, abstract no blood. Depletion is forbidden, when mucous membrane is dis-ordered. The first thing is a large loose box. Into this is put the machine repre-sented in the annexed engraving. It is a portable boiler, having a covering of iron wire. The steam, generated by the char-coal fire, soon renders the air of the place moist and warm. It must be kept boiling day and night. It is of more service during night than day, and it should be very grad-ually withdrawn.

STEAMING APPARATUS FOR HORSES WITH BRONCHITIS.

The water, as it is exhausted in the above boiler, should be supplied with more at the full temperature. Very little fire will then keep up the steam, though, as the fumes of charcoal are decidedly unhealthy, it is always well when those fumes can, by means of a pipe, be conveyed to the outside of the building; if that be impossible, let every door and window be left open; the necessary admission of air may impoverish the steam, but the vapor is too dense to be entirely dispelled. The steam acts upon the lungs; warm, moist air being soothing and curative to the thorax affected with bronchitis. When the apparatus cannot be obtained, the large nose-bag should be frequently applied during the day.

Some scalded hay is also to be fixed under the throat by means of an eight-tailed bandage. A macintosh jacket is then laid on the floor, and the horse gently led forward till one leg rests within one armhole. The opposite leg is to be raised and put through the other opening; the cloth is next lifted up and temporarily fixed upon the animal; after-wards, have six pieces of flannel, two three yards long and the entire

EIGHT-TAILED BANDAGE FOR RETAINING ANY SUBSTANCE AGAINST THE THROAT OF A HORSE.

width of the fabric, the others half a yard long and a foot wide. Satu-rate three of these with cold water; having folded the long piece, apply it over the back, equally to either side; the short pieces place upon the sides of the chest; fasten the jacket over the spine. When the flannel is

warm, remove it; replace it immediately with other flannels, which should
be ready for this purpose. Do this continuously for at least a couple of
hours, after which time the flannel may remain on; but must, on no
account, be suffered to become dry. The jacket and flannel should be
worn for a week subsequent to restoration.

Then prepare the following :

Burgundy pitch	Half a pound.
Powdered camphor	Two ounces.
Powdered capsicums	Half a drachm.

Melt the pitch. Take the vessel which contains it off the fire ; throw
in the other ingredients, stir well, and apply while warm to the front of
the neck, as low as the jacket will permit.

For bronchitis, consisting principally of aggraved congestion, prepare

A HORSE DRESSED FOR BRONCHITIS.

the following drink, and repeat it every half hour, until the pulse has
regained its tone; then give the drinks at longer intervals, and ultimately
reduce them to three during the day, which continue till restoration is
perfected :—

Sulphuric ether	One ounce.
Laudanum	One ounce.
Water	One pint.

Should no effect be produced after the third drink, discontinue the
frequency of the ethereal medicine, and substitute the following :—

Infusion of aconite	Half an ounce.
Extract of belladonna (rubbed down with one ounce of water)	Half a drachm.

Persevere with the above till the pulse amends, when withdraw the
aconite, but keep on with the belladonna, half a drachm of which may be

added to each dose of the ethereal drink; which ought to be resumed, should amendment ensue upon the administration of the aconite draught.

Let the food consist entirely of thick gruel. The appetite occasionally is unaffected during bronchitis; but, however pleasant it may be to behold a horse masticate, all solids should be withheld, especially during the acute stage. Nothing is so injurious to respiration as a loaded stomach, and a single meal (if permitted) would speedily aggravate the symptoms of this disease. When the disorder has subsided, food must be carefully introduced; the water should be, as grooms say, "chilled," or, in ordinary language, should have the chill removed. Boiled roots or crushed and scalded oats should constitute the earliest approach to natural diet. Hay should be given with extreme caution, the desire being to nourish the body, not to load the stomach. A bundle of grass each day may be allowed upon recovery being assured; and when hay is at length presented, mind that for the first month it is thoroughly damped; for nothing more retards recovery after bronchitis than the inhalation of those dusty particles with which hay too often abounds.

THE COUGH OF INCURABLE BRONCHITIS,

When the disorder is to terminate fatally, the proprietor, in the majority of instances, speedily learns the fact. The pulse continues unamended at first, but soon grows very quick and tremulous; the breathing becomes more painful even to the spectator. Every inhalation appears to shake the body; yet, so eager is the desire for air, that the haste and violence of the respiration evidently defeat their object. The nasal membrane assumes a bluish tint, a foul, bloody froth hangs about the nostrils; the eyes are dull and fixed. The cough is the most distressing symptom. It occurs in fits, and during the paroxysms the wretched animal reels about. The noise cannot now be restrained; the horse has no strength to struggle with disease. The sound which shakes

9

the sore lungs and checks the breathing that was already short to suffocation, cannot now be suppressed. It continues until a quantity of discolored fluid is ejected from the nostrils, then a brief respite ensues; but, as time progresses, the fits grow more severe and much longer, while the strength to endure them even more rapidly decreases.

It reads sadly, that hundreds of horses have thus perished without making any impresssion upon either masters or men. The directions, which have been given at some length, will probably be discarded by grooms as far too troublesome; they like the man who can give physic to a horse when the animal is sick, and "wants no more bother made." The proprietors will object to the expense and the personal superintendence which is necessitated. Most gentlemen hurry through the stable as though they were intruders upon their own premises, and expected all business there transacted to be dispatched most expeditiously. The master, when in the stable, is never at home; he is generally very much abroad; the groom, if a horse dies, always knew of something which must have saved the life, only it wasn't tried; and to prove his comprehension of the malady, in answer to inquiries, he says, thereby showing the real extent of his information, "The horse caught a cold and died of an inflammation." The employer commonly follows a system which custom approves; he does not trouble himself to hire a better qualified or a less prejudiced attendant for his stables. The place and all that is in it continues the same, only it contains one life the less. The lesson is thrown away, and all this great suffering in a huge animal has produced no more than a passing regret for the pecuniary loss.

PNEUMONIA.—INFLAMMATION OF THE LUNGS.

Under this title our grandfathers congregated all affections of the lungs. Congestion, bronchitis, pleurisy were all regarded as stages of

THE COMMENCEMENT OF PNEUMONIA.

pneumonia. This error, even at the present time, confuses the descriptions of most authors. True pneumonia is, consequently, now more rarely encountered; such a result accords with the knowledge gained by anatomical investigation concerning the structure of or the substance of the lung. The bronchial tubes constitute a large portion of these organs, but their disease is termed **bronchitis.** The pleura covers the lungs, but its inflammation is called **pleurisy.** The blood is affected during all disorders; but the vessels themselves are rarely implicated; involvement of the absorbents constitutes glanders and farcy. Yet, when the tubes, covering, veins, arteries, and absorbents are abstracted, there remains only cellular tissue; that structure is not apt to take on inflammation, and when it is so implicated, the inflammation of cellular tissue is regarded as **rheumatism:** consequently, there remains only a species of general disorder of all the constituents to stand for pneumonia.

Horses supposed to have perished from pneumonia, not unfrequently, when examined after death, present hydrothorax or dropsy of the chest; thus proving the pleura to have been affected. However, such vivid descriptions of pneumonia are bequeathed us by our ancestors, that we are, to a certain degree, overpowered by the authority of assertion. Too many are actually overawed by the positiveness of the dead; thus, in many instances, influenza is treated as inflammation of the lungs; dropsy of the chest, brought on by weakness, naturally ensues.

When **acute pneumonia** (as it is called, which really represents a sub-acute disorder of all the contents of the lungs) does occur, it is rather lingering in its development; the breathing is labored and slightly accelerated; the pulse is less increased than would be expected; the artery is full, and the beat seems driven by some hidden force through a gelatinous obstacle; it bulges out, and then all is still for an interval, after which the operation is repeated. The horse has lost all spirit, indeed, a considerable portion of its consciousness has evidently departed; it stands as though from giddiness it feared to fall; its legs are separated and strained outward to the furthest limit.

The head and ears are dejected; the coat rough; the extremities cold; the body without

THE POSITION ASSUMED BY THE HORSE DURING AN AGGRAVATED ATTACK OF PNEUMONIA.

warmth; the visible membranes discolored, and the bowels costive; in short, the animal appears oppressed by some heavy misfortune. Feeling seems half dead; thus we are warranted in imagining that the attack has embraced all the component structures of the lungs, and that it consists in no small degree of congestion.

The general practice is to bleed, and to bleed largely; to let the current run till the animal is on the point of fainting; then, as bleeding always quickens the pulse, more blood is abstracted to lower it; this not answering, the same plan is adhered to. The vein is tapped and the liquor drawn, as though the vital fluid were table beer, and the animal an inanimate cask. At last, nature resents such repeated depletion. No sooner is the fleam struck than weakness is alarmed; then the eyes and nostrils are sponged with cold water, to procure a *little more* blood; until, at last, the animal dies, as practitioners have said, because the horse could not bear bleeding enough!

The writer does not advise to destroy the strength, which is now essential to surmount disease. Bleed only once, then take no more than will afford ease to the sufferer; if a pint accomplishes that object, a pint is sufficient. Be guided neither by the quantity abstracted nor by the faltering of the pulse; watch the head of the animal; so soon as that is raised and the general aspect denotes a sense of life, pin up the orifice; but think twice before you bleed once, and shun the operation if it can possibly be avoided, or if the fluid has a thick and black appearance, dribbling down the neck, not spirting from the vein.

When you first behold the horse, carefully examine it; place your ear to the side; in health there is only a gentle blowing sound audible; if more than that is heard; if something within the chest seems to grate or suck; if, in addition, any noise, as of a huge pair of bellows at violent work, is detected, make up your mind to a case of pneumonia. No time is to be lost; procure a large and airy loose box; strew it thickly with tan; do this, because pneumonia has an aptitude "to fall into the feet," as grooms say, or, in other language, the disease is subject to metastisis, and the inflammation will sometimes quit the lungs to reappear in the feet; something soft and cool is most likely to prevent such a mishap; therefore, when the tan is strewn upon the floor, moisten it with a watering-pot, and have the iron shoes taken off the animal.

A STEAMING APPARATUS.

Place a pail of water within easy reach of the horse. Food—even gruel—is not now required. If it is winter, put a hood upon the head and throw a loose cloth over the loins and quarters; then introduce the steaming apparatus, and set it to work with all speed, leaving every window and door open, while the vapor is generated. The air being loaded with vapor, take off all clothing; but give, in the first instance, so soon as it can be procured, the following drink:—

Solution of aconite root	Half an ounce.
Sulphuric ether	Two ounces.
Extract of belladonna (rubbed down in half a pint of water)	A drachm.

Repeat this dose three times in the course of the day and once during the night, keeping up the steam all the time. Watch the pulse and observe the breathing. When the first amends, the quantity of aconite may be diminished; when the last grows easier, the amount of belladonna may be decreased.

These medicines should be persevered with, increasing the ingredients or diminishing them, as the symptoms warrant. Thus, if the pulse prove very obstinate, six, or even nine doses of half an ounce of solution of aconite in a little water, without other ingredients, may be exhibited in the twenty-four hours. Should the breathing be severe, the belladonna may be augmented in a similar proportion. Until the symptoms are more than merely amended, the nourishment ought entirely to consist of hay-tea, with a little oatmeal boiled in it. When improvement decidedly takes place, the hay-tea may be made a little thicker, and a couple of pounds of boiled potatoes allowed per day. So soon as the appetite seems to be eager for food, a pint of crushed oats, thoroughly scalded, may be given six times during the day. Great care, must, however, be taken not to overload the stomach, or to permit a full meal: a single gorge is likely to provoke a return of the disorder. Little and often must be the rule at first; and the quantity may be increased while the frequency is diminished, as recovery is confirmed. Let some days elapse, however, before any hay is presented: this substance rather amuses the horse and fills out the stomach, than nourishes the body. Allow to enter the stable none of the groom's favorite drink, which consists of a handful of flour stirred into a pailful of cold water. The flour is not in solution —it soon sinks to the bottom; and the horse, which you intend should in some degree be nourished, receives nothing but water.

Order the cook to prepare the gruel, and see that she does it with as much care and cleanliness as she would exercise for any Christian. The groom's gruel is hot water, which may or may not be boiling, stirred upon a certain quantity of meal. A lady may conjecture how she would relish such a composition sent to her sick chamber; and the horse is as nice in its taste as any human being possibly can be.

Neither permit any grass to be put before an animal which is recovering from pneumonia. Grasses of all kinds contain the least possible nutriment in the largest possible bulk. The object now is to accomplish the introduction of nutriment in the most concentrated form. A distended stomach impedes the action of the diaphragm, and thereby is most injurious to the breathing.

A MUCH-WISHED FOR SIGHT DURING DISEASE OF THE LUNGS.

The first marked sign of improvement, during pneumonia, is the animal lying down. When this wished-for sight is before your eyes, do not enter to disturb the prostrate horse. It has, under disease, stood for several days. Its limbs must ache and its feet feel sore : make no noise, therefore. Respect the repose of the sufferer, and be grateful that your horse, probably, has escaped from danger.

If, subsequent to recovery, the restoration to perfect health is not so rapid as you could desire, be very particular about the feeding. At the same time apply a strong blister upon the front of the throat, down to the chest and between the legs. That blister having worn itself out, apply another upon the sides of the throat and the *upper part* of the ribs; but respect the sides of the thorax; because the animal rests on these parts, and, during recovery, rest is of more value than medicine. Nothing, therefore, should be permitted that is likely to prevent so beneficial a state from being indulged in. Abjure all purgatives—these favorite potions are too debilitating for pneumonia ; forbid all mashes ; nature, as she permits recovery, will, at her own time, relieve the body ;

adhere to the treatment which has been laid down; permit no tonics; care and good food are the best restoratives. But, above all things, be certain the health is thoroughly recovered before the horse, which has been seriously ill, is again compelled to labor.

Several states are mentioned as the consequence of pneumonia. Adhesion of the lung to the covering of the thorax is alluded to as one result of this disease; but before adhesion could take place, inflammation must have existed in the pleura, which lines the interior of the chest and envelops the lung itself; consequently, pleurisy must have been present before the pleura could be sufficiently inflamed for adhesion to ensue. The other condition is the result of congestion; the tubes and vessels alike are clogged, the lung is converted from its soft and spongy natural texture to a firm and solid substance resembling liver. But congestion is not pneumonia, neither is a solid state of the bronchial tubes by any means good evidence that pneumonia has provoked the morbid alteration.

ADHESION 1. THE PLEURA PULMONALIS UNITED BY DISEASE TO THE PLEURA COSTALIS.

a a. The pleura pulmonalis, or the natural covering of the lung.
b b. The pleura costalis, or the lining membrane of the chest.
c. The false adhesion, fixing the lung and preventing its full expansion.
d. The divided surface of the lung.

HEPATIZATION 2. OR THE LUNG BY DISEASE CONVERTED INTO A SUBSTANCE RESEMBLING LIVER.

Now, in conclusion, we must answer the important inquiry,—what is the cause of this affliction? Poverty, without dependence, inherits few disorders. Nature, in mercy, spares the peasant those visitations which are heaped upon the nobleman. To what, then, shall we attribute the ailment of a life so entirely in possession of another as that of the horse? Is it untruth to point to that which in ordinary language passes for the master's thoughtlessness? The creature is often worked, not to the point of fatigue, but is goaded to the possibility of exhaustion; fed upon the cheapest sustenance, and lodged according to the proprietor's convenience; made subservient to the whims of vanity, and forced to conform to the habits or the caprices of fashion; now, waiting patiently in the storm; then, hurried along the dusty roads through the parching heat; now, stopped during a long journey and expected hastily to consume the provender which shall support life the remainder of the distance: treatment like this will provoke more acute evils than pneumonia. The last disorder is of too dull a type to be begotten by so harsh a parent.

The horse which is pampered, or has much to eat and little work to do; the creature which for days may stagnate in the stable and then be suddenly brought forth to extraordinary exertion; the horse whose

owner is capricious; the animal whose work is uncertain; the quadruped which now is idle, and now is required to make good the lost
time,—is the living being prepared to exhibit any slow disorder—to
consume itself with the disease which an existence, properly treated,
would possess the energy to resist.

Is it strange, that a creature doomed to so much and such deep sub-
serviency, occasionally fails, even when possessed by what men call the
best of masters ? Is it just reason for wonder, that flesh occasionally
rebels against the treatment which human ignorance subjects it to ?
Were the horse not a very hardy animal, were not the life implanted
as firmly as the frame is set, it would not survive a tithe part of the
usage it now endures, and, notwithstanding, continues to live on and to
obey.

PLEURISY.

This most painful disease, like those of the lungs generally, visits
valuable horses during the years when they are most esteemed. The
unbroken colt is seldom attacked, and the aged animal is, to an almost
equal degree, exempt. The young steed, newly stabled, is liable; and
that liability remains up to the sixth year, when it gradually subsides.
It is a terrible affliction. Its anguish is localized and concentrated. It
is inflammation of the fine, glistening membrane covering the lungs and
lining the inside of the chest. At every inspiration and at every expiration the inflamed surfaces must move upon each other. To breathe is
the primary necessity of the creature's life It cannot exist and refuse
to inflate the lungs; yet is existence purchased at a price worth many
years of happiness. The inflamed surfaces cannot remain quiet; yet, to
render the condition of motion the more acute, inflammation stops the
secretion, which, during health, smoothed and lubricated the passage of
the membranes. During disease, the pleura is swollen, rough, and dry;
it grates or scratches as one surface is, by the necessity to breathe,
dragged over the other.

Membranes are sensitive in disease in proportion to the fineness of
their structure, and to their insensibility during health. The pleura
belongs to what are termed serous membranes. These line closed
cavities; as the chest, the abdomen, and the joints. Of the existence
of none of these are we conscious while they are free from disease ; but,
let the inflammation set in, and it would be difficult to decide which of
them is the most painful. Fortunately, however, **pleurisy**, when concentrated or singly present, terminates generally by the second day.

The symptoms, therefore, are quickly developed. The violence on
their first appearance has been so great, that an attack of **pleurisy** has

been mistaken for a fit of spasmodic colic. A little care will guard against so fatal an error. The pulse, in colic, is always natural at the commencement, and the fits, when they first occur, are invariably of short duration. In pleurisy, the vessel *strikes* the fingers; the blow is strong, and the artery is thin; the pain is continuous; the agony never remits or ceases; the horse never feeds; the body is hot, and indicates the fire within; the feet are icy cold; the muscles are frequently corrugated in patches, and partial perspirations break forth upon the surface; a cough is often, not invariably, present; it is always suppressed and dry; it suggests no notion that the intent is to clear the throat; the inclination to cough, from the larynx sympathizing with the lungs, is great; the feeling cannot be entirely mastered,—but the horse is fearful of indulging an impulse, which would violently shake the inflamed chest. The ear, placed against the ribs, detects a grating sound, and the respiratory murmur is less clear than usual. Pressure made on the free interspaces between the ribs sometimes deprives the animal almost of consciousness; it shrinks, and were the torture continued, it would fall. At other times anguish maddens even timidity,—the foot is lifted or the teeth are displayed, to repel the tormentor. When left alone, the head is frequently turned toward the side, with a piteous stare of wonder and inquiry. Altogether the animal is, as it were, inspirited by the disorder.

A HORSE SUFFERING UNDER PLEURISY.

The fore foot is scarcely ever quiet; it constantly paws, which action, in the horse, always expresses impatience or pain. The breathing, of course, is peculiar; a full inspiration the animal dare not take. Before inhalation is half completed the ribs fly backward. However, the backward action has hardly been accomplished before anguish once more compels a change; thus the breathing, to a looker-on, appears short, jerking, quick, and always imperfect.

The treatment must be active, as it is likely to be short. At the first outbreak, abstract enough blood to ease the horse, but take no more; place the sufferer in a cool, loose box; put woolen bandages upon all the legs, but leave the body unclothed; give, every quarter of an hour, a scruple of tincture of aconite in a wineglass of warm water. Feel the pulse before each dose; when that has softened, discontinue the aconite; every second hour then administer one ounce of sulphuric ether and of tincture of opium in a tumbler of cold water, to dispel any congestion that may lurk about the pleura, and also to lend smoothness or fullness to the pulse.

Pursue these measures for the first day and night. On no account be tempted to bleed a second time, for fear of that weakness which generates hydrothorax. When the pulse and pain are amended, should the cough remain, introduce the steaming apparatus twice described under the headings of the two previous articles The bowels are generally costive; be not alarmed; with the departure of the disorder they will relax. Place lukewarm water within the easy reach of the horse; but before the symptoms abate, introduce nothing of a more stimulating nature. When the disorder lessens, hay-tea may be allowed; as improvement increases, the diet may be gradually augmented after the manner described, when considering the treatment of pneumonia. Such care is essential, because any violent disorder in a confined part of the body has a tendency to involve other structures, and the danger of this increases as the inflammation is removed from the surface.

The tranquilizing of the respiration, the softness of the pulse and the return of the appetite will announce the departure of pleurisy. When these longed-for indications are remarked, blister the throat and chest: should any seeds of the malady appear to be not entirely removed, repeat the blister to the throat and chest. Should the bowels not be relieved, throw up copious enemas of blood-warm gruel; nothing more must be attempted. Aloes or salts are poisons during pleurisy; wait patiently, and in time the establishment of health will restore all the natural functions, or if they are very confined, a bundle or two of cut grass may be presented with the usual food

A yellow, transparent discharge from the nostrils, occasionally streaked with blood, and more or less otherwise discolored, a horrible anxiety of countenance, which seems to appeal mutely to every human being the saddened eye rests upon; quickened breathing, a more rapid but a sinking pulse, and a leaden state of the nasal membranes declare the probability of a fatal termination. Pleurisy, however, mostly ends in hydrothorax, for the character of which the reader is referred to the succeeding pages.

Now comes the sad inquiry, what is the cause of pleurisy? All kinds of things may excite it; but those things which lead to so much suffering in an inoffensive animal, are under the control of man. Overexertion, being driven or ridden far and fast, the spirit being stimulated, and the energy promoted by potent drinks; for men will give the contents of the public-house to the horse when a wager is at stake, and will lash, while the limbs can move, to win any pitiful bet,—these circumstances not unfrequently provoke pleurisy. Injuries received externally not unseldom start up internal inflammation. Hurts calculated to lead to so serious an evil, together with broken ribs, will not be surprising to those who have seen the unseemly instruments which man will, in his rage, seize upon to strike the animal with Colds, aggravated by change of temperature, as waiting long in the rain and being flurried home afterward; inattention in feeding, thus generating a plethora, is apt to disorder any internal organ, and many other such like causes will generate the disease.

And what right has man to inflict so much agony upon any life intrusted to his care? What right has humanity to complain of tyranny in its superiors, when the human race can neglect and entail such anguish upon the beings beneath them? The greed of gain or the pride of winning are the first motives assigned as the promoters of this terrible affliction; next come the gratifications of passion; then follows carelessness for another's welfare, etc. Which of these several causes is worth the torture of a living body? such torture, too, as the rack cannot equal, and human malice is happily forbidden to rival!

A little self-restraint instilled by a better plan of education, a little more humanity enforced by the teachers of religion, to instruct that man should not view himself as the owner of the earth which he temporarily inhabits, that man should not consider himself the proprietor of the lives which share the globe with him; that man should be actuated by genuine CHRISTIAN LOVE toward all animated nature, feeling kindly for the lives akin to his own, and acknowledging, as fellow-sojourners, the creatures by which he is surrounded,—then, how much affliction might be eradicated from that which wickedness alone renders a "vale of tears!"

HYDROTHORAX.

This is the consequence of the latter stage of pleurisy; or rather, to speak with caution, we fear it is often the result of the severe treatment adopted to dispel that malady.

Man leaves his property, which is very ill of pleurisy over night, hopeless that the animal can survive till morning. On returning, however,

to the stable early on the following day, to his surprise he beholds the
horse actually looking better. The pain has evidently abated, if not
altogether departed; the eye is more cheerful; the manner more en-
couraging. Having observed this, attention rests upon the flanks. The

A HORSE DYING OF HYDROTHORAX.

motion of these parts is greatly increased. They are now forcibly
brought into action. The suspicion is awakened. The ear is applied
to the chest. Near the breast bone, or low down, all is very quiet. A
little higher up nothing can be heard; but rather past the middle of the
ribs the sound of breathing is once more detected. Again and again is
the experiment repeated, until the disappointed proprietor is forced to
believe that which is against his hope.

Still clinging to chance, after conviction has gained possession of his
mind, there is another trial he will make to render despair a certainty.
He seeks some man—any one will do; and having found a loiterer, he
returns with him to the stable. He places this individual upon one side
of the horse, and tells the man to slap the side of the animal with the
open palm, when the word "now" is spoken. This being arranged, the
master goes to the opposite side. He puts his ear to the place where
the silence ceased. Having assured himself the spot he has chosen is
correct, he pronounces the monosyllable "now." Directly afterward a
dull sound is heard, and a metallic ring or splashing noise is soon afterward audible.

All now is confirmed, yet, "to make assurance doubly sure," the owner
tries to take the pulse at the jaw. There is none to be felt! The hand
is then placed near the chest, upon the left side and over the region of
the heart. The sensation of a throb, coming through water, is percepti-

ble. The last requirement is confirmed. The horse has **dropsy of the chest,** and the termination of the disorder is all but certain.

The first thing to be done, in these cases, is to draw off the liquid before it soddens the pleura and further distresses the already labored

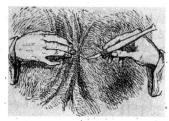

MAKING THE PRIMARY INCISION FOR TAPPING
THE CHEST.

A TROCAR WITH THE STILET UPON IT.

REMOVING THE FLUID IN
HYDROTHORAX.

breathing. The manner of performing this operation is very simple, and the operation itself remarkably safe. A spot near the inferior margin of the chest being selected, a small portion of skin, between the eighth and ninth ribs, is pulled forward, and then a narrow slit with a sharp knife is made upon the place which the skin originally covered. A trocar, armed with a stilet, is then inserted into the opening, and so much force applied as suffices to propel it onward. The moment all resistance ceases, the trocar is within the cavity of the thorax. The stilet is then withdrawn, and the water usually flows forth.

There is in this operation no danger of piercing the lung. The trocar must be driven upward and onward, very far and very forcibly, to induce such an effect. The lung is protected from all lawful violence by the water, on the top of which it floats.

There is, however, a dispute concerning how much of the fluid should be extracted. It is a good rule to take all you can get, or all the condition of the horse will permit to be abstracted. Do not commence the operation with any determinate quantity in your mind. Take all, if the horse will suffer so much to be withdrawn; but if the animal, after the loss of a quart, shows signs of approaching faintness, withdraw the trocar, let the skin fly back, and wait a more favorable opportunity for the next attempt.

In an hour or two the trial can be repeated. Make a new opening (for never risk exciting irritation in the original wound, by again thrust-

ing the trocar through it) There are but few precautions to be observed during the performance of tapping the chest. It is usual to
teach, that the posterior border of the ribs is to be avoided, because this
portion of the bones is grooved for the reception of the artery. Anatomy,
however, shows that such vessels are amply protected by the grooves in
which they travel.

There is also some selection to be made in the trocar which shall be
employed. If the tube be of too great a size and permits the fluid to
gush quickly out, nature may sink under the sudden change induced: the
water, consequently, ought to be very gradually abstracted. For this
purpose, the instrument cannot well be too small. The most diminutive
of those made for human practice will be quite large enough, so that the
bulk of liquid within the chest may be insensibly removed, and the horse
be scarcely aware of the change. Those trocars, however, which are
made for the human practitioner will not be long enough; therefore one
must be procured longer, but of the like bore.

Sometimes, after the trocar is properly inserted, no fluid will pour
forth: the operation is then all but hopeless. It must have been so
long delayed that various substances have been secreted. These cover
the interior of the chest. They obstruct the mouth of the cannula and
prevent the liquid issuing by the tube.

It is customary, in these cases, to employ a whalebone probe. This
is inserted up the trocar, and then moved about in different directions.
The intention is to break down the layer of pus or lymph lining the
thorax, and to allow the water to leave the cavity. But this is almost
needless, as the author does not recollect a single case of this description
which ultimately survived.

It is also advisable to draw off the fluid from both sides at the same
time, so there may be no pressure upon the delicate divisions of the
chest, and upon the important vessels within them. But happily the
fluid is, in the first instance, generally confined to one side only.

Always pull a piece of skin either backward or forward, before the
incision is made through the integument. The reason for doing this is,
because, when the trocar is removed, the skin may resume its proper
place, and act as a valve, keeping out the atmosphere from the cavity;
for external air, getting into the interior of the chest, is proved to be
most injurious to life.

There is to be tendered but one last admonition; even this has been
in a great measure anticipated by the previous observations. The
animal must not be left during the operation. Whatever time may be
consumed by the withdrawal of the liquid, the operator must remain a
patient spectator of the slow abstraction; for if the horse should be

left, syncope may come on during such absence, and the animal, on the person's return, be found prostrate upon the ground. On the first sign of weakness, the cannula should be at once removed; for, should it be suffered to remain, regardless of this caution, the horse may even die through sudden collapse.

The treatment, after the withdrawal of the fluid, is entirely changed; pleurisy has now departed, and weakness is left behind. The most nourishing but carefully-prepared food must be given; boiled oats and beans may be allowed in any quantity which the animal will consume, while the following ball should be administered, night and morning:—

Iodide of iron	One drachm.
Strychnia	Half a grain.
Sulphate of zinc	Half a drachm.
Extract of gentian and powdered quassia .	Of each a sufficiency.

That which will denote a fatal termination is restlessness; neighing; partial sweats; swellings under the region of the chest, and a distressed breathing, which nothing can relieve. The death struggle is as short as the disease has been painful.

DISEASE OF THE HEART.

This affection is characterized by various names in scientific books, as carditis, pericarditis, hydrops pericardii, inflammation of the pericardium, etc. All such conditions in the horse were discovered by examinations instituted after death, when, unfortunately, all opportunity of observing the symptoms had ceased. Veterinary science cannot distinguish one state from another, while life exists. Probably this deficiency may be attributed to the inutility of such discrimination. **Disease of the heart** in horses is incurable. In man, who can strictly conform to his physician's orders;

DISEASE OF THE HEART IN THE HORSE.

avoid excitement; abstain from exertion; eat only such a quantity of such a food, prepared after such a manner; feed at such an hour and rest at such a time; who can live by rule;—in man, the diseases of the heart are only to be delayed, not driven from their certain issues.

Practically, therefore, so the heart be diseased, it is of small import what shape the disorder may assume. The death is always sudden; it is likely to occur when the horse is journeying at its topmost speed; when accident generally follows. Consequently, it is perhaps wiser to take the life, thus afflicted and thus dangerous The horse may appear blooming, may even be skittish; yet, the existence shall at any moment be cut short. Auscultation affords the surest means of detection. Place the ear close to the left side and lower part of the chest; if any unusual sound be audible, conclude the heart to be diseased.

The signs visible, externally, are sometimes sufficiently emphatic to admit of no doubt The eye is expressive of constant anguish; the countenance is haggard; the pulse is feeble and irregular, but the heart throbs; its throbs are visible, and frequently they are to be seen as plainly on the right side as on the left The beat is occasionally so violent as to shake the body. The carotid artery can be felt to pulsate in the neck. The regurgitation, within the jugular vein, is nearly always excessive,—it often reaches almost to the jaw. It takes place by jerks, which ascend high and higher, each becoming less and more weak, as it mounts upward.

An attempt to represent this has been hazarded in the illustration. It is, however, impossible to truthfully depict action; and the reader will comprehend the jerks, in nature, do not occur all at the same period; but the first subsides before the second can be exhibited.

The appetite is sometimes ravenous ; more often it is fastidious The breathing is not accelerated, excepting during the existence of pain; lameness is occasionally witnessed in one fore leg; dropsical swellings and abdominal pains have been observed. The animal, when progressing, will suddenly stop, tremble, and appear about to fall; as suddenly, it will recover and proceed upon the journey. Noises, expressive of acute anguish, are, under the impulse of the moment, occasionally uttered. Sometimes the horse cannot be made to move, and it is always averse to turn in the stall. Often it is seen to yawn; but more frequently has been known to heave long and deep-drawn sighs. No ascertained sign, however, announces the climax of the disorder to be near at hand. Death is always unexpected, and, therefore, is a surprise.

The cause of heart disease is unknown. It may, however, be surmised from the fact that it is most common in gentlemen's stables, and is all but engrossed by the animals which have for years been subjected to the abuses therein practiced. It is incurable; and all physic is thrown away upon this disorder.

CHAPTER VII.

THE STOMACH, LIVER, ETC.—THEIR ACCIDENTS AND THEIR DISEASES.

SPASM OF THE DIAPHRAGM.

THIS is generally provoked by the heedlessness of the rider. A horse is "overmarked," as the condition is technically called, when the animal is urged onward to the point of falling. The person who may occupy the saddle then becomes conscious of a strange and loud noise coming from the body which he strides; it appears to the equestrian as though

THE YOUNG GENTLEMAN AND THE OLD HORSE.

some demon were located within the carcass, and were violently striking the sides. Should the indication be observed, the noise will be found to proceed from behind or immediately under, rather than from any part anterior to the rider.

The noise is produced by **spasm of the diaphragm.** The horse must, as the word "overmarked" seems to imply, have been pushed far beyond the point where man should have pulled the rein. A little distance farther, after the symptom is devoloped, will bring the animal to the ground; let the check, therefore, be immediately given; the rider should

10 (145)

dismount; the loins be covered with the gentleman's coat, if nothing better be at hand; he who has caused the misery is bound to make any sacrifice for its alleviation.   The girths should be loosened, the bridle removed, and when time has passed for the system to become slightly tranquilized, the sufferer should be very gently led to the nearest shelter. So soon as it is under cover, the following drink should be administered, but time should be taken to give the medicine, as the condition of the horse forbids all haste :—

Sulphuric ether	Two ounces.
Tincture of camphor	Half an ounce.
Tincture of opium	One ounce.
Cold water or gruel	One pint.

This should be repeated every quarter of an hour, till four drinks are swallowed; then the intervals should be lengthened to half an hour, and, as the symptom decreases, the medicine ought to be administered at still longer periods, and ultimately, but gradually, withdrawn

There are, however, other things to be done   When the animal is first brought in, procure five quiet assistants; give a leg-bandage each to four of the helpers, and a sponge, with a basin of cold water, to the fifth.   Order the men to perform their ministration silently; the four are to bandage the four legs while the fifth sponges out the mouth, nose, eyes, and anus; this done, the body is to be superficially cleaned   Sweat is to be removed and dirt taken off; the ears pulled, and the head made comfortable; the tail and mane having been previously combed, a hood and body clothing should be put on.

All this should be well understood beforehand; while it is being accomplished not a word should be spoken; nothing is more soothing to an agitated system than perfect silence.   Wet swabs should then be placed upon the feet, a pail of gruel suspended from the manger, and a man left to warn off all noisy strangers from the exterior of the building; for during spasm from overexertion perfect quietude is quite as essential as medicine

Spasm of the diaphragm, if taken in time, is not generally fatal; and no man, however determined a " Nimrod" he may be, is justified in proceeding after having recognized so mysterious a warning.   The sound before alluded to must emphatically inform him all is not right with the animal on which he is seated.   It is folly to urge that the horse enjoys the chase as much as the rider; no life would, for its own pleasure, run itself to a spasmodic exhaustion.   Old hunters may have left the field to follow the hounds; the animals, however, obey only the impulse of education, and did what they imagined would gratify their superiors. The horse is given as a servant to man; the creature is obedient to its destiny; to serve is its lot, to please is its reward. Body and soul it devotes to the heartless being who is assigned its appointed lord; it will spend its last breath in the gratification of its master; such affection surely merits better treatment than the quadruped generally receives.

When spasm of the diaphragm terminates fatally, approaching dissolution is announced by easily recognized signs. The pulse cannot be felt at the jaw; the heart only flutters; the feet are icy cold; a yellow discharge drains from the nostrils; the breath becomes fetid; the pupil of the eye enlarges; the horse wanders round and round its box; it soon sinks and perishes.

ACUTE GASTRITIS.

This most painful affliction is only known in the horse as the consequence of some poisonous substance being swallowed. Poisoning entire teams of valuable horses has followed the use of certain powders, these being mixed with the corn; the intention was to improve the personal appearace of the animals to which the drug was administered. Carters have a large faith in condition powders, and a distant belief in the *magic* of medicine; in their ignorance, they spend their hard-earned wages to procure the stuff, too often compounded of agents which never should be trusted in the hands of the uneducated. The men argue, if these powders, say one spoonful given each night, will make the horse bloom in a fortnight, two spoonfuls must do the same thing in a week; the spoonful

A HORSE SUFFERING FROM ACUTE GASTRITIS.

possibly contains the utmost limits of the dose; that quantity exceeded may endanger or destroy life. But ignorance is always impatient; it ever desires the speediest results; and if accident attends its eagerness, indignation should be visited upon those who put responsible trusts in such keeping; upon the men who for gain sell poisonous drugs to the obviously uninformed

Books and charts are published, explaining the various antidotes and tests to be employed for the detection and counteraction of the different poisons. Such authorities are of little service in the stable; the tests require care and time for their application; the symptoms are mostly so urgent as to permit no leisure for scientific inquiry. In an acute case, dependence must be placed on general principles, and fortune must be relied on to guide the result.

Certain poisons act instantaneously and without any warning sufficiently energetic to be interpreted, as the twigs or leaves of the yew-tree.

Other agents immediately establish the lesson which sometimes speedily kills, but more often produces consequences which will ultimately destroy life, though death may be some time before it occurs, as the mineral acids, etc.

The presence of particular kinds is announced only by violent disorder, as powerful diuretics and potent purgatives.

The symptoms, therefore, are not decided; the carter has his motives for silence, and the inability of the horse to vomit forbids the earliest announcement of deranged stomach The time for antidotes has generally passed before attention is excited; to support the life, in the hope that it may survive the destroyer, is evidently the best thing which can, under such circumstance, be adopted Chloroform, ether, and opium render the body insensible, and, by sparing the nervous system, certainly existence will be prolonged Purgatives had better be withheld; they may already have been administered in enormous doses; fearful amounts of aloes destroy life without purgation being exhibited.

Against alkalies there does not exist the same objection; carbonate of magnesia, carbonate of soda or of potash may, in quantity, be mixed with gruel and horned down; both opium and ether may be blended with the drink. Should the pulse be low, a drachm of carbonate of ammonia may be added to each dose of the other ingredients Should corrosive sublimate be in any degree suspected to be the agent employed, mix one dozen eggs with the other components; these will in no way detract from the operation of the drench.

The mixture should be given in as large quantities as the animal can be induced to swallow. The gruel should be quite cold, and one quart should constitute a dose. No bleeding should be permitted; the abstraction of blood promotes absorption; to prevent the absorption of the poison is the present endeavor. The following draught contains all that can be recommended, so long as ignorance of the actual poison it is desired to counteract, exists. When the information is positive, of course Morton's Toxological Chart will be a far better guide than any observations the author has ability to offer.

   Sulphuric ether and tincture of opium . . . Of each three ounces.
   Carbonate of magnesia, of soda or potash . . Four ounces.
   Gruel (quite cold) . . . . One quart.

To these may be added, should the pulse be of a sinking character :—

   Carbonate of ammonia . . . . One drachm.

If corrosive sublimate is known to have caused the agony, one dozen raw eggs ought to be blended with the drench.

Use discretion in the administration; but repeat the drinks as often and as quickly as can be accomplished without adding to the distress of the horse. Regard the state of the animal, and, if weakness be present, take time when giving the drench. Should delirium be displayed, do not trust to the natural functions; employ Read's pump, with the horse catheter attached, and inject, with all dispatch, the whole quantity at once through the nostril.

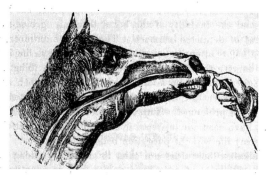

HOW TO GIVE PHYSIC, WHEN THE USUAL MODE OF ITS EXHIBITION IS ATTENDED WITH DANGER.

The symptoms of poisoning are various; they are also modified by the strength upon which they act. The annexed list, however, contains the general appearances by which poisoning is announced, though the whole of the symptoms are never simultaneously exhibited: Loathing of all food; extreme thirst; redness of the nasal and conjunctival membranes; discharge of ropy saliva; frequent eructations, which smell pungently fetid; colic, rolling on the ground, pawing, striking at the abdomen, etc.; tucked-up flanks; heaving; panting; small, quick pulse; superpurgation; violent straining; passing of mucus in large quantities; protrusion and inflammation of the opening; glances at the abdomen; prostration of strength; convulsions; madness and death.

And now, whence is derived the source of this evil? It springs from the ignorance of the age. Is it not, at the present day, a common saying, that "intelligence goes begging, while handicraft finds employment?" Goodness, education, and industry cannot, at this time, insure the bread which will support existence The cunning and the knowingness of the uninformed is much preferred. There is no mystery in the groom's office which might not be acquired in a week. The horse would fare better and be more safe in the custody of a person who possibly might sympathize with its solitude and appreciate its disposition. A higher class of servants would involve a higher rate of wages. But these might be paid, and notwithstanding, the horse proprietor be, in the long run, an evident gainer To put the wounds inflicted on the sensibility of a feeling man out of the question, it is a heavy misfortune to look upon three or four valuable horses stretched out in death. Add to this, there are other accidents that ignorance, without malice, commits, and all of which must be paid for by the master. Then there are the petty frauds and understandings in which cunning delights, and all of which are indulged at the master's cost. On the other hand, there is the certainty, or all but certainty, that intelligence would perform its duty. The horses would thrive better and last longer when confided to proper custody. The losses, attendant upon ignorance, would be avoided,—not to mention the ease of mind secured by confidence in the probity of the person to whom authority is intrusted. What a mockery it is, to cry up education and then to shun the educated! A stimulus would be given to the ignorant, when it is recognized that the informed will be alone engaged to fill offices of trust.

CHRONIC GASTRITIS.

This affection is more general than is commonly understood. The horse being unable to vomit, of course the first positive proof of disordered stomach cannot be exhibited. Thus, little attention is generally paid to its digestion, when primarily diseased.

Chronic gastritis is usually said to be provoked by rearing upon sour or soft land; but well-bred animals are very often subject to the malady. The ailment is frequently first displayed at the period when the services are esteemed most valuable, or between the fifth and sixth years, long after the mode of rearing must have ceased to operate. The symptoms are various, and hardly ever alike. The stomach may affect the nervous symptom; then, its complications become difficult to disentangle. The affection is mostly declared by an irregularity of bowels and a capriciousness of appetite. The animal starts off violently purging. The looseness stops as suddenly as it commenced Obstinate costiveness then sets in, and each state can be traced to no obvious reason. The straw or litter may be eaten ravenously, but all the wholesome provender obstinately refused. The dung shows the condition of the appropriating functions; it crumbles upon the slightest force being imposed; it appears to consist of fibers not agglutinated together. Sometimes it is coated with mucus, and always smells abhorrently. A dry cough may be present; the visible membranes are pallid; the mouth feels cool; the breath is tainted; the eyes are sunken; the respiration is catching; the belly is pendulous; the anus is lax and prominent; the coat dry and ragged; while the body quickly becomes emaciated.

A HORSE WITH CHRONIC GASTRITIS INDULGING ITS MORBID APPETITE.

The slightest exertion produces a thick and copious sweat. The symptom, however, which is most remarkable, when the cleanly habits natural to the animal are considered, is the peculiarity of the appetite. The rack and manger are generally neglected; but every unnatural or offensive substance, within reach of the extended jaws, is devoured with avidity. Woodwork has largely disappeared. Soil and stones have been removed from the stomachs of creatures destroyed for incurable disease. Either of the substances last named, however, are usually spared, so long as a morsel of plaster, a portion of mortar or of brick, is within reach. Animals, when in the field, will leave the grass and enter any ditch to gnaw at bricks and mortar. When confined, they will, under the morbid influence of this affection, employ themselves for hours searching for a morsel of either among the straw.

The old custom of purging and bleeding for a case of this kind is positively injurious. It is better to administer bitters, alkalies, and sedatives;—the first, to amend the appetite; the second, to correct the acidity of the morbid secretion; the third, to destroy the uneasy sensation which provokes too many of the symptoms.

Powdered nux vomica	One scruple.
Carbonate of potash	One drachm.
Extract of belladonna	Half a drachm.
Extract of gentian and powdered quassia	Of each a sufficiency.

Or,

Strychnia	Half a grain.
Bicarbonate of ammonia	One drachm.
Extract of belladonna	Half a drachm.
Sulphate of zinc	Half a drachm.
Extract of gentian and powdered quassia .	Of each a sufficiency.

    Give, morning and night.

One of the above balls may be given daily. When their benefits seem exhausted, give, instead of a ball, half an ounce each of liquor arsenicalis, the same of tincture of ipecacuanha, with one ounce of muriated tincture of iron and of laudanum, in a pint of water. Also, damp the food and sprinkle magnesia freely upon it. Then, as the strength improves, introduce sulphuric ether, one ounce; water, one pint, daily; and ultimately change this last for a quart of good ale or stout.

Before concluding, there remains to point out the cause of this lamentable affection. Ignorance views each part of the body as distinct; it cannot see the various components are connected, and, in the mass, constitute one whole. Thus, medicine appears to the uninformed as thrown away, when internally administered for a skin disease. So it may to such persons appear strange how the air inhaled can disorder the digestion! To those better informed, however, it will only seem a natural consequence that impure atmosphere, inspired day and night, should impair the body's health. It will, with such people, be recognized as likely that the disorder should break forth when the frame is on the eve of being matured. The cause of indigestion is close and unhealthy stables. What loss will instruct mankind, that they cannot enslave life and treat it according to their convenience? Life has its natural rights: these cannot be disregarded—the requirements of breathing creatures must be fulfilled. The ability of the enslaver to use according to his pleasure, must not be selfishly regarded; else nature is outraged, and in its deprivation, pride learns the impossibility of forcing all things to conform with its inclinations.

BOTS.

No animal which has not been turned out to graze during the summer months can possibly be troubled with these parasites. Such annoyances form no light argument against the benefits accomplished by that which is in slang phrase termed *"Dr. Green."* The appearance of the coat and aspect of unthriftiness, after a run at grass, generally declare bots to be present within the body.

Uninformed persons are always desirous to possess some medicine which will destroy bots; they wonder that science lacks invention sufficient to compound such an agent. An anecdote may probably dispel such astonishment.

A patron of the Royal Veterinary College was once conducted by a pupil through the museum belonging to that establishment; the pair at last stood before the preparation of a horse's stomach, eaten through by, and also covered with, bots.

"God bless my soul!" exclaimed the visitor, after the nature of the specimen had been explained "What a spectacle! What a myriad of tormentors! And have you no medicine to remove such nuisances? Can veterinary science discover nothing capable of destroying those parasites?"

"Why, sir," replied the student, "only look at that preparation. To my knowledge, it has been put up in spirits of wine, and corked air tight for two years. The creatures must be either very dead or very drunk by this time; yet, as you witness, they hold on. What sort of physic could accomplish more than is already effected by the spirits of wine and close confinement? I am at a loss to conjecture!"

For the above, the author is indebted to the admirable lectures delivered by Professor Spooner; but the conclusion drawn by the student must be more than satisfactory. Bots, once within the stomach, must remain there till the following year, when, being matured, their hold of the lining membrane of the viscus will relax, and, in the form of a chrysalis, they are ejected from the system. No medicine can expedite the transformation. It has hitherto appeared easier to kill the horse than to remove the parasite.

To the investigation of Bracy Clark, Esq , V. S , the public owe all their knowledge of the fly whence the bot is derived. The common parent, according to the above authority, is the œstrus equi; and the author gladly avails himself of the original description by the above-named talented gentleman

"ON THE ŒSTRUS EQUI, OR THE STOMACH BOT.

"When the female has been impregnated, and the eggs sufficiently matured, she seeks among the horses a subject for her purpose, and approaching him on the wing, she carries her body nearly upright in the air, and her tail, which is lengthened for the purpose, curved inward and upward: in this way she approaches the part where she designs to de-

posit the egg; and, suspending herself for a few seconds before it, suddenly darts upon it, and leaves the egg adhering to the hair: she hardly
appears to settle, but merely touches the hair with the egg held out on
the projected point of the abdomen. The egg is made to adhere by
means of a glutinous liquor secreted with it. She then leaves the horse
at a small distance, and prepares a second egg, and, poising herself
before the part, deposits it in the same way. The liquor dries, and the
egg becomes firmly glued to the hair: this is repeated by these flies till
four or five hundred eggs are sometimes placed on one horse.

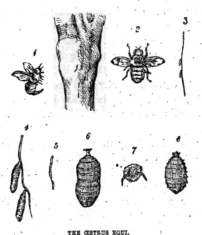

THE ŒSTRUS EQUI.

Copied from the Work on Bots, by Bracy Clark, Esq.

1. The female fly about to deposit an egg.   5. The newly-hatched bot.
2. The male fly.   6. The bot full grown.
3. The egg, its natural size.   7. The head of a bot magnified.
4. The egg, magnified.   8. The chrysalis.

" The skin of the horse is usually thrown into a tremulous motion on
the touch of this insect, which merely arises from the very great irritability of the skin and cutaneous muscles at this season of the year,
occasioned by the heat and continual teasing of the flies, till at length
these muscles appear to act involuntarily on the slightest touch of any
body whatever.

" The inside of the knee is the part on which these flies are most fond
of depositing their eggs, and next to this on the side and back part of
the shoulder, and less frequently on the extreme ends of the hairs of the
mane. But it is a fact worthy of attention, that the fly does not place
them promiscuously about the body, but constantly on those parts which

are most liable to be licked with the tongue; and the *ova*, therefore, are always scrupulously placed within its reach.

"The eggs thus deposited I at first supposed were loosened from the hairs by the moisture of the tongue, aided by its roughness, and were conveyed to the stomach, where they were hatched: but on more minute search I do not find this to be the case, or at least only by accident; for when they have remained on the hairs four or five days, they become ripe, after which time the slightest application of warmth and moisture is sufficient to bring forth in an instant the latent *larva*. At this time, if the tongue of the horse touches the egg, its *operculum* is thrown open, and a small active worm is produced, which readily adheres to the moist surface of the tongue, and is from thence conveyed with the food to the stomach.

"At its first hatching it is, as we have observed, a small active worm, long in proportion to its thickness; but as its growth advances, it becomes proportionably thicker and broader, and beset with bristles.

"They are very frequent in horses that have been at grass, and are in general found adhering to the white insensible tissue or coat of the stomach.

"They usually hang in dense clusters to this white cuticular lining of the stomach, and maintain their hold by means of two dark-brown hooks, between which a longitudinal slit or fissure is seen, which is the mouth of the larva. When removed from the stomach by the fingers by a sudden jerk, so as not to injure them, they will, if fresh and healthy, attach themselves to any loose membrane, and even to the skin of the hand. For this purpose they sheath or draw back the hooks almost entirely within the skin, till the two points come close to each other; they then present them to the membrane, and keeping them parallel till it is pierced through, they expand them in a lateral direction, and afterward, by bringing the points downward toward themselves, they include a sufficient piece of the membrane, to remain firmly fixed for any length of time as at anchor, without requiring any further exertion.

"These bots, as is also the case with two or three other species, pass the autumn, winter, and spring months in the stomach, and arrive about the commencement or middle of the summer at their full growth, requiring a twelvemonth fully to complete their structure."

"ON THE ŒSTRUS HEMORRHOIDALIS, OR FUNDAMENT BOT.

"The part chosen by this insect for this purpose is the lips of the horse, which is very distressing to the animal from the excessive titillation it occasions; for he immediately after rubs his mouth against the ground, his fore legs, or sometimes against a tree, with great emotion; till the animal at length finding this mode of defense insufficient, enraged he quits the spot, and endeavors to avoid it by galloping away to a distant part of the field; and if the fly still continues to follow and tease him, his last resource is in the water, where the œstrus never is observed to pursue him. These flies appear sometimes to hide themselves in the grass; and as the horse stoops to graze, they dart on the mouth or lips, and are always observed to poise themselves during a few seconds in the air, while the egg is preparing on the extended point of the abdomen.

THE ŒSTRUS HEMORRHOIDALIS.

Copied from the Work by Bracy Clark, Esq.

1. The female fly about to deposit an egg.   3. The bot.
2. The egg, magnified.   4. The chrysalis.
      5. The male fly.

"When several of these flies are confined in a close place, they have a particularly strong, musty smell; and I have observed both sheep and horses, when teased by them, to look into the grass and smell it very anxiously; and if they by these means discover the fly, they immediately turn aside and hasten to a distant part of the field.

"I once saw in a meadow or field, upon the cliffs at Margate, a fly of this sort teasing a horse that was confined to a small space by a spike stuck in the ground, to which a cord was tied. He could not get away from its attack, and became quite furious, for in kicking at the fly with his fore foot, which he did vehemently, he often struck the bone of the lower jaw, creating excessive pain; for in that direction while grazing, the fly comes to the beard of the lower lip.

" The eggs of this species are difficult to be seen upon the horse's skin or beard, owing to the agitation of the beast, and from the color of the egg being dark like that of the skin of the horse The animal has been generally too impatient, while undergoing this operation, to let me examine them very well. I ascertained, however, its form by pressing one of these eggs from the abdomen.

" The larva or grub of this species inhabits the stomach as the former, generally adhering to the white lining, and is disposed promiscuously in dense clusters, after the same manner; they may, however, be distinguished from them by being in general smaller and longer in proportion to their bulk

" The larva of this species may be obtained from almost any horse that has been much the preceding year at grass, and exposed to these flies, and will be found during the summer months sticking more or less within the verge or opening of the anus, adhering to its soft lining, and producing considerable irritation and uneasiness. Indeed, I once well remember being on a tour of pleasure in the Isle of Wight, and experiencing much annoyance from these larvæ The little horse I had hired for the journey became so lazy and unwilling to go on, and moved so awkwardly, that I could not keep pace with my company, and I was at a loss how to proceed ; but on casually taking up the tail, I discovered three or four of these insects hanging to the rectum, and their removal instantly proved a cure "

For more ample particulars, the reader is referred to the book itself, which is entitled " AN ESSAY ON BOTS IN THE HORSE AND OTHER ANIMALS." It will, in the pages of the original work, be seen that Mr Clark more than suspected the existence of other species of the same family ; but, as no positive knowledge has yet been gained, we must await patiently the inquiries of those to whom this branch of science belongs

However, the writer must dissent to Mr. Clark's conclusion, that " bots are harmless, if not beneficial." How far does such a supposition agree with the perforated stomach, preserved at the Royal Veterinary College ? How far does it accord with the ragged coat and unthrifty aspect by which the presence of the parasites is ascertained ? How, when crediting such a conjecture, are we to account for the horror exhibited by the horse at the approach of the fly ; and how can we interpret Mr. Clark's experience in the Isle of Wight ?

Bots are known to be injurious ; healthy bodies are seldom troubled with parasites. The parched and innutritious grass of the summer's heat cannot support the life accustomed to artificially saved and carefully prepared food. It is the meanness of the master which dooms the slave

to starvation; he begrudges the keep of the animal, therefore, he dis-
guises the ugliness of his feeling under a pretense of giving the horse a
month's freedom and its natural food ! In spring, when the herbage is
young, one hour night and morning might be excused; but those hours
must be before the flies are up, and after these pests are asleep. In the
height of summer, when the grass has perished and the ground is hard,
the health soon yields to constant exposure and to unwholesome food.
The flies torment the animal, and from the shed it is often driven by its
companions in the field. A large portion of the accidents which horses
are liable to, occur while out at grass; many an animal is released from
the stable blooming and valuable; it is, at the expiration of the month,
brought home looking ragged, with a huge belly, and is never fit for a
day's service subsequently. If the matter is to be regarded only in a
money point of view, it would have been a saving to the owner to have
paid a twelvemonth's keep, rather than lose his servant, and notwithstanding, afterward have to pay for food and treatment till experience
had instructed him in the inutility of expecting restoration But when
the matter is considered in a moral sense, what right has that individual
who has, for his own pleasure, accustomed a life to a particular form of
diet, at his will, or for his convenience, to snatch the food from the creature and drive it forth to gnaw at stalks which had shed their seeds, and
to be exposed to all the variations of the season ? It is no excuse to
talk about there being no work to be done while the master is at the
sea-side; the devotion of a life should have earned a brief support, and
the gentleman whose avarice thinks otherwise has no just reason to
complain of the punishment which the indulgence of his greed will
probably insure.

CHRONIC HEPATITIS.

Acute hepatitis is unknown among horses in England. The late
Professor Sewell thought he had witnessed one case Other people
know they have not seen a single instance of such a disease

Chronic hepatitis is peculiar to maturity. Brewers' horses—huge
animals, fattened upon refuse of the mash-tub, and which are paraded,
in all the pride of obesity, drawing one small cask over the stones of
London—are often attacked by this malady. All horses which consume
much provender, without absolute regard to work, are exposed to it.
Gentlemen's carriage horses are very liable to it. A private vehicle is
started, and at first much used; but after a time it is equally neglected.
The individual does not want the carriage to-day, when the coachman
comes round "for orders." Neither is it required on the next occasion.
Often a week passes without the fashionable plaything being uncovered.

The animals, during that time, depend on the groom for exercise. The coachman may be fond of his horses, and, in his ignorance, may think they cannot have too much rest, or himself too little work. Let the master neglect his duty, and the servant soon follows the example.

The word "duty" was employed in the last sentence. It is of an unpleasant signification, and was used in its harshest sense. Kings owe a duty to their subjects; the rich owe a duty to the poor. All authority has some obligation connected with it. There is nothing like perfect freedom in this world of dependence. Man is the king over living things. He may claim his rights, but he at the same time must adopt the weight of his office : he cannot assume the one and discard the other. A monarch is invested with dominion and authority over men ; but the stability of the throne is dependent upon the righteousness of the ruler. If he who wears the crown abuses his trust, he may possess "a right divine," but he is speedily without subjects. So, if man is unjust to the creatures ever which he is placed, nature snatches them from his grasp ; and he may be invested with every power, but he soon wants animals upon which to exercise it.

View the matter in another light, as an affair only of worldly prudence. Knives, formed of the hardest steel, if purchased and put away, in a short time are worthless, because of rust. A house wears faster when untenanted than when properly inhabited.

A horse cannot remain for days in the stable and retain its condition. The carriage proprietor has not only to find food, but he is equally bound to support the health of his animals, or the service for which he bargained will be rudely terminated. Too many do not think of this. Too many take out the carriage to-day, only because it accords with their convenience. All, however, complain of the uncertainty which appertains to horse-flesh. The frame of the horse is stronger than machinery; but it cannot resist the willfulness of human misrule. Let that man, whose stable troubles him, question his own conduct. Let him examine the house in which he has thrust life. Let him see to the servants he has engaged, and to the food for which he pays; and after all, let him inquire into his own behavior: the error will be found, not in the creatures over which he exercises dominion, but in those who are invested with authority.

If people will start carriages, the vehicle must be taken out every day, let the weather freeze, rain, or shine. The hard earth of sunshine is frequently more injurious to the feet than either cold or wet are to the body. The lady, when out visiting, has more than her own pleasure to consult; for all horses fed on the best and underworked, or retained standing long before the street door, are exposed to chronic hepatitis

The gentleman's delight is almost as liable as the brewer's pride.   Even moderate food and too little work will engender the disease.   The author, when he quitted the veterinary college, left in that establishment an Arab, which, from a year's stagnation, was obviously thus disordered

The primary symptoms are not well marked, and do not, generally, attract attention.   The animal is dull and averse to move.   It appears to have imbibed a fondness for the inactivity to which it has been accustomed.   The appetite is either nice, altogether lost, or unscrupulously ravenous; the bowels are constipated; the dung is black, and coated with bilious-looking mucus; it is friable, and imperfectly digested.   If a white paper be pressed upon it, a greenish-yellow stain is imparted. The urine is scanty, and, commonly, highly colored; while the pulse has a heavy beat, as though treacle, instead of blood, circulated within the artery.

The signs which indicate a confirmation of the disorder are : the mouth feels cold; the nasal membranes are unnaturally pallid; the whites of the eyes are ghastly, displaying a yellow tinge; sometimes the horse looks at the right side; usually, it lies upon the left ribs, but never for any long time; tenderness may be exhibited, if the right side be pressed upon.   However, the last symptom is rarely present, and lameness in either fore leg is seldom witnessed.

The disease is, for the most part, obscure, and is best recognized when medicine has become powerless.   If early detected, a limited, but suffi- cient supply of nutritious food; plenty of, but not exhausting labor, with a long course of iodine in alterative doses, are calculated to work some beneficial change.

> Iodide of potassium   . . . .   Two ounces.
> Liquor potassæ   . . . .   One quart.

Mix, and give two tablespoonfuls night and morning, in a pint of water.

Commonly, however, bleeding from the liver is the earliest recognized indication of disease.   Then the horse, with depressed head, is found standing before untouched food; often it staggers, sometimes it sup- ports itself against the partition to the stall; it always maintains the erect position with extreme difficulty; the pupil of the eyes are enlarged; if the hand be moved before the sight, the lid does not close; the vision is lost; the pupils are much dilated; the breath, denoting weakness, is. short and catching; the jaw is pulseless, and the heart flutters; the visible membranes are deathly; and the bilious nature of the disorder is, in these last parts, apparent.   Should the head, only for a minute, be raised, the animal threatens to fall

The first attack is seldom fatal, and possibly might, by proper usage, be recovered from.   The bleeding, then, is from the substance of the gland, and does not generally burst Glisson's capsule, or the first and fibrous covering of the liver. Glisson's capsule, however, is, by the pressure of fluid, bulged out. The hemorrhage stretches the peritoneum, which is the second or last envelope; and nature, striving to repair the injury, causes the serous investment to inflame,—to become white, opaque, considerably thicker, and altogether stronger than in its normal condition.

THE HEAD OF A HORSE SUFFERING FROM INTERNAL HEMORRHAGE.

THE TEST FOR HEMORRHAGE FROM THE LIVER.

There may be an indefinite number of attacks; or the horse, possibly, may succumb to the first assault. Commonly, there are several fits of the same character. Treatment is generally adopted. A dose of aloes is given, though with what intention the author is not aware. Quiet is enjoined; and styptics, as sugar of lead, alum, etc., are administered; and the horse, commonly, under such treatment, seems to recover.

It is, however, difficult to change a fixed habit, or to perceive the reason for an alteration after all danger has disappeared. The gentleman again indulges his inclinations. The coachman, to keep up his horse's flesh, fills the manger; the master very rarely orders the carriage; now he can ride, walking is preferred for his own exercise. Soon, a second fit takes place; this time, Glisson's capsule usually yields; but the thickened peritoneum, although pushed farther out, still resists, and now remains the single stay between human perversity and certain death.

With recovery, the former custom is again resumed; the man chooses to think a sick horse must require support; the master pleases to imagine rest must be beneficial to an animal which has been seriously ill. Another fit ensues; no one is much alarmed this time. The people have become accustomed to the sort of thing; men soon grow used to other's

11

agony. However, something is now present which has not been witnessed before; that circumstance rather disturbs the reigning equanimity;
the horse is evidently much disposed to quietude, but some hidden cause
excites it; it rolls, flings itself down, struggles up again, paws with the
fore feet, kicks with the hind legs at the belly, and breathes with much
more difficulty than formerly.

Often it lies upon the back for some minutes; the result, when such
symptoms are observed, generally is invariable. After death, the abdomen is opened; the cavity is full of black blood, which, commonly, does
not coagulate; though, should death occur upon the first attack, dark
clots may be found among the intestines.

With regard to the treatment, which the author approves, it consists
of the drink previously recommended; sufficient but nutritious food, and,
above all things, abundant exercise. The horse should also be removed
from the heated stable and allowed a large, roomy, loose box. Purgative medicine is too debilitating for such a disease; but the bowels
should be regulated by green meat or by bran mashes, when such agents
are required.   •

CRIB-BITING.

Nothing more forcibly illustrates the ignorance by which the horse is
surrounded, than the manner any trivial but visible fact is magnified into
vast and mysterious importance. The untutored always have active
imaginations; thus, what is at worst, in the author's opinion, the declaration of acidity within the stomach, is by most horsemen dreaded more
than an actual disease.

Cribbing is very common among horses which have been long inhabitants of the stable; the many hours of stagnation the domesticated horse
is doomed to pass, may induce the animal readily to seize upon any solitary pastime Or the perpetual consumption of oats and hay may disarrange the digestion, which, experience teaches, is in ourselves much
benefited by a moderate change of diet. Or, the constant inhalation of
close and impure air, such as will taint the clothes of the groom, who is
much exposed to it, may disorder that part of the body which is the
most sympathetic of the entire frame

Adopt which of these theories the reader may be inclined to, all of
them can be brought to bear upon the horse so affected. That cribbing
is a habit is seemingly proved by the young horse, stalled next to an
old cribber, soon acquiring the custom That cribbing is provoked by
idleness, appears to be in some measure confirmed by the horse never
exhibiting the peculiarity before it has been handled and become an
occupant of the stable. That it arises from acrimony, induced by the

food, is apparently shown by the colt, while at grass, never displaying the symptom. That it will be witnessed in the old horse, when turned out for a month's run at grass, establishes nothing. The temporary visitor to the field may often be seen galloping toward some gate, which, having reached, the horse there commences a long game at crib-biting. This circumstance can settle nothing, except that the digestion is chronically deranged—the stomach, when thus affected, being peculiarly retentive of its morbid condition.

Crib-biting consists in resting the upper incisor teeth against any solid or firm substance; a fixed point is thus gained, and, after much effort, a small portion of gas is eructated. The perpetual emissions of heated air is, in man, one of the symptoms attendant on indigestion ; and the act, in the horse, appears to be impelled by something stronger than habit; since the animal will leave the most tempting provender for its indulgence.

A HORSE IN THE ACT OF CRIB-BITING.

The premonitory symptoms, moreover, seem to declare heartburn to be the cause of this much-dreaded indulgence. The custom is always preceded by licking of the manger. If on that there should be iron, or should any part be cooler than the rest, to that particular spot attention will be paid. The licking of cold substances is a symptom of disordered stomach with other dumb creatures. It is prominently displayed by the dog when the viscus is inflamed. But crib-biting may be prevented, if attacked during the premonitory stage. Any substance, which acts as a stimulant to the stomach, is said to be beneficial. Salt is known as an almost necessary condiment, aiding the healthfulness of human food. The deprivation of salt was an old criminal punishment among the Dutch ; and a lump of rock-salt placed in the manger will often enable the horse's digestion to recover its lost tone.

Crib-biting has, in submission to general opinion, been alluded to as a habit, learned within the stable. But may not that which man designates a habit in a dumb creature, be no more than the influence of one atmosphere acting similiarly on two bodies, both caged in the same stable ? The air is much more than inhaled. A large quantity is swallowed with the saliva. No slight amount is deglutated with the masticated food. The water is generally kept in the stable some hours before the horses are permitted to imbibe it. Water has a large affinity for atmosphere. Air, therefore, enters largely into the body, besides being continually absorbed by the blood during respiration   And moreover, is it not strange that all horses, when indulging an imitative faculty, should always precede the display by the same licking of the manger, which assuredly is not learned, because that stage has passed before the young horse is placed near the one it is supposed to imitate ?   Is it not also surprising, that applying the tongue to cool substances should, in other domesticated but dumb creatures, be a symptom of derangement of the stomach ?

When the horse cribs, the manger is not bitten.   The upper incisors are merely placed against the wood-work, and, from this fixed point, the animal strains backward the body; thereby, the muscles of the neck are the more readily excited, and a small portion of air, accompanied by a slight sound, is forced up a canal which does not of itself favor regurgitation.   When the inability to vomit is considered, the necessity of some such stratagem, to relieve the stomach of its burning acidity, must at once be admitted.   We are still further reconciled to the necessity which prompts the action, when the ease afforded to human dyspeptic subjects, by the expulsion of "the wind," is properly regarded

To relieve crib-biting, first attend to the atmosphere of the stables; render that pure by ample ventilation.   Place a lump of rock-salt in the manger; should that not effect a cure, add to it a large piece of chalk; should these be unavailing, always damp the food, and, at each time of feeding, sprinkle magnesia upon it, and mingle a large handful of ground oak-bark with each feed of corn.   Should none of these measures prove beneficial, treat the case as one of **chronic indigestion or gastritis.**

Let every reader, however, remember dyspepsia is far easier acquired than eradicated or even relieved ; still, the vast majority of the fears entertained concerning crib-biting are perfectly groundless.   The habit, certainly, does not round the edges of the front teeth; neither does it predispose to spasm or to flatulent colic ; a horse that cribs may have either diseases ; so, also, do many animals which are free from the peculiarity. Cribbing can be no recommendation to a purchaser, although the writer cannot honestly point to the direction in which it is detrimental to the usefulness   The late Mr. Sewell had a brown horse : this creature was eighteen years old, and an inveterate cribber; yet, it would trot nine miles an hour, for its own pace, without ever needing the whip.   More than this, no horse master should require ; but let those who entertain a horror of crib-biting, pay extra attention to the means by which the indulgence can be prevented

CHAPTER VIII.

ENTERITIS.

THE nose turned forcibly upward in horses is only expressive of general abdominal disease. The author has witnessed this symptom during the earliest stage of enteritis. It is frequently exhibited when no disturbance calling for treatment is known to be present, or can be subsequently observed. Still, because it is sometimes the earliest warning of intestinal disorder, all horses displaying such a peculiarity should receive pointed attention.

THE NOSE STRAINED VIOLENTLY UPWARD IS A GENERAL SYMPTOM OF ABDOMINAL IRRITATION.

Enteritis is a fearful disease, creating the greatest possible agony. Aged horses are specially exposed to this scourge, which can rage with ungovernable fury from the commencement, and consume the life in eight hours. Its causes, unfortunately, are in a great measure purely conjectural; such as drinking cold water, etc. etc.

These incentives are formally recounted in books; but surely something is wanted to complete the catalogue. If all the animals exposed to the operation of such provocatives were to have enteritis, two-thirds of the horses inhabiting Great Britain would be dead by to-morrow morning. The principal thing, therefore, is the predisposition; incline toward a particular malady, and any triviality may start up the disease; yet this predisposition we at present are too ignorant to recognize.

A severe fit of colic, long continued, may end in enteritis. This is well known; yet it was not the colic which induced enteritis; but the real cause was that which originated the first affection. The predisposition must be present before the bowels would exhibit that inflammation into which the colic merged; the injudicious and cruel treatment most horses receive from those to whose service the life is devoted, may probably be accused as the root of all these evils; disease is the loudest proof that the life is stinted in some essential particular. The same food is placed before all horses; one animal will, however, purge upon

(165)

exertion; labor, on the other hand, may constipate the fellow occupant of the same stable. When the same effect has produced such opposite causes, all the bodies cannot be alike; an old proverb asserts "that which is one man's food is another man's poison " The diet which supports one animal in health may loosen or constringe its companion; yet we are too ignorant to practically use such distinctions.

Again, there is no practice more general than to load the rack and pile the manger after any uncommon toil has been endured. The practice may originate in the best intentions; but no intention can convert that which is evil into a positive good The wretched animal is tempted to cram the stomach when excessive labor has weakened the vital func-tions Horses which are brought home late at night do not usually receive much notice, the grooms are sleepy and eager for their beds. The dressing of the animal, however much such attention might conduce to health, is consequently left to the following morning Rapid motion quickens the circulation; the blood is sent to the skin, and copious per-spiration is the result However warm the stable may be, warmth only promotes evaporation; cold of the lowest degree results from evapora-tion; the consequence is, the body of the quadruped speedily shivers; the blood is repelled to the internal organs, the bowels are prepared for inflammation, and thus enteritis often follows upon the midnight return from a long journey.

Moreover, when the frame is exhausted, rest is far more essential than food, the nourishment then should be very light, and such as can be quickly swallowed. A quart of thick flour or of oatmeal gruel should be first offered after the return. When the cleansing of the animal's body is finished, another quart should be given; these will occupy little time in being put out of sight, and the administration need not interfere with the repose which is desired The gruel being swallowed, a feed of crushed and scalded oats may be placed in the manger; no hay should be allowed; the wish is to sustain a debilitated body, not to blow out an idle stomach Then the creature should, after being fully clothed, be left to itself, and no more nourishment be provided for that night. The danger of introducing substances into a stomach dead to its functions would thus be avoided; nothing likely to irritate or to operate as foreign bodies upon the bowels would be set before the debilitated horse. Besides, the groom would be obliged to remain up for some space, and, as a good servant always finds time hang heavy when without occu-pation, the animal is more likely to be dressed before the man retires. Moreover, the clothes would prevent the cold which ensues upon unchecked evaporation

Constipation, if permitted to exist for any period, is always dangerous; hardened feces are one of the surest causes of enteritis. Disregarding this fact, the endeavor of the immediate age seems to be to keep horses cheap. Strange mixtures are now substituted for wholesome corn, in which the grain and husk are mingled, the one supporting the strength, the other stimulating the bowels. It is folly to seek for profit from a life, and to stint the nourishment which feeds the strength, or to view cheapness as desirable where the service is unlimited. It is wicked to imprison a living being and then to regard it only in connection with our conveniences; "much care and no spare" is a good stable proverb. The food makes the work; omnibus masters know this fact, their horses perform hard work and eat of the best, however abominably the generality of these slaves were once lodged. The home of a London horse is mostly a miserable hole: heated only by fermentation; too often undrained; nearly always without sufficient ventilation. The stall of such a building is large enough for the animal to stand in and not wide enough for the recumbent frame to rest in, the roof is low, and the refuse of the body is piled near the entrance. When will man learn that his interest is best consulted by the proper observances due to vitality in every form? A horse cannot be treated as though it were a jug; it cannot be placed upon a shelf and taken down when required. The functions which nature has placed within a beautiful and exquisitely framed body will, if thus regarded, soon become deranged Sickness will soon cost more money than health would have required for its sustainment; and, in the end, he who strives to blend the animate and the inanimate will speedily find himself possessed only of the latter description of property.

The predisposing cause may, in most instances, be difficult to discover; but the premonitory symptoms of enteritis are well marked. The animal is dull and heavy. It may not notice aught about it, or it picks at its food; repeated and violent shivering fits usher in the attack. When the above characteristic signs are observed, at once take away all hay and corn. Bandage the legs, which will be cold; clothe the body, and, if already dressed, loosen the surcingle. Litter well the stall or remove the horse to a loose box; give two or three drinks, one every quarter of an hour, containing sulphuric ether and laudanum, of each one ounce; water, half a pint; and observe the animal without disturbing it. These symptoms are, however, generally unseen, because the groom is between the bedclothes while his charge is suffering.

The primary symptoms of decided enteritis are termed "**colic**" or "**fret.**" Such words simply represent bellyache; but harm is done and valuable time lost, if the terms of the stable are accepted in any absolute signification. Grooms always have some invaluable nostrum hoarded up; such people are proud of and confident in their secret knowledge; they will lie rather than communicate the contents of their charm. With the best hopes the foolish servant will waste precious moments in useless expectation, and watch for results from an injurious or worthless potion till the time when curative measures could have been effective has passed. Never permit the men who clean the horses also to administer to their diseases; the poor fellows may mean well, but they can have no knowledge which, in the presence of danger, can be beneficial.

The primary symptom, to an uninformed observer, may simply announce a mild fit of gripes. When the shivering has subsided, the horse rolls, plunges, kicks, etc. etc., as he does in spasmodic colic. The struggles, however, are less abandoned and far more mannered in inflammation of the bowels, than in genuine spasm. The pain, moreover, which in enteritis accompanies all movements of the diaphragm, throws the labor of respiration upon the walls of the thorax. The ribs can only partially dilate the lungs; nature endeavors by quickening the motion to supply the deficiency. In colic, the breathing is at first only excited by the exertion; it is deep and full. At the commencement of spasm, the mouth is moist and in temperature natural; during enteritis, the breathing is very short and the mouth is always hot and dry.

THE TEST FOR ENTERITIS AT THE COMMENCEMENT OF THE ATTACK.

The pulse is disturbed only as colic progresses; in enteritis it is quick, hard, and wiry, before the disorder is fully established. The term "wiry" well represents the kind of pulse which accompanies enteritis. If a thin metallic cord were to strike the finger ends somewhat gently, and about seventy times in a minute, it would impart the same sensation as is communicated by the beat of the artery during inflammation of the bowels. Besides, pressure in colic seems to ease the anguish; in enteritis, the horse often cannot bear to have the abdomen touched. The last symptom, however, is not always present, neither is there one, save those characteristic of general inflammation, which is invariably to be observed. In abdominal disease, so many organs are influenced that everything becomes, in a vast degree, mystery and confusion. Notwithstanding this, pressure, in enteritis, never affords relief; sometimes, however, the hand placed upon the belly will elicit the most energetic response. The horse will kick with the hind leg, turn round the head, and violently snap the jaws together. Then he who applied so rude a test must stand out of the reach of the hind foot, at the same time watching the head. Thus all

·danger is readily avoided; because the ears, the eyes, and nostrils of the horse express its intentions before these are carried into effect.

THE TEST OF PRESSURE TO THE ABDOMEN FOR ENTERITIS.

All the tests will, however, not warrant certainty. The heat and dryness of the mouth may proceed from bodily exhaustion; the pulse, though highly suspicious, may merely denote general disturbance rather than declare the particular locality of a disorder. The peculiarity of the breathing may only express temporary faintness; the resistance to pressure is common to many horses while in health, and the restrained method of the plunges may be consequent upon the absence of any incitive to greater energy; still, when all are put together, they imply a great deal. Faintness and exhaustion are not to be reconciled with a hard·pulse; the heat of the mouth and the resistance to pressure, especially when united to the voluntary restraint imposed upon the motion, certainly warrant a strong inference, and sanction no belief that colic is the sufferer's complaint. Happily, however, there remains a mode of assuring the most hesitating individual. The coat must be pulled off, the shirt-sleeves rolled up, and the arm be well greased or thoroughly soaped. About this there must be no false delicacy: in human surgery and in veterinary practice many things have to be surmounted which do not read well when described in cold print. In

A CERTAIN TEST FOR ENTERITIS.

this instance, the intention is to relieve a suffering life; the motive will elevate the act. The fingers of the right hand are to be compressed, while the left hand raises the tail; the position is on the left side, as near

to the feet as may be possible. Being there, the points of the compressed
fingers are brought to bear upon the center of the anus; gentle and
equable pressure is maintained until the resistance of the sphincter muscle is tired out; even then, no haste is warranted. Upon the hand
penetrating the body, a cavity is entered; here there is generally some
dung, the removal of which constitutes what is called "back-raking."
In enteritis, the excrement is hard, dry, offensive, in small and dark
lumps, upon the surface of which lie streaks of white mucus. This being
done, the arm must be regreased or again moistened with water, and the
hand gradually advanced to ascertain the temperature of the intestines.
If the health be undisturbed, the operator will be conscious only of a
genial glow; should inflammation exist, the augmentation of the natural
heat will be most decided.

All is then certainty; no further doubt is justifiable, and no additional
symptom need be looked for. The nature of the case is determined,
and should it be enteritis, every moment is indeed precious. Firstly,
neither bleed nor purge. A particular kind of venesection, however,
is allowed. Extract one quart of blood, and inject into the vein one
pint of blood-warm water; a profuse purgation and perspiration almost
immediately follows the disappearance of the fluid. Much uncertainty
is thus spared; and two conditions, both favorable to recovery, are
induced.

For this operation a quart syringe should be employed; a fine curved

nozzle should be affixed to it for the convenience of insertion down the vein; the tube connected with the handle
should be marked to show when a pint has been forced out
of the instrument.

The reason for using a larger and a less handy machine
than seems absolutely necessary to perform a delicate operation is, because nearly all syringes suck up a portion of
air, which, when the instrument is almost empty, comes
forth. Now breath or atmosphere, or gas of any kind injected into a living vessel, speedily destroys life. To prevent so fearful an accident the enlarged capacity of the
syringe is recommended.

THE SYRINGE TO
INJECT INTO
THE JUGULAR
VEIN DURING
ENTERITIS.

The water being injected, should the pulse regain its
inflammatory character, mingle half a drachm of aconite
root, in powder, with every subsequent antispasmodic
draught. The ethereal drenches must be continued, because pain of the intestines is always obstinate, and we cannot be certain how far spasm may cause the agony, seeing that a form of colic
always attends on enteritis.

Aconite root, in powder . . . . Half a drachm.
Sulphuric ether . . . . Three ounces.
Laudanum . . . . Three ounces.
Extract of belladonna . . . . One drachm.
(Rubbed down in water) . . . . . . One pint and a half.

These drinks should be administered as the pain, pulse, and the general appearance seem to demand them; they may be employed every quarter of an hour if requisite. When the pulse is quiet, withdraw the aconite; should the pain subside, remove the belladonna. The ether and laudanum may be diminished as the horse appears to be more comfortable.

Should the symptoms denote a dead, lingering pain in the abdomen, after the administration of the eighth drink, procure some strong liquor ammonia. Dilute this with six times its bulk of cold water. Saturate a stout-cloth with the dilution; lay the cloth upon several folds of rug;

THE APPLICATION OF AN AMMONIACAL BLISTER IN ENTERITIS.

obtain four resolute men with not very sensitive eyes or noses, and let them hold the cloth close to the animal's abdomen.

The action of the ammonia must be from time to time observed. It is a most powerful agent; in certain states it can blister in ten minutes; in other conditions, it requires half an hour to take that effect. It is very uncertain; but, if held too long, it may dissolve the skin and leave behind a fearful sore, which will establish a lasting blemish. He who employs it will understand he is using that which must not be abused. The removal of the cloth allows the ammonia to evaporate, and, consequently, at any moment effectually checks all further action.

When all is accomplished, should the progress of the disease be effectually stayed, but the cure not be complete, sprinkle on the tongue the following powder every second hour :—

Calomel . . . . Half a drachm.
Opium . . . . One drachm.

But stop all the other medicine as soon as the subsidence of the symptoms will permit. The food is now of all importance: bran, in enteritis, is positive poison; mashes are not to be thought of; linseed is too feeding for an inflammatory subject The same objection may be taken to gruel; hay tea, or pails of boiling water poured upon a pound of flour, must sustain the body for the first day after recovery; on the next day, a feed of boiled roots may be introduced, but not the whole quantity at once; that must be divided into three meals. Then the amount may be doubled, and thus the full bulk of provender be by degrees attained, afterward a few crushed and scalded oats may be mixed with the rest at each meal; but it should be some time before hay is permitted to irritate and distend the lately inflamed surfaces.

Enteritis is a fearful disorder; he who has witnessed one death by that terrible malady should have received an awful rebuke. The *post-mortem* examination best describes the violence of the affection. The intestines, generally the large intestines, are black and swollen; often in color they approach to a green Their structure is destroyed; they tear upon a touch, and are so loaded with inflamed blood that one division of the bowels may form no inconsiderable burden for a strong man.

The above directions, the intelligent reader will fully comprehend, are not pronounced in any absolute sense. No two cases of any violent disorder are precisely similar; the forms, therefore, prescribed in these pages admit of variations. They are given only as suited to the generality of attacks; they may be lessened or augmented, as circumstances demand or as discretion dictates. It would be as easy to make a shoe which should fit all feet, as to name medicines or point out the quantities which should be adapted to all maladies.

ACUTE DYSENTERY.

Diarrhœa may be banished from the list of diseases to which horse-flesh is liable. Certain animals will purge during work; others will scour upon the smallest change of diet; such peculiarities, however, mostly check themselves; they demand very slight or no remedial treatment. Unlike diarrhœa in the human subject, they never terminate in death, but dysentery is as violent as diarrhœa is mild. The length and size of the intestines render any disease within them a very serious affair. There are two kinds of dysentery, the acute and the chronic; the acute form of disease will constitute the subject of the present article.

The cause of **acute dysentery** is always some acrid substance taken into the stomach—generally aloes, combined with some preparation of croton; other substances will, however, induce an inflammatory purgation. Such a result may ensue upon the injudicious use of arsenic, corrosive sublimate, tartar emetic, blue-stone, etc. etc. Many of these substances will be eaten if mixed with the corn—the instinct which protects the lives of other animals being destroyed in the horse by ages of domestication. Others may be ignorantly administered with the very best of intention.

The symptoms often are obscure at the commencement; there is abdominal pain; so there is in most intestinal disorders. The agony may readily be mistaken for the pangs attendant on spasmodic colic. On other occasions, the suffering may be slight, not even sufficient at first to destroy the appetite. No poison acts upon two bodies in precisely the same manner; violent purgation is generally the first marked sign which makes known the nature of the disorder. The feces soon become mere discolored water; the thirst is then excessive; the stench is most offensive; the pulse, from being hard, shortly becomes thick and feeble, and ultimately it is intermittent; the countenance is haggard; the position of the body expresses abdominal pain. Perspirations break forth in patches; tympanitis starts up, and death speedily ensues.

It is of little use to inquire, while the animal is suffering, what has

A HORSE SUFFERING FROM DRASTIC POISON.

provoked the superpurgation; it is then most desirable, if possible, to remove the effect. The best chance of accomplishing this is by destroying the pain that exhausts the strength, thereby affording nature the better chance of vanquishing the irritation Ether, opium, belladonna, chalk, and catechu present the best means of doing this These agents, when combined, support the body, allay the anguish, and check the purgation; blended with thick linseed tea, which will in some measure supply the mucus lost to the bowels, they therefore form a good drink for most occasions.

Sulphuric ether	One ounce.
Laudanum	Three ounces.
Liquor potassæ	Half an ounce.
Powdered chalk	One ounce
Tincture of catechu	One ounce.
Cold linseed tea	One pint.

Give, throughout the acute stage, every quarter of an hour.

At the same time cleanse the quarters, plait up the tail, and throw up copious injections of cold linseed tea.   Expect the horse to become greatly prostrated when amendment commences The entire of the irritating agent must be expelled from the body before improvement can be witnessed The subsequent recovery is announced by a pause in the symptoms; the disease appears to be stationary, whereas previously everything denoted a hastening termination.

That pause is one of suspense, for no one can say what will follow; sometimes the cessation of agony precedes immediate dissolution; sometimes recovery dates from that event. The animal, upon the slightest change being exhibited, must still be assiduously attended. Care must never cease; and, after recovery is confirmed, the food for a week must consist of linseed tea, hay tea, and gruel. On the expiration of the week, a few boiled roots may be added, three of the drinks previously ordered being administered every day. Do not bother about the bowels; no matter, should the animal be constipated for a fortnight subsequent to the thorough emptying of acute dysentery. Upon the termination of a fortnight, stop all medicine, and allow some crushed, scalded oats and beans; withdraw some of the slops as the solids advance; but let a full month expire before a drop of cold water or a mouthful of hay are permitted to be swallowed

To escape the loss of so large a piece of property as a living horse, it is imperative the notion should be abandoned which asserts that because the horse can swallow most opening medicines with impunity, a strong purgative cannot otherwise than benefit the animal; the deduction is not fairly drawn But not to follow up too closely so lame a prey: aloes is the general purgative in the stable; it is a drug which should never be intrusted to the hands of the groom The difference between the necessary and the poisonous dose is too close for the un-educated to comprehend it; more horses have been slaughtered with aloes than have perished from all the other poisons conjoined   Yet grooms are particularly fond of this medicine; the dangerous drug enters into every ball which is popular in the stable; no matter how opposite the end desired may be, in the groom's opinion aloes must produce it. . Like the majority of the uneducated, the stable-man re-joices in a strong purge   Tenesmus is his delight, he loves to see six-teen or eighteen full motions, and then he cannot comprehend why the horse is weak, since the physic passed beautifully through him!

Of all persons living, grooms generally are the most prejudiced and the worst informed   All advice is disregarded; should the master speak, the groom shakes his head, and, after the lecture is ended, in-quires of himself, "what the old buffer can know about it?"   Here is the curse of horses! Gentlemen–transfer them to the custody of the uneducated.   The groom is accepted as an authority; the master asks for and is mostly governed by the opinion of an inferior.   No other servant possesses such a power; no domestic more abuses his position; the carriage and the harness maker, the corn merchant, and the veteri-nary surgeon all pay this person five per cent. upon the employer's bills; nothing comes on to the premises but the man claims a profit from it; nothing leaves the stable but is regarded as his perquisite.   He thus, while occupying a situation of trust, has an absolute interest in the ex-travagance of the expenditure   .Wear and tear of the articles over which he watches brings to him actual emolument; his interest and his duty are at war, and when a weak person has to decide the battle, it is easy to understand on which part the victory will be declared.

CHRONIC DYSENTERY.

This affliction is not so common among horses as it is with cattle; neither is it so frequent at the present day as it appears to have formerly been.   Once it was termed "molten grease," from an unfounded notion that liquid fat was discharged with the feces. Now it is known that what our ancestors took for grease is no more than the mucus, which is ex-pelled during every form of severe intestinal irritation

The cause of **chronic dysentery** among horses is not well understood It is said to follow diarrhœa; but such an explanation seems to con-found the commencement of one disorder with the establishment of another disease.   Horses having chronic dysentery are, generally, old animals, which are subject to the will of a very poor or a very penurious man.   They are badly kept, and may have to grub a scanty living from lanes and hedgerows; also, they are goaded to hard work upon watery food and sour grass. In such cases, disturbance of the bowels should be early attended to. The food should be immediately changed. Good sound oats and beans should be freely given, while the following drink is administered thrice daily:—

Crude opium	Half an ounce.
Liquor potassæ	One ounce.
Chalk	One ounce.
Tincture of all-spice	One ounce.
Alum	Half an ounce.

Mix with a quart of good ale, stir briskly, and give.

Should the primary symptom not be attended to, profuse purgation may ensue without excitement; but always will happen upon any exertion or the drinking of cold water. Violent straining often follows; the belly enlarges; the flesh wastes; the bones protrude; the skin is hide-bound; the visible mucous membranes become pallid; weakness increases; perspiration often bursts forth without occasion; the horse will stand still for hours, not grazing, nor seemingly being conscious that grass was within its reach.

At length a living skeleton alone remains of that which was a horse. The eyes have a sleepy, sad, and pathetic expression; the head is often

A HORSE SUFFERING UNDER CHRONIC DYSENTERY.

turned slowly toward the flanks; the sight remains fixed for some moments upon the seat of pain; the horse stands on one spot, or only changes it when the bowels are about to act; colic at length sets in, though frequently it is present earlier; and the wretched quadruped then fades speedily away.

It is a general practice to turn animals suffering from chronic dysentery upon some village common   The horse is, put there with scanty food and no shelter, under a plea of humanity, or "to give the old 'oss a last chance."   There can be no feeling in placing a diseased animal far away from sight or help, where it must pine, shiver, and starve, in a dreary solitude.

Supposing the affected life to be claimed by a generous master, either of the following drinks may be given, thrice daily :—

Sulphuric ether	One ounce.
Laudanum	Three ounces
Liquor potassæ . . . ⟍	Half an ounce.
Powdered chalk	One ounce.
Tincture of catechu . . ⁻ ⌐.	One ounce.
Cold linseed tea	One pint.

Choloroform	Half an ounce
Extract of belladonna	Half a drachm.
Carbonate of ammonia	One drachm
Powdered camphor	Half a drachm.
Tincture of oak bark	One ounce.
Cold linseed tea	One pint.

The above drinks may be changed, as either appears to have ceased to operate.   The food should be of the best and lightest description.   Boiled roots, boiled linseed, boiled rice, crushed and boiled malt, etc etc.; no hay.   The body should be frequently dressed, and always clothed.   A good bed ought to be allowed.   The lodging must be well drained and roomy.

Yet, after all this trouble, a speedy cure is not to be expected; and rarely does an old horse, should it recover, prove highly useful.   How sad, however, is that condition where the continuance of the life is made conditional upon the service of the body—where interest is the only motive which permits existence !   No sympathy to be anticipated in suffering; no pity in disease !   The only feeling that actuates the custodian is a cold regard for the gain which the jaded being can yet bring him.   A life of usefulness, years of toil, injuries sustained and accidents surmounted,—all cannot win a day's respite from the doom which attends the creature whose exertions in man's service have led to the disablement of its powers   Such, however, is the fate of the horse in England, which land specially boasts it is a "Christian country."

Chronic dysentery is the inheritance which the horse earns from being subjected to the dominion of man.   Excessive labor, filthy lodging, and innutritious diet are the causes.   Each of these causes increases as the age advances.

Prior to its domestication, the horse might not have found on every spot an abundance of excellent fodder; but then it was at liberty to seek a better fare in another place.   Man has taken away all power of choice; he forces the creature to toil, and obliges it to eat only that which parsimony may afford to place before it   When so vast and so absolute a power is claimed, it becomes a positive duty to see the mere animal necessities are satisfied: it is cruel folly to tax the powers and to stint the body   It is a crime to undertake a trust and then confide the fulfillment of its responsibility to an ignorant inferior.   It is a sin to seize on life and to neglect the prisoner you hold in captivity.   Where existence is claimed as a property, and animation is forced to wear out being in labor for the master's profit, surely the least obligation the superior could own should be the provision of ample lodging and fitting sustenance! Both are withheld from the aged horse.

ACITES, OR DROPSY OF THE ABDOMEN.

In the horse, **acute peritonitis** is unknown, save as the result of operation, then its fury takes possession of the cavity and generally refuses to yield to medicine.   It is different, however, with chronic peritonitis, which, though not a common disorder, is too often encountered to be esteemed a rare disease.   It is, when early noticed, tractable; but the earlier symptoms are generally not understood.   The first sign is a ragged coat and a tender state of the abdomen; the horse, which was passive previously, now shrinks from the curry-comb; snaps and kicks at him who dresses it   Such actions are viewed as denoting a return of spirit. Intending to encourage the favorite quality of the stable, the flank is violently struck or slapped by the servant; and the indication forced from a dumb animal by agony, is by grooms regarded as the proof of reviving animation

Masters should, in justice to themselves if from no higher motive, visit the stable more frequently than is their custom.   The horse is all gentleness and simplicity; a groom only knows less about the animal than a child, for he has acquired notions which induce him to misinterpret plain actions   Every owner of a stable should learn to feel and count the horse's pulse, he should be acquainted with the normal standard and its healthy character; chronic peritonitis might then early be discovered The pulse under this disease is hard and small, it vibrates about sixty times in a minute   The head is pendulous; the food is oftener spoiled, rather scattered about than eaten; the membranes are pale and the mouth is dry; pressure upon the abdomen elicits a groan, and turning in the stall always calls forth a grunt.

When such symptoms are observed, the food should be small in bulk, but nutritious in quality; no work should be imposed; the medicine should be tonic and alterative.

Strychnia	A quarter of a grain, worked gradually up to one grain.
Iodide of iron	Half a drachm, worked gradually up to one drachm and a half.
Extract of belladonna . .	One scruple.
Extract of gentian . .	A sufficiency.
Powdered quassia . . .	A sufficiency

Make into a ball; give one at night and at morning.

Small blisters should succeed each other upon the abdomen; but as these cases are always tedious and very much depends upon the constitution of the animal, charity alone should propose such a disease for treatment, as the general termination of the malady is incurable dropsy of the abdomen.

Acites offers a good illustration of the loss inhumanity brings down upon man, and of the gain which would attend a loftier conduct. Chronic peritonitis attacks aged animals; such horses are used only for harness purposes. Few masters inquire what propels the carriage, so the vehicle gets over the ground. The affected quadruped cannot drag its own body; thus more than double duty is cast upon the sound steed. The single horse has not only to draw the entire carriage and its load, but it also has to pull along its disabled companion. Servants frequently hide defects, hoping that time will remedy them, or dreading the reception proverbially given to the bearer of bad tidings; thus the sound horse ultimately fails, while the sick animal is rendered worse by violent exercise.

However, with the honesty which seems to prevail in and around the stable, the diseased horse is often sent to the nearest market. The proprietor, under some strange quibble of conscience, sells to another that which he is convinced is worthless. A rich master vends and a poor man buys; the cheatery of such a bargain is obvious, but to such results always tend a violated contract. The natural contract between man and horse is outraged; a conditional gift is construed to imply an unconditional bestowal. The terms are warped according to the convenience of the receiver; the possibility of any obligation being implied is never suspected. A few, and very few good people, from feeling only fulfill the conditions of the bond; but kindness, when bestowed upon the horse, is regarded as a weakness and a gratuity. From the highest to the lowest, none think that all of animated creatures are born with rights; no one behaves as though domesticated animals were only intrusted to the care of man. Violation of moral conditions begins the evil, which ends in cheatery and robbery of one another.

The symptoms which announce that the serous membrane has effused water into the abdomen are a want of spirit; constant lying down and remaining in one position for a long period; perpetual restlessness; thirst; loss of appetite; thinness; weakness; enlarged abdomen; constipation and hide-bound.

The enlargement of the belly has something peculiar in it; the swelling lies toward the inferior portion of the abdomen. Near the loins there is apparently an empty space; if the hand be placed on the enlargement, and another person strikes the belly on the opposite side, a sense of fluctuation can be distinctly felt. If the horse be thrown upon its back, the swelling will, with the change of position, gravitate toward the loins. At length small bags containing fluid depend from the chest and the inferior surface of the belly. Should the disease be suffered to progress, the sheath and one leg generally enlarge; the hair of the mane

A HORSE WITH ACITES, OR ABDOMINAL DROPSY.

breaks off and is easily pulled out. Where once hung the tail now remains little more than the dock with a few scattered hairs. Ultimately purgation starts up, which terminates the suffering.

Of course, after effusion, all treatment is powerless—creatures in the last stage of dropsy presenting sights which the mind shudders to contemplate; objects of this kind are sometimes to be seen on commons in the neighborhood of London. They are turned out to die miserably under the plea of humanity; the utmost limit of cruelty is justified or made pleasant by a pretense to sympathy. The poor horse literally starves; were there food to eat, the remaining strength would not serve to collect it. Still the proprietor is so very humane he cannot endure to destroy the property he has paid for; the poor animal is therefore thrust forth to cheaply live, or to die without trouble to its owner.

INFLUENZA.

This affection may rage throughout the kingdom, or it may be located upon a very circumscribed spot. In a disorder so eccentric, it is very difficult to decide the question whether or not it is contagious; it commonly runs through the stable in which it appears; but it does not invariably attack every animal within the building. It may, in a large edifice, first seize the horse nearest the door, then travel to the stall farthest from the entrance;'thus it skips about without regularity, and often spares many individuals.

Occasionally **influenza** fixes upon an animal when in the field; but it is a more probable visitant of the stable: this is a seeming proof that the contagion does not reside in the air, since the atmosphere is as much as possible excluded from every mews. We may conjecture it is not dependent upon any vapor exuding from the earth, since the creatures whose noses are nearly always in contact with the herbage are, of all others, least liable to the affection.

It is terrible to contemplate the suffering and loss of life which have been consequent upon the errors of mankind Influenza is regarded as a new disease, a new name deceives the world, though it is more than probable that a disorder of a low, febrile, and typhoid character has prevailed among animals for many ages. Nature has, for thousands of years, been striving to enforce the self-evident truth that man is by moral obligation bound to provide for the welfare of the animal he enslaves His gain or the inclination of his will can be no argument against the fulfillment of so plain a duty; the implied contract, the common parent of all living things, has been emphasizing with sickness and with death; all has been to no purpose. Cunning men have been employed, and nostrums have been invented to maintain misrule; wealth has been sacrificed and ruin endured, to uphold an unrighteous cause; but the voice of nature pleading for her children has not been understood.

Even at this day the old fault is to be met with on every hand; it is exhibited by the rich as well as by the poor, by the highly educated and

by the very ignorant. In every place exist horses of fabulous excellence ,
in the master's opinion, imprisoned within walls which exclude the vital
air.   The roof may not permit the animal's head to be raised, the sides
may not allow the body to be turned; the fumes within the walls shall
oppress the lungs and sting the eyes of the man who enters the building; yet within a circumscribed space, so foul and pestilential, the horse
is doomed to exist   Then the animal's disease is heard of with surprise,
and its death is lamented as a misfortune!

What cause is there for grief or for wonder, if impurity does generate disease and death?   What need has man to ape the martyr, because
influenza starts from the contamination which by human will has been
created? The pest once originated sweeps onward, nor can mortal exclamation nor mortal sorrow check the course of the destroyer, all fall
alike before the scourge.   The filthy and the cleanly alike are stricken;
yet neither masters nor legislators can draw wisdom from the visitation.

In influenza there is no difficulty in pointing to the structure affected;
it would, however, be hard to allude to the part which was not involved.
The weakness and stupidity which accompany the affection declare the
brain and nervous system to be diseased.   Local swellings show the
cellular tissue to be deranged; heat and pain in the limbs and joints
announce the serous, the ligamentous, and osseous structures implicated.
The muscular and digestive functions are acutely disordered; the rapid
wasting of the flesh demonstrate the absorbents are excited.   There is
no portion of the body which can escape the ravage of influenza.

Youth, or rather the approach of adultism, is the favorite season of
the attack, which is most prevalent during the spring time of the year
There is, however, no period or any age which are altogether exempt
from its influence.

All kinds of treatment have been experimented with.   Bleeding,
purging, blistering, setoning have all been tried, and each has destroyed
more lives than the whole can boast of having saved; experience has by
slow degrees shown the inutility of active treatment.   *Bold* measures,
as those plans are termed which add to another's suffering, commonly
end in hydrothorax or water on the chest.

It is difficult to determine when the first symptom of influenza is
present   The author is indebted to the acuteness of Mr. T W Gowing, V. S , of Camden Town, for a knowledge of a marked indication
declarative of the presence of influenza.   A yellowness of the mucous
membranes, best shown on the conjunctiva or white of the eye, is very
characteristic.   Whenever the sign is seen and sudden weakness remarked, caution should be practiced, for it is ten to one that the pestilence is approaching.   Influenza is a very simulative disorder; it has

appeared as laminitis; disease of the lungs is, perhaps, its favorite type. Bowel complaints are apt to imitate each other; blowing generally commences such disorders. But when influenza is prevalent, let the body's strength and the yellowness or redness of the membranes be always looked to before any more prominent indication is particularly observed. The other symptoms—which, however, are very uncertain, as regards any of them being present or absent—are pendulous head, short breath, inflamed membranes, swollen lips, dry mouth, enlarged eyelids, copious tears, sore throat, tucked up flanks, compressed tail, filled legs, big joints, lameness and hot feet. Auscultation may detect a grating sound at the chest, or a noise like brickbats falling down stairs at the windpipe; whenever this last peculiarity is audible there is a copious nasal discharge. Sometimes one foot is acutely painful, and, notwithstanding the weakness, the leg is held in the air. Purgation has been witnessed, although constipation usually prevails, and the animal generally stands during the continuance of the disorder.

Move the horse slowly to a well-littered, loose box; mind the door

CONFIRMED INFLUENZA.

does not open to the north or to the east. No food will be eaten; but suspend a pail of well-made gruel within easy reach of the animal's head. Let the gruel be changed or the receptacle replenished at stated periods, thrice daily; sprinkle one scruple of calomel upon the tongue and wash it down with a drink composed of sulphuric either, one ounce; laudanum, one ounce; water, half a pint; do this night and morning. Should the weakness be excessive, double the quantity of ether and of laudanum contained in the draughts. Watch the pulse—it always is feeble, but at first has a wiry feeling. So soon as the character of the pulse changes or the wiry sensation departs, which generally happens when the nasal discharge becomes copious and cough appears, one pot of stout may be allowed, and some nourishing food, as bread, on which a very little salt has been sprinkled, may be offered by hand. The horse feels man to be its master and appreciates any attention bestowed upon it in the hour of sickness. It will stand still to be caressed, and advance its hanging ears to catch the accents of sympathy.

Beware of what is termed active treatment; a purgative is death during influenza. It generally will induce the prostration from which the animal never recovers. Formerly it was common to see four strong men propping up a horse during its endeavor to walk. But the lower class are fond of joking one with another. Such was the usual result of their employment on these occasions. In the fun the horse got but partial support, while the noise distressed the diseased sensibilities. Horses

A COMMON SIGHT DURING RECOVERY FROM INFLUENZA, WHEN ACTIVELY TREATED.

have large sympathies, and readily comprehend the attentions dictated by kindness. The disregard which people too often display toward sickness in an animal acutely pains the creature: its effects may be told by the altered character of the pulse. Whereas the voice, when softened by pity, often causes the heavy head to be turned toward the speaker; and the muzzle of a diseased inmate of the stable has frequently reposed long upon the chest of the writer.

ABDOMINAL INJURIES.

These are of various kinds. They differ materially, but they all provoke inflammation of the vast serous membranes lining the abdominal cavity; and their symptoms are therefore too nearly alike to be distinguished from each other. A mere list of such perils must astonish the reader; and his pity will be excited when he learns that such accidents, numerous as they are, generate the most violent agony. These injuries consist of ruptured diaphragm, ruptured stomach, ruptured spleen, ruptured intestines, strangulation, intro-susception, impactment, and calculus.

Ruptured diaphragm is attended with a soft cough, and symptoms of broken wind—occasioned by the almost sole employment of the abdominal muscles—with sitting on the haunches. Still, Professor

AN UNNATURAL ATTITUDE, INDICATIVE OF SOME ABDOMINAL INJURY.

Spooner, of the Royal Veterinary College, mentioned in his lectures that an animal belonging to the Zoological Society lived two years with a ruptured diaphragm, through which the bowel protruded into the thorax. In the horse such a lesion is speedily fatal.

A position so unnatural as that of sitting on the haunches may

A POSITION OFTEN ASSUMED BY THE HORSE SUFFERING FROM ABDOMINAL INJURY.

denote something very wrong to be present; but it gives no definite direction to our ideas. Animals are known to have assumed it, and

subsequently to have recovered. The diaphragm when it yields generally gives way upon the tendinous portion. Through the opening the
peristaltic action soon causes the bowels to obtrude; and death is produced by displacement and strangulation of the intestine. The posture
previously delineated is common to all injuries of the abdomen; so is
the opposite peculiarity—or the horse remaining upon its chest. The
last attitude may not, to most persons, appear so strange, seeing that
the creature assumes it whenever it rises or lies down. Then, however,
it is only momentary. When it denotes abdominal injury, it is comparatively of long continuance. At the same time the breathing and
the countenance bespeak the greatest internal anguish.

Ruptured spleen is the gentlest death of all those which spring from

abdominal injury. The spleen
is at present a mystery to veterinary science. It has been discovered after death of enormous
size; but the symptoms during
life had not led to the expectation of any very serious disorder.
Ruptured spleen and ruptured
liver are both productive of
similar symptoms; both answer
to the same tests, and the termination of each is alike.

TEST FOR HEMORRHAGE FROM THE SPLEEN.

Ruptured stomach mostly
happens with old and enfeebled

horses. Night cab-horses are very liable to it; so also are animals of
heavy draught. The drivers often neglect to take out the nose-bags.
The horse's most urgent necessities always yield to man's passing con-

venience; so the creature has to journey
far or to remain out till the empty stomach
grows debilitated. It is then taken home
and placed before abundance. Elsewhere
this folly has been commented upon. It
was shown that light food and perfect rest
were the best restoratives for an exhausted
frame. The drivers, however, refuse to be
taught. The horse eats and eats. No contraction of the exhausted stomach warns

A RUPTURED STOMACH.

the animal when to stop. The viscus is crammed. Then digestion
endeavors to commence. With rest the organ recovers some tone. The
muscular coat of the sac starts into action, and, encountering opposition,

the vital powers exert themselves with the greater energy. The stomach is thus burst by its own inherent force; the largest division of its various structures always being exhibited by the elastic peritoneal covering —the lesser rent being left upon the inelastic mucous lining membrane. Excessive colic, followed by tympanitis, are the only general symptoms which attend ruptured stomach. The history of the case, if it can be obtained, is, however, a better guide; but there are too often interested motives for distorting the facts. Vomition through the nostrils has been thought to particularize ruptured stomach; but experience has ascertained that vomition may be induced by any lesion which is sufficiently great to cause revulsion of the system.

Intro-susception is always preceded by colic. The last-named affection causes portions of the bowels to contract. Such contracted intestines become small, firm, and stiff. They are, while in that condition, by the peristaltic action readily pushed up other portions of the canal, which are of the natural size. The entrance of the contracted bowel acts upon the healthy tube as if it were a foreign substance. Contractibility is excited. The displaced and intruding bowel is grasped as by a vice, and the accident is of that kind which provokes its own continuance. Cure is hopeless,

THE INTESTINE DIVIDED SO AS TO CLEARLY SHOW THE NATURE OF INTRO-SUSCEPTION.

while consciousness remains; the only hope is the administration of chloroform in full and long-continued doses; thereby to arrest vitality and chance the release of the imprisoned gut. While intro-susception lasts, all passage is effectually stopped. Inflammation soon commences, and the symptoms of outrageous colic are exhibited. However, such is not always the case. Mr. Woodger, veterinary surgeon of Bishop's Mews, Paddington, attended a case of this description, in which the symptoms present seemed to denote congestion of the lungs.

Invagination is here used to express the entrance of one entire division of the bowels within another. In this sense it is chiefly witnessed upon the large intestines; whereas intro-susception is mostly

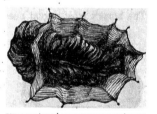

THE CÆCUM INVAGINATED WITHIN THE COLON, AND BLACK FROM INTENSE INFLAMMATION.

present upon the smaller bowels. The mesentery must be ruptured before such an accident can take place; but then the agony attendant upon the previous derangement is so powerful that it is impossible for the hugeness of this lesion to increase the violence of the torture; nor is there any sign by which so sad a catastrophe can be predicated.

Before **strangulation** can possibly occur, the mesentery must be sundered. It almost always happens to a portion of the small intestines. The bowel, freed from its support, soon involves itself with numerous complications; or the rent membrane may twine round a knuckle of the gut.

A KNUCKLE OF INTESTINE STRAN-
GULATED BY THE RUPTURED
MESENTERY.

RUPTURE OF THE SMALL
INTESTINES.

The above illustration, however, shows one of the simplest forms in which the accident can possibly take place; but no person, however acute, could distinguish between strangulation from rupture of the intestines. The last generally occurs upon the smaller bowels, and happens to the interspaces upon the superior portion of the tube, between the vessels which nourish the digestive canal. The ingesta is consequently forced between the layers of the mesentery. The most intense anguish, inflammation, and death are the consequences.

Calculus or stone may be present, either in the stomach or in the canal. Those in the stomach are of small size; those within the intestines may attain the weight of more than twenty pounds. Those of the stomach are always smooth, as also may be those of the bowels. To the intestines, however, there are common three kinds of, or differently composed calculi: the triple phosphate or the earthy; one formed of the minute hairs which originally surrounded the kernel of the oat; and another composed of dung, held together by the mucous secretion of the bowel. Any of these calculi may, as the

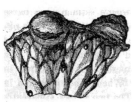

THE SAC FORMED IN THE BOWEL; THIS THE
CALCULUS HAS QUITTED, WHILE ANOTHER
PORTION OF THE INTESTINE HAS SO
FIRMLY GRASPED IT AS TO RUPTURE IT-
SELF.

size increases, gradually stretch the intestine; thus forming a living sac within which the stone abides. While it remains there, the food passes over it and no injury is occasioned. But by any movement it is likely to be dislodged and thrown into the healthy channel. There it is firmly grasped with such force as to produce rupture of the intestine, and the hold is only relaxed after inflammation has ended in mortification and in death. The bowels, in truth, are impacted by calculus. The passage is stopped However different the causes of abdominal injury may appear, they are each generally characterized by the severest possible abdominal pain. This symptom is often so violent that the agony conceals all other indications, or if any others can be exhibited, they are so partially shown and displayed for so very brief a space as not to permit of their being rightly interpreted.

It is very desirable that every one should witness a powerful horse in its agony. No stronger means could be found for enforcing such a lesson than the sufferings which spring from abdominal injuries. When this is proposed it is not intended the person should look on misery only so long as the spectacle stimulated his feelings; but that he should watch hour after hour and behold the afflicted life resigned under the pressure of mighty torment. Were such a sight once contemplated— were man fully conscious of how brimming with horrible expression every feature of the horse's frame can become—the thought of anguish wrenching life out of so huge a trunk would surely compel the better treatment of a gentle, inoffensive, and serviceable slave. Ruptured stomach a little forethought would prevent. The triple phosphate calculus is common among millers' horses, which are foully fed from the sweepings of the shop But if man will oblige duty to bow before convenience, or make it secondary to expense, the misery he inflicts will surely in justice recoil upon himself

Abdominal injuries are probably the sources of the greatest agony horse-flesh can endure. To account for the generality of such lesions, it is merely necessary to regard the places in which horses are housed and the manner in which they are fed. In the owner's estimation a horse seems to be a horse, in the same sense as a table is a table. Both objects are necessary to his comfort, to his pride, or to his profit Neither have higher claims. Both are to be used and to be flung aside. The one is to be cleaned and repaired at the cheapest rate; the other is to be lodged and supported at the lowest cost. When either grow old in his service, each is equally to be discarded. The two things apparently rank in man's estimation as simple chattels subject to his will and made to please his fancy. That there is a huge life, a breathing sensibility attached to one of these articles; that it delights in its master's pleasure, and, if properly trained, it is capable of sharing its master's emotions, is so preposterous a sentimentality as to be "with scorn rejected."

Nobody speaks of the horse as a creature enjoying man's highest gift—as a *living* animal. Everybody talks about his or her constitution; but no one imagines the horse has a constitution which can be destroyed. All horses are expected to thrive equally. They are regarded as things to be used, and to be sold or packed away when not required. They are obliged to live by man's direction, and are expected to display the highest spirit whenever they are taken abroad. Should it be astonishing if the framework nature has so exquisitely balanced occasionally becomes deranged under man's barbarous and selfish sway? Is it cause for legitimate wonder if, under so coarse a rule, disease sometimes assumes strange forms, or attacks parts which are beyond the reach of human science?

WORMS.

Worms are of various kinds; but all, according to the notions of ignorance, announce their presence by particular symptoms. The parasites, when really present, can, however, cause no more than intestinal irritation, the continuance of which may give rise to several disorders. Chronic indigestion is by the groom always recognized as a "wormy condition."

The only certain proof of the existence of such annoyances is visible evidence. Upon suspicion, careful horse proprietors may administer certain medicine, because some physics only cool the body and cleanse the system. The generality of worm-powders are, however, too potent to be safe. Like all drugs sold as "certain cures," they are so powerful that they frequently do more than remove the disorder which they pretend to eradicate—for they also destroy the animals to which they are administered.

Having premised thus much, the author will now commence to describe the usual form of irritation to which worms of different kinds give rise.

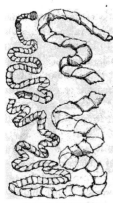

THE TÆNIA OR TAPE-WORM.

The parasite especially inimical to colts is the **tænia** or **tape-worm**. It is mostly perpetuated by the farmer's prejudice, which procures foals from dams that are done up for work: which starves the mother till her produce runs by her side, and which attempts to rear young stock upon the sour grass of a public common. Both sire and dam should be in perfect health if a valuable colt is desired: neither can be too good. The mare should not, during gestation, be "turned out" to distend the abdomen with watery provender—to have the stomach and intestines filled with bots—to allow filth and excretions to accumulate upon the coat and to check the healthy functions of the skin. Gentle work, only sufficient to earn the stable-keep, will injure no animal. The mare

.will rather be benefited by *moderate* exercise, and by also having all the food and attention to which she has become habituated. But to expose a mare during the summer months, and to stint the animal during the winter season, can produce nothing which shall repay the expense of rearing. The little progeny before it sees the light is the inhabitant of an unhealthy home; after birth the mother's secretion is thin, poor, and watery. It neither satisfies the cravings of hunger nor can nourish a body into growth. Ill health in the young encourages parasites. The colt soon becomes the prey of the tænia.

The young when afflicted with the above parasite may not die, but they are reserved for a miserable and a useless life. The developments are checked. The foal grows up with a large head, low crest, tumefied abdomen, and long legs. If it be a male it cannot be operated upon before the fourth year; even then it is cast only because there is no hope of further improvement. The appetite during the long time of rearing is more than

IRRITATION CAUSED BY WORMS. THE NOSE RUBBED VIOLENTLY AGAINST A WALL.

good; the ribs, nevertheless, are not covered with flesh; the dung is not well comminuted—it is friable and sometimes partially coated with slime; the anus projects—occasionally it is soiled by adherent strips of tenacious mucus, almost like to membrane; the coat is unhealthy; the breath fetid; the animal may rub its nose violently against a wall or remain straining it upward for a considerable time; the eye becomes unnaturally bright; the colt begins to pick and bite its body, often pulling off hair by the mouthful.

All this agony and the deprivation of a life depends on the parsimony of man. Women

A COLT PICKING THE HAIR FROM ITS LEG BECAUSE OF WORMS.

know that the body during certain times requires extra nutriment. Thus delicate ladies in peculiar states are accustomed to take "hearty pulls" at porter or at stout. It is very general for physiologists to

argue from animals up to man. Why should not the custom be reversed?
Why should not veterinary science reason from the human being down
to the horse, and thereby instruct the stolid in the necessary requirements of the mare during particular states? "Stint the dam and starve
the foal" is certainly a true proverb.

Tænia is best destroyed by the spirits of turpentine in the following
quantities:—

A foal	Two drachms.
Three months old	Half an ounce.
Six months	One ounce.
One year	One ounce and a half.
Two years	Two ounces.
Three years	Three ounces.
Four years and upwards	Four ounces.

Procure one pound of quassia chips. Pour into these three quarts
of boiling water. Strain the liquor. Cause the turpentine to blend, by
means of yolks of eggs, with so much of the quassia infusion as may be
necessary. Add one scruple of powdered camphor to the full drink, and
give every morning before allowing any food.

This probably may kill the worms; but as every link of the tænia is
a distinct animal of both sexes, and capable of producing itself, the eggs
must be numerous. For the destruction of these, nourishing prepared
food is essential, such as gruel, scalded oats, etc.; but little or no hay.
At the same time a tonic will be of all service. Take

Liquor arsenicalis	From one to eight drachms.
Muriated tincture of iron . . .	From one and a half to twelve drachms.
Extract of belladonna	From ten grains to two drachms.
Ale or good stout	Half a pint to a quart.

Mix. Give every morning to the animal—strength being proportioned to age—
till the coat is glossy.

Lumbrici are more dreadful to contemplate than they appear to be

THE LUMBRICUS, A WORM NOT
PECULIAR TO HORSES. ONE-
FOURTH OF THE NATURAL SIZE.

AN ASCARIDIS,
NATURAL SIZE.

A STRONGULUS,
NATURAL SIZE.

fearful in reality; specimens are not rare which measure eighteen inches,

This worm preys upon the weakly, be they old or young. One tænia will produce immense disturbance; whereas numbers of the lumbrici will cause little or no effect. Whoever has remarked the dunghill in a knacker's yard has seen it to consist quite as much of lumbrici as of excrement. Mr. Woodger, of Bishop's Road, Paddington, removes these pests with ease and certainty. The above-named veterinary surgeon gives two drachms of tartarized antimony with a sufficiency of common mass, as a ball, every morning, until the parasites are expelled.

ASCARIDES AND STRONGULI.

These parasites inhabit the large intestines. They produce extraor-

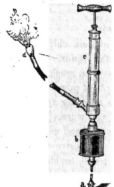

a. The sole opening by which air can enter. It is placed upon the ground and guarded by a valve; so that air, after having entered, cannot leave the instrument by this opening.

b. The box containing lighted tobacco, through which all air drawn into the instrument must necessarily pass.

c. The pump.

d. The end of the tube through which the fumes are driven.

To load the instrument: unscrew the lid of the box. Fill that with lighted tobacco. Fix on the lid again. Rest the air entrance upon the ground, and move the handle of the pump up and down. By this movement the air is first drawn through the lighted tobacco into the pump, and is then sent through the tube.

THE APPARATUS BY MEANS OF WHICH A TOBACCO SMOKE ENEMA IS ADMINISTERED.

dinary ravages, notwithstanding their insignificant appearance. The last is difficult to eradicate because of the extent of bowel which it infests. The **stronguli** will sometimes eat through important structures, but the **ascarides** are always located within the rectum. Then, most medicines being deprived of activity, are inoperative before they reach the last locality. For this reason it is best to commence the treatment with injections of *train* oil. Should these be followed by no result at the expiration of a week, resort to a solution of catechu —one ounce to the quart of water: give that for seven mornings. Upon the eighth, give the animal a mash, and at night administer a mild

A HORSE THAT HAS RUBBED ITSELF VIOLENTLY AGAINST A WALL.

physic ball; about four drachms of aloes and one drachm of calomel. Repeat the medicine if required; but if not, resort at once to the arsenicalis and ale or stout, which was recently recommended.

Tobacco smoke enemas are sometimes efficacious when all the previous measures are powerless. Frequently the posterior irritation is distressing. It is sometimes so provoking that the horse will thereby be induced to destroy its personal appearance by rubbing the tail and quarter violently against the wall, or any rough surface within its reach. In such cases the injections of train oil are most likely to prove beneficial; the local itching may be in some measure removed by inserting up the anus a portion of the following ointment night and morning :—

Glycerin	Half an ounce.
Spermaceti	One ounce.

Melt the last and blend. When nearly cold, add—

Mercurial ointment (strong)	Three drachms.
Powdered camphor	Three drachms.

SPASMODIC COLIC.—FRET.—GRIPES.

Spasmodic colic is an affection which every loiterer about a stable, from a postboy to a farrier, imagines he is able to cure. Many attacks no doubt would depart of themselves; others might be removed by simple motion. Nevertheless such possible remedies should never be trusted. Neither should gin and pepper, red pepper and peppermint, hot beer and mustard, rubbing the abdomen with a broomstick, kneading the belly violently with a man's knee, or any popular measure be permitted. Such remedies are likely to get rid of colic by causing enteritis. When inflammation of the bowels thus originates, it is generally fatal, the strength being exhausted and the powers of nature worn out by the previous disorder—not to mention the prepossession of the spectators, which prevents the more serious disease from being early recognized.

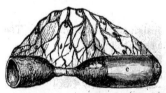

DIAGRAM EXPLAINING HOW THE BOWELS ARE
AFFECTED BY SPASMODIC COLIC.

a a. The healthy intestine rendered much more vascular by the blood being spasmodically driven out of other portions of the tube.
b. A portion of the tube much diminished by the presence of abdominal spasm.
c. The pallid appearance, denoting the place which colic has recently attacked.

Any cause may kindle colic. It is common after fast driving; hence many gentlemen take colic drinks to Epsom races. That affection which in ladies is designated spasms, in gentlemen is called pain in the bowels, and in children is known as the bellyache, is, in the horse, colic; and from the largeness of the animal's intestines, the affection probably provokes more anguish in the quadruped than the same disorder does in the entire human race. Under whatever term it may be recognized, spasmodic colic is never more than partial contraction of the muscular coat of the intestines. The action so compresses a part of the tube as to expel the blood and render the natural pink of the tissues, for some time after the disorder has departed, a glistening white. The blood, driven from particular spots, is forced into those parts in which no disease exists. Excess of blood predisposes to inflammation; hence we probably trace the reason why, if spasmodic colic be suffered to continue, the affection is so apt to end in incurable enteritis.

Colic most often attacks the small intestines, though the disease is by no means confined to those parts. It first occurs on a limited space; presently it vanishes altogether, and afterward reappears on some distant portion of the alimentary canal; or, in other words, colic dodges about, its attacks becoming more numerous and the intermissions shorter as the period of its commencement grows more distant. Change of water, change of food, getting-wet, fatiguing journeys, are all likely to originate it; but, perhaps, it is most frequently exhibited when no known cause is in operation. Aloes, however, are proved to be among the surest provocatives of this disease. Many horses cannot swallow pure aloes in any form, without being severely griped. For such animals, the following drench is recommended, instead of the above-named drug in substance:—

Sulphuric ether and laudanum, of each . . . . One ounce.
Compound tincture of aloes made with diluted spirits of wine . Five ounces.
Cold water . . . . One pint.

THE FIRST STAGE OF SPASMODIC COLIC.

If greater strength be requisite, obtain it by the addition of tincture of gentian, every ounce of which is equal, when combined, to one drachm of aloes.

Colic always commences suddenly; it starts into life ready armed for mischief. The animal may be apparently well and feeding. Without visible cause the head is raised and the occupation ceases. Should the pain last, the hind foot is lifted to strike the belly, and the fore leg begins to scrape the pavement. The groom, who has merely left to procure a pail of water from an adjacent pump, on his return discovers his charge exhibiting evident signs of uneasiness. As the man stares, wondering what can be the matter, the horse is pawing and the nose slowly points to the flank. All then is explained. **Fret** is the matter, and it would be "*fret*," should the disease prove to be of a very different nature.

While the horse is being watched, every indication of disturbance may disappear. The countenance tranquilizes and the nose is again inserted into the manger. A few minutes elapse and the pangs are renewed. The second fit may last longer and be slightly more severe. Then another, but a shorter period of ease follows: thus the visitations will ensue upon spaces of entire exemption from anguish. The recommencement of agony usually is denoted by a disposition to lie down. The animal crouches; next it turns round as though the intention was to stretch out the limbs; but suddenly the erect attitude is assumed—the design, lately so nearly executed, having been forgotten. Then pawing and striking at the abdomen quickly follow; and while the horse looks toward the flank, a morbid fire is perceptible in the eye.

THE SECOND STAGE OF SPASMODIC COLIC.

No relief being afforded, the pains lengthen, while the intervals of tranquillity become shorter. The action grows more fierce and the aspect more wild. The pawing is more brief, but more energetic; often during its continuance the foot is raised and violently stamped upon the ground. The animal now does not attempt to feed, but stares for a minute at a time, with an inquiring gaze, toward the abdomen. At length, without warning or preparation, the body leaps upward to fall violently upon the floor. The shock is often fearful; but the animal in its torment appears to derive ease from the violence. Being down, it rolls from side to side and kicks about, until one of its feet, touching the wall, enables the horse to poise itself upon the back.

Should relief not be quickly provided, colic soon passes into enteritis. The pulse, from being unchanged at first, then simply quickened by pain,

THE THIRD STAGE OF SPASMODIC COLIC.

grows harder and more wiry. The intermissions are lost, and though the anguish may for a space be less, yet in its continuity it is more exhausting.

On the appearance of colic, the morbid action ought to be immediately counteracted. Aloes in solution is generally administered; such a medicine, unless guarded as before recommended, is by no means advisable. Sulphuric ether and laudanum should be in the possession of every horse proprietor. One pint of each—the two being mixed together, with one ounce of rank oil floating on the top to prevent evaporation or mistakes—will be perfectly safe in any household. The mixture should, however, be well shaken before it is employed: two ounces of the combination in half a pint of water constitutes an excellent colic drink. Give three of these, one every ten minutes. If no improvement be displayed, double the quantity of the active agents and continue the drenches at the period stated: these medicines should be persevered with until the symptoms disappear.

Turpentine, as an enema, is an excellent adjunct. Mr. T. W. Gowing, of Camden Town, cured a lingering fit of colic by administering a pint of turpentine mixed with a quart of the solution of soap. The strong liquor of ammonia, diluted with six times its bulk of water and applied by means of a saturated cloth, held to the abdomen in a rug several times doubled, is likewise frequently beneficial. If these means, used simultaneously, produce no amendment in two hours, watch the pulse, for there is most probably something beyond simple colic to contend with.

Upon the earliest symptom the horse should be removed to a loose box amply protected by trusses of straw ranged against the walls. Into this the animal should be immediately led—for the reader must under-

APPLYING AN AMMONIACAL BLISTER.

stand colic does not always observe the stages in which it has been described. Occasionally it commences in the wildest form; and if a loose box be not at hand, one can always be extemporized by removing the carriage from its house, by throwing the doors wide open and by placing a bar across the entrance.

No disease is more quickly dispelled if treated at the commencement; nor is there one which, being left to run its course, occasions greater agony, is more fearful to witness, or leads to more terrible results than spasmodic colic. A single dose of ether and of laudanum may vanquish the malady at the commencement; yet if the attack be allowed to progress, the fit may set all skill and remedial measures at defiance. The principal attention of the proprietor must be given to prevent the administration of the "groom's favorite" or other ignorant nostrums. The case, when properly treated, is cured for a few shillings; and a horse cannot be killed with decency for less money.

Besides, let any human being, having feelings capable of impression, regard an instance of spasmodic colic which has been aggravated by mistaken treatment; and as he views the fibers of a living body quiver, sees the frame bedewed in sweat and wrenched in mighty torture, contemplates the sad condition of the companion of his pleasures, and hears vented from its throat sounds expressive of agony,—let him, having the image present to his eyes, ask himself whether any man, possessing means at his command, has a right to make a money question of the creature's suffering, which exists in a state of dependence on his bounty.

Horses must be gifted with a certain amount of reason. However furious may be the attack of colic, the mute expression of anguish is quieted when preparation is made for the administration of medicine. The most nauseous drenches are swallowed with a patience that speaks a perfect comprehension of their intent. The most wonderful proof of reason is, however, given by the manner in which the horse will recognize the veterinary surgeon. The author has known animals, in the intervals of spasmodic colic, walk close up to him, look full into his face with an eye beaming with intelligence, and a strain upon the features as though the creature "did so wish to speak;" then finding utterance impossible, the nose has mutely directed attention to the flank.

Every assistance is, by the animal, afforded to him who displays a desire to alleviate its distress. Where language is denied, motives appear to be the more quickly comprehended; and he who wishes to mingle safely among horses, may best protect himself by treating them gently and sympathizing with their emotions.

FLATULENT COLIC, WINDY COLIC, TYMPANITIS, ETC.

This is peculiarly the affection of old age. Horses, though not so liable to hoven as are horned cattle, nevertheless may be blown out if permitted to gorge upon moist, green food. Flatulent colic in the vast majority of instances, however, is not caused by any special fodder, but

THE FIRST STAGE OF FLATULENT COLIC.

springs from disordered digestion; living for years upon stimulating diet, breathing a tainted atmosphere, being now weakened by a long fast, then distressed by a too abundant supply; next exhausted by a tedious journey, and subsequently cramped by days of enforced stagnation,—all of these things ultimately tell upon the strong body of our domesticated quadruped. The stomach, as the earliest evidence of general debility, loses its tonicity. It cannot digest a full meal; the provender ferments, gas is released, and flatulent colic is the consequence.

A traditionary belief in the stable asserts this disorder is provoked by crib-biting, wind-sucking, etc. etc. The author is indebted to Mr. Ernes, a most successful veterinary surgeon of Dockhead, for the earliest comprehension of the impossibility that such causes should operate. Let the reader endeavor to swallow air; the mouth being deprived of all saliva, the attempt at further deglutition is fruitless; besides, to use the words of Mr. Ernes, "though the stomach or the bowels do contain a small portion of atmospheric air, flatulent colic is generated by carbonic acid or sulphureted hydrogen gas, the products of decomposition; either of which, if respired, destroys vitality."

The horse which is to be oppressed by flatulent colic exhibits uneasiness after feeding; it hangs the head; breathes laboriously; fidgets; rocks the body, and rests first on one leg then on the other. These

A HORSE DYING OF FLATULENT COLIC.

symptoms are exhibited before any enlargement of the abdomen is to be detected. With the swelling of the belly pawing commences; that action is, however, far too leisurely displayed to be for an instant confounded with the same energetic movement which characterizes spasmodic colic.

W. Percivall asserts that animals roll and kick at the abdomen during flatulent colic. Every fact requires to be respectfully considered which is recorded by so estimable a writer; but the author has never witnessed such symptoms in genuine flatulent colic. The horse will stand in one spot throughout the day; even the movement of the foot, before noticed, appears to be an exertion. The eye is sleepy, the pulse heavy, wind frequently passes from the body, and in such a condition the animal remains, slowly becoming worse.

Almost in the same place the horse may stand three or four days; then the abdomen is much increased in size; the animal is restless; the pulse is extremely feeble; the breathing is very fast; the pupil of the eye is dilated and the sight is lost. A walk as in a mill is commenced; obstacles are run into or upset; delirium begins; weak neighs are uttered in reply to visionary challenges; the coat is ragged; copious and partial perspirations break forth; the beat of the artery is lost at the jaw; an intermittent flutter is to be indistinctly felt at the heart. At last the limbs fail; the body falls; struggles ensue, and the creature dies in consequence of the distended abdomen compressing the lungs, thus preventing the breath being inhaled.

Relief should be afforded before the distress grows urgent; when the flatulence comes on without green provender being consumed, the chances favor recovery; even then, however, the gas may be confined to the stomach, which obliges entire dependence to be placed upon internal remedies. In the beginning, a ball composed of two drachms of sulphuret of ammonia, with a sufficiency of extract of gentian and powdered quassia, may be repeated thrice, half an hour being suffered to elapse between each administration. No benefit ensuing, one ounce of chlorate of potash, dissolved in a pint of cold water and mingled with two ounces of sulphuric ether, may, at the expiration of the time named, be horned down. After another hour, should no amendment be perceptible, two ounces each of sulphuric ether and laudanum, half an ounce of camphorated spirits, and one drachm of carbonate of ammonia may be given in a pint of cold water. Should no good effects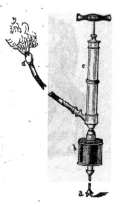
THE TOBACCO-SMOKE ENEMA. WORMS.
ensue, in another hour throw up a tobacco-smoke enema by means of the machine here represented.

As a last resort, should the previous remedies prove of no avail, procure a stick of brimstone; light it and let it fill the place with the sulphurous fumes which are the product of its combustion. However, mind that the air is not too strongly impregnated, though, at the same time, it should be so pungent as to allow a human being to breathe with difficulty. This last measure ought to be continued for two hours, at the end of which period repeat the remedies already recommended, resorting to each by turns; and do not fear being active, for flatulent colic becomes more difficult to remove as the period of its origin grows more distant. Should the affection appear to be approaching a fatal termination, and the size of the belly convince the spectator that the gas has entered the intestines, a desperate remedy remains. The situation where the vapor has accumulated may be ascertained by percussion; gently cut the skin which covers the abdomen on the left side, over those places indicated by white spots in the second engraving. A hollow sound will be emitted when the proper point has been struck; be certain of the last fact, as mistakes made in this operation are very awkward affairs. When assured, take a sharp-pointed knife, and, drawing the skin tight over the place selected, nick the integument slightly; then take a fine trocar and push it through the opening which has been made.

A TROCAR ARMED WITH A CANULA FOR PUNCTURING THE ABDOMEN.

This being accomplished, withdraw the stilet, and the gas should rush out with violence; be provided with a small probe to clear the canula in case it should become impacted. The gas being released, the abdomen is reduced; withdraw the canula and the skin will fly back, effectually excluding all atmosphere.

The gas, on rare occasions, will be generated a second time; therefore the points where other punctures may be made are indicated; for it is never well to interfere with those openings which in the first instance were instituted. However, should the operation have to be repeated, pull the integument in the opposite direction, so as not to disturb the original wounds into the abdomen.

Puncturing the abdomen for flatulent colic has been practiced both in this kingdom and in foreign lands; it is by no means a certain success, neither is it a certain failure. It assuredly requires boldness to perform it; but probably it is quite as beneficial and far more speedy in its effects than the great majority of medicinal remedies.

THE PLACES WHERE THE ABDOMEN MAY BE PUNCTURED IN THE LAST STAGE OF FLATULENT COLIC.

The duration of flatulent colic cannot be absolutely stated; it may continue for days, it may be cured in a single hour. However, should the abdomen be rapidly distended, then the termination will be sooner reached; but be the attack quick or slow, neither food nor water should be allowed during its continuance. The groom, while the disease lasts, should occasionally sponge out the eyes, mouth, nostrils, etc. Indeed, humanity would dictate such relief during every serious affection. Subsequent to recovery, feed for a few days on gruel and mashed oats; give a ball night and morning, composed of extract of gentian and powdered quassia, of each a sufficiency; of extract of belladonna and of sulphate of copper, half a drachm Continue this medicine and the above food until the stomach has regained its tone.

Is flatulent colic a disease provoked by domestication? Certainly! The wild horse would have to travel for his food; in domestication it is placed ready gathered before the animal Besides, the free animal being ever with his provender, the temptation to gorge the stomach would be absent; moreover, the untrained creature is protected by its instincts, which the care of man destroys Little, however, is thought of this; the fact even may be unknown to the great majority of educated horse proprietors. The sense of repletion is no longer indicated with such force as to warn the stabled animal. The responsibility thus cast upon the master has possibly never occurred to the mass of mankind. So entirely has the notion of any duty being due to the animal been ignored by society that, notwithstanding nature in the above fact asserts the obligation, its announcement most probably will be received with laughter.

CHAPTER IX.

NEPHRITIS OR INFLAMMATION OF THE KIDNEYS.

THE straddling gait is not peculiar to any one disorder. It denotes no more than the region in which the affection is to be sought; but it does not characterize any special disease. Therefore so general a trait is

THE GENERAL SYMPTOM WHICH ATTENDS ALL DISEASES OF THE URINARY ORGANS.

placed at the head of the chapter treating of ailments confined to the urinary organs, so that he who perceives the horse assume this position may at once recognize that part of the body in which the disorder resides.

Nephritis is not so common at the present time as it used to be formerly; the growing information of the people has in some measure altered the practices of the stable. The master is not quite so much the slave of a groom's ignorance as was once universally the case; the animal is no longer regarded as a mysterious creature which it required a particular education to understand. Urine balls, therefore, are no longer regularly kept in every loft. Niter—one ounce of "*sweet* nitre," or, to speak correctly, an overdose of *harsh* saltpeter—may, however, be still permitted, and by particular horse proprietors regarded as a charm against every

(204)

ill. It is true that such a dose of a powerful diuretic is four times the strength which science would, under any circumstances, approve; but certain people in remote parts are happy in the conviction that an ounce of "*sweet* niter" can *possibly* do no harm.

The urinary organs of the horse must be little disposed to disease; they must be capable of surmounting a vast quantity of ill treatment Were not ignorance thereby protected from the consequences which it provokes, half the horses in England would be disabled; inflammation of the kidneys would become the most common of equine disorders

The horse has small need of diuretic medicine; it is much exposed in that direction Every purge, should it not act as intended, passes out of the body by stimulating the kidneys; the ordinary provender of the animal may operate in the same manner. Foxy oats, kiln-dried oats, new oats; musty hay, mow-burnt hay, new hay, beans in particular conditions; grasses, when first in season, and water of any novel kind, will all operate energetically upon the renal glands; therefore the horse, in its ordinary food, will possibly imbibe more than a sufficiency of a most debilitating medicine; and the knowledge of such a liability may induce some men to withhold "*sweet* niter" from the future diet of the creature.

It may be necessary to inform men and masters that a horse needs rest when under the operation of diuretic, quite as much as when subject to the action of purgative medicine. It is never safe to take the horse from the stable while the animal is passing any unusual amount of water Excess of secretion proves the eliminating organs are excited. Before any part can exhibit excitement, an extra quantity of blood must circulate within it, or it must be in a condition bordering upon inflammation The urine is secreted from the blood by the kidneys; therefore before a greater bulk of water can be passed, of course more blood must flow through the glands.

The animal in such a state is not fit for work; every step taken brings into action muscles which pass directly under the kidneys, and which must, therefore, when contracted, compress those organs During labor, in proportion to the force required must be the power of the contraction exerted by the organs of motion; in a healthy state, such exertion is not always free from danger. Excitement is, however, far from a healthy state. Then the glands are gorged with blood; being squeezed for an hour or two while thus swollen or plethoric, they are very likely to be bruised; inflammation may thereby be engendered, or renal abscess may possibly ensue.

Agriculturists are entreated to pause over the above statement Such persons often possess a well-bred and promising colt. The farmer, however, is mostly uneasy until he has, according to his own notions, "tried the beast." He may be a personable man, riding fully "eighteen stun." The colt, probably, would be taxed to carry a third that load. The "*sweet*-niter" dose is administered over night to take all fever out of the body; and, while the kidneys are excited, the animal is saddled, mounted, and ridden to the hunt. Everybody knows the manner in which most farmers ride. The horse may have a hard run and be kept out for a long day. On the return, a full rack and a heaped manger

A COLT BROUGHT HOME AFTER THE FARMER HAS TRIED "WHAT KIND OF STUFF IS IN IT," BY A HARD
DAY WITH THE HOUNDS.

are placed before the overridden quadruped. Neither are touched. The saddle is removed and the back appears to be "queerly sticking up." The large full eyes are repeatedly turned round; and the renter of land is in doubt whether the creature is staring reproachfully at him or is simply inspecting its own quarters. However, with the apathy which too many agriculturists habitually display, the colt is left for the night. By the next morning the animal is ruined, even should it survive an attack of acute nephritis.

The symptoms of inflammation of the kidneys are a hard pulse, decidedly accelerated; quickened and short breathing, suggestive of pain; pallid mucous membranes; frequent looking toward the seat of anguish; head depressed; back roached; hind legs straddled, and the urine scanty. The animal almost refuses to "come round" in its stall, seldom lies down, and crouches beneath pressure when made upon the loins.

Subsequently, as the symptoms alter, pus or matter may subside in the water. It is indicative of an unfavorable termination should a fetid odor attend the secretion, and should it be deeply tinted by the blood. Death is generally close at hand when the pulse grows quicker but more feeble, when pressure elicits no response, when the body is covered with perspiration, and when a urinous smell is perceptible on approaching the animal.

The treatment of nephritis consists in applying fresh sheepskins to the loins. Should the case be urgent, a quantity of lukewarm made mustard may be first rubbed in and the sheepskin placed over it; or mustard poultices in any case may be employed and covered over to prevent them becoming dry, till sheepskins can be procured. Injections of warm linseed tea should be thrown up every hour, as these are the nearest approach that can be made to actual fomentation. Two scruples of croton farina, mixed with half a drachm of belladonna, may be given immediately in the form of a ball, the bulk of which should be made up with crushed linseeds and treacle. One scruple of calomel, with one

THE TEST FOR NEPHRITIS OR INFLAMMATION OF THE KIDNEYS.

drachm of opium, may be sprinkled on the tongue every hour while the acute stage continues. A pail of good linseed tea should be kept before the horse; but as for more substantial provender, none is requisite during the agony of the disease.

Should the slightest doubt be entertained concerning the nature of the affection, immediately insert the arm up the rectum. This intestine is anatomically spoken of as "a floating gut." It is suspended from the spine by mesentery or a loose fold of thin membrane, and, therefore, is easily raised or depressed. It is situated under the kidneys, and nothing consequently interposes between the diseased organ and the inserted hand but the pliable coats of the bowel and the fatty substances which immediately surround the glands. The hand is not conscious of the soft wall of the intestine which covers it. The motion is so free, and the fingers are so readily moved, that previous knowledge alone assures the operator his arm is within a circumscribed canal, and not located in a free space.

By inserting the hand and moving it gradually upward, an approach
can be made to the immediate vicinity of the inflammation. Sensitive-

a a a. The spine.   *b b b.* The mesentery.   *c c c.* The rectum.
A. The extent to which the rectum may by very gradual force be depressed without injury to the
animal.
B. The rectum, with the natural length of mesentery, when not depressed.
C. The rectum raised, showing that the mesentery is very pliable.

ness will be exhibited as the seat of disease is touched. Heat will also
be felt. A fore leg should, however, be held up on the same side as the

operator stands. Should the horse struggle violently and denote positive agony
when the hand is approaching the region
of the kidneys, the signs may be considered
conclusive without attempting farther exploration. Should the animal remain quiet
at first, nevertheless let the operator be
cautious, as the too near vicinity to the inflamed part provokes resistance, which, in
its utter heedlessness, is closely allied to
madness.

A CERTAIN TEST FOR INFLAMMATION
OF THE KIDNEYS.

Several reasons will suggest the point at
which the hand should pause. In the first
place, pressure cannot benefit a delicately-formed and a diseased organ.
In the second place, the agony of the animal may endanger the safety of
the operator. In the last place, anything approaching to downright
resistance brings the muscles that pass under the kidneys into energetic action, which circumstance is by no means favorable to ultimate
recovery

Many men can speak of the pain induced by affections of the kidneys.
The torture consequent upon disease of an internal organ appears to
be so excessive as at times to destroy reason in the human being. No

one can look upon a horse suffering from nephritis, without feeling that, in sensibilities at all events, the two creatures are alike. Sympathy has been interpreted to mean no more than a conscious similarity of emotion Such a definition must be erroneous, or more sympathy would actuate man toward his slave. The life is devoted to the service of the master. The body is disabled before its time for the pleasure of mankind. The horse is such a slave as no words can express. It lives but to obey Its master's whim is the animal's joy It is happy to exist where and how its superior may appoint. Still there is no sympathy felt toward its tortures, no feeling evinced for its sufferings: its life is one long solitude, its death is the degradation of misery. Were man to read of some wild beast capable of such sincere docility, what pains would not be spent to secure so valuable a companion! The animal is beside him and it is disregarded; or its goodness is converted into the means for its mutilation.

The additional treatment of nephritis consists more in the food than in the physic; linseed, both the seeds and the infusion, may be given for the body's support. The best oats should be procured upon recovery, and the quality of the hay also should be attended to; as for physic, that is almost limited to belladonna and to aconite Belladonna is administered mixed with four times its amount of opium, so long as the pain is acute.

Extract of belladonna	. Half a drachm.
Crude opium	. . . Two drachms.

Make into a ball with linseed meal and honey; give three daily while the symptoms require them; or, should the pain be excessive, administer one every hour.

The aconite root is intended to lower the circulation When the pulse is quick and hard, a scruple of the powder may be thrown upon the tongue every half hour, till the beat of the artery soften, or till the animal appear to be affected by the medicine. The above measures are to be adopted without regard to. the calomel and opium previously recommended.

A horse having survived one attack of nephritis, can scarcely, however successful may be the treatment, be restored to its original condition. The glands which have suffered inflammation must be left in an irritable state.

CYSTITIS—INFLAMMATION OF THE BLADDER.

This disorder is somewhat rare in the horse. Few cases have occurred; even those were not strongly marked. Besides the general indications present during nephritis, such as quickened breathing, accelerated pulse, straddling gait, etc. etc., the most prominent sign concerns the emission of the urine. The bladder is irritable at the commencement; the kidneys have not secreted half a pint of. fluid before it is violently expelled, and much straining, accompanied by sounds expressive of pain, follows the act. As the disease progresses, the bladder is contracted, and the water issues drop by drop, or as a constant dribble. This particularity marks the disease, which is also distinguished from nephritis by the roached back being absent; the spine rather being hollowed more than is usual in cystitis.

Most lecturers direct the student to insert the arm up a horse affected

A DANGEROUS TEST FOR INFLAMMATION OF THE BLADDER.

with cystitis and to feel the compressed bladder; this is easily accomplished, as the engraving demonstrates; but is the operation perfectly safe? White muscular tissue, when inflamed, becomes acutely sensitive. The bladder possesses a thick coat of that substance, and the hand, grasping an organ of this formation when in a state of disease, would probably torture the sufferer to frenzy. It is not wise to excite a creature commanding so huge a strength. There is, however, a test which yields as certain a response, and, at the same time, is far less hazardous. This consists in placing the hand under the flank and keeping it there till all the action which could be attributable to skittishness has disappeared; then press the abdomen, which, should it be hard and resistant, is a convincing proof cystitis is not present; for contraction of the recti abdominis muscles would force the contents of the cavity into violent contact with the inflamed bladder. Should any doubt be entertained concerning the condition of the muscle named, a little more pressure will soon ascertain the fact. However, let the person who applies the test be prepared for the consequence, as the application of pressure to a diseased organ provokes a sudden and energetic resistance, intended to strike the tormentor backward.

The treatment for inflamed bladder and diseased kidneys is alike as regards the administration of aconite root, extract of belladonna, calomel and opium. The reader is, therefore, in some measure referred to the article upon nephritis; there is, however, a difference in application of counter-irritation by means of a rug doubled over a cloth, which last is saturated with strong liquor of ammonia diluted with six times its bulk of water; should this not be within reach, hot cloths retained under the belly are the next best application; but these require constant change and a larger supply of heated fluid than most private establishments can command. Should both recommendations prove useless, then apply cloths dripping wet from a cold bath, and keep renewing them so often as they become warm.

A SAFER TEST FOR INFLAMMATION OF THE BLADDER.

The cause of cystitis is the same as produces many cases of inflamed kidney, namely, the abuse of medicine, or new and unwholesome food; blows likewise may induce it. Kicks under the belly, the too common mode of expressing impatience among carters, are very likely to provoke

APPLICATION OF THE AMMONIACAL BLISTER.

it. Horses are frequently seen in the streets of every town now whipped to make them proceed; then the rein jagged to command the animal to "stand still." Next the whip is again applied; afterward the animal's

belly is spitefully aimed at with the heavy boot of the countryman. The
horses know not how to interpret these different signs: they become
confused, they turn various ways, as if they hoped by such devices to
please their chastiser. All is in vain! At length the animals burst
into perspiration and shiver violently; by their alarm they are rendered
stupid But so disgusting an exhibition of folly and of cruelty on the
part of the driver mostly creates small indignation in the wayfarers who
behold it The spectators generally look on with smiling countenances,
and for the most part move onward without a word of displeasure or
rebuke. To the human mind a man appears invested with absolute
authority over the life which he has bought. So also no man risks
reprobation, who keeps his animals upon poisonous provender. The hay,
oats, and beans may be of a character calculated to engender disease.
But has not the owner purchased the right to treat his property as he
thinks proper? It is true, religion teaches that life is not in the custody
of man, and that health is not at mortal command; but where horses are
involved, all restraints appear to be forgotten, and mankind seem leagued
together to inflict suffering on the dumb. For, is it not universally
agreed that heavenly precepts were intended for man alone, and do not
stoop so low as to include all the creatures the existence of which dates
prior to the origin of the human being? Animals, according to modern
interpretation, are excluded from the ample embrace of Christian charity.
An all-merciful power looks down with pity only upon one inhabitant of
earth!

SPASM OF THE URETHRA.

This affection is commonly designated **spasm of the neck of the bladder.** The part named, however, has no fiber capable of excitation; and
it is difficult to understand how the elastic tissue at the opening of the
receptacle can display a condition which is inherent only within the
contractibility of muscle The compressor urethræ muscle, however,
being morbidly excited, is more than capable of preventing all discharge
of urine

The causes which provoke the spasm are not thoroughly understood.
The affection is mostly attributed to some acridity existing in the food
or water; else the supposed agent is said to be developed during the
process of digestion

The symptoms are: a widely straddling gait; total suppression of
urine, or small portions forcibly ejected at distant intervals. The suffering attendant on distention of the bladder is sometimes so violent
that the affection has been mistaken for phrenitis. At other times the
horse has been imagined to be griped. Both these blunders are unpar-

donable. The haggard countenance, copious perspirations, and the frequent glances toward the flanks, joined to the straddling gait and to the desperate but at the same time guarded struggles, are all opposed to such conclusions. Were a proper examination instituted, the real nature of the affection would at once be made apparent, beyond the possibility of error.

Insert the greased arm up the rectum, and, when fully advanced, make pressure downward; the dilated bladder will then be under the hand. The best remedies are sulphuric ether and laudanum, which should be given in large quantities. Four ounces of each should, in a quart of cold water, be administered by the mouth: the like quantities, blended with three pints of cold water, ought to be thrown up as an injection. The last being given, the hand should be placed over the opening and pressed upon it for ten minutes. Should one dose not succeed, in a quarter of an hour the injection may be repeated. Again and again it must be had recourse to; till the spasm is vanquished or till the urine flows freely forth.

MODE TO ASCERTAIN THE DISTENTION OF THE BLADDER.

Should the horse be seized where no medicine can be obtained, then extract blood from free openings till fainting takes place. Several small depletions are very weakening, and a large quantity of the vital fluid drawn at different times is far less likely to overcome the disease than one full venesection. Open both jugulars: allow the blood to flow from both veins till the water rushes forth or the animal falls, when, insensibility being produced, everything like spasm disappears, and the bladder will mechanically empty itself. Should not such a relief ensue, the greased arm may be inserted up the rectum, and gentle pressure made upon the gorged viscus. Advantage is thus taken of the animal's insensibility to adopt a mode of relief which we dare not hazard while consciousness is retained.

CALCULI.

Stones within the urinary apparatus are designated by various names, that are derived from the situations in which they are found. Thus renal calculus represents a stone which has been discovered within the pelvis of the kidney. Uretal calculus implies a stone found within the tubes leading from the kidneys to the bladder; but calculi of this kind are as yet unknown in the horse. **Cystic calculus** signifies a stone which resides in the cavity of the bladder. **Urethral calculus** denotes a stone which was detected within the passage leading from the bladder. Of these the cystic are altogether the largest, and the renal, at a considerable distance, rank as the next in magnitude. All consist of carbonate of lime or of common chalk, held firmly together by the secretion of the mucous membrane.

The symptoms which characterize renal calculus are not well marked. The urine may become purulent, thick, opaque, gritty or bloody. Exertion may provoke extreme anguish, resembling a severe fit of colic; but the attack is distinguished from genuine gripes by the back, during the pain, being always roached. However, the most decided symptom is of a negative nature; being the absence of stone in the bladder to account for the diseased urine. The inference is, moreover, strengthened if, when the hand within the rectum is carried upward, pain and alarm are elicited; or if pressure made upon the loins causes the animal to shrink.

Cystic calculus is denoted, as is the previous kind of stone, by certain conditions of the urine. Added to these general signs, the water, when

flowing forth, will often be suddenly stopped, and every emission is followed by violent straining. Abdominal pains also are present; but the back is rather hollowed than roached. The point of the penis is, in particular instances, constantly exposed; and the horse, when going down hill, sometimes pulls up short, either to recover from torture or to relieve the bladder.

The way to ascertain the presence of cystic calculus is to make an examination per rectum. Make the investigation with all gentleness. The foreign body may then be distinctly felt; even its size, form, and irregularities can by this means be discovered.

A CERTAIN METHOD OF ASCERTAINING IF THERE BE CALCULUS IN THE BLADDER.

Urethral calculus is a small stone which, during the flow of urine, has been carried out of the bladder and is spasmodically grasped by the muscle of the urethra. The passage is effectually closed and great suffering is induced. Should the stone be impacted within the exposed part of the canal, the precise situation is easily told. Behind the stoppage the passage is distended by fluid; while before it all is natural. The calculus should be cut down and removed; the wound being afterward dressed with a solution of chloride of zinc—one grain to the ounce of water. This is an easy and by no means a dangerous operation. Any person of ordinary skill having a sharp knife may undertake it.

For renal calculus little can be done. That little, however, consists in mingling two drachms of hydrochloric acid with every pail of water, and allowing the animal to imbibe as much as it pleases. Should the medicated drink be refused, the horse must be starved into accepting it. With this liquid, however, the stone must be small to be dissolved; but it effectually checks the further increase of the calculus.

Lithotomy is the name given to that operation by which large stones are removed from the bladder of the horse. It is far too complicated and too serious a proceeding to be entrusted to any general reader. No direction which possibly could be misconstrued shall, therefore, be attempted. When an operation is required for stone in the bladder, a qualified veterinary surgeon had better be employed. Mr. Simmonds, of the Royal Veterinary College, Camden Town, however, deserves praise for having invented an instrument by means of which stone can generally be removed from the bladder of the mare without resort to the knife being necessary.

HEMATURIA, OR BLOODY URINE.

The name fully characterizes this affection. The blood emitted may consist of small clots; it may congeal after it has left the body; or it may be entirely mingled with—giving a brownish tinge to—the water.

Upon the exhibition of this disorder, always treat the symptoms first; when all chance of immediate danger has disappeared, examine the body to ascertain whence the hemorrhage proceeded, because in this affection the symptoms really constitute the disease; and when the first has disappeared, the last is cured.

A HORSE SUFFERING FROM HEMATURIA, OR BLOODY URINE.

The extent of the bleeding, of course, regulates the symptoms. When that is copious, the breathing is short and quick; the pupils of the eye are dilated; the pulse is not to be felt at the jaw; the head is pendulous; and the visible mucous membranes are cold as well as pallid. Lifting the head produces staggering; if continued, the animal would fall. The back is roached; the flanks are tucked up, and the legs widely separated, as though the horse was aware of its inability to support its body.

The treatment consists in disturbing the sufferer as little as possible; in acting upon the report received, for in a case of this kind it is hardly credible there should be any mistake. Administer, as gently as it can be done, two drachms of acetate of lead in half a pint of cold water, or as a ball, if one can be delivered. If this has no effect, in a quarter of an hour, or sooner should the symptoms demand haste, repeat the dose, adding, however, one ounce of laudanum or two drachms of powdered opium. Give two more drinks or balls of the like composition; but should these be followed by no beneficial result, change the medicine after the administration of one ounce of acetate of lead.

When the indications are not alarming, the horse may be left for a couple of hours, with strict orders that the animal be watched, but on no account disturbed. Should, however, activity be required, obtain some of the coldest water, and have several pailfuls dashed from a height upon the loins. After this inject some of the same fluid, allowing the water to flow freely forth from the anus—the object only being to procure the advantages of excessive cold. For medicine, a trial may be made of the ergot of rye. Pour on to four drachms of the drug half a pint of boiling water, and, when cold, add one ounce of laudanum and four ounces of dilute acetic acid—not vinegar, as that always contains sulphuric acid, which would counteract the action of the lead Two drinks, two enemas, (each lasting twenty minutes,) and any quantity of water upon the loins will serve for the second hour.

If these remedies have produced no change, all further treatment must be suspended for eight hours, at the expiration of which period the treatment may be resumed, and the previous measures repeated.

Should the hemorrhage have ceased, leave the horse undisturbed for the night. On the following day, if no blood has been noticed, have the animal gently led under cover. Then proceed to examine the horse per rectum. If the kidneys are not enlarged, hardened, or sensitive, and if the bladder is without stone, but of its natural thickness, there is every prospect of a favorable termination.

Should the bladder be thickened, adopt the treatment laid down for cystitis; if stone is discovered, an operation is indicated; be the kidneys disorganized, the case is hopeless. If none of these are present, then any of the following medicines may be experimented with, it always being uncertain which will prove beneficial :—

Extract of catechu . . . . In one-ounce doses daily.
Strong infusion of oak bark . . . . Three pints daily.

```
Alum  . .  . . . . . . . . .  One ounce daily.
Sulphate of iron or of copper  . . .  One ounce daily.
Muriatic acid . . . . . . . . .  Six drachms daily.
```

DIABETES INSIPIDUS, OR PROFUSE STALING.

In this affection, which, properly treated, is but a passing annoyance, the thirst is enormous; but more fluid is voided than the animal drinks. The strength and condition are quickly lost, while the flesh fades rapidly away.

Either the horse has been tampered with by the groom, or the hay, oats, or beans are unsound. A sudden change of water is said to produce the disorder; but that, probably, is far more a stable excuse than an established cause. However, change both food and water. Take into the stable two slips of blotting-paper. Dip the ends of them into some of the urine, which will always be retained in the interspaces of the brick flooring. Smell one piece. If it communicates a scent resembling violets, that is proof positive turpentine has been administered. Dry the other piece. Should that, when perfectly dry, and a light is applied, prove to be touch-paper, the evidence is conclusive: "sweet niter" has been secretly given to the animal. Should both these tests fail, the groom is innocent, as other diuretics are unknown in the stable.

The horse should not be taken out while the prominent symptom lasts; it is languid; is unfit for work or even exercise. No brutality can quicken the body when the vital powers are exhausted; but inattention to the suggestion of mere humanity may change a slight and temporary evil into a severe and critical disorder—nephritis.

A pail of good linseed tea, made by pouring boiling water on whole linseeds, and afterward allowing the infusion to stand till lukewarm, should be constantly before the manger. The animal may drink according to the dictates of its condition. The linseed, when strained off and mixed with sound bruised and scalded oats, may be given as food. No hay or grass should be allowed. Attend to the grooming, although it is a sick horse and does not go out. Nothing relieves the kidneys more than the restored action of the skin. A ball may be given every day. It should consist of—

```
Iodide of iron . . . . . . . . . . . . .  One drachm.
Honey and linseed meal  . . . . . . . . .  A sufficiency.
```

Or, should a drink be preferred, dilute—

```
Phosphoric acid . . . . . . . . . .  . .  One ounce.
Water  . . . . . . . . . . . . . . .  . .  One pint.
    Give night and morning.
```

The author was once prepossessed in favor of iodide of potassium for the cure of diabetes. He is indebted to Mr. Woodger, the excellent practical veterinary surgeon of Paddington, for a knowledge of the very superior efficacy of the drug just named. It exercises a potent action over the kidneys, at the same time it is a first class tonic, and in a surprising manner reduces the desire for fluids. It is in all respects the exact medicine which could be wished for in a case of **diabetes insipidus.**

ALBUMINOUS URINE.

Two cases of this description occurred in the extensive practice of the late William Percivall, Esq. They are narrated in the admirable work entitled "Hippopathology," bequeathed to posterity by the estimable author. The present writer having been honored by the friendship of the gentleman named, is, from frequent conversations upon the subject, the better able to describe and to depict the disorder.

The positions of both horses were remarkable. One stretched the fore and hind legs out, as though it were about to urinate; the other roached the back and brought the hind feet under the body as far as possible. Turning in the stalls was, in each case, accomplished with difficulty; and the straddling gait remarkable in both, indicating the seat of the affection.

THE POSITIONS ASSUMED BY HORSES HAVING ALBUMINOUS URINE.

Some urine being caught by the groom, it was thick but clear—like melted calves' foot jelly—and, when cold, the surface was uneven. Bichloride of mercury being added to a portion of the fluid, caused a thick, colorless, opaque substance—resembling coagulated white of egg—to be thrown down, leaving a clear straw-colored liquor above the settlement. Another portion being first treated with acetic acid, afterward mixed with prussiate of potash and subsequently boiled, became in appearance like to milk. With time, however, a white sediment occurred, leaving the fluid perfectly clear.

Mr. Percivall's treatment was mildly depletive. He bled moderately, gave a laxative, and applied mustard to the loins for a brief space.

Perfect rest, strict attention to diet, and repeated doses of opium, constituted the after-measures. It is also mentioned that diuretics, tonics,

THE TESTS FOR ALBUMINOUS URINE.

A. The appearance of the urine when cold, being partially rough on the surface. Sometimes, however, the fluid is merely thicker than usual, appearing like water in which a portion of gum has been dissolved.

B. The white precipitate produced by the addition of a portion of the solution of bichloride of mercury.

C. Some urine to which a little acetic acid was first added. A portion of the solution of prussiate of potash was subsequently introduced. The liquid was then boiled, when it became thick, white, and opaque, like milk.

and stimulants were tried, but all proved injurious. Both animals ultimately recovered.

Those who desire ampler details are referred to "Hippopathology," by W. Percivall, published by Longman & Co.

CHAPTER X.

THE SKIN—ITS ACCIDENTS AND ITS DISEASES.

MANGE.

THIS troublesome disease, which is the itch of the stable, generally preys upon the poorly nurtured, the aged or the debilitated. Neglect is the almost necessary associate of poverty; loss of pride attends loss of means, for seldom can the spirit of man brave the frowns of fortune. The want of emulation is always seen most emphatically without the

SYMPTOMS OF MANGINESS WHEN CAUGHT IN THE FIELD.

doors of the home; the garden denotes the failure of industry, and the stable languishes under an absence of activity. The grooming is avoided; the horse's food is proportioned to the master's means, and is not given at regular hours; coarse diet and a filthy abode generate that weakness which will assuredly breed **mange**.

The disease, once developed, is highly contagious; all horses standing near the one affected, all that may touch it, or the shafts to which it was harnessed, or anything that has been in contact with the contaminated body, are inoculated. The very robust, to be sure, may escape; but this circumstance is to be regarded as the most stringent test of actual

.(220)

health rather than as the declaration of that state which the majority of mankind are pleased to term perfect condition. The animal which escapes must be of so sound a body as to afford no nutriment to the disorder which preys upon debility. Probably not one horse in ten thousand could resist so searching a test; the trial, however, after all, would be no more than a negative proof; and it is to be much regretted that science, up to the present time, has not discovered any means by which the presence of established health can be demonstrated.

Mange depends upon the presence of an insect which is classed with spiders, though to the uninitiated it looks, under the microscope, far more like a deformed crab. A representation of this parasite, very highly magnified, is here given, from Dr. Eras-  mus Wilson's paper upon the subject; and the reader may indulge his ingenuity by discovering its likeness to the spider.

The parasites are, when attentively searched for, to be recognized by the naked eye. Any man, by scratching the roots of the hair upon the mane of a mangy horse, may loosen a por- tion of scurf; let this scurf be received or cast upon a sheet of white paper. The paper then should be subjected to a strong light; the glare of the noonday sun is to be preferred, as warmth greatly influences the activity of the parasites. Numerous very small shining points may thus

THE MANGE INSECT.

be seen moving about the mass in all directions. Those points are the insects, and, considering the easy means we now possess of demonstra- ting their existence, it seems astonishing that veterinary science was so long before it recognized the true source of the contagion. Even at the last moment, the sight was quickened by the research of a human physician, Dr. Erasmus Wilson; but after that gentleman soon followed Mr. Ernes, veterinarian, of Dockhead.

Mange would be far less general than it is, did not the convenience or the prejudice of mankind predispose them to favor a "run at grass." The horse there placed is all at once taken from a stimulating diet, while, the groom being relieved of his charge, foulness accumulates upon the coat. The animal, instead of standing still and feeding upon nour- ishing provender, has to travel far and to distend the stomach with a watery substance before the cravings of hunger can be appeased and satiety impress the creature with a consciousness that existence has gathered a sufficient support. The quadruped while at grass is neces- sitated to be eating the major portion of both day and night; little leisure is left from the cravings of appetite for rest or for repose. No comfortable bed is placed beneath the jaded limbs. There may be an open shed under which all the inhabitants of the field are free to shelter themselves from the storms of autumn and from the colds of early morning. That building is, however, generally taken possession of by horned cattle, or by the victor of the steeds, and none but favorites are allowed to share the comfort of the tyrant.

It is assuredly true that the horse, in its primitive state, must have galloped over the plains free from human care and without a roof to harbor it. In a similar state man also must once have existed. The early Britons are described as walking about in painted costume, and as living on acorns and wild berries Which of her Britannic Majesty's present subjects would like for six weeks in every year to return to the habits of our ancestors? The horse is even more artificial than man himself. It proves nothing, therefore, that the creature has existed upon the plain; any more than the possibility of rearing human beings apart from civilization can establish that the latter mode is beneficial to the body's development. Man has lost the desire for a wild existence. Then, why is the horse expected to be benefited by a return to the so-called natural state, although securely fenced from that freedom and extent of choice which primitive nature would have afforded?

Horses, when huddled together, often commit fearful injuries upon their companions. The creatures are unused to the society into which they are forced, and awkwardness is apt to be rude Any want of manners in the heels of a horse is a serious business. But, to put upon one side so weighty an argument against the grass field, as foreign to the present subject,—all sorts of animals are there congregated. Some are turned out "to regain condition;" some to become "fresh upon the legs;" and some to live cheaply till their services are required. Others are allowed "a run," after some virulent disorder; and others merely to afford time for the eradication of obstinate disease The pony, the cart-horse, the thorough-bred, and the roadster,—all are crowded together. All sizes and conditions meet as at a common table. Is it very wonderful, or much out of the scope of ordinary probability, if one of the creatures so exposed, so fed, and so tended, should engender mange? A few years back, the children kept at Yorkshire schools were much exposed to a similar affection Those babes, however, had not been more accustomed to cleanliness than the horse, nor were they exposed to half the neglect which the animal at grass is obliged to endure. Is it then surprising that the lower creature should breed a disease like to that which afflicts the human being? Let mange appear in one, and the rest are prepared by exposure and unwholesome food to imbibe the disorder;

the contagion rapidly spreads; posts and rails are loosened or over-thrown by horses rubbing against them; or, should such things be want-ing, constant irritation instructs instinct, and the miserable animals scrub one against the other in the open space

Besides the grass field, foul lodging or filth and poor provender will breed mange in the horse, as the same causes operating upon the human subject will engender a like disorder. It is sad to think that with the horse, as years increase, ailments accumulate and strength departs; it is sad to think, that as the animal's life becomes more hard to sustain, its food is always the less nourishing and its labor the more exhausting; that as care is necessary, so is neglect encountered; that the wretched quadruped at length is sold to some costermonger, who, when he makes the purchase, nicely calculates how many days of labor the emaciated life is capable of before it is turned over to the knacker   Many a noble-man must have looked upon an animal in the last stage of a weary life which was formerly the companion of his pleasures.   The rusty, lean, and worn-out carcass most probably was not recognized, or how must reflection have whispered that power was not given to turn away exist-ence into wretchedness after willfulness had rendered the body less capable of sustaining suffering!

In the vast majority of cases this disease first appears in the mane, among the hairs of which a quantity of loose, dry scurf is perceptible Before such a sign, however, is to be recognized, excessive itchiness is exhibited.   The disease, once established, soon extends to the head, to the neck, to the withers, to the sides, to the loins, and to the quarters; only in very exceptional cases are the legs exposed to its attacks.   As the disorder proceeds, the hair falls off, leaving vacant places upon the body; these have a peculiar, dry, acrid, and irritable appearance; they suggest that portions of the body have been scorched with quick-lime, so irregular, patched, and scabby are the parts just referred to.   The integument in these places greatly thickens and is no longer soft and pliable as a lady's glove, but becomes corrugated or thrown into well-defined folds.

The hairs, however, are not all removed; a few and only a few re-main; these cling with exceeding tenacity to the surfaces which their fellows have quitted   The force required to pull out one of these remaining hairs is somewhat surprising, and the hair being extracted, the roots, upon close examination, will be discovered enlarged and far more vascular than is usual.

The above are the broad and more obvious indications of mange. However, should the diseased locality be more minutely inspected, a number of small pimples are discerned; these elevations are clustered upon different spots. As they mature, the point of each contains a very slight quantity of gelatinous fluid; the vesicles ultimately burst; the contents exude and become dry through the absorption of the atmosphere, forming incrustations upon the surface. Add to this, the irritation provokes the diseased animal to scrub itself against any irregular, projecting surface which may be at hand. Raw places, frequently of magnitude, are often occasioned by the friction so rudely applied; from this source another set of crusts spring up. The places which are denuded, therefore, may present a very varied aspect, but still the parched appearance of the scurfy and dry skin affords the best external evidence of the presence of mange.

An animal, which from being gray in youth has grown white with age,

A MANGY PIECE OF SKIN.

THE HEAD OF AN OLD, MANGY WHITE HORSE.

still retains to its death the signs of its youthful color upon its skin. The integument is dark, although the hair may have lost the last vestige of its original hue; the checkered appearance established by mange gives to the white horse a particularly ragged and dejected aspect.

Unfortunately, man is not, at the present moment, sufficiently enlightened to recognize the symptoms which indicate an approaching attack of mange; but the animal energetically announces the malady so soon as the contamination is established. The disorder being confirmed, its existence is

THE TEST FOR MANGE.

readily ascertained; the fingers have only to be inserted among the roots of the mane, and the part titillated with the nails. The horse thus treated will stretch forth the head and neck, will compose its features into an expression of excessive pleasure, and will continue motionless so long as the hand remains upon the crest.

This sign, being witnessed, may be esteemed conclusive. Let such an animal be placed in the sunshine for an hour, should the weather permit; otherwise allow it to stand in the warmest house which is unoccupied; then have the coat thoroughly dressed or whisked, until all the loose scurf and incrustations are removed, afterward have the following ointment well rubbed in. Mind the man who whisks the horse goes near no other animal for eight and forty hours See that every portion of the skin, from the tip of the nose to the point of the tail, is anointed; mark that no crevice or irregularity escapes, from the bottom of the coronet to the apex of the ears.

Liniment for Mange.

Animal glycerin	Four parts.
Creosote	Half a part.
Oil of turpentine	One part.
Oil of juniper	Half a part.
Mix all together, shake well, and use.	

It is impossible to state accurately how much will be required to dress the horse—the disease, the coat, and the size vary so materially in different animals About one pint and a half is, however, the general quantity employed for one application; every portion of the coat must be saturated, and in that condition the animal should be left till two clear days have expired. Thus, supposing the liniment to be used upon a Monday, it is left on until the following Thursday. Then have the surface washed with soft soap and warm water; dry the body and allow the animal to stand in a warm spot as before, so that every portion of moisture may evaporate. Afterward employ the whisk as has been previously directed; subsequently repeat the anointing That operation must be again gone through for the third and last time after two clear days have once more expired, when the disease ought to be cured; all the insects should have perished, and the skin have been benefited by the stimulation to which it has been subjected.

There are many preparations employed to cure mange All have some repute, though all (save that already given) are attended with some danger. The author, however, will recite two, at the same time warning the reader that neither of those which follow can be sincerely recommended.

Ointment for Mange.

Strong mercurial ointment	Three ounces
Soft soap	One pound and a half.
Mix.	

15

Wash for Mange.

Corrosive sublimate . . . . One drachm.
Spirits of wine . . . . One ounce.
Tobacco (made into an infusion) . . . . One ounce.
Hot water (which is to be poured into the tobacco) . . One quart.

Dissolve the corrosive sublimate in the spirits of wine. Soak the tobacco in the boiling water. When cold, mix.

The question has been much debated, "whether man can derive the itch from an animal?" Imaginary proofs favoring the possibility are every now and then confidently promulgated; but all doubts seem to have been put to rest by the investigations conducted by M. Bourguignon. That gentleman demonstrated the unfitness of one creature to support the parasite generated by another. Horses may be violently irritated by insects bred by fowls; but, remove the birds, the supply ceases, and the irritation dies away. So an individual handling mangy horses may get some of the acari upon him and cause vexatious itching; but let the man keep away from the contaminated stable, and the sensation is quickly lost. The repeated and repeated renewal of the pest gives a seeming warranty to the popular belief. Certain disorders assuredly are communicable throughout every species of life, as though to prove to the stubbornness of mankind that all nature is akin. Such are hydrophobia in the dog, and glanders in the horse; were all affections, however, equally interchangeable, the inhabitants of this world would speedily become one breathing mass of disease.

PRURIGO.

This affection may lead many a gentleman to imagine his horse has

THE PROOF OF PRURIGO.

caught the mange; the leading symptom in each disorder is the same. Excessive irritability of the skin is, in **prurigo**, generally exhibited during the spring of the year; the animal will rub itself with a fury which often removes portions of the coat, but which never exposes the dry and corrugated patches that characterize genuine mange. It is very annoying to behold the horse, when in the stable, scrubbing its neck upon the division to the stall; it is provoking to witness the animal leave its corn for the same employment. It excites the fancy of the master and conjures up the dread of every cleanly horse proprietor; the symptom is, however, easily eradicated. It only denotes heat of body; let a portion of the hay be abstracted and a couple of bundles of cut grass be allowed each day; let a mash be given night and morning, until the bowels freely respond, and, without further measures, the annoyance usually ceases.

The irritation may not, however, subside so quickly as shall be desired; to hasten its departure, either of the annexed may be applied externally:

Washes for Prurigo.

Animal glycerin . . . . One part.
Simple water or rose-water . . . .   Two parts.
   Mix.

Sulphuric acid . . . . One part.
Water . . . . Ten parts.
   Mix.

Creosote . . . . One part.
Oil . . . . Eight parts.
   Mix.

Either of these probably will answer, but the writer strongly recommends the first; at the same time it is well to try and reach the source of the disease, or to improve the blood. For this purpose the following drink should be given every night after the last meal:—

Drink for Prurigo.

Liquor arsenicalis . . . . One ounce.
Tincture of muriate of iron . . . . One ounce and a half.
Water . . . . One quart.
   Mix, and give half a pint for a dose.

A week after the irritation has subsided, all medicine may be withdrawn; but it is always well to see that a sufficiency of exercise be given, and to allow an extra feed of oats with a pot of porter every day. These last will restore the strength; for every form of disease is to be regarded as the most emphatic testimony of weakness.

RING-WORM.

This affection at first is simply a disfigurement; but, if neglected, it becomes a troublesome disorder. In the primary instance, the hair falls off in patches, leaving visible a scurfy skin; some say there are pimples under the scurf, but the author must confess he was unable to discern them in those cases which he examined. The scurfy particles, however, are somewhat large, and resemble, in no little degree, the scales which form the bulk of bran. At first, these pieces or flakes of cuticle cover the entire surface; but ultimately they congregate upon the circumference, which, by their numbers, is made to assume a raised appearance. Should the **ring-worm** not be attended to, the outward margin at last begins to ulcerate, becoming the more difficult to eradicate in proportion to the time of its continuance and the extent of the ulceration.

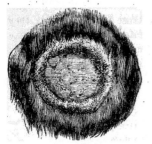

A REPRESENTATION OF A RING-WORM ON A HORSE.

For the cure of ring-worm, a rigid attention to cleanliness is imperative; the parts should, at all events, be washed night and morning with mild soap, and hot, soft water; to the places—these having been rendered perfectly dry—one of the following preparations must be applied and laid rather thickly upon the denuded spot:—

Ointments for Ring-worm.

Animal glycerin	One ounce.
Spermaceti	One ounce.
Iodide of lead	Two drachms.

Rub the glycerin and spermaceti together, and, when thoroughly incorporated, add the iodide of lead, or use any of the appended:—

Nitrate of lead	Two drachms.
Simple ointment	Two ounces.
Mix.	
Oil of tar	Half an ounce.
Simple cerate	One ounce.
Mix.	
Creosote	Two drachms.
Simple cerate	One ounce.
Mix.	
Oil of juniper	One drachm.
Simple cerate	One ounce.
Mix.	

Besides the above, which are not one-half of the remedies in general use, some parties are loud in the commendation of a saturated solution of a sulphate of iron. Others are strongly prejudiced in favor of pure liquor plumbi; another class protest they employ nothing but compound alum-water, which invariably and speedily affords relief. There are people who regard a strong infusion of tobacco as a charm for ring-worm; while another set will hear of nothing for that purpose but hellebore ointment.

The author, however, has always employed the first preparation, which, in his hand, has never occasioned disappointment. It has, however, always been aided by the following drink, administered every night No medicine could possibly act better than those here proposed; they seem to go directly to the skin; but as the state of the integument may be accepted as evidence with regard to the condition of the entire body, a most powerful alterative may not, in this instance, be out of place.

Drink for Ring-worm.

Liquor arsenicalis . . . . One ounce.
Tincture of the muriate of iron . . . . One ounce and a half.
Water . . . . One quart.
    Mix, and give every night half a pint for a dose.

This drink must be continued till every vestige of the disease has disappeared. However, it frequently happens that, after the central bare spot has been cured, ulceration remains about the circumference. Treat this with either of the following lotions :—

Permanganate of potash . . . . . . Half an ounce.
Water . . . . Three ounces.
    Mix, and smear gently over the part six times daily. Or—
Chloride of zinc . . . . Two scruples.
Water . . . . One pint.
    Mix.

The ulcers should be punctually moistened with the last preparation at the periods already stated, and the horse should be thrown up during the treatment. The food should be of the best, and a month ought to be allowed for the cure.

SURFEIT.

Old practitioners generally entertain very false opinions concerning the importance of **surfeit**; they being inclined to employ more stringent measures for its eradication than the real nature of the disease demands. The affection is rather annoying than dangerous; it makes its appearance suddenly, and seldom involves the entire body. It is a sudden rash or a quantity of heat spots bursting out upon the skin; the spots are round, blunt, and slightly elevated; they resemble the blotches which, during hot weather, often appear upon the human countenance, only the horse's integument being so much more active than the skin of man, the outward affection in the animal may be regarded as proportionably the more severe Frequently, during the eruption, the pulse is tranquil, the spirit and appetite being good; when such is the case, the lumps mostly disappear in a few hours Still the food should be looked to; about eight pounds of hay should be abstracted and two bundles of cut grass allowed per day; the corn should be kept up or even increased, and a handful of sound, old beans, which have been properly crushed, should be mingled with each feed. The stable should be airy, and the following drink should be given every day for a month:—

> Liquor arsenicalis . . . . One ounce.
> Tincture of the muriate of iron . . . . One ounce and a half.
> Water . . . . One quart.
>   Mix, and give once daily, one pint for a dose.

A HORSE AFFECTED WITH SURFEIT.

Should the horse be young, and have been neglected throughout the winter, a surfeit sometimes appears which is of a different character. The lumps do not disappear; but an exudation escapes from the center of each. The constitution is involved in this form of disease, and the malady, if unattended to, is apt to settle upon the lungs.

Should the attack assume the last appearance, on no account take the animal out, not even for exercise. Attend to the perfect cleanliness of the bed, and keep every door and window in the stable open during the day. Feed as directed for the previous form of surfeit, and allow two or three bran mashes whenever the bowels appear constipated; but do not give mashes after the constipation is removed. The desire is not to weaken the system by purgation, but simply to relieve the body; administer the drink recommended above only, giving one night and morning, but, should the appetite suffer, reduce the quantity, or withhold all medicine.

Clothe warmly; bandage the legs, and remove from the stall to a loose box; if the pulse suddenly sink, two pots of stout may be given at different times during the day. If the appetite is bad, good gruel instead of water must be constantly in the manger; cut carrots, if presented a few at a time, will generally be accepted. However, with all such care, a very speedy termination is not to be expected; nature is casting forth something imbibed during a winter of neglect, and no art can quicken the process. The shortest cases of this kind mostly last a fortnight, during which time the treatment, and the entire treatment, merely consists in good nursing and in liberally supporting the body.

HIDE-BOUND.

Strictly speaking, the condition signified by the above term is not so much a disease as the consequence of exposure, of poor provender, and of neglect. Thrust a horse which has been accustomed to wholesome food and a warm stable, thrust such an animal into a straw yard and leave it there through the long and severe winter of this climate. Let

ONE OF THE CAUSES OF HIDE-BOUND IN HORSES.

the creature which has been used to have its wants attended to and its desires watched—let it for months exist upon a stinted quantity of such hay as the farmer cannot sell—let it go for days without liquid, and at night be driven by the horns of bullocks to lie among the snow or to shiver in the rain—let an animal so nurtured be forced to brave such vicissitudes, and in the spring the belly will be down, and the harsh, unyielding skin will everywhere adhere close to the substance which it covers.

Straw yards are abominations into which no feeling man should thrust the horse he prizes; and no feeling man should long possess a horse without esteeming it. The docility is so complete, the obedience so entire, and the intelligence so acute, that it is hard to suppose a mortal possessing a creature thus endowed, without something more than a sheer regard for property growing up between the master and the servant.

Every amiable sentiment is appealed to by the absolute trustfulness of the quadruped. It appears to give itself, without reservation, to the man who becomes its proprietor. Though gregarious in its nature, yet, at the owner's will, it lives alone. It eats according to human pleasure, and it even grows to love the imprisonment under which it is doomed to exist. Cruelty cannot interfere with its content. Brutality may maim its body and wear out its life; but as its death approaches, it faces the knacker with the same trustfulness which induced it, when in its prime, to yield up every attribute of existence to gain the torture and abuse of an ungrateful world.

Liberal food, clean lodging, soft bed, healthy exercise, and good grooming compose the only medicine imperative for the cure of **hide-bound**. The relief, however, may be hastened by the daily administration of two of those tonics and alterative drinks which act so directly upon the skin :—

Drink for Hide-bound.

Liquor arsenicalis . . . . Half an ounce.
Tincture of muriate of iron . . . . One ounce.
Water . . . . One pint.
    Mix, and give as a dose.

LICE.

These parasites are the consequences natural to the states of filth and debility. Insects, which have been mistaken for **lice**, sometimes infest large stables and almost drive the horses frantic with the itching they provoke. Application after application, intended to destroy lice, is made use of. Every recognized source of contagion is exterminated. Internal as well as external medicine is resorted to, but every endeavor to remove the annoyance signally fails. The horses are fat and feed upon the best; yet they seem to breed the parasites peculiar to the opposite condition. At last some one points to the hen-roost which leans against the stable. That building is pulled down, and with it the nuisance disappears.

It may to the reader appear strange that the application which killed lice did not destroy the insects derived from fowls. Those parasites which were upon the horse doubtless perished; but the dressing being washed off, the pests came again and again, being supplied by the source of all the mischief.

Insects breathe through the skin. On that account, a hornet is more readily destroyed by dropping a little oil upon the exterior surface than by immersing the head in hydrocyanic acid. All, therefore, requisite for the removal of lice is smearing the entire body with any cheap oil or grease. But when the skin is washed, the business is not ended. Generally the horse troubled with lice is hide-bound, and may have various other affections derived from the debility which generated the parasites.

LARVA IN THE SKIN.

These annoyances are another result of turning an animal out to grass, the fly whence the trouble is derived never entering the stable. The insect rejoices in the freedom of the field; and man, by turning out his horse, finds the creature a fitting spot for the deposit of its eggs. This body is carefully deposited upon the back or sides. The warmth

a. The winter residence of the larva.
b. The summer abode of the insect.
c. A drop of tallow falling upon the center of the abscess.

of the animal hatches the **larva**; no sooner is it endowed with life, than, with the instinct of its kind, it burrows into the skin. The integument of the horse, however thick it may appear, is soon pierced by the active little maggot, which, thus snugly housed, retains its lodging until the following spring. During the winter, a small lump denotes its abiding place; but as the second summer progresses, a tolerably large abscess is instituted.

The interior of the abscess, of course, contains pus. Upon that

1. The spot through which the larva breathes.
2. The insect, full size.
3. The mouth of the parasite.
4. The pus surrounding the body, and upon which the creature lives.
5. The sac of the abscess.
6. The fat of the horse, or the adipose tissue much swollen and inflamed.
7. The skin.
8. The superficial muscle.
9. The muscle proper to the body of the animal.

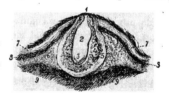

DIAGRAM OF THE LARVA ABSCESS, DIVIDED THROUGH ITS CENTER.

secretion the insect lives and thrives. The inhabitant of a warm abode, and surrounded by its food, the early period of life no doubt is, for an inactive being, highly agreeable. A division of one of these abscesses, when fully matured, is represented in the second cut, page 233.

Such swellings are acutely painful and prove the sources of much annoyance They mostly occur upon the back. The saddle cannot be laid on one of these tumors, and, as the spine supports much of the harness, the proprietor has the vexation of beholding his horse rendered perfectly useless; for suffering, should service be exacted, occasions the creature to excite displeasure; besides, the pranks thus provoked by torture often continue after the cause has been removed

Upon the summit of the abscess appears a black spot. It is at this spot the larva receives the air needed to support a dormant existence. This fact being known to certain people, the knowledge is employed to destroy the parasite. The swelling is first slightly greased, and then a drop of melted tallow is let fall upon the breathing place. By such means the insect is effectually suffocated, and assuredly dies.

Others employ a darning needle as the instrument of execution. The needle is thrust through the central spot into the swelling for three-eighths of an inch The larva thereby is pierced, and the life certainly is sacrificed.

Neither method occasions at the time the slightest pain to the horse, and therefore may by some persons be esteemed highly humane; but, in the end, such plans of cure prove the very reverse In either case the maggot dies; but the business, unfortunately, is only rendered worse by killing the source of evil The dead body putrefies. A foreign and corrupting substance beneath the skin may enlarge the abscess to many times its original dimensions. After all, the system has to cast forth the irritating matter, and for that purpose inflammation, with its attendant fever, must be perfected. Much suffering is thus occasioned, and the proprietor is, for several weeks, forced to forego the employment of a valuable servant.

The safest, the surest, and the quickest manner of eradicating these parasites is, with the point of a lancet, slightly to enlarge the central opening, and then with the finger and thumb, applied on either side of the swelling, to squeeze out the intruder The abscess rapidly disappears; and it only requires a few dabbings with the solution of chloride of zinc, one grain to the ounce, to close the wound However, the best manner to avoid such annoyances is not to endeavor at saving money by treating a domesticated animal as though it were an untamed quadruped.

WARTS.

A wart, when of a fixed cartilaginous nature, should, in the horse, be eradicated immediately upon its appearance; being permitted to exist, such growths always increase in number and in magnitude. By certain people, or rather by a tradition, these excrescences are imagined to breed, or it is thought that one can produce many. That warts are possessed of any such inherent property science refuses to acknowledge; but the same system which has generated one may generate several. The faculty of casting forth such growths may even be encouraged by allowing them to remain; and it is possible that the slight shock occasioned by their removal may alter the tendency of the body. Certain it is that, by some mysterious law, nature refuses to build up only for human agency to destroy. Youatt asserts that it was once fashionable to crop the ears of horses until animals were ultimately born with the ears ready shortened.

A portrait of an extraordinary instance of warty disposition, showing the imprudence of permitting such accumulations to continue, is here given. The writer's experience cannot at all equal the disfigurement there represented; the animal was the favorite saddle-horse of a lady who could not bear the idea of the creature being put to pain. One wart first appeared upon the inside of the thigh; the motion of the legs used to chafe the excrescence, and frequent discharges of blood were the consequence. The growth increased in size, and three times was it "charmed." However, the cure, said to be potent over the human being, was inoperative upon the horse; housewife's remedies were next resorted to, but all of these proved equally unsuccessful.

PORTRAIT OF THE HEAD OF A HORSE WITH WARTS.

At length, smaller warts began to show; it would have been easy to have removed the original excrescence, but the numerous after-growths assumed a form which would have rendered them difficult to destroy. Many of them came with wide bases and slight elevation; to have attempted the excision would have almost necessitated the flaying of a living body. The remedy, which at first was easy, was by time rendered impossible; the horse being permitted to exist, could only see imperfectly. It could not move or feed without hemorrhage being provoked. The animal, of course, became useless; but still its kind mistress could not consent to its destruction. A country farrier, previous to the author seeing the animal, had slit up one nostril to relieve the breathing, which before was much impeded.   Of course nothing could be done for such an object.

There are three different sorts of growth, all of which are recognized under the term "wart"   The first is of a cartilaginous nature and is contained in a distinct sac or shell, which last is entirely derived from the cuticle of the skin.   Upon the sac being divided, the substance drops out, leaving behind a perfectly clean cavity, which soon disappears. Little hemorrhage and less pain attend upon this trivial operation.   The second sort also is cartilaginous, but, unlike the first, is not contained within a cuticular sac.   It adheres firmly to the skin, and is apt to grow large; sometimes it becomes of enormous bulk, when regarded simply in its character of a wart.   The crown is rough and unsightly; the body is vascular, and the growth, from its magnitude and uneven texture, is apt to be injured, when it never heals, but invariably exhibits the ulcerative process in a tedious form   This species of wart is often to be found, though of a smaller development, upon the human hand.   The third variety is hardly to be esteemed a true wart, and would not here be named, were it not universally accepted as one of these abnormal growths   It consists of a cuticular case, inclosing a soft granular substance.

It is impossible always to distinguish the first and third from the second; therefore, in a case of this kind, it is advisable to cut into the excrescence as soon as it is large enough to be operated upon   When the warts are ascertained to be inclosed in a defined cuticular shell, the quickest and the more humane practice is to take a sharp-pointed knife and impale them, or run the blade through each in succession   The edge should be away from the skin, and the knife being withdrawn with an upward, cutting motion, the sac and substance are both sundered.   This accomplished, the interior is easily removed; and all that can subsequently be necessary is to occasionally touch the part with the solution of the chloride of zinc, one grain to the ounce of water.

When the growth proves of the fixed cartilaginous kind, no time should be lost in its removal.   The quickest plan—and not, perhaps, the most painful method—of doing this is by means of the knife.   The excrescence should be thoroughly excised, being sundered at the base Some bleeding will follow.   This may be readily commanded by having at hand a saucepan of water boiling on a small fire   Into the heated liquid a budding-iron should be placed, by which artifice sufficient heat is obtained to stimulate the open mouths of the vessels when the instrument is applied to the bleeding surface, without any danger being incurred of destroying the living flesh.

Should excision be objected to, the next best plan is the use of caustic. Strong acetic acid, only to be generally obtained as aromatic vinegar, is the mildest cautery; the next in strength is butter of antimony; after that, ranks nitrate of silver, or lunar caustic; and lastly, comes a preparation invented by Mr. Woodger, to whose perceptions the veterinary profession is so largely indebted. It consists of sulphuric acid, made into a paste with powdered sulphur, and applied by means of a flat piece of wood.

Whichever remedy is adopted, it must be remembered that the application will occupy time in exact proportion to the mildness of the means employed. It may also be proper to hint to the reader that, as an animal has no foreknowledge to alarm its anticipatory fears, and as, the anguish past, the mind of the creature does not linger upon painful recollections, probably the knife is to be very much preferred.

Some people remove warts by ligatures. To this custom the author strongly objects, for the following reasons: Because the process is slow; because the pain is great and continuous, till the removal is accomplished; because the ligature soon becomes filthy, the wart, when large, often turning putrid before it falls off; and because, when small, the breadth of base and the slight projection render fixing a ligature an utter impossibility.

TUMORS.

It is impossible to particularize the nature of every **tumor** to which the horse is subject, such formations being so very various. Seldom are two cases met with in which a precisely similar structure is developed. More seldom are two cases encountered located upon the same part. These growths are liable to every possible change. One may be very small, but extremely malignant, or of that kind which seems to resent the slightest interference. Employ the knife to this last sort, and incurable ulceration may start up. All remedies may be powerless and the life may be sacrificed. Such growths are, happily, rare in the equine species; but the author has heard of their occurrence, although it has not been his misfortune to encounter one. Another shall be of such enormous size as to impede the motions, yet will be perfectly bland in its nature. A portrait, not of the largest tumor which the writer has witnessed, but of the most awkwardly situated, is represented herewith.

AN ABNORMAL GROWTH UPON A HORSE'S CHEST.

It was not malignant. The horse which carried about this burden was brought to the veterinary college during the time when the author was attached to that establishment. The animal had previously been under the treatment of various veterinary surgeons. All had cut and cauterized the enlargement, but without reducing its magnitude. The wounds healed quickly, and the constitution appeared not to be in the slightest manner affected.

Why was not the swelling removed with the knife, when the kindly nature of the growth had been ascertained? For good and sufficient reasons. No operation could, with the slightest prospect of success, be hazarded. In the first place, nature is apt to resent the loss of so large a substance, or, in other words, although the surgery may be perfect, the life, from some unexplained cause, is likely to depart before the operation is finished. In the next place, most bland tumors, when of magnitude, are of a semi-cartilaginous nature, and spring either from tendon or from bone—usually from the latter. This tumor impeded the action; hence it was inferred that the substance ramified among the fibers of the pectoral muscles. Those fibers are large, and are divided; they present interspaces, between which the abnormal growth might readily penetrate. Now, unless every portion of the tumor were excised, the enlargement would sprout again, and the surgeon would be disgraced. To remove the pectoral muscle of a man, would be esteemed of little consequence, so that the life was preserved. But the limbs of the horse constitute the value of the creature's existence; and to disable these from being safely moved, would be to return a burdensome life to the proprietor. Therefore that which is compatible with human surgery could not be entertained in veterinary science

A tumor may be small and soft, yet it must be respected It may be hard, or even ulcerated and large, still its excision may be readily accomplished. The majority of these growths which appear upon the horse, however, are not malignant Nevertheless, let every man consult some duly qualified veterinarian of experience before he resorts to measures which, possibly, may lead to the acutest regret

One caution must be given before the subject is concluded. Gray horses, which have grown paler with age, or have become white, are liable to an incurable and malignant disease termed **melanosis**, which hereafter will be fully described. The presence of this disorder is generally testified by the appearance of some external tumor. Unless that enlargement be of great size and admirably situated for removal, it on no account should be interfered with Let, therefore, every light-gray or white horse having a tumor be submitted to some experienced judgment, and let the owner be guided by the opinion he receives.

SWOLLEN OR FILLED LEGS.

These are one of the most common troubles of the stable; the coach-man is very apt to complain piteously that in the morning he is sure to find such and such a horse with the legs filled. Commonly the hinder limbs below the hock are thus affected; sometimes the fore legs below the knee will be involved. The coachman mostly bandages the parts. In mild cases this resort may answer; but in bad instances the leg

THE HORSE'S LEG OF A NATURAL SIZE.   THE HORSE'S LEG WHEN FILLED.

above the bandage is apt to enlarge. The cloth or flannel, before ap-plied, should be wetted; this, however, affords but a temporary relief; the wet often causes the hair to curl, and the uniformity of the appear-ance is thereby spoiled. After some time, the bandage frequently leaves its impress upon the leg, and it is astonishing how long in peculiar cases this impress will continue.

Swollen legs mostly occur in heavy animals and in overgrown carriage horses; such creatures are of weakly or soft constitutions. They have a vast tendency to become partially dropsical. Fast work exhausts the system of the carriage horse, while high food stimulates its natural dis-position toward disease. With heavy horses, the prolonged hours of labor are equally debilitating, and the Sunday's stagnation generates disorder; neither have any innate hardiness to withstand injurious in-fluences; both, when highly fat, have the weakness inherent to their constitutions greatly increased. The quadruped, loaded with the accu-mulations of many months' repletion, may please the eye of the master; but it is rendered more subject to disease, and less capable of labor or of activity.

Persons who require fast work, should employ light vehicles and small horses; the creatures should be principally supported by grain— a little hay may be allowed during certain times, when the animal's attention requires to be engaged, but the chief sustenance ought to consist of oats and beans When the carriage is not wanted for the day, care should be taken to see the groom gives at least four hours' exercise

With regard to the heavy animals, the custom of blowing them out with chaff or hay is not to be commended. A good horse is surely deserving of good provender, and the best manger food is not generally deserving of any higher character than the word "good" may convey. A horse for work should be in sound flesh without being fat; when not required, it should not be allowed to remain in the stable all day. Who, however, ever saw a cart-horse being exercised? These animals have to stand in the stall of a heated stable throughout the Sabbath; the excuse is, that the creatures may enjoy a day's rest. But four hours' easy exercise given at different times, although it might occupy the time of the attendant, would assuredly greatly add to the comfort of the quadrupeds which he is paid to look after.

When a horse is troubled with swollen legs, take it from the stall and place it in a roomy, loose box; nothing more quickly removes this affection than easy and natural motion. At grass, dropsy generally attacks the abdomen; but the author has not heard of the legs being affected in the field, the limbs there being in constant action. Having placed the animal in a loose box, abstain from giving hay for some weeks; procure some ground oak-bark; having damped the corn, sprinkle a handful of the powder among each feed of oats Particularly attend to the exercise; and should the legs still enlarge, do not allow bandages to be employed, but set both groom and coachman hand-rubbing till the natural appearance is restored

SITFAST.

This, whenever it occurs, provokes great vexation. Generally it affects animals of the highest value or of fast capabilities, which are used only for saddle purposes. The affection consists of a patch of horn, resembling a corn upon the human foot. These patches are not absolutely large, though of course in size they vary. Neither are they all similar in form or in thickness. In one respect, however, a family likeness runs throughout the kind They are not simple corns, but their different nature is shown by a margin of ulceration. The situation which they invariably occupy is under the saddle-tree. Their presence, of course, obliges the horse to be disused; and they are the more annoying, since there is no chance of these comparatively trifling ailments disappearing without-treatment. The treatment, moreover, cannot be speedy. Whatever measures may be resorted to, time is necessary for the cure; and, during this space, the proprietor sees his horse in high health and spirits, but is forbidden to mount it because of a petty blemish which, in his eyes, is perfectly contemptible.

Sitfasts, though all said to be caused by the friction of the saddle, have several distinct excitants. The saddle is without life, and cannot of itself injure the quadruped. It is common to account for a sitfast by saying the saddle does not fit. Such may occasionally be the case; for a saddle, if badly made, will chafe the skin and produce a sitfast. But this cause is in operation less often than is imagined. A retired surgeon, whom the author had the honor of visiting at Reigate, wore a cork leg. That gentleman stated that, whenever the leg used to chafe the stump to which it was attached, he always considered his body

A SITFAST, AS IT APPEARS UPON A HORSE'S BACK.

was out of order. Medicine then was taken, and the symptom disappeared. We mortals refuse to think the horse ails anything unless the animal is alarmingly prostrated. All smaller ills are disregarded; yet that derangement of the stomach which caused the stump of a man's leg to become painful from pressure may, if not attended to, also cause the skin of a horse to exhibit a sitfast.

An awkward horseman is the more frequent source of the complaint. There are gentlemen so very energetic as riders that the best of saddles may be readily moved under them. The saddle must be well made indeed which can, under no circumstances, be stirred upon the back to that extent which is required to generate a sitfast. Loose girths will likewise establish the nuisance, and so also may the saddle-cloth whenever it is hastily put on so as to become thrown into a fold when the horse is mounted.

The speediest cure for a sitfast is the knife. The excrescence is quickly removed; and the wound, if treated with the solution of chloride of zinc, one grain to an ounce of water, soon heals. A more tedious plan of removal, and one not recommended by any proper feeling, is to rub into the sitfast, every night and morning, a small quantity of blistering ointment. Such is the usual direction; but the ointment may be applied, for some time, to a layer of compact horn, before the true skin or flesh beneath is affected. The unguent must therefore cover the perhaps ulcerated margin of the sitfast; and even then it is a tedious and a painful operation, not likely to improve the disposition of an animal which it is so desirable to keep free from every excitement.

While the sitfast is being operated upon, the bowels should be rendered pultaceous by bran mashes. Four of these per diem will usually loosen the most constipated body in two days. That effect being gained, while the food is liberal and the animal is led to plenty of exercise, give one of those drinks, night and morning, which are tonic to the system, but seem to exhaust their virtue upon the skin.

Drink for Sitfasts.

Liquor arsenicalis	Half an ounce.
Tincture of muriate of iron . .	Three-quarters of an ounce.
Water	One pint.

Mix, and give

GREASE.

This filthy disorder is a disgrace to every person concerned with the building in which it occurs; it proves neglect in the proprietor, want of fitness or positive idleness in the groom, and culpable ignorance or the absence of the slightest moral courage in all people entering the doors of the stable It is one of those disorders which it is easier to prevent than to cure. By an ordinary regard to cleanliness, and by an average attention to the necessities of the animal, this taint may be avoided; wherever it is witnessed, it not only argues the human being to whom the building belongs to be in the lowest stage of degradation, but it also testifies to the sufferings endured by the poor creatures which are compelled to drag out life in such custody.

The **grease** is, in the primary instance, inflammation of the sebaceous glands of the legs; but it soon extends beyond the limits of its origin, and involves the deeper-seated structures. A white leg is more subject to the disorder than one of another color, and the fore limbs are almost exempted from the ravages of grease The reason of that exemption is found in the greater proximity of the anterior extremities to the heart or to the center of the circulation. Consequently the vitality in the fore legs is more active, and the flow of blood much more energetic; hence the anterior extremities can resist that ailment which fixes with impunity upon the posterior limbs. Added to this, in the fore legs the vessels describe almost perpendicular lines, whereas in the hind members the arterial current is impeded by numerous angles; these conditions doubtless operate upon the health of parts, but, above everything else, ranks the fact that the front legs are not subject to the same external causes as are the members more backwardly located The stalls are drained from the manger to the gangway; consequently all the contamination of the space in which the horse is confined flows toward the hind feet; there are, moreover, other reasons, which the intelligence of the reader will not require should be particularized.

Grease is banished from every decent stable; it may, however, be occasionally encountered in situations very much secluded; there yet remain places whence so foul a disgrace is never absent The wretched animals which are employed in brick-yards, in dust-carts, and in drawing canal boats are hardly ever free from this loathsome disorder. These creatures labor incessantly, and are removed far from the wholesome check which brutality receives from public opinion; they are resigned to the mercies of men who, as a class, are certainly not the most refined, and are seldom inconvenienced by any excess of feeling. The places, not stables, into which the miserable quadrupeds are thrust can rarely be entered without the peculiar smell which announces the existence of grease almost overpowering the stranger The fact is unpleasant to human sense, but it is only right that the probable effect upon the creature, which is doomed for the duration of its weary life to inhale such an atmosphere, should be considered

Smell is perhaps the most acute sense with which the equine race are endowed; the horse can appreciate that in which the human being vainly endeavors to detect even the slightest odor. Not only is the scent far more acute than that of man, but the two beings have to be compared as regards their habits; the animal is most cleanly in its tastes Flesh it abhors, and all fatty substance it shrinks from; men eat such things with appetite. Then, the human subject can dwell, and even labor, in a tainted atmosphere with comparative impunity. A quadruped may be forced to toil in such a place, but those who oblige the creature to do this kind of work know the certain consequences of the act They buy cheap and old horses—animals which have suffered much, and have but a year or two longer to exist. Were younger or dearer quadrupeds purchased, in which an energetic constitution would render disease more malignant, and were such animals obliged to breathe such contamination, the loss in every way would be fearful.

There is, at present, a great fuss made about sanitary laws; but the attention of those to whom such subjects are confided seems to be engrossed by man and his excretions. No one yet appears to have imagined that the subject involves life in all its varieties; the horse cannot exist in the air which human lungs have exhausted; man cannot live in the atmosphere in which the horse has perished The two creatures are not, therefore, entirely distinct; but the open nostrils and huge lungs of one horse can consume the oxygen which would support many men Then, the dung of the horse, which is always exposed, gives off fumes only slightly less dangerous than those which emanate from the human body. Yet officers pry into alleys and into courts; they enter the habitations of the poor, and count the number of those who *sleep* in each,

room. The impacted people are pointed to as the source of certain diseases, and society shudders as the medical report is circulated. No one,
however, visits the stable; no one inquires whether horses *live* in the
space which affords sufficient atmosphere to support existence; no one
has yet traced disease in man as probably originating in the close and
contaminated fumes of nearly every London mews. Still, if the over-
crowded rooms of the poor merit an elaborate report as so very danger-.
ous to society, may not the stifling and reeking condition of the stables
deserve a passing comment in its relation to the same effect?   . :

Cutting the hair from, and thereby exposing the hinder heels to the
operation of cold and of wet is no unfrequent cause of grease Such
is a common practice with lazy horsekeepers when not stimulated by the
proprietor's eye. In winter, when the legs most require warmth and
protection, the heels are deprived of the covering which nature intended
should protect them; and parts where the blood flows most tardily are
laid bare to the effects of evaporation and of frost. When the animal
returns soiled from work, most grooms will sluice a pail of cold water
over the legs; the dirt is thereby washed off, but the legs are suddenly
chilled, and soon become more cold, because of the moisture which they
retain and of the evaporation which ensues; for very few stablemen,
finding the appearance pleasing to mortal perceptions, think about the
comfort of the creature which is principally concerned

Sudden chill striking a part, and followed by gradually-increasing
cold, will certainly induce congestion; the foundation of disease is thus
laid The better plan would be to instruct the groom that appearance
is secondary to the welfare of his charge. Order the man not to mind
about leaving his horses so very clean and tidy, never allow the hair, -
which grows long and luxuriant about the heels, to be cut off. Leave
strict orders that, when the animal returns with dirty legs, the stableman
is to take several wisps of straw and rub them until the surface is quite
dry. The absence of wet will greatly add to the comfort of the horse,
while the friction will increase the circulation and prove the very best
preventive to disease With the moisture, of course, much of the dirt
must be removed; any which is left behind will readily fall out on the
following morning, upon the hair being carefully hand-rubbed and
combed. However, mind and see this is done, for it entails some
trouble; and, if you are content with merely giving orders, the "old
buffer's megrims" are sure to be laughed at and disobeyed.

Turning out to grass, especially during the colder months, when the
wet is particularly abundant, and the bite peculiarly short, is another-
fruitful source of this affection If a well-bred, aged animal, which has
done its work, after a life spent under the protection of the stable and

in the enjoyment of its carefully-prepared diet, is, from mistaken motives, turned into the field, life may be prolonged, but it is at the expense of much suffering, with the almost certain visitation of grease in a virulent form.

The earliest symptom of approaching grease is enlargement of the legs, accompanied by considerable heat of the skin. If the animals be now observed, they will be seen to be uneasy in their stalls; the hinder feet are occasionally noisily stamped upon the pavement. Should the hair be examined, it will be discovered loaded with scurf about the roots, while one hind foot will be frequently seen employed to scratch the back of the opposite leg.

A HORSE SCRATCHING ONE LEG WITH THE OTHER FOOT—A SYMPTOM OF THE EARLIEST APPEARANCE OF GREASE.

Should these indications attract no attention, the hairs soon begin to stand on end or to project outward, as though each was actuated by a separate purpose, and each desired nothing so much as to avoid its fellows. At the same time, the part begins to exude a thick, unctuous moisture, from which the disease derives its name. This hangs upon all the hairs of the heel in heavy drops. It is an offensive secretion. It emits a remarkably pungent and a very peculiar odor, which, once inhaled, is never afterward to be forgotten.

Should no regard be now bestowed upon the sufferer, and should the horse be worked on despite the lameness which it now exhibits, the skin

FIRST STAGE OF CONFIRMED GREASE.
EXUDATION.

THE SECOND STAGE OF CONFIRMED GREASE.
CRACKS.

swells, while cracks, deep and wide, appear upon the inflamed integument. The lines of division ulcerate, sometimes very badly; a thin, discolored, and unhealthy pus mingles with the discharge; the odor grows still more abominable, while the wretched animal becomes yet more lame.

Should, even at this period, no proper remedy be applied to check the disease, the leg enlarges. Proud flesh, or fungoid granulations, sprout from the lines of ulceration. The granulations grow in bunches, and have a ragged surface. Often the masses are of great size, and shake, as though about to fall, with every movement of the foot. The points, from exposure, become dry and hard; their nature, from that of fungoid granulations, changes to a substance resembling horn, like which, they are without sensation. These bunches have been named "grapes," which they are vulgarly thought to resemble. The likeness, however, is very distant—the one being pleasant to look upon, the other forming a painful and disgusting spectacle.

THE THIRD STAGE OF CON-
FIRMED GREASE. HORNY
BUNCHES WHICH ARE COM-
MONLY CALLED GRAPES.

However insensitive the points of the bunches may become, the limb itself, throughout the disorder, possesses a morbid sensibility. The gentlest touch occasions exquisite torture, and the animal will tremble lest the agony should be repeated. Upon the slightest impression, the leg is instantly snatched up, nor is it trusted again upon the earth until fatigue necessitates rest or till the cause of suffering has departed. Horses have even suppressed their urine, lest the fluid, splashing upon the seat of disease, should provoke any access of the infliction. Few greasy animals ever have a bed under them, the straw of which might arrest the liquid in its flight. Indeed, such a luxury might save them from one source of torture, but assuredly would start up another. The ends of the straw, pricking or even touching the disorder, would cause such agony as must occasion the animal constantly to stand in terror.

One peculiarity, witnessed during grease, has not been indicated in the above illustrations. It has been purposely omitted, because, though invariably attendant upon the disorder, it in reality forms no part of the malady, being only a sympathetic effect. The cutis is continuous with the coronet and lamina, which secrete the outward horn of the hoof. Any disease fixing upon the one, of course cannot but affect the other. The irritation which involves the skin of the leg, therefore, necessarily stimulates the growth of the foot. The hoof of a greasy leg, from this cause, often becomes of enormous dimensions; but this peculiarity has not been noticed, because it was desired to keep the attention of the reader fixed wholly upon the more immediate symptoms of the loathsome affection.

The remedy for grease is simple enough. Indeed, did not a sense of duty oblige it to be resorted to, the smell would, in the majority of persons, induce it to be employed In the first place, clip off the hair—if any remains to be cut off. The natural protector of the heels now can conserve nothing. It can only heat the skin and retain the discharge. This being accomplished, if the leg merely be hot and scurfy, have it thoroughly cleansed with curd soap and warm water. Then a cloth, saturated with the lotion for the earliest stage of grease, should be laid upon the inflamed integument. This should be removed so soon as it becomes warm, and another, also dripping, should immediately supply its place. Thus a wet, cold cloth should constantly cover the part till the heat is destroyed, or at all events is greatly mitigated.

For this purpose, two men are required, one to remove and the other to apply. Four old cloths will be necessary. These, when removed, should be flung over a line, so that as large a space as possible may be exposed to the cooling action of the atmosphere There is nothing so disagreeable in performing this office as might at first appear. The active agent of the lotion is a powerful disinfectant and deodorizer. The first cloth removes almost all the fetor, and hanging the wrappers subsequently over the line effectually purifies the atmosphere. The part being reduced to a comparatively natural temperature, the after-treatment consists in renewing the cloths so often as the heat returns; and in otherwise moistening the limb with some of the subjoined lotion thrice daily :—

Lotion for the earliest stage of Grease.

Animal glycerin . . . . Half a pint.
Chloride of zinc . . . . Half an ounce.
Water . . . . Six quarts.
To be employed after the manner already directed.

When the cracks, with ulceration, appear, the previous lotion is too weak to be of much service; but the same treatment must be adopted: only one of the lotions subsequently given should then be used :—

Lotion for the ulcerative stage of Grease.

Permanganate of potash or phosphoric acid . . . . . One pint.
Water . . . . Six quarts.
Or—

Chloride of zinc . . . . One ounce.
Creosote . . . . Four ounces.
Strong solution of oak bark . . . . One gallon
Both to be used after the manner of the previous solution.

Should the spurious granulations have begun to sprout, lose no time in having the horse cast. Have near at hand a small pot, with a charcoal fire beneath it. Let the vessel be full of boiling water Within the fluid, previous to the casting, insert several irons; then throw the

animal. With a keen knife excise the external bunches of proud flesh.
As each lump is removed, much bleeding will ensue; therefore, before
using the knife again, take an iron and lay it flat upon the raw surface.
Should one not check the hemorrhage, return the first to the saucepan
and apply a second   It is necessary to operate with as small a loss of
blood as possible; for horses having grease are always old and debilitated.   In this manner proceed till all the external growths are cut
away.   Then let the animal rise.   Enough has been suffered for one
occasion; more agony the exhausted system of the animal might not
sustain.   Besides, with every attention concerning the irons, the bleeding, generally, will not permit more to be accomplished

One thing has been forgotten   When removing the fungoid excrescences, it is always well, for the comfort of the operator, to have the leg
previously saturated with chloride of zinc; also to have a man, with a
sponge and a quart of the solution, ready to bathe the limb as fresh surfaces are exposed   Subsequently wet the leg frequently with the lotion
last recommended.

In another three days the animal may, a second time, be cast.   The
operation being again confined to the crop of growths which on the
former occasion were exposed; all the previous directions should also
be strictly carried out   After three days have once more been suffered
to elapse, the horse, if necessary, should be thrown for the last time, and
the knife once more employed.   The after-treatment will depend much
upon circumstances.   If the ulceration predominates, employ the last
lotion   Should the granulations appear likely to grow, make use of the
first solution of chloride of zinc—only it should be double the strength
which was originally recommended.   When both ulceration and granulation appear equal, the first and last lotions may be alternated

Such are the chief remedies necessary for the cure of grease.   The
other measures are : the removal to a loose box thickly bedded with
refuse tan; the food should be liberal—old beans are now of every service, each feed of oats should be rendered damp, and a handful of
ground oak-bark ought to be thoroughly mixed with it.   For medicine,
those excellent tonic and alterative drinks may be thus prepared, and
given daily :—

Drink for Grease.

Liquor arsenicalis	One ounce.
Tincture of the muriate of iron	One ounce and a half.
Porter or stout	One quart.

Mix, and give one pint night and morning.

Chopped roots, speared wheat, hay tea, and a little cut grass, should
it be in season, are all proper in this disease.   At the same time, walk-

ing exercise is much to be commended. Motion quickens the circulation; but in grease, it seems, in a manner which is not understood, also to allay pain. A horse having grease will be led out of the stable limping lame; but after an hour's exercise it may return walking firmly and almost soundly. After cleanliness, good food and medicine, nothing is so beneficial to grease as moderate exercise.

MALLENDERS AND SALLENDERS.

These names are to be traced to no derivation, but in their arbitrary signification they denote a certain condition of the parts situated on the points of principal flexion in either limb. **Mallenders** appear upon the back of the knee; **sallenders** are located in front of the hock. Both, in the first place, are scurfy patches exhibiting a roughened state of hair and suggesting considerable irritability. Either, if neglected, will degenerate into a troublesome sore from which a foul discharge will issue.

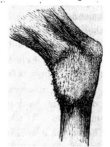

MALLENDERS, OR A SCURFY PATCH AT THE BACK OF THE KNEE.

SALLENDERS, OR A SCURFY PATCH IN FRONT OF THE HOCK.

With ordinary care they neither do much harm; but are rather regarded as proofs of idleness and as eyesores, than as actual diseases, to which importance they now seldom attain. For their relief it is essential to pay scrupulous attention to cleanliness; as, when the coat suffers from neglect, it is very probable the same cause may likewise influence the constitution. Therefore, always begin the treatment with the tonic alterative drinks described on the previous page; at the same time applying with friction a little of the annexed ointment thrice daily :—

Ointment for Mallenders and Sallenders.

Animal glycerin	One ounce.
Mercurial ointment	Two drachms.
Powdered camphor	Two drachms.
Spermaceti	One ounce.

Incorporate all thoroughly together, and apply as directed.

When the scurf, through neglect, degenerates into a sore, treat after the manner subsequently advised for cracked heels. But in every case of this kind always begin the treatment with a change of stable attendant; for where certain diseases appear, these are conclusive proof that duty is neglected. No remonstrance, no chiding, can amend the habits of the groom, who has, from drink or other indulgence, lost pride in the stable over which he should reign supreme.

CRACKED HEELS.

This is, save where very wrong-headed measures are pursued, the affection peculiar to the cold and wet months of the year. Even during the inclement weather of the summer, however, the horse may, if badly managed, exhibit this form of disease. Should the hair, which nature with kind intention placed upon the fetlock, be ruthlessly cut away, the animal is thereby rendered liable to **cracked heels.** The wet very rarely penetrates that designed defense. When it does, the ample covering of hair falling over the skin prevents evaporation, and the moisture rather promotes warmth than causes any excess of cold. The dirt of the road always lodges upon the surface of the hair, and if the horsekeeper exercise only ordinary care it can never soil the flesh.

THE HEEL OF A HORSE IN A
CRACKED CONDITION.

The liability induced by removal of the natural covering exemplifies the folly of those practices which have lately become so very fashionable as at the present time to be almost universal. But there has always appeared to exist in the human mind a restless desire to improve the beauty of the horse. Now the tail has been docked; then the ears have been cut. A short space prior to these amendments, the skin was tampered with to produce a star, as a white spot upon the forehead was termed. At the passing hour almost every man who owns a horse must have the body clipped or singed. The length of hair is given in this climate as a necessary provision. Nature never forms anything without its use; though man in his ignorance may not always be able to comprehend her intention. Were finer coats desired, it would probably be wiser to obtain them by warming the stable, increasing the clothing, and avoiding those long stagnations during which the animal has to remain motionless before street doors. A long coat is a defense against a cold winter; and unless man provides against the consequences of our climate, it is evidently flagrantly wrong to deprive a dumb creature of the protection which nature has bestowed.

Shortening the coat, if anywhere justifiable, is certainly most pardonable among hunters. Animals used for this purpose always have, or should have, plenty of attendance; these creatures also are mostly required during the autumn and early winter. Removing the coat certainly does stimulate the body. The horse assuredly is capable of greater exertion immediately after the deprivation. At the same time, however, a greater susceptibility to disease is engendered, and often the deprived animal falls a victim to man's fancy, notwithstanding all the care and attention which the hunting-stable can command. A burst and then a check, when a piercing wind blows from the northeast, invariably produces sad effects among the horses, especially at the commencement of the season. A gentleman who prizes the animal he rides should take it to "the meet" unclipped; and, perhaps, should the run be long, the quadruped may hold a better place at the death than horses adorned after the prevailing fashion.

The folly of the custom is shown in the animals attached to London vehicles. These horses are mostly wanted for spring service. The stimulant of the autumn is purchased at the cost of debility during the spring. The coat is shed the later because of the previous deprivation. When the summer hair is growing, the creature presents a very uneven and ragged appearance in consequence of the points of the new and the roots of the old coat being of opposite colors. The gentleman who, therefore, has his nag and carriage horses shorn of their natural coverings at the time when hunters are thrown up, beholds the objects of his pride deficient in animation and beggarly in aspect, while the animal that has been allowed to wear its native garments dashes past him in all the briskness of the season and the smartness of new apparel.

The question of clipping and of singeing is simply this. Do you require your servant's services all the year round, or do you want its utmost exertions for a comparatively short space immediately subsequent to the removal of the outer hair; and, at how great a hazard are you prepared to purchase your wish?

Were the legs of horses allowed to retain that adornment which nature gave, and were the parts not shorn of their shaggy beauty— were men not inclined to confound the different breeds of horses, and, because the thorough-bred has clean legs, to imagine the cart-horse can be artificially made to display members equally fine—were masters more resolute in resisting the selfish suggestions of lazy grooms, who love to have the bushy heels clipped—were the stable-keeper not afraid of doing his duty, but would go down upon his knees and rub the fetlocks dry, instead of drenching them with water, and then leaving them to chap in moisture and in cold,—were these things attended to, there is no reason why cracked heels should not speedily become a thing which has been, but no longer is.

However, if animals are exposed throughout the wintry season, under the pretense of being placed in a straw-yard, the proprietor must expect to take the creatures up with some defect The worst case of cracked heels the author ever looked upon, was produced after the last-mentioned method; the skin was much thickened and deeply marked by fissures. In places it had sloughed, and where the integument was absent fearfully deep ulceration was established Fortunately, the absorbing process had reached none of those important structures which are situated about the heel of the horse; and the animal, after lengthened treatment, was cured

For cracked heels, if bad, the animal must rest, at all events till the parts are improved. When slight, always wash them with tepid water and mild soap, upon the animal's return to the stable; dry them thoroughly with a soft leather; then damp them with the following .—

Wash for Cracked Heels.

Animal glycerin	Half a pint.
Chloride of zinc	Two drachms.
Strong solution of oak-bark	One pint.

Dissolve the zinc in water, then mix, and use thrice daily.

Should sloughing and ulceration have commenced, that condition claims the first attention as being the most dangerous

Forbear all exercise while such a state exists Throw up the animal. Allow it to rest in the stable. Give a few bran mashes or a little cut grass to open the bowels; but do not take the horse out even for exercise while such an unhealthy action is in existence. Ulceration is too dangerous and morbid a process not to be treated with every consideration; and it is far too irritable and painful a state not to necessitate perfect inaction for its relief Apply the following to the heels:—

Wash for Ulcerated Cracked Heels.

Animal glycerin or phosphoric acid	Two ounces.
Permanganate of potash or creosote .	Half an ounce.
Water	Three ounces.

Mix, and apply six times daily.

Upon the ulceration being arrested, the last prescription may be discarded, and the former recipe resorted to; with these, however, it is always well to attend to the constitution. A drink, each day, composed of liquor arsenicalis, half an ounce; tincture of the muriate of iron, one ounce; water, half a pint, should be given every night. This composition has been often recommended, but the author knows of none which is more beneficially tonic to the general system, and which, at the same time, acts so directly upon the skin.

Stablemen are fond of urging various excuses to hide their disinclination for exertion. Thus it is common for such people to assert that the horse's heels cracked while the animal was out on a cold, a wet, or a windy day: this is nonsense. Stablemen, of course, do not desire the creatures which they look after to be exposed to that soil which it is their duty to remove; but nature, that ordained the climate, formed the animal to endure it.

Were not the heels clipped, nothing short of extreme stable neglect could occasion those parts to crack. If the hair is removed, nothing but excessive good fortune will prevent this affection. The groom in the last case is not to blame, should the heels become sore. However, the best method of avoiding this affection, where the hair is cut short, experience has proved to be the following: Upon return to the stable, wash the feet scrupulously clean with cold water; then dry them thoroughly. Use several cloths to effect the latter purpose, and do not relinquish the object while the slightest moisture remains; nor cease to rub them until the parts are in a glow. Subsequently, smear over the heels a little glycerin; but even this will not in every instance prevent the affection. No care can render safe that which human folly has exposed.

CHAPTER XI.

BROKEN WIND.

Broken wind in the horse approaches very nearly to dry asthma in the human being. Man, however, can suit his work to his capabilities; but all horses have only one employment, which, to be sure, may differ

CONVULSIVE SPASM, INDUCED BY FATIGUE, IN A BROKEN-WINDED HORSE.

in its intensity; still, the most afflicted animal always has to perform the severest kind of draught. Let any person propose that individuals having dry asthma should pull loaded trucks, to earn their bread or to purchase a right to live; the cruelty of such a proposition would be apparent to the dullest sense. Yet is it the horse's doom that, no matter with what disease it may be afflicted, the animal must work or die. Old or sick, weak or disabled, still the body's toil must earn the creature's food and the master's profit. Spasm or agony can excuse no pause; let the sufferer even slacken the space sufficiently to mitigate in some degree the pangs it endures, and the long whip, aided by the harsh voice of the driver, will urge the flagging cripple onward. The horse has no words to plead with; the signs of its distress are not understood; the law

(254)

which assumes to protect it is a delusion; the animal is given up, help-less, friendless, and unpitied, to the almost unrestrained barbarity of its master. It is born doomed to live in solitude, to wear its life out under the goad, and to yield up existence in a knacker's yard.

"Broken wind" is a sad affliction; it is the more sad because no men but the very careless or the very poor will keep an animal thus diseased. The author has known it to be a frequent reason given by the better class of horse proprietors for having the life destroyed; which decision may have been quickened by the fact that the horse is generally old before this disease appears. In the knowledge of the writer there is no recorded instance of a colt having "broken wind" The malady is usually witnessed after the adult age has been attained, or during the latter period of life, whether the affection has been naturally induced or aggravated by the cruelty of man

It is said to have been produced suddenly; thus a man has been reported to have ridden an untrained horse after the hounds, and so have provoked the disorder. Another is asserted to have galloped a nag with a stomach loaded either with food or water, and thus to have broken the wind. Doubtless the seeds of the disorder may by either process have been sown; but that the disease was fully developed after either incident, is more than doubtful

The seat of this affliction is not confined to any one organ; its ravage is universal No part escapes; that the entire animal economy can change all at once, like a trick in a Christmas pantomime, is a circum-stance which has yet to be established The malady is most general among the agricultural districts; the farmer's poor team, in many parts of England, seldom tastes much of that which can be taken to market. Cut grass constitutes its chief summer food; the coat is rarely groomed; the stable often left open, and only cleaned when manure is wanted. During the winter months the animals have to luxuriate in the straw-yard; the body's abuse, in such horses, may readily lead to the body's degeneration Green-meat will not support the strength, though upon it the life may be sustained. The occupiers of the soil would find it to their account, could the class be brought to bestow a little more atten-tion upon their living property. The years of labor would be prolonged, and the activity of the laborer be quickened; fewer horses need then be kept, and the anxieties of the farmer would be lightened. Agricultural teams would not then be encountered slowly creeping along the high-way, and sleeping as they journeyed Care naturally begets pride, and worth generally resides where pride is exhibited. Increased value would reward the farmer, whose animals would not then so often present the spectacle of horses doing slow work, being touched in the wind.

Broken wind is evidently a disorder of slow and of long growth; any abuse may lay the foundation of such an affliction. Where abuse of life is possible, there folly is too often habitual; thus repetition may hasten the development of broken wind, but no one act could provoke so lamentable a consequence.

There is some dispute whether broken wind originates in the stomach or in the lungs The mass of evidence would favor the opinion that originally it was a disease of the digestive organs; but, as the disorder proceeds, all parts of the body appear to be involved.

The symptoms of broken wind are a short, dry cough, which is described as "*hacking*," and which may be readily imitated by any person making a coughing noise while he withholds from enlarging the mouth, moving the lips, or employing the tongue, but at the same time endeavoring to pronounce the word "hack."

The cough arises from irritability of the larynx, the mucous membrane of which is directly continuous with that proper to the lungs, and is joined to that of the stomach, any disease of which organ is frequently accompanied by cough.

The appetite is ravenously and unscrupulously morbid; the thirst is insatiable; the flatus is most abundant; the dung is but half digested; the abdomen is pendulous; the coat is ragged, and the general aspect is dejected.

The leading symptom, or that which is looked for as indicative of broken wind, is found in the breathing. Respiration is accomplished by a triple effort: inhalation is quick and single, expiration is slow and double The air is drawn upon the lungs as by a gasp This being quickly accomplished, the ribs commence to expel the vapor, and move laboriously to their utmost extent without being able to effect the purpose. The movement of the chest and the inhalation are counted as two efforts. Then ensues the third. The abdomen begins to rise, with an evident desire to aid in emptying the lungs by driving forward the diaphragm, and thereby diminishing the capacity of the thorax These two last efforts are comparatively laborious; but the double effort is only partially completed before a sense of suffocation forces the animal to gasp once more for breath.

There certainly are several circumstances which favor the opinion that broken wind is a disease of the digestive organs In the first place, the great majority of broken-winded horses are to be found in those stables where the animals are badly fed; moreover, it is no unusual thing for a gentleman to turn his nag out to grass, or into the straw-yard, and to take it up broken winded Then, again, low dealers, who frequent fairs and public houses, have a method of what they term "setting broken wind;" this consists in pouring into the stomach various substances which cause the indicative symptom of the disease to be for a time concealed. Grease, tar, shot, and many filths are used for this purpose—anything which seems to induce nausea appears capable of producing such an effect. These things may conceal, but they cannot destroy, the characteristic cough; a copious draught of cold water, by refreshing the stomach, will induce the restoration of all those signs natural to the disorder.

Formerly there was very generally accepted a supposed cure for broken wind. The flatus is one of the most marked and troublesome symptoms of the disease; that, when coaches had possession of the roads, rendered a broken-winded animal unsuited to run in such vehicles. To master the objection, and also, by relieving the intestines, to enable the broken-winded horse to live through the pace, a hole was bored into the rectum from without by means of a heated iron; into this hole a leaden tube was inserted, and by that the flatus found egress without the outside passenger being unpleasantly aware of its perpetual escape.

For broken wind, prevention is far more easy than cure; in fact, the utmost which science can at present accomplish is to relieve the distress. To effect this, water should be given only at stated times, and never immediately before work. Four half pails may be allowed each four and twenty hours; one the first thing in the morning, another the last thing at night, and the other two at convenient times during the day. Into every drink of water it is likewise well to mingle half an ounce of dilute phosphoric acid, or half a drachm of dilute sulphuric acid.

Besides this allow oats and beans, five feeds each day, with only five pounds of hay; two pounds in the morning, when being dressed, and the remainder in the rack at night. Crush the oats and beans; thoroughly damp all the food before it is presented to the horse, and also scald the corn.

Remove all bed by day, and muzzle when littered down for the night. Place a lump of rock-salt at one end of the manger, and at the other put a block of chalk.

Such is the little science can propose for the alleviation of an incapacitating disorder. All other recommendations rather concern the owner than the stable. A horse thus afflicted should never be pushed hard or called upon for any extraordinary exertion. Fatigue, when severe, is apt to provoke alarming spasm; a spectacle which the author once witnessed, of an animal which had journeyed far, pulling a heavy load, is represented at the head of this article. The horse had only paused while the carter took his beer, and had received nothing but hay upon the road. It had traveled all night, and it was still in the chains when the writer beheld it on the afternoon of the succeeding day.

After death, the body which has suffered from the disease declares the ravage of the malady. The lungs are larger than usual, and always pallid; small bladders containing gas are upon their surface, and when taken from their cavity the organs do not collapse as do the healthy lungs, nor can the air by compression be entirely driven forth. The hand being forced upon the surface elicits crepitation, or provokes a crackling sound, induced by the vapor passing out of one cell into another; for broken wind causes the terminations of the bronchial tubes to give way or to freely communicate one with another. Now, it is within these air-cells that the blood absorbs the oxygen from the inhaled atmosphere, and purifies itself by yielding up carbonic acid. How much must the destruction of their integrity, therefore, affect the entire body! Impure blood cannot nourish a healthy life; and the reader, after the above explanation, will easily account for the ragged and dejected aspect of the horse with broken wind.

The diaphragm is also disintegrated; the fibers of its tendinous portion are separated. The stomach is distended and thin; the bowels are enlarged and blown out with gas; the muscle of the anus is flaccid; the visible mucous membranes are of an unhealthy tint; the lining of the windpipe and the bronchial tubes is greatly thickened; the muscles are soft and deficient in color; and, where fat should have been, is only found a gelatinous fluid.

Having related the living and the morbid changes which characterize the malady, it remains now to inform the reader how so terrible a scourge

may be avoided. The horse is so valuable a helpmate that it merits, for its own sake, man's greatest care. Never, for any reason, therefore, drive the animal from the shelter of the stable to the exposure of the field; never turn the steed which has thriven upon prepared food to the starvation of a "run at grass," or rankness of the "straw-yard." Never, for cheapness, buy damaged provender; never load a famishing stomach; be generous in all provision for those creatures which devote their lives to your service.

HOW TO HEAR THE SOUND MADE WITHIN THE HORSE'S WINDPIPE.

Never, where such a thing is possible, permit the groom to ride or exercise the nag out of your sight. Be very attentive that the times of watering are rigidly observed. Never suffer an animal to quit the stable soon after it has drank or eaten. Be very attentive to all coughs; accustom yourself to the sound of the healthy horse's windpipe, that when the slightest change of noise indicates the smallest change of structure, you may be prepared to recognize and to meet the enemy before disease has had time to fix upon the membrane.

Having laid down the above rules, it may, to the ignorant, appear that every possible movement of the proprietor has been interfered with; that, in fact, the horse owner has been left no freedom of action. To the informed, however, it will seem that nothing more than every gentleman should observe has been proposed; and the horseman will smile when he learns that by such trivial matters can so heavy an affliction as broken wind be avoided.

MELANOSIS.

A quantity of black deposit, accumulated in large quantities upon certain parts of the frame, and contained within an increased amount of cellular tissue, constitutes this disease. At an early period swellings may be detected externally; they may be as small as a millet-seed, or as large round as a plate. These may remain dormant for years, or, if cut into before they start into activity, are almost white, and very glistening in parts, much resembling cartilage.

A MELANOTIC TUMOR DIVIDED, SHOWING THE INTERIOR IN THE MIDDLE STAGE OF DEVELOPMENT.

As time progresses, however, all the white disappears, and its place is filled by a material not unlike lamp-black when thoroughly incorporated with water. These growths increase both in number and in size. Should one be cut into after it is

THE SPLEEN OF A HORSE LOADED WITH MELANOTIC TUMORS. THE BLACK SPOT TOWARD THE RIGHT HAND REPRESENTS ONE OF THE GROWTHS DIVIDED.

fully matured, an inky fluid follows the knife. The disease is not confined simply to external tumors; the coverings to nerves, the coats of arteries, and the recesses of the closest bones, are each found to bear minute evidences of a melanotic tendency. The deposit, however, seems principally to attack the internal organs. The interior of the sheath is not unfrequently clogged to that degree which forbids the passage of the natural emission; while the preceding engraving of a loaded spleen by no means represents an extreme case.

A tumor should be admirably placed for operation, and its removal should be almost imperative, before the surgeon presumes to meddle with it. As a general rule, the best treatment for **melanosis** is to let it alone. Our present knowledge points to no medicine which can prevent or disperse such deposits, and the tumors appear to resent the slightest interference. The integrity of one swelling being violated seems to start off the disease with enraged intensity. If let alone, melanosis may exist for years, and cause little inconvenience to the body in which it resides. The horse is, by its daily service, exposed to various accidents. The large majority of the tribe perish before their youth has passed. The animal may, therefore, cease to live by other causes than disease, or die before disease has become formidable. But irritate the system by employment of the knife, and a lamentable malady may speedily render the knacker's office an act of charity.

Above all, let the master not permit any man to blister, seton, rowel, fire, stimulate, or slough out the tumor; such deeds are cruel folly. Bleeding is worse than useless. Purging weakens the body which disease is sapping. All medicines used in ignorance are probable hazards. Let such things, therefore, be discarded; but if something must be done, let the animal have daily an eight-ounce dose of any bland vegetable oil. Some linseed may likewise be mingled with the corn, or a decoction of the whole linseed may be presented as drink before the seeds themselves are given with the oats.

It is but natural to connect melanosis with the changed aspect of the

THE COLORED HORSES WHICH ALONE ARE EXPOSED TO MELANOSIS. TO THE LEFT IS THE OLD HORSE, WHICH HAS BEEN GRAY; TO THE RIGHT IS THE YOUNG ANIMAL, WHICH WILL WITH AGE BECOME WHITE.

skin. A young gray horse seems to be exempt; but as the dark hairs disappear from the coat, and the animal with age turns white, a black deposit accumulates upon various parts of the body. Creatures of other colors are not liable to so terrible a scourge; and seeing that the disease is in some manner connected with a change in the skin, probably some attention to the integumental covering might be of service.

All use of the curry-comb should be forbidden. The dressing should be long continued, only with the brush; but it cannot, at the same time, be too gentle. Twice a week the body should be anointed with the following :—

Animal glycerin . . . . One part.
Rose-water . . . . Two parts.
    Mix.

A brush should be moistened with the liquid, and the hair of the body should be rendered thoroughly damp, not wet, with the fluid. The after-dressing should consist in the long employment of the brush, so as to carry the glycerin from the hair and to lodge it upon the cuticle.

Glycerin has the peculiar property of destroying scurf; therefore, if glycerin be used, the curry-comb may be dispensed with. It likewise renders soft and moist the cuticle, which invariably becomes harsh and dry with age. Acting thus, it will, in the human subject, so far restore the color to the hair as to conceal the presence of the gray or white ones common to advancing years. The effect on one animal argues favorably for its action in another direction.

A dappled gray is perhaps the most beautiful covering in which boun-teous nature could invest a graceful body. Creatures so clothed are usually the favorites of their owners, as well as generally the pets of the stable. Therefore the author may assert there are more than a few horse proprietors who would not bestow a thought upon any expense which could secure to them the services of their much-prized steeds.

When melanosis threatens, a tumor no larger than an egg generally appears upon some part of the body. It may show on any locality. It has no fixed abode· It is hard to the touch, and apparently devoid of sensibility. In this state the disease may remain for one, or it may continue stationary for six, years. When the next and the more active stage commences, the tumor suddenly enlarges. It becomes soft in places, and will fluctuate under the pressure of the fingers. The horse, at the same time, grows slothful. The tumor, which previously seemed in no way to affect the animal, by its enlargement marks the departure of all spirit. This sluggishness rapidly increases till the poorest owner becomes dissatisfied with the perpetual use of the goad.

The body, when opened, generally displays a condition which, from the outward signs, was far from expected. The internal organs are covered with tumors. Numberless morbid growths, of various dimensions and in every stage of development, crowd upon every part. These readily account for that disinclination to move which characterized the latter days of existence.

There is one test for melanosis which does not invariably meet with a response, but which, when successful, seldom deceives. This is a pim-ple near to the root of the dock; it is very rarely of magnitude; there may only be one or there may be several, and the largest may not exceed the dimensions of half a pea. When, however, such an indication can be detected upon a gray horse which is turning white, the evidence is almost conclusive. The author does not know an instance, where it has suggested the presence of melanosis, that the post-mortem examination has contradicted the indication.

THE SIGN THAT TELLS OF THE EXISTENCE OF MELANOSIS.

With regard to the ultimate termination of this disorder, the author has no experience. Horses thus affected are always slaughtered when the second stage interferes with their utility; but, judging from the similarity of the disease in man and in the animal, it is conjectured the last stage in each would be alike.

WATER FARCY.

Water farcy, like so many equine disorders, is the offspring of weakness. Man, having a servant willing to work and incapable of complaining, too often proportions the toil only to the master's desire or the master's convenience. Many horses—which perform slow labor—are in harness eighteen hours out of the four and twenty; their rest is while the carter drinks, eats, and sleeps. No, not even can they enjoy such brief respite as is afforded by avarice to the laboring fellow-being; often is one of the drivers seen soundly sleeping on the top of the load which the stiff and jaded animals are compelled to draw. Thus the horse's toil is almost constant; wagoners are well aware that many horses sleep while in the shafts or in the chains. Overcome by fatigue, the animals doze, but continue to walk and to pull the burden onward. Who, knowing such a fact, can wonder that a living frame thus abused should often bow beneath its yoke, and, through death, set torture at defiance?

Water farcy is a warning which nature gives to human selfishness; it is, when rightly viewed, an intimation that, if the owner does not use the life intrusted to him more gently, the common parent will speedily take the sufferer to its rest. The complaint proceeds from debility; should the cause of exhaustion be continued, the affection soon changes its character. Water farcy is dropsy of one hind leg; very rarely does the malady involve two members. Such is the form of the admonition; but the labor undiminished, or the dropsy removed by means of coarse and drastic medicines, the local affection speedily becomes a constitutional disorder; and true farcy releases an ill-used slave from custody of the tyrant who has abused his power.

Horses that are liable to water farcy are mostly of the heavy breed, or are animals which perform slow work. It is usual, on a Saturday night, for the driver to throw much provender before such creatures, and then to lock the stable door, satisfied he has discharged his duty.

Often he does not visit them on the Sunday; the creatures pass "the best of all the seven" confined in a close atmosphere, and eating food which they have contaminated by breathing upon. The man observes the day of rest himself, and takes his ease; for the "brutes" he has heaped up rack and manger—so they have to eat; what more can dumb animals require? Upon opening the door on Monday morning, he may see one horse with a swollen leg. The drudge generally, not invariably, is lame, and holds the enlarged member in the air; the coat stares; the aspect is dull; and much of the abundance which was

THE CARTER'S FIRST APPEARANCE IN THE STABLE ON A MONDAY MORNING.

placed before the animal remains untouched. The poor creature was too tired and in too much pain to eat; but agony has created a consuming thirst, and it will drink the foulest water.

The horse doctor is sent for. In the opinions of veterinary surgeons there are two kinds of water farcy—one springs from debility, the other is accompanied with irritable symptoms. It, however, requires no vast knowledge of physiology to recognize debility and irritability as the children of one parent; indeed, most veterinarians admit the sameness in practice, however much they may dispute it in theory. They bleed, purge, and send in half a dozen diuretic balls, when, the swelling having been removed by such coarse measures, the horse, still further weakened, is once more put to its work.

Let every man who keeps cart-horses view a case of water farcy as a caution, proceeding direct from nature, that the management of his stable requires immediate change. The work is too heavy; pecuniary loss will soon follow, if the system be not amended; true is it, the writer has known men rated "good" in the world's report, and who were very "professing Christians" in their own esteem; he has known these men never to give more than ten pounds for a horse, and, at the time of purchase, the premeditated sin was to work out the life over which money had established authority. It is the most offensive feature of what is termed modern civilization that, rarely as individuals, never as a society, do mankind entertain the slightest sympathy for the animals by which they are surrounded. Most men are only eager for the services of the horse; they do not regard its ailments with the smallest feeling; they seek a veterinary surgeon merely to restore their animal to labor, and care only for a fellow-creature's sufferings as these disable it from toiling for their profit.

Water farcy is, however, an admonition which all men should understand; the horse, when thus attacked, announces that farcy hovers over the stable. Let the work of the team be made less prolonged and less exhausting; let the provender be improved. Green food is no sufficient sustenance for a working horse; it may fill the stomach, but it brings down the belly, and it impoverishes the blood. The team may not travel fast, but they are out for many hours; generally they cover more ground than horses of a quicker pace; they also pull weights before which none but a cart-house would be harnessed. On the appearance of water farcy, therefore, let the distances be shortened and the loads lightened.

Then, for remedial measures, let the diet be nourishing, the bed cleanly, the house drained and airy. As for exercise, let the horse, so soon as it can bear the motion, be gently led out morning, noon, and night, for one hour each time. Do not turn the creature from the stable to the field. Grass may be the cheapest food; but it never yet did a domesticated animal good "to blow itself out" upon such a diet.

As for medicine, when the limb can bear friction, let it be well and often hand-rubbed; the oftener and the longer the better. Every morning saturate it with pails of cold water; wipe it dry immediately, and then set to work hand-rubbing the leg. This is all that is absolutely necessary, save that if the lameness continues longer than the first day, a few punctures may be made through the skin. These should be equally distributed, each being about three-eighths of an inch deep, and one inch long, so as to divide the skin but not to wound the muscles beneath. Through these incisions the fluid, by which the limb is distended, will escape. As for physic, the following ball should be given every morning, if the proprietor can think a sick servant merits such trouble and expense:—

Iodide of iron . . . . One drachm.
Powdered cantharides . . . . Two grains.
Powdered arsenic . . . . One grain.
Cayenne pepper . . . . One scruple.
Sulphate of iron . . . . One drachm.
Treacle and linseed meal . . . . A sufficiency.
    Make into a ball, and give.

This should be made as it is wanted, for, by keeping, the ingredients become hard, and are apt, when given in that state, to cause injury to the animal.

By such slight and simple means, water farcy has generally been removed; but no delay should occur in having recourse to them, as some cases will set all endeavors at defiance, and delay is always dangerous where health is concerned. A few days of neglect will often permit the limb to become organized. It ceases to pit on pressure. Fibrin has been effused under the skin. The swollen leg is even harder than is the healthy member. Then the horse, should it escape true farcy, will carry about an enlarged member for the duration of its remaining life.

PURPURA HEMORRHAGICA.

This disease formerly was unknown, though at present it appears to be rather common. What is there can shut up the sight of man like ignorance? It is but fair to conclude that **purpura** was as frequent in past times as it now is; yet men, having professional zeal to quicken their recognitions, could not read what was before their eyes, because they had not been tutored to know and to understand it. It was so with our forefathers, and, we may not deny, it is so with the existing generation. Science begets an infatuation. Men, because they have learned much, imagine nature has no more lessons to enforce. At all events, they act as though such were their convictions; else why is it that genius every now and then startles pedantry, by widening the sphere of human perceptions?

A HORSE'S HEAD DEFORMED
BY PURPURA HEMORRHAGICA.

The cause of this terrible affliction is a mystery. The horse has worked, fed, and looked well, when locked up for the night. The next day the animal is discovered breathing with difficulty, and having several parts of the body greatly enlarged. The creature appears, by the disorder, to be rendered stupid rather than insensible. It stands erect, but seems not to be acutely conscious of its condition. Not only are several portions of the horse's frame swollen beyond all recognition, but through the skin there

issues streams of serum fearfully variegated by the admixture of blood.
The openings to the nostrils and the lips soon enlarge; then the tongue
likewise increases in size, a portion of it hanging out of the mouth.
The appetite is never entirely lost, though the affliction prevents deglutition. In this lamentable state the wretched horse may continue for
several days, or the disorder may reach its termination in a few hours.

As the horse begins to recover, extensive sloughs occur, generally in
those parts which have been much enlarged.

Recovery appears to restore the consciousness in some degree, and
the life is prolonged at the expense of much suffering The appetite
remains The power to eat is, nevertheless, slowly attained. The desire
for fluids, however, appears to exist throughout the attack, and should
be taken advantage of to nourish the patient, by presenting thin gruel in
the place of water

Purpura hemorrhagica is universal congestion If the body of an
animal which has succumbed to this disease be examined, the cellular
tissue will be found distended with serum and with blood of a dark
venous character. In this case, therefore, a blood-letting judiciously
managed may be beneficial. No pulse can be felt, nor is any needed to
guide the surgeon. So soon as the heaviness is ameliorated, the can is
to be withdrawn, and the orifice is to be pinned up. The smaller the
quantity taken the better, as the patient has no strength to spare.
Should the congestion return, a second venesection may be imperative
to relieve the vessels; such a resort, however, should be practiced only
upon the conviction of its absolute necessity

. Mr. Gowing, of Camden Town, in two cases reported in "Blain's
Veterinary Art," gave turpentine with success Turpentine is, however,
a potent diuretic to the horse, and therefore, the writer thinks, not the
best diffusible stimulant in these cases. Preference would, by him, be
given to sulphuric ether or to chloroform. Half an ounce of the last,
blended with a pint of linseed oil, should be given in the earliest stage.
Half an hour having elapsed, the dose may be repeated No amendment being witnessed, discard the chloroform and administer two ounces
of sulphuric ether in one pint of cold water. After a little space, as in
the previous instance, more diluted ether may be administered, though
it will seldom be required.

It is imperative to be speedy in adopting the measures intended to
relieve purpura; for the disease rapidly attains its termination For
that reason, if the breathing is distressed, as is pretty certain to be the
case, at once perform tracheotomy. Impure oxygenation of the blood
is one of the most active causes of congestion; indeed, that state
appears only possible during impeded respiration.

The tongue often becomes infiltrated, and, hanging out of the mouth, renders the appearance of the head most unsightly. It is, when thus enlarged, a fixture, and is in danger of being injured by the teeth. So soon, therefore, as the member is protruded, several free incisions should be made through its integument. The organ should then be manipulated, so as to cause the fluid to exude. These processes should again and again be had recourse to so often as they are required to return the tongue to the mouth.

The sloughing of the skin is a serious matter. It is treated by the solution of the chloride of zinc—one grain to the ounce of water—applied by being squeezed from a sponge on to the denuded part. This lotion will not only promote healing, but it will also destroy the fetor which results from decomposition.

After all, however, these cases are mostly very unsatisfactory. They would prove less so were tracheotomy more generally resorted to; but, in some instances, the horse seems to be rendered stupid by the disease. Instead of courting man's assistance and yielding up itself to his will, it appears to resent every effort made for its relief, as though all it desired was permission to die in peace. The beautiful resignation and the pleading solicitude for human sympathy appear to be lost. The brain evidently is affected; and when it is known the purpura hemorrhagica consists in universal congestion, no wonder will be expressed that an organ so sympathetic as the brain is affected during this disease.

THE HIND LEG OF A HORSE ENDURING PURPURA HEMORRHAGICA.

The condition of the animal suffering from this terrible disorder is indeed dreadful. If the brain be oppressed, the body is deformed out of all recognition. The beauty of the animal is lost, and the carcass becomes so misshapen as to be commonly compared to a hippopotamus. The legs share with the trunk the general disorder; and from these, as from other parts, blood and serum will exude.

STRANGLES.

Strangles, in its effects upon the body of the horse, is similar to measles in the human being. Both are diseases peculiar to the young; both sometimes occur after the attainment of maturity; and both are dangerous in proportion as their advent is delayed. Both, also, are attended with evil consequence if driven inward, or if any irregularity warps the even tenor of their course.

Here, however, the similarity ends. Strangles is developed as an abscess under the jaw; measles appears as a rash all over the body. Both, however, are eruptive, and both are cast outward at some expense to the system.

Strangles is peculiarly the property of the rich man's horse. It is spoken of as relieving the body of some matter prejudicial to the after-health. The author has known several poor men's horses which never exhibited strangles. Those animals certainly seemed none the worse for escaping the disorder. Nevertheless, it may relieve the body of the high-bred and tenderly-nurtured animal of something which might prove injurious if retained, although every quadruped does not appear to need such a cleansing. And the man must have some extraordinary faculty who would enter a certain stable, and point out the creatures which had suffered and which had escaped the strangles. Still, it may be, and probably is, an effort of nature to adapt the body to a sudden change of circumstances, though whether these circumstances are natural or induced remains to be proved.

Highly-bred horses are cared for from the moment of their birth. Up to a certain period—varying in different parts of the country and in different animals—the colt is allowed to roam the field. All at once, however, it is taken up, and its education commences. From the dew, and from the grass under its feet and within its mouth, the colt is suddenly removed to dry food, and is imprisoned inside a hot and fetid stable. Nature rebels against such treatment. The strangles is the consequence, after which the poor captive becomes better adapted to its unnatural situation.

Strangles is ushered in by slight general indisposition, which, however, does not pass away. Sickness rather hovers over the colt than

THE HEAD OF A HORSE WITH STRANGLES.

plumps directly upon it. The animal is then, in stable phraseology, "breeding strangles." After a few days, a stiffness of the neck is conspicuous; subsequently an enlargement can be perceived. It is, at first, very hard, hot, and tender. A discharge from the nose appears. The symptoms of general disease become aggravated. The throat is sore; the breathing is oppressed; the discharge is copious; the coat stares; the appetite is lost; the creature stands, with eyes half closed, the picture of mute distress.

At length the tumor softens. It becomes prominent at a particular spot. Upon this place the surgeon makes an incision. A pint or more of pus escapes, and the animal quickly recovers.

Such is the history of a case of strangles, as the disorder generally develops itself. Of course it will vary in degree, though in every instance a sufficient similarity will be apparent to guide the student.

With regard to treatment: never purge or bleed a colt when it exhibits a dubious sickness It may be "breeding strangles," and the strength then will be needed to cast off the disease. Give all the nourishment the animal can imbibe If food should be rejected, whitened water, or *boiling* water into which some flour has been stirred, or thin gruel, is useful for that purpose A little green-meat is generally relished. But, if the colt is not frightened at the approach of a stranger, the food should be offered, little at a time, by the hand—not forked into the rack or cast upon the ground, for the animal to breathe upon and then turn from with disgust Corn, crushed and scalded, may be allowed, if it can be eaten No grooming must annoy the feverish body; the clothing must be light; the bed should be ample, and scrupulously clean; the loose box ought to be large, perfectly well drained, with every door and window open during the day, and only partly closed at night

Some persons blister the abscess, and then apply a poultice over the blistered part: to this practice the author objects In the first place, sufficient friction cannot be employed to insure the effects of a blister. In the second place, a blister is said to be endowed with the properties of bringing forward or of dispersing a tumor. In strangles, one of these processes alone is desirable, the dispersion being much to be dreaded. In the third place, though oil and water are in their natures antagonistic, yet water will creep through a coating of oil, and warm water, especially, thickens the cuticle. This action may possibly prevent the vesicatory from reaching the cutis, should the emollient be applied immediately after the blister In the last place, the weight of the poultice is likely to stretch the cloth in which it is applied; when, being removed from the skin, the cold air of course finds its way between the poultice and the tumor. Cold is not desirable where we seek to promote suppuration; but cold is increased by damping a surface, and allowing it to be swept by a current of air. Evaporation then takes place, and the warmth is decreased by many degrees.

The writer prefers gently stimulating with the following mixture :—

Spirits of turpentine	Two parts
Laudanum	One part.
Spirits of camphor	One part.

This may be applied, by means of what cooks term a "paste brush," morning, noon, and night, until soreness is produced. It will, at first, seem cool, and be grateful to the part. After every application, have

A HORSE WITH STRANGLES WEARING AN EIGHT-
TAILED BANDAGE.

ready three pieces of flannel—no house-cloth, no open and thin stuff, which some economical housewives presume to think is good enough for the stable, but soft, thick, and warm, new flannel, such as any feeling person would bind around a sore and inflamed part. Put these over the embrocation, and bind all on with a flannel eight-tailed bandage. An eight-tailed bandage is simply a long piece of flannel having three slits at either end. Its use, and the manner of applying it, is shown in the above illustration.

When the tumor points, the surgeon takes with him two assistants into the box where the horse is confined. One proceeds to apply the twitch; this twitch is an instrument of torture—it is a strong stick, having a short loop of cord at one end. The sensitive upper lip of the horse is grasped by the assistant's left hand, which has previously been thrust through the loop of the twitch. The loop is next slid over the left hand, and with the right hand placed upon the lip, while the fellow-assistant, by twisting the stick round and round, tightens, and thus pinches into a ball this most sensitive lump of imprisoned flesh; for in the upper lip of the horse resides the sense of touch—anatomy shows us it is more largely supplied with nerves than any other part in the body.

The attendant, who had first put on the twitch, gives the stick to his companion, and lifts up one of the animal's legs. The horse, with its attention engrossed by the agony of its lip, is rendered disinclined to motion, and is comparatively powerless while standing on three legs. The surgeon then takes an abscess knife, not a lancet, which is a coarse and clumsy instrument—the lancet simply punctures, whereas in an abscess more is desirable. A free opening is always wished for; and where living flesh is to be operated upon, it is, for very many reasons, preferable to do all the cutting at once. The knife is held lightly in the hand, with the thumb resting on the back of the blade. The horse, when it feels the incision, is apt, spite of the twitch, to drag suddenly backward. Thus it pulls against the back of the knife, and no injury can occur; whereas, with a double-edged lancet, an ugly and a danger-ous wound has, by the motion of the animal, been inflicted. The thumb, in this situation, also serves another purpose. It allows only so much of the blade to enter the abscess as is above the nail of the member—this is usually about three-quarters of an inch. The thickness of the skin, increased by disease, requires so much; and if not, the pus, accumulated beneath the skin, will save the more important parts from being injured.

The leg being raised and the head guided upward by the elevation of the twitch, the operator approaches the horse. He looks well at the

OPENING THE ABSCESS OF STRANGLES.

part he has to open, and mentally determines where to make his incision. He also ascertains the extent of the tumor. This is necessary; for if the swelling be to one side, a single incision will be sufficient; but if this extend (as is usually the case) from right to left, two incisions are requisite. In either case the surgeon seizes the left rein with the left hand, and, placing his right hand in a proper position, by a short and simple motion of the wrist the knife is driven through the skin.

The horse, during every operation, is usually blinded. Darkness invariably increases terror, and is unnecessary, since the horse cannot see what is being done under its jaw; nevertheless, the creature is obviously amused by watching the people about it. From the behavior, we have no reason to imagine the animal draws any conclusions. To blind the horse is, therefore, to increase to fears of excessive timidity. It is easily accomplished. Double a handkerchief into close longitudinal folds; then tie either end to the sides of the bridle, so that the handkerchief may rest upon the eyes, and the object is attained.

Every case of strangles will not be settled so readily. Occasionally the soreness of the internal throat will cause much annoyance. The animal is continually gulping its saliva. When it attempts to drink, the fluid flows back through the nostrils. The animal will not eat, and the strangles or tumor may threaten to be absorbed. In such cases the food must be carefully prepared. No mashes, made by merely pouring hot water into a pailful of bran, stirring it round once or twice and splashing the mess into the manger, will now do. Even malt mashes will not answer the purpose. Good gruel must be carefully prepared and frequently changed. The drink must also be varied, so as to tempt the sick stomach,—as a general rule, equal parts of grits, (not oatmeal,) linseed meal, bean or pea flour, may constitute the ingredients. Let the drink be always just warm when placed before the animal. Sometimes clover-hay, or simple hay tea, may form the basis of the drink; sometimes one or other of the constituents may be withdrawn. Too much care cannot be taken of the horse at this period. Good nursing is now the most effectual, as well as the cheapest medicine; and all warranted expense at this time is a saving in the end. The breathing also is frequently most acutely distressed. In severe cases the symptoms are so alarming as to demand the immediate performance of tracheotomy. This the surgeon is forced to have recourse to, although at the time he knows it will only be temporarily required. When, though distressing, the disease is not of so fearful a character, relief may be sometimes obtained by mingling steam with the air which the animal inhales, and casting upon the source of vapor ten or fifteen drops of the etherial tincture of phosphorus. This last artifice may be renewed every quarter of an hour should it appear to afford even the slightest relief.

Avoid physic as much as possible. In strangles, purge and kill is the rule. Open the bowels, if it be imperative, by green-meat; if that should not answer, let them alone, however confined they may be. Let the fever rage, but do not potter with one drug and another "*to cool*" the body.

Some horses suffer terribly when they have strangles. The reasons

for such a difference have not hitherto been ascertained; but doubtless science will one day discover them. In bad cases the tumor appears under the throat, but it is larger than usual, and longer in maturating than is customary. Tears, frequently mingled with pus, flow from the eyes; a copious discharge runs from the nose; the pendulous lips are disfigured by long bands of thick saliva; the coat is dull, erect, and rusty; the heavy lids close the sight; often the nostrils become dropsical; the breathing is fearful; the tumor presses against the larynx, and a roaring sound is audible at each inspiration.

A BAD CASE OF STRANGLES.

For this case no more must be done than was directed for the milder form of the disease. The animal may be gently cleansed, but this office must be tenderly performed; for the filth will do far less harm to the horse than the provocation of irritability. Gruel, repeatedly changed, should always be within easy reach of the mouth; the pail should be hung upon a hook, so that the head may not be necessarily raised to reach the nourishment A little of the sediment, strained from the gruel, should be placed in the manger, as some quadrupeds will only eat; others will only drink; a third class will be content with such nourishment as they can suck up from the more solid form of slops, a fourth may all but starve, yet no coaxing will induce the sufferers to look at aught but the dry, hard food, which they dare not swallow.   Most, however, will feed on green-meat, and this should always be at hand.   Should the animal become worse, tracheotomy may be necessitated.   Then stout and treacle should be liberally horned down—half a pound of treacle being mingled with the quart of stout, and the whole mixed with a quart of good thick gruel.   However, give at one time only so much as can be taken without distress being occasioned.

Such cases, bad as they may appear, are not to be despaired of; nor are the tumors, on any account, to be opened before they have thoroughly maturated   Hasty incisions may throw the abscesses back upon the system   When that is the case, real danger is provoked; the horse seldom thrives afterward.

In some instances the tumor will burst internally.   It may find egress through the nostrils; but if it burst into the large guttural pouches of the animal, the pus may be there imprisoned until it becomes inspissated, and, by the motion of the jaws, kneaded into numerous distinct masses, resembling small sea-side pebbles   Such has been witnessed, but should hardly now occur; since Professor Varnell, of the Royal Veterinary College, has invented an instrument by means of which these cavities can be effectually injected, and even washed out.

Besides those varieties already mentioned, there is yet another form of strangles: that is, where no tumor appears beneath the jaws, but several form on other parts of the body.   The greatest number of abscesses the author has heard of, being developed on one body, is seven. They generally contained about a pint of pus; and, if the direction given for the treatment of strangles be observed, the animal will usually recover upon these being opened.

The great danger of strangles is in the disease fixing upon any internal organ; the horse is of no use afterward.   It sinks from bad to worse, till it resembles the illustration appended to " Chronic Indigestion."   The best thing which can happen in such a case is the death of the wretched creature.   To prevent so lamentable a termination to a

18

generally mild affection, nurse with every possible care, and begrudge no
expense which can add to the comfort of the patient.

GLANDERS.

This is the most loathsome disease to which the horse is subject. It
is provoked by stimulating food combined with exhausting labor. It
was formerly very common in posting stables; long stage teams were
seldom free from it. The London omnibuses, by night, are said to drive
glandered horses, and the proprietors of those vehicles are reported to
keep glandered stables.

In all of such cases the food is of the best and most stimulating
description—twenty pounds of oats and beans with five pounds of hay,
per day, are needed to keep a glandered horse in working condition.
Gentlemen formerly used to fee the post-boy to "push along." We well
remember the quivering forms of gasping flesh which were unharnessed
whenever the old coach changed horses.

Omnibuses are very heavy, the constant stoppages make the draught
still more severe The animals which appear in front of these vehicles
are small in size, rarely sixteen hands high, but the best and strongest
their proprietors can afford. A little breed is desirable, as a coarse
horse would lack the courage to take the collar and to persevere. The
age of these horses is generally three years when first bought in. Some
animals have worked through many seasons, but such instances are ex-
ceptions. Numbers annually yield to the drag upon the constitution.
These are sold for what they will fetch But several, either from weakness
or some other cause which our science yet lacks perception to discover,
annually become glandered

Youth and high feeding, conjoined with excessive labor and damp
lodging, will certainly produce **glanders**. Age, starvation, and ceaseless
toil generally induce farcy. The glanders and the farcy, however, are
one and the same disease, modified by the cause which originates them.
Glanders is the more vigorous form of the disorder, farcy is the slow
type, fastening upon general debility.

These disorders have been the scourges of horse-flesh. They still are
the inheritance which man's willing slave gains by service to a harsh and
cruel master Men, to their fellow-men, sometimes confess, without any
sense of shame, that they buy cheap horses to work them up It is, in
some cases, esteemed more economical to exhaust the life than to purchase and to maintain that number of animals which would be equal to
the labor. This horrible system is in daily operation in a country
professing Christianity !

Glanders is provoked by human depravity. Had people common feeling for the life over which they are given authority—would they only admit, in its largeness and its truth, that "the laborer is worthy of his hire"—the disease might, in one year, become a tradition.

At present the affection exists as the dread of every horse proprietor It is highly contagious—all owners of horses know this The stable may be scrupulously clean, yet the poison may have been lodged there by the last inhabitant. It is not only contagious to horses, but it is equally dangerous to men. Three sad instances of this fact have come to the author's knowledge. Two respectable gentlemen, moving in good society, were each contaminated, and both pitiably perished of this terrible disease. They were no stable-helpers, moving and living among suspicious beasts, but individuals whose avocations did not oblige them to mix with horses—gentlemen of professional standing, who were inoculated they knew not how. Mr. Gowing, of Camden Town, informed the writer, of a boy who once went from a shop to stand at the head of a pony the master of which wished to make a purchase. The animal, while the boy was so placed, cleared its nostrils, and a portion of the ejected matter flew into the lad's eye. The handkerchief removed the soil, and the accident was soon forgotten. However, the poor youth was glandered, and became a patient in the University Hospital.

Such facts sufficiently prove all men have an interest in opposing any conduct likely to generate so horrible a scourge. Man, as a community, is answerable for the comfort of every creature intrusted to his charge He may refuse to accept the conditions of the trust, but he cannot escape the responsibility. In proof of the truth of this conclusion, glanders is now recognized as one of those incurable diseases, generated by neglect, to which the human being is liable, in every hospital throughout the kingdom.

Why is the legislature behind the medical profession in the extent of its recognitions? Any man may now, according to law, drive or ride a glandered animal through the crowded streets of any town in the three kingdoms He may, without fear of punishment, endanger the lives of the unsuspecting wayfarers, whom it is the especial province of the Parliament to protect Why should not the glandered stable be detected, and the animals, dangerously diseased, be slaughtered? Why should any man be allowed to retain, and openly use as property, that which is perilous to society; and wherefore should law protect him, when harboring pestilence for the sake of profit?

That the foregoing observations are correctly based, is proved by the pest becoming less common as the public have morally improved—only, why leave so immediate an evil to be cured by so slow a process? Years ago, an affected horse, led through the streets, was an almost hourly occurrence. Since that time we have improved, and such sights are no longer common. Therefore the morality here alluded to is not of limited meaning. It implies improvements in drainage, and all those innovations by which life has been made more secure. He is the truest benefactor of mankind who lessens the ills to which existence is exposed.

Glanders is the phthisis of the horse. Phthisis is, in some countries, esteemed even more dangerously contagious than glanders and farcy are in England admitted to be. Man, however, employs a handkerchief; the plates off which he feeds are washed. The manger is never cleansed; and the discharge soils the boards on which the corn reposes.

The lungs of very many horses, however, which have perished of the pest, will exhibit numerous tubercles; these, in the human subject, are considered conclusive evidence as to the existence of phthisis.

THE LUNGS OF A HORSE WHICH HAD PERISHED FROM GLANDERS.
(A portion of the left lung has been excised, to show the ravage of the disease.)

By some practitioners glanders is esteemed a purely local disorder. In books, schools, and elsewhere, the running from the nose has been pointed out as the disease itself; and the situation of the affection is said to be the frontal sinuses—hence the dependence placed in various caustic injections forced up the nostrils.

A very little reflection will, however, enable the reader to take a more extended view of the malady. When glanders exists, a staring coat generally declares the skin affected; and the customary termination of the disorder—farcy and dropsy—proves more than the surface of the body to be implicated. The lungs—or, at all events, the air-passages— never escape. Loss of flesh and swelling of the glands demonstrate the absorbent system to be involved. Absence of spirit and inability to work, toward the close of the affection, are evidence the nervous system does not escape. The secretions are derived from the blood; and the blood, it has been shown, by a silly experiment, is capable of generating the malady. Their pallid aspect, after death, convinces us the muscles were far from healthy. Of all parts, perhaps, the abdominal contents are least diseased, though the marked decay of appetite does not favor such an opinion. What disease, then, can be considered a constitutional disorder, if one which involves so many and such various structures is to be regarded as a strictly local affection?.

A horse, full of corn, and in the prime of health, if unfortunately inoculated with the virus of glanders, generally has the disease in its acutest form: the animal may be dead by the expiration of a week. Other quadrupeds, in which the disorder is provoked by natural causes, may, on the contrary, exhibit glanders in the most chronic shape. If the exciting cause has a strong constitution to act upon—especially if the horse, soon after imbibing the poison, be removed to easier work or a more dry abode—the malady may exist for years in a subtle, undeveloped form. A thin discharge only may run, irregularly, from one nostril. At times no fluid may appear, nor is the

THE HEAD OF A HORSE WHICH HAD BEEN SLAUGHTERED FOR GLANDERS.
1. The lymphatic gland enlarged, hard, and adherent firmly to the interior of the jaw-bone.

liquid ever copious. One of the kernels, or lymphatic glands, situated between the branches of the channel, may be more or less fixed. But, otherwise, the horse is active, full of fire, and exhibits nothing to excite suspicion. During all this time the creature may be endowed with a fatal power of communicating the disease. Horses, having received the taint from such a source, may die within the week, while the cause of the mortality eats well, works well, delights the master's eye by its thriving appearance, and in such a condition even may exist for years.

In the early stage it is difficult to pronounce positively upon a case of glanders. Ulceration of the nasal membrane would be confirmation of the worst doubt; but the ulceration may be situated so high up as to defy all our efforts to distinguish it. Yet running from the nose may be perceptible, and the gland may be fixed to the jaw. Both of these symptoms, although lawfully provoking our fears, are frequently attendant upon aggravated or upon prolonged colds. The only lawful test, in such cases, is the administration of three doses of solution of aloes, eight ounces to the dose—allowing three days to elapse between each. If the horse be glandered, before the last purgative has set the real nature of the malady will be apparent in the aggravation of the symptoms. If glanders be not present, a little careful nursing will generally remove all effect of the medicine.

The glanders is mostly ushered in by febrile disturbance. The appetite is bad, the coat stares, and the pulse is quickened. A mash or two, however, apparently sets all right, and the matter is forgotten. Soon afterward a slight discharge may issue from one nostril; but it is so very slight, it excites no alarm. One of the lymphatic glands, on the same side as the moist nostril, alters in character. It may remain loose and become morbidly sensitive. Usually, however, it grows adherent to the jaw, turns hard, insensitive, and, from being wholly imperceptible in the healthy animal, enlarges to about the size of half a chestnut.

THE PRIMARY DISCHARGE OF GLANDERS. SIMPLY A SLIGHT WATERY DEFLUXION.

THE SECONDARY DISCHARGE. A THICK AND COPIOUS BUT STILL TRANSPARENT EXCRETION, CONTAINING PIECES AND THREADS OF MUCUS.

At a later period the discharge, retaining its clear appearance, becomes more consistent, and, to a slight degree, the hairs and parts over which it flows are incrusted. It subsequently adheres to the margin of the nostril, and then, in the transparent, albuminous fluid may be seen opaque threads of white mucus. This marks the second stage.

The next change takes place more rapidly. The transparent fluid entirely disappears, and in its place is seen a full stream of unwholesome pus. At this time there is some danger of glanders being mistaken for nasal gleet. A little attention will, however, rescue any person from so imminent a peril. The smell of glanders is peculiar. It is less pungent but more unwholesome, suggesting a more deep-seated source, than characterizes the disease with which it has been confounded. The ejection of glanders, moreover, is obviously impure; whereas that of nasal gleet generally flows forth in a fetid stream of thick and creamy matter.

THE THIRD, OR SUP-PURATIVE STAGE OF GLANDERS.

When the third stage is witnessed, the disease is rapidly hurrying to its termination. The membrane of the nose changes to a dull, leaden color. The margins of the nostrils become dropsical, and every breath is drawn with difficulty. The defluxion exhibits discoloration. Scabs, masses of bone or pieces of membrane, mingled with patches of blood, next make their appearance; and the internal parts are evidently being broken up by the violence of the disorder.

THE FOURTH, OR LAST STAGE OF GLANDERS.

The above description of filthy facts is, probably, sufficiently explicit; but to render the foregoing more clear, the following diagram is appended. The reader will perceive there are two kinds of tubercles—

the large and the small. One is no bigger than a grain of sand; the other is as large as half a pea. The disease which follows both is the same,—is equally contagious and is equally fatal. It will also be remarked, the membrane appears swollen and partially discolored in the case of glanders. It loses its bright, fleshy, or healthy hue; and it assumes a dull, heavy, and dropsical aspect. It will likewise be observed that comparatively few blood-vessels are ramifying upon the affected membrane, which sign, in a well-marked case, is often so obvious as to become a leading indication of the disorder.

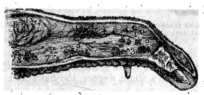

THE SEPTUM NASI OF AN OLD HORSE, SHOWING THE DIFFERENT KINDS AND STAGES OF GLANDERS.

1. A large tubercle.
2. The same in the ulcerative stage, pale in the center and dark at the edges.
3. The same ulcers after they have united, sloughed in one another, or become confluent.
4. The roughness which announces granular tubercles to be beneath the skin.
5. The slightly elevated condition of the membrane when granular tubercles appear.
6. Granular tubercles in the vesicular stage.
7. Granular tubercles in the ulcerative stage.
8. Granular tubercles after they have ulcerated and assumed the confluent form.

It is usual for low dealers, when a tubercle in the vesicular stage is detected, to assert that it is only a piece of mucus. To test such assertion, wrap a portion of tow, or anything soft, round a small stick, and wipe the place. If it be mucus, it will be removed; but if it remains, the reader may rest assured as to its nature. When an ulcer is seen, the dishonest salesman will laugh, and ask if that is all the inspector

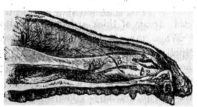

THE TURBINATED BONES OF A YOUNG HORSE WHICH WAS FREE FROM GLANDERS, SHOWING THOSE APPEARANCES A GLANDERED NOSTRIL IS OFTEN ASSERTED TO EXHIBIT.

1. A punctured wound, the skin removed, but darkest toward the center.
2. A lacerated wound, with a flap of pendant membrane.
3. A scratch—long and rough—having the edges slightly raised.

can discover—declaring the horse recently hurt itself against a nail. The interior of the nostril is a very sheltered part, and, therefore, very unlikely to be wounded. Yet so that the reader may be prepared to recognize such reality, in spite of the hard swearing and loud jocularity which is designed to confuse him, a diagram of a portion of the nostrils, covered with healthy membrane and showing the veins natural to the part, also displaying the shapes and appearances of wounds—when they occur—is inserted.

The reader has been told what constitutes glanders. He has been instructed how to recognize its more marked indications. There, however, remains to teach him the manner in which a suspected horse should be handled or examined.

The animal's head should be turned toward the strongest light obtainable; if toward the blaze of the noonday sun, so much the better. The examiner should then place himself by the side of the creature's head, not in front, but in a situation where, though the animal should snort, he is in no danger of the ejected matter falling upon him. With one hand the upper and outer rim of the nostril should be raised; when, grasping this part between the finger and thumb, no fear need be entertained. The case would be something more than suspicious, were any risk of contamination incurred.

The wing of the nostril being raised, the examiner must note the appearances exposed; this he will best do by knowing where to look

THE PROOF OF GLANDERS.

1. Termination of the lachrymal duct—a natural development.
2. A discolored membrane, disfigured by ulcerative patches.

and what to expect. His eye has nothing to do with the skin nor with the marks that appear upon it. The opening of the lachrymal duct often challenges observation by being well defined and particularly conspicuous; but that natural development does not concern him; to that no attention must be given. The inspection must be concentrated upon the membrane more internally situated than the skin seen at the commencement of the nostrils. The skin, moreover, suddenly ceases, and is obviously defined by a well-marked margin; there is, therefore, no difficulty in distinguishing the membrane by its fleshy and moistened aspect, as well as by its situation. If, on this membrane, any irregular or ragged patches are conspicuous, if these patches are darker toward their edges than in their centers, and if they, nevertheless, seem shallow, pallid, moist, and sore, the animal may be rejected as glandered. Should any part of the membrane—after being wiped as before directed—seem rough or have evidently beneath its surface certain round or oval-shaped bodies, the horse assuredly is glandered. The membrane may present a worm-eaten appearance, or be simply of a discolored and heavy hue. In the first case, the animal ought to be condemned; in the second, it is open to more than suspicion.

No animal should be permitted to slowly perish of glanders. The disease, as it proceeds, affects the fauces, phaiynx, and larynx; all become ulcerated. Not a particle of food can be swallowed; not a drop of saliva can be deglutated; not a breath of air can be inspired, without the severest torture being experienced. As the disease proceeds, the obstruction offered to the breathing grows more and more painful. Farcy breaks forth, and, as a consequence, superficial dropsy is added to the other torments. The edges of the nostrils enlarge; the membrane lining the cavities bags out, while the fauces and larynx contract: the discharge becomes more copious and the breathing is impeded Thus the difficulty of respiration is increased, just as the condition of the lungs renders the necessity of pure air the more imperative. Ultimately, however, laborious breathing induces congestion of the brain, and the wretched sufferer falls insensible—it is hoped—to die of actual suffocation.

Such is a brief description of glanders, to cure which every now and then pretenders arise. No medicine, however, can restore the parts which disease has disorganized. There is no cure for glanders, which is essentially an ulcerative disorder. Every horse being thus contaminated should be at once destroyed: it is now lawful to do this when animals are taken in Smithfield market; but what is just in one place is surely not unjust in another. Moral rectitude resides on no particular spot. The blackguards who deal in contagion, driven from the public market, now reap a rich harvest by private sales. A chronically-glandered horse is an actual property to these rogues. It is sold No sooner is the money paid and the vendor out of the way, than an accomplice appears and points out the nature of the bargain. The unfortunate purchaser seeks advice, and finds his worst fears confirmed. The accomplice offers to buy the horse at a knacker's price. It is obtained; and again it is advertised as "a favorite horse, the property of a gentleman deceased."

Any person ought by law to be empowered to give any man, driving or riding a glandered horse, into custody. There should be appointed certain qualified practitioners who should have authority to enter any stable at any time Those abominations, where numbers of glandered horses are now stived together, whence they only are taken out to draw public vehicles by night, would then soon cease to exist Were glandered horses by law condemned, men, from mercenary motives, would soon cease buying cheap life for the purpose of working disease to utter exhaustion. Such proprietors, were glanders declared just cause for slaughtering any horse wherever found, would soon discover their cheap purchases to be dear bargains. It is terrible now to witness animals, in almost the last stage of a most debilitating malady, goaded through the public streets with cruel loads behind them. It is horrible, when we reflect that every citizen in a large town is, by the avarice of unscrupulous people, exposed to a most loathsome disease, and to a most torturing death.

FARCY.

When the horse, which has been the pampered favorite in its youth, grows old, it generally becomes the half-starved and over-worked drudge of some equally half-starved proprietor. In the fullness of its pride and the freshness of its strength, it had to canter under the airy burden of my lady's figure. When the joints are stiff—when accident, disease, and sores, have rendered every movement painful; and when its energy is poorly fed upon the rankest provender—then the wretched animal is,

THE OLD FAVORITE AND THE NEW PET.

by the whip of a thoughtless hireling, forced to toil between the shafts of some creaking cart. It is sad to watch the vehicles on a London road, and speculate upon what has been the past fortune and will be the future fate of the animals which propel them!

Farcy is peculiarly the lot of the poor man's horse. It is the consequence of utter exhaustion. It is the horrid friend—the last and dreadful rescuer of the thoroughly wretched. No one cause will produce it. To generate farcy, there must be a congregation of evils: the constitution must be weakly; the grooming must be neglected; the food must be stinted; the bed soiled; the dwelling small; the drainage bad; the master unfeeling, and the work excessive. All of these things, or so many of them as nature can endure, must exist before farcy can be generated.

It is true the disease can be communicated by inoculation. But that source of farcy is of very small importance. Not one case in a thousand thus originates. Farcy is essentially a skin disease. It commences with specific inflammation of the superficial absorbents. This inflammation leads to suppuration and to ulceration. Abscesses first appear. They may come on any part of the body. They seem to be, in the primary instance, lumps or hard enlargements. Something of the annexed form is first observed. There may be one of these, or there may be many. Ultimately they burst or are opened. Apparently healthy matter then issues from the interior. But the first discharge being released, the wound does not heal. The edges grow rough, the center of

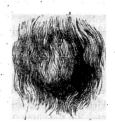

A FARCY BUD.

the sore becomes pale, and moistened by a thin, semi-transparent fluid. Then, if the neighborhood of the sore be felt, cords, more or less thin, will be discovered running from it toward some other lumps on the body.

Such is the distinguishing sign by which to recognize farcy. Lumps appear, which prove to be abscesses. They, after discharging, do not heal; they become ulcers. From them run certain cords, which are the swollen lymphatic or absorbents. Till the enlargement of the absorbents is discerned, a man, from the other signs, may suspect, but he cannot pronounce with certainty, the disease to be farcy.

If a recent case of farcy be slaughtered and dissected, the affection appears to go no deeper than the skin. The cellular tissue will exhibit indications of dropsy, which invariably is present. The muscles will be pallid and flabby, suggesting bodily debility; but, to most observers, such signs will be all that is discernible.

Is farcy, then, strictly, a local disorder? Can such be asserted of a malady which appears to be so constitutional in its origin? Is there nothing continuous with the skin? Yes, there is. Intimately connected with the outward covering of the body, imperceptibly blending with it, and capable, after exposure, of assuming its appearance, is the mucous membrane. Mucous membrane lines the interior of the body, and is very abundantly supplied with absorbents. The French, who are far more minute observers and more accomplished dissectors than the generality of English surgeons, have, in cases of farcy, detected signs which assure us the disease is not strictly an external affection. It has an internal and a deep-seated origin, as is evidenced by the discovery of a few tubercles upon the mucous membrane of the interior.

The course of the disease would likewise teach us to arrive at this conclusion. The appetite often fails; sometimes it becomes voracious. The matter is, by pressure, to be squeezed through the skin. The thirst becomes torturing; the horse will cry for water. All it drinks, however, passes quickly through the body, and the desire for fluid cannot be satisfied. At last—as though to prove the correctness of our opinion concerning the constitutional nature of farcy—glanders breaks forth.

Glanders and farcy seem to be the same disease, modified by certain circumstances to which the animal is exposed. Thus a horse, inoculated with the matter of glanders, may become farcied; or an animal, infected with the taint of farcy, may exhibit glanders. These results, together with the fact of a glandered horse displaying farcy prior to death, and of a farcied animal exhibiting glanders previous to decease, are pretty conclusive evidence.

Farcy is of two kinds, the large and the small. The large may appear as one or more abscesses. Generally it is disposed to select, in the first instance, those places where the skin is thin and the hair all but absent. It breaks, and becomes shallow ulcers, which, however, may heal upon the application of any escharotic. The abscesses are not, in every instance, of one absolute figure. They vary in such respect, and have a tendency, if neglected, to generate large ulcers, from which spring unsightly bunches of fungoid granulations.

FARCY ON THE INSIDE OF THE HORSE'S THIGH, WHERE THE SKIN IS THIN AND THE HAIR ALMOST ABSENT.

The smaller description of this disorder has no preference for any particular locality. It appears, like surfeit, in small lumps all over the body. These lumps, from their size and uniformity, have been likened to buttons—hence the term "button farcy." Cords soon connect them; they maturate and burst, like the larger sort. The "button farcy," however, leaves a deeper and a more painful ulcer. It yields less readily to treatment, and seems to exhibit itself before the body is utterly exhausted.

A PORTION OF SKIN, TAKEN FROM A FARCIED HORSE, INJECTED WITH MERCURY.

How very numerous the absorbents of the skin are, may be conjectured from the subjoined engraving of a prepared specimen—and not a very successful one either—of a piece of farcied skin, when deprived of hair. In this case, the animal suffered under the large or common form of the disease. In the button variety, the tumors would only be smaller, of a more even size, and far more numerous.

Farcy is, by the generality of practitioners, regarded as a more tractable disease than glanders. Certainly the course of the disorder is arrested much easier; but, to cure the malady, there is a constitution to renovate and a virus to destroy. Is it in the power of medicine to restore the health and strength, which have been underfed, sapped by a foul atmosphere, and exhausted by overwork? Tonics may prop up or stimulate for a time; but the drunkard and the opium-eater, among human beings, can inform us that the potency of the best-selected and the choicest drugs, most judiciously prescribed and carefully prepared, is indeed very limited. What, then, can be hoped for in an animal whose treatment is generally an affair of pounds, shillings, and pence? Sulphate of copper or of iron, oak-bark, Cayenne pepper, and cantharides, probably, are the chief medicines the practitioner will give. With such the horse may be patched up; it may even return to work. But at what a risk! It carries about the seeds of a disorder contagious to the human species, and in man even more terrible than in the quadruped. Is it lawful, is it right, to save an avaricious master the chance of a few shillings, and to incur the risk of poisoning an innocent person? The author thinks not. Therefore he will give no directions how to arrest the progress of farcy. The horse, once contaminated, is, indeed, very rarely or never cured. The animal, after the veterinary surgeon has shaken hands with the proprietor and departed, too often bears about an enlarged limb, which impedes its utility, and, at any period, may break forth again with more than the virulence of the original affection.

A GENTLEMAN'S SERVANT OUT OF PLACE.

CHAPTER XII.

LIMBS—THEIR ACCIDENTS AND THEIR DISEASES.

OSSEOUS DEPOSITS—SPAVIN.

"ONE horse could wear out two pairs of legs," is an old jockey's phrase. Most men, when purchasing a dumb slave, pay great attention to the lower extremities. If an animal be used up or has performed hard work, the indications are sure to be found on those parts; but what a comment does the language and the act referred to pass upon the conduct of those masters, the history of whose treatment, or rather

A PARK NAG WITH BONE SPAVIN LED OUT OF THE STABLE.

whose abuse of a living creature, is thus sought for and often found upon a breathing frame!

Before the strength has departed, or the legitimate number of years are exhausted, cruelty deprives a most obedient drudge of its power to serve. The history of almost every horse in this kingdom is a struggle to exist against human endeavors to deprive it of utility. Nature, when she made the animal, formed a creature hardly second to her master-piece in anatomical perfection; the legs are strong, but, in his impatience and in his blind obedience to the dictates of fashion, man *will* put them to their fullest use before their structure is confirmed. Racers go into training when one year old Carriage horses, omnibus machiners, cart horses, nags, roadsters, may-birds, and park hacks generally come into work about the third year. The animal, however, does not cut all its teeth till the completion of its fifth birthday. It requires to look upon eight seasons before its adult period is entered upon; and yet at the third year, or before that period, it is put to such work as only a horse can or does perform.

When the horse was designed to be only matured, the frivolity of mankind pronounces the creature to be *aged*. The life is, indeed, generally worthless before the eighth year is entered upon. The young flesh, bones, and sinews, long before that time arrives, are made the seats of poignant diseases. Work, not in the first instance laborious, but sudden and energetic beyond what the frame of the young horse can endure, casts it out of the gentleman's stable. Once removed from that place, its descent is rapid From the carriage to the cab is a leap often cleared in equine history; but every change adds misery to its lot. It fares worse, lodges worse, and works harder with every new proprietor, till at length, as its years and wretchedness accumulate, Nature interposes and takes the sufferer to herself.

At the head of this article stands an engraving of the mildest form of reward which docility reaps by service unto cruelty When will this land, which so loudly boasts its Christianity, apply in its fullness and its strength the sacred maxim—"Do unto others as you would others should do unto you"? When will churchmen teach that the religion which does not enlarge the heart toward every breathing life upon the earth, is unworthy of the *Christian* title? Men who would rage to hear their faith called in question, nevertheless feel no shame when they urge the young steed to that act which probably will cripple the animal for the short remainder of its life.

Spavin, splint, or **ring-bone** are no more the legitimate consequences of equine existence, than nodes and anchylosis are the natural inheritances of human beings; yet what would the world look like, if men had their motions impeded and their joints firmly locked by bony deposits in anything like the proportion which such misfortunes are witnessed in the inferior life? The most useful, the most trusting, and the most joyous of animals is the one toward which man acts as though his study was to abuse the authority intrusted to him. Its utility lies in its legs; its play also is a canter; but before its body is set, its limbs are disabled. Kindness can subdue the creature, which, however, is never taken out of its prison without the whip; it is treated as a thing without feeling: but its body is not more impressible to brutality than its feelings are sensitive to gentleness. The one is often injured, and the others are frequently vitiated by the master it too literally obeys.

Spavin and splint both are the change of ligamentous structure into bone: spavin occurs at the inner and lower part of the hock; splint also may be sometimes found at the same part of the knee. The name

splint is likewise applied to any bony enlargement upon the shins or below the hocks and the knees.

Splints in the fore leg are mostly seen on the inner side. On the hind limb, however, such growths principally favor the outer side. The advent of splint, when near the knee, is generally accounted for by saying the inner side of the joint lies more under the center of gravity;

BONE SPAVIN.
A swelling or bony tumor, situated upon the lower and inner part of the hock-joint.

and, therefore, is the more exposed to injury. Such an interpretation, however, leaves the preference for the outer locality—when splints are witnessed on the hind leg—unexplained. Perhaps the reader will—after having contemplated the two following engravings, and subsequent to having observed that the artery of the hinder limb crosses the inferior part of the hock, to take its course down the outer side of the leg, while in the fore extremity the vessel continues along the inner side of the shin-

THE *inside* OF THE FORE LEG, SHOWING THE VESSELS PROPER TO THAT PART OF THE LIMB GENERALLY AFFECTED BY OSSEOUS DEPOSITS.

THE *outside* OF THE HIND LEG, DISPLAYING THE VESSELS NATURAL TO THAT PART OF THE LIMB WHICH IS COMMONLY THE SEAT OF OSSEOUS DEPOSITS.

bone—conclude with the author that, in splint, the distribution of the blood is more to be regarded than the weight, which, originally conveyed through a ball-and-socket joint, can hardly afterward affect one part to the release of the rest.

Having explained the peculiarity attending some bony tumors on the hind extremity, it now becomes our duty to explain what actually constitutes a spavin. Any bony growth or bony enlargement, however small, which is to be seen or felt upon the inner side of the hock, is a "spavin." But of spavins there are three kinds. The low sort, or the "Jack" of the horse-dealer's phraseology. This answers to the splint of the fore leg, and originates in the top of the splint bone.

A SHIN-BONE HAVING AN OSSEOUS DEPOSIT UPON ITS HEAD AND ON THE INNER SIDE, WHICH MIGHT BE A SPLINT OR A SPAVIN, AS IT OCCURRED UPON THE FORE OR HIND LEG.

THE INNER SIDE OF THE HOCK AFFLICTED WITH HIGH OR INCURABLE SPAVIN.

The bony enlargement, should it be located comparatively high upon the joint, often produces acute and incurable lameness. When low down, the granules of bone have little to interfere with. Being placed higher up, the tendons have to play over the osseous deposit; and, when that happens, the cure is hopeless.

The above form of disease, however, does not ensue upon every case of spavin. Many good racers, and most seasoned hunters, have spavins, which do not in any way detract from their speed, however much these growths may interfere with their action.

Bony spavin does, when the quadruped starts, sensibly deteriorate that

THE NATURAL POSITION OF THE HEALTHY FOOT WHEN RAISED FROM THE EARTH DURING AN EASY TROT.

THE FOOT, INCAPABLE OF BEING FREELY RAISED FROM THE GROUND, BY A HORSE WHICH IS BADLY SPAVINED.

grace of motion which should characterize the action of the perfect horse. During the trot, the leg should be lifted clear of the earth,

19

while, by an involuntary movement within the hock-joint, the hoof is inclined outward. This peculiarity is exhibited in the engraving on page 289, which supposes the spectator to be standing by the side of the animals.

Exostosis, formed on any part, locks together the bones which the deposit may involve, or it unites the several distinct parts into one osseous mass. By the bones of the hock being thus joined, all movement of the shin is effectually prevented; the foot of a spavined horse is, to a spectator who is laterally situated, always presented in a side view. Moreover, when severe spavin is present, the entire flexion of the lower portion of the limb is rendered impossible.

The toes being moved along, instead of being lifted from the ground, occasions the hoof and shoe to suffer wear. The hoof generally presents a toe blunted by perpetual friction; while the shoe of a spavined horse is, in front, worn to a state of positive sharpness. These indications of disease should always be sought for, and, when present, they are so obvious as hardly to be mistaken.

THE FOOT OF A SPAV-
INED LIMB, SHOWING
THE WEAR OF THE
TOE OF THE HOOF AND
SHOE; BOTH ARE CON-
SEQUENT UPON DRAG-
GING THE MEMBER
UPON THE GROUND.

Another test for spavin consists in observation made upon the manner of going. A horse thus affected comes out of the stable always stiff, and sometimes lame. Exercise, by warming the body, seems to soften the stubbornness of the disease; and the same animal, which left the stable in a crippled condition, may return to it in a state which, to the generality of gentlemen, would represent soundness. So well are dealers acquainted with this fact, that it is a custom with these folks for a spavined horse to be warmed before it is shown to a probable purchaser. No person, however, should hazard an opinion on any quadruped which is not perfectly cool, especially when there is a motive to be suspected of the slightest desire for a favorable judgment. The horse which, after exercise, should trot past with no obvious sign of spavin, having stood for an hour in the stable, would come forth a decided cripple, or, at all events, with such faulty action that a novice would immediately detect something wrong about the legs. This peculiarity is illustrated by the engraving which heads the present chapter.

Should the dealer refuse to exhibit the animal when cool, such refusal would be convincing evidence as to the condition of the horse. The sale should, under such circumstances, be at once repudiated.

However, when judging of disease, it is always well to divest the mind of every kind of prejudice. Animals of a certain kind of conformation are said to be disposed, or to be more than ordinarily subject, to spavin. Creatures of the foregoing sort show what are denominated sickle-hocks, or cow-hocks. A sickle-hock is not a diseased joint, but it is one which the majority of horsemen have stigmatized as very liable to become diseased. Weakness, it

it is only natural to imagine, such a malformation indicates; but, so far as the author's experience goes, creatures thus formed often continue sound when limbs of model shape give way.

It is now our duty to inform the reader how to examine a horse for spavin. In this operation there are four points of view to be taken —behind the animal, though always at a safe distance from the heels; in the front, but not close to the horse, yet so near that the examiner must bend to view the hocks between the fore legs; and

A SICKLE-HOCKED OR COW-HOCKED HORSE.

from both the sides. In all these positions, it is prudent now to elongate the distance and now to approach nearer; then to move the head about, and occasionally to step to the right or to the left. In short, it is advisable to get as many different points of sight as possible; for in one, and only in one, may a spavin be detected on the hock, which, seen from any other spot, shall look perfectly clean. At the same time, from every point care should be taken to compare one hock with the other; if the slightest difference in point of size can be detected, it is fair to suppose one is enlarged by the commencement of disease. Any indication of this sort is always to be sought for. The disease may have just begun; but it is impossible to say where it may stop. The spavin may be very small; yet who can assert its growth is perfected? In the examination for spavin, however, allowance should be made for the age of the horse. Spavins, in young horses, may be regarded with alarm; in old animals, they generally are perfected, and, however large they may be, probably they will grow no bigger—on the contrary, as the years increase, they are usually diminished, being absorbed; but the bones, once locked together, are never subsequently unloosed, although all the swelling should entirely disappear.

The examination having been up to this point properly performed, there is yet another test to be adopted before the animal is trotted forth; here a well-trained and attentive groom is of every value—one who will keep on the same side as you may be upon, and who will follow your footsteps whenever you change from right to left. The duty of this groom is to hold up the front leg; the more stress is placed upon his attention, because no horse can kick with the hind foot of that side upon

THE POINTS OF VIEW WHENCE TO LOOK FOR SPAVIN IN A HORSE.

which one fore leg is off the ground. The attempt would deprive the body of all lateral support, and a fall would ensue; whereas many quadrupeds can, for a short time, balance themselves upon two legs, each being on opposite sides of the body: therefore the examiner, probably, engrossed in his occupation, would be in considerable danger, should the groom forget to follow his movements.

Most horses are averse to having the hocks fingered; such liberties are apt to call up vehement indignation; it is necessary, therefore, to guard him who undertakes to inspect them. This the groom does most effectually; but the examiner should also take some caution—he should stand as close to the foot of the horse as may be convenient. Thus, should the animal kick out, he may escape, or, at most, be very rudely pushed on one side. The horse's kick is only severe after the heels have reached some distance, or have obtained power by propulsion; for that reason is the advice given to stand as near the hind foot as may be convenient.

Being in this situation, one hand is laid upon the top of the hock, and

the entire weight of the body is brought to bear upon that part. The object is three-fold—to obtain, by this means, the earliest intimation of any design on the part of the animal to use the limb; to impede in some measure the extension of the leg; and to gain a point of rest on which to lean, while the head is bent forward to inspect, the free hand being employed to feel the part appropriate to spavin. Afterward comes the trot, the peculiarities to be detected in which have been anticipated.

THE MANNER IN WHICH TO FEEL FOR A SPAVIN.

Now we encounter the important question, What can be done for a spavined horse? If the animal be not lame, let it alone. However large, however unsightly the deposit may be, do not run the chance of exciting a new action in a part where disease exists in a quiescent form.

The regular treatment is to purge, give diuretics, bleed, blister, rowel, seton, periostotcomy, neurotomy, fire, and punch. The bleeding may be great or small, local or general; the blister, mild or severe, applied over half the joint at a time, or rubbed in after the limb has been scored by the iron. Rowels and setons may also be simple, or they may be smeared with irritants, which are made of different strengths. Periostoteomy may be single, or may be made compound by the addition of a seton and a blister. Neurotomy is very unsatisfactory, and very often a most tedious affair when employed to cure spavin The fire may be down to the true skin; it may be through the skin, and on to the tumor; or it may be inflicted by means of a blunt-pointed instrument, which, when heated, burns its way into the bone itself. The punch also admits of variety; it may be with or without a blister; it may be holes made in a living body, which holes are filled with a corroding paste Or the operation may consist of the exposure of the bone, and cutting off the offending portion with a saw, or knocking away part of a breathing frame with a chisel and a mallet

All these tortures have for centuries been inflicted; they have been practiced upon thousands of animals, only for men, at this day, to doubt whether the cruelty has been attended with the slightest service. Flesh, as capable of feeling as our own, has been cut, irritated, burnt, and punched for hundreds of years; and now, at the twelfth hour, such operations are not discarded, but their efficacy is mildly questioned.

Reader, if you have a horse which is lame from spavin, and your calculations tell you it will not pay to nurse the cripple, have it slaughtered. Do not consent to have it tortured for a chance; do not sell it to the certainty of a terrible old age and of immediate torment

The cure for spavin is good food and rest — perfect rest: such rest or stagnation as a healthy horse submits to in the stable. This, enjoined for months, with the occasional application of a mild blister, with the best of food, to enable nature to rectify man's abuse, will do more good, cost no more money, and occupy no more time than the devilries usually adopted, and very often adopted without success. As an additional motive on the side of humanity, it may be stated that the horse suffers much more when disease is located in the hind than when it is exhibited upon the fore leg. The ravages which, in the first case, would endanger the life, in the last would be borne with comparative tranquillity. The posterior parts of the animal seem to be endowed with exquisite sensibility; yet, in spite of this, the so-called cure for spavin, and the boasted treatment for ages, only consists in torturing the hocks of the animal.

While inflammation exists, apply poultices, and well rub the part with a mixture of belladonna and of opium—one ounce of each drug rubbed down with one ounce of water. Or place opium and camphor on the poultices; or rub the enlargement with equal parts of chloroform and camphorated oil. The pain having subsided and the heat being banished, apply, with friction, some of the following ointment. It may reduce the disease by provoking absorption; at all events, it will check all further growth by rendering further deposit almost an impossibility.

Iodide of lead . . . . One ounce.
Simple ointment . . . . Eight ounces.
    Mix.

SPLINT.

The horse, could it only speak, would have sufficient cause to overwhelm man with its injuries. It is to be hoped that He who heeds not language, but reads the heart, will not peruse the horror written on that of the most contented and sweetest-dispositioned of man's many slaves. It is true, colts have spavin and splints. Creatures, whose days of bitterness are as yet to come, exhibit exostoses; but these blemishes are the sad inheritances of the cruel service exacted by thoughtless masters from the progenitors of the deformed. Nature gave the horse a fibro-cartilaginous or elastic union to particular bones, so that all its motions might be bounding and graceful. The animal, thus formed, was presented to man; but the gift was not prized by him to whom it was given. The authority possessed was abused. The capability of the horse was only measured by what it was able, at the risk of its life, to perform. The most humane of modern proprietors is an ignorant tyrant to his graceful bond-servant. The most meek of owners likes his horse to possess high action. The consequence is, the leg, lifted from the ground to the highest possible point, is forcibly driven again to the earth. This pace is imposed upon a creature so docile, it only seeks to learn that which pleases its master, and, in the entirety of its confidence, never mistrusts its instructor. The lesson is learned. The animal soon becomes proud to exhibit its acquirement. High action, however—especially that kind of action the horse is taught to exemplify—soon deranges the system. It breeds inflammation in the fibro-cartilaginous tissues, upon which its chief strain is felt. The union between the splint bones and the cannon, or between the shin-bone and the accessories, one on either side, speedily becomes converted into osseous matter.

However, man cannot say to nature, "Thus far shalt thou go, and no farther;" otherwise the alteration of structure, if unseen, might distress the horse, but would little affect the owner. A diseased action, once started up, is apt to involve other parts than those in which it originated. Thus, a splint is strictly an exostosis or bony tumor on the inner and lower part of the knee-joint; but there are found to be others which this definition will not embrace. Here, for instance, are the ordinary kinds of splint to be seen, more or less, in every animal subject to man's usage. Number 1 is unsightly. Moreover, it gives an unpleasant jar to the rider of the poor horse thus deformed; and few men, when they state this fact, ever think of what sensation that which jars the equestrian must occasion to the steed. It will produce lameness at first; but, this surmounted and the tumor fully formed, it causes no inconvenience beyond a loss of elasticity when in motion; and because it provokes no lameness, man says it is unattended by feeling.

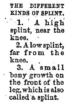

Figure 2 is a splint on the side of the leg. It also is unsightly, and produces a disagreeable sensation to the person in the saddle. Moreover, it is exposed to accidents. If the horse has high and close action, the tumor may be struck when the foot is being raised. Such a possibility is not altogether free from danger. The horse, having grazed the swelling, will often fall down as though it were shot. That circumstance warrants the supposition that these growths are not quite so devoid of sensibility as most horse owners are pleased to assert they are.

THE DIFFERENT KINDS OF SPLINT.
1. A high splint, near the knee.
2. A low splint, far from the knee.
3. A small bony growth on the front of the leg, which is also called a splint.

The slight enlargement, opposite which stands figure 3, denotes a growth of small size. It may be of no great consequence, if it appear on a vacant part of the bone, or on a place over which no tendon passes; but it is of serious import, if situated beneath a tendon, as then it causes incurable lameness.

Man having provoked these blemishes, Nature generally strives to remove the effects of his stupidity. She will smooth the top of the tumor by the interposition of cartilage and of ligament, that the skin may not be irritated when passing over these enlargements. She will also develop a false bursa on the top of each, thereby causing the integument to move with an approach to ease.

Yet there are other sorts of splints which often are very serious affairs. That the reader may comprehend these, let him attend to the next engraving.

1—Represents a splint which has involved the bones of the knee, and which has left the horse only the joint formed by the lower end of the radius to progress with. This is a sad business. The action is injured for life; and death, or a cart, is the lot of the wretched animal so diseased.

2—Shows fine points of bone, so placed that they would impinge upon the suspensory ligament, if not upon the flexor tendons. Lameness, in its acutest form, would thereby be caused wherever the limb was bent. The lameness, probably, would last till death, as splints in this situation are rarely discovered during life.

3—Denotes an enlargement, probably produced by a blow received during a leap, or given by an impatient groom. It is placed directly under one of the extensor tendons. In consequence of this minute substance, the severest agony is endured, or the most marked lameness exhibited, whenever the leg is advanced.

SPLINTS OF A SERIOUS KIND.

1. A splint involving the bones of the knee-joint.
2. A splint interfering with the action of the back sinews.
3. A small splint situated under the tendon of an extensor muscle.

The great majority of these maladies may result from the present rage for high action, and the too general practice of pushing the horse beyond his speed. Racers and hunters commonly have splints: almost every roadster exhibits them. Few draught-horses are without them: they are all but universal. It may be easy to detect or to feel a full-sized splint; but it is rather difficult to discover these tumors when they are small, or when they are just beginning to develop themselves. At that period they are most painful. They may be mere deformities when fully formed; but, when growing, though not to be seen, they are apt to cause decided lameness.

The cause of such failing action very often can only be guessed at. To detect a fully-developed splint, stand at the side of the animal's leg and grasp the posterior part of the shin; then, by running the thumb down on one side and the fingers on the other, in the groove formed by the junction of the two small splint-bones with the cannon-bone, the examiner may recognize enlargement or feel heat, should either exist. By making pressure where the heat or swelling is perceived, he may cause the leg to be snatched up. Should nothing result from this trial, the animal is trotted gently

A HORSE "DISHING," OR CARRYING THE FRONT LEG OUTWARD, WHEN ON THE TROT.

up and its action is observed. Horses with splints, when lame, generally "dish" or turn the leg outward, when it is raised from the ground. That is done because the bending of the limb pressed the splint-bone downward, the outward carriage of the shin being an endeavor to lessen the pain which attends upon the natural action.

Should no "dishing" be remarked, next observe whether the leg is fully flexed or advanced; and, after the hints thus received, the investigation may be resumed with a better-prospect of success. .

The treatment of splint is conveyed in the old maxim, "time and patience." Rest will do more than physic A man, therefore, may as well let his horse rest in his own stable, as pay for rest, lodging, and useless treatment in another place Splints, moreover, if only subjected to rest, accompanied with liberal feeding, are likely the sooner to attain their maximum magnitude If they are interfered with under the pretense of treatment, the irritation may cause them to increase; thus the proprietor, through his impatience, may purchase an injury.

When they are acutely painful, a poultice, on which one drachm of opium and one drachm of camphor is sprinkled, will frequently afford relief. They may also, at such times, be rubbed with a drachm of chloroform combined with two drachms of camphorated oil.   These measures, however simple, aim at mitigating the present symptoms—they do not even infer the possibility of curing the disease.   Periostoteomy pretended to do something of that sort; but has failed so often, it is now seldom recommended by practiced veterinarians

When, however, a particle of the bone interferes with a tendon, the lameness is so acute that often the choice lies between cure and death; for some, even of present proprietors, scorn to sell a favorite horse which has become sick in their service.   In these cases, it is lawful to open the skin, and with a fine saw, a chisel or a sharp knife, to remove the offending growth; after the operation, leave the skin open and dress the wound with a lotion made of chloride of zinc one grain, to water one ounce. This application has the great merit of keeping down granulations; but employ nothing irritating to the bone, or the result may be worse than the injury which has been removed.

Splints sometimes occur on the outer side of the hind leg; there, however, they are little thought of. The hind leg propels the horse, but does not support its body; therefore, splints of this last sort are less unpleasant to the rider. The hind leg, not bearing much weight, splints, when situated on that member, do not occasion very severe lameness, and the enlargement being located upon the outside of the shin, is thereby removed from the possibility of being struck by the opposite hoof. For these reasons, splints of the foregoing nature are considered trifles, and are rarely esteemed worthy of much notice.

To check the further enlargement of a splint with a fair chance of also removing the deformity—though with no hope of releasing the parts locked together by bony union—employ the ointment already recommended for spavin:—

>Iodide of lead . . . . One ounce.
>Simple ointment . . . . Eight ounces.
>   Mix, and apply with friction thrice daily.

RING-BONE.

The whole soul of the horse seems devoted to man's will; who has not seen a team of small but sturdy horses contrive to drag a heavy load up a steep hill, as though nothing could afford them such content as to

leave their hoofs behind them! What Londoner but has witnessed the cart-horse dig its toes into the stones of Ludgate Hill, and make the muscles bulge out upon the glossy coat as though life had but one object, and to that object the animal was straining every nerve!

A sight such as this, when properly contemplated, cannot otherwise than teach man to esteem his fellow-laborer; for what creature on earth toils so

A HORSE STRAINING TO
MOUNT A STEEP HILL.

willingly in the service of humanity as the horse? At any hour it is ready—in health it is willing, and in sickness it is obedient; even when worn out, entirely used up and driven to the slaughter-house, it looks upon its slayer with large placid eyes, stands quietly in the place where it is bid, with no mistrust in the kindness of its abuser, and ends a life of devotion by accepting the blow almost as a favor. It is the only animal which lives but to more than share the burden of its owner; yet, of all existing quadrupeds, the horse is the most ill treated.

Ring-bone is an osseous deposit; so far it resembles splint and spavin: it differs, however, in the kind of horses it attacks. Splint and spavin are principally witnessed upon quadrupeds of speed. Ring-bone is all but confined to the cart-horse. It is caused by those violent efforts this animal makes, in obedience to the voice of the driver, when dragging a heavy load up some sharp ascent. The entire force is then thrown upon the bones of the pastern; inflammation ensues; lymph is effused; the lymph becomes cartilage, and the cartilage is converted into bone. Then an exostosis is established, and a ring-bone is the consequence.

The disease may implicate one or more bones; it may involve one or more joints; it may also be confined to one bone; it may be either partial or complete. It may exist as a slight enlargement in front of the bone, or it may quite encircle it. On page 299 is a specimen of the disease. The exostosis, as in this case, was prominent during life. The disease

..did not quite encircle the bones, and though, when the preparation was dried, the different parts could be slightly moved one upon another, yet, during life, the joints were firmly locked.

THE PASTERN AND PEDAL BONE OF A HORSE AFFECTED WITH SEVERE RING-BONE.

1. The joint between the pastern bones, showing the groove in which the tendon of the extensor pedis muscle reposed.
2. The joint between the lower pastern and the bone of the foot.

THE FOOT OF A LIVING HORSE WITH AGGRAVATED RING-BONE.

The animal, from which the above sketch was taken, although used to propel a cart, was by no means of a cart breed. The creature rather hobbled than went lame; but all flexion was entirely lost in the pastern bones.

One of the above sketches depicts this disease as it appeared prior to death. The reader has now to consider the consequences of such a deformity; it materially interferes with the value. The hind limbs are the instruments of propulsion in the horse; these are much incapacitated by the presence of ring-bone. An animal thus affected might move an easy load upon even ground; but when the weight had to be drawn up hill, the creature would obviously be unable to use the toe; the foot, placed flat upon the ground, or so shod as to have an even bearing, would perceptibly be of comparatively little use in such a case. So, also, in descending an inequality, the horse with severe ring-bone will be unable to bite the earth. Ring-bone, therefore, does incapacitate the animal for many uses, besides interfering with the free employment of the muscular energy; no persuasion or brutality can induce a maimed animal to cast its full weight upon a diseased limb. The pace may be quickened by the lash; but the horse will, nevertheless, continue to hop when the affected member touches the earth.

Let mankind, therefore, reflect that the horse is given as their fellow-laborer. The life of the quadruped is the property of the master; but who, being sane, would abuse his own property? The being who should destroy chairs and tables—although such things can be mended—would be speedily confined as mad. Yet it has not entered the mind of man, as a reasonable idea, that to deface a living image—to destroy the value or to deteriorate the property which is present in the animal—deserves more than the very mildest of punishments. The breathing creature, when defaced, cannot be made sound again ' Horse property is notoriously hazardous. It should be the care of men to use a tender thing with a greater gentleness. Instead of which, horses are galloped till they become blind, and lashed to drag weights beyond the proper limits of their strength. Men, who never think in whom the fault really lies, complain that Providence has not suited the horse to purposes such as would derange most iron-wrought machines!

When a horse first shows ring-bone, seek to allay the pain Apply poultices, on which one drachm of powdered opium and one of camphor has been sprinkled. Rub the disease with equal parts of oil of camphor and of chloroform The pain having ceased, have applied, with friction, to the seat of enlargement and around it, some of the following ointment, night and morning :—

Iodide of lead	One ounce.
Lard	. . Eight ounces.
Mix.	

Continue treatment for a fortnight after all active symptoms have disappeared, and allow the animal to rest—being liberally fed for at least a month subsequent to the cessation of every remedy. When work is resumed, mind it is gentle, and be very careful how the horse goes to its full labor

STRAIN OF THE FLEXOR TENDON.

The flexor tendons of the legs are liable to a variety of accidents. Injuries to these structures, according to their severity, are denominated: **strain of the flexor tendon, clap of the back sinews, sprain of the back sinews, and breaking down.**

The first accident is common enough, and springs from the horse being forced to perform extraordinary work on uneven ground. Else it is caused by the irritability of the rider, tugging now at one rein, then at the other; forcing a timid animal into strange contortions, and at the same time elevating the head, thereby throwing all the strain upon the muscles This is a spectacle repeatedly presented to him who walks about town An angry rider is seen sawing, without compunction, at the mouth of some patient horse. The spectators look on complacently. There is nothing offensive to them in an enraged man venting his anger on an unoffending creature. Were the act generally reprehended, it would not be so frequently exhibited; but the only emotion the contemplation of another's brutality appears to elicit, is a desire in the passengers to provide for their own security.

The main cause, however, of the most prevalent of these sad deformities is that of the shaft-horse descending a steep declivity with a load behind it The weight would roll down the descent: this the horse has to prevent, and the chief stress is then upon the back tendons. The injuries to such parts are generally of a chronic character. The strain seldom occasions decided lameness. But the horse being harnessed to the shafts, the cause is in daily operation. The part injured is being constantly excited. Thus, without the development of a single acute symptom, the tendons are stretched—a low kind of inflammation is generated—and this action being kept up, the sinews gradually lose their elasticity, and shorten.

When strain of the fore leg is received, the animal goes oddly, but is not lame. However, if put into the stable and taken out the next morning, the horse is found to be stiff and apparently very cramped The halting action may disappear upon exercise, but assuredly it will again be present on the following dawn The proprietor may resolve to work "the brute" sound. Such a speculation with disease may occasionally answer; but, on the large scale, it is a losing game, for it more often fails than succeeds : the limb, on work, commonly does not amend. The symptoms are aggravated in every way; and what was curable in the first stage is apt, after the lapse of time, to degenerate into an intractable malady. The many horses to be seen in the London cab ranks, with the fore limbs permanently contracted, are evidences as to the result of such very knowing treatment.

When a horse slightly strains the flexor tendon, do not expect to discover the seat of the affection till several hours have elapsed Then pass the hand gently down the injured limb A small swelling may be detected. The enlargement may feel soft, slightly warm, but hardly tender Bind a linen bandage round the leg rather tightly, and keep this constantly wet with cold water. For the three first nights, have men to sit up in the stable and perform that operation After that time, if everything goes on well, wet the limb only during the day.

· Throw up the horse till more than recovered, and do not put it to full work till some period after that event Give immediately four drachms of aloes. Allow only two feeds of corn per day; but do not turn out to graze under the idea that it saves cost and gives a chance that the animal may be taken up sound. At grass, the horse must walk many miles to eat poor food, sufficient to support life. This kind of motion will not suit a strain, which does best with absolute rest. Keep, therefore, in a stall, and do not begrudge the necessary meat to support the life which has suffered injury, and is now enduring pain, in consequence of exertion made in your service.

CLAP OF THE BACK SINEWS.

When the accident is more severe, and the sprain more decided, it is spoken of as "**clap of the back sinews;**" this is a serious affair. The usual fate of the wretched animal thus maimed is to be sold to the highest bidder. It passes from a carefully-tended stable to some wretched out-shed; and its new master is made happy, if the crippled horse can only limp, and somehow get through a day's labor. No pity is wasted upon agony; "the beast," as it is now called, has to live worse, work harder, and drag out a miserable existence with the heavy burden of an almost useless limb.

Clap of the back sinews results from exertion; it may be the work of an instant. The horse sometimes is pulled up, or, in severe cases, it falls. If it be pulled up, it refuses to move at a quicker pace than a hobble, and stands still again so soon as whip or spur are not applied to the sufferer's body. The maimed limb is flexed, and rests upon the toe of the injured leg. There can be no mistake now about the seat of lameness; the foot of the affected limb will hardly be put to the ground. The seat of the malady is soon declared. In a short space a tumor displays itself; it

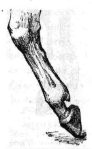

THE EARLIEST SYMPTOM OF CLAP OF THE BACK SINEWS, OR SEVERE SPRAIN OF THE TENDON.

is small, hot, tender, and soft, in the first instance, though it soon enlarges, and grows very hard. The animal does not exhibit much constitutional distress, for it requires excessive pain to call forth such a display in the patient and most enduring horse.

Physic is necessary in this case; a gentle blood-letting, even, may be required, followed by a few doses of febrifuge medicine; but the treatment should be carried no further than is necessary to reduce the pulse to fifty-five degrees. The leg should be wrapped in a stout linen bandage; day and night the part should be saturated with the coldest possible water until the primary symptoms have abated. Cut grass should be the food while any fever rages, but no longer, for the wish is not to destroy the powers of reparation by weakening the body. The cold water should be continued till recovery appears confirmed; but it will be many months before the horse, thus disabled, will again be

THE BLEMISH LEFT BY CLAP OF THE BACK SINEWS.

fit for full or energetic work. Commonly, however, this accident takes place in the hunting-field; and sportsmen, silly as may be their amusements, are no niggards. If they occasionally injure a horse, they will spare no expense that can aid its restoration; and a summer's rest may not be thrown away upon the favorite which has met with such a mishap. However, the mark will remain for life— an obvious swelling will, during existence, denote the place where clap occurred to the back sinews.

SPRAIN OF THE BACK SINEWS.

Sprain of the back sinews of the hind legs is very general among animals which have to perform slow work upon hilly roads. People in the carrier trade can afford to bestow small attention upon the lameness which does not incapacitate. Every journey, however, aggravates the disease. The horse works on till his owner is told by the blacksmith the animal's legs are contracting, and higher calkins are given as a cure.

HIGH CALKINS.
The earliest attention commonly paid to sprain of the back sinews of the hind leg.

At length, however, calkins become of no use. The work continues, and the disease progresses. The position of the foot is now so altered, that the smith discovers his office is unable to render the animal useful. Perhaps these circumstances would little affect the owner, but the horse evidently loses power. At first it is longer on the road. The passengers grumble at the delay, (for country carriers reap no little profit by carrying passengers;) and the driver, flog as he may, can oblige the horse to move no faster. Excessive beating is apt to provoke pity; and every word of pity which is lavished on the evidently eager animal is distasteful to the carrier, who vents his anger upon the wretched cause of all "this rumpus."

At last the horse cannot guide the cart down hill, even when lightly loaded. Assistance is at first procured; but very soon the assistant has to do all the labor. The proprietor cannot imagine what ails his horse; it keeps getting worse and worse. He takes the animal to a farrier. Remedies—oils and blisters—are applied to no effect. A veterinary surgeon is consulted, and the master learns that the only hope left him lies in division of the tendons of the hind leg.—(*See operation.*)

THE SURE RESULT OF CONTINUED WORK AFTER STRAIN OF THE BACK TENDONS.

When a cart-horse's heel heightens, always attend to the back sinews. Feel them gently, to discover if one place is more tender, harder, softer, or slightly warmer, than the rest. Should this not succeed, pinch them hard, and run the fingers down them, marking the part at which the animal flinches. Healthy tendon will endure any amount of pressure; diseased tendon is acutely sensitive Having discovered the locality of the injury, order the hair to be cut short Put a linen bandage round the lesion, and see that it is constantly kept wet; but do not expect a speedy cure. Those structures which are slow to exhibit disease are always tardy in resigning it. Bone and tendon are of this kind.

Therefore do not expect any relief before three months have expired, and it will certainly be six months before the horse is fit to resume labor. Do not blister, bleed, seton, or fire : these things are expensive, and occupy much time. Have patience. Grant the time which the supposed specifics would employ, and the effect, with or without their use, is very likely to be the same. The only remedy for a badly-contracted tendon is an operation, and to that subject the reader is referred.

The horse, however, which has been subjected to such a remedy will never be fit for its former uses No art can restore the primary strength of nature, although human intelligence may arrest the progress of disease. The thought, that the consequences of ill treatment are not always to be eradicated, should surely induce greater care of that property which, once lost to man, can never be replaced.

When a tendinous structure is injured, the best treatment is gentleness and patience. Blisters, setons, etc can only change an acute disorder into a chronic deformity. Entire rest, with such applications as ease the attendant agony, and a sympathy that can afford to wait upon a tardy restoration, are better than all pretended specifics.

BREAKING DOWN.

Breaking down is the severest injury which the tendons can endure. In proof of this may be cited the general notion that, when a racer breaks down, some of the back sinews are ruptured. This, however, does not often occur; but though the tendons are, generally, only severely sprained, some of the finer tissues, which enter into the composition of the leg, are in all cases actually sundered

The animal is at its full pace—doing its utmost, and delighting its rider, who feels confident of coming in first Instantaneously the horse loses the power of putting one fore leg to the ground. The jockey knows what has taken place He flings himself from the saddle, and hastily glances at the animal's foot. It probably is distorted; or, perchance, the accident may have taken effect higher up, and the injury merely be severe clap of the back sinews. Be it which it may, with a heavy heart at loss of money and credit, thus suddenly snatched from him, the jockey leads the horse toward the stand, or, by the shortest road, to the stable.

BREAKING DOWN.

Many horses, after encountering this accident, are instantly shot. The poor animals, by such a proceeding, are saved from a painful cure and a crippled existence. Such conduct is, however, seldom actuated by thoughts of mercy. Nevertheless, to an animal of motion, whose every feeling is displayed by means of its limbs, and which is instinctively more perfect in action than the most accomplished ballet-master, the incumbrance of a leg mis-shapen, callous, and unwieldy, must be a serious affliction. The limb is spoiled for life in the horse which has broken down. The pain in time departs; the breathing becomes quiet; the pulse sinks to the normal point; the appetite returns, and the spirits grow to be as high as ever. But no art can replace the structures which have been disorgan-ized; and the limb, after everything approaching to inflam-mation has subsided, remains a huge, unsightly object—an affliction to its possessor.

THE CONSEQUENCE OF "BREAKING DOWN" IN THE HORSE.

The treatment of breaking down has not been much experimented with. However, constitutional measures are, at first, imperative. At the same time, a bandage should be applied to the injured limb, and this bandage should be kept constantly wet with cold water. A high-heeled

20

shoe should be put on as soon as may be possible; but no treatment can hope to restore the horse to its departed agility, or even to fit it for ordinary usefulness. However, should it be a stallion or a mare, it may be as valuable as a sounder animal for stud purposes. Accidents are not hereditary; nor is there any reason why the foal of a horse which has broken down should not excel the progeny of a more fortunate sire. Among racers, emasculation not being the general practice, this opinion may probably save many a favorite from the doom which a disappointed proprietor now too often inflicts.

CURB.

This is one of the evils which chiefly are the property of the better breed of horses. Man delights to show off the animal he is mounted upon. Be it male or female, old or young, the equestrian is always pleased by the prancing of the horse. The creature seems to comprehend, and to derive gratification from obeying the wish of its superior. It enters into the desires of its dictator, without a thought of prudence or a care for its personal safety. In hunting or in racing, the simple horse more than shares the excitement of its rider, and often encounters the severest accidents in consequence of these amusements. That which is pastime to man frequently proves death to his amiable servant. Often is the animal so maimed by these sports as to necessitate its life being taken upon the course or in the field.

These reflections are very painful to any body who appreciated the loving and devoted character of the quadruped. Among the least of its sufferings probably may be reckoned **curb**, although the mark of the affection nearly always remains for life, and the misfortune sometimes quite disables the horse which incurs it. It consists of an enlargement, or a gradual bulging out, at the posterior of the hock.

There is some dispute about the seat of curb. The author examined a hock which had chronic curb, and found the perforan tendon disorganized. The late Mr.

A CURB.

W. Percival (the respected originator of the very best work upon the horse and its diseases which is extant in the English language) also inspected a hock, and found the sheath of the tendon more involved than the tendon itself. However, a slight acquaintance with the mystery of anatomy assures us that the tendon must have been stretched when the sheath was injured, since the first invests and is inserted into the last. It is well known that synovial membrane is far more sensitive than tendon. It is therefore probable that the membrane would exhibit disease before the tendon displayed the slightest symptom of being affected. The membrane is also capable of displaying the signs of injury long after every trace may have disappeared from the tendon itself.

The effect of the treatment at present adopted is to confirm the enlargement, or to change the swelling into a lump of callus, which will accompany the sufferer to its death. Curbs are said to be the inheritances of animals of a certain conformation. Horses born with what are termed curby hocks are asserted to be much exposed to this kind of accident. The author has, for many years, particularly inspected animals of this description; and he never recollects to have seen a curb upon a hock of that peculiar conformation. To be sure, no man is likely to select either a hunter or a racer from a tribe thus bearing upon their limbs the signs of weakness. The creatures are consequently exempted from the great provocatives of the accident. However, that the reader may fully comprehend what is meant by a curby hock, one is here represented, together with a sound or naturally-formed, clean joint.

A CLEAN HOCK.   A CURBY HOCK, SLIGHTLY
BULGING OUT BEHIND.

The custom of blistering a horse the instant a curb appears is most injurious. Harm is done, in every point of view, by such a habit. The animal should have a high-heeled shoe put on immediately, so as to ease the overstrained tendon. The part ought then to be kept constantly wet with cold water, so as to lower or disperse the inflammation. It should not be blistered, to heat and increase the vascularity of the structures. A cloth, doubled twice or thrice, is easily kept upon the hock by means of an India-rubber bandage, of the form delineated in the accompanying engraving. Such a cloth, so placed, is afterward to be made constantly cool and wet.

AN INDIA-RUBBER
BANDAGE, FOR KEEP-
ING WET CLOTHS
UPON A CURB.

This treatment should be continued; the animal being confined to the stall and made to move as little as possible, until the heat and swelling are diminished and the leg is almost sound. The part being quite cool, a blister should then be rubbed all over the joint; and with that this treatment, in the great majority of cases, is ended. On no account should any man allow his horse's hock to be fired for curb. This is a very general practice; but the author has never witnessed any good result therefrom. He has, however, seen much agony ensue upon the custom. The form of the marks perpetuated upon the skin of a living creature is shown herewith, and were plainly visible in the case of curb, which the writer dissected.

THE LINES MADE, FOR SOME IMAGINARY BENEFIT, WITH A HEATED IRON, UPON THE HOCK OF A HORSE HAVING CURB.

Pulling horses up on their haunches is asserted to be a frequent cause of curb; yet curb is not an accident commonly met with among those animals which drag London carriages. These creatures are being constantly thrown upon their haunches, it being, by ladies, considered "very pretty and very dashing" to make their servants tug at the reins, regardless of the living mouths on which these operate.

THE SUREST MANNER OF PRODUCING CURB.

Pulling suddenly up, however objectionable for other reasons, does not seem to induce curb, as London carriage horses are all but free from that affection. The disease is mainly caused by uneven ground wrenching the limb; by galloping at the topmost speed; by prancing when mounted, or by leaping when after the hounds. Perhaps more curbs are to be seen in a district on which several packs are kept, than in any other part of the country.

OCCULT SPAVIN.

The horse is subject to many fearful maladies, but to none which is more terrible than ulceration between the bones composing the joints. Synovial membrane, cartilage, and bone are without sensation during health. The author hopes his reader is not conscious of a bone in his body; it is also wished that he may read with surprise, that the ends of bones are covered with cartilage, and that many are invested with synovial membrane. As has already been observed, these structures in health are not sensitive; but when disease starts up, be it only the slightest blush of inflammation, the acutest anguish is thereby occasioned.

Ulceration of the joints is, unfortunately, rather common among

horses; the animal, while being ridden, usually drops suddenly lame.
It has trodden on a rolling stone, or made a false step, or put its foot
into some hole, and injured the bone. After a little time, continuance
of the impaired gait causes the rider to dismount; nothing is to be
found in the foot, yet the animal is taken to the stable decidedly lame.
The foot is searched, the limb is examined, pressure, even of the hardest

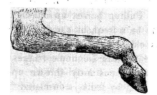

THE EXTENT TO WHICH THE LEG IS CAUGHT UP WHEN OCCULT SPAVIN EXISTS; ALSO THE VIEW OF THE FOOT
PRESENTED TO THE SPECTATOR WHO IS PLACED AT THE SIDE OF THE HORSE, WHEN, DURING THIS DIS-
EASE, THE LEG IS IN MOTION.

kind, is endured with provoking complacency. No heat or swelling can
be discovered; but one thing is to be discerned, the lameness is most
emphatic. After some time, a peculiarity in the trot may be remarked;
the lame foot hardly touches the earth before it is snatched up again,
and that very energetically. Then, closer observation notes that the
leg, when flexed, is always carried in a direct line, as it is when displaying the symptoms of bony spavin. The hoof is never even partially
turned outward. Still, neither of these traits is always displayed in
so prominent a manner as to force attention; frequently, a conclusion is
to be drawn only from negative testimony—as the duration of the lameness, the soundness of the foot, and the perfect condition of the tendons;
these evidences, taken with the suddenness of the complaint, cause the
practitioner to comprehend he has a case of **occult spavin** under treatment.

Such is the origin of the disease: some authors assert the synovial
membrane has been ruptured; some, on the contrary, say the bone has
been injured. The author, knowing nothing, cannot tell how the disease
begins, but he knows that from the date of its origin the horse is lame;
very bad one day, but better, probably, the next. Generally improved
after rest, and always badly limping subsequent to work; never to be
depended upon, for proprietors say the animal is sure, wherever its services are required, to be obstinately lame.

Usually the wretched horse is blistered; setoned; blistered again;
and, at last, fired. All failing to do the smallest good, the horse is next
turned out for three months; while at grass, the poor animal, with an
acutely diseased joint, which is enlarged and stiffened by mistaken treat-

ment, has to take one step for every morsel it bites of poor and watery
food. It is forced to travel long and far, or literally to starve; its body
must rest upon the ulcerated bone, and the weight even be increased by
the pendulous head before enough herbage can be cropped to sustain the
life. At every step two ulcerated surfaces grate upon each other and
are forced violently together; while anguish consumes the flesh, the
nature of the food may keep in the life, but cannot otherwise than
depress the spirits. Besides, the horse has been turned from a sheltered
stall where it was daily groomed, into a field where it has to brave the
utmost stress of the elements, uncared for and unnoticed.

At the end of three months the horse is taken up: to the master's
disgust, it is found to be not looking smarter and not to be going
sounder. More routine treatment is now permitted, and the diseased
limb undergoes further torture; another three months is passed, and the
lameness becomes worse than ever. The proprietor is loath to part with
his property; but he often says "he wishes the animal were dead." At
last, losing all patience, and never having possessed any care for the life
which had suffered injury in his service, the horse is lent to some carter,
who undertakes to "work it sound " This process never, in occult spavin,
succeeds; the wretched quadruped gets worse day by day, till neither
oaths nor lashes can prevent misery from limping on three legs.

At length, worked to a skeleton, the horse is returned to its proprietor, who, inviting pity upon *his* misfortune, that life will feel, and that
horse-flesh is subject to the ailments affecting all creatures which breathe,
orders his servant to take "the beast" to the knacker's and to get what
he can for it

Such is the history of ulcerated joint. All joints are exposed to
ulceration; every bone in the fore and hind leg may be thus affected.
The small bones of the hock are those most commonly diseased; whenever this is the case, the only termination which can reasonably be hoped
for is that the inflamed surfaces may be united The bones are then
bound together by osseous union, and are, of course, firmly locked;
they are no longer capable of the slightest movement one upon the
other; but this is no vast evil: many animals are now at work having
the smaller bones firmly united by osseous deposit Horses in that condition are far from useless, even for the highest purposes

The man whose animal gets ulceration of the hock-joint ought to
allow the injured quadruped even twelve months of uninterrupted rest
The first thing is to get the sufferer into slings; the earlier this is done
the better; it takes off the weight from the affected joint, relieves the
pain, and gives the system full opportunity to rectify the lesson To
draw blood to the part and so promote deposit, rub in, once every two

days, some of the embrocation recommended in the article on "Rheumatism," which is thus composed: of soap liniment, sixteen ounces; liquor ammonia, tincture of cantharides, and of laudanum, of each two ounces. There need be no fear of applying friction; the utmost pressure made upon an ulcerated joint can call forth no response. When the joint is embrocated, wrap the part loosely in flannel, using an elastic webbing to fasten the portion above and below the hock, and not tying any fastening around the painfully-diseased member; give three feeds of corn, a few old beans, and sweet hay for each day's support, while the treatment lasts.

The improvement will be denoted by the animal bearing upon the affected limb; after three months or longer, the slings may be removed; in another three months, the horse, should the pace be sound, may perform gentle work. However, the first three months must be reckoned from the date when the animal commenced to bear continuously on the ulcerated joint; in short, the slings are not to be removed until long after the quadruped has, by its carriage, declared them to be useless. Then, for the three subsequent months, the work must not be violent; time should be allowed for the union to be confirmed, for, among the many diseases the horse is exposed to, there is not one more treacherous or more liable to relapse than occult spavin.

Such is all that is necessary for the treatment of this disorder; rest—perfect rest, with food capable of supporting nature in the reparative process—is everything which is absolutely necessary. A loose box even does injury, so entire must be the rest, which should be as near to stagnation as it is possible to make it. The embrocation is simply recommended to draw blood to the part, and promote the required deposition. One caution only is necessary—give no purgative; keep the bowels regular by means of cut grass and bran mashes.

If the above measures fail, as in the majority of cases they certainly will, nevertheless good will have been done by abating the violence of the ulcerative process. Before the last resort of all is adopted, another chance remains, which, as an experiment, is justifiable. Puncture the joint—a very small incision will be required; have the limb forcibly retracted or pulled backward; then inject, with a syringe having a fine point, about one ounce of dilute spirits of wine, in which is dissolved half a drachm

THE DISEASED BONES OF THE HOCK. THE DARK PLACE INDICATES WHERE THE ULCERATION IS GOING FORWARD.

of iodine. Immediately afterward place the animal in slings, and apply cold water to the hock by means of the India-rubber bandage described in the preceding article. Keep the horse liberally so soon as the pulse becomes quiet, and do not allow it to leave bondage till the tread is firm; as exercise is endured, work may be very gradually resumed.

Remember, the above is proposed only as a last experiment; the design is to change the ulcerative action to one of a secretive character, and thereby promote union of the diseased bones. A trial of this kind has never been instituted; but, certainly, judging from the result of a similar operation upon the human subject, there are the best grounds for anticipating good effects. That it may be known where to make the puncture, a drawing made from the bones of a diseased hock is inserted on page 311; the darker line marks the place where the ulcerated surfaces existed, and into which the fluid should be injected. This, however, is so nice an operation that, although unattended with any immediate danger, none but a skilled anatomist should undertake it. In proper and judicious hands it is perhaps as safe, and more likely to be accompanied with benefit than the great majority of veterinary remedies.

RHEUMATISM.

This form of disease in the horse is commonly known as following more serious affections. After influenza it is very frequent; it is not rare as coming in the train of thoracic disorders; most important organs, being acutely affected, will leave it behind them. On rare occasions it may appear without any forerunner.

Its advent is announced by swelling about the joints, accompanied by the most painful lameness; the animal may not dare to put its foot to the ground. Often the disease flies about, now seizing upon one or two joints, next attacking the hitherto free members, and generally clinging to similar parts, as the hocks, knees, etc. Then it will return to its former abode—thus shifting about, to the torture of the animal and the confusion of him who may undertake its relief.

One almost constant symptom is an increase of synovia. For synovial membrane, whether in the sheaths of tendons or on the heads of bones, rheumatism always displays a marked partiality. This structure is, as has been already noticed, without sensation during health; in disease, however, its involvement communicates extreme agony. The afflicted horse stands with difficulty; its pulse and its breathing declare its sufferings—both are quick and jerking; the limbs may be greatly swollen; and the parts secreting joint-oil bulged out, soft, and puffy, from the increase of their contents.

No disease is accompanied with such long and extreme pain as rheumatism; the remedies, therefore, should be quick and effective. Procure

the steaming apparatus recommended for bronchitis ; fill the warm, loose box, into which the horse should be brought, with vapor ; while that is being accomplished, get ready the slings ;
put the belly-piece under the animal, and fix
them so as not to take the entire bearing
from the ground, but so as to relieve the diseased joints of some portion of their burden,
and allow the horse to rest its body when it
is disposed to repose.

Keep up the steam for one hour ; at the
end of that period, have several men ready
with dry cloths—wisps would be too exciting ; let the men wipe the horse quite dry,
with as little noise and as much speed as
possible? This over, order some of the as-

THE STEAMING APPARATUS USED IN
BRONCHITIS.

sistants to put on the hood and clothing, also wrapping the sound limbs in flannel ; the disengaged helpers are to go upon their knees and rub into and about the seat of disorder a liniment thus composed :—

Compound soap liniment	Sixteen ounces.
Liquor of ammonia	Two ounces.
Tincture of cantharides	Two ounces.
Tincture of opium	Two ounces.

When the liniment has been applied, incase the affected limbs in warm flannel.

Many persons are at a loss to comprehend this last direction ; it is easily accomplished. Have ready some rings of elastic webbing to fasten over the members ; also procure four pieces of flannel, each rather more than the length of a limb. To the small ends of two pieces of flannel, one yard and a half long, attach a band of broad, elastic webbing, and fix a buckle and strap at the other terminations ; at similar points of the other two pieces of flannel, only these last are to be two yards long, like-wise fix broad elastic bands, and also append a buckle and strap. Place the long pieces of flannel by the hind limbs ; put the shorter flannels by the fore legs ; buckle the straps, the fore ones over the withers, and the hind straps over the loins. This will keep the flannel up to its proper height ; fasten it with the rings of elastic webbing to the hoofs, while the assistants are wrapping it loosely round the limbs.

The horse being in the slings, no surcingle can be put on, nor is any needed. The animal with acute rheumatism is certain to stand quiet enough. So much being accomplished, give the horse a bolus formed of powdered colchicum, two drachms ; iodide of potassium, one drachm ; simple mass, a sufficiency.

These measures are to be taken regardless of the condition of the body; if the attack, however, follow another disease, the bodily support must not be too low. It should be all prepared or softened by the action of heat and water; the oats should be of the best description;

A HORSE DRESSED FOR RHEUMATISM.

they should be crushed and boiled; a few old beans, also boiled, may be added, and a malt mash occasionally will do no harm. To open the bowels, and likewise to allay excitement, give green-meat when required; but do not make a practice of allowing this sort of food in quantity, as it blows the animal out, weakens the digestion, and soon loses all laxative effect.

Next morning repeat the steaming, etc., and give a ball composed of a scruple of calomel and two drachms of opium; allow only five pounds of hay during the day. At night, again steam, etc., and give the ball which was recommended on the first occasion.

When the horse begins to bear upon its legs, should the liniment not have blistered the joints, the following may be applied with a soft brush, but without friction :—

Tincture of cantharides . . . . One ounce.
Camphorated oil . . . . Half an ounce.
Tincture of opium . . . . Half an ounce.

The horse may be of a full habit when affected; in that case, pursue the measures already recommended, but do not give the food before advised; instead, allow bran mashes twice a week, and a bundle of green-meat once a day, and sweet hay must make up the sustenance for twenty-four hours. Should the horse, however, appear to lose flesh and spirit, boiled corn must form a portion of the diet, and the quantity can be regulated only by him who has charge of the case

One caution must be given before concluding this article. A sick animal is very sensitive as to noises; a door banged to will excite the terror of the poor creature, which, probably, was half asleep, with the head hanging down. A loud word or an energetic action will not unseldom call forth symptoms of such alarm as may threaten, through their utter recklessness, to demolish the structure in which the horse is confined. For these, if from no purer motives, respect the sufferings and wisely try to soothe the animal. As the creature is devoid of reason to shape its fears, approach it noiselessly; speak softly at first; ascertain—although the eye be closed—by the motion of the ears, whether your voice is heard. Then lay the hand upon the neck and gently caress the sick body; after that you may do what you please, so nothing be very sudden or very loud.

Such slight considerations will not be thrown away, even in a medical point of view. A moment of excitement may do the injury which no physic will remove; nay, in critical stages, many a life has been lost from want of thought in the attendants about a diseased horse.

DISTENTION OF SYNOVIAL MEMBRANE—WIND-GALLS

Man treats the horse after a strange fashion. He buys the animal for a large sum, because it possesses some particular quality; but, hardly has he obtained it, before he behaves as though he desired only to destroy the property he has so dearly purchased. A horse, for private use, is generally bought for its beauty; in a short time afterward it is sold as having become too deformed for its master's service. A year or two commonly suffices to spoil the most perfect animal. Many are ruined in their colthood; many more are made worthless by the trainer Of all creation, the horse is most abused. So universal is this custom that the marks of ill usage are in the market even regarded as if they were natural consequences. Those affections designated **wind-galls** are generally lightly esteemed by most horsemen when the animal is required for actual service—as hunting, racing, coaching, etc.

Such marks, however, are evidences of hard work having been performed. They are not natural formations; but are blemishes, which man, in his consideration for a dumb servant, is pleased to make light of. They do not generally impede the action—and lameness is the only fact a true horseman cares to notice. He will not stay to inquire what must have been the kind of work which could occasion the **synovial**

membrane to bulge out upon a living body. He does not care to ask whether Nature, when deformity first appeared, instituted the fact without intention. He will not condescend to question whether every unnatural appearance is not designed to be a warning. But he views windgalls rather as a proof that the poor animal exhibiting them is a seasoned horse, and, therefore, is bettered by the distortion of a sensitive structure.

Wind-galls are the result of severe work. The back sinews are incased in a fine sheath which contains synovia, or, as it is commonly termed, "joint oil." The use of the synovia is to facilitate the motions of the two great flexor tendons one upon the other; so, when the pace is too fast or the labor too energetic, the delicate membrane which secretes the synovia becomes irritated. The consequence of irritation is increased secretion. More joint oil is poured forth than the natural sac can contain. The membrane, therefore, bags out at those parts which are weakest. Two such places are situated above the fetlock and one below it. The localities, with the size of the tumors, as they generally are exhibited, the reader will find delineated in the following engravings.

THE SITUATIONS AND SHAPES OF WIND-GALLS.   WIND-GALLS, AS THEY APPEARED TO THE AUTHOR, UPON DISSECTION.

Wind-galls generally appear on the hind leg. They used to be regarded as swollen bursæ; but Mr. Varnell, Assistant Professor at the Royal Veterinary College, by careful dissection, first pointed out their real character. He proved them to be synovial enlargements; and the writer, benefiting by Mr. Varnell's instruction, has verified the fact.

Very slight physiological knowledge was required to detect they were not bursæ. Bursæ are little round sacs, secreting a fluid like synovia, but always placed so as to facilitate motion. Now, wind-galls appear close to a synovial sheath ordained to serve the same purpose. They, moreover, start up in the hollow between the flexor tendons and the suspensory ligament, in which arteries, veins, nerves, and absorbents reside. The merit in discovering they had been misnamed was, perhaps, small; but the credit of demonstrating what they actually were—which demanded a more elevated talent—remains with Mr. Varnell.

Wind-galls are fond of the hind leg; or rather, the hinder limbs do the heaviest portion of the horse's work; therefore these deformities are commonly found on those members. There may be one or three on both sides of each leg: they generally are quiescent; but occasionally they prove wind-galls to be something more than the simple blemishes which man is pleased to esteem them. After a hard run it is not unusual to hear a huntsman complain that the wind-galls have disappeared and the back sinews of his hunter have become puffy. When that occurs, the entire sheath suffers excessive irritation, and has enlarged. The horse is then very lame, but a day or two of rest reduces the sudden enlargement, and the animal recovers its soundness.

THE DISAPPEARANCE OF WIND-GALLS AND THE PUFFINESS OF THE SYNOVIAL MEMBRANE, PROPER TO THE FLEXOR TENDONS, WHICH ENSUES UPON EXCESSIVE LABOR.

Sometimes, however, repeated irritation starts up a new action; the secretion becomes turbid, displays enormous floating threads of cartilage and occasional sanguineous infiltration; the sac enlarges; the walls begin to thicken; the tumor feels less pulpy and more firm; it grows harder. First becomes cartilage, and ultimately may be converted into bone. Mr. Gowing, of Camden Town, has a fine specimen of this species of disease.

During these changes the animal is very lame; yet wind-galls are so lightly esteemed by horsemen as scarcely to lessen the price of a steed; they are, in general, accounted hardly worth mentioning, although men have been known to be strangely anxious to have them removed. This, however, is not easy to bring about; all the common methods are worse than useless; the only treatment which promises any benefit is the application of pressure. Fold a piece of soft rag several times; saturate the rag with water; lay upon the wetted rag one drachm each of opium and of camphor; put these upon the enlargement. Upon the moistened rag place a piece of cork big enough to cover the wind-gall, and of such a thickness as may be necessary; above the cork lace on a vulcanized India-rubber bandage. Constant and equal pressure will by these means be kept up; however, mind the groom be strictly ordered to take the bandage off the leg the last thing when the horse leaves the stable, and to put it on again immediately on the animal's return; otherwise, the proprietor may chance to enter the building and find his steed without an application, which, to be beneficial, should be perpetually worn.

Such is the history and the occasional termination of wind-galls. What kind of man is he who, when purchasing a horse, can confidently assert the animal will not exhibit the worst stage of the affection? A horse displaying wind-galls is prepared for the advent of the more serious form of disease; still, horsemen will persist in deeming synovial enlargements a trivial affair, when seen in the body of a creature whose utility resides in its power to move the limbs with agility.

BOG SPAVIN.

Bog spavin is a mark which man makes to signalize his authority over breathing flesh; man, in his stupidity, will form notions of what animals should be; he will not learn from nature. Thus the horse, which is made up of timidity and affection, he loves to chronicle as fierce, fiery, noble, and courageous; he talks largely of having mastered such or such a creature; he boasts highly of having laid whip and spur to a "brute" which, had he courted with gentleness, and wooed with sympathy, might not have been subdued so quickly, but assuredly would have been attached to him for life.

The hocks suffer severely through such erroneous opinions. These convictions are widely spread and influence every horseman; they control the breaker, who acts as though he had a wild beast to conquer into a show of submission, not to train a living animal which is naturally willing, only afraid to submit. Instead of courting such a being, the bit, the lash, and the cold steel are brought to bear upon a frame every fiber of which already quivers with alarm; many a colt, consequently, is ruined by the breaker. The creature is pulled up with a tug at the reins; and pain never yet enlightened an understanding; the horse is

forced to do what he would cheerfully perform, if man would only take necessary trouble to communicate his wishes to a creature which, not comprehending words, is naturally somewhat slow to interpret heavy chastisement.

The breaker, however, is considered equal to his office, if he be a light weight and a very resolute man. The young colt is sprained and jarred in every possible manner; it is at last returned to its master more than half broken—in the literal sense—for the seeds have been sown which, in time, will assuredly crop into a host of virulent diseases.

BOG SPAVIN, OR DISTENTION OF THE PRINCIPAL SYNOVIAL MEMBRANE OF THE HOCK-JOINT.

This affection is an increase of synovia in the upper or chief joint of the hock; it lies upon the most inward and forward portion of that part. The increase of the contents causes the membrane to bulge out after the manner represented in the wood-cut on page 318.

It is produced by repeated shocks to the limb, and in this respect resembles wind-galls; though situated in a different locality, it is also liable to the same changes. In short, the affections are the same, and are dissimilar only with regard to their relative situation.

Bog spavin is thought slightly of by professed horsemen; however, the reader must ask himself, if it be viewed as no deterioration, can it be also regarded as a recommendation? Is a blemished leg, or a limb with disease, which is liable to assume an aggravated type, properly considered a sound member? The writer thinks not. Bog spavin does not, in its ordinary stage, lame the horse; but can such an unnatural enlargement add to the pleasure of the animal's existence? Were pain in man judged of entirely as it affected the walk of the human being, the disorders of how many people would the doctor esteem of little consequence! Such a standard of agony is ridiculous. It is most difficult to say when no anguish is felt by the life which is denied the faculty of announcing its sensations through the medium of speech.

THOROUGH-PIN.

This disease is so called, because in some cases it pierces right through the thinnest part of the hind leg, or appears on either side immediately before the point of the hock. It, however, is often single. It is rarely present without bog spavin; and in every instance which the author has examined, it communicated with the large synovial articulation of the joint.

THOROUGH-PIN.

It is provoked by the same causes as generate bog spavin; it is similar to that disorder in not being generally accompanied by lameness, and in being liable to the same fearful changes. Pressure and rest are the best remedies; pressure, applied after the manner recommended for wind-galls, may in some cases answer. The bog spavin and the **thorough-pin**, however, should not in every case be treated at the same time; as a general rule, it is prudent only to attack one affection by means of an India-rubber bandage. This should be so cut as to release the bog spavin from all pressure; and where the slightest uneasiness is evinced, all bandages should be instantly removed, while the corks and cloths—employed as for wind-galls—are taken off the thorough-pin.

It is never well to attempt to cure the bog spavin first; the treatment

ought always to commence with the thorough-pin; therefore, for a horse
which will not endure the bandage, a truss must be procured from the
instrument-maker. The truss is of the ordinary description, only adapted
to bear upon the parts. This will probably act with efficacy equal to
the bandage. When the truss has performed its office, then a perfect
India-rubber bandage may be safely applied. Only, mind and also
employ with the last the corks and cloths; else, when endeavoring to
remove one disorder, you may reproduce another. Watch the animal
while wearing the bandage; on the slightest change, either in habit or
appearance, remove the India-rubber. Should the pressure affect the
skin, (as it will in certain cases,) rags, thoroughly wetted, should be
wrapped round the hock before lacing the bandage up. If the rags
appear to be of no avail, it is better to forbear for a time, and to renew
the attempt hereafter.

The horse which exhibits bog spavin and thorough-pin also generally shows wind-galls on the hind legs. Let the reader consider the

hard usage the limb must have undergone before
it could have become thus deranged. Here is a
specimen, demonstrating the connection which exists between thorough-pin and bog spavin. It was
made in consequence of Mr. Varnell having informed the author that thorough-pin was a bulging
out of the synovial sheath, proper to the flexor
tendon; and was not, as is generally taught and
credited, an enlarged bursa. The author found
them to be in accordance with the description he
had received: the enlargement called thorough-

DISSECTION OF THOROUGH-PIN
AND BOG SPAVIN, DEMON-
STRATING THE JUNCTION OF
THE TWO AFFECTIONS.

pin, and the synovial membrane of the hock, had united, and free communication existed between them, in the joint which the writer examined.

Nature formed the synovial cavity of the joint as a distinct and
separate part. It is usual for teachers to promulgate a maxim that
Nature is all-wise. Man, however, it appears, can violently disarrange
her provisions; yet, by his fellow-men, he is accounted to have done no
wrong who destroys the harmony of Nature. Thorough-pin is not, in
popular estimation, essentially unsoundness. A horse thus disfigured is
believed, nay, professionally pronounced to be, perfect, although two distinct parts are battered into one. If two are beneficial, why was one
only created? The horse may not be lame; but, granting Nature to be
all-wise, must not the uses for which the limb was designed be injured?
The question is not, whether an animal trots sound; but it is, whether
it really is sound. What sane man would assert such to be the case,
where the anatomical structures have been disorganized?

CAPPED KNEE.

Capped knee, in the fore limb, answers to bog spavin in the hind leg; the diseases are alike in most respects. Both affect the principal articulation of a complicated joint; both may be provoked by the like causes; but the fore leg, being less exposed to shocks than the hinder member, must have been much abused before it could become thus deformed.

Blows, also, are common originators of capped knee. This disorder is likewise peculiar for a course it takes. The fluid within the swollen joint is, upon excitement, secreted in such quantity as to tighten the enlargement. Ultimately it lames the horse, and at length bulges out, or points, after the manner of an abscess. If let alone, it would burst. Much of the surrounding parts would have to be absorbed or would be effectually destroyed before such a termination could ensue. The life would be endangered, or a lasting blemish would be left behind. To prevent this, the surgeon draws the skin to one side, and, holding the

THE SYNOVIAL MEMBRANE OF THE KNEE-JOINT ENLARGED.

point of his lancet upward, opens the capped knee upon its lower surface. A quantity of synovia, more or less in a turbid state, escapes, and an open joint remains. For the treatment of this contingency, the reader must turn to "Open Joint." (*Injuries.*)

Capped knee is, by certain persons, viewed as a trivial accident. Generally, however, it is regarded in a more serious light, because it is *more conspicuous* than bog spavin. We also should object to it, because, while liable to the same changes as wind-galls, etc., it is also likely to expose the horse to an open joint. It is, like wind-galls and bog spavin, to be reduced by pressure, though sometimes pressure will call up aggravated symptoms. Rest is the best treatment; during the rest pressure may be safely applied. Pressure does not answer, however, while the limb is exposed to the irritation of work. The horse must be thrown up during treatment, and gently used after the animal has been patched up or "cured."

CAPPED HOCK.

When an injury is formed near an important part, Nature is so conservative of her creature's welfare that she always has some means ready to preserve the utility of the structure. Thus when, from external violence, the hock becomes capped, or a swelling like to that represented in the following engraving ensues, to prevent the joint being thrown out of use Nature allows the skin to enlarge. The cap of a hock, originally, was a bursa. A bursa is a little bladder or round sac, formed of the finest possible membrane, and filled with a fluid similar to joint oil. Its use is to facilitate motion; hence it eases the tightened skin over the points of the bony hock. But when it becomes deranged and swollen, the skin, which was dense, hard, and solid, stretches so as to cover the increase of bulk.

The tumor, however, having been produced, may in time subside, should the injury which provoked it not be repeated. Too often, however, the cause springs from motives over which the animal has no control; and the violence being renewed again and again, the swelling enlarges, and that which was soft and pulpy at first becomes hard to the feel, while all

CAPPED HOCK.

THE LARGEST SPECIMEN OF CAPPED HOCK WHICH
THE AUTHOR HAS MET WITH.

sensation of fluid disappears. The provocative being repeated, the part first grows firm, then solid, while its bulk also enlarges to a fearful magnitude. There appears to be no limit to the size; but the largest the author has encountered was nineteen inches in its greatest circumference, and seriously interfered with progression. Above, on the right hand, is a portrait of the tumor.

These unsightly growths have two causes—the ignorance of the groom and the timidity of the animal. To speak of the last first: Dogs will dream; often, as they lie before the fire, they work their legs and utter suppressed noises, being at the time soundly asleep. Dogs also have imagination. Almost everybody must have remarked the dog slink away from some object which is to be indistinctly seen in the dusk of evening. Nobody, however, seems to have credited the horse with either of these faculties. Because it is of service to man, it is appropriated, and the attributes belonging to the creature are overlooked; the groom locks the stable door, and, having bedded the horses down, leaves them in the dark, "comfortable" for the night. One dreams—awakens in terror, similar to that which causes children to start out of their sleep with terrible crying. The hind legs are the means of defense with the horse; it has no other, for it seldom, and not habitually, employs its teeth. The animal, in alarm, begins kicking, for terror becomes powerful as the reason diminishes. Animals have passions; these man can, in himself, subdue with reason; but the poor horse has no reason to restrain its emotions. Fear, once awakened, unopposed, possesses it; it begins to kick before it knows why. Bodies of men are exposed to panics. Can we wonder, therefore, at a timid and unreasoning animal being subject to the same influences? The kicking commenced, terror spreads; and a whole stable full of horses, each chained to its stall, each alone, forbidden the consolation of society, and prevented from scampering from the unknown horror, takes up the action; thus thirty or forty horses may be heard, in the depth and darkness of a night, kicking at the same time. The hind legs, when forcibly projected, are apt to hit the point of the hock; the bursa there developed is injured by the blow, and a capped limb is the consequence.

Another cause is kicking while in harness. This habit is always attributed to vice: to speak of vice as associated with the ideas of a simple animal is purely ridiculous. Fear is a much more probable cause, if man would only expand his understanding to comprehend the motives likely to actuate an unreasoning creature; vice is far too heroic an impulse, far too human a failing, for the horse to embody. Fear is essentially an animal passion; that some mighty influence agitates the quadruped, when it begins to kick in harness, is proved by the serious accidents the horse encounters through this habit. No life can be careless of its own existence; all creatures are conservatives where their own being is concerned. Would mankind only admit this fact, and seek to gain the confidence of, as they now labor to establish authority over, the horse, gentle words, spoken when the impulse was awakened, might reassure the animal, and would thus frequently save the owner from impending danger.

A third cause is lazy drivers riding on cart-horses, when unhooked, as leaders of the wagon; the poles, called spreaders, which keep the chains asunder, frequently hang so low that, at every movement of the leg, they strike the point of the hock. The uneven paving of some stables is likewise said to produce the disease; in short, anything which may cause the point of the calcis to suffer violence will produce a capped hock.

The cure for capped hock has been differently directed. Some hobble the hind legs of the horse, to prevent its kicking in the night; some fasten a chain and a log to one hind limb, for the same purpose; others suspend a piece of loose cloth at the back of the horse; but the best plan is always to leave a lantern lighted in the stable. The power to see around reassures timidity, while darkness is an awful instigator of terror; horses often fly back in their stalls, but never kick, during daylight.

Then, as to the cure: Such a tumor, when recent, is hot and somewhat painful; at this time, keep it wet with cold water or with a lotion formed of spirits of wine and water in equal parts; when the tenderness has subsided, procure some men who want employment and have strong arms; set these fellows to rub the cap of the hock constantly, and the tumor, in three or four days, or in less time, will have disappeared.

Should the enlargement, however, have become hard, the knife then must be employed; the horse must be cast, and the substance must be

THE SKIN FROM BENEATH WHICH THE TUMOR OF CAPPED HOCK HAS BEEN REMOVED.

carefully dissected out without opening the sac. This being done, remove none of the skin; leave that bagging about the hock; simply treat it with a lotion composed of chloride of zinc one grain, to water one ounce, and the integument will contract. Ultimately there will remain no more than will be required to cover the part, whereas, if any be taken away, the wound, which in these cases never heals quickly, will be very long before it closes, and, in proportion to the skin which has been removed, there will remain a lasting blemish.

There is another caution we have to give the reader before leaving this subject; let no advice persuade, no temptation induce him to puncture, seton, or merely to open capped hock. The membrane lining the swelling is, when diseased, so extremely sensitive that the writer has known the lives of animals endangered by these so-called remedies. The author, moreover, never knew the enlargement to be much reduced by these means; neither has it been the author's lot to witness much good follow the application of blisters. No; extirpation is the only remedy, and it should be accomplished without puncturing the sac; this is as safe an operation as there is in the entire range of veterinary surgery. There is neither nerve, muscle, membrane, vessel, nor any important structure to avoid; with ordinary care, the removal is most easy. There is but one thing annoying connected with the business, and that is, the length of time which the healing of a necessary wound, made upon a point of motion, almost invariably occupies.

CAPPED ELBOW.

This is very common, especially among cart-horses; it is attributed to the calkin of the fore foot; to the point of the hind hoof; or to a stable floor, thinly bedded, and composed of sharp stones. So, likewise, blows with the butt-end of the whip will induce it; but the harness probably guards the elbow, which therefore can be struck only in exceptional cases.

It consists of a bursa, which, as in the former instance, has been injured, and has consequently enlarged; in appearance and in its subsequent course it greatly resembles capped hock, from which it differs only in a greater liability to ulcerate and become sinuous when allowed to remain until it is of extreme magnitude. It is said to derive that unenviable peculiarity from being situated nearer to the center of circulation. Capped hock is so little disposed to take on such a form of disease that the author cannot remember having seen a case of the

A CAPPED ELBOW.

kind; with a tumor on the elbow, however, ulceration is unfortunately too common. That probability should forbid the owner to allow the tumor to attain any great size; when large, moreover, it is apt to encircle the elbow-joint, and then its size seems to render the removal apparently impossible. It, however, may be extirpated. All said of capped hock applies to capped elbow.

LUXATION OF THE PATELLA.

That is displacement of the whirl-bone of the stifle, (which answers to the knee-cap of the human being.) Such an accident, fortunately, few horses incur; there are many veterinary surgeons who, during a practice extending over many years, have not encountered a single case; whereas other gentlemen will have hardly started in their profession before **luxation of the patella** is submitted to their notice. It is not peculiar to any district, it is not confined to any special breed; it may affect all kinds of horses in all sorts of places; for it is produced more by the parsimony or the uncharitableness of mankind than by any fault in the structure of the animal.

In several localities throughout the country agriculturists, under the notion of saving money, determine to rear horses on short grass. The creatures are out in the fields during all kinds of weather; the body becomes debilitated under such a starvation system;- those parts which are naturally weak become weaker, while those structures which were originally endowed with strength grow comparatively stronger. The beautiful balance of nature is overthrown, and each portion becomes at discord with all the rest; any trivial disease may destroy the life thus at war within its own-dominion. Colts frequently exhibit luxation of the patella before they are broken; but it is always provoked by weakness, and commonly only seen where the management is faulty or. the food is stinted.

When the whirl-bone is displaced, it is always found as an unnatural lump upon the outer side of the thigh; it cannot, for three sufficient reasons, be drawn to the inner part of the leg. The inner condyle of the humerus, over which the patella plays, is sufficiently large to oppose any unnatural motion in that direction; the inner ligaments are the weakest, and are, therefore, most readily stretched in the outward direction; the circumstances permit the bone to be displaced from the inside of the leg. Then, moreover, the muscles are altogether more powerful upon the outer side. Any force acts more energetically as debility increases, and, to favor it, there is less resistance in the direction opposite to which the force pulls; for these reasons the bone is invariably luxated upon the outer side of the animal's haunch.

The symptoms denoting luxation of the patella are: the leg thrust out behind, and remaining fixed; the horse's entire frame is affected; the

head is erect; the muscles quiver; the pastern of the protruded leg is violently flexed; there is an unnatural swelling upon the outer and lower part of the buttock. If the animal be forced to move, it can only imperfectly hop upon three legs; such an accident may occur at any time, and never be repeated. It may, however, become so common as to be mistaken for a species of habit; for luxation of the patella, when by frequency confirmed, will take place upon the slightest possible cause.

THE PATELLA, OR WHIRL-BONE DISPLACED.

In stinted colts the most trivial motion will often give rise to this accident; the creature can hardly move without its leg being thrust out behind it. The cure is, in these cases, anything which may flurry the animal. A noise, made by moving the hand quickly and rather energetically from side to side within a hat, the crack of a whip, or any sudden and loud sound, will occasion the bone to return, with apparent ease and the utmost rapidity, to its natural situation. The colt, however, may the next moment exhibit the misfortune which, in young life, can only be cured by kindly treatment and liberal sustenance.

Probably the author will best describe the nature of the affection in old animals, by narrating a case which a few years ago happened to himself.

At the request of a friend he visited one of those auction marts for the sale of horses which in London are somewhat notorious. The object of his visit being, if possible, to purchase, his attention was directed to certain animals. As usual, a glance enabled him to pass by all the marked "lots," and he had reached the third stable, when his eye rested on a horse which seemed wrongly placed among such companions. It was lively, young, clean legged, short backed, well ribbed up—in fact, one of those rare creatures every inch of which seems made for service. The height was fifteen hands three inches; the color was a dark brown The author tried in vain to discover if it had any "vice." It appeared perfectly quiet. He examined the feet; he could detect no unsoundness He went to the office and ascertained the price—twenty-four guineas! It was too cheap! Such an animal would be thrown away if sold for fifty guineas. "Would they give a warranty?" "It was not their custom to give any warranty." "Had the horse megrims?" "No." "Would they grant a trial?" "It was contrary to their rules." Still the author wanted to buy; he would "deposit the cash, and if all proved right take the horse." "They never granted trials; but there stood the owner—the writer could talk to him "

. The person alluded to was lounging close to the writer's elbow, and was habited in that half-blackleg, half-blackguard costume which characterizes the low London dealer. The contemplation of this individual did not improve any previous opinion of the matter. However, the man's eye was firmly fixed upon that of his would-be customer, and, rather than encounter a disturbance, the author approached the fellow, to whom he repeated his request. The answers given were too similar to those received from the clerk for the likeness to be purely accidental. The dealer nevertheless saw a trial was imperative to convert the inquirer into a purchaser; and, rightly judging from appearance that there was little of the jocky in the writer's attainments, reluctantly consented to afford the demanded test.

The horse was speedily between the shafts of a very light gig. The man took the reins, placed the whip behind him, and we moved off at the gentlest of possible trots No objection was taken to the pace; it gave the better opportunity of examining into the soundness. All was right in that particular. The steps were loud and even. After some time, during which the man frequently inquired if "I had had trial enough *now?*" we left the paved streets, but no entreaty could cause the pace to be improved. At length we came to a rise in the ground, and, as it was approached, my companion turned sulky. Hardly had the horse began to ascend the inequality, before it suddenly stood quite still The gig was brought to with a jerk, which almost threw both of its occupants upon the footboard. The author was the first out of the vehicle; there stood the horse—the leg out, the foot flexed, the head erect—displaying the evident symptom of luxation of the patella.

An inn was fortunately near the spot. To the yard of the hostelry the animal was with difficulty led. Being sheltered in an unoccupied building, a groom was placed at the horse's head. A long rope, thrown over a beam, was fastened to the fetlock of the protruded limb. By this rope the owner stood; and while he pulled the leg upward and forward, the writer was by the quarters, with both hands pushing the luxated bone inward. The patella soon slipped into its situation; and the horse was afterward sold by auction for four guineas more than the author had refused to pay for it.

Mr. Spooner, in his lectures at the Royal Veterinary College, always

THE MANNER OF RETURNING THE PATELLA OF AN ADULT ANIMAL.

recommends his hearers, after this bone has been returned, to place an assistant by the horse's side, with strict orders to hold the patella in its situation for some hours. Such advice is most excellent; to which we can only add, perfect rest, and as much strengthening food as the animal can consume. If such measures are pursued, and the horse be not used for six weeks subsequent to the accident, there need be little fear entertained of a second luxation of the patella.

BLOOD SPAVIN.

This disease is, happily, with the past: the writer has not seen an instance. Neither had the late Mr. Percival—the highest veterinary authority—after a life laboriously passed in scientific research. It is described to have existed as varicosity of the vena saphena, where the vessel crosses the hock. The cause is said to have been bog spavin when of magnitude: this, it is asserted, opposed circulation within the vessel; but the author conjectures the swelling must have assumed the callous state, before it could have offered sufficient resistance to the flow of blood to occasion the vessel to enlarge or to become varicose.

There is no cure for such a disease. The knife may remove the deformity; but a larger blemish was often left as the consequence of the operation. Should such a case be known to any of the present readers, the author would advise the enlargement should be left alone, and trust placed in the absorbing powers of nature for its removal.

A BLOOD SPAVIN, AS IT IS REPORTED TO HAVE ONCE EXISTED.

CHAPTER XIII.

THE FEET—THEIR ACCIDENTS AND THEIR DISEASES.

LAMENESS.

OF all inventions intended to mitigate the sufferings of the horse, none, perhaps, is so generally useful as the foot-bath; certainly, not one is so decidedly beneficial in its operation. It consists merely of a wooden or iron trough, one foot deep; the shoes of the animal should, if possible, be taken off before the hoof is allowed to tread within the

A READY MEANS OF SOFTENING THE HORN, WHERE PRESSURE OF THE HOOF AGGRAVATES THE LAMENESS.

bath; or, if such a measure be not possible, then the burden of the horse's body should be counterpoised by means of weights. This precaution is always prudent, for, should the shod horse occasion fracture or breakage, an alarm might be excited which probably would ever after prevent the employment of the foot-bath with the same quadruped.

The water should always be mixed without the building; it is never well to excite an animal's fears by allowing it to witness unnecessary preparation. The author is fully aware that most people assert the horse has a very limited comprehension: so it may have; but it has an active terror, which is apt to misconstrue the simplest of motives. Whoever has seen the busy eye of the quadruped watching all that takes

(330)

place around it, and noting every triviality whenever any unusual movement gives intimation to the animal that something is about to be attempted, will readily allow the need there is for excessive caution. The
horse may comprehend nothing, but it is not, therefore, the less to be
propitiated. Its terror has to be soothed and its confidence has to be
gained; the last is soonest won by avoiding anything which possibly
might excite the first

Always have the heat of the water ascertained by a thermometer.
Sensation is only a relative test with regard to the presence or absence
of warmth; were it not so, the coarse hand of a groom, nevertheless,
might easily endure that degree of temperature which should pain the
foot and leg of a horse Let the fluid in the first instance stand at 70°;
after the animal has entered the bath, gradually and without noise increase the temperature up to 90°.

At that standard the water ought to be maintained; the hoof should
remain soaking from four to six hours at each operation; the groom,
doubtless, will complain of having frequently to fetch warm water, and
when not so employed, of being obliged to watch a thermometer; but
the present book is not written to please the likings of any individual.
To contribute to the welfare of the horse is the object of the writer;
that he has not unnecessarily imposed an irksome duty upon any human
being, the purpose for which the bath is introduced into the stable should
be sufficient evidence

The horse's hoof is of considerable thickness; it is far from unusual
with stablemen to saturate the healthy hoof with various greasy preparations; therefore it will require some time before the heat and water
can soften that which is, as it were, prepared to resist their action. The
hoof should be rendered perceptibly soft when the object is to relieve a
painful **lameness**; the warmth and moisture should not only saturate
the covering to the foot, but should also soothe the internal structures.
The pressure of the horn may thus be mitigated, and the deep-seated
inflammation likewise be ameliorated

When the bath is removed, the foot should not be left exposed to the
air, as the horn then quickly dries; it soon becomes harsh and brittle.
In this condition, it is likely to do more injury to the sensitive parts
than good was anticipated as the consequence of its immersion. The
hoof, when taken from the water, should be incased in warm and air-
proof bandages—the intention being to retain the heat, while evaporation is prevented   The bandages likewise answer another purpose;
they protect the foot, which, being without a shoe, and covered by horn
that has been deprived of its resistant property, is therefore much exposed to accidents.

To obtain the full benefit of the bath, the foot should enter it night and morning; the animal should be subjected to its operation for at least four hours each time, and the ingenuity ought to be exerted to prevent the hoof from becoming dry in the interim. Perhaps nothing is better for this purpose than the leather case, which is lined with sponge, and which can be procured of most tradesmen who deal in veterinary instruments; it is made to fit the foot, also to envelop the pastern. The bottom portion is formed of the stoutest leather, and will afford all desirable protection; while the sponge will retain the moisture, which this material permits to be renewed, should circumstances, such as the heat of the hoof or the warmth of the weather, cause the fluid to evaporate. However, such additions must always be made with warm, cold water being unsuited for the purpose.

These particulars have been thus fully detailed because lameness constitutes no inconsiderable portion of equine misery, and because such ailments are more frequently encountered than special forms of disease. To judge quickly and surely of such affections proves in no small degree veterinary proficiency; in every shade of lameness, the gentleman, unless more than usually practiced in such ailments, had better be guided by an educated opinion. Where it is possible to mistake another's misery, it displays no boldness to risk chances upon our own judgment.

Lameness is simply the difference of bearing cast, during progression, upon the several legs. Pain in the joints, bones, or tendons is most severe. It is even more terrible when inflammation of such structures is confined within the horny hoof; of this torture man can know nothing—he may rest the angry limb, may recline the body, or may seek consolation in friendly converse and in mental diversion. From all the higher pleasures the horse is excluded. It cannot rest the leg; and the instinctive dread which the sick animal displays of being unable to rise again prevents the quadruped seeking that relief a change of posture might afford.

The horse always stands when seriously diseased; often the erect position is continued to the last, for the sufferer ceases to maintain it only with the relinquishment of life. During severe lameness in one foot, the animal seldom lies down; it stands and stands, often for months. How the limbs must ache! Yet the relief which the slightest motion might induce is avoided with the tenacity which pain begets when operating upon excessive timidity. Often one spot is occupied for months! During this tedious period one foot is held from the earth. The mind shrinks from conjecturing the torture which could prompt such an act; the reason retreats from contemplating the agony by which the deed can alone be occasioned; we shudder as the imagination remotely pictures the pains by which it must be accompanied! Yet who has been much among stables, and has not witnessed many such sights?

It requires small knowledge to recognize those lamenesses to which the heavy breed of horses is particularly exposed. Agony, being excessive, always obliges this species of animal to indicate the limb, or to attract the attention of the spectator toward it. These creatures, when thus affected, if compelled to move, hop onward upon three legs; the weight is never thrown upon the foot which has been severely injured.

Illustrating this subject is the annexed figure of a horse which has been hurt upon the off fore foot; the figure is supposed to be desirous of progressing, or to be in the act of bringing the hind limbs forward. The entire weight having for a certain space to rest upon a single support, some time is spent in accurately balancing the body before this action is hazarded. The slightest mistake would

THE MANNER IN WHICH THE HORSE PROGRESSES WHEN ONE FORE LEG IS INCAPACITATED.

necessitate a fall, of which it has been observed the sick horse is endued with a particular dread. Therefore, after a certain time spent in preparation, the legs are, with much muscular exertion, lifted from the ground, and the sufferer hops onward.

The wretchedness of the quadruped, however, is not complete until one or both hind legs are implicated. From some hidden cause, the anguish of the animal, great as it may be, is not perfected while the lameness resides in front. The horse, suffering in a fore limb, has even laid on flesh during the period of enforced idleness. But when the posterior extremities are injured, the constitution is involved. The body wastes rapidly, and every fiber within the huge framework seems to quiver with sensibility.

If the creature, thus disabled in one leg, is obliged to advance, the chief difficulty is to so place the sound limb upon the earth that the balance shall not be destroyed. There are the two fore legs to rest upon, and the head to act as a kind of counterpoise; therefore there is little impediment to raising of the trunk; but the obstacle consists in the peril to be surmounted when the sound member reaches the ground. A certain shock has then to be

THE MANNER OF ADVANCING THE HIND MEMBERS WHEN ONE POSTERIOR FOOT IS INJURED.

sustained, and the fear apparently is lest the slightest want of preparation should bring the body to the earth.

The next motion delineated necessitates the greatest care and the
mightiest exertion. There are several signs which declare such to be
the case. To advance the two sound

A HORSE, HAVING ONE HIND LEG RENDERED
USELESS, BY A SUDDEN EFFORT ADVANCES
THE FORE LIMBS.

fore legs is an effort of despair always
preceded by a pause. During the time
the feet are from the earth, the entire
weight, unrelieved by the slightest counterpoise, must be supported by one sound
limb. The muscles on that side have
to raise the trunk, or to perform double
labor, for the step invariably is a species
of leap. The body has not only to be
lifted, but the strain must be maintained
to continue or rectify the balance. A
pause of more than ordinary length declares the magnitude of the approaching
struggle. The teeth are clinched; the head is thrown backward; a deep
inspiration is inhaled; the muscles are powerfully excited; and, with a
spasmodic suddenness, the feet are projected onward.

The step accomplished, the breath is released in a kind of heavy sigh;
the animal remains quiescent for a brief space, as though the greatness of
the late effort had partially deprived it of consciousness. It is, however,
an exceptional case for a horse of the lighter breed to be thus "hopping
lame." In all animals, nevertheless, lameness is a heavy affliction; in
all, the manner of progressing is characteristic of pain. Suffering, more
or less intense, is declared every time the injured foot touches the
ground.

One fore foot being affected, the head and body drop, or slightly sink,

A HORSE, IN THE ACT OF TROTTING, BEARS THE
WEIGHT UPON THE SOUND FORE FOOT.

whenever the sound member rests upon
the earth. This peculiarity a little reflection will readily account for. Of
course the desire of a lame animal is to
spare the disabled foot as much as possible. The injured part scarcely touches
the earth, before, with an effort which
raises the head and body, it is lifted
again into the air. The least possible
burden is thrown upon the disabled foot.

However, the weight must be cast somewhere; and by how much less
one leg has to carry, so much more must the other support. Conse-

quently, when the sound hoof comes to the ground, the extra burden rests upon it; the head and body perceptibly drop, and the footfall emits an emphatic sound, the accent of which is increased by the all but inaudible tread of the opposite member.

The indication, however, is in some measure reversed when the lameness is situated behind. The movements of the head no longer accompany those of the fore legs; for, although the head be not steady, it evidently is not influenced by the forward members. If, however, the motion be closely observed, it will be found to be regulated by the movements of the posterior extremities, only with a difference. When the sound hind limb rests upon the earth, the head is raised; but the sinking or elevation of the whole body is never so marked as it is in the previous case

A HORSE, BEING LAME IN ONE HIND FOOT, RESTS THE WEIGHT UPON THE SOUND LIMB WHILE TROTTING.

of anterior injury. The movements characteristic of posterior lameness are, however, well shown in the haunches. When the sound limb reaches the ground, the hind portion of the body obviously drops upon that side; when the painful member is caught up, that side of the haunch on which resides the disabled foot is also jerked upward.

There are other sorts of lameness to be described. A horse is sometimes returned by the smith lame all round. The gait is peculiar, because it is caused by the shoes being too small or tight. It has been likened to skating; and the author thinks the term so applicable that he has no desire to change it. There can, however, be then no difficulty in detecting the cause of the affliction. The horse was, a short time before, sent to the forge a sound animal, and it has been returned a positive cripple.

It is lamentable to remark the number of horses which are driven through the streets of London in a disabled condition. People appear to be without feelings or recognitions when the sufferings of horse-flesh are before them. An animal with scarcely a sound limb, or else "hopping lame," may frequently be seen, in broad daylight, attached to some gentleman's carriage or tradesman's cart, to a hired vehicle or a costermonger's "all sorts." From the highest to the lowest, all are equally disgraced; the toil of a life seems incapable of purchasing a day's commiseration. A little forbearance might be a profitable investment in these cases; but no person seems able to keep a horse and to allow the animal a day of rest. So long as it can crawl, so long must patience work!

Other forms of suffering than those confined to the feet affect the progression of the horse; the "whirl-bone" or hip-joint is sometimes visited by ulceration. The symptoms then in a degree resemble those exhibited when occult spavin is present; the affected limb is, however, after touching the earth, caught up more sharply when the hip is diseased. The hoof, moreover, is presented more fully during motion in the last-mentioned affection. The best method, however, to ascertain the existence of the ulceration, is to hold some soft substance over the joint, then to strike it with a mallet; the shock will be communicated to the seat of lameness, and elicit an energetic response.

ACUTE LAMENESS CAUSED BY ULCERATION WITHIN THE HIP-JOINT.

Nothing can be done for such a condition; certain barbarities are proposed as experiments by continental veterinarians; but man obviously has no right to run chances with cruelty practiced upon breathing life. Hip-joint disease is decidedly incurable, and renders every step a separate agony.

The shoulder is a very favorite seat of injury with those who pretend to a knowledge of equine ailments; with such simple folk, if a horse be lame behind, the cause is always traced to the whirl-bone; should an animal have partially lost the use of an anterior limb, the injury is invariably found in the shoulder. The proof of their correctness is always exhibited in the lessened bulk of the parts referred to; but throw a limb out of use, as lameness in the horse always does, and the absorption of the whole extremity,

DRAGGING THE LIMB, THE INDICATION OF SHOULDER LAMENESS.

from want of exercise, naturally ensues.

The shoulder-joint is occasionally ulcerated; but more often disease is found upon the tendon of the flexor brachii, a muscle which, arising from the shoulder-joint, is of service in flexing the radius. In both cases the seeming length of the arm is remarkable; so also is the fixedness of the shoulder, and the obstinate refusal to advance or to flex the arm. The consequence is, that a horse with disease of the shoulder drags the limb, and never lifts the toe from the ground.

Ulceration is sometimes, though rarely, witnessed within the elbow-joint; a case of this description is recorded by the late W. Percival.

The chief symptom indicated subacute laminitis; the affection appeared gradually, and, without intermission, proceeded from simple bad to the very worst. The foot was, however, neither hot nor tender; by this sign the affection was distinguished from every form of fever in the feet, although the animal endeavored to bear only upon the heels of the fore extremities, and brought the hind legs as far under the body as was possible.

THE MANNER IN WHICH A HORSE HAVING ULCERATION OF THE ELBOW-JOINT ENDEAVORS TO PROGRESS.

Disease of the knee-joint is far from unusual. Mr. Cherry first directed attention to this fact; for, although dissection had frequently exhibited the carpal bones united, no one prior to Mr. Cherry drew any inference from the obvious indication.

Mr. Cherry describes the symptoms of the affection to be a stiffened protrusion of the fore leg, a long step, and an entire want of flexion in the diseased limb.

The author is unable to corroborate the above observations, possibly from his attention only having been directed to a few cases, and those not of a very acute character. The writer has, however, remarked, in certain instances, a perpetual knuckling over, without deposit in the knee or contraction in the tendons being present to account for the assumption of so uncomfortable an attitude. A want of power to bend the leg was noted in a few animals. Such horses either placed the limb outside the body when they lay down, or rested upon their sides; and lameness, though always present, was never witnessed in an aggravated shape.

No human lamentation could embody the deep sorrow which the crip-

THE HEALTHY LEG WHEN THE HORSE IS LYING DOWN.

THE NEAREST APPROACH MADE BY THE HEEL TO THE ELBOW IN CERTAIN CONDITIONS OF THE KNEE-JOINT.

pled condition of one leg occasions to the horse. The creature thereby is left a clog upon the earth. Its existence is deprived of the power which alone made it pleasant. Progression is laborious, and even rest is painful. The quadruped, thus disabled, stands motionless on one

22

spot; the head is lowered; the eyes are dejected; the breathing is fit-
ful; and the entire frame is apparently resigned to a huge sense of
degradation All the pride of life is lost.   Every trace of animation
has fled.   The animal evidently is, in its own conviction, useless and
disgraced.   A horse in such a state is, indeed, a melancholy spectacle;
and the feelings of that man who, understanding the image, can contemplate it unmoved are not to be envied.   Still, for how many years
has such a sight been before the eyes of mankind, without any individual
possessing the heart to interpret it!

Surely in all life there exists no other creature so willing to obey—
so happy in its labor, and so entirely obedient under command—which
is equally subjected to abuse! All the horse demands, in requital for its
manifold services, is food and shelter: kindness it does not insist upon,
and even bad usage it submits to.   For permission to live, it mildly
pleads; and in return for the liberality which merely supports the
strength, it contentedly resigns its body and relinquishes its intelligence.
Yet the natural wants are often stinted, although the toil is always bit-
terly exacted.   Surely in all life there exists no other creature equally
subjected to abuse!

The patience of the reader is solicited, while the author notices a
circumstance connected with the present subject, which has repeatedly
come under his observation.   Nothing can so entirely subdue the spirit
of a horse as an acute lameness: the suffering must be intense.   To a
distant conception of the agony endured man cannot excite his imagination.   Still, all of the effect upon the quadruped is not to be attributed
to that cause.   Other diseases are painful, but by them the constitution
is affected Lameness, generally, is a local affliction—it is not a general
involvement; it leaves the constitution healthy.   Yet a high-mettled, or
even a savage animal, is often quieted as by a charm when the foot is
disabled.   The intractable of the species has, by a sudden visitation of
this nature, been rendered passive.   The existence seems then to be
given up to misery, and the horse becomes disregardful of whoever
approaches it.   On such a sufferer expend but a little time striving to
convince it of your intent.   It is astonishing how quick affliction is to
comprehend humanity; and the painful foot is given up to man's desires
—nay, sometimes it is even advanced for his inspection.

The writer has applied to the crippled feet of horses certain remedies
which must have augmented what previously appeared to be the extreme
of anguish.   The author has been painfully conscious of the agony
attendant on the operation; but to his surprise the animals have not
flinched, neither have the feet been withdrawn. The quadruped appeared
to suffer torture with the patience of stoicism, influenced by the aban-

donment of utter confidence. The most caustic dressings have been freely employed upon the most sensitive part; yet the creature which, when in health, seemed made up of the acutest sensibilities, has submitted to the torture with more than mortal fortitude. Once win the reliance of timidity, and so beautiful, so entire, so self-nugatory is its confidence.

Little can be said concerning the cure of lameness. The causes are various, and, of course, the remedies are as numerous as the provocatives. One thing may, however, be advised: have the shoe taken off and the foot searched. Never mind the horn being pared away—many a horse limps upon a whole hoof; and it is astonishing upon how small a portion of horn an animal may go sound. The seat of the injury being ascertained, and so much of the inorganic covering removed as may be necessary to afford some relief, always soak the foot in the bath' before permitting the final use of the knife. The water cleanses the part, favors the discharge of pus, lowers the inflammatory action, softens the anguish, and destroys the harsh character of the dry horn. This last substance, as was observed, by the united action of warmth and moisture loses its resistant property. It cuts easily when newly released from the bath; and if the knife be sharp, it may be excised without any of that dragging sensation which frequently provokes the animal to snatch away the member while it is being operated upon.

PUMICE FOOT.

Pumice foot is a deformity produced by hard work; it does certainly appear strange, when we regard the beauty and strength united in the frame of the horse, that man's barbarity should exceed Nature's ingenuity. A more captivating present—heightening human pleasures, lessening human toil—than the horse, it is impossible to imagine, but its beauty seems only given for man to deface. A stronger helpmate, when speed is considered, it appeared beyond the most excited imagination to fancy. But the cruelty of the master found it easy to incapacitate the power so exquisitely endowed. The speed was too slow for the eagerness of the rider; the docility was not apt enough for the impatience of the possessor; in every particular the servant seems to have been at fault; and now we hear men gravely lamenting the invention of railroads, because these will interfere with the breeding of horses. Let us hope the establishment of railroads may supply a deficiency which the willingness of flesh and blood was unable to gratify.

Animals bred on a marshy land, and of a loose habit of body, are apt to have weak feet, a specimen of which is given on next page, though not of one belonging to the heavy cart-horse. All the delineations inserted in this book are necessarily extreme cases; it is easy for the imagination to soften the evil when the mind is impressed with characteristics of the thing which is depicted; but not always so free from difficulty for an untutored imagination to magnify a reduced portrait.

A weak foot has a long, slanting pastern; the hoof is marked by rings, showing the irregularity of the horny secretion, and the crust is broken in those places where nails have been driven to fasten on the shoe, proving the brittle nature of the hoof.

Such are the outward signs of a weak hoof; but if the person behold-

A WEAK FOOT.

THE SOLE OF A WEAK FOOT.

ing that sort of foot be in any doubt, let him lift it from the ground and inspect the sole. That part will also present peculiarities which can hardly fail to attract attention.

The sole of a weak foot has a thin and irregular margin of crust; a flat surface; well-developed bars, and a healthy frog. Creatures with this kind of hoof, when brought to work upon hard roads or London stones, are apt to throw the foot down with heedless force at every step, and thereby soon to bruise the sole. These horses generally have high action, and this circumstance lends additional force to the blow; the injury reaches the coffin-bone, which begins to enlarge, and ultimately forces the horny sole outward. A pumice foot has the appearance of the member represented on the next page, though the reader must not anticipate the illustration will accurately indicate every stage of the disorder.

Feet of the above description generally have very weak and brittle crusts; but the frog almost invariably is large and prominent; there is no kind of foot which so generally exhibits a healthy frog, and the next page shows an engraving of the ground surface of a pumice foot, in illustration of the fact.

There are many methods proposed for amending a pumiced foot. One is the removal of the shoe; then allowing the deformed foot to stand a certain portion of time upon flat flag-stones. But as stamping the foot upon stones produced pumice foot, prolonged stress thereon does not seem calculated to remove the deformity. A pumice foot is not a lump of pudding, to be flattened by simple pressure. In the horse's hoof there is bone and flesh to operate upon. Even supposing the standing upon flag-stones was beneficial, what immediate result could be anticipated from a medicine which was to be administered once in three weeks, and for half an hour only at each application?

THE SIDE VIEW OF A PUMICED FOOT.
Showing the swollen or rounded state of the sole, with the brittle and uneven condition of the crust.

THE SOLE OF A PUMICED FOOT.
Displaying a ragged wall, and exhibiting a very healthy frog and a bulging sole.

Another artifice is to draw a hot iron over the sole at every shoeing. The intention is to stimulate the horn and thus render the sole of greater thickness. But that which may affect the secreting membrane of the foot may also stimulate the bone to which that membrane is attached. Thus the intended remedy may turn out to be a positive aggravation.

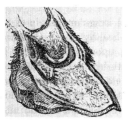

A PUMICED FOOT DIVIDED.
Showing the altered state of the internal structures.

A DISH SHOE.
Employed in cases of severe pumice foot.

There are also other methods of intended relief, but all are equally useless.

The only means of real benefit lies in the treatment of the hoof and in the mode of shoeing. For the last, select what is denominated a "dish" shoe; that is, a bar shoe, having the web hollowed out like to the sides of a pie-dish. The only part of this shoe which touches the ground is the rim of the inner circle.

This kind of shoe will protect the bulging sole, and if shod with leather, the protection will be greater, though the shoe will, in that case, be more difficult to retain. The flat surface at the posterior part of the shoe presents a point for the bearing of the frog, which can afford almost any amount of pressure. The many nail holes made around the shoe denote the difficulty the smith encounters when fixing a protection of this sort upon the pumiced hoof The crust of the foot is always brittle, and the weight of iron employed being greater than usual requires an extra number of nails to fasten it securely The smith consequently, in such cases, has no choice. He must drive a nail wherever he can find the horn which will sustain one.

With regard to the horn, keep that continually dressed with equal parts of animal glycerin and tar Moisten the hoof with this mixture twice a day No improvement may be remarked in a week; but in two or three months the crust will have become perceptibly less brittle, and the labor of the smith will be rendered far less perplexing. For the abnormal condition of the foot—that is permanent and nothing can be done beyond employing such artifices as are calculated to relieve the affliction.

SANDCRACK.

Any cause which weakens the body of the horse by interfering with the health of its secretions may induce **sandcrack.** Treading for any length of time upon ground from which all moisture is absent, by rendering the horn hard or dry, may cause the hoof to be brittle and give rise to sandcrack However, this last provocative seldom operates in this country; when sandcrack occurs in an English horse, it is generally generated by debility, which leads to the secretion of faulty horn. So far, however, is this from being the prevailing opinion, and so little sympathy does the horse receive in its diseases, that the endeavor, indeed the custom, of all veterinary surgeons is to continue at work the horse having a division running completely through the hoof

Sandcracks are of two sorts. Quarter crack, which chiefly happens among the lighter breed of animals; toe crack, which occurs principally with cart-horses, and mostly with those which work between the shafts

Quarter sandcrack is of the least importance of the two It is oftenest seen upon the inner quarter of the hoof, where the horn, being thinnest, is most subjected to motion. Usually it commences at the coronet, extending to the sole, and also to the sensitive laminæ.

A horse thus affected should be thrown up; should be placed in a large, loose box, and receive soft, nutritious food, such as boiled oats, boiled linseed, and scalded hay. A little green-meat occasionally should be allowed to regulate the bowels; greased swabs should be placed over the hoof and under the sole. A bar shoe should be worn upon the affected foot. : This treatment should be continued till the horse has recovered from its debility.

With regard to the crack itself, take a fine knife and gradually scrape off the sharp edges till the division assumes the appearance of a groove. If the crack does not reach through to the flesh, no fear need be entertained concerning the lower edges of the crack, because the horn secreted by the laminæ is of a soft nature, and will most readily yield. Besides, paring the outer horn often prevents the inner layer being cracked by the motion of the foot; this being done, should the division not descend the entire length of the hoof, or reach from the ground to the

QUARTER SANDCRACK.

Generally met with, in fast horses, upon the inner side of the fore foot.

coronet, with a firing-iron, heated to redness, draw a line at each extremity of the fissure. The line need not be made so deep as will occasion pain; it is only necessary that the mark should go through the hard outer crust of the foot to prevent extension of the division.

Should the separation be the whole way down the hoof, it is as well to adopt either the plan followed by the late Mr. Read, or the mode pursued by Mr. Woodger, the clever practical veterinarian, well known in Paddington. Mr. Read used to make a semicircular line near the coronet with the hot iron: Mr. Woodger has for years been accustomed to draw lines from the coronet to the crack in the shape of a V, with the same instrument. Both methods have a like intention, namely, to cut off the coronet from the inferior portion of the hoof, thereby preventing the movements of the foot from operating upon the newly secreted horn. However, Mr. Woodger's plan being the easiest, and quite as effective as that of the late Mr. Read, is certainly the best.

A PARTIAL QUARTER SANDCRACK DRESSED AND SHOD.

THE METHODS OF ERADICATING A SANDCRACK: EITHER THE SEMICIRCULAR OR THE ANGULAR LINES ARE EQUALLY EFFECTIVE.

Sandcrack, when it occurs at the toe, usually extends the entire length of the foot, and leaves a portion of bleeding flesh exposed. The laminæ, being opened to the stimulating effects of the air, are very apt to throw out a crop of luxuriant granulations. These, of course, are pinched between the two sides of the division. They bleed freely; often, from the pressure, they turn black, and then smell abominably. The putrid action, having once commenced, is apt to extend, and portions of the coffin-bone are likely to exfoliate.

· A FOOT WITH TOE SANDCRACK.

Illustrating the mode of shoeing with clips, and of easing off at the toe; also exemplifying the manner of paring down the hoof, and showing the part where granulations are likely to appear.

Now to prevent this, so soon as the horse is brought in with a sandcrack, wash the part thoroughly with the chloride of zinc lotion, one grain to the ounce of water. The bleeding having ceased, pare down the outward edges of the separation, and put on a bar shoe, eased off at the toe, and with a clip on either side of the division. If the injury has not extended the length of the hoof, you must make a line at each extremity with a heated iron, as in quarter crack, than which it is also of more consequence that the coronet should be isolated; because the external horn being thickest at the toe, is the more likely by its movements to be influential upon the new and plastic horn of the coronet.

Should, however, the granulations have appeared, and the horse, with appetite lost and the head dejected, the pulse thumping and the injured foot held in the air, appear the picture of a living misery, first cleanse the wound thoroughly with the chloride of zinc lotion. Then apply a firing-iron, of a black heat, to the hoof, near to the crack. The intention, in doing this, is to warm and thus to soften the horn. This effect being accomplished, pare down or scoop off the edges—using the heated iron again, if necessary. Do all this leisurely, and with every consideration for the animal, which endures intense agony; for anything like violence or impatience tells fearfully upon the sufferer's system.

The horn being lowered, take a very sharp drawing-knife, and, with one movement of the wrist, excise the granulation. Set down the foot, and leave it to bleed; the loss of blood will lower the inflammation and will benefit the internal parts. Give a little green-meat to cool the system and act upon the bowels. Then, with the constant use of the lotion, enough has been done for one day.

The following morning you may again apply the lotion, and continue to use it afterward thrice daily. Any further lowering may also be accomplished to the edges of the crack, as well as the coronal portion of the horn be separated from the lower part of the hoof, by means of lines drawn as before illustrated.

If the horse must go to work, remember, it should not be in the shafts, upon long journeys, or with a heavy load behind it. Before the animal quits the stable, lay a piece of tow saturated with the lotion within the crack, and bind that in with a wax-end; tie a strip of cloth over all; give this bandage a coating of tar; and, when the horse returns, be sure to inspect the part. Should any grit have penetrated, wash it out with the lotion, and do not begrudge a minute or two to remove that which, if allowed to remain, may cause the animal much additional anguish. Then give the suffering creature a nice, deep bed, some scalded hay, and a mash made of bruised oats, into which has been thrown a handful each of linseed and of crushed beans; moisten these last constituents with the water drawn from the scalded hay, and, if the horse should not appear hungry, throw among the hay half a handful of common salt.

A HORSE'S FOOT DRESSED FOR THE SANDCRACK.

Showing the way in which it should be bound up when work is imperative.

The poor man may have some excuse for working an animal with sandcrack; such a person cannot afford to keep the horse in idleness for the months which the cure will occupy. But the worst cases of this kind the author ever beheld have always been in quadrupeds belonging to wealthy tradesmen, who had ample means to gratify their desires, but wanted the heart to feel for mute affliction.

FALSE QUARTER.

False quarter is the partial absence of the outer and harder portion of the hoof; the consequence is, that the sensitive laminæ, in the seat of the false quarter, are only protected by their own soft or spongy horn. This is frequently insufficient to save the foot from severe accident; it is apt to crack, being strained by the motion of the hoof. The fleshy parts are then exposed; bleeding ensues, and fungoid granulations sometimes spring up; these are often pinched by the two sides of the divided horn, between which they protrude. When such occurs, the treatment should be the same as that recommended for sandcrack.

FALSE QUARTER, OR A DEFICIENCY OF THE OUTER WALL.

THE ONLY POSSIBLE RELIEF FOR FALSE QUARTER.

No art can cure a false quarter; a portion of the coronary substance has been lost, and no medicine can restore it. All that can be done is to mitigate the suffering ; a bar shoe with a clip at the toe may be used, the bearing being taken off at the seat of false quarter. The portion of crust near to the weakened part should be beveled off, so as to join the soft horn with an insensible edge. Some persons recommend a mixture of pitch, tar, and rosin to be poured over the exposed quarter; the author has not found this compound to answer ; it peels and breaks off upon the horse being put in motion. A piece of gutta-percha, of proportionate thickness, fastened over the place, has sometimes remained on for a week, and answered to admiration.

SEEDY TOE.

It appears not to have occurred to writers upon veterinary subjects that the horse, which breathes but to work—for the instant its ability to toil ceases the knacker becomes its possessor—that an animal which exists under so severe a law, should occasionally be "used up ;" that a creature which is sold from master to master, all of whom become purchasers with a view only to "the work" each can get out of the "thews and muscles," should occasionally be debilitated to that stage which might interfere with the healthiness of its secretions, is a notion that seems to have been beyond the reach of those writers who have hitherto

SECTION OF A HORSE'S FOOT
AFFECTED WITH SEEDY
TOE.

composed books upon the equine race. A separation between the union of the two layers of horn which compose the crust has been long known ; it has been much thought about, and the fancy has been somewhat racked to account for its origin. Still, although the human physician has recorded the brittle state and abnormal condition of man's nails in peculiar stages of disease, no one seems thence to have argued that a certain condition of body might possibly affect the hoofs of our stabled servant.

The method of cure which the author adopted, led thereto by the admirable lectures of Mr. Spooner, and the success it met, soon made apparent the fact of its origin ; but, before describing this, it may be as well to inform the reader in what consists a seedy state of the horse's toe.

The wall of the foot is composed of two layers—the outer one, the hardest, the darkest, and the thinnest, is secreted by the coronet ; the inner layer, the softest, thickest, and most light in color, is derived from the sensitive laminæ. These different kinds of horn, in a healthy state, unite one with the other, so that the two apparently form one substance. The junction makes a thick, elastic, and strong body, whereto an iron shoe can be safely nailed, and whereon the enormous bulk of the horse's frame may with safety rest.

But when overwork affects the natural functions of the body, the two kinds of horn do not unite; their division invariably begins at the toe, as it always commences in the nail of the human being at the outer margin. If the seedy toe be tapped or gently struck, it emits a hollow sound; and if the shoe be removed, there will be found a vacant space between the two layers of horn; into this space a nail, a piece of broom, or a straw is commonly pushed, to ascertain the depth of the lesion.

THE APPEARANCE PRESENTED BY SEEDY TOE WHEN THE SHOE IS REMOVED, AND THE GROUND SURFACE OF THE WALL IS INSPECTED.

Mr. Spooner advised that the whole of the detached horn should be cut away. The writer, however, insists that the horse should be thrown up—not turned out to grass, but placed in an airy, loose box, and liberally fed, or otherwise so treated as its condition may require. Once every fortnight, for two months, the smith should inspect the foot, and should cut away so much of the outer wall as may still be disunited. It commonly takes three or four months for the hoof to grow down or to become perfect; and rest, with liberal feeding, during this time, is sufficient to renovate an exhausted frame. A new and sound covering for the hoof of the invigorated horse is secreted by the expiration of the period named; nor has it reached the knowledge of the writer that any animal, after such a mode of treatment, has been liable to a second attack.

THE APPEARANCE OF THE HOOF AFTER THE SEEDY TOE HAS BEEN REMOVED WITH THE KNIFE.

The ordinary method of cure is to cut away the hoof; then, having nailed a shoe on, to send the disfigured horse to resume labor. Under this form of treatment, the seedy division, once confined to the toe, has extended to the quarters; the structure of the hoof being destroyed, the horn was unfitted for its purposes. The weight of the body forced the sensitive laminæ from the coronary secretion, and the foot, after long treatment, became a deformity. The author has never beheld so lamentable a termination; but it is described by writers upon seedy toe with a complacency which seems to regard so grievous a result as the natural consequence of an intractable disorder.

TREAD AND OVERREACH.

Tread is a very rare occurrence with light horses; the author has met with but one instance. Then, from the horse being a good stepper, and from the accident happening toward the end of a long journey, as well as from certain indications of the wound itself, it was conjectured to have occurred in the manner depicted below.

TREAD IN LIGHT HORSES.
The hind foot, from fatigue, not being removed soon enough, is wounded by the heel of the fore shoe being placed upon its coronet.

TREAD UPON THE HIND FOOT OF CART-HORSES.
The animal become unsteady from exhaustion; the feet cross, and a wound results.

However, among cart-horses such a form of injury is more frequent; these poor animals have to drag heavy loads, at a slow pace, it is true, but to long distances; they are generally badly fed. Farmers' horses, especially during the spring and summer months, being supported upon green-meat, the watery nourishment impoverishes the blood, and the exhausting labor undermines the system. Often the load has to be taken down hill, toward the end of a tedious journey; the whole burden then rests upon the shafts, and the wretched horse which is between them rocks under the weight like a drunken man. The legs cross, till at last the calkin belonging to the shoe of one hind foot tears away a large lump of the opposite coronet. A piece of flesh is commonly left upon the ground; the hemorrhage is extreme, and the wagon is brought to a stand.

The worst case of the kind the writer ever saw occurred after the preceding fashion; and the carter—who, by-the-by, was proprietor of the sufferer—left the poor horse in a forge, giving orders that the smith was to do what he could, or to have it killed, as he pleased. The smith consulted the writer, and he treated the wound after the method recommended for open joint, or by bathing it thrice daily with the solution of chloride of zinc, one grain to the ounce of water. In a week a large slough took place; this opened the coffin-joint, and left a portion of the extensor pedis tendon hanging from the orifice. The treatment was continued; the lameness, which at first was excessive, gradually grew less; the piece of tendon sloughed out, and the wound began to heal. It had closed when the animal was fetched away by the owner; but the writer was unable afterward to learn whether false quarter ensued upon the injury. This, from the extent of the wound, the writer would conjecture to have been probable; indeed, false quarter and quittor are the general consequences of severe tread.

Overreach is confined to fast horses; it happens to those which are good steppers. When tired, the feet are apt to be moved irregularly; thus, one foot is often in its place before the other has been lifted; the result is, that the inner part of the hind foot strikes the outer side of the fore coronet. A wound, and frequently a severe one, is the consequence. False quarter or quittor is likely to ensue; the treatment must be the same as was before described. No poultices are required; these only add to the weight of the injured limb, and augment the distress of the animal. No harsh measures should be allowed; the horse has enough to bear; a slough has

OVERREACH OCCURRING DURING THE EXHAUSTION OF LIGHT HORSES.

to take place. This is a severe tax upon the strength; all the good food and prepared water the animal can consume will not now be thrown away; the treatment is materially shortened by the nourishment being sustaining of its kind, and liberal in quantity; but the injury should be treated only with the knife, and the chloride of zinc lotion described in the course of this article.

CORNS.

Corns are of four kinds—the old, the new, the sappy, and the suppurating; all are caused by bruises to the sensitive sole. The shoe is the passive agent in their production, when they occur in large, fleshy feet; the thick, unyielding, horny sole is the passive agent, when they are present in contracted feet. The coffin-bone, in both cases, is the active agent; the wings, or posterior portions of this bone, project backward nearly as far as the bars, or immediately over the seat of corn. When the horse is in motion, the coffin-bone can never remain still; it rises, or rather the wings are drawn upward by the flexor tendon, every time the foot is lifted from the earth, and sinks, because of the weight cast upon it, every time the foot touches the ground. The wings of the bone, thus in constant action, when the horny sole is weak, often descend upon the fleshy sole, and bruise that substance upon the iron shoe; what is called a corn is the consequence. In contracted feet, where the sole is high, thick, and resistant, the horny sole does not descend, even when the immense weight of the horse's body rests upon it. It remains firm and fixed during every action of the animal—not so, however, the coffin-bone, which is in continuous motion. The result, of course, is, the imposed burden forces the wings of the coffin-bone downward. The horny sole

DIAGRAM

Showing the position of the hindermost part of the coffin-bone when in a passive state; also portraying the shoe in the fleshy or flat foot.

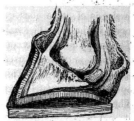

DIAGRAM

Illustrating the relative positions of the wings of the coffin-bone, and the thick, concave, horny sole of the contracted foot when not in motion.

will not yield, and the fleshy sole is therefore bruised between the wings of the coffin-bone and the horn bottom of the hoof; a corn is thereby established.

Corns in a horse do not answer to those excrescences found upon the feet of man; being bruises, they consist of effusion in every instance. The effusion may either be of blood or of serum; blood constitutes the old and the new corn, serum gives rise to the sappy corn. The suppurative corn is an after-consequence of either of those just named; when the effusion has been so large as to defy absorption, a new action is started up—pus is secreted, and a suppurative corn is then created.

An old corn is the least serious, especially when it is easily cut away; it appears as a black mark upon the surface of the horny sole, and is little thought of when it can be speedily removed by the knife, because this shows the horse had a corn, but at present is free from such an annoyance. When, however, a superficial corn cannot be scooped out

THE SITUATION AND ASPECT OF AN OLD CORN UPON A LARGE, FLAT FOOT.

THE DEEPLY-SEATED AND SMALL, SCARLET SPOT WHICH DECLARES THE PRESENCE OF A NEW CORN.

with the drawing-knife, but becomes brighter and brighter as more and more horn is cut away, till it assumes the scarlet aspect of a new corn, the matter is rather grave, because it denotes the horse to have had, and not to have been free from, corns during the growth of the present sole.

The new corn, as has been just intimated, consists of a portion of blood effused into the pores of the horn, and is of a bright-scarlet color. The size is of some consequence, as it best intimates the extent of the injury; if the stain be small and deep seated, it is of least moment.

The sappy corn is the consequence of a more gentle bruise, when serum and lymph only are effused—the horn being thereby merely rendered moist, not discolored. This species of corn is not very common, and by proper shoeing is readily removed.

The suppurating corn is the worst of all; it engenders heat in the foot, and causes excessive lameness; it creates all that anguish, a shadowy taste of which the human being endures when pus is confined beneath the substance of the finger-nail. The foot cannot be put to the ground; the arteries of the pastern throb forcibly; the countenance is dejected; and every symptom of acute suffering in a large body is exhibited.

Corns, which in man are found on the lower members, in the horse are generally witnessed only upon the fore feet. The writer has rarely seen an instance of their presence behind; but in whichever foot they appear, they must be the production of an instant, though, probably, the suppurative may be an exception; yet from these always being suddenly observed, even this species are said to be of instantaneous origin. A horse, when progressing, makes a false step; a sanguineous or sappy corn is by that faulty action established. The same horse may trot home perfectly sound, and be put into the stable for the night a healthy animal; but on the following morning it may be discovered standing on three legs. Pus may, in the interval, have been secreted, and the corn may have assumed the suppurative character.

The manner to examine for corn is, in the first place, to mark the age of the horse; then observe if, in the trot, either leg is favored. The animal being young, splint is the common cause of uneven action; if old, corns are more generally expected; the horse is brought to a stand and the smith sent for. The man raises the fore foot, and, taking a portion of crust and sole between the teeth of the pincers, gradually increases the pressure; he thus proceeds till he has by successive trials squeezed the sole all round. If the

THE SOLE OF THE HORSE'S FOOT BEING TESTED FOR CORNS.

leg, while undergoing the operation, be withdrawn near either of the nails, the ideas take a different direction to that of corn; but if the foot

be held steady, the seat of corn is lastly squeezed.   Should no flinching
be witnessed, the examination is not esteemed satisfactory until the smith
has, with a small drawing-knife, denominated a searcher, cut away a portion of the sole at the seat of corn

The sensibility will be extreme should suppurating corn be present;
in that case the sole must be gradually removed until the pus is released
That being done, the shoe should be taken off and the foot put into a
bran poultice   By this means the horn will be rendered more soft and
the wound cleansed.   The smith, on the following day, must again cut
the foot, every portion of detached horn being very carefully excised.

The horn is itself a secretion, and, in a healthy state, is intimately
united with the source of its origin   When, however, pus is effused,
this always lies between the secreting membrane and the horn, which
has been already secreted.   The horn so displaced by the presence of a
foreign substance is called under-run or detached; and all horn, so
under-run or detached, must be removed   When this operation is properly performed, all signs of lameness will have generally disappeared.
It is usual, however, to tack the old shoe on again; and having dressed
the injury with chloride of zinc and water—one grain to the ounce—
there remains only to examine the foot from time to time till new horn
covers the surface; merely taking precaution for the present to shield
the wound with a little tow, fastened in its place by a couple of cross
splints.

When sanguineous or sappy corns are found, the method is, firstly to
thin the sole, so as to render it pliable, especially over the seat of corn.
Should a sappy corn have rendered the horn moist for any space, or
should the discoloration caused by sanguineous corn be of any size, it
is as well always to open the center of the part indicated: no matter
should the cut release only a small quantity of serum or a little blood.
Take away a small portion of horn; pare the sole till it yield to the
pressure of the thumb   When such a proceeding is necessary, the bars
may be entirely removed, and the wounds should be covered with some
tar spread upon a pledget of fine tow   As soon as the orifice is protected by new horn, the horse may be shod with a leathern sole and
returned to its proprietor

Such a course would occupy little time—a week at most.   Yet the
great majority of horse proprietors appear to have 'flinty hearts," as
nearly all of them begrudge the necessary day of rest to the maimed
animal which has been injured in their employment.   The cry, where
the horse is concerned, is "toil, toil!"   The veterinary surgeon is often
asked "if *absolute* rest is imperative."   He is frequently solicited to
patch up the poor animal, so that it may do a *little* work   As day after

day passes onward, the tone becomes more and more authoritative. The horse is at last too often demanded from the hospital, and taken to resume ordinary labor before the injury is effaced. Should no evil effect ensue on such a culpable want of caution, the proprietor is apt to chuckle over his daring with another's sufferings, and to blame the science which would not incur risk, even to propitiate an employer.

. Corn is not generally reckoned unsoundness. If a horse be lame from corn, the lameness renders the horse unsound; but the corn does not. Such is the beauty of horse logic when pronounced in a court of justice! A corn may suppurate, or may provoke lameness at any moment. Still the corn, in the bleared eye of the law, is no sufficient objection to the purchase of a horse. The suppurated corn may lead to quittor—still, corn is not legal unsoundness. It is a pity such is the case, since it leads men to neglect that which is removable. When the sole is high, the shoe should always be accompanied by a leathern sole. Liquid stopping should be poured into the open space at the back of the foot; and at every time of shoeing, the smith should pare the sole quite thin, even until drops of blood bedew the surface of the horn. When corns appear in flat or fleshy feet, as shoeing

THE POSTERIOR OF A HORSE'S FOOT SHOD WITH LEATHER.

The central angular mark indicates the place into which the liquid stopping should be poured.

time comes round, only have the very ragged portions of the frog taken away. Have the web of the shoe narrowed so as to remove all chance of pressure against the iron. Lower the heels of the shoe, or try a bar shoe with the bearing taken off over the seat of corn; should that not answer, next put on a three-quarter shoe: many horses, however, will go sound in tips, that cannot endure any other sort of protection to the foot. By resort to one or the other of these measures, that injury, which in the learned eye of the law is of no consequence, but which, nevertheless, may lead to terrible lameness, or even lay the foundation for a quittor, may be greatly mitigated.

Bruise of the sole is an accident leading to effusion of blood—so far it resembles corn; but it is dissimilar in not occurring on a part subject to the same degree of motion, and, therefore, is not so severe in the consequences to which it leads. It is caused by treading on a stone, and is removed by paring off the horn which has been discolored or lies immediately beneath the injury. It seldom leads to great lameness or gives rise to serious results. It is treated after the manner directed for corn; but it is always advisable to shoe once, with leather, the horse which has suffered from bruise of the sole. The difference between

23

corn and bruise of the sole is simply this: the first is an injury produced by a cause which is always within the control of the proprietor,
and which, if neglected, is likely to lead to the most disastrous maladies; the last is purely an accident, to which any horse at any time is
liable, and with ordinary care is not likely to give rise to any serious
consequences.

Prick of the foot is an injury incurred while the horse is being shod.
There are two sorts of this accident: one, when the nail penetrates the
fleshy substance of the sensitive laminæ and draws blood; the other
is when a nail is driven too fine, or among the soft horn which lines the
interior of the hoof, and consequently lies near to the sensitive laminæ.
The first is of the more immediate importance; but the last may be
equally serious in its effect. As the horse works, the strain upon the
shoe bends the nail fixed into soft horn. It thus is made to press upon
the sensitive laminæ, and may provoke suppuration.

To detect whether the smith is at fault, the foot should be first

PRICK OF THE FOOT AND BRUISE
OF THE SOLE.

The smaller opening represents
prick of the foot: the larger
space indicates bruise of the
sole. The extent to which
the horn may be removed, in
the generality of cases, is also
indicated.

squeezed between the pincers as for common
corn; then have the nails withdrawn one by
one, and mark each as it is removed. If one
appears moist or wet, have the hole of that nail
freely opened. Let the shoe be replaced, leaving that nail out. Put a little tow, covered
with tar, over the wound, and shoe with leather.
If, however, lameness should still be present,
the shoe must again be taken off and the injury treated as recommended for suppurating
corn.

Blame the smith who pricks a horse and conceals the fact; punish the fellow to the extent
of your power. But the man who pricks a foot
and acquaints you with the circumstance, de-
serves civility. The last enables you to take proper measures, such as
paring out, etc., and thereby you avoid all unpleasantness. The first
braves chances with your living property, and deserves to suffer if the
hazard go against him.

QUITTOR.

This is a severe and painful disease. Many a horse is, at the present
moment, working with a suppurative wound above the hoof, within the
interior of which run numerous sinuses. The police arrest the driver
of the horse when the condition is so bad as permits the collar to wring

the shoulders. Of all other shapes of misery they seem ignorant. Animals limp over the stones, every step being an agony; but the policemen look on at such pictures with placid countenances   Horses are driven at night in a state of glanders which renders them dangerous to mankind; yet no officer thinks of looking at the head of an animal for the sign of suffering or the warning of public peril. Creatures, in every stage of misery, may be seen openly progressing along the streets of the metropolis; but so the shoulders be sound, the brute who goads them forward performs his office with impunity. Still, it is something gained, that the law has recognized the want of man's *absolute* power over the feelings of those creatures intrusted to his care   Let us hope, as knowledge extends, the legal perceptions will be quickened. It is partly with this view that the present "illustrated work" is published.

Quittor is a terrible disorder. To comprehend thoroughly the pain which accompanies it, the reader must understand the structures through which it has to penetrate, and the substances it has to absorb All parts are slowly acted upon in proportion as they are lowly organized. Cartilage is the structure into the composition of which no blood-vessels enter. Next to cartilage is bone, which, though supplied with vessels, is, on account of its mixture with inorganic matter, exposed only to slow decay, and the exfoliation of which is effected at a vast expense to the vital energy. These substances mainly compose the foot of the horse. In addition, there is ligament, almost as slowly acted upon as bone; disease in which substance is accompanied by the greatest anguish   Horn is an external protection; but that material, though an animal secretion, is strictly inorganic: when cut it does not occasion pain—neither does it bleed. If a portion of horn should press upon the flesh it must be removed by the knife; for, unlike the more highly-gifted structures, there is no chance of its being absorbed.

The hoof, therefore, being the external covering to the foot of the horse, and not being liable to the same action as organic secretions, serves to confine pus or matter when generated within its substance Pus could work through the largest organized body; but it cannot escape through the thinnest layer of horn   Now, most of the other substances which enter into the composition of the horse's foot are such as slowly decay; but those parts which slowly decay being without sensation during health, occasion the most extreme agony when diseased.

The cause of quittor always is confined pus or matter, which, in its effort to escape, absorbs and forms sinuses in various directions within the sensitive substances of the hoof. In the hind feet of cart-horses quittor generally commences at the coronet; the coronet is wounded or bruised by the large calkins or pieces of iron turned up at the back of the hind shoes, which are universally worn by animals of heavy draught. Any one who has punctured or cut the coronet of a dead horse knows this structure is as difficult to penetrate and as hard to divide as cartilage itself; the consequence of an injury to such a part is, the bruise produces death of some deep-seated portion of the compact coronet. Nature, after her own fashion, proceeds to cast off that which is without vitality, or, in other words, she divides the dead from the living tissues by a line of suppuration; but the matter thus located cannot readily escape through the harsh material of the horse's coronet. It is confined and becomes corrupt, while the constant motion of the foot and the higher organization of the secreting membrane of the horn inclines the pus to take a downward direction. However, it is more difficult for pus to pierce the horny sole than to penetrate the coronet; so the effort is renewed above; numerous pipes or sinuses are thus formed upon the sensitive laminæ; the fleshy sole is often under-run, and this mischief goes on until the coronet, which becomes of enormous size, at last yields to the increasing evil.

Another cause is pricking the sensitive part of the foot with a nail during shoeing; the wound generates pus, the pus cannot penetrate the horn, and the motion of the coffin-bone causes it to absorb upward, until after some time it breaks forth at the coronet.

DIAGRAM.

Which supposed the outward covering of the coronet and the horny wall of the hoof removed, to expose the ravages of quittor, when commencing in the coronet of a heavy horse.

DIAGRAM.

The covering of the coronet and horny crust supposed to be absent, and exposing the manner in which any suppurating injury to the sole of the foot ultimately causes a wound above the hoof.

Another cause is corn; the horse's corn is nothing more than a bruise; the bruise, in some instances, is severe, and takes on the suppurative action. The pus, as before, is confined, and by the motion of the coffin-bone it is propelled upward till it breaks forth at the coronet, which, as before, enlarges to deformity; in short, any injury done to the sole of the foot or to the coronet above it may produce quittor.

The leading sign of quittor, before it breaks, is a large swelling at the coronet, attended with heat and excessive lameness. In cart-horses, it is usually present in the hind feet; but in the lighter species it more frequently occurs in the fore feet. It generally appears upon the inner side of the hoof, though, of course, it has often been witnessed upon the outer coronet. Quittor becomes a huge swelling before it breaks. The amount of tumefaction symbolizes the amount of anguish; it is, indeed, a most painful disorder.

A QUITTOR, AS IT DENOTES ITS EXISTENCE BEFORE THE PUS ABSORBS ITS WAY THROUGH THE CORONET.

A QUITTOR, AFTER THE PUS HAS FOUND AN EXIT AT THE CORONET.

The animal, after the pus has found vent, becomes easier; fever departs; the appetite returns, and the enlargement greatly diminishes.

In the cure of a quittor, all depend upon the time during which the disease has been allowed to exist; if brought under notice at first, and from an examination a belief is confirmed that the sinuses are wholly superficial, no treatment is comparable to the plan of slitting them up, the method of doing which will be described in a subsequent chapter; this at once affords relief. The horse, which was limping lame, upon getting up puts the foot fearlessly to the ground, and trots sound.

If we have reason to believe the matter has burrowed inwardly, and that one or more sinuses have penetrated the cartilages and threaten the deeper-seated parts, still we should settle with the knife all those pipes which are superficial. This gives a better view of the structures supposed to be diseased; then, if among the matter thrown out by the healing wounds there is seen a speck or two of fluid, which, being gelatinous and transparent, looks dark among the opaque, creamy pus, be sure there remains further work to be accomplished.

DIAGRAM.

An attempt to depict the small size of the transparent fluid, indicating the existence of a sinus, when it appears at the wound whence issues the stream of thick and creamy pus.

Cut a small twig from the stable broom; this is pliable, and, where a sinus is concerned, makes the best possible probe. With a knife, render it perfectly clean, as well as round or blunt at one end; then, while an assistant holds up the foot, insert it in the center of the dark fluid. If it should not at first detect an opening, you must not give up the trial; the probe must be moved about, and even a smaller one procured. A sinus does exist; of that you have positive proof; the pipe being found, mix some powdered corrosive sublimate with three times its bulk of flour; then wet the probe; dip the probe into the powder and afterward insert it into the sinus. Do this several times till you feel certain that every portion of the pipe is brought in contact with the caustic.

The horse, subsequently, will become very dull, the foot will grow very painful : thus it will continue for two days. About the third day, a white, curd-like matter is discharged from the orifice. The lameness disappears, and the spirits are regained

It is against our inclination to publish such directions; but the author has knowledge of no gentler or more speedy measure. The better plan for the gentleman who is tender of his servants' feelings, and infinitely the cheaper for the person who is regardful of his pocket, is to have every animal inspected by a qualified veterinary surgeon so soon as it displays acute lameness. Were such the practice, corn, prick of the foot, or wound of the coronet need not run on to quittor. That is an affection which loudly pronounces man to utterly disregard the welfare of his most willing slave. It always originates in neglect: It always requires time for its development. It springs from that idle and silly maxim which, when a horse falls lame, treats the circumstance as though the honest animal were shamming, and teaches a hard-hearted proprietor to work the poor drudge sound again.

CANKER

Thrush is a disease that causes a certain liquid to be secreted which has the property of decomposing the horn. **Canker** is a disease which not only is attended with a liquid having a like property, but the last-named affection also causes fungoid horn to be secreted. Canker, therefore, appears to be an aggravation of thrush; and anybody who has been much among the animals of the poorer classes may have observed these diseases lapse into each other : thrush will, through neglect, become canker

Thrush appears to be the commencement of the disorganization of the food. Canker is the total perversion of the secreting powers belonging to the same organ. In thrush, a foul humor having a corruptive property is poured forth In canker, something is superadded to this. The horn itself is sent forth in large quantity as a soft, unhealthy material, totally divested of elasticity and devoid of all healthy resistance.

Any animal, being exposed to the exciting cause, may exhibit thrush; but, before canker seems capable of being produced, poor living must have undermined the constitution. Old horses—pensioners, as they are humanely termed—when turned out to grass, frequently have canker, which otherwise should be confined to the animals of poverty, on which bad lodging, no grooming, stinted food, and hard work produce sad effects. The stable in which a case of canker occurs is lamentably disgraced. Every attendant in it ought to be discharged, as the surest evidence of a gross want of industry is thereby afforded.

A horse, perhaps once the pride of the favorite daughter, may descend to be the hack of some bawling dust collector. Its wants increase as age progresses; but with the accumulation of years its hardships augment. It is sad, very sad, to stand within the shed of some corn-chandler, and witness, as the day draws in, ragged boys advance and shout out, "Three pen'orth o' 'ay bunds" Upon those hay-bands it is even more sad to reflect what creature will be obliged to subsist—probably the darling once of some aristocratic children! Now, cramped and diseased, it may receive no other food between this time and the following evening. The diet being meager, all the rest is on a parallel The wretched animal is purchased only for such a space as it may pull through before it passes to the knackers Every day of life is looked upon as a clear gain, for the carcass may be sold for very nigh the price which has been paid for the living body. The commonest attention is denied; its bed is filth, and its nightly hay-bands are cast upon the flooring.

What, the humane reader may inquire, can be done to prevent such a state of things? Something surely might be accomplished. To make men good, it is first necessary to educate them by communicating knowledge and also by preventing the commission of wickedness. Were the sanitary laws enforced in their spirit, no man would keep an animal who had not proper accommodation for the creature he possessed as a property. A horse or a donkey consumes much more air than any human being. The air ejected from the lungs of a quadruped is deprived of all life-sustaining qualities. The filth of a stable is as corruptive as any cess-pool connected with a laborer's cottage. The atmosphere which can in the horse engender disease cannot promote health in the superior animal. Yet how does it happen that, while sanitary reports are eloquent upon filth and fluent about cess-pools—while they descant learnedly upon foul abodes, and enter into all particulars concerning corrupted atmosphere—the close, contaminated stables in which all costermongers, and some gentlemen, shut up their drudges when the labor of the day is over, are never alluded to, are altogether abjured, as though such nuisances had no existence?

Canker, like thrush, is not generally attended with much lameness. It often astonishes us that, with a foot in such a condition, the animal can progress so soundly. It invariably commences at the seat of thrush or in the cleft of the frog. A liquid more abominable than that of thrush, and rather more abundant, issues from that part. Likewise it frequently exudes from the commissures, which unite the horny sole to the frog. The horn, also, becomes not only disorganized, but more ragged than in thrush. It bulges out at first, and ultimately flakes off, exposing a substance not much more resistant than orange-peel. The substance is horn in a fungoid state. Its fibers run from the center to the circumference; and between the space of each fiber is lodged a clear liquid, which becomes tainted and dark colored by mingling with the horn that it dissolves and corrupts.

The fungus is secreted in quantity, and always is most abundant when located about the edge of the sole. Here the papillæ are largest, and

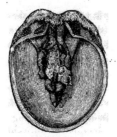

THE PRIMARY ESTABLISHMENT OF CONFIRMED CANKER.
The horn turned back, so as to display the altered state of the frog, which indicates a severe attack of the disease.

THE SECOND STAGE OF CANKER,
Showing the great abundance of fungoid horn secreted around the margin of the foot. No notice is purposely taken of the frog in this illustration.

here the granulations attain their greatest magnitude. The unresistant horn of canker becomes somewhat hard upon the surface of the sole, and large flakes peel off. Cut into, it displays no sensation; and this is fortunate, inasmuch as it considerably reduces the difficulties surrounding the treatment of a badly-cankered foot.

Concerning treatment, when the disease is confined to one hind foot, or even affects both posterior feet, the case may be undertaken with some degree of confidence. When it has involved one or more of the fore feet, it is always difficult to eradicate; and, in the majority of cases— being guided by the age of the animal — a cure had better not be attempted.

When a horse is cankered all round, the disease is apt to seem capricious. It may be cured in three feet; but it will linger in the fourth, resisting art's resources. Suddenly measures before tried in vain seem to be endowed with marvelous efficacy. The diseased member, which hitherto no treatment could touch, now heals as by its own accord. However, before we can express the full of our satisfaction, canker once more breaks out again in one of the feet which had been cured; thus the affection dodges about till patience is exhausted.

Canker has hitherto been reckoned an intractable disorder. It is mostly seen in heavy horses, with weak, flat feet These creatures proverbially receive but little grooming. They are esteemed only for their labor, and honored with small attention, which does not decidedly fit them for their work. Their stables are seldom to be cited as examples of what a horse's home should be. Their beds are never too clean; and a number of foul disorders, as thrush, grease, etc., are located among them. Their food is generally measured by the scale of profit and loss; for few cart-horses, in the generality of establishments, can boast of any extraordinary care being lavished on their comfort.

For the treatment of canker, the first thing is to attend to the stable. See that the building is lofty and well drained; that the ventilation is perfect, and the bedding unexceptionable. Then inspect the water, the oats, and the hay. Allow the horse a liberal support, and with each feed of oats mingle a handful of old beans. These things being arranged, order the animal into the forge. Cut away every portion of detached horn. When that is done, pare off carefully so much of the soft, diseased horn as the knife can readily separate. Then apply a dressing of the following strength to the diseased parts :—

Chloride of zinc . . . . Half an ounce.
Common flour . . . . Four ounces.
    Mix, and apply dry on the foot.

To the sound parts use—

Chloride of zinc . . . . Four grains.
Flour . . . . One ounce.

Cover over the sound parts before you begin to dress the fungoid granulations.

Afterward tack on the shoe. Pad well, so as to obtain all the pressure possible; and fasten the padding on the foot by means of cross pieces of iron driven firmly under the shoe. Let the horse be carefully groomed, and receive four hours' exercise daily.

On the second day remove the padding Cut off so much of the granulations as appear to be in a sloughing condition. Repeat the dressing, and continue examining and redressing the foot every second day. When some places appear to be in a state of confirmed health, an application of the following strength should be employed to such parts; but where the granulations continue to sprout, or the horn appears to be of a doubtful character, the caustic mixtures of the original strength must be used :—

| Chloride of zinc | . . . . | Two grains. |
| Flour | . . . . | One ounce. |

After some time, the dressings may be lengthened to every third day, but should not be carried to the distance which some practitioners recommend. When so long a period elapses between each examination,

THE BOTTOM OF A HORSE'S FOOT
WHICH HAS BEEN DRESSED FOR
CANKER, SHOWING HOW THE
CROSS PIECES ARE PLACED AND
FIXED.

AN IMPROVEMENT IN A CANKERED FOOT.
1. That portion of a cankered foot which is advancing toward a healthy condition.
2. Canker in a mitigated form, but still present.

the foul and irritating discharge, being confined, does more injury than the delay can possibly produce good.

In the plan of treatment here proposed, the chief reliance is placed on the action of chloride of zinc. It is the peculiar property of that agent to suppress fungoid granulations. The author has some experience in the use of this salt. Whenever he gave it to a groom to apply, and subsequently he found the wound clogged with proud flesh, the man was accused of having neglected to employ the lotion. The evidence on which the charge was made never, in a single instance, proved erroneous. To suppress fungoid granulation is to cure canker.

The application here advised is, moreover, cleanly. It is the most powerful disinfectant. It does not discolor, like the messes now in general use. It is more gentle in its action than undiluted sulphuric acid, etc. etc. It will cause none of those terrible fits of agony, during which all applications have to be removed, while the foot has to be bathed and poulticed. Notwithstanding all authors agree that the absence of water and the presence of pressure are indispensable to the cure of canker, the frequent dressings will not endanger the life, nor leave the foot in that condition which entails a deformed hoof upon the horse for the remainder of its existence.

THRUSH.

Veterinary writers are very fond of splitting hairs about words. **Thrush,** therefore, in most books, becomes "frush;" notwithstanding, if the reader should consult any professional authority, or a professor at either of the colleges, the person so appealed to will decidedly designate the disease as it is here spelled. The disorder therefore bears, in these pages, the name it carries in ordinary speech, and all far-fetched distinctions are discarded.

Thrush is a foul discharge issuing from the cleft of the frog, and attended with disorganization of the horn. It is derived from two causes—either internal disease or bad stable management. When internal disease gives rise to thrush, it is present in the fore foot. The quarters of the

THRUSH IN THE FORE FOOT, WITH A THICK CRUST, A CONCAVE SOLE, AND A SMALL FROG.

hoof are strong and high; the sole is thick and concave; the frog small and ragged. When bad stable management provokes the disorder, it shows itself in the hind foot, which may be of any shape; but the frog is generally large, while the discharge is more copious than in the former instance.

It is sad to think that the creature which lives but to toil, and whose existence is a type of such slavery that its greatest freedom is to labor, should be begrudged the bed whereon it reposes, or be doomed to stand in filth which will generate disease. The horse's foot is not very susceptible to external influences. It is incased in a hard and inorganic, yet elastic substance. Thus protected, it appears like praising the ingenuity of man when we say such a body is not proof against his neglect. The hoof is made to travel through mud and through water; it is created to canter over sand and over stones. It is capable of all its purposes; but it only seems not fitted to be soaking days and nights in the filth of a human lazar-house. The drainage of the stable is too often clogged; the ventilation bad; the bedding rotten, and more than half composed of excrement. All that passes through the body, from the inclination of the flooring, tends toward the hind feet. Over this muck the animal

THRUSH IN THE HIND FOOT.

breathes. In it the creature stands, and on it the victim reposes.

No wonder the horn rots when implanted in a mass of fermenting filth. The fleshy, secreting parts, which it is the office of the hoof to protect, ultimately become affected; they take on a peculiar form of irritation; from the cleft of the frog a discharge issues; it becomes colored and offensive through being mixed with the decaying horn ; the smell is most abhorrent ; frequently it taints the interior of the place, and to the educated nose thus makes known its presence.

The first thing is to clear the stable, then to cleanse it thoroughly.

Bed down the stalls with new straw, and attend to the animals themselves. Wash the feet well with water, in every pint of which is dissolved two scruples of chloride of zinc. The fetor will thus be destroyed, and the animal be made approachable. Place some of the fluid, to be used as required, near the smith, while the man cuts away the diseased frog. All the ragged parts are to be excised. The knife is to be employed until all the white, powdery substance is effectually removed.

AN ILLUSTRATION OF THE ABUNDANCE OF WHITE POWDER INVESTING DECAYED HORN, AND OFTEN FOUND AFTER THE RAGGED PORTIONS OF A THRUSHY FROG HAVE BEEN REMOVED.

The knife must then be used fearlessly. Every particle of the colorless investment of the frog must be excised. This is absolutely necessary toward the cure.

It must be accomplished, although the flesh be exposed, or a large, bulging frog be reduced to the dimensions indicated in the annexed engraving.

Then the shoe is to be nailed on, and the horse to be returned to a clean stall.

The cause being removed, the effect will soon cease. No ointments are required. A little of the chloride of zinc lotion, three grains to the ounce of water, may be left in the stable, and the keeper should receive directions to bathe the frog with this once a day, or oftener if required. A piece of stick, having a little tow wrapped round one end, should also be given to the man, so that he may force the fluid between the cleft of the frog. No greasy dressing need be employed. The ordinary shoe is to be used. The diseased part is to be left perfectly uncovered, so that it may be the more exposed to the sweetening effects of pure air, while the earliest indication of any further necessity for the knife may be readily perceived. When the stench has disappeared, a little of the liquor of lead, of its original strength, will perfect the cure ; and all that is requisite to prevent a return of the disorder is a reasonable attention to the cleanliness of the stable.

At this place, however, the reader may well reflect that, if the filth of the stable is capable of rotting the resistant and insensitive horn of the horse's foot, how much more is it likely to affect some of those delicate structures of which the bulky frame of the animal is composed ! The air in which a man might object to live is altogether unfit for a horse to inhale. It is true, animals have breathed such an atmosphere, and continued to exist So, also, is it true that men have been scavengers, and have followed that calling on account of what they esteemed its extraordinary healthfulness Neither case establishes aught. The animal is by nature formed for large draughts of pure air. All other sustenance is as nothing, if the primary necessity of life be withheld. Tainted atmosphere is the source of more than half the evils horse-flesh is exposed to Glanders, farcy, inflammation of the air-passages, indigestion, bowel complaints,—in fact, all diseases save those of a local character may spring from such a parent. Let every horse-keeper, therefore, if from no higher motive, at all events to conserve his property and to promote his pecuniary interest, be especially careful about the purity of his stables.

When thrush occurs in the fore feet, it is generally significant of navicular disease, and is most frequent in horses which step short or go groggily. The hoof feels hot and hard; a slight moisture bedews the central parting of the very much diminished frog. No odor may be smelt when the foot is taken up; but by inserting a piece of tow into the cleft of the frog, the presence of the characteristic symptom will be made unpleasantly apparent

In this case, it is best to remove the ragged thrush and unsound horn, doing so, if required, even to the exposure of the sensitive frog. Afterward, simply wash the part with a little of the chloride of zinc and water, previously recommended. Repeat the cleansing every morning; the intention being, not to remove the thrush, as the horse mostly goes lame the instant that is stopped, but merely to correct the pungency of the morbid discharge, and thus prevent it in some measure from decaying the horn.

Clay, cow-dung, and other favorite filths, employed for stopping the horse's feet, if long continued, will produce thrush.

The worst specimen of the affection the author has encountered, was in a horse which had been turned into a moist straw-yard and neglected. The thrush generally witnessed in the hind feet may be present in all four; but the writer knows of no instance in which the thrush peculiar to the fore feet was also observed in the posterior limbs.

Thrush does not generally provoke lameness In its more aggravated forms, however, it interferes with the pace; and the horse having only incipient thrush is liable to drop suddenly, if the foot be accidentally placed upon a rolling stone Now, knowing our roads are made of stones, and that the bottom of the horse's foot is, in the ordinary manner of shoeing, entirely unprotected, it is curious to state that this disease is commonly not esteemed unsoundness Any thrush, when present, may lead to acute lameness; then the lameness would be unsoundness;

if thrush simply interferes with the action, although it endanger the
safety of the rider, it is, by the code of veterinary legislation, esteemed
no reasonable objection to the soundness of a horse.   In the author's
opinion, any animal should be esteemed unsound which has suffered
from loss of or from change of any structure that ought to be present,
or has any affection which reasonably could subject it to remedial
treatment.

OSSIFIED CARTILAGES.

  This signifies a conversion into osseous structure of the cartilages
naturally developed upon the wings of the coffin-bone, or the bone
of the foot.   Here is a drawing of the largest specimen of this transformation which the writer ever witnessed.
This was borrowed from the museum of
T. W. Gowing, Esq.; and, from the magnitude of the disease, the writer should
imagine the posterior of the pastern must
have been in the living animal somewhat
deformed.

OSSIFIED CARTILAGES.

The lateral cartilages of the horse's foot
have undergone change and become
bone; being now continuous with the
os pedis.

In heavy horses, working upon London
stones, so certain are the cartilages to become ossified that several large firms pay
no attention to this defect.   They prefer
an animal with a confirmed disease to a sound horse, which will be certain to be ill during the change, and the extent of whose subsequent
alteration no one can predicate.   So far these purchasers act wisely;
but, in horses designed for fast work, **ossified cartilages** are a serious
defect.   They frequently occasion lameness, and always interfere with
the pleasantness of the rider's seat.   When accompanied by ring-bone,
ossified cartilages give rise to the most acute and irremediable lameness.
  Ossified cartilages are incurable.   No drugs can force Nature to restore the original structure which has been destroyed.   Once let a cartilage become ossified, and it remains in that condition for the creature's
life.   There is little difficulty in ascertaining when this change has taken
place.   The hand grasps the foot just above the coronet; the fingers are
on one side, and the thumb upon the other.   The cartilages lie at this
place, immediately under the skin.   Cartilage is soft, pliable, and semi-
elastic.   It yields very readily to pressure.   However, when the thumb
and fingers forcibly press the part, if, instead of feeling the substance
under them yield, the hand is sensible only of something as hard as stone,
or any way approaching to such a character, that is proof positive the

cartilages are ossified, or are approaching change. If the horse has recently gone lame, and the seat of cartilages feels of a mixed nature—partly soft and partly hard—apply a blister to the coronet, so as to convert that which is a subacute process into an acute action, and with the cessation of activity hope to stop the deposit. Repeat the blister if absolutely necessary; but there is no occasion to subject more than the coronet, and a couple of inches above that structure, to the operation of the vesicatory. Indeed, blisters act more effectually upon confined spaces. This

THE CERTAIN TEST FOR OSSIFIED CARTILAGES.

is all that can be accomplished, save by good feeding and liberal usage: these are essential, because every abnormal change denotes a deranged system; and this is, in the animal, soonest mended by generous diet. Perfect rest and two pots of stout per day may even be allowed, should the pulse be at all feeble.

ACUTE LAMINITIS, OR FEVER IN THE FEET.

This term implies that the disease is confined to the laminæ; the word certainly warrants an inference that the other secreting surfaces within the hoof are not implicated; such a meaning is generally conceived to be intended. The name, by inducing erroneous opinion, does much injury; the old appellation of fever in the feet is, therefore, much more characteristic and altogether more correct.

The entire of the fleshy portion of the foot is involved in this terrible affliction; any man, who has had an abscess beneath some part where the cuticle is strong, or who has endured a whitlow, may very distantly imagine the pain suffered by the horse during fever of the feet. Such an individual, if his creative powers be very brilliant, may vaguely conjecture the torture sustained by the quadruped; but no power possibly can realize to the full the anguish sustained by the animal. Man does not, like the horse, rest upon his finger's end, and, if he did, the pain he would then suffer could not be likened to the terrible affliction borne by the animal, for the following reasons: What is the weight of any man to that of a quadruped? What is the thickness of his skin or the substance of his nail to the hardness and stoutness of the horse's hoof? The human skin is elastic, and the end of the finger permits some swelling of its fleshy portion; but the secreting membrane of the horse's foot lies between two materials almost equally unyielding. Bone is within,

and horn is without; the heat soon dries the last and deprives it of its
elasticity; the first is naturally unyielding; thus the secreting substance,
largely supplied with blood, because of inflammation, and acutely endowed with sensation when swollen and diseased, is compressed between
the two bodies as in a vice. To conceive the amount of anguish and to
imagine the violence of the disorder, we have only to recognize the
pathological law, that Nature is conservative in all her organizations;
she protects parts in proportion to their importance to the welfare of her
creatures, and reluctantly allows injury to be inflicted on any vital organ,
though she may even permit deprivation of those members which are
not essential to the animal economy.

A man may lose a leg; he can live, enjoy life, and to a certain extent
effect progression with a wooden substitute. Touch the heart of a man,
however, and being ends The heart is guarded by the ribs, and so
securely is it protected that, even in battle, the organ is seldom punctured; the hoof of the horse is almost as important to the animal as is
the heart to the human being. In a free state progression is necessary
to the support of the body; when domesticated, the horse is valued
according to its power to progress

Yet, the member so important to the creature is, by the nature of
laminitis, frequently disorganized, and a valuable quadruped, by the
affliction, may be reduced from the highest price to a knacker's purchase
money.

There is some dispute about the kind of hoof most liable to this disease English authors incline toward the weak or slanting hoof Continental writers, however, suppose the strong or upright hoof is most
exposed to the affliction. Neither party, however, assert any kind of
hoof to be exempt; therefore, it may be supposed, were all circumstances similar, every kind of foot would be equally subjected to
laminitis

There is but one cause for acute laminitis—man's brutality. Horses
driven far and long over hard, dry roads, frequently exhibit the disease.
Cab and post, as well as gentlemen's horses, after a fine day at Epsom
or at Ascot, not unfrequently display the disorder Animals which have
to stand and strain the feet for any period, as cavalry horses upon a long
sea voyage, if, upon landing, they are imprudently used without sufficient
rest, will assuredly fail with this incapacitating malady. Any extraordinary labor may induce laminitis. Hunters, after a hard run, and racers,
subsequently to heats, are liable to be attacked; especially should the
ground be in the state we have before intimated.

Acute laminitis does not immediately declare itself; the pace of the
animal, when its work is drawing to a close, may be remarkable; but

this is attributed to the effects of exhaustion. The creature reaches the stable; the surface of the body is rubbed over; the manger and the rack are filled; a fresh bed is quickly shaken down, for, in the opinion of grooms, quiet does horses extreme good. The animal is left for the night, under the impression that it has everything one of the race could require.

The next morning the horse is found all of a heap, and the food untouched; the flesh is quivering; the eyes are glaring; the nostrils are distended, and the breath is jerking. The flanks are tucked up, the back is roached, the head is erect, and the mouth is firmly closed; the hind legs are advanced, to take the bearing from the inflamed fore members; the front feet are pushed forward, so as to receive the least possible amount of weight, and that upon the heels; but the feet thus placed are constantly on the move. Now, one leg is slightly bent; then, that is down and the other is raised; the horse is, according to a vulgar phrase, "dancing on hot irons."

The first indications—food untouched, glaring eyes, etc.—represent only excessive agony; the position of the body is symptomatic. The hind feet are thrust under the body in order to take the weight from the front, or the diseased organs; the fore feet are thrust forward and the head held erect, that the inflamed parts may be as much as possible beyond the center of gravity. In this attitude the wretched quadruped will stand, its sides heaving and its flesh creeping with the pain within the hoofs, and with the fire that burns within the blood. The teeth are occasionally heard to grind against each other; ex-

ACUTE LAMINITIS, OR FEVER IN THE FEET.

pressive sounds sometimes issue from the throat, and partial perspirations burst forth upon the body; it is a horrible picture of the largest agony!

The fore feet are mostly the seat of the disorder; all four may be involved, but the author has only witnessed the two front affected. The implication of the others are rather recorded wonders than general facts. The writer, in his professional experience, has met no one to whom a case of laminitis involving all four hoofs has been submitted.

Everything concerning laminitis is in confusion. It is not yet authoritatively ascertained whether horses lie down or stand up—whether the

shoes should be taken off or left on—and what kind of treatment it is
proper to adopt. Any dispute about general facts pronounces both
parties wrong; it assures us that the experience of the disputants is
somewhat limited. The circumstances cannot be very marked where the
recognition is not universal: the treatment can only be not confirmed,
because none attended with conspicuous benefit has been proposed.

Horses do often lie down in laminitis; but they more generally stand.
When down, they should be suffered to remain; and when up, the first
thing done should be the employment of slings. Place the cloth under
the belly with the least possible noise; the man the horse is accustomed
to, with orders to soothe the animal when alarm is excited, should be
stationed at the head. The men who are arranging the slings should
pause on the slightest sign of fear, and only resume their labor when

A HORSE IN SLINGS, WITH THE FORE FEET IN HOT WATER, FOR ACUTE LAMINITIS.

confidence is restored. The ropes, however, must not be drawn tight
and fixed. The ends of the cords should, by means of two extra pulleys, be carried to some distance from the animal. To the end of each
rope ought to be fastened a stout ring, and on this, by means of hooks,
weights should be suspended. As the weights are added, the man should
caress the sufferer till sufficient counterpoise be attached to take the
principal bearing from the feet without offering much obstacle to the
breathing.

With regard to the shoes, we should first soften the hoof by allowing
the feet to soak in warm water in which a portion of any alkali has been
dissolved. The slings being applied, the fore feet are to be placed in a
trough of hot, soft water, and allowed to remain there till the hoof is
quite pulpy. Then one foot is to be gently raised and the trough par-

tially removed. All this must be done very quietly—not a word being spoken—and all operation suspended at the appearance of the smallest alarm. The man at the head must not for an instant quit his post.

The foot being released from the water, a sharp-pointed knife is to be employed and the horn cut, so as to free every nail, till the shoe drops off; but the iron should not be allowed to clatter on the ground.

This method is infinitely better than the common practice of taking off the horse's shoe. The smith removes the shoe by a wrench, using his pliers for the purpose of gaining extra power. No doubt the metal had much better remain on than be thus rudely displaced. But, in removing the shoe from a softened foot, no smith is necessary, and no smith should be employed: the veterinary surgeon should himself cut out the nails; and no matter if an hour or two be occupied over each foot. In laminitis there must be no hurry.

THE MANNER IN WHICH THE NAILS, WHICH FASTEN ON THE SHOE, ARE TO BE RE-LEASED FROM THE HORSE'S HOOF DURING ACUTE LAMI-NITIS.

Before the shoes are removed, half a drachm of belladonna and fifteen grains of digitalis should be placed in the horse's mouth. Both drugs should be gently introduced, not as a draught or a ball, but in substance; or in the smallest possible bulk. These medicines should be repeated every half hour, till the breathing is easier and the pulse somewhat altered in character. Then some additional weight may be added to the slings; and, by taking advantage of similar opportunities, the animal may be eventually lifted almost off the ground without displaying any inclination to resist.

When the horse is in this position, open the jugular vein with a lancet, making the least possible flurry. Abstract one quart of blood,

THE SYRINGE TO BE EMPLOYED TO INJECT BLOOD-WARM WATER INTO THE VEINS DURING ACUTE LAMINITIS. THE MARK ON THE ROD DENOTES HOW FAR THE HANDLE IS TO BE PUSHED DOWN. (See *Enteritis*, p. 170.)

which may be obtained with the greatest ease. Have ready a quart syringe filled with water; inject one pint into the orifice whence two pints of blood have been abstracted. The effect will be produced in a few minutes. Copious purgation and perspiration will ensue, and the fever will be greatly abated. Clothe the horse well up. Place before him a pail of thin gruel with a bundle of green-meat, and enough has been done for one day. But mind and leave two men to watch in the stable throughout the first three nights.

On the following morning give a dose of ether and laudanum—two ounces of both in a pint of water. Let the horse take his own time in swallowing: do not care if half the drink should be lost. In fact, if the attempt to give the physic should call forth much opposition, abstain from administering it: quiet is of more importance than medicine. On that account, strict orders should be given to admit no visitors, and the strictest injunction concerning silence should be enforced.

The pulse and breathing must be watched; and, as either appear to augment, the drugs before recommended must be introduced. Should the artery on either side of the pastern throb, that sign indicates the foot to be congested. This condition must be relieved. With a lancet open both pastern veins, which are sure to be in a swollen state, and plunge the foot up to the fetlock in warm water A little blood abstracted by this method does more good than the ample venesections so generally advised, but which, from their tendency to lower the system, are apt to prepare the way for the worst terminations to acute laminitis. Our object should be to conquer the disease without reducing the strength; had the horse ten times its natural vigor, such an affliction as acute laminitis would more than exhaust it all. The failure of former practitioners has been chiefly owing to their inattention to this fact.

While the affection lasts, these measures must be pertinaciously adopted; the feet, the entire time, must be repeatedly put in warm water, not only to soften the horn, but because the chief pain is caused by the congested or swollen condition of the secretive portion of the foot; congestion, likewise, induces the terminations to be most feared; heat or warmth is perhaps the best means of relieving loaded vessels. Cover over the water or blind the horse's eyes while in the slings, because acute disease is likely to disorder the vision, and a sick, imprisoned animal is too apt to be startled by the reflection of its own image The author has had reason to lament the neglect of such necessary precaution.

The termination to be feared is disorganization—either from the casting of the hoof or the descent of the coffin-bone from its natural situation. The first result is preceded by chronic suppuration. A slight division is observed between hair and horn; and from the opening thus occasioned a small quantity of unhealthy pus issues, mingled with much bloody serum Ultimately the entire hoof loosens and drops off, exposing the fleshy parts beneath Now, all these fleshy parts must have been diseased before they could have separated from their secretion, and such fleshy parts are not the laminæ only, but all those represented in the engravings on page 373.

The sudden exposure of parts which, during health, are covered and protected, cannot otherwise than cause an extraordinary effect upon the body of the sufferer. Persons who have lost a nail seldom have that substance renewed in all its original integrity. Deformity or an imper-

THE SENSITIVE LAMINA AND CORONET DIVESTED
OF THEIR HORNY COVERING.

THE SENSITIVE SOLE—FROG AND BARS DI-
VESTED OF THEIR HORNY COVERING.

fect secretion is generally retained to mark the deprivation. Nature appears averse to the restoration of any of her original structures.

Such a catastrophe is denominated sloughing of the hoof. After that has occurred it is useless to prolong the suffering by permitting the horse to live. Doubtless in time a sort of new hoof would be produced, but it would only be a deformity. It would want the toughness and strength of the original formation.

Such was the hoof which used to succeed sloughing under the old plan of treatment; the author is happy to state he has not witnessed such a misfortune since he has followed the practice which he here recommends.

DIAGRAM.
The new horny cover-
ing which invests the
foot of the horse after
sloughing of the hoof,
as a termination to
acute laminitis.

The suppuration just spoken of was not of the copious kind, but was a tardy secretion mingled with bloody serum; it is astonishing such a fact should not have warned veterinary surgeons against following depletive measures. The effusion, however, of which the writer has next to speak is entirely the result of weakness. It does appear most strange that exhausting treatment should have been pursued as with infatuation, despite of so evident a warning. The parts which in health only secrete horn, during exhaustion throw out serum, or the thinner portion of the blood. This separates the coffin-bone from its attachments, while the imposed weight forces the loosened bone from its natural position. To make this more clear, diagrams of a natural foot, and of one which has suffered distortion from acute laminitis, are represented on page 374. In the natural foot, the pedal bone is situated close to the outer crust; in the laminitic foot, the bone is forced down-ward toward the sole, which it ultimately penetrates. There is an artery running around the lower edge of the coffin-bone; upon this artery the animal, if suffered to live, would, after displacement of the coffin-bone, be obliged to tread. The consequence is that a horse, having a foot thus distorted, cannot by any possibility take a sound step; it lives in torture and moves in anguish.

This formation has been too generally spoken of as pumice foot, whereas that peculiarity is altogether distinct. Pumice foot does not

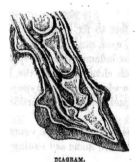

DIAGRAM.

A section of the horse's foot, showing the natural and relative situations of the bones which enter into the formation of the horse's foot when in a healthy state.

DIAGRAM.

A section of the horse's foot after one of the terminations to acute laminitis, exposing the interior of the hoof when the coffin-bone has fallen from its original situation.

entirely incapacitate the horse for labor; it is a chronic disease leading to a very opposite species of distortion, or to a bulging of the sole such as is here illustrated.

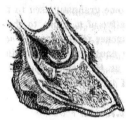

A SECTION OF THE HORSE'S FOOT, ILLUSTRATING THE DISTORTION WHICH CONSTITUTES PUMICE FOOT.

THE DEFORMITY WHICH ENSUES UPON DROPPING OF THE COFFIN-BONE.

After dropping of the coffin-bone has taken place, it is commonly said that the hoof, struck upon the spot once occupied by the coffin-bone, emits a hollow sound; such is not the fact.

The space supposed to be empty is immediately filled by an impure horn—a soft, transparent substance, which, if the animal be permitted to live, dries, or diminishes in bulk, and the front of the hoof falls in. The author once beheld, working in a lime-pit near Reigate, an aged animal which, some time previous, had suffered dropping of the coffin-bone; the animal was shod with leather, and had a shoe lifted from the ground by means of large calkins both before and behind. The hoof, however, was terribly misshapen; it hardly admits of such a description as would be readily understood; therefore the hoof is represented from a sketch made upon the spot.

The other terminations to acute laminitis are metastasis and mortification.

Metastasis is when the fever leaves the feet to fix upon some other and remote part, as the lungs, bowels, brain, eyes, etc. Or, fever of the feet is frequently asserted to be caused by the inflammation "dropping" from those parts into the hoofs; when such changes ensue, the body being already weakened, the attack is seldom of a very acute type; but, nevertheless, it may be attended by disorganization, by distortion, or even by death.

It is a bad symptom should no change be observed in the course of the disorder before the expiration of the fifth day; some sad ending may then be expected, but it does not invariably follow. The animal should be watched night and day; all that can possibly be done to alleviate its suffering should be put into practice. For that end, the writer has found nothing equal in its soothing effects to perfect quietude, and good gruel made with a portion of linseeds and of beans mixed with oatmeal But be sure that laminitis has departed from the feet before the slings are removed; then, even supposing no metastasis to have occurred, do not suddenly take all support from the horse, but remove a weight every day, so that the restored parts may become gradually used to their original functions. On the first sign indicative of a return to the disorder, restore the full counterpoise and recommence treatment; for acute laminitis is somewhat treacherous. Very cautiously exercise the invalid upon a piece of meadow land; and, as the health appears restored, gradually return to the usual method of treatment.

SUBACUTE LAMINITIS.

This is a variety of the former disease; the characteristic differences between the two are thus stated by the esteemed late William Percival:—

"In neither form is laminitis the disease of the unbroken or unused horse Now and then acute laminitis will appear in the four or five year old horse when newly taken into work; more commonly it is witnessed incapacitating the horse when at work, and during the middle period of life. **Subacute laminitis,** on the other hand, is very apt to select the aged and worked animal. Secondly, acute laminitis is the immediate effect of labor, hard either from its distressful character or its endurance. Subacute laminitis, on the contrary, will make its appearance in the stable where the horse has been for some time living in a state of idleness or absolute rest. Thirdly, acute laminitis makes its attack directly or shortly after the application of the exciting cause; subacute laminitis approaches so gradually that it is often present some days before its existence is discovered. Fourthly, acute laminitis is marked by great suffering and accompanied by raging fever; in subacute laminitis fever is not to be detected, and the mode of progression alone indicates suffering. Fifthly, acute laminitis may terminate in metastasis, suppuration, and mortification; in subacute laminitis neither of these issues is to be dreaded, for, if we do not succeed in producing resolution, dropping of the coffin-bone is the customary ending to the disorder."

The above, quoted from memory, presents a graphic contrast and an admirable portrait of the disorder. It is so eloquent in its brevity that it leaves nothing to be added; therefore the author will at once proceed to state his views of the subject.

Subacute laminitis is always first noticed in the manner of progressing. The master complains that the horse has become slower; that the whip has lost influence over the body; and that the animal, when progressing, appears to jolt more than usual. This last observation indicates the kind of horses to which subacute laminitis is principally confined. Acute laminitis is almost the property of fast saddle-horses; the subacute variety more especially belongs to harness-horses. The author

THE MANNER OF PROGRESSING WHEN SUFFERING UNDER SUBACUTE LAMINITIS.

has lately seen specimens of the subacute disease tugging those vehicles which were once fashionable and which were called "cabriolets." The animal suffering this disorder endeavors to bring the heels only to the ground. All its fumbling gait, its supposed sluggishness, and want of appreciation for the whip are to be attributed to this desire—to take the weight as much as possible from the seat of agony.

The success of treatment, in a great measure, depends upon the disorder being early detected. Get the horse immediately into slings, as was directed for acute laminitis, and proceed in the same manner with the removal of the shoe. Omit all bleeding. If the bowels are costive, allow a portion of green-meat until the evil is removed; but do not produce purgation All medicine of a debilitating character must be withheld. Give, night and morning, a quart of stout; allow two drinks, each containing one ounce of ether, in half a pint of water, during the day. This, with half-drachm doses of belladonna as needed to allay any symptoms of pain, will constitute the whole of the treatment.

As regards food, it should consist of sound oats previously ground, and a moderate allowance of crushed, old beans The water should be whitened, and all hay strictly withheld. The animal should not be left night or day, and gentleness should be enjoined upon its attendant. The food, however, should not be without limit; five feeds of corn are enough for one day, if the horse will eat so much

Should dropping of the coffin-bone end the attack, it is only charity to terminate the existence. In Mr. W. Percival's admirable work the reader will find described at length a method proposed for restoring the bone to its original position. The author has seen that plan tried more than once, but never beheld any good result. The knacker has, in every case, been called in to finish the unsuccessful experiment.

The horse, however, which recovers from an attack of laminitis, either in the acute or subacute form, should ever after be shod with leather; and were this admirable practice universal, probably, by deadening concussion, it might altogether eradicate the disease. The expense is the objection to its adoption; but against the cost, the horse proprietor has to ask himself, What are a few shillings extra, at each shoeing, to secure immunity from that horrible disorder to which the servant of his pleasure is exposed?

NAVICULAR DISEASE.

This is the scourge of willing horse-flesh; it is the disease from which favorite steeds mostly suffer; it is not less fatal in its termination than vexatious in its course and painful during its existence.

The malignancy of the disorder is expended upon the substances which in health are without feeling, but which occasion the most acute anguish when affected by disease—namely, bone, tendon, and synovial membrane Strictly confined to these structures, and frequently limited to a space not half an inch in diameter, the suffering it occasions is such as often provokes the sacrifice of the life, and invariably renders the animal next to useless.

It is confined to the interior of the foot, being, as its name implies, strictly located upon the navicular bone. The navicular bone is a small bone attached to the posterior portion of the os pedis, and resting upon the perforans tendon, which is inserted into the inferior surface of the coffin-bone. A synovial sac is placed between the navicular bone and superior surface of the tendon, on which the ossoeus structure reposes. Synovial sacs are only found in places where motion is great and almost incessant; thus the existence of this formation apprises us that the bone and tendon, in a healthy state, are designed to move freely upon each

A DIAGRAM TO EXPLAIN THE SEAT OF NAVICULAR DISEASE.

a. The perforans tendon running beneath the bone, and on which the bone reposes.

b. The comparative size and relative situation of the navicular bone.

c. The synovial sac which facilitates the motion of the bone on the tendon; upon the superior surface of this sac navicular disease is alone exhibited.

other. They do this while unaffected by disease; the foot, indeed, cannot be flexed, extended, retracted, or placed upon the ground without this busy little joint being put into motion. It is, perhaps, as essential a part—though of small size—as any of the larger structures which enter into the horse's body.

Navicular disease, however, affects only the lower surface of the bone; the upper surface shares another synovial sac, which lubricates the articulation of the coffin-bone with the lower bone of the pastern. This upper surface is never affected; the navicular bone may diminish or wither through disease, still the affection remains confined to its original situation; disease may lead to fracture of the bone or to rupture of the perforans tendon, still the superior portion of the navicular bone to the last exhibits a healthful condition.

This most annoying and terrible disorder springs from two causes. The first was a very favorite crotchet of the late Professor Coleman, who was always theorizing to the injury of the animal it was his office to cure. The disease is now largely distributed through that gentleman's favorite maxim concerning the absolute necessity that there should be pressure upon the frog. Every smith thus instructed tried to bring the frog as near the ground as possible, and the consequence was the spread of navicular disease. It is true, the frog, in a state of nature, was designed to bear pressure; but surely it is folly to talk about the natural condition of the horse when nothing like a wild horse exists. Here was Coleman's error; he legislated for the most artificial of living creatures, which consumes only prepared food, and which moves only over laboriously manufactured roads, as if it had been in an undomesticated condition, gamboling upon the untilled earth.

The second cause is, the parsimony of most horse proprietors. Would these gentlemen have their favorites shod with leather, the smith would be obliged to slightly raise the frog; while the leather—if good, stout, sole leather—and the stopping would protect the seat of navicular discase from injury. With regard to the first cause, it was recognized by the late W. Percival, one of Coleman's most enthusiastic pupils; and, as concerns the last, its efficacy as a preventive needs no pleading nor any reference to establish its merits.

The horse, when attacked, commonly has a good open foot—in fact, before disease commences, the foot is healthy. An animal in this condition is being ridden or slowly led out of the stable. In the last case it, being fresh, may rejoice to feel and sniff the cool air of heaven. It may prance about, and we may admire its attitudes; but in an instant it becomes dead lame. So a horse may be mounted by a kind master; the creature may be going its own pace, when, of a sudden, the movement shall change, and the rider will be made conscious that his steed is lame.

In either case the foot is examined It is cool, quite cool; no stone appears to have injured it—nor is any pebble sticking between the web of the shoe and the sole. Yet the lameness is acute and does not pass off. Now, to explain this, let the reader turn to the illustration which was last presented.

The portion of the foot, immediately under the navicular bone, has been placed upon a stone; the stone has been forced against the foot by the immense weight of the horse imposed upon it The stone, under this impulse, has bruised the navicular bone. But the fleshy frog and the perforans tendon would have to be passed before this effect could reach the bone Are neither of these also hurt? Doubtless they are. But the fleshy frog is a highly organized, secretive organ, and probably, by its innate energy, soon recovers from the effect. The tendon is, on the contrary, too soft and yielding to retain any harsh impression. The bone is firm and solid; and thus that which failed to act upon either of the intervening parts, leaves a lasting injury upon the osseous structure, which, moreover, is held stationary by the coronary bone, and which is disposed to display injury, being covered by synovial membrane.

The navicular bone belongs to a peculiar class called "sesimoid, or floating bones." These are more highly organized than the generality of osseous structures—in short, quite as much, or rather more, than the human tooth. Everybody must be acquainted with the anguish occasioned by unexpectedly biting upon a hard substance. The tooth, however, is coated with crystalline enamel The bone is covered by delicate synovial membrane. The impression is, therefore, more likely to be lasting with the last than the first.

After the expiration of a week, however, the lameness disappears, and the proprietor fondly hopes all is over The animal may work soundly for months—sometimes it never fails again. Generally, however, after some period, extending from six to nine months, the lameness reappears. This time the treatment occupies a longer space; and the subsequent soundness is of shorter duration. Thus the malady progresses; the period occupied in curative measures lengthens, while the season of usefulness diminishes; till, in the end, the horse becomes lame for life.

The worst of it is, that the pain in the lame foot occasions greater stress to be thrown upon the sound member; the result generally is that both legs ultimately become affected with the like disease: such is ordinarily the case. The horse with a tender foot will always bring it gently to the earth; but this circumstance obliges the animal to cast the other foot to the ground with heedless impetuosity. The consequence is, the sound foot is sooner or later forced upon some stone or other inequality; from the law of sympathy, the disease subsequently makes rapid strides; for at death both feet are usually found in a similar condition.

The effect of these repeated attacks is soon shown. The anguish has been likened to toothache, only it must assuredly be a toothache twenty

A HORSE, WITH NAVICULAR DISEASE, POINTING IN THE STABLE.

times magnified. All people know "there never yet was philosopher who could withstand the toothache;" but think of the poor horse with twenty toothaches compressed into one agony! The man can seek a thousand changes to divert his suffering; the simple horse cannot even drink intoxicating fluids, and has hitherto not learned to smoke. The suffering, therefore, continues. And as man strives to spare a decayed tooth by masticating on the other side of the mouth, the horse endeavors to ease an aching foot by leaning all its weight upon a sound limb. Thus it learns to point in the stable or to advance one leg beyond the center of gravity, leaving the healthy member to support the entire weight of the body.

A foot thrown out of use decreases in size. Nature has given certain parts for certain purposes; and if these purposes are avoided, those parts diminish in bulk. Wear the arm in a sling for any extended period, and the arm will sensibly grow smaller, or become withered. So the horse's foot, spared in progression and pointed in the stable, obviously changes its shape. The quarters draw inward; the heels narrow; the frog hardens and decreases; the sole thickens and heightens; the crust becomes marked by rims and grows considerably higher. In fact, the foot, from being

THE UPRIGHT PASTERN AND HARD, UNYIELDING HOOF, INDICATIVE OF CONFIRMED NAVICULAR DISEASE.

an open, healthy foot, becomes a strong, contracted, or diseased member.

The effect of the disease is speedily shown by the animal progressing entirely upon the toe, whereby the front of the shoe becomes much worn, as shown in the following engraving. Indeed, it is not unusual to see shoes taken from horses having navicular disease with their front edges worn positively to a cutting sharpness. When the animal is in

THE TROT, PECULIAR TO NAVICULAR DISEASE, GENERALLY TERMED GROGGINESS.

this stage, the mode of progression is usually what is termed groggy— that is, the hind feet, which are never affected, step out as boldly as ever; but the fore feet are limited in their action. They cannot be advanced far, because extension causes the perforans tendon to press upon the navicular bone; the leg cannot be bent, because flexion moves the perforans tendon upon the navicular bone. The animal, thus doubly disabled, endeavors to make up by quickened movement for that which it lacks in perfect action. It dare not bring the heel to the ground or take long steps. It therefore progresses upon the toes, and indulges in very short but quick movements of the fore feet; and a horse thus affected may be challenged, though unseen, by the "*patter, patter! clatter, clatter!*" which it makes.

Navicular disease appears to the author to have been entirely mistaken
as regards its treatment. It is administered to as though it consisted in
violent and acute inflammation, whereas it is caused by a different process—namely, ulceration. Inflammation excites the whole system, and
occurs in strong bodies: ulceration is a diseased condition peculiar to
the aged and to the weakly. Navicular disease is, so far as the writer's
knowledge extends, unknown in the unbroken animal. It mostly affects
the adult or the aged. It is not inflammatory; for the foot, in the first
instance, exhibits no heat, and, in the after-stages, never becomes more
than warm. Often the warmth is so very slight that practitioners have
to adopt a kind of stratagem to determine which is the more hot of the
fore feet. A pail of water is brought forward, and sufficient to thoroughly wet both hoofs is thrown over the feet. The parts are then
watched; and that which becomes dry the sooner is reasonably considered the warmer hoof of the two.

Moreover, the consequences of this disease are absorption, which it
takes years to effect—not deposition, which is accomplished in a few
days. The bone lessens in size, sometimes grows thin, till ultimately it
may fracture; the tendon loses in substance, and its fibers separate, till
at length they may rupture. All internal structures which enter into
the composition of the foot grow less and less, till the hoof becomes
obviously small or contracted; for it is a law of nature that, in the living
creature, the contents should govern the covering: thus the brain con-
trols the skull, the lungs regulate the chest, etc. etc. The horn alone
increases; but it is a curious fact that Nature always endeavors to protect the part she allows to suffer from disease: thus in rickets, with

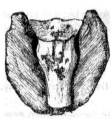

A MORBID PREPARATION, KINDLY
LENT TO THE AUTHOR BY T. W.
GOWING, ESQ.

The diseased surface of the navicular bone exposed, and the
affected tendon turned back upon the lower part of the os pedis.

children, the bones of the legs frequently curve;
but Nature, true to her principles, strives, by
extra deposition, to strengthen the parts which
threaten to break through weakness.

All tokens declare the navicular disease to
be a chronic affection, attended by symptoms
of bodily weakness. The accompanying example of the disorder, taken from the body of a
horse which was killed for incurable lameness,
will illustrate fully this fact.

In this specimen, the navicular bone occupies
its natural situation between the wings of the
os pedis. That portion of the tendon which
once shared and concealed the disease is turned

back upon the sole of the coffin-bone. What does the inspection dis-
close? Three small holes within the bone, and a few stains of blood,

which denote irritation upon the tendon. For, as the disease progresses, synovia ceases to be secreted, the navicular joint becomes dry, and is subject to the most torturing irritation every time the leg is moved.

That the one presented may not by the reader be supposed an extreme case, produced to support the writer's opinions, another specimen of the disease is given; but, on this last occasion, both sides of the navicular bone shall be exhibited. The upper surface appears perfectly healthy; the lower surface only displays a large clot of blood, and a small but comparatively a deep hole.

THE SUPERIOR SURFACE OF THE NAVICULAR BONE.   THE INFERIOR SURFACE OF THE SAME BONE.

Supposing the reader to be convinced of the justness of the writer's views, the treatment which these recommend shall be stated. Ulceration in any form proves the body to be weak or exhausted. Feed liberally, chiefly upon crushed oats and old beans. Attend to any little matter in which the horse's body may be wrong; but do little to the foot beyond, every other night, soaking it one hour in hot water, for the first fortnight. Afterward apply flannel bandages to the leg, put tips upon the hoofs, and wrap the feet up in a sponge boot, having first smeared the horn with glycerin. This, with a very long rest, is all it is in our power to accomplish. The rest, however, should be proportioned only to the proprietor's pocket or to his powers of endurance. In the first instance, six months' rest in a well-aired stable, and three subsequent months at slow agricultural employment, will not be thrown away, but will be likely to prevent future annoyances. After one relapse, the treatment is all but hopeless. The horse may be again restored to soundness; but the disease, which has with time gained strength, will be all but certain to reappear.

This, probably, may be the fittest place for stating the writer's reason for objecting to the treatment generally adopted.

Bleeding from the toe is decidedly objected to, because there never are any signs of inflammation present, but rather those symptoms which favor the belief that too little blood circulates within the foot. Blistering the coronet is more likely to augment the crusts than to reach the disease; and the tendency of navicular derangement is to thicken the horn. The same reasoning applies to paring out the foot and placing the hoof in poultices; it is more likely to act upon, and lead to activity in, the secreting membrane, which is near the surface, than to operate

beneficially upon a remote joint   Objection is taken to the feet standing
in clay, because the cold produced by evaporation is disposed to drive
blood from the parts, which already have too little.

In extreme cases, neurotomy, or division of the nerve, is the only
resort   For a detailed account of that operation the reader is referred
to the next chapter.   It permits the horse to be of some service to the
master, and allows the animal an escape from the agonies of a cruel disease ; it is, however, not final.   It conceals the lameness ; it rarely cures
the disorder.   The internal ravages may still go on ; and, though the
nerve of the leg has been properly divided, yet at an uncertain period
nerves generally reunite, and the part which was deprived of sensation
may become once more sensitive to pain.   Moreover, no eye can look
upon the internal ravage.   Sensation destroyed in a foot tempts the
horse to throw even more than its proportion of weight on a part weakened by disease   The bone has fractured, or the tendon has ruptured,
under too sudden a test of their integrity.

For the above reasons, neurotomy is always most successful when
early performed   In the primary state of the disorder, a restoration
of the foot to its healthy functions has seemed to banish the affection.
Pressure being given to the neurotomized organ, health has occasionally returned ; and when the time has arrived for the reunion of the
nerve, that event has been signalized by no reappearance of lameness.

But when the disorder has continued so long as to weaken the structures of the foot, operation is always attended with hazard   The nerve
may be properly divided ; the operation shall be admirably performed ;
still the parts, weakened by the joint actions of active disease and of
long rest, have become disorganized   Pressure being suddenly restored,
the debilitated structures could not sustain the restoration of that burden
they were originally formed to endure   Rupture or fracture was the
result , and the veterinary surgeon, despite his admirable talent, is disgraced by being obliged to order the immediate destruction of that
animal which it was intended he should have benefited.

For the above reasons, and because the sound member is always disposed to exhibit the disorder which incapacitates one foot, never delay
adopting the only chance of certain relief.   If from pecuniary motives,
or from better but mistaken feelings, the proprietor hesitates to subject
his dumb companion to the surgeon's knife, never afterward should he
repent of such a resolve.   With delay the opportunity of benefit has
passed ; the operation, to be successful, should be resorted to upon the
second appearance of acute and decided lameness.

CHAPTER XIV.

INJURIES—THEIR NATURE AND THEIR TREATMENT.

POLL EVIL.

Poll evil consists of a deep abscess, ending in an ulcerous sore which has numerous sinuses. The situation of the affection is the most forward portion of the neck, near the top of the head, which part is peculiarly liable to injury, especially in agricultural horses.

The gentlemen who superintend the laying down of stable floors always make the pavements of the stalls to slant from the manger to the gang-

THE POSITION OF THE HEAD BEFORE AN ENLARGEMENT ANNOUNCES THE EXISTENCE OF AN ABSCESS ON THE POLL.

way. They either know nothing about the habits of the horse, or they disdain to think about so trivial a matter as the convenience of an animal. Their stables are built for men; and it is sufficient if the places will hold whatsoever man chooses to put into such out-buildings.

The horse is most at ease when the position takes the strain off the flexor tendons. That end is accomplished when the hind legs are the higher portion of the body, or when the ground slants in precisely the opposite direction to which the flooring of all present stables incline. The animal, finding the slope which is most convenient for the builder's purposes adverse to its comfort, endeavors to compound the matter by hanging back upon the halter, thus getting the hind feet into the open drain which always divides the stalls from the gangway.

The rope should be stout which has to sustain the huge weight of the horse; in proportion to that weight, of course, must be the pressure upon the seat of poll evil. Pressure, as a natural consequence, stops circulation. Upon circulation being freely performed, health, secretion, and even life itself is dependent The flow of blood to any part of the body cannot be long prevented without unpleasant sensations being engendered. Numbness and itching are the first results. The horse tries to master these by rubbing its head violently against the trevise or division of the stall. Friction, when applied to an irritable place, is never a soothing process; when instituted by the huge strength of a horse, its probable ill effects may be easily surmised. It is, therefore, no legitimate cause for wonder if some of the fleshy substances, compressed between the external wood and the internal bones of the neck, become bruised, and deep-seated abscess is thus provoked

This, however, is not the sole cause; there are others equally potent and generally springing from the same source—namely, from human folly. How much of animal agony might be spared if man, in the pride of superiority, would deign to waste an occasional thought upon the poor creatures which are born and live in this country only by his permission and to labor in his service! Stable doors are commonly made as though none but human beings had to pass through them The tallest of mankind, probably, might enter a stable without stooping; but does it therefore follow that a horse can pass under the beam without assuming a crouching position? Many horses learn to fear the doorway. They shy, rear, or prance, whenever led toward it. Man, however, refuses to be instructed by the action of his mute servant, those symptoms of fear, which are the bitter fruits of experience, are attributed to the patient and enduring quadruped as exhibitions of the rankest vice.

Low doors, such as usually belong to stables, are among the most frequent causes of poll evil The horse, when passing through them, is either surprised by something it beholds outside the building, or checked by the voice of the groom The sudden elevation of the head is, in the animal, expressive of every unexpected emotion Up goes the crest and crash comes the poll against the beam of the doorway. A violent bruise is thereby provoked, and a deep-seated abscess is the sad result.

The horse likewise suffers from the representatives in brutality of him for whose benefit it wears out its existence. Carters display their ignorance by getting into violent passions with their teams. "Whooay" and "kum hup" are shouted out; the huge whip is slashed and snaffle jagged, till mute intelligence is fairly puzzled. Were mortals in the like position, subject to the same terrible chastisement, and, at the same time, forbid to inquire the wishes of their commander, théy would be in no better condition. The panting, sweating, and starting of the poor, confused quadrupeds announce their terror. The driver, too enraged to understand himself, and too impatient to delay punishment upon the objects of his wrath, resorts to the butt-end of his heavy whip. Some wretched animal is struck upon the poll, for the head is always aimed at when stupidity quarrels with its own ignorance, and a dreadful disorder is established.

All the causes of poll evil may, however, be reduced to one—namely, to external injury. The first result of such a cause is pain whenever the head is moved. Motion enforces the contraction of the bruised muscles; and the agony growing more and more acute, the sufferer acquires a habit of protruding the nose in a very characteristic manner long before the slightest symptom of the malady can be perceived. When forced to bend the head toward the manger, it generally hangs back to the length of the halter; for although so doing occasions pain, the position renders the necessary angle of the head upon the neck as little acute as possible. The anguish attendant upon the earlier stages of the disease is exemplified by the length of time occupied in emptying the manger. At this stage nothing is apparent; at this period also great cruelty is too often exercised when the collar is forced over the head regardless of the struggles of the acutely-diseased animal.

Should the seat of poll evil at this stage of the disease be particularly examined, the most lengthened inspection, when prompted by expectation, may fail to detect even an indication of probable enlargement. Pressure, or enforced motion of the head, excites resistance. A few weeks in some cases, and the swelling becomes marked or prominent. In others, the enlargement is never well developed: instances of this last kind invariably are the most difficult to treat, for in them the seat of the disorder is always most deeply seated. The size of the tumor is therefore always to be hailed as a promise that the injury is tolerably near the surface, and, consequently, more under the influence of remedial measures.

After pressure has been made, the agony occasioned causes the animal to be difficult of approach. The common method of examination is, however, very wrong. No good is done by inflicting torture. Something, on the contrary, is concealed. Place the fingers lightly on the part, and allow them to remain there till the fear, excited by a touch upon a tender place, has subsided. Then, and not till then, gradually introduce pressure. The more superficial the injury, the more speedy will be the response.　The longer the time and greater the force requi-. site to induce signs of uneasiness, the deeper, as a general rule, will be the center of the disease.

In either case there is little good accomplished by those applications which are recognized as mild measures.　Fomentations and poultices commonly waste valuable time, and, at last, prove of no avail. There-fore, blister over the place.　Obviously, the employment of more active treatment is at present forbidden.　Do not, however, give the carter so much liquid blister, to be rubbed in by his heavy and coarse hand; but lightly paint over the seat of the supposed hurt with spirituous or acetous tincture of cantharides.　Do this daily till copious irritation is produced, and, before that dies away, repeat the dressing. Keep up the soreness, but do no more.　Never apply the tincture upon active vesication, otherwise a foul sore, ending in a lasting blemish, may be the result. Make the poll merely painful.　An additional motive will thereby be instituted to keep the head perfectly quiet, for constant motion pro-vokes the worst consequences of poll evil, causing the confined pus to burrow, or to form sinuses.

The foregoing treatment has been proposed because the tincture, when applied by means of a brush, penetrates the hair more quickly, acts quite as energetically, and is less likely to run down upon other parts than the oil of cantharides, which the heat of the body always renders more liquid.　It is advised to be used, because it establishes an external inflammation.　Inflammations in living bodies, like fires prey-

ing upon inanimate substances, have an attraction for each other. All injuries which lead to suppuration likewise have a tendency to move toward the surface; and these two laws, acting together, very probably may tend to the speedier develop-ment of poll evil, thereby shorten-ing the sufferings of the animal. Should they not have that effect, the vesicatory is beneficial. About the head of the horse are numerous

POLL EVIL DURING THE FIRST STAGE.

layers of thin tendon, which are termed fascia.　Through this substance matter absorbs its way with difficulty.　It is, therefore, almost impris-oned, and motion always disposes the pus to seek new outlets.　Thus pipes or sinuses are formed; these constitute one of the worst symp-toms attendant upon poll evil.

As soon as the swelling appears, watch it attentively.　Wait till some particular spot points, or till it feels softer, if it be not more prominent than the surrounding substance. Then have the animal cast. Being down, take a keen knife and open the spot before indicated. That being accomplished, pause while the secretion flows forth. Afterward insert into the cut a small, flexible probe. When its progress is impeded, employ the knife with a director. Continue doing this till the seat or center of the disease has been gained.

Remember, however, you are not hacking at the family loaf; it is living and sensitive flesh you are wounding Therefore, be very careful your knife is thoroughly sharpened, and is of sufficient size; mind, also, that all the cuts run smoothly into one another, so as to leave clean surfaces for the healing process to unite. Having reached the heart of the disorder, proceed to empty out all the concrete matter. That done, wash out the part with a syringe and the coldest spring water. Afterward examine the cavity Excise any loose pieces of tendon or of ligament, and cut until a healthy aspect is everywhere presented. Then rub the sides of the deep-seated wound with lunar caustic Let the horse rise, giving orders that the sore is to be thoroughly moistened thrice daily with the solution of the chloride of zinc, one grain to the ounce of water, and, placing a rag dipped in a solution of tar over the wound to keep off the flies, return the horse to the stable

If the disease be left to run its course, the swelling generally increases, while numerous openings at last disfigure the enlargement. From such drain a glairy discharge. This adheres to the surrounding parts, and, joined to the miserable expression of the countenance, gives to the horse a peculiarly unpleasant appearance. The flesh wastes under the perpetual anguish, and the half-conscious aspect of the creature justifies a suspicion that the brain is affected.

In that case, proceed as before directed concerning casting the horse and the knife with which you operate. Have the blade rather too large than too small. Most veterinary instruments are mere adaptations of those employed by the human surgeon. The author never remembers to have seen anything approaching to the magnitude of a proper horses operating knife in the hands of his fellows. A small blade compels numerous small cuts. The part is rather snipped asunder than divided by one clean incision The recovery is thereby materially delayed; and the lengthened operation greatly deteriorates from its chances of success, not to dwell upon the increased suffering occasioned to the quadruped

The horse being down, do not attempt any display of your proficiency. Look well and long at the part intended to be operated upon Decide in your own mind the course in which the knife is to move. That course should be influenced by the direction in which you may probably separate the greater number of sinuses. In the engraving inserted below there are four holes, each indicating the presence of a sinus. The supposed direction of the knife is laid down by dotted lines. The primary and lower incision includes three of the pipes. That made, another connects the other sinus with the longer incision ; the after-labor necessitates the cleaning of the central sac, removing all the hanging pieces, also probing

the sinuses, and making sure all are fairly opened. If any are found unopened, a director should be inserted, and the channel should be connected with the chief wound by means of a smaller knife.

Two cautions are necessary to be given with regard to the treatment of poll evil: Never permit the knife to be applied

POLL EVIL IN ITS SECOND STAGE, OR WHEN READY FOR OPERATION.

upon the root of the mane. Underneath the hair which decorates the neck of the horse lies an important ligament, by means of which the head is chiefly supported. All the evils which might be anticipated may not spring from the division of that development; but it is well to spare it, although the prostrate animal should have to be turned over, and the operation have to be continued on the other side. Also, when working the creature subsequent to its recovery, never use a collar. Wounds, although perfectly healed, are apt to remain morbidly sensitive ; serious accidents, over which the reader would deeply grieve, may occur from the harness touching the part which once was diseased. A breast strap is, therefore, to be much preferred.

There are several popular methods of treating this disease. All, however, are cruel; one is barbarous; when properly conducted, none are efficient under the direction of a person possessing the smallest feeling. The injection of potent caustics in solution, or violent compression upon an exquisitely tender swelling even until the force employed amounts to that power which can bring the sides of a distant internal cavity together, drive out the corruption, and hold the part in that position while healing is established, have been largely advocated. Whoever could increase the suffering of a mute and patient life to that degree which the last method necessitates would merit a much severer punishment than the writer can afford space to detail. Of these modes of cure the author can profess no experience. He has, however, seen injections used; in no instance have they been successful. The time which they occupied was enormous, and the expense with which they were attended by no means small. The man who hopes, to eradicate this disease should never have recourse to them.

Another process, formerly very popular, consisted in slicing the living flesh in a very coarse and vulgar manner; that, however, was merely preparatory. The chief dependence was placed in boiling liquor, which was inhumanly poured into the wounds After such a method were all sinuous sores treated by an ignorant and uneducated quack, who especially delighted in eradicating such forms of disease The writer has heard terrible descriptions given of the agony produced, and equally revolting has been the picture of the filth employed by this unqualified horse doctor. While, however, the course which has been mentioned is reprobated, our heaviest condemnation should alight upon those persons who could so violate the sacredness of their trusts as to surrender any creature to the torments of so horrible a remedy

In poll evil, the only certainty reposes on the knife. When properly employed, the operation is brief; the temporary agony bears no proportion to the years of subsequent relief thereby secured. To be properly employed, however, it should be used as though the person invested with it was, for the time, divested of all feeling. He who accepts it must think only upon what he is about to perform, and must summon resolution to do it quickly. In surgery, hesitation is positive cruelty; the knife, to be curative, should be gracefully moved through the living flesh. All notching and hacking are tortures, and worse than folly; the blade should sweep through the substance; and, to prevent the struggles of the quadruped from interfering with the intentions of the surgeon, all that will be necessary is for some person to sit upon the cheek of the prostrated animal.

FISTULOUS WITHERS.

This disease, in its chief characteristics, closely resembles poll evil. It, however, differs from that disorder in one fortunate particular; poll evil must come to maturity before its cure can be attempted with any hope of success. Injury to the **withers** is easiest eradicated when attacked upon its earliest appearance; both, however, in their worst periods, proceed from pus being confined, from it decomposing and its establishing numerous sinuses When disease has reached this stage, the only certain cure is the free but skillful use of the knife.

Fistulous withers, in the first instance, is an injury to one of the superficial bursæ which nature has provided to facilitate the movement of the vertebral, points spinal under the skin ' The hurt is occasioned by badly-made saddles, but more especially by the ladies' saddles Some fair equestrians delight to feel their bodies lifted into the air, and enjoy the trivial shock of the descent; such movements, however, necessitate the weight should be leaned upon the crutch and stirrup. This kind of exercise is never indulged in by good female riders, as no saddle, however well constructed, can resist the constant strain to one side. Friction is produced; a bursa is irritated, and the animal will, under the best treatment, be rendered useless for a fortnight. Rolling in the stalls is also reported to have occasioned this affection; so likewise is the heavy hammer of the shoeing smith, intemperately employed to chastise the transient movement of an observant horse.

When first produced, the remedy is certain and easy. A swelling about the size of an egg appears near the withers, upon the off side of the body. Go up to the horse upon that side; have with you a keen-edged and sharply-pointed knife of pocket dimensions. Stand close to the animal; then impale the tumor, and, having the back of the blade toward the quadruped, cut quickly upward and outward. Mind, and stand very close to the center of the body, as the pain of this trivial

THE SLIGHT ENLARGEMENT WHICH, BADLY
TREATED OR UNATTENDED TO, MAY END
IN FISTULOUS WITHERS.

operation is apt to make the creature lash out and prance. At the spot indicated a person is perfectly safe; neither hoof nor leg will touch that particular place, or even come near it. Rest one hand on the back, and by your voice reassure the startled creature.

The swelling being divided, exchange the knife for a lunar caustic case; smear over the interior well with the cautery, and all the business is over. Never, however, attempt to pass by the heels of a steed which has been pained. The animal may suspect your motives, and the hind feet of the horse are the most powerful weapons of offense and of defense. Have the creature backed from the stall ere you attempt to quit it. Subsequently keep the wound moist with the lotion composed of chloride of zinc—one grain to the ounce of water; also have the part covered with a rag, moistened with solution of tar. In nine or ten days the incision will have healed, and after the lapse of a fortnight the animal may return to its ordinary employment.

Should this remedy be neglected, pus is soon formed within the enlargement, and the formation is accompanied by swelling, heat, and pain. The horse is useless, and continues thus till the affection is eradicated. The animal cannot wear a collar; it cannot endure a saddle; at length numerous holes are formed upon the enlargement. These are the mouths of so many sinuses, and from each exudes a foul discharge. The poor quadruped evidently suffers greatly; it will almost stand still and starve rather than brave agony by violent motion.

The only remedy is by operation; make an incision so as to embrace the greatest number of holes. Then cut from the other-openings into the main channel; this done, have the sides of the wound held back, while the center of corruption is cleaned out. Such is a very filthy and unpleasant office; if the bones are affected, all the diseased parts must be removed. When slight, the tainted portions may be scraped away; when of long standing, the spines of the vertebræ have

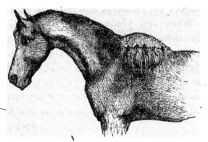

A HORSE WITH FISTULOUS WITHERS IN THE WORST STAGE.

been sundered with the saw and thus taken from the body. At any risk, none but healthy bone must be suffered to remain; all discolored or white portions of the bony structure must be extirpated, and none but that which is of a healthy pink color suffered to continue. If a particle of unhealthy, osseous growth is left behind, the wound may close, but it will break out again, and the disease become as bad as ever.

The cleansing being accomplished, apply the cloth over the wound, and keep wet with the lotion formerly directed to be used.

Sometimes the sinuses will take a dangerous direction, and, favored by the action of the shoulder, will burrow from the withers to the chest or elbow. Then the knife cannot be employed. Should a pipe incline to this course, but be of comparatively short extent, insert a little bichloride of mercury down the channel. This is best done by powdering some of the salt. Dip the elastic probe, which has recently been down the sinus, into the powder. Reinsert it, and continue to repeat this action till all the bichloride is expended.

If the sinus should have run its entire course, but not have found an exit below, then employ a long guarded seton needle, such as can be purchased at all veterinary instrument makers. Insert this in its guarded state, and, having pushed it as far as it will go, give, upon the end of the handle, a moderately sharp blow; this will force out the cutting edge and drive the point through the flesh. Pass a long tape, with a knot at the further end of it, through the opening near the point, and withdraw the instrument, leaving the tape in after another knot has been tied at the other extremity.

Thus a seton is established, and a depending orifice is instituted. The tape will act as a drain to the morbid secretion, while the irritation produced by it will also remove the callous lining of the pipe. A healthy action will thereby be established; and so soon as the inferior wound discharges a full stream of thick, creamy pus, the seton may be cut out, with a conviction that its office is fulfilled.

A GUARDED SETON NEEDLE.

THE SETON NEEDLE PROTRUDED, AND SECURED WITHIN THE HANDLE BY MEANS OF A SCREW.

The screw being loosened, the button is struck, and the sharp needle shoots forward, cutting its way through any interposing obstacle.

However, never turn animals afflicted with fistulous withers or with poll-evil out to grass. In the last disease, the motion of the head, the outstretching of the neck, and movement of the jaws occasion agony; and in the first instance, the necessity for perpetual action entails so much misery as soon renders the life worthless. The horse which is not worth the best of food in the best of stables, should not be doomed to a life of starvation and of torture. It is the shame of society that rich men are tempted by a few pounds to dispose of the creature which has been maimed in their service. Wounds endured when obeying the wishes of the master should endear the slave unto his lord. In the case of the willing steed, the law is reversed. The owner blemishes; and instead of nursing the wounded life, he disposes of it. The injured animal is sold to the first purchaser for so much as the damaged article will fetch.

FISTULOUS PAROTID DUCT.

This is a most serious evil, rather than a quickly-killing disease. The animal which is thus afflicted may endure for years; but each meal consumed and each day survived rates as a period of misery. When it is considered how much the happiness of the lower order of beings depends on merely feeding and living, it will be at once apparent how much the horse has lost when all enjoyment has departed from eating; when mere existence is embittered by being a prolongation of the suffering. The digestion becomes deranged, because the saliva, or a valuable secretion imperative to the proper performance of the function, is absent; while every movement is a pain occasioned by the agony of a diseased stomach and the anguish attendant upon a fistulous sore. The wretched creature, in this condition, speedily becomes an object of disgust to the most humane master; and, according to the convenient morality of modern times, is therefore sold to the highest bidder. Purchased only for the work which remains in the carcass, a fearful doom lies before the sick and debilitated quadruped. It rapidly sinks lower and lower, at each stage of its descent the food growing more scanty as the labor becomes more exhausting.

The **parotid duct** is the tube by which the saliva secreted by the gland is, during the act of mastication, conveyed into the mouth and mingled with the food. The parotid gland lies at the spot where the neck joins the jaw; within the interior of that body numerous fine hollow vessels connect and unite. These at each junction become larger and fewer in number, till at length they all terminate in one channel, which is the duct immediately about to be considered. It leaves the gland and travels for some space upon the inner side of the jaw; after which it curls under the inferior border of the bone and runs in front of the large masseter muscle of the horse's cheek.

Its injury is frequently occasioned by hay-seeds or particles of food, during the process of comminution, entering the open mouth of the duct; these, subsequently becoming swollen, prevent the free egress of the saliva. The secretion, nevertheless, goes forward and accumulates within the tube, which it greatly distends. A confined secretion produces the most exquisite agony. The motion of the jaw stimulates the gland to pour forth its fluid; thus every mouthful which the animal is forced to eat not only is the cause of suffering, but likewise occasions additional pressure to a channel already enlarged to bursting, and which at length bursts.

THE PAROTID DUCT DISTENDED BY A SALIVARY CALCULUS.

Another provocative is calculus, or stone, which is sometimes taken from the cheeks of horses, they being of enormous comparative magnitude; the natural tube would not admit a pea. Concretions have been removed from this narrow passage as large as a pullet's egg. Such an obstacle not only impedes the flow of saliva, but produces additional anguish by the distention it occasions, and by the hinderance so hard a substance offers to every motion of the animal jaw during the necessary period of mastication.

Every puncture made into the substance of the duct, and every rupture of the canal, speedily becomes fistulous sores. The saliva constantly pours through the opening thus instituted; the healing process is thereby prevented, and the edges of the wound rapidly become callous. It is, however, painful to be obliged to state that the stable fork, in the hand of an intemperate groom, is the instrument by which these punctures are too frequently occasioned.

Gentlemen when engaging people to attend upon their animals should always be very particular concerning temper. An irritable person, however smart he may appear, is obviously disqualified for such an occupation. A man of an evil temper should never be engaged. Still, the great majority of present grooms are rather conspicuous for an exuberance of conceit, than remarkable for any openness of countenance. Smartness may gratify the pride of the master; but it is difficult to comprehend in what manner it possibly can benefit his horse.

There is an old proverb which, being "the condensed wisdom of ages," teaches that "the master's eye fattens the steed." Most of modern masters dislike nothing so much as trouble. The stable is given over to the servant. No Eastern despot is so absolute as the groom in his dominions: he kicks and abuses its inhabitants at his pleasure. If the free exercise of his will occasions injury, a lie is easily invented and readily believed by the lazy superior. All that comes into or passes out of the building pays toll to the invested ruler. Five per cent. is levied upon the hay and corn merchant; the dung is sold as a legitimate per-

A HORSE, HAVING A FISTULOUS PAROTID DUCT, IN THE ACT OF EATING.

quisite; the bills of the harness and the coach makers are taxed one shilling in the pound by the most ignorant groom, and often much higher by the properly initiated. Thus the idle man pays dearly for his ease. There is no luxury so expensive as a want of wholesome energy.

The process of mastication causes the saliva to be secreted. At each motion of the jaw it is squirted forth with violence; every drop of the fluid passes through the false opening—no portion finds its way into the mouth. The running of the stream down the cheek wears away the hair, while the absence of a valuable constituent toward perfect digestion occasions the diet not to nourish the body. The animal loses flesh, and quickly assumes a miserable appearance, which makes the proprietor long to rid his sight of so pitiable an object.

The cure for this disease was aptly illustrated by Mr. Gowing, the excellent veterinary surgeon of Camden Town. That gentleman made an adhesive fluid, by either saturating the strongest spirit of wine with gum mastic, or dissolving India-rubber in sulphuric ether. Then, when the horse was not eating, he pared off the hardened edges of the wound till blood issued therefrom. He subsequently allowed the bleeding to stop, and placed over the orifice a piece of strained India-rubber. Over that he put a thin layer of cotton; fastened one end of the cotton to the hair of the cheek by means of the adhesive preparation. That being dry, he tightened the cotton and glued down the opposite extremity. Next he attached another layer of cotton, and subsequently another   Afterward he fastened more cotton, some of it crossways; and, having added as many layers as would make a good body, saturates the whole with the adhesive solution before alluded to

The hair affords a good ground to which any other substance can be fastened; but it is rendered better by being thoroughly washed with soft soap and warm water. The ablution deprives the skin of the horse of its naturally unctuous secretion, and permits the adhesive application a better chance.

The horse should be allowed no food which necessitates mastication The head should be fastened to the pillar-reins during the process of cure. Thin gruel only should be presented while treatment is progressing, and that should be continued until the covering falls off. Should the wound not be healed, allow a couple of days to elapse; but give no solid food   Permit the horse to rest on refuse tan—not straw, which might be eaten—during all this time. Afterward renew the attempt, and repeat it again if necessary—though the first trial generally succeeds

Before concluding, it may be well to arm the reader against those practices generally adopted by horse doctors   These practices consist in the use of the red-hot budding iron, which is among them a very popular application to a **fistulous parotid duct**. The theory which induces this resort is, a belief that the heated iron induces an eschar, and the wound closes before the crust falls off   Red-hot iron is, however, far more disposed to destroy substance than to favor growth; and, probably, its curative properties could have gained faith among no other class   Possibly there exists no other body which would credit that, to burn a hole larger, was the best way to close it. Another artifice is to inject caustic lotions up the duct, and thereby occasion the gland to slough out. Against such cruelty the author is pleased to think little need be said. The operation, when successful, causes so much irritation as endangers the life; for the body of the gland is permeated by so many and such important vessels as render the termination always very dubious.

PHLEBITIS, OR INFLAMMATION OF THE VEIN.

Formerly it was the custom to bleed horses for everything and for nothing. It was not even suspected that a creature which exists only to labor unto the limit of possibility is far more likely to be the victim of debility than of repletion It never occurred to any master that his wretched animal wanted blood putting into it rather than abstracting the smallest quantity of blood from it. However, formerly bleeding was a favorite resort with the apothecary, and the old veterinary surgeon seems to have followed the bad example. Aged people have informed the writer that they remember the time when, on a Sunday morning, a long shed was filled with agricultural horses standing in a row. These victims were all waiting to be bled The veterinary surgeon's assistant used to take the fleam, and to open a vein in the first animal's neck Then he would proceed to the second; and thus, in turn, he would open the jugulars of the entire number. No account was taken of the quantity of blood lost; that flowed forth till the last had been operated upon, when all the creatures stood simultaneously draining forth their lives

The veterinary surgeon's assistant subsequently returned, and pinned up the orifice of the first horse; then he went and performed that office for the succeeding animal. Thus he, a second time, progressed down the row, pinning up as he proceeded, and the poor horses often tottered before he came. All this was done for a human fancy: man thought the loss of blood, at spring and autumn, beneficial to all kinds of life. The writer has heard of old ladies who were very skillful in bleeding cats Most cats, however, resist such an application of medical talent; not so the horse: this animal submits itself patiently to the master's will. The creature seems to recognize that it has no right to exist except by the permission of its owner. There is no living being which acknowledges so abject a dependence

In return it is made a sport of the idlest whims. Hence horses, after bleeding, were all thought to be much benefited They were expected to perform greater labor and to continue in sounder health. In vain did the disease visit the stable more frequently; to no purpose was diminished capability displayed. The ungrateful bodies of the "plaguy beasts" were blamed, which would go wrong even after mortal science had expended its wealth upon them Man never doubted his own wisdom; he never questioned his own conduct; and it is astonishing the quantity of prejudice which is from year to year perpetuated for the want of a small amount of so cheap an article as mental inquiry.

The worst of the evil still remains to be told. The creatures, being bled, were esteemed so greatly benefited as to require no subsequent attention. **Phlebitis** was consequently, in other days, a rather common affection. If neglected, the disease may terminate in death In cases aggravated by mistaken measures, the disorder mounts to the brain, and occasions awful agonies. Taken early and properly administered to, this disposition is easily arrested. It was formerly wrongly treated, and was traced to an erroneous origin. Phlebitis was, to the perfect satisfaction of learned judges seated on the bench, attributed to the surgeon's want of care. So serious an evil was imagined to be caused by culpable neglect during a trivial operation. It was thought to have been provoked by the use of a foul instrument, or by employing anything else to strike a fleam than a properly-made blood-stick

Experiments, however, which were instituted at the Royal Veterinary College, have proved that no want of care, during the performance of bleeding, can provoke the disorder. Wretched horses, in that establishment, have been punctured with dirty, rusty, blunt, and jagged fleams; all manner of blood-sticks have been employed in every description of way These have been struck violently and tapped in the gentlest fashion. Every possible sort of pinning up has been adopted; but the utmost endeavor of intentional perversion could not produce inflammation of the vein. There appears to be only one ascertained cause: that is, bleed; do not tie up the head, but turn it into a field, or present fodder to be eaten off the ground, and the animal will have phlebitis The pendulous position of the head and the motion of the jaws alone seem capable of starting inflammation in the jugular vein Therefore, should the reader ever permit a horse to be bled—which, save in extreme cases, is perfectly unnecessary—let him remember to place the animal subsequently in the stable, to tie the halter to the rack for twenty-four hours, and, during the same space, to abstain from allowing any food. These injunctions, however, do not refer to the bleedings sometimes adopted to counteract acute disease

There is one circumstance which should always be well considered before any horse is bled : Certain animals have a constitutional predisposition toward this peculiar form of disease The horse whose vein shall inflame no man can, by sign, mark, or investigation, pick from a herd It is, however, an ascertained fact that particular animals, of no fixed breed, and apparently characterized by no recognized state of body, have a mighty tendency to exhibit this particular disorder., The horse may appear unexceptionable as regards health ; but, nevertheless, strike

it with a fleam or puncture it with a lancet, and phlebitis will undoubt-
edly be generated; none of the usual precautions can *always* prevent
the misfortune Such predisposition evidently depends on a determinate
condition of system which science has hitherto failed to recognize.

This fact, or eccentricity in the constitutions of isolated horses, ought
to be generally known Men have recovered heavy damages in courts
of law, and blameless veterinary surgeons have been ruined, by circumstances over which the utmost stretch of human precaution could possibly exercise no control However, a more extended knowledge concerning the real origin of this disorder may do some good, since it will guard
juries from delivering wrongful verdicts, and may tend to check that
love of venous depletion which is still too prevalent with ignorant horse
owners

There was formerly a great diversity of opinion concerning a supposed
eccentricity in the facts observed during this disease If a horse was
bled in the neck, and subsequently exhibited phlebitis, the brain became
affected. If an animal was depleted from the fore leg, and displayed
the disease, the heart became involved In one case, the disorder proceeded from the center of circulation; and in the other, it mounted
directly toward the organ A great many hypotheses were published to
explain or to account for this imaginary peculiarity. Much nonsense
was spoken, and more was written, to point out the real cause of an
imaginary difference Yet, calmly viewed, the seeming diversity appears
to agree with the commonest law of nature Phlebitis always closes the
vessel at the seat of injury. The disease, therefore, in each case, is prevented from descending, and consequently ascends above the orifice—
the only peculiarity being the relative situations of the structures involved.

This affection is most common after blood has been taken from the
neck. That seeming preference for a particular part may, however, be
nothing more than a circumstance dependent upon the greater number
of animals which have their jugulars opened Were the brachial or the
saphena veins punctured as frequently as the vessel which carries the
blood from the brain, the apparent difference might appear in the opposite direction. However, from whichever vessel the depletion is effected,
always tie the quadruped's head up, and present no food A stall is to
be preferred to a loose box, as the confined space is more likely to prevent action. Motion is the source of all danger. This fact was aptly
illustrated by an anecdote which used to be related by the late Mr Liston, the eminent surgeon In his lecture, that gentleman surprised his
class by stating that the last person whom he bled perished of phlebitis.
Bleeding is the most simple operation in human surgery. Most surgeons

leave this office to the apothecary; consequently it was rather a conde-scension in one who deservedly ranked so high in his profession to stoop to such an act. What, therefore, could possibly cause disease to follow the operation, when performed by him who was accustomed to surgery upon its grandest scale?

The cause was soon explained. The person operated upon chanced to be a lunatic. This insane individual embraced the notion that the healing process was much favored by constant motion; consequently he kept on flexing and extending his arm with all the violence which is natural to the demented. In vain was every effort made to persuade him from so mad an action. He clung with extraordinary pertinacity to his unwholesome theory. On the following day, Mr. Liston was sur-prised to find his patient in bed, but still moving the arm in which disease had already declared itself. Measures were taken to keep the limb quiet, but it was found impossible to accomplish this in a satisfactory manner; and when Mr. Liston again called, the patient was no more!

A vein being about to inflame, the earliest intimation of the fact is given by the separation of the lips of the wound, while through the opening drains a small quantity of a thin discharge. Should this warn-ing excite no attention, a round and hard swelling appears. That may be like a hazel-nut in size, or it may resemble half a chestnut in magni-tude; and this is soon followed by a swollen state of the vein superior to the orifice.

Then supervenes the sec-ond stage of the disorder. Unhealthy abscesses are formed along the course of the vein. As these mature, they burst, and send forth an unsightly and filthy liquid resembling thin, contamina-ted pus. On examination, these tumors are found to be united.

A HORSE WITH PHLEBITIS, OR INFLAMMATION OF THE VEIN, IN THE SECOND STAGE.

They penetrate to the interior of the vessel, and are joined together by numerous si-nuses. They literally con-stitute so many holes in the neck.

If no attention be now paid to the aggravated symptoms, worse speedily ensues. In the direction

THE THIRD STAGE OF PHLEBITIS.

26

formerly indicated the vessel feels hard under the skin. Supposing this sign to be neglected, unhealthy pus issues in quantity from the wounds and soils the neck. This secretion is soon converted into a dark, impure, and fetid discharge resembling decayed blood. The horse grows dull and stupid; the inflammation ultimately affects the brain, when the suffering and the life are extinguished in the violent agonies of phrenitis.

The cure is easy, but everything depends upon the energy of him who undertakes it. When the lips of the wound which have been brought together by means of the twisted suture—as the "pin with tow wrapped round it" is professionally termed—display a tendency to separate, and, instead of being dry, appear moist, let no prejudice incline toward the ancient practice of fomenting and poulticing the injury. Without the loss of a moment in hesitation, withdraw the pin; remove the substance which was twined round it, and apply a moderate-sized blister immediately over and around the puncture. Should the disease have ascended up the neck, still rub in a blister; only a proportionate amount of surface must then be acted upon. If the case be as bad as possible, and yet the animal is alive, still a blister is indicated.

THE TWISTED SUTURE.
A pin is first stuck through the lips of the wound; a portion of tow, thread, or hair is then wrapped round the pin, and, to complete all, the point of the pin is lastly clipped off.

With the progress of the disease a larger space should always be subjected to irritation, so as to cover every part the most active imagination could suppose to be involved. One blister, moreover, will not suffice; another, and another, and another must be employed, till every sign of disorder has vanished. They must, however, be applied in quicker succession as the symptoms are more urgent, while a greater interval may be allowed between each when the affection is less serious. In the worst stage of phlebitis, another blister must be put over the part upon which the irritation of the first has not entirely ceased to act. In the second stage, the surface must have been barely healed before another vesicatory is resorted to. During the primary symptom, a single application frequently is sufficient; or, at most, two blisters generally suffice.

When the vessel assumes the corded state, a blister can effect no more than to check the progress of the disorder; no agency, however, which science has placed at the disposal of man can restore the uses of the vein. The vessel is lost, and lost forever. If a foul and black discharge issue from the openings, insert a director and enlarge the wounds, joining the holes by slitting up the sinuses which unite them; but do not cut the entire extent of the hardened vessel, as in that case you may be deluged in blood. The employment of the knife and the free use of blisters constitute the chief means toward the cure of phlebitis. The sinuses must be laid open. The probe should then be most patiently employed, for every sinus *must* be slit up. This may be done at once, when the hardness indicates the vessel to be closed above the part which the incision interferes with. To such an extent the knife may always be employed, while blisters after blisters are used, regardless of the severe wounds over which they are applied.

Much relief is afforded by the large and pendulous incision, through which the corruption freely finds an exit Some horses, however, from the pain occasioned by the raw and inflamed condition of the neck, will not allow the blister to be rubbed in after the ordinary fashion, especially when the irritation caused by the former application has not thoroughly subsided. In cases of this sort, do not employ the twitch or resort to greater restraints. Exercise your reason. Regard the painful aspect of the wounds Ask yourself how you should enjoy the hard hand of a groom violently scrubbed over such a part, were the soreness upon your own body Act upon the response. Procure a long-haired brush, such as pastry-cooks use to egg over their more delicate manufactures. Go then into the next stall. Speak kindly to a sick inferior that is at your mercy Have the creature led forth, and, with the brush just described, smear the part with oil of cantharides or liquid blister The extract of the Spanish fly does not occasion immediate agony, and the application of oil will cool or soothe the anger of the wounds.

With the jugular vein inflamed, the horse, during the period of treatment, should consume no solid food. Hay tea, sloppy mashes, and well-made gruel should constitute its diet. However, the gruel must not be given in such quantities or made so thick as the same substance would be allowed to a healthy horse. Gruel may not be very sustaining to the human being, but it is nothing more than the oat divested of the shell or refuse part. To the equine species such food, whether given dry or boiled in water, is highly stimulating; and, as fever invariably accompanies inflammation, oats in any form evidently are contraindicated. Should the animal, however, become ravenous, a portion of potatoes, being first peeled, may be boiled to a mash. Some water and a sufficiency of pollard ought to be added, and the whole presented in such a state as requires no mastication, but in a condition that will allow the mixture to be drawn between the teeth The same thing may be done with carrots and with turnips, only all mashed roots, except potatoes, should be passed through a colander, and moistened with some of the water in which they are boiled.

Any animal, during treatment, should be placed in a loose box. No creature should be turned into the field. It is cheaper to pasture than to stable a horse; but the constant motion of the legs, as the field is traversed, is injurious to the punctured vein of the limbs, while the pendulous state of the head and the perpetual movement of the jaws are most prejudicial when venesection has been performed upon the neck The stable is, in every point of view, the cheapest and the best residence The head of the animal must be tied to the rack throughout the day; while, at night, the halter may be lengthened, permitting the creature to lie down; but the floor should be littered with tan, as straw might be eaten.

Let the horse remain thus for six weeks subsequent to the completion of a cure Then give gentle exercise to the extent which it can be borne—the quantity being small, and the pace very slow at first, but gradually augmented This exercise should be maintained for three months. The animal may afterward return to slow work; but if the neck is the place affected, it must not wear a collar or be harnessed to the shafts for the next six months. At the end of that time the horse may return to its customary employment; but, if ridden or driven, it is always well to bear in mind the late affliction, and to grant more than the usual time for the performance of the journey. At the expiration of the year, the smaller veins, having become enlarged, have adapted themselves to the loss which the circulation has sustained, and the horse may resume full work

For the first year, gruel, crushed and scalded oats, with two bundles of cut grass per day, should constitute the diet. The manger should be heightened, and the halter be so arranged as to prevent the head being much lowered Do all in your power to render useless violent mastication, and, as the horse never chews when the operation is unnecessary, the animal will obviously second your endeavors.

At the expiration of twelve months the animal which has lost a vein may be sold, and, *in law,* has been accounted sound. Such a blemish, however, is far from a recommendation; in this case law and common sense may be at variance. The reader, therefore, is advised never to purchase a nag in such a condition without insisting upon a special warranty, in which it is provided that the animal is to be taken back should the loss of a vessel be productive of any evil effects within the space of one twelvemonth.

BROKEN KNEES.

These accidents affect the exterior of the central joint of the fore legs They may be very trivial or very serious: they may simply ruffle the hair or scratch the cuticle covering the integument; the same cause may, however, remove the hair and lay bare the cutis Moreover, the wound is often aggravated by the nature of the road on which the animal is traveling. A fall upon a very rough surface might even destroy a portion of the skin, and deprive more or less of the cellular tissue of vitality.

BROKEN KNEES OF VARIOUS DEGREES OF INTENSITY.

| The hair ruffled and the cuticle scratched. | The hair removed and the true skin exposed. | The skin destroyed and the cellular tissue injured. |

Accompanying such accidents there is generally some amount of contusion. When it falls, the horse is in motion, and the impetus lends violence to the descent. Probably the animal is being ridden when it comes to the ground. The weight of the blow is not only then proportioned to the heavy body of the horse and the rate at which it is progressing, but its effect is augmented by the load upon its back. These considerations render **broken knees** the proper dread of every horse proprietor. An animal may stumble and come down which, prior to the mishap, would have been sold cheap for several hundreds. It may be raised from the ground with almost all its worth demolished. The nature of the hurt is not, however, always shown at first. The chief danger, in broken knees, lies in the accompanying contusion. The horse which rises without a hair ruffled, but which fell with violence, is always, with informed persons, a cause of considerable anxiety. Contusion is to be more dreaded in its consequences than is the largest wound when devoid of anything approaching to a bruise.

The reason why contusion is thus gravely regarded is because, when that occurs in severity, the vitality of all the coverings to the knee is destroyed, and, in very bad cases, even the bones are materially injured. All dead parts must be cast from a living body; and no man can predicate how deep may be the injury, or how important may be the structures which shall be opened, when the slough takes place.

Proprietors of horses thus injured are commonly very earnest in their solicitations for a professional opinion as to the extent and probable consequences of the accident. No certain judgment can, however, be pronounced, nor should one be given. Any surgical calculation, notwithstanding it may be most prudently qualified, is apt to be misconstrued by the anxiety of distress. The most guarded hint at a proba-

bility of recovery is too likely to be seized upon as a positive guarantee
of perfect restoration; and the possible evils which may have been
alluded to, confusion causes the individual not to remember Therefore
silence is wisdom in these cases, however slight the broken knee may
appear in the first instance

Broken knees are principally caused by the imprudence of him in whom
authority is invested. Certain people imagine the public admire the man
who chastises a horse Such persons slash away for every trivial error.
Every imaginary fault is punished with the whip, which too often curls
around parts that should be respected The animal, pained and frightened, thinks only of the slasher behind it, and entirely disregards the
path upon which its eyes should be directed The cutting is incessant,
and the horse's pace is incautiously fast. An impediment is encountered;
the animal trips; it is cast to the ground with violence, while the man
is probably rendered fitter for a hospital than for the continuance of his
travels.

Other riders and drivers always visit with severity the slightest indication of weak limbs A sudden drop or a false step is, to such people, the
signal for the reins to be jagged, the voice to be raised, and the whip to
be freely exercised upon all parts of the animal's body, but mostly about
the face and ears. The man likes to behold the poor creature shake its
head, and loves to imagine he is then teaching the terrified quadruped
to be careful Equine pupils, no more than human scholars, are to
be tutored by barbarity, which may slay the reason long before it can
instruct the mind Composure is imperative to the acquirement of any
knowledge. Thrashing calls forth terror, and alarm is synonymous with
confusion of mind. The horse is susceptible of a fear which humanity,
happily, finds it difficult to conceive; and how far such a creature is
calculated to be educated by cruelty, the intelligent reader is left to infer.

Could the animal argue, it might plead that the weakness objected to
was caused by exertion made in man's service; that the stumbling gait
was consequent upon no negligence on its part; that it afforded the
beaten wretch no pleasure to have the knees broken, but, if the quadruped might profess a choice, it would prefer not falling down, etc etc If
such pleas were properly considered, they perhaps might still the turbu-
lence of the punisher.

The great majority of these injuries are consequent upon the prejudice
or thoughtlessness of mankind Popular admiration is, in this country,
much in favor of a good crest. Every animal, no matter how nature
may have formed the neck, must carry a good head. The rider, therefore, drags upon the bridle, while the form of nearly every gentleman's
harness-horse is distorted by the bearing-rein. The constraint thus

enforced not only obliges additional muscular action, but it disqualifies the animal to see the ground. In England there should be no objection to a blind horse, since such of the species as have eyes are, by the prejudices of society, seldom permitted to use them. The horse, being urged on when virtually blindfold, must of necessity stumble upon any unusual impediment being encountered. Such an accident shows no fault in the quadruped; but the man is truly responsible for those consequences which his folly has induced.

When a horse stumbles, never raise your voice—the creature dreads its master's chiding; never jag the reins—the mouth of the horse is far more sensitive than the human lips; never use the lash—the horse is so timid that the slightest correction overpowers its reasoning faculties. Speak to the creature; reassure the palpitating frame; seek to restore those perceptions which will form the best guard against any repetition of the faulty action. When the legs are weak, the greater should be the care of him who holds the reins. No cruelty can restore the lost tonicity of the limbs; therefore all slashing is utterly thrown away. If the reader regard his own safety, let him not, when riding, hold the head up, or, when driving, sanction the employment of a bearing-rein. No inhumanity can convert an animal with a ewe neck into the creature with a naturally lofty crest. The disguise of such a defect as a head badly placed on the neck is an impossibility. Therefore, if you are desirous of a well-carried head, think of it when making the purchase. Pay something more, and any kind of quadruped is obtainable; but be above the meanness which purchases for a low figure, and then endeavors to palm off its cheap article as a jewel procured at the highest price.

When a horse has been down, never judge of the injury by the first appearance. While the animal stands in the yard, order the groom to fetch a pail, with milk-warm water and a large sponge. With these he is to clean the knees—not after the usual coarse and filthy fashion now universal; not by first sopping the part, and then squeezing the soiled sponge into the pail whence more fluid is to be abstracted. The dabbing and smearing a wound simply irritates it; and the dirt, having all entered into the pail, the fluid is rendered unsuited to after cleanly purposes. To perform the office properly, the knee should not be touched. The sponge should be saturated, then squeezed dry above the seat of injury. The water thus flows in a full stream over the part, and, by the force of gravity, carries away any loose dirt that may be upon

THE PROPER WAY TO WASH
A BROKEN KNEE.

the surface Sopping, dabbing, wiping, and smearing occasion pain, and can remove nothing which may have entered the skin and which is protected from the action of the sponge by a covering of hair; whereas by the plan recommended the dirt is removed, the part is not debilitated, neither is its natural energy destroyed. The last drop of water, moreover, is as clean as was the first, and the animal is not irritated immediately prior to a surgical examination.

The wound being cleansed, a certain time should be allowed to elapse for the horse to recover its composure. It should return to the stable, have a feed of corn, and be watered Then the real business commences The animal should be gently approached; its condition should be observed. If any nervousness is exhibited, the person ought to retire, and a further pause should be allowed If, on the second visit, any unusual symptoms are displayed, have the quadruped led into the yard and blindfolded. Let a man take up the other fore leg, when the knee may be examined with safety.

Place the palm of the hand over the joint Hold it there to ascertain if any heat or swelling is to be detected. Should there be swelling, make gradual and gentle pressure upon it with the thumb or one finger. If, upon suddenly removing the hand, an indent is conspicuous, it argues considerable effusion, and justifies fear as to the result. Should neither heat nor swelling be remarked, further pressure is to be made with the thumb upon the knee. The force should be gentle at first and gradually increased. If the action is sustained well, or even moderately endured, it allows of hope being entertained. But should the horse attempt to rear upon the first impress of the thumb, the result is very dubious. The absence of agony is far from anything approaching to a positive proof, as bone and synovial membrane, tendon and ligament, do not take on acute inflammation when first injured; but, from the response thus elicited, a fair inference as to the probability may be drawn.

Should the skin be lacerated, the probe must be employed. Such injuries are very deceptive. They may be much more extensive than the size of the wound would indicate The probe being of metal, ought not to be thrust violently against every exposed part. This kind of proceeding can effect no good The probe should be held lightly between the thumb and fore finger; no pressure should be made upon it —the instrument ought rather to fall of its own gravity than be forced into the flesh. A thin piece of wire can be readily driven into soft structures; but where an actual division exists, no opposition necessitating force will be encountered.

Broken knees always happen when the horse is in motion. The onward impulse is not by the fall immediately destroyed; but after the horse is down there always exists an impetus which has a tendency to propel the body forward. Should the skin of the knees be divided by the fall, the after-force obviously cannot affect the upper line of such division; but the lower edge of skin will present an acute obstacle to the roughened ground, and will, by the grating of the body, in all probability be rent from its attachments. When the animal rises, the action and the elasticity natural to the integument will occasion the torn portion of the skin which has been driven backward to once more assume its original position. By this means a kind of bag or purse is formed upon the knee. Grit, mud, and all kinds of impurities may be retained and concealed within this pouch. These will be disposed to irritate the structure with which they are in contact; suppuration is certain to be established, and sad consequences have followed such sacs not being early detected.

Such a cavity having been discovered, the next object is to ascertain its dimensions. That is done by gradually moving the probe along its sides. Should it be small, it will be sufficient that a hole be made through its most depending portion with a sharp seton needle. If it be large, the needle should be armed with a piece of tape knotted at one end. The sac being punctured, the needle is to be drawn through the opening, the tape being left in the cavity, and a seton is thus formed.

PROBING THE SAC OF A BROKEN KNEE.

A SETON BEING INSERTED THROUGH
THE SAC OF THE KNEE.

The seton should be knotted at the other end, and moved its entire length every night and morning. It will prevent all premature attempts to heal, will stimulate the soft parts to suppuration, and will remove the dirt, as the tape affords a guide to the secretion. When inserting a seton into the knee, always use a large curved needle. The size of the instruments should never be regulated by any foreign standard, but should always be proportioned to the magnitude of the patient and the intention of the operator.

Three days subsequent to the full establishment of suppuration, cut off one of the knots, and, laying hold of the other knot, withdraw the seton Its advantages by this time are gained, and its longer stay, by hardening the opening through which it passed, would occasion lasting blemish.

The reason of its insertion is thus explained Where foreign matter is confined, no wound will heal; the orifice may close, but soon after abscess forms This process is repeated until the suffering is long protracted. Danger is generally proportioned to the duration of the evil, where wounds not of a mortal character are concerned. By the agency of the seton, the foreign matter is removed and the healing process thereby considerably expedited. After the above plan, all blemish may be lost by the expiration of the third month, and the once injured knee restored to its uses, being as fine as any other part of the body.

Everything being accomplished as it is here directed, no attempt must in the first instance be made to poke out any particle of dirt which the probe may touch The bagging skin being divided by the seton having been established in the sac, no further thought need, for the present, be given to a common but most vexatious attendant upon the customary treatment for broken knees

The animal should be returned to its usual stall and have the head "racked up." Some cold water should then be procured, with every quart of which two ounces of tincture of arnica should be blended A portion of this fluid ought, with a clean sponge of moderate size, to be poured into a saucer; the groom must have strict orders to take the sponge, and, having saturated it with the fluid, to squeeze it quite dry, allowing the liquor to run over the injured knee—after the manner previously illustrated, as washing the wound. Two men are required for this office, which should be performed every half hour throughout the day and night for half a week. The injury being thus made continuously wet, the cold produced by evaporation keeps down inflammation, while the arnica is a potent remedy for bruises and all kinds of contusions or lacerations.

If at the expiration of the period named no swelling appears, and suppuration seems to be thoroughly established by means of the seton, the halter may be released to a great extent, a cradle being merely fixed upon the horse's neck; the animal will thereby be permitted to lie down and to enjoy its natural rest.

But should the joint be much enlarged, should the part have become acutely sensitive, while the horse resolutely refuses to bear any weight upon the injured limb, then withdraw the seton, give the animal two pots of stout per day, and all the oats mingled with old beans which it will consume. Untie the head and place the horse in slings; employ the arnica lotion night and day, until the slough is thrown off, which, having taken place, change the liquid application for the solution of chloride of zinc—one scruple to the pint of water—and continue to employ this last lotion after precisely the same manner as has been previously directed.

Probabilities, however remote they may seem to be, are here endeavored to be anticipated; although the author's experience cannot recall a single case where the arnica lotion has been used with proper assiduity, and any but the most happy results have followed. When an animal has fallen violently to the earth, and has been, in the first instance, shown to the writer with much tumefaction and excessive tenderness, a slough has in exceptional cases followed; but never has the enlargement or the sensitiveness increased under the proper use of the arnica lotion. The slough, moreover, in such instances, has been superficial, only entailing loss of hair, and never occasioning open joint.

All horses are exposed to these accidents for the reasons already stated. Whenever such misfortunes occur, employ the arnica lotion. Should the skin be divided, still use the arnica lotion until copious suppuration is established. The secretion once seen, resort to the lotion formed of chloride of zinc and water—one grain to the ounce—which operates most marvelously upon all suppurating wounds.

No absolute period can be stated which a case of broken knees, when severe, ought to occupy. The danger, however, is generally passed by the expiration of a week, and the cure commonly entails loss of services for a couple of months.

AN ORGANIZED KNEE, ENSUING AFTER
A LONG COURSE OF THE ORDINARY
TREATMENT.

THE APPEARANCE OF THE KNEE SUBSEQUENT
TO THE HEALING OF THE WORST CASE THE
AUTHOR EVER HAD UNDER HIS CARE.

When adopting the foregoing mode of treatment, no bandages are to be employed. Such wrappers only augment the heat inherent in every species of inflammation. They dam up the pus and speedily become foul and offensive rags; cleanliness is one of the primary requisites toward good surgery.

No caustics of any kind are imperative or even necessary   The two lotions, if used with proper zeal, will accomplish all that can be desired The arnica lotion should, however, be in all cases applied night and day during the early stage; the chloride of zinc lotion ought to be employed only during the time man is usually out of bed

The wound, in ordinary cases, should not be washed or touched. Should proud flesh start up, such is positive proof of the negligence of the groom, whose duty it was to apply the chloride of zinc lotion. If the mode of treatment here laid down be strictly pursued, the author can with confidence promise a satisfactory and a speedy cure   To enforce the value of the measures recommended, the portraits of two knees, which were subjected to the opposite processes, have been presented.   Both were copied from living subjects in the sixth week after the misfortune had occurred

OPEN SYNOVIAL CAVITIES

The primary cause of these fearful accidents is the pride of mankind; gentility is always striving to impose upon credulity.   It loves to be mistaken for something better than it really is.   After all, this vice of society is nothing more than the child's game of "Lords and Ladies," played by grown-up persons.   A horse having a naturally defective neck is obtained; no barbarity is too abhorrent to repress the hope of making people believe the steed thus deformed is a creature of extremest value.   The animal, if ridden, has the chin pulled in close to the neck; if driven, the free carriage of the body is prevented by the cruel bearing-rein.   The horse progresses in agony, while gentility sits smiling at the result of its artifice   The horse cannot see the ground before it, because of the constraint imposed upon the head; it cannot fix attention upon its duty, because of the agony which the cunning of gentility inflicts upon the lips   The pace is always rapid; the action is high as in the case of blindness; and the animal generally comes to the earth with violence   The skin upon the knees is divided, and the structures beneath are penetrated.   One or more **synovial sheaths** are opened, while the cavities formed by the junction of the separate bones may be lacerated.

Sheath or joint may not be immediately opened by the fall, but either may have their integrity destroyed through the slough induced by the contusion consequent upon a broken knee   Moreover, various accidents will occasionally happen—misfortune is of infinite variety.   The synovial bursæ, sheaths, or cavities of the hind legs are occasionally punctured by the quadruped kicking violently while in harness   The capsule, embracing the tendon of the flexor brachii upon the point of the shoulder, has been opened by the animal drawing a vehicle being run into; or by the horse running away and coming in contact with some obstacle. Any synovial cavity within the body may be penetrated by an unfortunate combination of circumstances; or by the unbridled passion of the groom, who may have a pitchfork near at hand. So also they have been cut into by the arrogance of unskillful operators However, it matters not how the misfortune may arise, the mode of treatment and the manner of cure is in all such cases exactly the same.

Neither, as regards the primary effect, is it of subsequent importance whether air be admitted into an opened bursa or sac, a synovial sheath, or the interior of a joint. All of these structures are formed into bladders or closed cavities They all contain a similar secretion, which is a transparent, albuminous fluid, resembling white of egg. They all are of one use, or all serve to facilitate motion The bursa is the smallest; the synovial sheath is the next in magnitude; and joints may be much the largest. The secondary effects are proportioned to their size, but in the first instance much constitutional disturbance will attend the opening of each.

These structures are not formed to endure the presence of atmosphere; air is admitted a short time after each displays inflammation This creates symptoms of irritability, and air will enter before we see the wound. The secondary effect is, however, most to be dreaded. Bursæ are small bladders, or closed sacs, distributed over the body, and located wherever the natural motions possibly might originate friction. Sheaths always embrace tendons, being essentially closed sacs. The secondary effects of tendinous sheaths are so much the more to be dreaded than those attending punctured bursæ, because the last generally lie loosely between highly-organized parts; whereas a sheath is partly fixed upon a tendon, and tendon, being lowly organized, is more difficult to cure when it is diseased. However, joints are much worse than the preceding two, because in these the synovial membrane is partly spread over the cartilage, which lies upon the articular surfaces of bones Now, cartilage is the most lowly organized substance in the entire body. When disease fixes upon it the morbid condition is so slow, so irritating, and so difficult to eradicate, that science almost despairs of the issue

The results indicated show that every effort should be made to ward off the secondary effect. Therefore, when an accident of this nature occurs, proceed with the utmost gentleness. Having procured a large sponge and a pail of milk-warm water, saturate the sponge and squeeze it dry, above the injury Do not touch the sore, but allow the fluid, as it gravitates, to wash off all or any foreign matter. With regard to the wound, dirt seldom enters that. When it does, the suppuration which must ensue upon the accident will more effectually remove it than could hogsheads of water, however unfeelingly it might be employed.

The part having been rendered clean, the wound is to be attentively observed. When nothing but blood or serum, or thin, discolored fluid can be seen, this argues the more important structures are entire. Should there be among, and yet distinct from, those discharges, a transparent, glairy liquid flowing forth, such is absolute proof some synovial membrane has been severed. The size of the current and the abundance of the secretion are also evidences not to be despised. Probabilities may be inferred from these circumstances. If the amount of the synovia be small, there is hope that a bursa only has been interfered with; when the amount is large, it demonstrates that either a sheath is punctured or the joint itself may have been opened. Synovial cavities between bones may be larger, and are much more active than the sheaths of tendons; therefore the magnitude of the current should be observed; although, when the integrity of many parts has been destroyed, little absolute dependence will be placed upon the comparative quantity of the synovial secretion.

Anatomy is, under the circumstances, a fair guide. Where numerous structures are involved, a well-grounded learning is requisite for accurate judgment; but as regards the knee of the horse, the spot whence

No. 1.

No. 2.

THE TENDONS WHICH CROSS THE OUTSIDE OF THE KNEE-JOINT.

THE TENDONS WHICH CROSS THE INSIDE OF THE KNEE-JOINT.

Explanation of No 1.
1. The extensor metacarpi tendon.
2. The extensor metacarpi obliquus tendon.
3. The extensor pedis tendon.
4, 5, 7. Connecting and restraining bands between the tendons.
6. The extensor suffraginis tendon.
8. The flexor metacarpi externus tendon.
9. The back sinews.

Explanation of No. 2.
1. The extensor metacarpi tendon.
2. The extensor metacarpi obliquus tendon.
3. The flexor metacarpi internus tendon.
4. The back sinews.
The letter a denotes the only spot where the knee-joint could probably be opened by a fall without lacerating a synovial sheath or injuring a tendon.

the synovial discharge issues is of all importance. The incision must either be very deep and gaping, (all subjacent structures being divided before the knee-joint can be exposed,) or else the wound must affect a very circumscribed place. The reader, by consulting the above anatomical engravings of the horse's knee, will remark how closely it is laced about with tendon. Each of the tendons, when crossing the joint, is embraced in a synovial sheath. From such information, it will instantly be seen how far more likely a sheath is to be lacerated than the joint is to be punctured.

The single point where the joint could be entered without severing tendon, lies rather on one side than directly in the center. The vulnerable spot is therefore not exposed to the full force of the blow. To lay bare the joint by an ordinary fall several parts must be divided. Rarely is an accident witnessed of so fearful an extent. Generally that which is spoken of as open joint proves to be no more than punctured sheath, the presence of synovia being commonly accepted as the proof. But when the joint is really laid open, the immense flow of synovia—so many sheaths being severed—should at once prove the fact.

The probe must next be used. In the first instance it should be employed to ascertain whether the fall has left any purse or sac at the inferior part of the joint. All which was enforced respecting the use of metallic wire to a raw wound must here be observed. The probe had better be altogether

PROBING BROKEN KNEE.

discarded than employed with the smallest approach to rudeness.

The suspected sac having been discovered, a large spatula is placed below the knee. A knife with a keen point, but with the edge only sharpened for one-third of its length, is to be used. Upon the cutting point of the knife a piece of beeswax is firmly moulded. The wax answers the purpose of a temporary probe; the blade, thus guarded, is cautiously inserted beneath the loose flap of skin. When the bottom of the pouch is reached, a certain amount of resistance will be encountered; through this the knife is driven. The force cuts in twain the wax, and pushes through the integument the blade,

THE MANNER OF OPENING THE DIRT SAC, IN CASE ONE SHOULD BE PRESENT WITH OPEN JOINT.

which the spatula guides from the leg. This operation should be performed quickly; the hand should simply be carried downward, and then brought upward when all is concluded; care, however, being taken that the withdrawal of the knife does not injure any part save those it was designed to cut.

Should the horse be nervous, it is desirable to blindfold the animal and order the groom to hold up the sound leg; the creature can then only rear. When thus disabled, that movement is rendered difficult, and it is proportionably slow. The operation, if properly performed, should be over before action can be prepared for; and by the knife a considerable incision is made in the bottom of the sac, through which all grit or dirt can, with the pus, readily pass.

The examination concludes with a second resort to the probe. The instrument is in surgery of great use; but as it is commonly employed, reason may doubt whether injured life has been much benefited by its invention. It generally is raked and poked about as though the person holding it was determined, at all hazards, to ascertain the length, breadth, and every irregularity of the wound he is asked to cure; much harm is thereby done. Delicate attachments which, if not interfered with, might induce speedy reunion, are thus broken down, and the injury aggravated; while the operator thinks he ought to know all about the lesion he is to treat, and supposes that he can possibly do no harm with an instrument which the best schools order to be employed.

A good surgeon has no curiosity to gratify; all he desires to know is

PROBING AN OPEN JOINT.

so much as will enable him to benefit the patient placed under his care. Therefore never abuse the probe in cases of open synovial cavities. Imagine the distance the bones are from the surface; and, if the probe can enter a very little beyond that distance, such a fact demonstrates the cavity to be exposed. When a horse is before you with synovia running from a wound upon the knee, have the leg slightly flexed; look for the most free space, and into that insert the probe. The bones of the knee-joint are directly under the skin; and, when no opposition is encountered for three-quarters of an inch, be sure the joint is exposed.

Most of the cases narrated as opened joints were simply punctures into synovial sheaths; as such, they were sufficiently serious, but not of so important a character as is assumed for them. Synovia is placed between the ends of bones, its use being to prevent the friction which otherwise would be occasioned by the movement of one hard body upon another. Being confined in a circumscribed sac and incapable of much compression, the liquid performs all the uses which could appertain to the most solid substance. When the fluid—which, from its thick appearance and unctuous feel, was formerly termed "joint oil"—has escaped, the bones grate against each other, inflammation ensues, all neighboring parts sympathize, and the constitution suffers from intense irritation.

Something of this kind happens when a synovial sheath is punctured. The tendon comes in contact with its investing synovial membrane; but there are reasons why that circumstance is not so serious as when the lubricating fluid is released from the cavity of a joint. Tendons support no weight, and their motion is, with the sick, almost optional. The bones are the pillars on which the body rests; even while the frame is prostrated, a certain degree of pressure is upon them; for that reason, and also because tendon is more highly organized than cartilage, the first-mentioned substance is endowed with the greater renovating energy. An open joint is consequently far more serious than a punctured sheath.

Notwithstanding the serious nature of these accidents when wrongly treated, few injuries yield more kindly to proper measures than open joint. However, should the ordinary treatment of caustics and bandages be adopted, the entire limb, before the expiration of a week, will be hot, hard, and tense. The health of the animal will be seriously affected by the continued irritation, and the body will rapidly become emaciated. The foot of the limb will with evident difficulty be held from the ground. Should not death interpose—the animal being unable to lie down, and the entire weight being cast upon the sound limb—the foot attached to the healthy member frequently becomes affected with the worst form of incurable laminitis.

THE INJURED LEG, HARD, HOT, TENSE, AND SWOLLEN—ALL RESULTING FROM THE INJUDICIOUS EMPLOYMENT OF BANDAGES.

Even should such a misfortune as laminitis not occur, the after-deformity and blemish renders the horse almost worthless. The bones sympathize in the general disease,

OSSEOUS STRUCTURE HAS BEEN THROWN OUT, CAUSING ENLARGED KNEE AND PERMANENT BLEMISH—THE RESULTS OF USING BANDAGES.

EXTENSIVE LOSS OF HAIR, GENERAL ENLARGEMENT OF THE KNEE, AND ORGANIZED THICKENING OF THE SCAR—RESULTING FROM THE USE OF BANDAGES.

and a large osseous deposit is engendered to mark the surgical inaptitude. When bony growth does not follow, the parts lying immediately over the knee thicken; the skin sloughs, and, the integument never being restored, a full knee with a lasting blemish is the consequence.

OPEN SYNOVIAL JOINTS.

The more favorable terminations are never to be anticipated when the barbarity of bandages and the cruelty of caustics are sanctioned. The horse which recovers from such treatment is, by an enlarged and blemished limb, rendered an object painful to contemplate, and is entirely unsuited to any gentleman's uses, while the life of the creature is rendered burdensome. There is nothing in the proper treatment which a child might not safely apply. The measures create no pain and require no force; they rather soothe than irritate, and therefore are always submitted to with complacency.

OPEN JOINT ENSUING UPON BROKEN KNEE, AND SOLELY CAUSED BY THE ABUSE OF BANDAGES.

THE GENERAL APPEARANCE OF AN OPEN JOINT WHEN FIRST SUBMITTED TO THE NOTICE OF THE SURGEON.

The animal, when first brought in, never displays symptoms indicating the full extent of its injury. The part which has been wounded generally presents something like the aspect represented in the engraving on the right. Commonly there is an evident flow of synovia, but the most careful examination can seldom detect positive evidence of an open joint.

The full extent of the evil cannot be known before the slough takes place. This is certain to follow upon the customary bleeding, physicking, low diet, bandages, and caustics being employed. As recovery is wished for, all such aggravations must be rejected. Proceed, in the first instance, as has been directed for broken knee; and these things being done, give the following drink :—

> Sulphuric ether . . . . One ounce.
> Laudanum. . . . . One ounce.
> Water . . . . Half a pint.
> 　Give this without noise or violence.

Treat the frightened animal with even more gentleness and patience than would be bestowed upon a sick child. A harsh word may now, when the system is shaken and every nerve unstrung, do that harm which no medicine can repair.

Having given the drink, look at the animal and take the pulse. Should the appearance denote inward comfort, should the pulse be natural, give no more drinks; but if the eye is in constant motion, if the horse breathe hard and start at sounds, if the head is held high and the ears are active, repeat the ethereal draught, and continue repeating it every hour until the foregoing symptoms abate

The object of the medicine being gained, have the horse quietly led into a stall; the stall it has been used to is the best, and the favorite neighbor need not be removed   But all other quadrupeds which might disturb the sick animal should be taken out of the building. A good, clean bed should be shaken down, and the diet must be suited to the symptoms. If the pulse is at all low, no hay should be allowed till it amends; should the arterial beat denote oppression, a rather large proportion of beans may be blended with the oats   If the breathing is short, the countenance unhappy, and the eye sleepy, while a very quick and feeble pulse only is to be detected, give four of the ethereal drinks in the twenty-four hours. Also allow two quarts of stout daily.

All horses should be accustomed to drink beer; with very little teaching they abandon their teetotal habits, and will.by very expressive action signify delight at the sight of a pewter pot   The best means of introducing the beverage to their notice is, in the first instance, to break a penny loaf into pieces, to soak the pieces in the beverage, and then to offer them, one by one, from the hand of the master or the favorite attendant   Animals quickly learn to recognize their owners. The dog will bestow such a welcome upon its proprietor as is never lavished upon any stranger. The horse also learns to recognize the individual whose property it has become   See the animal which has carried the groom without excitement to the door, and which has walked before the house with pendant head and listless ears : the moment the door opens and the master appears, all dejection is cast off; the creature cannot stand still when the foot is in the stirrup; and, immediately the weight is felt upon the back, the happy quadruped prances gayly off, often at the risk of unseating him who has provoked this demonstration of excessive pleasure.

The master who is unknown has earned his fate by his neglect, and probably may live to repent his inattention to the duties which Providence has intrusted to his charge. The affections of the meanest creature that breathes are blessings which the highest and the proudest may well stoop to gain. The love of a horse is not to be despised; the noble quadruped is easier controlled by its uncultivated impulses than by all the restraints which brutes have invented or fools have adopted. It should enter into the considerations of every life assurance company, whether the man who takes out a policy is of a nature likely to be loved by the animals which he possesses.

Beer is everywhere procurable, and it is not to be altogether contemned as a medicinal stimulant. Many a horse which is now lost upon every hard field-day would have been saved if the animal had been pulled up at the nearest public house to be presented with a slice of bread and a pint of beer. Such nourishment would not load the stomach; but it would serve to keep off that utter exhaustion from which too many steeds fail.

The animal being in its stall, then apply the lotion, composed of tincture of arnica, two ounces; water, one quart. Use this by means of a sponge and saucer. Pour some of the liquor into the receptacle. Saturate the sponge and squeeze the fluid upon the leg; but above the injured knee. Do this after the manner which is illustrated as the proper mode of washing the wounded part.

Continue with the arnica lotion, night and day, for half a week. No periods can be named for applying the sponge, as inflammations, and therefore the drying powers, vary in different individuals; but the knee should be always wet. This should be attended to for the first three days and a half, during which the halter should be tied to the rack. At the end of that time turn the horse very gently round. Remember the condition of the limb, and allow time for the performance of an action which is always an effort to the most agile of the equine species, as few stalls are a single inch too wide.

THE MANNER IN WHICH LO-
TION SHOULD BE APPLIED
TO AN OPEN JOINT.

The animal being with its face to the gangway, and fastened by the pillar-reins, place the slings before it. Leave the creature to contemplate the apparatus for half an hour. Then take the cloth and hold it up to the inspection of the quadruped. Afterward place it between the fore and hind legs—pausing and speaking kindly should alarm be displayed. Thus by degrees fix it to the pulleys and bring it near to the abdomen, which, however, should by no means be touched. Then caress the creature's head, and present some of its favorite food: eating generally tranquilizes the mind of an animal. So much being done, proceed to fix the straps upon the chest and withers. Then fondle the sufferer again, and it will permit the hind tackle to be arranged.

When all is fixed, leave a pail of water suspended from one pillar, and put an elevated trough, charged with favorite provender, in front of the horse. · Let it be watched till a week from the date of the injury has expired, and never left during that period even for an instant. If any restlessness is exhibited, the attendant should approach and caress the creature. Quadrupeds—though none comprehend the precise meaning of the language—love to be praised. The hand, fondly applied to the skin, and the human voice, modulated by kindness, seem to convey a purport to animals which they will suffer pain to deserve. The writer lately had a favorite dog, whose aversion was dry bread. It would hold the detested morsel in its mouth for hours, looking most uncomfortable, but making no attempt at mastication. Yet, upon praise being lavished, the eye would brighten, and, rather than prove unworthy of so much commendation, the hardest and stalest crust would be chewed and swallowed.

Watching is necessary, because many horses when thus imprisoned, being left alone, grow terrified and injure themselves by struggling their bodies out of the slings. The presence of any human being assures the timidity and checks the active imagination of a solitary animal. The author well knows that the learning of the present time denies imagination to animals. Shying, is only the creature imagining something which is not actually before it. What are dreams but positive evidences of imagination? All people have heard the suppressed bark and seen the excited limbs of the dog as it slept upon the hearth rug. How many grooms have been surprised, upon their earliest visit, to see the stable knocked to pieces and the horse prostrated amid the ruin it has created! How is this to be explained if imagination be not present in the animal? This is the author's interpretation of the mystery. Dreams are active, in proportion to the immaturity of the reason. Children often

A HORSE IN SLINGS FOR OPEN JOINT.

wake up in tears, and continue screaming in terror for long periods if unattended to. The horse starts out of a fearful vision; darkness is about it; the fear augments; the animal begins kicking; the sound made by its own feet increases the creature's alarm; it lashes out frequently until it has pounded part of its dwelling into atoms and disabled itself to that degree which makes the highest punishment the greatest mercy.

A high trough is required to guard against the effects of that itching which attends the healing process, and provokes the animal to strike its knees. This it would do against the manger were its head in the customary position. Were a wall before it, the knees might still be laid open; but with a high trough nothing is within the reach of its injured joint. Even supposing one of the slender supports, by the cunning of excitement, to be struck, the substance should be too light to offer any dangerous resistance, the blow being far more likely to overturn the machine than to lacerate the limb.

When the quadruped has remained sufficient time in the slings to have become familiar with them, pull up the cloth so that it may slightly touch but not press against the belly. Then well secure it, and leave the animal to rest its wearied limbs, or not, as it pleases. Its suffering joints will soon teach the horse to bear the entire weight upon such a support, and to sleep comfortably in the contrivance. With a few, and only a few examples, living in slings has induced such confirmed constipation as necessitated a daily resort to bran mashes. Most horses, however, speedily accept and grow fat, enjoying the relief thus afforded. Only one caution need be given—look well to the tackle. The horse is very heavy, and should a single fastening prove insecure, the result might convert a healing wound into a hopeless injury.

With the employment of slings, change the lotion for one composed of chloride of zinc, one scruple; water, one pint; this need be applied

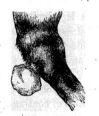

only during the day. It is too weak to occasion pain, and should be used with the saucer and sponge, after the manner of washing a broken knee or open joint, which has been previously illustrated. The strength, nevertheless, is sufficient to coagulate the albumen of the synovia. Thus it forms a species of natural bandage which excludes the air, while at the same time it stimulates the flesh and causes that to heal under the protection of its own albuminous secretion.

THE ALBUMINOUS BALL, WHICH FORMS IN SHAPE OF AN OPEN JOINT WHEN TREATED WITH A SOLUTION OF CHLORIDE OF ZINC.

The coagulated albumen frequently accumulates in front of the knee. The author has seen it attached to the part quite of the size and very near to the form of the largest apple. It must on no account be touched, however large it may grow or however

insecure it may appear. Respect it, and it will fall off when its service
is accomplished. The cure is nearly completed when the white ball
falls. Shortly after the wounds being closed, and pressure made with
the fingers—not with the thumb—can be endured, the slings may be
removed; though the healing should be further confirmed before the
horse is allowed to stand opposite to any substance against which it
may strike what recently has been a fearful open joint.

WOUNDS.

To this species of injury the horse is much exposed from the recklessness or incompetence of those who assume to hold the reins of authority.
Occurrences which are politely termed "accidents," generally entail
suffering upon the blameless animal. The common provocatives of such
accidents are either the drunkenness of man or his utter ignorance of
the mental attributes of the quadruped he has possession of. The first
cause shall be passed over in disgust; the second merits some consideration, being rather a universal than an individual fault.

When a horse pauses, always endeavor to ascertain the motive; the
reason may be groundless. By gentleness, convince the creature that
its fears are without foundation, and you earn a supremacy as well as
win a gratitude which will always be cheerfully acknowledged. Never·
employ the whip to correct "the obstinacy of the brute." The horse
is naturally very fearful; were it not so, man would never have obtained
that mastery which is imperative for domestication. Elderly gentlemen
should never thrust their heads out of carriage windows and shout to
the driver to "go on" Such implied chiding may urge the coachman
to display severity, and the horse is dangerous when alarmed. So long
as the animal continues calm, the superiority of man is submitted to;
but once excite the terror of the quadruped, and all earthly restraint
is powerless. Dread assumes the form of the wildest fury, and the
horse tears onward, insensible to mortal punishment and blind to every
danger

It is in this manner the most terrible wounds are produced. Such
injuries, in surgical language, are defined to be "solutions of continuity,"
or "separations of the skin and soft parts underneath." Neither of
these definitions, however, includes a bruise or a contused wound. Therefore, for the present purpose, a **wound** will be interpreted an injury inflicted by external violence.

A **lacerated wound** may be too trivial to attract the surgeon's notice,
as a scratch. It may also be a very serious affair, as when a cart-wheel
runs against a horse's thigh, tearing the flesh asunder. Laceration is

generally accompanied by contusion, though contusion forms no necessary part of a lacerated wound. When such injuries are inflicted, they are mostly followed by little hemorrhage; yet it is

far from unusual for an animal thus hurt to perish. Shock to the system is the most serious of the primary effects. Beyond that the immediate consequence appears to be insignificant. Little blood is lost, for the vessels are stimulated by the violence which rends these tubes and the soft structures asunder. Stimulation causes the torn mouths of the arteries and veins to close or to retract. The ragged coats of the vessels, the loose fibers of the flesh, and the jagged cellular tissue likewise fall over the orifices, and help to stay the flow of the vital current.

DIAGRAM OF A SEVERE
LACERATED WOUND.

The dangers attending lacerated wounds spring, in the first instance, from collapse. This possibility being overcome, the immediate peril has been surmounted; all injuries of this nature are commonly attended, however, with more or less contusion. The force necessary to tear open a portion of the body will, of necessity, bruise or kill some part of the flesh. Any animal substance, when deprived of vitality, must be cast off by a living body; a slough must follow. Now that process is attended with hazard in proportion as it is tardily accomplished. The period of its occurrence is always one of anxiety; for when this process takes place, the stimulation that originally caused the vessels to retract no longer exists. All mechanical opposition to hemorrhage is, with the loss of the dead matter, generally removed. Everything, therefore, depends upon the fibrinous deposit—a sort of glutinous material secreted by the body, which is commonly largely poured forth when any slough by natural and speedy action is effected. Should the frame be so far debilitated as to prevent all secretion of fibrin, the most frightful bleeding must ensue.

The horse which has not recovered from the original injury will then sink under the terrible depletion. Therefore, it is impossible to form any opinion of the injurious effects or of the consequences likely to follow a lacerated wound before some time has elapsed.

An **incised wound** implies a division, more or less deep, of the soft parts. This form of injury produces less shock to the system, and generally heals more quickly than any other. The principal danger is encountered at the moment when the wound is inflicted; vessels may be sundered, and they are cut in twain with the least possible irritation to the parts within which they are situated. The veins and arteries, therefore, do not generally retract any more than do the soft structures. A gash into a fleshy substance always produces a gaping wound, which is wide in proportion to the depth and length of the injury. From that hurt the dark-colored venous blood drains in a stream, while the bright scarlet or arterial blood is propelled forth in jets, sometimes to a considerable distance. These jets correspond with the pulsations of the heart; but as syncope or fainting takes place, the emission ceases with the beating of the circulatory center.

DIAGRAM OF AN INCISED WOUND.

The danger consequent upon an incised wound is ever measured by the extent of the hemorrhage. When large arteries are divided, that fact is easily told by the size and the force of the jets sent forth. A strong horse may, from that cause, be dead in ten minutes. To enforce the difference between a lacerated and an incised wound, the reader is reminded of those painful cases, frequently recorded in the newspapers, where a limb is by machinery torn from a poor man's body, and scarcely a drop of blood marks the deprivation; also of death by severing a throat, when sensation ceases ere the stream has flowed forth. The last is an incised, the first is a lacerated wound.

An abraded wound, in its mildest form, is simply a graze. The reader will, however, remember how acutely painful such accidents always are. The horse's sufferings are not highly estimated by the generality of people; nevertheless, an injury of this description is not to be despised, even when witnessed on the animal. A broken knee, as it generally is exhibited, is nothing more than an abrasion. An abraded wound may simply mean that the

DIAGRAM OF AN ABRADED WOUND.

insensible outer covering of the skin has been injured; it may also imply that the soft structures beneath have been sundered. Wounds of this kind are not free from danger when of magnitude. Little blood may flow, but the cutis is the most sensitive structure of the entire body. A needle's point cannot enter any part of the skin without sensation warning the person of a puncture. In human operations, division of the skin, or separation of the cutis, is known to constitute the major portion of the patient's agony.

The suffering attendant on the latter class of injuries is increased by almost every abrasion forcing grit or dirt into the substance of the cutis. This, of course, is generally washed out. The torture accompanying a large abraded surface is, therefore, very great; and horses when suffering from accidents of such a nature sometimes sink from the irritation consequent upon the injury. When the animals survive, the roots of the hair too often have been destroyed, and a perpetual blemish is the result.

A **punctured wound** is always dangerous; the hazard in this, as in every species of injury, is greatly increased when inflicted on parts liable to any vast amount of motion. Thus, punctures occurring over the stifle-joint too often set our best surgery at defiance. The muscles of the hind leg contract with every movement of the body. Added to that, the part abounds with fascia.

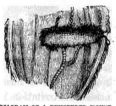

DIAGRAM OF A PUNCTURED WOUND.

The engraving supposes the soft parts to have been divided, in order to show the ragged nature and large extent of the injury, with the comparatively small opening by which this amount of harm is characterized.

The majority of these wounds heal by suppuration. Fascia is a substance no pus can penetrate, and which is more easily rent than punctured. The exit of the secretion, therefore, is opposed in many directions, while the ceaseless motion occasions the matter to burrow. The sinuses thus produced are by the fascia guided to the stifle-joint; and, when once the synovial cavity is polluted by the intrusion of the unhealthy pus, all the best efforts of science are useless.

When a punctured wound occurs, the skin, being elastic, stretches before the instrument by which the wound is inflicted. The soft parts beneath the skin, not being elastic to the same degree as the integument, break down before the penetrating force. They are torn or lacerated; for generally the muscles receive a larger injury than would be calculated from the size of the instrument by which the blow was inflicted. The rent flesh must be cast off by a slough—corruption generally attends that process. Much of the pus secreted cannot find an exit through the opening in the skin; a large portion of it is confined within the puncture. There it decays, and, being impelled by the motion of the limb, readily finds its way in all directions save the upward one.

No judgment approaching to accuracy can be formed at the first sight of a punctured wound. The probe may ascertain the depth of the injury, but it cannot tell the extent of damage done to the interior of the body. Therefore, whether the hoof is pierced by a nail, or the muscles are lacer-

ated by the shaft of a cart—be the instrument large or small—the consequences likely to follow upon the injury cannot be foretold.

A **contusion, in** its mildest form, is simply a bruise. Injuries of this
class, when of magnitude, are very deceptive; the surface is unstained
by blood, and there is no flesh exposed. For these
reasons the ignorant are apt to disregard such accidents, and to express surprise when they terminate
otherwise than kindly. When a bruise happens, blood
is effused in smaller or larger quantities according to
the extent of the injury. A small quantity of effused
blood, sufficient to discolor the human skin, may be
absorbed; but when the amount is large, the powers
of nature are defied. The blood thrown out, not
being taken up again, congeals, and ultimately cor-

DIAGRAM OF A CONTUSED
WOUND.

rupts. Then an abscess or a slough is necessitated; both are attended
with danger: the first may be deep seated or superficial; either form is
attended by much weakness. That generates considerable irritation, and
may even be the cause of fatal hemorrhage; or it may lead to sinuses,
the direction, the number, or extent of which, when they do occur, is not
to be predicated. A bruise is, consequently, not to be judged of hastily.
The amount of pain which it provokes is even unworthy dependence, as
the injury may have hurt the bone or the tendon; and then, though the
accident is rendered very serious, in the first instance no sign of agony
announces the extent of the evil.

With regard to treatment, when a **lacerated wound** occurs, the first
attention should be paid to the system, which has always been much
shaken. Give, therefore, the drink composed of one ounce each of laudanum and sulphuric ether, with half a pint of water; repeat it every
quarter of an hour till the shivering natural to the horse on these occasions has disappeared, and the pulse has recovered its healthy tone.

Avoid all poultices of the ordinary kind; one composed of one-fourth
yeast and three-fourths of any coarse grain, excepting bran, may be
applied. So also may a lotion thus composed :—

Lotion for Lacerated Wounds.

Tincture of cantharides	One ounce.
Chloride of zinc	Two drachms.
Water	Three pints.

Mix. Keep a rag constantly wet over the part.

Either will stimulate the parts, and probably prevent any tendency to
unhealthy action. The yeast poultice produces this effect by giving off
carbonic acid; the lotion accomplishes this intention by both its active

ingredients. Each is stimulating, also disinfectant, and will counteract any filthy odor which may attend the sloughing process; but the lotion is perhaps to be preferred, as it is more easily applied. When the slough has taken place, should hemorrhage ensue, dash upon the part jug after jug of the coldest water; or, should no very cold water be at hand, drive upon the mouths of the vessels a current of wind from the nozzle of the bellows. Continue to do this till the bleeding ceases, or until a surgeon can be obtained to take up the arteries.

The after-treatment is simple : apply frequently the solution of chloride of zinc, one grain to an ounce of water; that lotion will cleanse the wound and prevent unpleasant smells.

As respects feeding, this must be regulated by the character of the pulse. Should the beat of the artery be quick and feeble, no hay should be given; good, thick gruel should constitute the only drink excepting in extreme cases, when two pots of porter may be allowed each day. Good oats and old beans, both crushed and scalded, should then constitute the food, and the utmost gentleness should be exercised toward the animal.

Should the pulse be natural, allow three feeds of oats each day, as, in every kind of injury to the horse, more danger is to be apprehended from debility than from any excess of energy.

Incised wounds.—When these happen, always dash the part with plenty of cold water or blow upon them with the bellows. Place the horse in the nearest shed ; motion promotes hemorrhage, therefore a walk is not to be hazarded. The bleeding being arrested—for, in severe accidents of this kind, there is no time to send for assistance—let the animal remain perfectly quiet until the exposed surface has become almost dry, but on being touched by the finger feels sticky. Then draw the edges together, and keep them in that position by means of sutures.

FIXED SUTURE NEEDLE: VERY USEFUL FOR INCISED WOUNDS OF NO GREAT DEPTH.

The best means of inserting these sutures is with a curved needle fixed into a handle. The handle is wanted to obtain the necessary power, and the needle's point should be sharp to penetrate the hide of the horse, which in places is of considerable thickness. The needle is thrust through the integument about one inch and a half from one margin of the incision; it is brought out about the same distance within the divided soft parts. It enters the opposite side of the sundered flesh even with the place whence it came forth, and afterward it appears through the skin about equally distant from the opposite edge of the wound. There is a hole near the point of the needle; through this opening a piece of strong twine or narrow tape is threaded; when, the instrument being withdrawn, the twine or tape is pulled into the puncture which has been made. The needle is then released, the suture being left in.

So many sutures as may be necessary are thus inserted — in small wounds, these being about two inches asunder, but in larger injuries,

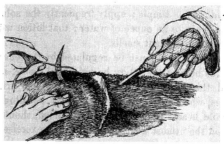

THE MANNER OF USING THE FIXED SETON NEEDLE.

A second person pushes the wound together, and, when the point of the needle appears, threads it with a piece of zinc wire or soft string. The needle is then retracted, and released from the wire or string, whereby a suture is left in the wound.

three inches apart. All are duly placed before any are tied; the whole being ready, the wound is forced together by an assistant, while the strings are fastened—care being exercised not to bring any of them actually tight, lest the motion of the body or the swelling of the part should drag the sutures through the flesh and thereby tear them out.

DIAGRAM OF SUTURES WHEN TIED AND LEFT IN A WOUND.

A wound thus united may possibly heal by first intention, or the divided parts, when brought together, may join, and give no further trouble to the surgical attendant.

Union by first intention is, however, somewhat rare in the horse; and should not that take place, suppuration will be established. So soon as the pus flows freely forth, and the sutures appear to tighten or drag, cut them out by snipping the twine; but allow the strings to loosen before you attempt their withdrawal.

If this is not done, the sutures will speedily find an exit for themselves by causing the flesh against which the tension acts to be absorbed; thus the original injury will be rendered more complicated, and the ultimate blemish must be altogether greater.

All that is required after the establishment of suppuration is to bathe

the part with the solution of chloride of zinc, one grain to the ounce of water. This lotion will suppress any fetor, and gently stimulate the healing process, as well as prevent the sprouting of fungoid granulations; it is necessary also to attend strictly to the directions laid down for feeding during the curing of wounds.

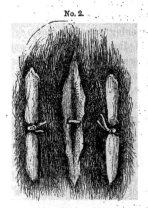

No. 1.

No. 2.

TWO KINDS OF SUTURES RARELY EMPLOYED UPON THE HORSE.

No. 1. The continuous suture, which is employed for sewing up portions of bowel when the intestines are injured and exposed.
No. 2. The deep suture or the quill suture. In the horse pieces of wood are substituted for quills. The wood is notched in the center; and upon the indentations the sutures are fixed, to prevent the movements of the animal from displacing them. It is sometimes employed to bring the sides of deep and gaping wounds closer together.

The treatment of an **abraded wound** chiefly consists in cleansing the surface with plenty of cold water, which should be allowed by its own weight to wash off any loose particles of dirt. No cloth or other aid should be employed to scrub the living flesh as though it were an insensitive board. The matter which cannot be removed by simply sluicing, had better remain to be expelled by the secretion of pus. The horse, especially when terrified, endures pain very badly; indeed, the animal is so timid and so delicately framed that it is always good surgery to spare all unnecessary suffering.

Support the body with laudanum and ether drinks, one ounce of each to the pint of water, as often as they may be needed. Let the food be generous, unless fever should arise, when the directions already given must be attended to.

Punctured wounds require only one kind of treatment, whether a nail be driven into the flesh of the foot, or the shaft of a cart be forced into the substance of the thigh. Here the knife must be employed; and, unless the animal shows evident symptoms of excessive weakness, it is better, perhaps, to operate while the parts are partially numbed by the shock, than to wait until a morbid sensibility is provoked. Always enlarge the opening; do this in the foot by cutting away the horn of the sole around the small puncture left by the nail. When the soft parts are penetrated, probe the wound first; then, if possible, insert a knife to the bottom of the puncture, and, with the edge downward, draw it forth. By this means a wound resembling a subverted < will be instituted. It will be narrowest toward the extremity, and widest at the mouth A free opening affords a ready egress for all sloughs and pus. It materially aids the healing process, and effectually prevents the establishment of sinuses; while the clean incision left by the knife is of small import, when taken into consideration with the other consequences of a punctured wound.

Support the animal if necessary, or regulate the food by the symptoms A **contused wound**, when slight, may be rubbed with the iodide of lead ointment, one drachm of the active agent to the ounce of lard; when all enlargement will sometimes subside, and the effused blood may be absorbed. However, the horse commonly receives injuries of magnitude. In the last case, take a sharp knife and draw it along the entire length of the swelling. Make a long gash, only through the integument, at every eighth inch, and be careful to carry the knife through the integument, or to the lowest portion of the detached skin Any sac that may be left is certain to retain corruption, and may produce fearful afterconsequences. The attendant measures consist in bathing the contusion with a lotion composed of chloride of zinc, one grain, water, one ounce, and diminishing the food or supporting the body as nature demands such treatment.

The after-treatment of all injuries consists in keeping any external orifices open till all sloughs and pus have disappeared In surgery, a large and depending opening, by means of which the interior may drain, is always to be preserved, and the knife, to this end, may be employed so often as the healing process threatens to prematurely close the wound.

Formerly it was the practice to bleed after every injury; this was done to prevent fever. However, observation has shown that the vital powers are more often weakened than increased by the shock attendant on severe accidents. Whenever the contrary happens, it is far better to lower the pulse by repeated doses of aconite, than to abstract that which will subsequently be necessary to repair injury.

It was also once the custom to fill wounds with tents or lumps of tow, and to bandage every injured part. These habits only served to confine that which nature was striving to cast out. They consequently did much harm; and are now happily discarded.

A piece of loose rag, saturated in the oil or the solution of tar, should, during summer, be suspended over the mouth of every wound, to keep off the flies. The only tent which the author approves of is when an incised wound happens where assistance is far away, and difficult to procure. Then, to arrest the hemorrhage, let the horse rug, a man's coat, or anything else be violently thrust into the gash, and forcibly held there until proper assistance can be obtained.

Such is the present method of treating wounds; this to the reader may appear very cruel; but could he have walked through and have inhaled the atmosphere of the wards in hospitals appropriated to such injuries as they existed in former times, he would thoroughly understand that apparent want of feeling is, in reality, the height of charity.

A BANDAGE DESIGNED FOR WOUNDS ON THE TRUNK OF THE HORSE.

To conclude this part, the author lays before his readers the following bandage, intended to meet an inconvenience hitherto experienced when a horse has the walls of the abdomen punctured. The constant motion of the part renders ordinary sutures of no avail, and for that reason bandages, unless so tight as to check circulation, are of little use. The annexed is made like a broad belt, and is buckled round the body. The bars are composed of vulcanized India-rubber; they will yield to the movements of the abdomen, and yet serve as sutures supporting any pendant flap, while at the same time they will allow the wound to be dressed without disturbing the bandage. They also offer the advantage of permitting the attendant to pull one support aside without removing the whole.

Every part in the horse subjected to much motion when wounded, should have an adhesive plaster placed over it, and retained there until the suppurative action is confirmed. By this means is excluded the atmosphere, which, when this precaution was neglected, has entered the wound, penetrated between the muscles, and by distending the body increased the suffering, as well as led to the worst of consequences.

Wounds in veterinary surgery rank among the most formidable cases with which the practitioner has to contend. They are not so because the flesh of the horse is slower to heal than that of the human being. Indeed, the scale in this respect inclines toward the animal; but they are rendered slow to heal and difficult to cure by two causes. The horse is always impatient of restraint; any effort to confine the creature is more likely to provoke dangerous resistance than to induce the slightest symptom of amendment. The quadruped naturally delights in motion. It was formed for activity. Even when in its stall the body is never absolutely still; the position is being changed; the legs are frequently stamped; the head, eyes, ears, and tail are never quiet. This innate quality retards the union of sundered flesh. It favors the gravitation of pus between the muscles, and thus generates sinuses. These are the torments of veterinary surgery. Could the sinus be anticipated, or in all cases eradicated, the principal difficulty would be removed; but intelligent as the horse is, it proves impossible to make the animal comprehend the necessity for quietude. Hence any trivial accident may lead to injuries of so extensive a character and so malignant a nature as will set the best endeavors or the most consummate skill at defiance.

28

CHAPTER XV.

THE veterinary art is by no means rendered more successful by the cunning of its stratagems. Many of its objects are accomplished after the rudest and the most primitive methods. Not one, perhaps, is more

THE PRESENT MANNER OF CASTING A HORSE FOR OPERATION.

coarse than the present method of casting or throwing an animal previous to an operation. The reader has only to ask himself what condition the body must be in when, with the sight blinded, it is suddenly jerked to the earth; and how far it is fitly prepared by so violent a practice to be submitted to the knife of an operator?

There are few operations in veterinary surgery which a person of moderate nerve and average intelligence might not himself perform. The author has seen gentlemen with titles, and others holding high rank in the army, indulge in the strange pleasure of singeing living flesh with the heated iron. But he has never beheld horsemen handling the knife. The latter would better become their hands than the first severe and disfiguring instrument, which, however useful it may have been found in

(434)

certain cases met with in human surgery, nevertheless would be well abolished from veterinary practice, because of its indiscriminate abuse. Firing is employed for every and for no reason. Now recourse is had to it because the joints are weak. Then it is adopted because a gentleman is fond of seeing his horses scored. Next, it is used to gain time, and thus prolong the treatment. Generally it is brought forward because the practitioner does not know what else to do. Lastly, it is esteemed the crowning measure of routine practice.

The author, however, has never been necessitated to resort to so violent an agent. It is a most unseemly ornament in unprofessional hands; in this book, which is intended for the general public, the use of the firing-iron is altogether omitted.

The knife, especially to the animal, is the most humane of remedies. It often affords instant or immediate relief. The animal seems to suffer more from the restraint imposed than from the wounds inflicted. The chief sensation, with all forms of life, resides in the skin; so that the integument be quickly and effectually divided, the soft parts underneath have but little feeling. The interference with these last rather produces faintness or sickness than acute suffering; the knowledge of which fact will embolden many a humane person, though the writer trusts it will not be credited by all who are of an opposite character, since boldness, unrestrained by humanity, only renders the individual a savage without the savage's excuse.

Such operations as embriotomy, castration, and lithotomy are intentionally omitted, from a conviction that no gentleman would undertake them; and because, in every instance, they had better be intrusted to a regular veterinary surgeon.

Before undertaking any operation, always reflect on what you are about to do, and make up your mind how you design to do it. Irresolution causes more suffering than the most perverted determination can inflict. It is always well (however much in practice the operator may consider himself) to first perform the intended operation upon the dead subject. This is a custom which the writer invariably adopted; and frequently it has supplied his memory with a refresher which, in the hurry of practice, was found a most timely warning.

Never use small knives. Such things look pretty. The sight of a large blade may appear very ugly; but it does at one movement that work which an instrument of notching smallness would not in twenty hacks accomplish. Understand thoroughly that which you are about to perform, and always choose the tool likely to get through the business quickly. Periosteotomy cases were formerly sold by veterinary instrument makers which contained a knife of moderate doll's dimension. The

writer, to accomplish the purpose which that little knife was specially
made for, was accustomed to employ a bistoury larger than those in
ordinary use among gentlemen of his profession.

Where you anticipate much bleeding, always endeavor, if possible, to
divide the main artery with the first incision.   This is by far the most
humane, and therefore the safest practice.   The vessel, being divided,
can be taken up, and all further flow of blood thereby checked.   But if
the artery be left to the last, it remains to fill the smaller branches.
These are of necessity frequently severed.   Each, as it is cut, bleeds
more or less freely; thus the hemorrhage is far greater, and the operation far more difficult, than if the main trunk had been secured at the
earliest possible period.

Always tie both ends of an artery; because, though the main stream
flows through that portion of the vessel nearest the heart, yet the other
half, being fed by the smaller trunks, and the current having a tendency
to regurgitate, a considerable quantity of the vital fluid may flow out of
the mouth, which, in general opinion, has no medium of supply.

If, during an operation, you make an accidental incision into a vessel,
either take it up, (which is the better way,) or cut it short off when there
is a chance of its retracting and of the bleeding being thus arrested.
Vessels of large size may, when requisite, be excised and tied; the
vital current being afterward carried on by the dilatation of the lesser
ducts.

To tie an artery it is imperative to secure the end of the vessel; this,
if possible, should be accomplished with the forceps.   When the mouth
of the vessel is much retracted, it may be necessary to employ the knife;
but that practice should be viewed only as the last resort of the profi-
cient surgeon.

The end of the artery being fixed and drawn forth, a piece of strong

silk, thrice twisted, (after the method represented in
the inferior circle of the annexed illustration,) is
passed over the vessel.   The silk is then drawn tight,
and will generally remain fixed.   However, sad accidents have occurred by operators trusting to so
doubtful a security; for that reason it is always
advisable to make another twist, (as shown in the
smaller circle of the illustration,) which will render
the knot secure.

THE LOUP BY MEANS OF
WHICH THE ENDS OF AR-
TERIES ARE SECURED.

Even a vessel of the second magnitude may be
obliterated, as the carotid artery or the jugular vein,
without life being necessarily sacrificed.   However,
it is always well to spare these parts, or when either is lost to arrange so

that the absence of them may entail the least possible inconvenience upon the animal. Thus, if the carotid artery be lost, place the food low down, and thereby aid the flow of blood to the head. If the jugular vein be destroyed, then put the fodder high up, that the current from the head may be facilitated.

Never, on any account, remove any portion of skin which is not involved in some fearful injury, or separated from its attachments by the action of disease.

Skin is the part of the body which is never reproduced, and even the place whence it is absent always heals slowly. However loose the skin may appear, however disproportioned it may seem after some tumor has been removed, respect every particle of it. Before the wound can heal, inflammation must set in. That process ended, the skin, under its action, will have contracted, and in the end there will be only sufficient integument to cover the part; whereas, if the slightest amount be excised, to such an extent there will for a long time remain a gaping sore.

Never spare the knife. Think well before you touch that tool; but, having it in hand, assure yourself its edge is sharp, and never do at two cuts that which might have been accomplished in one.

Always slit up a sinus where such a proceeding is possible. When the sinus is too long, supposing the pipe to take an internal direction, as from the withers to the chest, insert a seton with the guarded seton needle, a representation of which is given below.

THE GUARDED SETON NEEDLE.

The blade of this instrument is generally about two feet long. Before using it, the cutting head is always retracted by pulling back the nut at the extremity, and securing it in its place by means of the screw situated on the middle of the handle. The blade then reposes upon a blunt companion, and may with impunity be inserted down any sinus or false canal. Having reached the bottom of the pipe, and all important vessels being passed, the screw is loosened, and the projecting end of the blade at the extremity of the handle is struck forcibly, when the sharp point is driven forward, and this pierces the flesh.

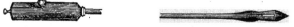

THE SETON NEEDLE PROTRUDED, AND SECURED WITHIN THE HANDLE BY MEANS OF A SCREW.

Behind the cutting head there is a free space. Through that opening a long piece of tape is threaded, and the instrument is withdrawn, pulling the tape into the sinus, in which it remains. A knot is made at either end of the tape; thus a seton is with safety placed in situations where the depth to be penetrated would defy ordinary measures, and the vessels to be passed would render such measures more than doubly hazardous.

The use of a seton is to act as a drain, or to stimulate an unhealthy canal—to provoke a sinus to secrete healthy pus, instead of a thin and often a foul discharge—and thus to cause the diseased pipe to heal or to become obliterated.

When operating, always make your first incision through the skin rather too large than in the least too small; remember, the division from within outward occasions much less pain than the separation, made after the ordinary fashion, from without inward.

Never spare hair; the substance is readily reproduced. It can be wished to be spared only to conceal the fact of an operation having been performed. Always refuse to become a party to dishonesty. Do what is necessary for the proper performance of your office. The removal of hair, which may otherwise interfere with your sight, is essential: therefore cut it off, regardless of any wish to the contrary.

Instruct your assistants beforehand how to cast the horse; leave that business to them: never meddle yourself. The writer has seen veterinary surgeons, in their operating dresses, push and haul with the utmost energy. Such silly people have doubtless thought themselves exalted by this exhibition of violence. It would have been more to their credit had they devoted half the energy to teaching their people beforehand. But in what condition must their hands and temper be after having taken a lead in a struggle with a horse for mastery !

A surgeon should always be cool. His head should direct his hand; his knife should be held lightly; his eye should be quick, and his mind prepared to meet any accident. He should do his office neatly, and, if possible, without soiling his person. The ripping cut and the bloody hands alone distinguish the ignorant butcher from the scientific operator.

During every operation enjoin the strictest silence upon the spectators. The horse is never vicious, but it is always timid. Sounds have a powerful effect upon animals which cannot understand speech. Every word uttered, even in a whisper, should be of assurance to the sufferer; for the horse is only to be feared in its efforts to escape from some supposed peril. It becomes mad in its alarm. It then puts forth its strength and exerts it without regard to consequences. Man has everything to hope from the fortitude and noble forbearance of the creature. It responds to kindness with something more than submission; it answers sympathy by the most entire confidence and utter dependence. The life, the feeling, the natural powers are all subservient to the great love which is embodied in a horse's attachment There is not among created beings one which has so large a sympathy; the horse must attach itself to something; to love seems essential to its being. The stable in which it is captive the patient prisoner learns to regard, as it were, a palace The pace is always more willing when returning to captivity; freedom has no charm; the field has no allurement to the horse which has lived any time in the most crimped, confined, and uncomfortable of stalls It will quit the spring grass to be fastened once more in the place to which it has been accustomed and has grown attached.

Then, however much removed from itself, it must pour the richest of its affections on some animal, should man, in pride, refuse to accept the offering. Creatures the most opposite have been the horse's favorite. How often do we hear of the liking formed between a goat, a dog, a cat, and the horse! Love has a strange freemasonry of its own; how else can we account for the larger creature being able to make its longing understood by the smaller life? There may, however, be between animals some substitute for language; but we can hardly suppose any recognized signs exist between birds and the equine species. Yet a famous animal-painter had a pony which formed a violent and lasting affection for a bantam cock. These two used to march side by side up and down the field in which the larger animal was confined; for so very expansive is the horse's love that it will embrace not only its abode, but some life, however distant apparently from its own.

The voice of the person who is accustomed to groom and feed the animal, if he has been only ordinarily humane in the performance of his office, will at all times reassure the beating heart of a prostrated horse. But vast injustice to the animal's better qualities is done by the mode of casting it. It is violently jerked off its legs; by a sudden pull it is thrown "with a burster" upon its side. There it struggles. If mastery sides with the animal, then let the men be speedy in their flight. The quadruped, in its fear, designs no harm to any person It means only to escape from the terrible danger which encompasses it. Still, it is regardless in its alarm, and may do more injury than the most evil intention could accomplish. There is an engraving of the method of casting horses commencing this chapter. Let the capable reader imagine the effect produced upon the timid quadruped when it is violently flung upon the earth with a sound well denominated "a burster"

The horse is much better made to lie down gently, after the method adopted by Mr. Rarey Half, and far more than half, the terror excited by an operation may thus be avoided. The confusion and bustle, conjoined with violence, which naturally attend "casting," must make a lasting impression upon the retentive mind of the animal, and, we may suppose, must aggravate the pain, thus materially endangering the result of an operation. The hobbles may be fixed quite as readily when the horse is down as when the animal is standing. Nay, they may be fixed more readily, as the horse, when down, has lost three-fourths of its power.

Mr. Rarey's method of throwing the most unruly animal is thus described by that gentleman:—

"Everything that we want to teach the horse must be commenced in some way to give him an idea of what you want him to do, and then be repeated till he learns it perfectly. To make a horse lie down, bend his left fore leg and slip a loop over it, so that he cannot get it down. Then put a surcingle around his body, and fasten one end of a long strap around the other fore leg just above the hoof. Place the other end under the surcingle, so as to keep the strap in the right direction; take a short hold of it with your right hand; stand on the left side of the horse, grasp the bit in your left hand, pull steadily on the strap with your right; bear against his shoulder till you cause him to move. As soon as he lifts his weight, your pulling will raise the other foot, and he will have to come on his knees. Keep the strap tight in your hand, so that he cannot straighten his leg if he rises up. Hold him in this position, and turn his head toward you; bear against his side with your shoulder—not hard, but with a steady, equal pressure—and in about ten minutes he will lie down. As soon as he lies down he will be completely conquered, and you can handle him as you please. Take off the straps, and straighten out his legs; rub him lightly about the face and neck with your hand the way the hair lies; handle all his legs; and, after he has lain ten or twenty minutes, let him get up again. After resting him a short time, make him lie down as before. Repeat the operation three or four times, which will be sufficient for one lesson. Give him two lessons a day; and when you have given him four lessons, he will lie down by taking hold of one foot. As soon as he is well broken to lie down in this way, tap him on the opposite leg with a stick when you take hold of his foot; and in a few days he will lie down from the mere motion of the stick."

What prevents the hobbles being buckled on? What prevents all necessary arrangements being carried out? What, indeed, but the stubbornness inseparable from ignorance! Veterinary surgeons, as a rule, are not an educated class. In proportion as their information is limited, so is their adherence to established custom likely to be intractable.

There are, besides the hobbles, two other inventions designed to limit the capability of resistance. One is the side line. A soft collar is put over the horse's head and a hobble is fastened to the foot it is desired to have elevated. From the collar is dependant a metal-loop, ring, or other contrivance. By the side of this a strong rope is attached. The cord is then passed through the D

of the hobble; afterward it is brought back and ran through the side ring or loop. A man then takes hold of the end of the rope, and, by gradual traction, causes the leg to be advanced. It is neither wise nor humane to drag the foot off the ground. A horse which will stand quiet with both feet resting on the earth, is rendered restless when one leg is fastened in the air.

THE SIDE LINE.

The occasion which makes it imperative to apply the side line is, when the hocks or hinder parts are examined. Many unbroken horses, though quiet in other respects, will not allow these portions of the body to be touched. By causing one leg to be advanced, the other is deprived of all power, as a weapon of offense. The horse would obviously fall, if he were to project the only free hind member; and the timidity of the creature indisposes it to incur so vast an indignity.

The other invention is the double side line. A rope is fixed to a loop on either side. The loop or ring is attached to a soft collar. The rope

is afterward threaded through a hobble on each pastern. Both legs are then gently pulled for-ward, and the animal, having its posterior supports drawn from under it, comes to the earth. The ropes are held tight while the horse is turned upon its back. The instant it is in that position, somebody seats himself upon the head, while the body of the animal is propped up by numerous trusses of straw.

This last is but an imperfect method of casting. In general

THE DOUBLE SIDE LINE.

it is rendered still more cruel by the abuse to which it is subject. The ropes are commonly pulled with an utter disregard to the living body upon which they operate. The hind legs are often drawn to the shoulders, and frequently additional cords are employed to make the poor creatures more distorted and more fixed. Has man any cause to wonder at a horse being occasionally what is called "vicious," when the unreasoning creature is thus fearfully operated upon? Is it not rather a proof of the horse's intelligence that it can recognize the cause of its suffering, and study ever after to repel its tormentor?

Let the horse be thrown down after the admirable method introduced by Mr. Rarey. Let it then be hobbled, and never, during the operation, hear any sound but soothing accents. Animals do not understand words, but they are quick readers of characteristics. The language itself these creatures may not be able to literally interpret; but they comprehend all which the manner conveys. When kindness is expressed, the meaning is felt, though the verbiage be lost: it is astonishing how animals will enter into the intention of speech! How home kind language seems to go to the ignorant heart, and how true it is that a gentle word is never thrown away! It is surprising to observe the affection by which the human race is surrounded; they live and walk among animals eager for permission to adore them, anxious to love and to serve them; but it is lamentable to see how an evil spirit repels the feeling which pervades all nature.

There is another point upon which the writer presumes to offer advice. Veterinary surgeons display ignorance in nothing more than in being servile copyists. They do not view their sphere of science as a separate and distinct branch. They always will strive to follow the example of human practitioners even to particulars. There is no difference in the dissecting knives used at the King's College and the Royal Veterinary establishment, though bodies of different bulks are studied in each school. The operating knives of most veterinary surgeons are ridiculously small for such purposes. The consequence is, the animal is much longer down than is absolutely necessary. The author has known one hour employed in dressing a quittor; whereas six sinuses ought to be laid open and dressed in less than five minutes. A vast deal of time is thus wasted; although the opposition to Mr. Rarey's method of throwing will, doubtless, be the length of time it would occupy. However, granting the objection; which is the surgeon bound to consider—the welfare of his patient or his own convenience? It is not every day that the gentleman who enjoys the largest practice has to cast a horse. It is, in fact, a somewhat rare and an exceptional occurrence. Could not the most engaged man devote an occasional half hour to the benefit of his profession?

When operating upon living flesh, always have your knives rather too large than in any measure too small. The work is performed quicker; besides, the hands are kept at some distance from the wound, and the eyes thereby are enabled to direct their movements. The probability of mistakes is thus lessened, and no man, with a knife in his hand and bleeding flesh under his eyes, has a right to expose himself to the possibility of an error which, of course, is not to be erased or atoned for.

Should a horse, when under the knife, struggle, do not attempt to contend with the animal. Immediately leave hold of your instruments, and withdraw your person out of danger. Allow your knife, etc. to remain; it will seldom be displaced, or, if cast out of the wound, can be easily reintroduced; whereas, did you endeavor to snatch away or to retain your hold, the most lamentable consequences might be the result.

Another caution, and this part of the writer's office is concluded. When you operate upon a leg, have that limb uppermost, unless your incision is made upon the inner side. Have the foot placed upon a pillow or sack stuffed with straw, and a strong webbing put around the

hoof. The webbing give to a man who is to pull at it. The dragging sensation renders the horse inclined to retract the member; therefore place yourself in front of the limb, or on the same side as the man who holds the webbing. The fore leg, when advanced, cannot be readily employed as a weapon of offense, and the hind limb is always, when used in defense, projected backward.

OPERATIONS—TRACHEOTOMY.

This operation is, perhaps, the most humane recourse of veterinary surgery. Neurotomy may save the horse from greater and longer suffering; but **tracheotomy** is performed, unlike the former operation, upon an animal in an unconscious state. Difficult respiration, either from tumor pressing upon the larynx, infiltration upon the lining membrane of the larynx, or choking from various causes, produces imperfect oxygenation of the blood. The vital current being impure, of course the brain which it nurtures is not in a condition of health or activity. The consciousness is impaired or altogether destroyed; and immediate relief is experienced after the performance of the operation. The recovery is as rapid as the previous symptoms were alarming. The altered aspect of the animal is as though the body were resuscitated. In certain cases, where every breath is drawn in pain, the ease afforded by tracheotomy is most marked. It makes little difference to Nature, by what means the air is inhaled, so that a sufficiency of diluted oxygen come in contact with the absorbing membrane of the lungs. This, when the larynx is closed or diseased, tracheotomy permits to be accomplished. It is equally beneficial, safe, and humane. However ugly its description may read, it is in practice to be strongly recommended.

The general fault with veterinary sugeons is the delay which commonly pushes off the operation to the last moment. In this delay the proprietor is, perhaps, equally or even more at fault. Hope leads the owner on to the very last, and even then it is with reluctant horror that consent is given "to cut the horse's throat." Such is the term by which certain practitioners characterize tracheotomy; and though it is uttered merely as a joke, yet it creates an impression which acts against a harmless operation.

In agricultural districts, the veterinarian is frequently knocked up at night by a messenger, who announces "Farmer Hodges's horse be a dying." The farmer may live several miles off in the country; and the reluctant sleeper hurries on his clothes to obey the implied summons.

In due time the pair reach farmer Hodge's homestead. It needs no finger to point out the stable. The sound of laborious breathing effectually notifies it. However, the practitioner, upon entrance into the place, is horrified to find himself there with no better company than a boy and a rapidly-sinking animal. The circumstances demand other assistance. The horse doctor cannot help giving voice to his requirements. The lad hearing this, says hastily he will fetch somebody very soon—hangs up the lantern and vanishes into the darkness.

Minutes pass and no footfall greets the ear. The divisions of the hour are struck by the village church, and still no sound of returning steps. The animal becomes worse and worse. In its disabled state it fears to lie down, as that position impedes the breathing. In its efforts to stand, it reels about—now falling to one side and then to the other. Yet the departed messenger does not return. The veterinarian finds the limits of delay are passed: ten minutes more and the quadruped will be down. He takes out his lancet. One foot from the breast-bone, and as near the center of the neck as the rocking motion of the horse or the flickering light of the lantern will allow him to aim, he plunges the blade deeply into the flesh, if possible at one cut dividing the cartilages of the trachea. He has little control over the incision. Frequently a gash results from the tottering of the animal. Mostly he divides more than he would have done had daylight and assistance been afforded him.

The incision, being made, the fingers are thrust into the wound to keep the division open. At first this may be difficult; but as time

TRACHEOTOMY, AS PERFORMED UNDER DIFFICULTIES—A COMMON OCCURRENCE.

proceeds, the standing of the horse becomes firmer and the breathing less noisy. The veterinarian is, however, impatient at the delay and his enforced position. He is just beginning to despair, when the messenger returns, accompanied by a sleepy companion. Both are surprised at the condition of the horse, and, not observing the wound, imagine the animal has been cured by magic. However, to the demands of the equine medical attendant, nothing like a tracheotomy tube is to be invented. At last the spout of the tea kettle is thought of; and the good dame awakens in the morning to find her kettle demolished and its spout thrust into the "plaguy horse's throat."

It is the curse of veterinary surgery, that nobody appears to understand when an operation is required. The practitioner, therefore, is seldom prepared for its performance. The circumstances allow him little time to think, and none to return or to fetch the necessary instruments.

However, when he has proper time and choice, he should always make a free incision through the skin and panniculus carnosus. Make this opening about one-third up the neck, measuring from the chest. It is more general to open the windpipe at a similar distance from the jaw, and, assuredly, the superior incision has this advantage, that there is less to cut through. But where no important nerves or vessels are endangered, surgery cares little about the depth of a wound, the chief attention being given to the probable after-consequences.

The superior portion of the neck is especially the seat of motion; it varies with every turn and movement of the head. Hence the end of the tube is apt to be brought into constant contact with the lining membrane of the trachea, and horses have been slaughtered with huge tracheal abscesses, to all appearance produced solely by wearing the tracheotomy tube.

To avoid this danger the author chooses for incision a spot nearer to the chest, where the motion is less constant and not so varied. Even at this last place all danger is not entirely surmounted, in consequence of which a horse, while wearing a tracheotomy tube, should never be permitted to feed from the ground.

DIAGRAM, SHOWING THE STRUCTURES TO BE INTERFERED WITH DURING THE PERFORMANCE OF TRACHEOTOMY.

THE MANNER IN WHICH THE CARTILAGES OF THE TRACHEA ARE TO BE EXCISED.

1. 1. The sterno-maxillares muscles—a pair—have to be separated, being joined by fine cellular tissue.
2. The sterno-thyro-hyoidei muscles, lying under the first pair, also have to be divided, being similarly united.
3. The trachea, which is fully exposed when the above muscles are disunited.

At the commencement, when the operator has leisure, he generally does not cut too deep. The first incision fairly divides the skin and panniculus carnosus quite in the middle of the neck, and is rather longer than a by-stander would deem to be absolutely necessary. The elasticity of the skin will somewhat shorten the opening; while the torture of repeated enlargements will be avoided, and the more important structures beneath the skin will be fairly brought into view.

In the center of your division will appear two long muscles, joined together by a fine cellular union; that union you are to separate; it consists only of cellular tissue, and will necessitate more care than exertion. Underneath the divided muscles will be found two others, smaller and paler, but also joined together by means of fine cellular tissue. These are also to be sundered, and then the trachea lies exposed. There is neither nerve, nor artery, nor vein to avoid, nor to take up in the performance of tracheotomy. All consists in making your primary incision large enough, and, subsequently, in not attempting more than the division of two pairs of muscles.

The commencement of the incision should be made at the spot already indicated. After the skin is cut through and the muscles are divided, two assistants should be obtained to hold them back, while a circular piece is excised from the cartilages of the exposed trachea.

The trachea is formed of numerous cartilaginous rings each half an inch wide, but so united by elastic tissue that the whole forms one continuous tube reaching from the head to the chest of a horse. If possible, only two of these rings are to be interfered with; that is, a half circle should be cut out of each, which, with the elastic connecting medium, will make an opening of one inch in diameter. Both the rings, however, should be perfectly divided; but a half circle should be excised from one, leaving a portion of cartilage to keep the remainder in its place. This matter, probably, may be made more clear by the engraving on the opposite page.

After the first half circle is made, or when a portion is cut off the first cartilage, that piece should be bent outward. The elastic connecting substance will readily permit this to be done, and the current of fresh air admitted will considerably refresh the animal. The cartilage being bent outward, it should be leisurely transfixed by means of a sharp needle armed with strong twine. The string may be fastened to the button-hole of the operator's waistcoat, and afterward the circle be leisurely completed.

The twine is necessary because the spasmodic breathing has drawn the excised portion of cartilage upon the lungs, and thereby done as much mischief as the operator designed to do good. By bending the half circle outward, some relief is afforded to the breathing, and the character of the respiration partially benefited. The process is, however, rendered more safe by the employment of the loop; but care should be taken, when subsequently using the knife, not to cut the string. Therefore, before the circle is completed, the cartilage should be bent backward, as shown in the previous engraving, then laid hold of, and, when firmly grasped, the excision ought to be perfected.

A tube has to be worn afterward; this is put into the opening, and fastened in by means of a strap or tape passed round the neck. There are many tubes sold by the instrument makers for this purpose; the majority, however, are far too large. None should be beyond one inch in diameter. The horse only requires to inhale part of the air through the canula, the remainder coming, as before, through the larynx. A free space of one inch is, therefore, plenty to admit the deficient oxygen; for no animal could live through an operation, were air, previous to its commencement or during its continuance, altogether excluded.

The best instrument for hasty and temporary tracheotomy is the invention of Mr. T. W. Gowing, of Camden Town. To insert this canula no cartilage need be excised; a puncture is made with a knife

MR. T. W. GOWING'S TRACHEOTOMY TUBE.

A. The canula, with a shifting shield, armed with the pointed trocar.
B. The trocar withdrawn from the canula, showing its peculiar construction.
C. The canula fitted into the horse's trachea, showing how the movable shield may be adapted, by means of a screw, to the size of the horse or the swollen condition of the parts.

through the connecting medium of the tracheal rings, and through this puncture the tube is driven. It is of all use for temporary or immediate service, but obviously would not do for a continuance.

The objection to tracheotomy, when designed to last for any period, is that the canula, by irritating the lining membrane of the larynx, is apt to provoke abscess, which impedes the breathing to a degree that destroys the life. The author has seen some fearful instances of this effect; but of all tubes, that invented by the French seems to be least open to this objection.

OPERATIONS—PERIOSTEOTOMY.

This operation was first applied to the horse by the late Professor Sewell. It is intended to relieve the lameness consequent upon exostosis

A PAIR OF ROWELING SCISSORS, FOR MAKING SMALL INCISIONS THROUGH THE HORSE'S SKIN.

A SETON NEEDLE ARMED WITH A TAPE, A, AND FIXED INTO A HOLLOW HANDLE BY MEANS OF A SCREW, B.

situated on the shin-bone. A pair of roweling scissors are first employed to snip the skin above and below the tumor. Then a blunt seton needle,

A BLUNT SETON NEEDLE.

A TUMOR BEING CUT WITH A PROBE-POINTED KNIFE.

being fixed into a hollow handle by means of a screw, and armed with a tape knotted at one end, is to be used. The needle is violently driven through, and breaks down the cellular tissue which attaches the skin to the tumor. The point is forced to enter at one snip and come out at the other, after which the needle is withdrawn by the first opening. A probe-pointed knife is then introduced into the space thus made; the tumor is sliced into as many pieces as may please the operator or the nature of the growth will admit of. The knife is afterward retracted, and the needle, released from the handle, is passed through the openings, or in at one snip and out at the other. The knot at the end of the tape prevents that being drawn after the needle. The unknotted end is next withdrawn from the needle and tied into a large knot—the whole forming a seton. The operation is occasionally varied by smearing the tape with terebinthinate of cantharides, and sometimes by blistering over

29

tumor, seton and all. This last practice may add to the severity of the operation, but it seems calculated to do little good. Breaking down the attachment of the skin and slicing the tumor appear designed to deprive the growth of blood, while a blister seems calculated to draw to the part an excess of that which the operation was intended to dispel.

Periosteotomy is not very highly esteemed by the vast majority of practitioners. It is, however, sometimes very successful. A horse is thrown, being dead lame; the animal gets up from the hands of the surgeon and trots sound. It is difficult, however, to predicate the quadruped on which it will thus act. Certainly the operation is best adapted to young horses; but even to all of these it will not prove beneficial. It is therefore looked upon as a surgical experiment, quite as apt to disappoint as to please. The seton, moreover, is disposed to cause the edges of the holes through which it passes to indurate. A blemish which it takes some months to eradicate is the consequence; and this, added to the expense attendant upon treatment, is not apt to prove pleasing to horse proprietors, especially when the operation altogether fails.

A HORSE'S LEG WITH TWO SNIPS UPON IT, C C, OUT OF WHICH HANG THE TWO KNOTTED ENDS OF A SETON, D D.

A modification of periosteotomy might perhaps be tried. Omit the seton altogether; make an inferior snip with the scissors; introduce a sharp-pointed needle, and cut a channel. Then insert a probe-pointed bistoury, and incise the tumor. If periosteotomy were to prove successful, it probably would be so in this shape. The author has seen small benefit result from the after-use of the seton, and by operating in the manner proposed all the subsequent blemish would be avoided. The cut would soon heal and leave no scar behind : thus the grand objection to the performance of periosteotomy, as it now stands, would be removed.

The motive for the above proposal is to spare the suffering of the animal. If the hair is cut short previously, and pressure made above the snip of the scissors, the wound need occasion little pain. A sharp point cutting its way through the cellular tissue would not cause one tithe of the agony which follows the use of a blunt instrument necessarily tearing, stretching, and breaking a passage through a living body. Cartilage or bone in a state of health has small sensibility. The employment of the knife would therefore provoke no struggle, while all the after-torture of a seton applied directly to the surface of a wound would be avoided.

Perhaps it would be best to bind a broad tape, with a cork under it

and upon the vessels, round the leg before the operation, thereby pressing on the nerve and cutting off the supply of blood. This would probably deprive the leg of all sensation. The most severe part of this
method of periosteotomy would be the after-consequences. The incised
tumor would inflame; the vacant channel would have to unite. The
one would occasion agony, the other be probably attended with violent
itching. The limb, therefore, should be bandaged, even though a wound
upon the horse's body does not do so well when covered up   The bandage, however, will prevent the animal from injuring the sore leg with the
opposite shoe, which a horse may be provoked to attempt by that irritation which attends the healing process.

OPERATIONS—NEUROTOMY.

Neurotomy is the division of the nerve which supplies the hoof of the
fore leg with sensation. The foot of the horse being moved through
tendons by muscles from above, and having in itself no muscular power,
obviously has no occasion for a motor nerve   Consequently the nerve
running to the foot is wholly sentient. It is the means of communication through which pain or pleasure is transmitted from the hoof to the
brain

To take away a portion of this nerve is evidently to separate the
medium of such communication. Feeling can no more travel along a
divided nerve than electricity can along a broken wire. The knowledge
of this fact has led to a portion of the nerve being excised; and the
doing of this has been named neurotomy.

A nerve is a very compound structure. It is composed of numerous
fine filaments or small threads bound together by a cellular sheath called
neurilema. Healthy nerve feels firm, and has a brilliant white appearance; unhealthy nerve is of a yellowish tint, and is of a less solid texture.

The operation of neurotomy is certain relief, but that relief is of uncertain duration. The divided nerve, after a time, reunites. The junction
thus formed carries on all the functions of the perfect structure; but a
bulb is left behind at the place of union. This bulb is to be easily felt
by pressing upon the seat of neurotomy externally with the points of
the fingers; and the bulb being felt leads to a knowledge that the horse
has been subjected to the operation. Neurotomy, therefore, can never
be concealed, if pains are bestowed upon its detection. The operation,
however, is not successful in every case.

In some animals, the wound has just closed when junction seems to
be formed between the divided ends of the nerve. The lameness then
returns as acutely as ever.

In others, the horse will proceed to work, and continue sound ever after—the restored power to use the foot having, in the last case, seemingly destroyed the affection.

Some animals are subjected to operation so late that disease has had time to weaken the pedal structures. The consequence is that no sooner does the absence of feeling tempt the horse to throw his entire weight upon the foot than the navicular bone fractures or the perforans tendon ruptures.

Certain horses, from a tingling sensation in the neurotomized foot—similar to that felt by men in the imaginary fingers of an arm which has been amputated—will stamp violently till they injure it and provoke suppuration; while other feet are so irritable that the head is bent downward and large pieces from the hoof literally bitten off. To account for this last circumstance the reader must remember that, though the foot seems to itch, it in reality has no sensation to preserve it from the teeth of the provoked animal.

Cases occasionally happen of horses having picked up nails, or having incurred wounds in the foot, which, being deprived of feeling, the animal wanted the power to recognize. No lameness was exhibited, and the injury was necessarily unattended to. The foot has been left alone till the hurt has induced mortification.

Weak feet have not been able to endure the consequences of operation. They have sustained no external injury, but the heaviness of tread attendant on a loss of sensation has so battered the senseless member that suppuration has been induced. The hoof has therefore been cast off and the horse been destroyed, although it was discovered in the stable standing with the utmost composure upon the bleeding and exposed flesh.

These are a few of the disagreeables attending a most humane and successful operation. The first requisite for the performance of neurotomy is a sound knowledge of anatomy. A familiar acquaintance with the course of the nerve is essential. It descends in two main branches from the knee, one on either side of the leg. It travels in company with and behind the artery and vein on the inner side of the fore limb. On the outer side it is accompanied by no vessel. About the center of the leg, however, the two nerves are united by a branch which travels over the perforans tendon, connecting the sentient fibers of either side. It is therefore essential, in the performance of neurotomy, to make the primary incision rather low down, especially if it is meant that the high operation should be accomplished, or that all sensation should be destroyed on one side by a single division.

At the pastern the nerve divides; the posterior branch runs direct to the frog. The anterior branch travels in front of the artery for some distance, when it takes a more forward course, dividing into several separate branches.

The generality of operators remove about an inch of the main trunk before the nerve divides, or above the pastern; and the result certainly confirms the soundness of such a practice.

The nerve of the frog is, however, frequently excised. The objection to this is the junction of a filament of the anterior branch with the nerve below the excision. That union should deprive the operation of all effect; but, notwithstanding, the division is sometimes beneficial. The operation is, however, never certain; and to that circumstance the proprietor must make up his mind when he sanctions its performance.

Always examine minutely any horse submitted to you for neurotomy. Do this to discover if the operation has been previously performed—the object being that you may thereby be prepared for some trouble in mastering the retentive consciousness of the animal; likewise, that by such inquiries you may decide upon the benefit likely to result from the operation; also, that you may be warned of a

THE COURSE OF THE NERVE EXPOSED.

a, Denotes the nerve of the frog.

bloody and tedious job. The leg which has previously been subjected to neurotomy becomes doubly vascular. We know of no reason to account for this phenomenon, excepting it may denote the cost at which nature repairs her higher order of structures.

A HORIZONTAL INCISION, WITH THE HAIR CLIPPED ABOVE THE OPENING.

A PERPENDICULAR INCISION, WITH THE HAIR CUT OFF ABOVE AND ON THE SIDES OF THE WOUND.

Before you consent to operate upon any animal, examine the feet. If the hoof is weak or even weakly, refuse at once. If the hoof be strong and thick, the wall upright, and the frog small, you may consent, with the best hopes of success. Have such a horse put into the stable, and the diseased foot or feet kept wet for a week prior to the operation. This frequently has the effect of constringing the arteries, greatly depriving the part of blood. That result renders the use of the knife more cleanly and more easy. Two days prior to the important one have the hair cut short over the place or places where you design to make your incisions. By so doing, all chance of hair getting into and irritating the wound will be effectually destroyed. This may happen, and, should the hair be left on, much delay will be occasioned, while the animal's sufferings must be augmented if the hair be clipped after the horse is down for operation.

Never operate upon a horse with the hair uncut—leave that to parties who league with the lowest class of horse-cheats. Cut off hair two days beforehand. Make an incision through the skin about three-quarters to one inch long. Have a needle and thread ready—a strong surgeon's needle and a stout twine. Pierce the divided skin from the inside to the outside, leaving a moderate piece of twine hanging out of the wound. Carry the twine under the leg, and pierce the integument on the other margin of the wound—also from the interior to the exterior. Then bring the piece of twine left hanging out of the first puncture and the needle together, at the back of the leg. Slightly tighten the twine; fasten these two ends in a bow, and the effect will be to keep the sides of the incision asunder.

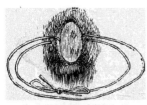

THE MODE OF FASTENING BACK THE SIDE
OF A PERPENDICULAR WOUND.

If you design to perform the high operation, choose a spot a little above the pastern, and incise the skin at one cut, if possible. The high operation is most approved of for general purposes, and, as before remarked, destroys sensation in the entire hoof. Some proprietors think it well to leave a little feeling in the forward portion of the foot, which is free from disease. This is done to escape those results that have already been enumerated as the effects of total insensibility. The high operation is, therefore, performed only on one side, and the posterior or low division on the other. There are two spots at which the low operation may be accomplished. The author has given the reader a representation of the anatomy of the leg. He presents a view on page 455, of the places where the incisions can be made.

Either of the lower operations, regarded by itself, is very uncertain in its effect; and, if taken both together, they present no advantage over the superior opening.

These remarks may be better comprehended, by comparing this

engraving with the course of the nerve shown in the previous illustration.

When the skin is divided—supposing the horse is neurotomized for
the first time—nothing is visible but white-looking cellular tissue. This
must be carefully dissected away with a pair of forceps and a scalpel.
Dissect on until the nerve and artery are exposed plainly to view.
Then take a crooked needle and thread. Pierce the nerve—this you
may do fearlessly. The author has not known it to produce pain.

The superior opening represents the place where one side of the foot may be deprived of sensation by
a single division.
The two middle incisions denote the part where either the fore or after portion of the foot may, perhaps, be rendered void of sensation.
The two inferior cuts suggest the situations where, probably, the parts of the foot toward which the
incisions point may be made insensible.

The fibers composing the nerve are so fine that the needle's point is
blunt when compared with them. It, therefore, glides through them
without pricking any of the filaments.

If the horse has been operated upon before, you must expect a tedious
and sanguinary business. It is then of all importance to obtain a very
attentive and equally nimble man to take the sponge. Blood will follow every movement of the knife. However, with each cut you must
retract the hand, and the man who has care of the sponge must quickly,
surely, and forcibly cleanse the wound. When the sponge is withdrawn,
for an instant, and for an instant only, is there a clear view of the part.
The operator must be ready to make the most of that glimpse; for, the
next moment, blood flows over the lips of the orifice and all is concealed
from view. Thus we proceed, rather snipping than cutting, taking
away particles instead of flakes of cellular tissue, till the nerve is exposed. Then it is fixed with the needle as before directed.

The nerve being caught, withdraw the needle, leaving the thread

behind.   Tie both ends of the thread together, and insert the first finger
of your left hand into the loop thus formed.   By gentle traction raise

the nerve a little, and with the
knife release its inferior attachments.   Then let the man who
held the sponge make pressure
with all his force upon the
artery and nerve *above* the incision.   After this has been
done about a minute, and by
the stoppage of the circulation
you may conclude the sensation
to be in some degree numbed,
insert the blade of the knife

THE LOOP RAISING THE NERVE WHILE THE KNIFE LOOSENS
ITS INFERIOR ATTACHMENTS.

under that portion of the nerve which is nearest the body, and cut
boldly upward.

A spasm mostly follows the division; but it is of short duration.
Afterward dissect about one inch of the nerve from its attachments,
and remove this inch from the main trunk.   No sign of feeling will
follow the excision when made lower down.   All communication with
the brain has been cut off by the previous division, and the sensorium
no longer takes notice of any violence offered to that part of the body
which has been isolated.

Next, having sponged the part, close the wound by means of a pin

forced through the lips of the orifice.   Then
twist a little tow round it in the form of a
figure of 8.   That being finished, so much of
the point as protrudes is to be removed with a
pair of wire nippers; a bandage is then put on;
and, if both sides of the limb are to be neurotomized, the horse is turned over.   All being
accomplished, return the horse to the stable,
but watch the pin which fastens the wound.   If

THE BEST WAY TO CLOSE THE WOUND   the incision continues dry, the pin may not be
CONSEQUENT UPON NEUROTOMY.
removed till six days have expired; but if the
slightest appearance of pus be suspected, immediately withdraw the pin,
and remove the tow, treating the part with solution of chloride of zinc,
as though it were a common wound.

There are various knives invented for the performance of neurotomy.
That the writer most approves of was the invention of Mr. Woodger,
the admirably practical veterinary surgeon of Bishops Mews, Paddington.   The author has used this instrument himself, and seen it guided,

by other hands. In every case it has expedited the operation and thereby shortened the period of the animal's suffering.

The after-treatment of neurotomy consists in letting well alone, if all goes on rightly. Should pus make its appearance, bathe the wounds, thrice daily, with the solution of chloride of zinc, one-grain to the ounce of water. Remove the bandages from the legs after the horse has

MR. WOODGER'S NEUROTOMY KNIFE.

To use this instrument.—After the nerve is raised, insert the crooked point, with the edge toward the body of the horse; then drive the knife forward. By this simple means the cutting portion of the blade is brought violently in contact with the nerve, which is excised at the proper point, and about an inch is left hanging out below the incision.

entered the stable. The incisions heal more readily when exposed to the stimulating effects of the air. Place a cradle round the horse's neck, and feed liberally. Avoid all pur-gative medicine; you now want an injury repaired, and do not desire to reduce the vital energy.

THE AWKWARD TREAD OF A HORSE WHEN NEWLY NEUROTOMIZED.

When the wounds have healed, the horse may be gradually taken once more to work, but it should not be fully used. Excessive and too early labor is the cause of the many serious objections taken to a merciful oper-ation. The horse for some period does not feel his foot. He does not flex the pastern as the hoof nears the ground. The foot is placed flat upon the earth, and with a kind of sen-sible jar, as though the animal had made "a false step." This pecu-liarity unfits the quadruped to trot upon stones, or hard roads, until it has learned "to handle its feet," or to accommodate the tread to the new condition of the hoof.

OPERATIONS—DIVISION OF THE TENDONS.

Many horses when standing knuckle over to such an extent as threatens to throw them upon their knees. Others can only put the toe of the hind leg to the ground. The natural use of the limb is equally injured in each case: the fore legs of the horse support the body and the burden; the hind legs propel the carcass and the load. Both are deformed by contraction of the perforans tendon; and both deformities are generally produced by excessive labor, inducing strain, though a few cases have come to the author's knowledge of animals being born thus afflicted. When we contemplate the huge frame of the horse, it seems more than fitted for all man's ordinary purposes. But country carriers have vans proportioned only to the extent of their custom; their carts are enlarged as their trade increases; but very seldom is the power which draws the load augmented in the same proportion. The horse, so agile and so beautiful, as long as it can move the cart is esteemed to be not over-weighted. It labors up hill, and then the carrier congratulates himself that the worst of the work is over; it may be for him, but it is not for his horse. All the stress in going down hill lies upon the back sinews; the animal has to put forth all its strength to check the downward impetus of the load. It is the same with other horses in the shafts of other vehicles. Three or four animals—according to the usual English fashion—may be attached to a load; but the weight which three strengths can draw upon level ground, when descending an inequality, then, never bears equally upon the leaders.

Clap of the back sinews is a common accident with all horses. The equine delight is the pleasure of the master. So entirely is the horse the slave of man, that it, by instinct, puts forth its utmost strength to attain anything in which its owner takes enjoyment. It does so regard-less of its own probable sufferings. In racing, in hunting, in all kinds of pastime the horse will strain every nerve and even burst its strong vessels laboring to gratify an ungrateful proprietor. Who does not remember the old coaching days? The animals then appeared happy in their vocation. A well-appointed coach, trotting by the White Horse Cellar, was a sight to contemplate. However, follow the vehicle to the termination of the first stage. See the poor panting carcasses un-harnessed—the perspiration lathering their sides, their veins swelling, their tails quivering, their nostrils jerking, and their limbs stiffened. Who then could regret that railroads were invented to indulge man's desire for speed? See, as the coach leaves the metropolis behind it, the cattle deteriorate. At last, behold life with swollen legs, stiff joints, and diseased feet made to propel the loaded vehicle. Who, properly regard-ing such a spectacle, and having a heart to feel, does not rejoice that a method of traveling has at length been invented which renders the employment of the lash to overcome the agonies of breathing flesh no longer imperative?

These fast abuses induced contraction of the perforans tendon in the front legs. There is, however, this difference between contraction in the anterior and posterior extremities—one hind leg only may be affected; but the author remembers no instance of one fore leg being alone involved.

When a tendon is sprained, it is usual to apply stimulating or fiery mixtures to that part, winding up the treatment with blisters and the heated iron. Notwithstanding such measures are very seldom successful, man seems incapable of learning anything where another has to bear the torture, and he will often endure a great deal of agony himself before an obvious idea can be awakened.

Such slowness is, however, very lamentable in the case of the horse. **Division of the tendons** was borrowed from the human surgeon by the veterinary practitioner. The operation, however, till very lately, remained as it was originally adopted. Human surgery had advanced; but veterinary practice stood motionless. At length, Mr. Varnell came from America, and instructed veterinarians in an improved mode of operating, which at this date should be universally practiced.

THE KNIFE EMPLOYED BY MR. VARNELL, ASSISTANT PROFESSOR AT THE ROYAL VETERINARY COLLEGE.

THE POSITION OF THE LEG WHEN THE KNIFE IS INSERTED.

A stout knife with a probed point, a curved blade, and a smooth, rounded back, is first obtained. Before the blade is inserted, the skin is divided, at the point selected for the operation, by the slight puncture of a lancet.

The leg is then flexed; the tendons are, by the position of the limb, rendered flaccid. The knife is next inserted sideways, behind the nerve and artery, under the tendons. This last act is not, however, in practice, very easy or very safe.

The edge of the knife is now toward the shoulder or haunch, and the vessels lie upon that side of the blade which is nearest to the bone. The operator now, by a simple motion of the hand, turns the cutting edge of the knife toward the posterior part of the limb. A man at the same

moment takes hold of the leg and forces it straight; the perforans tendon is thus dragged against the knife, while the suspensory ligament and vessels are safe at the back of the blade. If the tendon be not divided without any effort on the part of the operator, he makes a sawing motion as he withdraws the knife. A slight sensation or a feeble sound often testifies the separation of the structure.

Often, if the contraction be not chronic, the strength of the extensor pedis muscle, when released from its opponent's force, is sufficient to straighten the fetlock. When the disease, however, has existed for any time, it requires some violence to break down the false attach-

THE TENDON DIVIDED.

ments which have been formed. For this purpose the knee of a strong man is placed in front of the fetlock-joint, and the horse's foot is, by pulling hard, drawn forward.

The wound is then closed with a pin and twisted thread, as in neurotomy, and the animal, till junction is perfected, should be kept in the stable, as the shoe to be worn afterward is not favorable to progression. One week after the operation, a shoe, with a projecting piece at the toe about one inch and a half long, is to be put on the foot of the diseased limb. Five weeks after this, the shoe is to be replaced by one having the projecting point twice as long; and this last is to be worn till union

THE SHOE TO BE WORN ONE WEEK AFTER DIVISION OF THE TENDON HAS BEEN ACCOMPLISHED.

THE SHOE TO BE PUT ON SIX WEEKS AFTER DIVISION OF THE TENDON, AND TO BE WORN UNTIL UNION IS PERFECTED.

is supposed to be perfected — till the expiration of three months at least.

The horse, after having the tendon divided, is said to be as strong as ever. The author would, however, object to such an animal being put into the shafts with even a light load behind it, or to its being again used for saddle purposes. The animal, though forbidden these uses, has still a large field of service open to it.

This operation is alike effectual and humane. That the last assertion may not appear based upon a single opinion, the author presents the reader with an engraving taken from a park near Lewes. That animal seemed to have all four limbs contracted, or the hind limbs were flexed and much advanced, to take the weight off the fore members. A foal ran by the side of the creature thus crippled; though it would be supposed no sane person would select such a dam to breed from.

Now had this mare been operated upon, slight pain would have been inflicted. Tendon, unless in a state of inflammation, has no sensation. Relief would have been afforded for the remainder of the life, and though, from her make and shape, the animal might never have held a high station among her breed, still, with straight legs she must have been worth as much for work as with bent limbs she could be valuable for stock purposes.

LAYING OPEN THE SINUSES OF A QUITTOR.

Give no opening medicine to any horse previous to this operation. Every member of the equine race is more likely to be too low from excess of work, than in any degree inflammatory from over-indulgence. Therefore, discard the general practice of preparing the horse with a dose of compound aloes. If the bowels are costive, get them open. But before employing the drastic drug, try what bran mashes and green-meat can effect. The entire strength will be needed to repair the injuries effected with the knife.

Give tonics and high feeding where the symptoms declare the body to be enervated. It is at all times better to operate upon a system having a superabundance of vital energy than upon one in which the powers are at all tardy. Collapse is the greatest enemy the surgeon has to dread. It is true, animals do not, like men, often "shut up" or die while under the operator; but frequently the most skillful surgery is defeated by the horse, after it has been released from the hobbles, never thriving. There may be no disease to be detected; but the body seems to want the strength requisite for recovery. To make this apparent to the reader—two gentlemen shall each perform neurotomy. One shall bungle, yet his patient shall do well. The wounds shall heal by the first intention, and the horse in a fortnight be again delighting its owner. The other shall display the perfection of scientific attainment; yet the horse shall never thrive. The wounds shall ulcerate, and the animal either gnaw the foot or cast the hoof. How can such differences be accounted for but by believing the horse is subject to a peculiar species of chronic collapse?

Rasp the quarter of the horse's foot which has **quittor**, until the soft, light-colored horn of the laminæ is exposed. Then let the hair be cut off around the opening on the coronet, and the foot be carefully cleansed. Afterward throw the horse. Release the quittored leg from the hob-bles, and with a steel director probe each sinus. So soon as the instru-ment is well in, take a sharp-pointed knife and run it carefully down the groove of the director. Then ascertain, with a grooved probe, whether the sinus decreased in diameter, or whether the whole extent of the pipe be laid open. If the smallest portion remains, to which the knife has not reached, use the groove of the probe as a director, and slit it up. Do this to as many sinuses as may exist.

Next place in each sinus a small piece of tow. These pieces of tow should be already divided into short and thin skeins. They should be saturated with chloride of zinc dissolved in spirits of wine, one scruple to the ounce. Put one of these into each sinus, and let the horse up. In three days such of the pieces of tow as have not been removed by the sloughing process may be taken from the wounds, and the foot simply dressed with chloride of zinc and water, one grain to the ounce, squeezed from a sponge, as in the case of open joint.

THE QUARTER RASPED BENEATH THE OPENING OF A QUITTOR.

THE SINUSES OF A QUITTOR BEING OPERATED UPON.

This operation, when described, reads abhorrent; but it is really most humane. It is a common thing for a horse to be three, or even six months under treatment, on account of an ordinary quittor. During the entire space, the foot—the tenderest part of the horse's body—is burned with violent caustics, and has had heated wires thrust down its sinuses. By the operation proposed, the affair is settled in a few minutes. The horse seldom evinces much sensibility while the knife is being employed; in three days the animal is so far recovered as to allow the diseased member almost to be left to nature. The horse should, however, on no account do any work before the hoof is in some measure restored. Until the outer covering of dark horn has grown down, a bar shoe, well eased off the diseased quarter, should be worn. When the hoof is reproduced, instead of false quarter or other deformities, the usual results of quittor, it is all but impossible to decide which has been the affected foot, and which was operated upon.

The author has now stated at length that treatment which the horse for its own sake deserves, and which, for the honor of the being whom it serves, the animal should receive. He has, designedly, rather appealed to the reason of his readers than sought to enlist their feelings. The subject was, indeed, a wide one. Man has hitherto been too content to consider animals as something given absolutely to him to be treated according to his sovereign will or merest pleasure. He has not reflected that, when he was created lord of this earth, he was invested with a title which had its responsibilities as well as its privileges.

ALPHABETICAL SUMMARY.

A BRIEF SUMMARY

ARRANGED IN ALPHABETICAL ORDER.

THIS abbreviation is made for the purpose of hasty consultation, when the symptoms exhibited by the horse are so urgent as will not allow the owner to refer to the body of the book. That, however, he is earnestly recommended to do after the first anxiety has subsided; because what follows is to be regarded only as notes of cases, and by no means to be viewed as a substitute for the more detailed descriptions of diseases and their treatment.

ABSCESS OF THE BRAIN.

Cause.—Some injury to the head.

Symptoms.—Dullness; refusal to feed; a slight oozing from a trivial injury upon the skull; prostration, and the animal, while on the ground, continues knocking the head violently against the earth until death ensues.

Treatment.—None of any service.

ABDOMINAL INJURIES.

Ruptured Diaphragm generally produces a soft cough; sitting on the haunches or leaning on the chest may or may not be present; the countenance is haggard.

Ruptured Spleen answers to the tests described under "Hemorrhage of the Liver."

(467)

Ruptured Stomach is characterized by excessive colic, followed by tympanitis.

Introsusception possibly may be relieved by the inhalation of a full dose of chloroform; but the result is always uncertain.

Invagination is attended with the greatest possible agony.

Strangulation is not to be distinguished, during life, from invagination.

Calculus causes death by impactment; but however different the causes of abdominal injury may be, they each produce the greatest agony, which conceals the other symptoms, and makes all such injuries apparently the same while the life lasts.

ACITES, OR DROPSY OF THE ABDOMEN.

Cause.—Chronic peritonitis.

Symptoms.—Pulse hard; head pendulous; food often spoiled; membranes pallid; mouth dry. Pressure to abdomen elicits a groan; turning in the stall calls forth a grunt. Want of spirit; constant lying down; restlessness; thirst; loss of appetite; weakness; thinness; enlarged abdomen; constipation and hide-bound. Small bags depend from the chest and belly; the sheath and one leg sometimes enlarge; the mane breaks off; the tail drops out. Purgation and death.

Treatment.—When the symptoms first appear give, night and morning, strychnia, half a grain, worked up to one grain; iodide of iron, half a drachm, worked up to one drachm and a half; extract of belladonna, one scruple; extract of gentian and powdered quassia, of each a sufficiency; apply small blisters, in rapid succession, upon the abdomen: but if the effusion is confirmed, a cure is hopeless.

ACUTE DYSENTERY.

Cause.—Some acrid substance taken into the stomach.

Symptoms.—Abdominal pain; violent purgation; the feces become discolored, and water fetid; intermittent pulse; haggard countenance; the position characterizes the seat of anguish. Perspiration, tympanitis, and death.

Treatment.—Give sulphuric ether, one ounce; laudanum, three ounces; liquor potassæ, half an ounce; powdered chalk, one ounce; tincture of catechu, one ounce; cold linseed tea, one pint. Repeat every fifteen minutes. Cleanse the quarters; plait the tail; inject cold linseed tea. The whole of the irritating substance must be expelled before improvement can take place.

ACUTE GASTRITIS

Cause.—Poison; generally given to improve the coat.

Symptoms.—Excessive pain, resembling fury.

Treatment—Give, as often and as quickly as possible, the following drink: Sulphuric ether and laudanum, of each three ounces; carbonate of magnesia, soda, or potash, four ounces, gruel, (*quite cold,*) one quart. Should the pulse be sinking, add to the drink carbonate of ammonia, one drachm If corrosive sublimate is known to be the poison, one dozen raw eggs should be blended with each drench If delirium be present, give the medicine as directed for tetanus, with the stomach pump.

ACUTE LAMINITIS.

Cause—Often man's brutality. Horses driven far and upon hard roads are exposed to the disorder Any stress long applied to the foot, as standing in the hold of a ship, may generate the affection.

Symptoms—The pace seems odd toward the end of the journey; but the horse is placed in the stable with plenty of food for the night Next morning the animal is found all of a heap Flesh quivering; eyes glaring; nostrils distended, and breath jerking; flanks tucked up; back roached; head erect; mouth closed; hind legs advanced under the belly; fore legs pushed forward; fore feet resting upon the heels, and the limbs moved as though the horse were dancing upon hot irons.

Treatment—Put on the slings in silence. To the end of the cords append weights Soak the feet in warm water, in which a portion of alkali is dissolved. Cut out the nails from the softened horn. Before the shoes are removed give half a drachm of belladonna and fifteen grains of digitalis, and repeat the dose every half hour until the symptoms abate. When the slings are up, open the jugular vein; abstract one quart of blood, and inject one pint of luke-warm water. Clothe the body; place thin gruel and green-meat within reach, and leave two men to watch for the first three nights.

Next morning give sulphuric ether and laudanum, of each two ounces, in a pint of water. Should the pastern arteries throb, open the veins and place the feet in warm water While the affection lasts, pursue these measures; and it is a bad symptom, though not a certain one, if no change for the better takes place in five days.

ALBUMINOUS URINE.

Cause.—Unknown.

Symptoms.—These consist of the positions assumed by the horse. The legs are either stretched out or the hind feet are brought under the body. Straddling gait, and much difficulty in turning within the stall. Some urine being caught, it is thick, and answers to certain chemical tests.

Treatment.—Bleed moderately; give a laxative, and apply mustard to the loins. As after-measures, perfect rest, attention to diet, and repeated doses of opium.

APHTHA.

Cause.—Unknown.

Symptoms.—Small swelling on the lips; larger swellings upon the tongue. As the disease progresses, a clear liquid appears in each swelling. The bladders burst, crusts form, and the disease disappears.

Treatment. — Soft food, and the following wash for the mouth: Take borax, five ounces; honey or treacle, two pints; water, one gallon. Mix.

BLOOD SPAVIN.

A disease never encountered at the present time.

BOG SPAVIN.

Cause.—Brutality of some kind.

Symptom.—A puffy swelling at the front of and at the upper part of the hock.

Treatment. — Pressure, maintained by means of an India-rubber bandage.

BOTS.

Cause.—Turning out to grass.

Treatment.—No remedy. Wait till the following year, and the parasites will be ejected naturally.

BREAKING DOWN.

Cause.—Violent exertion; generally when racing.

Symptoms.—The horse, when going, suddenly loses power to put one leg to the ground. The foot is turned upward; pain excessive; breathing quickened; pulse accelerated; appetite lost. In time these symptoms abate, but the leg is disabled for life.

Treatment.—Bleed and purge, or not, as the symptoms are severe. Place a linen bandage round the injury, and see that this is kept constantly cold and wet; put on a high-heeled shoe, and leave the issue to nature. The animal is afterward serviceable only to breed from.

BROKEN KNEES.

Causes—Terrifying a horse, or rendering alive only to fear · Pulling in the chin to the breast, or driving with a tight bearing-rein.

Symptoms.—The horse falls; the knee may only be slightly broken, but deeply contused. A slough must then take place, and open joint may result. Or the animal may fall, and, when down, be driven forward by the impetus of its motion. The knee is cut by the fall, and the skin of the knee may be forced back by the onward impulse This skin will become dirty; but the removed integument will fly back on the animal's rising, thus forming a kind of bag containing and concealing foreign matter.

Treatment—Procure a pail of milk-warm water and a large sponge. Dip the sponge in the pail, and squeeze out the water above the knee. Continue to do this, but do not dab or sop the wound itself. The water flowing over the knee will wash away every impurity. Then with a probe gently explore the bag If small, make a puncture through the bottom of the bag; if large, insert a seton, and move it night and morning until good pus is secreted: then withdraw the seton "Rack up" the horse's head, and get some cold water, to every quart of which add two ounces of tincture of arnica. Pour a little of this into a saucer, and then dip a sponge into the liquid. Squeeze the sponge dry above the joint. Do this every half hour for three and a half days, both by day and night. If at the end of that time all is going on well, the head may be released; but should the knee enlarge and become sensitive, while the animal refuses to put the foot to the ground, withdraw the seton; give no hay, but all the oats and beans that can be eaten, with two pots of stout each day. Place the quadruped in slings; apply the arnica lotion until a slough takes place; then resort to the chloride of zinc lotion, one scruple to the pint, and continue to use this as has been directed.

BROKEN WIND.

Causes.—Old age, prolonged work, and bad food.

Symptoms.—Short, dry, hacking cough, caused by irritability of the larynx; ravenous appetite; insatiable thirst; abundant flatus. Dung half digested; belly pendulous; coat ragged; aspect dejected. Respiration is performed by a triple effort; inspiration is spasmodic and single; expiration is labored and double. The ribs first essay to expel the air from the lungs; these failing, the diaphragm and abdominal muscles take up the action. Broken wind can be set or concealed for a time by forcing the animal to swallow quantities of grease, tar, or shot. A drink of water, however, will always reproduce the symptoms.

Treatment.—No cure. Relief alone is possible. Never give water before work. Four half pails of water to be allowed in twenty-four hours. In each draught mingle half an ounce of phosphoric acid or half a drachm of sulphuric acid. Remove the bed in the day; muzzle at night; put a lump of rock-salt and of chalk in the manger. Never push hard or take upon a very long journey.

BRONCHITIS.

Causes.—Riding far and fast; then leaving exposed, especially to the night air; neglect and constitutional liability.

Symptoms.—Appetite often not affected; sometimes it is increased. A short cough, in the first instance; breathing only excited; legs warm; mouth moist; and nasal membrane merely deeper color during the early stage. When confirmed, the appetite is lost; the horse is averse to move; the cough is sore and suppressed; the breathing is audible; the membranes are scarlet; the mouth is hot and dry; the legs are cold; the body is of uneven temperatures.

Treatment.—Do not deplete. Place in a large, loose box; fill the place with steam; apply scalded hay to the throat; fix flannels wet with cold water to the back and side by means of a Mackintosh jacket. When the flannel becomes warm, change it immediately. Do this for two hours. After that space the flannel may remain on, but must not become dry. Prepare half a pound of melted Burgundy pitch, and stir into it two ounces of powdered camphor, with half a drachm of powdered capsicums. Apply the mixture to the throat. To restore tone to the pulse, give, every half hour, sulphuric ether and laudanum, of each one ounce; water, one pint. If no effect be produced by three of these drinks, substitute infusion of aconite, half an ounce; extract of belladonna, half a drachm, rubbed down in water, a quarter of a pint When the pulse has recovered, resume the former physic, only adding half a drachm of belladonna to each dose. Support with gruel. Introduce food gradually; "chill" the water; be careful of hay, and mind, when given, it is thoroughly damped.

BRONCHOCELE.

Symptom —An enlargement on the side of the throat.

Treatment.—Give the following, night and morning: Iodide of potassium, half a drachm; liquor potassæ, one drachm; distilled water, half a pint. Also, rub into the swelling the accompanying ointment: Iodide of lead, one drachm; simple cerate, one ounce.

BRUISE OF THE SOLE

Cause —Treading on a stone or some projecting body.

Symptom.—Effusion of blood into the horny sole.

Treatment.—Cut away the stained horn, and shoe with leather.

CALCULI.

Causes.—Unknown.

Symptoms of Renal Calculus. — Urine purulent, thick, opaque, gritty, or bloody; back roached. Pressure on the loins occasions shrinking; the arm in the rectum and the hand carried upward provoke alarm.

Treatment. — Two drachms of hydrochloric acid in every pail of water; but the result is dubious.

Symptoms of Cystic Calculus.—Same states of urine as in renal calculus. The water, when flowing forth, is suddenly stopped; every emission is followed by straining; the back is hollowed, the point of the penis is sometimes exposed, and, when going down hill, the animal often pulls up short.

Treatment of Cystic Calculus.—Examine per rectum An operation for the horse, or Mr Simmonds's instrument for the mare, is imperative. When the stone is small, hydrochloric acid may be tried.

Symptoms of Urethral Calculus —Suppression of urine; great suffering If the urethral calculus is impacted in the exposed portion of the urethra, the passage is distended behind the stoppage.

Treatment of Urethral Calculus.—Cut down upon and remove the substance.

CANKER.

Cause.—Old horses, when "turned out" for life as pensioners; aged and neglected animals will also exhibit the disease.

Symptoms.—Not much lameness. The disease commences at the cleft of the frog; a liquid issues from the part, more abundant and more abominable than in thrush; it often exudes from the commissures joining the sole to the frog. The horn firstly bulges out; then it flakes off, exposing a spongy and soft substance, which is fungoid horn. The fungoid horn is most abundant about the margin of the sole, and upon its surface it flakes off. This horn has no sensation. The disease is difficult to eradicate when one fore foot is involved. When all four feet are implicated, a cure is all but hopeless, and the treatment is certain to be slow and vexatious.

Treatment.—See that the stable is large, clean, and comfortable; note that the food is of the best; allow liberal support; pare off the superficial fungoid horn, and so much of the deep seated as can be detached. Apply to the diseased parts some of the following: Chloride of zinc, half an ounce; flour, four ounces. Put on the foot without water. To the sound hoof apply chloride of zinc, four grains; flour, one ounce. Cover the sound parts before the cankered horn is dressed; tack on the shoe; pad well and firmly. When places appear to be in confirmed health, the following may be used: Chloride of zinc, two grains; flour, one ounce. At first, dress every second day; after a time, every third day, and give exercise as soon as possible.

CAPPED ELBOW.

Cause.—Injury to the point of the elbow.

Symptom.—It is often of magnitude, and is liable to ulcerate and become sinuous.

Treatment.—The same as capped hock.

CAPPED HOCK.

Cause.—Any injury to the point of the calcis.

Symptom.—A round swelling on the point of the hock, which, should the cause be repeated, often becomes of great size.

Treatment.—If small, set several men to hand-rub the tumor constantly for a few days. Should the capped hock be of magnitude, dissect out the enlargement, without puncturing it. Remove none of the pendulous skin. Treat the wound with the lotion of chloride of zinc—one grain to the ounce of water—and it will heal after some weeks.

CAPPED KNEE.

Cause.—The same as the previous affection.

Symptom.—A soft tumor in front of the knee.

Treatment.—If let alone, it would burst and leave a permanent blemish   Draw the skin to one side, and with a lancet pierce the lower surface of the tumor.   Treat the wound as an open joint.

CATARACT.

Cause.—Looking at white walls, or receiving external injuries.   Specific ophthalmia generates a permanent cataract.

Symptoms.—When partial, shying; if total, white pupil and blindness

Treatment.—Color the inside of the stable green, as cataract, when not total, is sometimes absorbed.

CHOKING.

Causes —Something impacted in the gullet, either high up or low down.

Symptoms—High Choke.—Raised head; saliva; discharge from the nostrils; inflamed eyes, haggard countenance; audible breathing; the muscles of neck tetanic; the flanks heave; the fore feet paw and stamp; the hind legs crouch and dance; perspiration; agony excessive. *Low Choke.*— The animal ceases to feed; water returns by the nostrils; countenance expresses anguish; saliva and nasal discharge; labored by seldom, noisy breathing; roached back; tucked-up flanks, while the horse stands as though it were desirous of elevating the quarters.

Treatment.—Make haste when high choke is present   Perform tracheotomy to relieve the breathing; insert the balling-iron, or, with a hook extemporized out of any wire, endeavor to remove the substance from the throat   If the choking body is too firmly lodged to be thus removed, sulphuric ether must be inhaled to relax the spasm.   The ether not succeeding, an egg is probably impacted   Destroy its integrity with a darning-needle carefully inserted through the skin; then break the shell by outward pressure. *Low choke is seldom fatal before the expiration of three days.*   Give a quarter of a pint of oil every hour; in the intermediate half hours give sulphuric ether, two ounces; laudanum,

two ounces; water, half a pint; and use the probang after every dose of
the last medicine. Should these be returned, cause chloroform to be
inhaled; then insert the probang, and, by steady pressure, drive the
substance forward.

Subsequent to the removal of impactment feed with caution.

CHRONIC DYSENTERY.

Cause.—Not well understood; generally attacks old horses belonging
to penurious masters.

Symptoms.—Purging without excitement, always upon drinking cold
water; violent straining; belly enlarges; flesh wastes; bones protrude;
skin hide-bound; membranes pallid; weakness; perspiration; standing
in one place for hours. At last the eyes assume a sleepy, pathetic expression; the head is slowly turned toward the flanks; remains fixed
for some minutes; the horse only moves when the bowels are about to
act; colic; death.

Treatment.—Give, thrice daily, crude opium, half an ounce; liquor
potassæ, one ounce; chalk, one ounce; tincture of all-spice, one ounce;
alum, half an ounce; ale, one quart. Should the horse belong to a generous master, give one of the following drinks thrice daily, upon the
symptoms being confirmed: Sulphuric ether, one ounce; laudanum,
three ounces; liquor potassæ, half an ounce; powdered chalk, one
ounce; tincture of catechu, one ounce; cold linseed tea, one pint. Or,
chloroform, half an ounce; extract of belladonna, half a drachm; carbonate of ammonia, one drachm; powdered camphor, half a drachm;
tincture of oak-bark, one ounce; cold linseed tea, one pint. Feed
lightly; dress frequently; give a good bed and a roomy lodging.

CHRONIC GASTRITIS.

Symptoms.—Irregularity of bowels and appetite; pallid membranes;
mouth cold; a dry cough; tainted breath; sunken eye; catching respiration; pendulous belly; ragged coat, and emaciation. Sweating on
the slightest exertion; eating wood-work or bricks and mortar.

Treatment.—Do not purge; administer bitters, sedatives, and alkalies. Give powdered nux vomica, one scruple; carbonate of potash,
one drachm; extract of belladonna, half a drachm; extract of gentian
and powdered quassia, of each a sufficiency. Or give strychnia, half a
grain; bicarbonate of ammonia, one drachm; extract of belladonna,
half a drachm; sulphate of zinc, half a drachm; extract of gentian and
powdered quassia, of each a sufficiency. Give one ball night and morn-

ing; when these balls seem to have lost their power, give half an ounce each of liquor arsenicalis and tincture of ipecacuanha, with one ounce of muriated tincture of iron and laudanum, in a pint of water; damp the food; sprinkle magnesia on it As the strength improves, give sulphuric ether, one ounce; water, one pint, daily. Ultimately change that for a quart of ale or stout daily.

CHRONIC HEPATITIS.

Cause.—Too good food and too little work

Symptoms —Cold mouth; pallid membranes; white of eyes ghastly, displaying a yellow tinge; looks toward the right side; the right side may be tender for a long time, with generally repeated attacks of this nature, although the horse may perish with the first fit.

Treatment.—Hold up the head, and if the horse staggers, this proves hemorrhage from the liver. Give sufficient of nutritious food, but only enough of it, plenty of labor, and the following physic : Iodide of potassium, two ounces; liquor potassæ, one quart; dose, night and morning, two tablespoonfuls in a pint of water.

CLAP OF THE BACK SINEWS.

Cause.—Extra exertion.

Symptoms.—The maimed limb is flexed; the toe rests upon the ground. In a short space a tumor appears; it is small, hot, soft, and tender, but soon grows hard. Great pain, but attended with few constitutional symptoms.

Treatment —Administer physic, and bleed gently; then give a few doses of febrifuge medicine, but go no further than to reduce the pulse to fifty-five degrees. Put a linen bandage on the leg; keep this constantly wet until the primary symptoms abate Cut grass for food while fever exists; continue the cold water till recovery is confirmed The horse will not be fit to work for many months.

COLD

If mild, a little green-meat, a few mashes, an extra rug, and a slight rest generally accomplish a cure.

Symptoms of severe cold are dullness; a rough coat; the body of different temperatures; the nasal membrane deep scarlet, or of a leaden color; the appetite is lost; simple ophthalmia; tears; the sinuses are clogged, and a discharge from the nose appears

Treatment.—Give no active medicine. Apply the steaming nose-bag six times daily; allow cut grass and mashes for food, with gruel for drink. If weak, present three feeds of crushed and scalded oats and beans daily, with a pot of stout morning and evening. Good nursing, with pure air, warmth, and not even exercise, till the disease abates, are of more importance than "doctor's stuff" in a case of severe cold. Cold, however, often ushers in other and more dangerous diseases.

CONGESTION IN THE FIELD.

Cause.—Riding a horse after the hounds when out of condition.
Symptoms.—The horse, from exhaustion, reels and falls. The body is clammy cold; the breathing is labored; every vein is turgid.
Treatment.—Bleed, if possible; cover the body; lead gently to the nearest stable; keep hot rugs upon the animal; bandage the legs and hood the neck; warm the place, either by a fire or tubs full of hot water. Give, without noise, every half hour, one ounce of sulphuric ether, half an ounce of laudanum, half a pint of cold water. Should no chemist be at hand, beat up two ounces of turpentine with the yolk of an egg; mix it with half a pint of water, and repeat the dose at the times stated. Allow an ample bed, and place a pail of gruel within easy reach of the horse. Do not leave the animal for thirty hours, as in that time its fate will be decided.

CONGESTION IN THE STABLE.

Cause.—A debilitated, fat horse, unused to work, being driven fast with a heavy load behind it.
Symptoms.—Hanging head; food not glanced at; blowing; artery gorged and round; pulse feeble; cold and partial perspirations; feet cold; eye fixed; hearing lost; and the attitude motionless.
Treatment.—Give immediately two ounces each of sulphuric ether and of laudanum in a pint of cold water. Give the drink with every caution. In ten minutes repeat the medicine, if necessary. Wait twenty minutes, and give another drink, if requisite; more are seldom needed. Take away all solid food, and allow gruel for the remainder of the day.

CORNS.

Cause.—In a flat foot, the heels of the coffin-bone squeeze the sensitive sole by pressing it against the shoe. In a contracted foot, the sensitive sole is squeezed between the wings of the coffin-bone and the thick, horny sole. A bruise results; blood is effused; and the stain of this left upon the horny sole—generally upon the inner side and anterior to the bars—constitutes a horse's corn, which is mostly found on the fore feet.

Symptom.—If the stain is dark, and is to be removed with the knife, this indicates a corn has been, but no longer exists. The smallest stain of bright scarlet testifies to the existence of a new and present corn. Corns are of four kinds—the old, the new, the sappy, and the suppurative. The old and new are produced by the blood, and are judged by the scarlet or dark-colored stain. The old is generally near the surface, the new is commonly deep seated. The sappy is when the bruise is only heavy enough to effuse serum. The new corn alone produces lameness. The suppurating corn may start up from either of the others receiving additional injury. It causes intense pain and produces acute lameness.

Treatment.—Cut out the stain. If a suppurating corn, place the foot in a poultice, after having opened the abscess. Then, the horn being softened, cut away all the sole which has been released by the pus from its attachment to the secreting surface. Tack on an old shoe, and dress with the solution of the chloride of zinc, one grain to the ounce After-ward shoe with leather, and employ stopping to render the horn plastic

COUGH.

Causes.—Foul stables; hot stables; coarse, dusty provender; rank bedding; irregular work; while the affection may attend many diseases.

Treatment.—Crush the oats; damp the hay; give gruel or linseed tea for drink Clothe warmly, and give, thrice daily, half a pint of the following in a tumbler of water: Extract of belladonna, one drachm, rubbed down in a pint of cold water; tincture of squills, ten ounces; tincture of ipecacuanha, eight ounces. No change ensuing, next try— Barbadoes or common tar, half an ounce; calomel, five grains; linseed meal, a sufficiency: make into a ball, and give one night and morning. This being attended with no improvement, employ—Powdered aloes, one drachm; balsam of copaiba, three drachms; cantharides, three grains; common mass, a sufficiency. Mix, and give every morning.

A daily bundle of cut grass is good in the spring of the year. A lump of rock-salt has been beneficial. If the animal eats the litter, muzzle it. Roots are good. Moisten the hay; and, above all things, attend to the ventilation of the stable.

CRACKED HEELS.

Cause.—Cutting the hair from the heels, and turning into a straw-yard during winter.

Symptoms.—Thickened skin; cracks; and sometimes ulceration.

Treatment.—Wash; dry thoroughly; apply the following wash: Animal glycerin, half a pint; chloride of zinc, two drachms; strong solution of oak-bark, one pint. Mix. If ulceration has commenced, rest the horse. Give a few bran mashes or a little cut grass to open the bowels. Use the next wash: Animal glycerin, or phosphoric acid, two ounces; permanganate of potash, or creosote, half an ounce; water, three ounces: apply six times daily. Give a drink each day composed of liquor arsenicalis, half an ounce; tincture of muriate of iron, one ounce; water, one pint.

CRIB–BITING.

Cause.—Sameness of food and unhealthy stables, or indigestion.

Symptoms.—Placing the upper incisors against some support, and, with some effort, emitting a small portion of gas.

Treatment.—Place a lump of rock-salt in the manger; if that is not successful, add a lump of chalk. Then damp the food, and sprinkle magnesia upon it, and mingle a handful of ground oak-bark with each feed of corn. Purify the ventilation of the stable before these remedies are applied.

CURB.

Causes.—Galloping on uneven ground; wrenching the limb; prancing and leaping.

Symptom.—A bulging out at the posterior of the hock, accompanied by heat and pain, often by lameness.

Treatment.—Rest the animal. Put on an India-rubber bandage, (see page 307,) and under it a folded cloth. Keep the cloth wet and cool with cold water. When all inflammation has disappeared, blister the hock.

CYSTITIS, OR INFLAMMATION OF THE BLADDER.

Causes.—Kicks and blows under the flank. Abuse of medicine, and bad food, with the provocatives generally of nephritis.

Symptoms.—Those common to pain and inflammation. Urine, however, affords the principal indication. At first, it is at intervals jerked forth in small quantities. Ultimately it flows forth constantly drop by drop. A certain but a dangerous test is to insert the arm up the rectum, and to feel the small and compressed bladder. A safer test is to press the flank, which, should cystitis be present, calls forth resistance.

Treatment.—Give scruple doses of aconite, should the pulse be excited; the same of belladonna, should pain be excessive; and calomel with opium, to arrest the disease. Place under the belly, by means of a rug, a cloth soaked with strong liquor ammonia diluted with six times its bulk of water. Or apply a rug dipped into hot water or loaded with cold water; change when either becomes warm.

DIABETES INSIPIDUS, OR PROFUSE STALING

Causes.—Diuretic drugs or bad food.

Symptoms.—Weakness; loss of flesh; loss of condition.

Treatment.—Do not take from the stable; keep a pail of linseed tea in the manger; give no grass or hay; groom well. Order a ball composed of iodide of iron, one drachm; honey and linseed meal, a sufficiency. Or a drink consisting of phosphoric acid, one ounce; water, one pint. Give the ball daily; the drink, at night and at morning

ENTERITIS.

Causes.—Greatly conjectural. Prolonged colic may end in it. Constipation may induce it.

Symptoms—Dullness; heaviness; picks the food; shivers repeatedly; rolling; plunging; kicking, but more gently than in spasmodic colic; quickened breathing; hot, dry mouth; wiry pulse. Pressure to the abdomen gives pain. Remove your coat; insert the arm up the anus; if the intestines are very hot, all is confirmed.

Treatment.—Extract one quart of blood from the jugular, and inject into the vein one pint of water at a blood heat. Give aconite in powder, half a drachm; sulphuric ether, three ounces; laudanum, three ounces; extract of belladonna, one drachm, (rubbed down in cold water, one pint and a half.) As the pulse changes, withdraw the aconite; as the pain subsides, discontinue the belladonna. The other ingredients may be diminished as the horse appears to be more comfortable Should the pain linger after the administration of the eighth drink, apply an ammoniacal blister. Sprinkle on the tongue, if any symptoms declare the disease vanquished but not fled, every second hour, calomel, half a drachm; opium, one drachm. Feed very carefully upon recovery, avoiding all things purgative or harsh to the bowels.

EXCORIATED ANGLES OF THE MOUTH.

Cause—Abuse of the reins.

Treatment.—Apply the following lotion to the part: Chloride of zinc, two scruples; essence of anise seed, two drachms; water, two pints.

FALSE QUARTER.

Cause.—Injury to the coronet, producing an absence of the secreting coronet of the crust from the hoof.

Symptoms.—No lameness, but weakness of the foot. The soft horn of the laminæ, being exposed, is apt to crack. Bleeding ensues. Sometimes granulations sprout when the pain and the lameness are most acute.

Treatment.—In cases of crack and granulations, treat as is advised for sandcrack. Put on a bar shoe, with a clip on each side of the false quarter. Pare down the edges of the crack, and ease off the point of bearing on the false quarter. A piece of gutta-percha, fastened over the false quarter, has done good.

FARCY.

Causes.—Excessive labor, poor food, and bad lodging operating upon old age.

Symptoms.—It is at first inflammation of the superficial absorbents. Lumps appear on various parts. If these lumps are opened, healthy matter is released; but the place soon becomes a foul ulcer, from which bunches of fungoid granulations sprout. From the lumps may be traced little cords leading to other swellings. The appetite fails, or else it is voracious. Matter may be squeezed through the skin. Thirst is torturing. At length glanders breaks forth, and the animal dies. There is a smaller kind of farcy called button-farcy; the smaller sort is the more virulent of the two.

Cure.—There is no known cure for the disease.

FISTULOUS PAROTID DUCT.

Causes.—Hay-seeds or other substances getting into the mouth of the duct during mastication. Stones being formed within the canal. The stable-fork in the hand of an intemperate groom.

Symptoms —The duct greatly enlarges behind the obstacle, which, becoming swollen, prevents the secretion from entering the mouth. Great agony is occasioned by every mouthful masticated. The duct bursts, and a fistulous opening is established, through which the saliva jerks at each motion of the jaw. From the absence of a secretion important to digestion, the flesh wastes, and the animal soon assumes a miserable appearance.

Treatment.—Make an adhesive fluid with gum mastic and spirits of wine, or with India-rubber and sulphuric ether When the horse is not feeding, pare the hardened edges from the wound; cover the orifice with a piece of strained India-rubber; over this put a layer of cotton; fasten one end to the horse's cheek by means of the adhesive fluid; that having dried, fasten the other end tightly down. Place other layers of cotton over this, allowing each layer to cross the other, and fastening all to the cheek Fasten the head to the pillar-reins; allow the horse to remain till the cotton falls off, and give only gruel for food. Put tan under the feet; and should the first trial not succeed, repeat it.

FISTULOUS WITHERS.

Cause.—External injury, generally by the lady's saddle, which bruises one of the bursæ placed above the withers.

Symptoms.—When first done, a small, round swelling appears on the off side. If this is neglected, the place enlarges, and numerous holes burst out, which are the mouths of so many fistulous pipes.

Treatment—In the early stage, go to the horse's side, impale the tumor and divide it. Touch the interior with lunar caustic; keep the wound moist with the chloride of zinc lotion, one grain to the ounce of water, and cover it with a cloth dipped in a solution of tar. If the sinuses are established, make one cut to embrace as many as possible. Clean out the corruption. Scrape or cut off any black or white bone which may be exposed. Cover with a cloth, and keep wet with the solution of chloride of zinc Should there exist a long sinus leading from the withers to the elbow, insert a seton by means of the guarded seton needle. This seton should be withdrawn so soon as a stream of creamy pus is emitted.

FUNGOID TUMORS IN THE EYE.

Cause.—Unknown.

Symptoms.—Blindness; a yellow, metallic appearance to be seen in the eye.

Treatment—None of any service.

GLANDERS

Cause.—Bad lodging, stimulating food, and excessive work operating upon young life.

Symptoms—Staring coat; lungs or air-passages always affected;

flesh fades; glands swell; spirit low; appetite bad. A lymphatic gland adheres to the inside of the jaw; the membrane inside the nose ulcerates; a slight discharge from one nostril. This becomes thicker, and adheres to the margin of the nostril, exhibiting white threads and bits of mucus; then it changes to a full stream of foul pus; next the nasal membrane grows dull and dropsical; the margins of the nostrils enlarge; the horse breathes with difficulty; the discharge turns discolored and abhorrent; farcy breaks forth, and the animal dies of suffocation.

Treatment.—There is no known cure.

GREASE.

Causes.—Age; debility; excessive labor; neglect; filth. Cutting the hair off the heels; turning out to grass in the cold months.

Symptoms.—Scurfiness and itchiness of the legs. Rubbing the leg with the hoof of the opposite limb; hairs stand on end; moisture exudes, and hangs upon the hairs in drops. Smells abhorrently; lameness; cracks on the skin; swelling; ulceration; thin discharge; odor worse. Lameness increases; leg enlarges; granulations sprout in ragged bunches; their points harden and become like horn; pain excessive; horn of hoof grows long.

Treatment.—Cut off all remaining hair. If hot and scurfy, cleanse with mild soap and hot, soft water; saturate a cloth with the following lotion: Animal glycerin, half a pint; chloride of zinc, half an ounce; water, six quarts. Lay it upon the leg. When this cloth becomes warm, remove it, and apply another, also wet with the lotion; thus continue applying cool cloths to the limb till the heat abates; afterward moisten the leg thrice daily. When cracks and ulceration are present, adopt the wet cloths; but subsequently use one of the following to the sores: Permanganate of potash or phosphoric acid, one pint; water, six quarts. Or, chloride of zinc, one ounce; water, one gallon: employ thrice daily. If the granulations have sprouted, remove them with a knife, in three operations, (*full directions are given in the book;*) likewise always place in a loose box. Feed liberally; allow old beans; give a handful of ground oak-bark with each feed of oats. Night and morning exhibit liquor arsenicalis, one ounce; tincture of muriate of iron, one ounce and a half; porter or stout, one quart: one pint for the dose. Chopped roots; speared wheat; hay tea; cut grass, and exercise are all good for grease.

GUTTA SERENA.

Cause.—Over-exertion.

Symptoms —Fixed dilatation of the pupil; a greenish hue of the eye; total blindness. Active ears; restless nostrils; head erect; high stepping; occasionally a rough coat in summer and a smooth coat in winter.

Treatment.—No remedy is possible.

HEART DISEASE.

Symptoms —Auscultation. The beat of the heart to be seen externally; haggard countenance; pulse feeble; heart throbs; the beat of the carotid artery is to be felt; the regurgitation in the jugular is to be seen. The appetite is sometimes ravenous—often fastidious; the breathing is not accelerated excepting during pain; lameness of one leg; dropsical swellings; stopping short when on a journey, averse to turn in the stall; noises; yawns; sighs. Death always unexpected. No treatment is of any use.

HEMATURIA, OR BLOODY URINE.

Cause.—Unknown.

Symptoms. — Discoloration of the fluid. When the bleeding is copious, breathing is oppressed; the pupils of the eyes are dilated. Pulse is lost; head is pendulous; membranes are pale and cold. Lifting up the head produces staggering Back roached; flanks tucked up; legs wide apart

Treatment —Be gentle. Act upon the report given Give acetate of lead, two drachms, in cold water, one pint; or, as a ball, if one can be delivered. In a quarter of an hour repeat the dose, adding laudanum, one ounce, or powdered opium, two drachms. Repeat the physic till one ounce of acetate of lead has been given. Leave the horse undisturbed for two hours, if the symptoms justify delay. If not, dash pailfuls of cold water upon the loins from a height Give copious injections of cold water. Pour half a pint of boiling water upon four drachms of ergot of rye When cold, add laudanum, one ounce, and dilute acetic acid, four ounces Give two of these drinks, and two cold enemas, of twenty minutes' duration Suspend all treatment for eight hours, when the measures may be repeated (*For after proceedings, see the article which is presented in the body of the book*)

HIDE-BOUND.

Cause.—Neglect, or turning into a straw-yard for the winter.

Treatment.—Liberal food, clean lodging, soft bed, healthy exercise, and good grooming. Administer, daily, two drinks, composed of: Liquor arsenicalis, half an ounce; tincture of muriate of iron, one ounce; water, one pint. Mix, and give as one dose.

HIGH-BLOWING AND WHEEZING.

Habits which admit of no remedies.

HYDROPHOBIA.

Cause.—Bite from a rabid dog or cat.

Symptoms.—The horse is constantly licking the bitten place. A morbid change takes place in the appetite. Eager thirst, but inability to drink, or spasm at the sound or sight of water is exhibited. Nervous excitability; voice and expression of countenance altered. More rarely the horse—when taken from the stable—appears well. While at work, it stops and threatens to fall. Shivers violently, and is scarcely brought home when the savage stage commences. The latter development consists in the utmost ferocity, blended with a most mischievous cunning, or a malicious pleasure in destruction.

Treatment.—No remedy known. Confine in a strong place and shoot immediately.

HYDROTHORAX.

Cause.—Pleurisy or inflammation of the membrane lining the chest.

Symptoms.—The horse is left very ill. The next morning the animal is looking better; the pain has abated; the eye is more cheerful; but the flanks heave. A man is procured; he is told to strike the chest when the person listening on the other side says "now." The word is spoken, and a metallic ring follows. The pulse is lost at the jaw; the heart seems to throb through water. The horse has hydrothorax!

Treatment.—The first thing is to draw off the fluid. A spot between the eighth and ninth ribs is chosen, and the skin is pulled back; a small slit through the skin is made; into that opening an armed trocar is driven. When there is no resistance felt, the thorax has been entered; the stilet is withdrawn and the water flows forth. Use a fine trocar; take all the fluid you can obtain. Should the horse appear faint, withdraw the canula, and in two hours again puncture the chest Afterward the food must be prepared, and a ball administered .night and morning, consisting of iodide of iron, one drachm; strychnia, half a grain; sulphate of zinc, half a drachm; extract of gentian and powdered quassia, a sufficiency.

IMPEDIMENT IN THE LACHRYMAL DUCT.

Cause.—A hay-seed or other substance getting into and becoming swollen within the duct

Symptom.—Swollen lid and copious tears

Treatment.—Inject, forcibly, a stream of water up the duct.

INFLUENZA

Cause —Unknown; but suspected to be generated by close stables. It is also episotic.

Symptoms.—Weakness and stupidity; local swellings; heat and pain in the limbs. Loss of appetite; rapid wasting; every part of the body is diseased. Youth most exposed, but no age exempt. Spring-time the general season, but an attack may ensue at any period of the year. The following symptoms are somewhat uncertain: Pendulous head; short breath; inflamed membranes; swollen lips, dry mouth; enlarged eyelids; copious tears; sore throat; tucked-up flanks; compressed tail; filled legs; big joints; lameness and hot feet. Auscultation may detect a grating sound at the chest, or a noise like brickbats falling down stairs, within the windpipe When the last is audible, there is always a copious discharge. Sometimes one foot is painful; purgation has been seen; but constipation is generally present, and the horse usually stands throughout the disease Always suspect influenza when it is in the neighborhood, and the membranes are yellow or inflamed.

Treatment.—Move to a well-littered, warm, loose box. Suspend a pail of gruel from the wall; change the gruel thrice daily; sprinkle on the tongue, night and morning, calomel, one scruple; wash this down with sulphuric ether, one ounce; laudanum, one ounce; water, half a pint. If weakness increases, double the quantity of ether and of laudanum. When the pulse loses all wiry feeling, and the discharge becomes copious, give from the hand some bread, on which there is a little salt; when the cough appears, give a pot of stout daily. Beware of purgatives or active treatment.

INJURIES TO THE JAW.

Causes.—Pulling the snaffle; abuse of the bit; too tight a curb-chain.

Symptoms.—Discoloration before or behind the tush; bruise under the tongue or upon the roof of the mouth; tumor and bony growth upon the margin of the lower jaw.

Treatment.—Cut upon the discoloration till the knife reaches the bone; if fetor is present, inject the chloride of zinc lotion; keep the wounds open, that the injured bone may come away.

LACERATED EYELID.

Causes.—Nails in the gangway, or the horses playfully snapping at each other.

Treatment.—Bathe with cold water till the bleeding ceases; allow the separated parts to remain until the divided edges are sticky; bring together with sutures; place the horse in the pillar-reins till the healing is perfected.

LACERATED TONGUE.

Causes.—Sticking to a horse when giving physic; making a "chaw" of the halter-rope.

Treatment.—Insert no sutures; if the arteries are excised, cut off the hanging portion of the tongue; should the vessels have escaped, allow all to remain; feed on gruel and soft food; after every meal wash out the mouth with the solution ordered for aphtha, or with the chloride of zinc lotion.

LAMPAS.

A groom's fancy.

LARYNGITIS.

Cause.—Foul stables.

Symptoms.—Dullness; enlargement over the larynx; stiff neck; short and suppressed cough; breathing hurried and catching; pulse full; nasal membrane almost scarlet.

Treatment.—Give drachm doses of tincture of aconite, in wineglasses of water every half hour, to amend the pulse. Refrain from bleeding. Put on a steaming nose-bag, and keep it almost constantly applied, to amend the breathing. Fix some hay, soaked in boiling water, upon the throat, by means of an eight-tailed bandage. Give, very carefully, the following drink, thrice daily: Infusion of squills, two ounces; infusion of ipecacuanha, two ounces; infusion of aconite, half an ounce, extract of belladonna, one drachm, rubbed down with a pint of warm water. Place in a cool, well-aired, thickly-littered, loose box; bandage the legs; clothe the body; give only gruel for food, changing it thrice daily. On improvement, a little moist food may be allowed. When improvement is confirmed, put a seton under the throat. Blister the throat; pick and damp the hay; sift, bruise, and scald the oats. Employ no lowering agents.

LARVA IN THE SKIN.

Causes.—Turning out to grass. The fly lays its egg upon the hair, the warmth of the body hatches it, and the larva enters the skin. The next summer a tolerably large abscess is established, the insect occupying its center.

Treatment.—With a lancet open the abscess, and squeeze out the larva. Dab the wound with a lotion made of chloride of zinc, one grain; water, one ounce.

LICE.

Causes —Filth and debility.

Treatment —Rub the skin with some cheap oil or grease. Wash, and then look for other diseases, as hide-bound, mange, etc.

LAMINITIS, (SUBACUTE.)

Causes.—Age; long standing in the stable; over-work, and stinted diet.

Symptoms.—First noticed by the manner of going upon the heels of the fore feet.

Treatment.—Get into slings Remove the shoes Do not bleed. If costiveness is present open the bowels with green-meat, but do not purge. Give a quart of stout, night and morning. Allow two drinks per day, each consisting of one ounce of sulphuric ether and half a pint of water; half drachm doses of belladonna, to allay pain; sound oats and old beans, both crushed, for food; water to be whitened; no hay. No limit to this food, but five feeds to be given if the horse will eat so much.

LUXATION OF THE PATELLA.

Cause.—Bad food and constitutional weakness.

Symptoms.—The horse stops short, and has one of the hind legs extended backward. A swelling upon the outer side. The pastern is flexed, the head raised, and the animal in great pain. In colts it will sometimes appear on the slightest cause.

Treatment.—For colts, any flurry may restore the bone; but feed well, to eradicate the weakness. For horses, get into a shed, and, throwing a rope, one end of which has been fixed to the pastern, have the leg dragged forward while some one pushes the bone into its place. A man should be put to keep the bone in its situation for some hours. Give strengthening food, and do not use for six weeks subsequently.

MALLENDERS AND SALLENDERS.

Cause.—Neglect.

Symptoms.—Scurf upon the seats of flexion; mallenders at the back of the knee, and sallenders at the front of the hock.

Treatment.—Cleanliness. Give the liquor arsenicalis drink, recommended for grease; change the groom; rub the parts with this ointment: Animal glycerin, one ounce; mercurial ointment, two drachms; powdered camphor, two drachms; spermaceti, one ounce. If cracks appear, treat as though cracked heels were present.

MANGE.

Causes.—Starvation; bad lodging and no grooming; turning out to grass.

Symptoms.—Scurf about the hairs of the mane; the hair falls off in patches; the skin is corrugated; a few hairs remain upon the bare places, and these adhere firmly to the skin; scrubbing the body against posts; sores and crusts. To test its presence, scratch the roots of the mane and the horse will exhibit pleasure.

Treatment.—Place the horse in the sunshine, or in a heated house, for one hour; then whisk thoroughly, to remove scurf and scabs; then rub in the following liniment: Animal glycerin, two parts; oil of tar, two parts; oil of turpentine, half a part; oil of juniper, half a part. Mix Leave on for two days; wash; anoint again; wash; anoint and wash once more, always leaving the liniment on for two clear days.

MEGRIMS.

Cause —Unknown

Symptoms.—The horse suddenly stops; shakes the head; strange stubbornness may be exhibited, followed by a desire to run into dangerous places. Then ensues insensibility, accompanied by convulsions.

Treatment.—Throw up on the first fit. Give a long rest, and try to amend the constitution

MELANOSIS.

Cause —Unknown. The disease only attacks gray horses which have become white.

Symptoms —It appears as a lump of uncertain form, size, and situation. The swelling, if cut into, discloses a cartilaginous structure, dotted here and there with black spots. Do not use the knife unless the swelling impede the usefulness, or should be peculiarly well placed for operation Feel the tail. A pimple on the dock is an almost certain sign of melanosis, which disease affects the internal organ even more virulently than it attacks the external parts. As melanosis proceeds, all spirit departs, and the animal is at length destroyed as utterly useless.

Treatment.—Let the tumor alone. Forbid all use of the currycomb. Dress very long and very gently with the brush only Twice a week anoint the body with animal glycerin, one part; rose-water, two parts.

NASAL GLEET.

Causes.—Decayed molar tooth; kicks from other horses; injuries to the frontal bones.

Symptoms.—Distortion of the face; partial enlargement and softening of the facial bones; irregular discharge of fetid pus from one nostril. The discharge is increased, or brought down by feeding off the ground, or by trotting fast.

Treatment.—Surgical operation, with injection of a weak solution of chloride of zinc. Also give daily a ball composed of balsam of copaiba, half an ounce; powdered cantharides, four grains; cubebs, a sufficiency. If the foregoing should affect the urinary system, change it for half-drachm doses of extract of belladonna, dissolved in a wineglass of water. Give these every fourth day, and on such occasions repeat the belladonna every hour, until the appetite has been destroyed.

NASAL POLYPUS.

Symptoms.—An enlarged nostril; a copious mucous discharge; signs of suffocation, if the free nostril be stopped; a cough generally forces down the growth.

Treatment.—Surgical operation, which removes the tumor.

NAVICULAR DISEASE.

Causes.—Frog pressure, and not shoeing with a leathern sole. The unprotected foot treads on a rolling stone, and navicular disease is the result.

Symptoms.—Acute lameness; this disappears, but may come again in six or nine months. Acute lameness is then present for a longer time, while the subsequent soundness is more short. Thus the disease progresses, till the horse is lame for life. The pain in one foot causes greater stress upon the sound leg, and from this cause both feet are ultimately affected. The foot is pointed in the stable. The bulk diminishes, while the hoof thickens and contracts. The horse, when trotting, takes short steps, and upon the toe, going groggily.

Treatment.—Feed liberally upon crushed oats and old beans. Soak the foot every other night in hot water. Afterward bandage the leg, fix on tips, and having smeared the horn with glycerin, put on a sponge boot. Rest very long—six months in the first instance—and then give three months agricultural employment. In bad cases resort to neurotomy, but do so upon the second attack of lameness; because continued disease disorganizes the internal structures of the hoof, and also occasions the sound foot to be attacked by navicular disease.

NEPHRITIS, OR INFLAMMATION OF THE KIDNEYS.

Causes.—Bad provender, or niter in a mash, and long or fast work upon the following day.

Symptoms.—Hard, quick pulse; short breathing; pallid membranes; looking at the loins; depressed head; roached back; hind legs straddling; scanty urine; refusing to turn in the stall; and crouching under pressure on the loins. Subsequently, pus is voided with the water. If the urine has a fetid odor, if blood be present, if the pulse grows quicker, if pressure gives no pain, and if the perspiration has a urinous smell, death is near at hand. To be certain of nephritis, insert the arm up the rectum and move the hand toward the kidneys.

Treatment —Rub mustard into the skin of the loins. Cover it over to prevent it becoming dry Apply fresh sheepskins as soon as these can be procured. Inject warm linseed tea every hour. A ball composed of Croton farina, two scruples; extract of belladonna, half a drachm; treacle and linseed meal, a sufficiency, should be given immediately; one scruple of calomel; one drachm of opium should be sprinkled on the tongue every hour. A pail of linseed tea may be placed in the manger. Feed on linseed tea, and mind the oats—when allowed—are very good. While the pain is acute, give, thrice daily, a ball composed of extract of belladonna, half a drachm; crude opium, two drachms; honey and linseed meal, of each a sufficiency. When the pain is excessive, repeat the above ball every hour. Should the pulse increase and become wiry, a scruple of aconite should be thrown upon the tongue every half hour until the artery softens, or the animal becomes affected with the drug.

No cure is to be expected; the disease may be arrested, but the kidney must be left in an irritable state.

OCCULT SPAVIN.

Cause —Treading on a stone.

Symptoms.—Sudden lameness, which never departs, but in the end becomes very bad. The disease is always worse after work, and better after rest. The foot is without disease, and the leg is not hot or painful; yet the lameness continues and gets worse. The leg is snatched up in the walk, and the foot is not turned outward

Treatment —Get the horse into slings. Rub the front of the hock with an embrocation composed of compound soap liniment, sixteen ounces; tincture of cantharides, liquor ammonia and laudanum, of each two ounces. After the joint is embrocated, wrap it round with flannel, held upon the hock with elastic rings. Give three feeds of corn, a few old beans, and sweet hay daily. After the horse bears upon the diseased limb, allow the slings to remain for three months. Three months after it has left the slings, put to gentle work, but mind the labor is not in any way exhausting. The work must not be full till six months have elapsed · Keep the bowels regular with bran mashes and green-meat If all treatment fail, cast the horse; retract the injured limb; make a small puncture, and inject one ounce of dilute spirits of wine, in which half a drachm of iodine has been dissolved. Place the horse in slings, and apply cold water to the hock. When the pulse is quiet, feed very liberally.

OPEN SYNOVIAL CAVITIES.

Causes.—The pride of gentility, which apes what is not, and tries to pass off a horse with a ewe neck for an animal with a lofty crest. The quadruped, being in pain and constraint, necessarily trips, and cannot save itself from falling. Kicking in harness; running away and being run into.

Symptoms.—Air being admitted creates inflammation; inflammation causes constitutional irritability. Bursæ are attended with least danger when punctured; sheaths of tendons are more dangerous; joints are by far the most serious. Judge which is opened by the extent of the wound and the quantity of synovia released.

Treatment.—Exercise gentleness toward the injured animal. Wash as was directed for broken knees. Examine if there be any sac or bag into which dirt could have entered. If one exists, place a large spatula under the knee; then take a knife with a sharp point, but with its edge blunted the two posterior thirds of its length; guard the point with a lump of beeswax; introduce this into the sac and drive the point through the bottom of the bag. An opening will thereby be created, through which the pus and dirt will gravitate. If the probe enters the knee of the flexed leg, unopposed, three-quarters of an inch, push it no farther; be satisfied the cavity is opened.

OPEN SYNOVIAL JOINTS.

Treatment.—Proceed in the first instance as for broken knees. Then give a drink composed of sulphuric ether and laudanum, of each one ounce; water, half a pint; look to the comfort. Should the eye rove, the breathing be hard, ears active, and the horse start at sounds, hourly repeat the drink before recommended, till these symptoms abate. Then place in a stall and allow four drinks and two pots of stout daily. Use the arnica lotion as for broken knees, during the first three and a half days. At the end of that time turn the horse gently round in the stall, and let it stand with its head toward the gangways. Place the slings before the horse and leave the animal to contemplate them for half an hour. Then, with extreme gentleness, fix them; but do not pull the cloth up to the abdomen. Leave a pail of water suspended from one pillar, and feed from a high trough, supported upon light legs. Let the horse be watched night and day for the remainder of the week. When the animal is at ease in the slings, these may be heightened till the cloth lightly touches, but not presses, against the belly. With the slings change to the chloride of zinc lotion, one scruple to the pint of water; have this frequently applied during the day. It will coagulate the albumen and promote the healing of the wound. The albumen will accumulate as a large ball in front of the injury; do not touch it. Allow it to fall off. The cure is nearly perfect when it falls. When pressure can be endured, the slings may be removed; though the healing process should be confirmed before the animal is allowed to stand near anything against which it could strike the knee.

OPERATIONS.

Admit of no abbreviation; they should never be hastily undertaken; they should be only resorted to after time has been allowed for thought, and opportunity has been afforded for more than one perusal of the directions detailed in this book.

OSSIFIED CARTILAGES.

Cause —Battering the foot upon hard roads.

Symptoms.—Of little consequence in heavy horses unless accompanied with ring-bone. The disease causes lameness in light horses used for fast work.

Treatment.—Rest; liberal food; and small blisters to the foot immediately above the sides of the hoof.

OVERREACH.

Cause.—When a good stepper is very tired, this accident sometimes happens—the coronet of the fore foot upon the outer side being severely wounded by the inside of the hind shoe.

Symptom.—A severe wound and a large slough, probably followed by a false quarter.

Treatment.—Feed liberally, and bathe the injury thrice daily with the chloride of zinc lotion, one grain to the ounce of water.

PARROT-MOUTH.

Cause.—Natural malformation.

Symptoms —Projecting upper teeth; an inability to graze or to clean out the manger.

PARTIAL PARALYSIS.

Cause.—Violent exertion.

Symptom.—One hind leg gets in the way of the other, and threatens to throw the animal down.

Treatment.—A loose box; warm clothing; good grooming; warmth to loins; regulate the bowels with mashes and green-meat; absolute rest. Give the following ball night and morning: Strychnia, half a grain, (gradually work this medicine up to one grain and a half;) iodide of iron, one grain; quassia powder and treacle, a sufficiency

PHLEBITIS, OR INFLAMMATION OF THE VEIN.

Cause—Motion. Bleeding in the neck and turning out to grass; or from either of the limbs, and then forcing the animal to walk.

Symptoms.—The earliest indication is a separation of the lips of the wound and the presence of a small quantity of thin discharge. A small swelling then takes place, and the vein hardens above the puncture. Then abscesses form along the course of the vessel. These mature, burst, send forth a contaminated pus. The abscesses are united by sinuses. If these signs are neglected, a dark discharge resembling decayed blood issues from the numerous wounds and soils the neck. Dullness ensues; the brain becomes affected; and the horse perishes phrenitic.

Treatment.—Remove the pin and apply a blister. Another may be required. In bad cases, blister must follow blister, but not be rubbed in. A little oil of cantharides should be put over the sore with a paste-brush. Place in a loose box and litter with tan; feed on slops, which require no mastication. Let the horse remain there and be so fed for six weeks subsequent to the cessation of all treatment. Then give a little exercise at a slow pace, gradually augmented. At the end of three months the horse may do slow work. But the horse should not wear a collar or go into the shafts before the expiration of six months.

PHRENITIS.

Cause.—Unknown.

Symptom.—Heaviness, succeeded by fury in excess, but without any indication of malice.

Treatment.—Bleed from both jugulars till the animal drops. Then pin up, and give a purgative of double strength. Follow this with another blood-letting, if necessary, and scruple doses of tobacco; half-drachm doses of aconite root; or drachm doses of digitalis—whichever is soonest obtained. But whichever is procured must be infused in a pint of boiling water, and, when cool and strained, it ought to be given every half hour till the animal becomes quiet. But the probable result is by no means cheering, even if death is by these means avoided.

PLEURISY.

Causes.—Over-exertion; blows; injuries; cold.

Symptoms.—These are quickly developed. The pulse *strikes* the finger; pain continuous; agony never ceases; horse does not feed. Body hot; feet cold; partial perspirations. Muscles corrugated in places; cough, when present, suppressed and dry; auscultation detects a grating sound and a dull murmur at the chest. Pressure between the ribs produces great pain or makes the animal resentful. The head is turned very often toward the side; the fore foot paws; the breathing is short and jerking.

Treatment.—Should be active. Bleed, to ease the horse; place in a loose box; bandage the legs; leave the body unclothed. Give, every quarter of an hour, a scruple of tincture of aconite in a wineglass of warm water. When pulse has softened, give, every second hour, sulphuric ether and laudanum, of each one ounce; water, half a pint. Do not bleed a second time. When the pulse and pain are amended, introduce the steaming apparatus. Do nothing for the bowels. Place luke-warm water within easy reach of the head, and give nothing more while the disease rages. When the disease departs, return with caution to full food. After the affection subsides, blister throat and chest. If the horse is costive, administer enemas; or a bundle of cut grass may be presented with the other food.

PNEUMONIA.

Causes.—Fat; irregular work; and sudden exertion.

Symptoms.—Breathing labored; oppressed pulse; partial consciousness; giddiness. Standing with outstretched legs; head and ears dejected; coat rough; extremities and body cold; visible membranes discolored; bowels costive; feeling half dead; and general oppression.

Treatment.—Bleed but once; take only blood sufficient to restore consciousness; do not attempt to obtain blood, if the liquid flows black and thick. Place in a loose box strown with damp tan; take off the shoes; place water within easy reach; no food. If winter, clothe; then introduce steam; when the steam is abundant, take off the clothes. Give solution of aconite root, half an ounce; sulphuric ether, two ounces; extract of belladonna, (rubbed down with half a pint of water,) one drachm. Repeat the drink three times each day. When the pulse improves, withdraw the aconite; when the breathing amends, abstract the belladonna; or increase either as pulse or breathing becomes worse. Allow only hay tea, with a little oatmeal in it, until the disease abates. On amendment, cautiously increase the food. Lying down is the first sign of improvement. Do not disturb the animal: it must require rest, having stood throughout the attack.

POLL EVIL.

Causes.—Hanging back in the halter; hitting the poll against the beam of the stable door; blows on the head; and any external injury.

Symptoms.—The nose is protruded and the head kept as motionless as possible; the animal hangs back when it is feeding from the manger. Pressure or enforced motion excites resistance. Swelling: the swelling bursts in several places, from which exude a foul, fistulous discharge. Pus has been secreted; confinement has caused it to decay; while motion and fascia have occasioned it to burrow.

Treatment.—Paint the part lightly with tincture of cantharides, or acetate of cantharides. Do this daily till vesication is produced; then stop. When the swelling enlarges, open the prominent or soft places. Allow the pus to issue; then cut down on the wound till the seat of the disease is gained. Use a proper knife, and include as many pipes as possible in one clean cut. All others should join this. Empty out all concrete matter. Wash the cavity with cold water. Excise all loose pieces of tendon and all unhealthy flesh. Moisten the sore with the chloride of zinc lotion, one grain to the ounce, and cover the wound with a cloth dipped in the solution of tar. If the disease has burst, still include the pipes in one smooth incision; clean out the concrete pus, and treat as has been directed. Spare the ligament which lies under the mane; and work in a breast-strap after recovery.

PRICK OF THE SOLE.

Cause.—Generally the smith's carelessness when shoeing the horse.
Symptom.—Great lameness.
Treatment.—Withdraw the nails of the shoe. If one is wet, cut down on that hole until the sensitive sole is exposed. If not very lame, treat with lotion of chloride of zinc, one grain to the ounce of water. If very lame, treat as if the injury were a suppurating corn.

PRURIGO.

Cause.—Heat of body

Symptom —Itchiness   The horse rubs off hair; but never exposes a dry, corrugated surface.

Treatment.—Take away some hay.   Give two bundles of grass per day.   Allow two bran mashes each day till the bowels are open.   Apply either of the following washes: Animal glycerin, one part; rose-water, two parts   Or, sulphuric acid, one part; water, ten parts.   Or, acetic acid, one part; water, seven parts.   Drink: Liquor arsenicalis, one ounce; tincture of muriate of iron, one ounce and a half; water, one pint—half a pint to be given every night   Withdraw the drink a week after the disease has disappeared.   Allow a pot of porter and an extra feed of oats each day.

PUMICE FOOT.

Cause.—An animal reared on marshy land, having high action, batters the feet upon London stones

Symptoms.—Bulging sole; weak crust; strong bars, and good frog.

Treatment —The only relief possible is afforded by a bar shoe of the dish kind, and a leathern sole.   The constant use of equal parts of animal glycerin and tar is also beneficial to the hoof.

PURPURA HEMORRHAGICA.

Cause.—Unknown.   Universal congestion

Symptoms —The attack is sudden   The body, head, and limbs enlarge; consciousness is partially lost.   The horse stands, and the breathing is quickened.   Through the skin there exudes serum with blood. The nostrils and lips enlarge, and part of the swollen tongue protrudes from the mouth.   The appetite is not quite lost, although deglutition is difficult.   Thirst is great.

Treatment.—Bleed till the animal appears relieved   A second venesection may be demanded, but it should be adopted with caution.   Give half an ounce of chloroform in a pint of linseed oil, in the first stage Repeat the dose in half an hour.   No amendment following, give two ounces of sulphuric ether in one pint of cold water.   In half an hour repeat the dose if necessary.   Perform tracheotomy to ease the breathing.   Incise the protruding tongue.   Squeeze out the fluid and return the organ to the mouth   Should the skin slough, bathe the part with solution of chloride of zinc, one grain to the ounce of water.

QUITTOR.

Causes.—Confined pus from suppurating corn; or prick of the sole; matter results, and this issues at the coronet. Or from injury to the coronet, generating pus, and this burrowing downward, as it cannot pierce the coronary substance. The secretion may also penetrate the cartilage, and thus establish sinuses in almost every possible direction.

Symptoms.—The horse is very lame. The animal is easier after the quittor has burst. Probe for the sinuses. If, after the superficial sinuses are treated, among the creamy pus there should appear a dark speck of albuminous fluid, make sure of another sinus, probably working toward the central structures of the foot.

RHEUMATISM.

Cause.—Generally follows other disorders, as influenza, chest affections, and most acute diseases. Very rarely does it appear without a forerunner.

Symptoms.—Swelling of particular parts, generally the limbs; heat and acute lameness. The disorder is apt to fly about the body. The synovia is always increased when the joints are attacked. The pulse and breathing are both disturbed by agony.

Treatment.—Lead into a loose box; fill the place with steam. (See page 313.) Get ready the slings; put the belly-piece under the horse, but do not pull it up so as to lift the legs from the ground. Keep the steam up for one hour. Then have several men with cloths ready to wipe the animal dry; mind they are perfectly silent. Next rub into the diseased parts the following: Compound soap liniment, sixteen ounces; tincture of cantharides, liquor ammonia, and laudanum, of each two ounces. Afterward incase the limbs in flannel. (See page 314.) Then give a bolus composed of powdered colchicum, two drachms; iodide of potassium, one drachm; simple mass, a sufficiency. Should the attack succeed upon other diseases, the diet must be supporting, everything being softened by heat and water. Next morning repeat the steaming, and give calomel, a scruple; opium, two drachms. At night steam again, and repeat the first bolus. Should the horse be fat, withdraw all corn, if the strength can do without it.

RING-BONE.

Cause.—Dragging heavy loads up steep hills.

Symptoms.—A roughness of hair on the pastern and a bulging forth of the hoof. A want of power to flex the pastern. An inability to bring the sole to the ground only upon an even surface. Loss of power and injury to utility.

Treatment.—In the first stage apply poultices, with one drachm of camphor and of opium. Afterward rub with iodide of lead, one ounce; simple ointment, eight ounces. Continue treatment for a fortnight after all active symptoms have subsided, and allow liberal food and rest; work gently when labor is resumed.

RING-WORM.

Symptoms.—Hair falls off in patches, exposing a scurfy skin. The scurf congregates on the bare place about the circumference, which is apt to ulcerate.

Treatment.—Be very clean. Wash night and morning, and afterward apply the following ointment: Animal glycerin, one ounce; spermaceti, one ounce; iodide of lead, two drachms. Many other things are popular. For a detailed list of these, see the body of the book. A drink is likewise of use when employed with the ointment. Liquor arsenicalis, one ounce; tincture of muriate of iron, one ounce and a half, water, one quart. Mix, and give every night half a pint for a dose. Should the ulceration prove obstinate, apply permanganate of potash, half an ounce; water, three ounces. Or, chloride of zinc, two scruples; water, one pint. Moisten the parts with a soft brush six times daily. Feed well, and do not work for one month.

ROARING.

Causes —The bearing-rein; the folly of fashion.

Symptom.—A noise made at each inspiration.

Treatment.—No remedy. The cabman's pad is the only alleviation : that conceals and does not cure the disease.

RUPTURE, OR STRICTURE OF THE ŒSOPHAGUS.

Cause.—The use of the butt-end of a carter's whip, which either rends the lining membrane of or ruptures the gullet.

Symptom of Rupture —The body becomes distended with gas, and death ensues. *Of Rent Membrane* —This induces a disinclination to feed, as the first symptom. A stricture is formed. Excessive hunger. Distention of the tube. A large sac is developed out of the stretched membrane above the stricture. Then, after feeding, the animal fixes the neck, and returns the masticated food through the mouth and nostrils. Accompanying loss of condition and failure of strength.

Treatment.—Feed on prepared soft food : though the horse is generally not worth its ordinary keep at the stage when this is required.

SANDCRACK.

Causes.—Bad health, provoking imperfect secretion. Treading for any length of time upon a very dry soil.

Symptoms.—Quarter crack occurs on light horses upon the inner side of the hoof. It usually commences at the coronet, goes down the foot, and reaches to the laminæ. Toe crack happens in heavy wheelers, and is caused by digging the toe into the ground when dragging a load up hill. From the sensitive laminæ, when exposed, fungoid granulations sometimes sprout, which, being pinched, produce excessive pain and acute lameness.

Treatment.—Always pare out the crack, so as to convert it into a groove. When the crack is partial, draw a line with a heated iron above and below the fissure. If granulations have sprouted, cleanse the wound with chloride of zinc lotion, one grain to the ounce of water, and then cut them off. Afterward place the foot in a poultice. Subsequently pare down the edges of the crack while the horn is soft. Use the lotion frequently. Draw lines from the coronet to the crack, so as to cut off communication between the fissure and the newly-secreted horn. Shoe with a bar shoe, having the seat of crack well eased off and also a clip on either side. If the horse must work, lay a piece of tow saturated with the lotion into the crack : bind the hoof tightly with wax-end. Tie over all a strip of cloth, and give this a coating of tar. When the horse returns, inspect the part. Wash out any grit with the chloride of zinc lotion. Feed liberally on prepared food.

SCALD MOUTH.

Cause.—Powerful medicine, which burns the lining membrane of the mouth.

Symptom.—A dribbling of saliva, with constant motion and repeated smacking of the lips.

Treatment.—Give soft food, and use the wash recommended for aphtha.

SEEDY TOE.

Cause —Weakness, inducing an imperfect secretion of horn

Symptom.—A separation between the crust of the coronet and the soft horn of the laminæ, commencing at the toe of the foot.

Treatment.—Remove the shoe Probe the fissure,-which will be exposed. Cut away all the separated crust. Throw up until the removed portion has grown again. Feed liberally.

SIMPLE OPHTHALMIA.

Causes.—Slashing with the whip over the head; hay-seeds falling into the eyes; horses biting at each other in play; blows, etc.

Symptoms.—Tears; closed eyelid; the ball of the eye becomes entirely or partially white

Treatment.—Remove any foreign body; fasten a cloth across the forehead; moisten it with a decoction of poppy-heads to which some tincture of arnica has been added If a small abscess should appear on the surface of the eye, open it, and bathe with chloride of zinc lotion Should inflammation be excessive, puncture eye vein, and place some favorite food on the ground.

SITFAST.

Causes.—Ill health; badly-fitting saddle; too energetic a rider; loose girths; ruck in the saddle-cloth.

Symptom.—Like a corn on the human foot, but the hard, bare patch is surrounded by a circle of ulceration.

Treatment.—The knife should remove the thickened skin. Chloride of zinc, one grain; water, one ounce, to the wound. Attend to the bowels. Feed liberally; exercise well; and give, night and morning, liquor arsenicalis, half an ounce; tincture of muriate of iron, three-quarters of an ounce; water, one pint Mix, and give.

SORE THROAT.

Causes.—In colts, change from freedom to work, from the field to the stable, is the cause. Sore throat, however, may be caused by close stables, or be an indication of some greater disease.

Symptoms —Perpetual deglutition of saliva; want of appetite; inability to swallow a draught of liquid—the fluid returning partly by the nostrils, and each gulp being accompanied with an audible effort.

Treatment.—Forbear all work; clothe warmly; house in a large, well-littered, loose box. Gruel for drink; green-meat, with three feeds of bruised and scalded oats, also beans, daily. If the bowels are obstinate, administer a drink composed of solution of aloes, four ounces; essence of anise seed, half an ounce; water, one pint. Should the throat not amend, dissolve half an ounce of extract of belladonna in a gallon of water; hold up the head: pour half a pint of this preparation into the mouth, and in thirty seconds let the head down; do this six or eight times daily. No improvement being observed, try permanganate of potash, half a pint; water, one gallon: to be used as directed in the previous recipe. Still no change being remarked, prepare chloride of zinc, three drachms; extract of belladonna, half an ounce; tincture of capsicums, two drachms; water, one gallon.

All being useless, give two pots of stout daily, and blister the throat.

No alteration ensuing, cast the horse, and mop out the fauces with a sponge which is wet with nitrate of silver, five grains; water, one ounce. Give a ball daily composed of oak-bark and treacle.

If none of these measures succeed, the throat must be complicated with some other disease.

SPASM OF THE DIAPHRAGM.

Cause.—Imprudently riding too far and too fast.

Symptom.—Distress, and a strange noise heard from the center of the horse.

Treatment.—Pull up; cover the horse's body; lead to the nearest stable. Give as soon as possible a drink composed of sulphuric ether, two ounces; laudanum, one ounce; tincture of camphor, half an ounce; cold water or gruel, one pint. Give four drinks, one every quarter of an hour; then another four, one every half hour, and then at longer intervals as the animal recovers. When first brought in, procure five steady and quiet men; give a bandage each to four of them, and order them silently to bandage the legs; give a basin and sponge to the other, and bid him sponge the openings to the body. This done, and sweat and dirt removed, clothe perfectly after the skin is quite dry.

SPASM OF THE URETHRA.

Cause.—Acridity in the food or water.

Symptoms.—Small and violent emissions; straddling gait. Roached back; pain; total suppression of urine.

Treatment.—Insert the arm up the rectum, and feel the gorged bladder: Give, by the mouth, four ounce doses of sulphuric ether and of laudanum mixed with a quart of cold water, and, as injection, mixed with three pints of cold water. Repeat these medicines every quarter of an hour until relieved. If no physic be at hand, open both jugular veins, and allow the blood to flow until the horse falls. Should not the urine then flow forth, insert the arm and press upon the bladder.

SPASMODIC COLIC—FRET—GRIPES.

Causes.—Fast driving; change of water; change of food; getting wet; fatiguing journeys; aloes; and often no cause can be traced

Symptoms 1st *Stage.*—Horse is feeding; becomes uneasy; ceases eating; hind foot is raised to strike the belly; fore foot paws the pavement; the nose is turned toward the flank, and an attack of fret is recognized. 2d *Stage.*—Alternate ease and fits of pain; the exemptions grow shorter as the attacks become longer; the horse crouches; turns round; then becomes erect; pawing, etc. follow; a morbid fire now lights up the eyes. 3d *Stage.*—Pains lengthen; action grows more wild; often one foot stamps on the ground; does not feed, but stares at the abdomen; at last, without warning, leaps up and falls violently on the floor; seems relieved; rolls about till one leg rests against the wall; should no assistance be now afforded, the worst consequences may be anticipated

Treatment.—Place in a loose box, guarded by trusses of straw ranged against the walls. Give one ounce each of sulphuric ether and of laudanum in a pint of cold water, and repeat the dose every ten minutes if the symptoms do not abate. If no improvement be observed, double the active agents, and at the periods stated persevere with the medicine. A pint of turpentine, dissolved in a quart of solution of soap, as an enema, has done good. No amendment ensuing, dilute some strong liquor ammonia with six times its bulk of water, and, saturating a cloth with the fluid, hold it by means of a horse-rug close to the abdomen It is a blister; but its action must be watched or it may dissolve the skin. If, after all, the symptoms continue, there must be more than simple colic to contend with.

SPAVIN.

Cause.—Hard work.

Symptom.—Any bony enlargement upon the lower and inner side of the hock. Prevents the leg being flexed. Hinders the hoof from being turned outward. Causes the front of the shoe to be worn and the toe of the hoof to be rendered blunt by dragging the foot along the ground

Leaves the stable limping; returns bettered by exercise. Sickle hocks, or cow hocks, are said to be most subject.

Treatment.—View the suspected joint from before, from behind, and from either side. Afterward feel the hock. Any enlargement upon the seat of disease, to be felt or seen, is a spavin. Feed liberally, and rest in a stall. When the part is hot and tender, rub it with belladonna and opium, one ounce of each to an ounce of water. Apply a poultice. Or put opium and camphor on the poultice. Or rub the spavin with equal parts of chloroform and camphorated oil. The heat and pain being relieved, apply the following, with friction: Iodide of lead, one ounce; simple ointment, eight ounces.

SPECIFIC OPHTHALMIA.

Cause.—The fumes of impure stables.

Symptoms.—A swollen eyelid; tears; a hard pulse; sharp breathing; a staring coat; a clammy mouth; the nasal membrane is inflamed or leaden colored; the lid can only be raised when in shadow. The ball of eye reddened from the circumference; the pupil closed; the iris lighter than is natural. The disease may change from eye to eye; the duration of any visitation is very uncertain; the attacks may be repeated, and end in the loss of one or both eyes. If one eye only is lost, the remaining eye generally strengthens.

Treatment.—Remove from the stable and place in a dark shed. Open the eye vein, and puncture the lid if needed; put a cloth saturated with cold water over both eyes. If the horse is poor, feed well; if fat, support, but do not cram; if in condition, lower the food. Sustain upon a diet which requires no mastication. Give the following ball twice daily: Powdered colchicum, two drachms; iodide of iron, one drachm; calomel, one scruple; make up with extract of gentian. So soon as the ball affects the system, change it for liquor arsenicalis, three ounces; muriated tincture of iron, five ounces. Give half an ounce in a tumbler of water twice daily. See the stable is rendered pure before the horse returns to it.

SPLINT.

Causes—Early and hard work; blows, kicks, etc.

Symptom.—Any swelling upon the inner and lower part of the knee of the fore leg, or any enlargement upon the shin-bone of either limb. On the knee they are important, as they extend high up. On the shin they are to be dreaded, as they interfere with the movements of the tendons. All are painful when growing, and in that state generally cause lameness.

Treatment.—Feel down the leg. Any heat, tenderness, or enlargement is proof of a splint If, on the trot, one leg is not fully flexed, or the horse "dishes" with it, it confirms the opinion. Time and liberal food are the best means of perfecting them When they are painful, poultice, having sprinkled on the surface of the application one drachm each of opium and of camphor. Or rub the place with one drachm of chloroform and two drachms of camphorated oil Periosteotomy (see *Operations*) is sometimes of service When a splint interferes with a tendon, the only chance of cure is to open the skin and to cut off the splint, afterward treating the wound with a lotion composed of chloride of zinc, one grain; water, one ounce. To check the growth of a splint, rub it well and frequently with iodide of lead, one ounce; simple ointment, eight ounces.

SPRAIN OF THE BACK SINEWS.

Cause —Cart-work upon a hilly country.

Symptom.—Gradual heightening of the hind heel.

Treatment —The only possible relief is afforded by an operation— "division of the tendons."

STAGGERS.

Sleepy Staggers and Mad Staggers are only different stages of the same disorder.

Cause.—Over-gorging

Symptoms.—Excessive thirst; dullness or sleepiness; snoring; pressing the head against a wall Some animals perish in this state; others commence trotting without taking the head from the wall, and such generally die, but sometimes recover. Other horses quit the sleepy state; the eyes brighten; the breath becomes quick Such animals exhibit the greatest possible violence, but without the slightest desire for mischief.

Treatment.—Allow no water. Give a quart of oil. Six hours afterward give another quart of oil, with twenty drops of croton oil in it, should no improvement be noticed In another six hours, no amendment being exhibited, give another quart of oil, with thirty drops of croton oil in it After a further six hours, repeat the first dose, and administer the succeeding doses, at the intervals already stated, until the appearance changing indicates that the body has been relieved.

For the full development of the mad stage no remedies are of the slightest avail.

STRAIN OF THE FLEXOR TENDONS.

Cause.—Hard work on uneven ground, or the rider punishing a horse with the snaffle and the spurs.

Symptoms.—The animal goes oddly, not lame. The defective action will disappear upon rest, but stiffness is aggravated by subsequent labor. Any attempt to work the horse sound induces incurable lameness or contraction of the tendons.

Treatment.—Allow several hours to elapse before any attempt is made to discover the disease. A small swelling, hot, soft, and sensitive, may then appear. Bind round it a linen bandage, and keep it wet with cold water. Have men to sit up bathing this for the three first nights; afterward apply moisture only by day Throw up the horse. Give four drachms of aloes. Do not turn out, but allow two feeds of corn each day. Keep in a stall, and do not put to work till more than recovered.

STRANGLES.

Cause.—Something requiring to be cast from the system, so as to suit the young body to a sudden change.

Symptoms.—A slight general disturbance, which, however, remains. The colt continues sickly. After a day or two, the neck becomes stiff, and a swelling appears between the jaws. The enlargement at first is hard, hot, and tender. A discharge from the nose comes on. The symptoms increase; the throat becomes sore. Breathing is oppressed; coat stares; appetite is lost; tumor softens, and, being opened, the animal speedily recovers.

Treatment.—Neither purge nor bleed. Give all the nourishment that can be swallowed. If all food is rejected, whiten the water, and a little cut grass may tempt the colt. Corn, ground and scalded, may be offered, a little at a time from the hand. No grooming; light clothing; ample bed; door and window of loose box should be open. Gently stimulate the throat with the following: Spirits of turpentine, two parts; laudanum, one part; spirits of camphor, one part. Apply with a paste-brush morning, noon, and night, until the throat is sore. After every application, take three pieces of flannel, place these over the part, and bind on with an eight-tailed bandage. So soon as the tumor points, apply the twitch, and have one fore leg held up. Then open the swelling with an abscess knife. It may be necessary to make another incision. There are other occasional varieties of strangles, for which consult the substance of the work, pages 272, 273.

STRINGHALT.

Cause.—Over-exertion.

Symptom —Raising both hind legs, one after the other, previous to starting

Treatment —None is possible.

SURFEIT.

Cause —Heat of body.

Symptom.—An eruption of round, blunt, and numerous spots.

Treatment.—If the pulse is not affected, the symptom may disappear in a few hours. Look to the food. Abstract eight pounds of hay, and allow two bundles of cut grass per day. Even increase the oats, but with each feed give a handful of old crushed beans. The following drink will be of service: Liquor arsenicalis, one ounce; tincture of muriate of iron, one ounce and a half; water, one quart. Mix. Give daily, one pint for a dose.

Symptom.—If a young horse has been neglected through the winter, the surfeit lumps do not disappear. An exudation escapes; the constitution is involved, and the disease is apt to settle upon the lungs.

Treatment —Do not take out. Keep the stable aired, and attend to cleanliness. Feed as previously directed, and allow bran mashes when the bowels are constipated. Administer the drink recommended above, night and morning Clothe warmly; remove from a stall to a loose box. Should the pulse suddenly sink, allow two pots of stout each day. If the appetite fail, give gruel instead of water, and present a few cut carrots from the hand. The shortest of these cases occupy a fortnight.

SWOLLEN LEGS.

Cause —Debility.

Treatment.—Place in a loose box. No hay for some weeks. Damp the corn, and sprinkle a handful of ground oak-bark on each feed. Attend to exercise. If the legs continue to enlarge, hand-rub them well and long.

TEETH.

Cause.—A thickening of the membrane sometimes conceals the upper tushes and provokes constitutional symptoms.

Treatment —Lance the membrane.

Symptoms of Toothache.—Head carried on one side, or pressed against the wall; saliva dribbles from the lips; quidding or partial mastication of the food, and allowing the morsel to fall from the mouth. Appetite capricious; sometimes spirit is displayed—then the horse is equally dejected. The tooth dies; the opposing tooth grows long. The opposite teeth become very sharp, from the horse masticating only on one side. The long tooth presses upon the gum and provokes nasal gleet.

Treatment.—Chisel off projecting tooth; file down the sharp edges of the opposite teeth, and look to the mouth frequently.

TETANUS.

Causes.—Cold rain; draughts of air; too much light; wounds.

Symptoms.—The wound often dries up. The horse grows fidgety. Upon lifting up the head, "the haw" projects over the eye. The tail is raised; the ears are pricked; the head is elevated; the limbs are stiff; the body feels hard. Any excitement may call up a fearful spasm.

Treatment.—Give a double dose of purgative medicine. Place in solitude and in quiet. Put a pailful of gruel and a thin mash within easy reach of the head. Let nobody excepting the favorite groom approach the place; and allow him to enter it only once a day.

THOROUGH-PIN.

Cause.—Excessive labor.

Symptom.—A round tumor going right through the leg, and appearing anterior to the point of the hock. It is nearly always connected with bog spavin.

Treatment.—Never attack thorough-pin and bog spavin at the same time. Relieve the thorough-pin first by means of rags, cork, and an India-rubber bandage, cut so as not to press on the bog spavin. If the corks occasion constitutional symptoms, use a truss to press upon the thorough-pin, which, being destroyed, apply a perfect bandage and wetted cloths to the bog spavin. When attempting to cure bog spavin, however, continue the remedy to the thorough-pin; or the cure of one affection may reproduce the other.

THRUSH.

Cause.—Standing in filth, when it appears in the hind feet; navicular disease, when seen in contracted feet.

Symptoms.—A foul discharge running from the cleft of the frog.

This decomposes the horn The surface of the frog becomes ragged, and the interior converted into a white powder. The affection does not generally lame; but should the horse tread on a rolling stone, it may fall as though it were shot.

Treatment.—Pare away the frog till only sound horn remains, or until the flesh is exposed. Then tack on the shoe and return to a clean stall. Apply the chloride of zinc lotion—three grains to the ounce of water—to the cleft of the frog by means of some tow, wrapped round a small bit of stick When the stench has ceased, a little liquor of lead will perfect the cure. For contracted feet pare the frog, and every morning dress once with the chloride of zinc lotion; but do not strive to stop the thrush.

TREAD.

Cause.—Fatigue and overweight.

Symptom.—In light horses-it occurs toward the end of a long journey. The hind foot is not removed when the fore foot is put to the ground. The end of the fore shoe consequently tears off a portion of the coronet from the hind foot In cart-horses, after the horse is fatigued, the load has to be taken down a steep hill; the animal, being in the shafts, rocks to and fro; the legs cross, and the calkin of one shoe wounds the coronet of the opposite hoof.

Treatment.—Bathe the sore with the chloride of zinc lotion, one grain to the ounce of water. Continue to do this thrice daily; feed liberally. A slough will take place, and the animal be well in about a month; the only danger being the after-result of a false quarter.

TUMORS.

These are so various and of such different natures, that in every case a surgeon should be consulted.

WARTS.

Cause.—Unknown.

Symptom.—There are three kinds of warts. 1st. Some are contained in a cuticular sac, and, upon this being divided, shell out. 2d The second are cartilaginous and vascular. These grow to some size, and are rough on the surface. They are apt to ulcerate. 3d Consists of a cuticular case, inclosing a soft granular substance.

Treatment.—When of the first kind, slit up, and squeeze them out. The second kind, excise and apply a heated iron to stop the bleeding The third kind are better let alone.

WATER FARCY.

Cause.—Overwork and coarse feed, succeeded by periods of stagnation. It is the warning that true farcy threatens the stable.

Symptoms.—Load less and work less.

Treatment.—Improve the diet, and never allow the horse to remain a day in the stable without exercise. Saturate the swollen limb with cold water every morning, and have it afterward thoroughly hand-rubbed until it is perfectly dry. Should lameness remain after the first day, a few punctures may be made into the limb, but only through the skin. Give the following ball every morning: Iodide of iron, one drachm; powdered cantharides, two grains; powdered arsenic, one grain; Cayenne pepper, one scruple; sulphate of iron, one drachm; treacle and linseed meal, a sufficiency. Mix. The delay even of a day in treatment is attended with danger in this disease.

WIND-GALLS.

Cause.—Hard work.

Symptoms.—Small enlargements, generally upon the hind legs and below the hocks; no lameness; two wind-galls appear above the pastern, one beneath that joint; after extraordinary labor, the round swellings disappear and the course of the flexor tendons becomes puffy. Sometimes continued irritation will cause the wind-galls to greatly enlarge, and ultimately provokes their case to change into bone. During these changes the horse is very lame.

Treatment.—Fold pieces of rags; wet them; put these on the wind-galls; place on the rags pieces of cork, and over the cork lace on an India-rubber bandage. Mind this bandage is constantly worn, save when ridden or driven by the proprietor. Rest is the only alleviation for the change of structure.

WINDY COLIC.

Causes.—Gorging on green food; but more commonly impaired digestion, consequent upon severe labor and old age.

Symptoms.—Uneasiness; pendulous head; cessation of feeding. Breathing laborious; fidgets; rocking the body; enlargement of the belly; pawing. Standing in one place; sleepy eye; heavy pulse; flatulence; the abdomen greatly enlarged. Breathing very fast; pulse very feeble; blindness; the animal walks round and round till it falls and dies.

Treatment —Three balls of sulphuret of, ammonia, two drachms, with extract of gentian and powdered quassia, of each a sufficiency, may be given, one every half hour. Next, one ounce of chloride of potash, dissolved in a pint of cold water, and mingled with sulphuric ether, two ounces, should be horned down. In an hour's time, two ounces each of sulphuric ether and of laudanum; half an ounce of camphorated spirits; one drachm of carbonate of ammonia may be administered. No good effect being produced, throw up a tobacco-smoke enema. As a last resort, procure a stick of brimstone and light it Remain in the stable while it burns, or the sulphureous fumes may become too powerful for life to inhale them. Continue this measure for two hours; then repeat the remedies previously recommended. All being fruitless, a desperate resort may be adopted Puncture the abdomen with a trocar; but this operation can only be named here; the reader must turn to the substance of the book for its description.

WORMS

Are of four kinds: the Tænia, the Lumbrici, the Strongulus, and the Ascarides.

The *Tænia* mostly affect the young.

Cause.—Starving the mare when with foal, and breeding from old animals.

Symptoms —Checked development; large head; low crest; long legs, and swollen abdomen Appetite ravenous; body thin; coat unhealthy; breath fetid. The colt rubs its nose against a wall, or strains it violently upward; picks and bites its own hair.

Treatment —Give spirits of turpentine. To a foal, two drachms; to a three months' old, half an ounce; six months, one ounce; one year, one ounce and a half; two years, two ounces; three years, three ounces, four years and upwards, four ounces. Procure one pound of quassia chips; pour on them three quarts of boiling water. Cause to blend with the turpentine a proportionate quantity of the quassia infusion, by means of yolks of eggs; add one scruple of powdered camphor, and give first thing in the morning. Good food is essential afterward Subsequently give every morning, till the coat is glossy, liquor arsenicalis, from one to eight drachms; muriated tincture of iron, from one and a half to twelve drachms; extract of belladonna, from ten grains to two drachms; ale or stout, from half a pint to a quart.

The *Lumbrici* prey upon the old and the weakly.

Treatment.—Tartarized antimony, two drachms; common mass, a sufficiency to make one ball. Give one every morning.

The *Strongulus*, during life, is generally not known to be present.

The *Ascarides* cause great itching posteriorly, which provokes the horse to rub its hair off against the wall.

Treatment.—Try injections of train oil for one week. Then use infusion of catechu, one ounce to one quart of water. On the eighth morning, give aloes, four drachms; calomel, one drachm. Tobacco-smoke enemas are sometimes useful, and the following ointment may be placed up the rectum night and morning: Glycerin, half an ounce; spermaceti, one ounce; melt the spermaceti, and blend; when cold, add strong mercurial ointment, three drachms; powdered camphor, three drachms.

WOUNDS.

A *lacerated wound* is generally accompanied by contusion, but with little hemorrhage. Shock to the system is the worst of its primary effects. The danger springs from collapse. A slough may probably follow. The slough is dangerous in proportion as it is tardy. The horse may bleed to death if the body is much debilitated.

Treatment.—Attend-first to the system. Give a drink composed of sulphuric ether and laudanum, of each one ounce; water, half a pint. Repeat the medicine every quarter of an hour if necessary, or till shivering has ceased and the pulse is healthy. A poultice, made of one-fourth brewer's yeast, three-fourths of any coarse meal; or a lotion, consisting of tincture of cantharides, one ounce; chloride of zinc, two drachms; water, three pints, may be employed. When the slough has fallen, apply frequently a solution of chloride of zinc, one grain to the ounce of water; and regulate the food by the pulse.

An *incised wound* produces little shock. The danger is immediate, as the horse may bleed to death.

Treatment.—Do not move the horse. Dash the part with cold water, or direct upon the bleeding surface a current of wind from the bellows. When the bleeding has ceased and the surfaces are sticky, draw the edges together with divided sutures. When the sutures begin to drag, cut them across. After copious suppuration has been established, bathe frequently with the solution of chloride of zinc, one grain to the ounce of water.

An *abraded wound* generally is accompanied by grit or dirt forced into the denuded surface. The pain is so great, the animal may sink from irritation.

Treatment.—Cleanse, by squeezing water from a large sponge above the wound, as was directed for broken knees, and allow suppuration to remove any grit that is fixed in the flesh. Support the body, and use the chloride of zinc lotion.

A *punctured wound* is dangerous, as the parts injured are liable to motion. On this account those above the stifle are very hazardous. Sinuses form from the torn fascia opposing the exit of the pus; also because the small hole in the skin generally bears no proportion to the internal damage.

Treatment —Always enlarge the external opening to afford egress to all sloughs and pus. Regulate the food by the symptoms, and use the chloride of zinc lotion.

A *contused wound*, when large, causes more congealed blood than can be absorbed. This corrupts, and a slough must occur or an abscess must form Either generates weakness, produces irritation, and may lead to fatal hemorrhage. Or sinuses may form. Wherefore, such accidents are not to be judged of hastily.

Treatment.—When the contusion is slight, rub the part with iodide of lead, one drachm of the salt to an ounce of lard. When large, divide the skin, every eighth inch, the entire length of the swelling Bathe the injury with the chloride of zinc lotion, and support the body, as the symptoms demand liberality in the matter of food

In all wounds, gain, if possible, a large depending orifice, and cover the denuded surfaces with a rag saturated with oil of, or in solution of, tar.

The author, having now concluded his labors, cannot forbear from repeating the advice which was given to the reader at the commence-ment of the present Summary—always appeal to the body of the work so soon as the first danger has subsided. Many hints are therein contained which could not be embodied in anything deserving to be entitled an abbreviation. Ampler space there enables the writer to describe certain precautions and to suggest various stratagems which, of course, would be out of place in the pages where condensation was the professed characteristic. For these reasons the reader is most earnestly recommended never to depend longer upon the contents of the Summary, than the pressure of immediate danger shall render imperative.

INDEX.

INDEX.

THE END.

Gazetteer of the World.

Lippincott's Pronouncing Gazetteer of the World; or, Geographical Dictionary. Containing—

I. A Descriptive Notice, with the most recent and authentic information respecting the countries, islands, rivers, mountains, cities, towns, etc., in every part of the globe.

II. The Names of all important places, etc., both in their native and foreign languages, with the pronunciation of the same—a feature never attempted in any other work.

III. The classical names of all ancient places, so far as they can be accurately ascertained from the best authorities.

IV. It also contains a complete etymological vocabulary of geographical names.

By J. THOMAS, M.D., and T. BALDWIN. One volume of over 2000 imperial 8vo. pages. $6.00.

It has evidently been prepared with great labor, and, as far as I can judge, from the best materials and sources of information. . . . I have no doubt it will be found an extremely useful work, well calculated to supply a want which must have been severely felt by almost every class of readers.—From the Hon. EDWARD EVERETT.

Having long felt the necessity of a work of this kind, I have spent no small amount of time in examining yours. It seems to me so important to have a comprehensive and authentic gazetteer in all our colleges, academies, and schools, that I am induced in this instance to depart from my general rule in regard to giving recommendations. . . . The rising generation will be greatly benefited, both in the accuracy and extent of their information, should your work be kept as a book of reference on the table of every professor and teacher in the country.—From the Hon. HORACE MANN, LL.D., President of Antioch College.

It gives me pleasure to be able to say that I have found it, as far as examined, not only very correct, but very full and comprehensive; and that I consider it a desideratum alike to the scholar and the man of business, as well as a very valuable contribution to our American literature.—From ELIPHALET NOTT, D.D., LL.D., President of Union College.

This is a great work, and executed with immense labor and consummate ability. . . . It would be difficult to find another volume in the English language which contains, in the same space, an equal amount of important, well-digested, and clearly-expressed information. I see not how the office or the counting-room, the family or the school, can anywhere afford to do without this book.—From Prof. C. E. STOWE, Andover Theo. Seminary.

Goodrich's Man upon the Sea.

Man upon the Sea; or, A History of Maritime Adventure, Exploration, and Discovery, from the earliest ages to the present time: Comprising a detailed account of remarkable voyages, ancient as well as modern. By FRANK B. GOOD-RICH, author of the "Letters of Dick Tinto," "The Court of Napoleon," etc. With numerous illustrations, by Van Ingen & Snyder. One vol. 8vo. $3.00.

Ponce de Leon and the Fountain of Youth.

This popular work, which had reached its second edition a few days after publication, will always remain a favorite with the public. It is complete, covering the whole history of maritime adventure, and yet it gives lively details of the doings of celebrated voyagers, from the first navigator down to the celebrated voyagers who laid the Atlantic submarine telegraph cable. Mr. Goodrich's vivacity and agreeableness as a narrator are exhibited not less auspiciously here than in his celebrated "Court of Napoleon," which was recognized as one of the most delightful of court histories. The embellishments are very numerous, and strictly appropriate to the subject.—*Home Gazette.*

Waverley Novels.

I. **The Abbotsford Edition**, printed on fine white paper, with new and beautiful type, from the last English edition. Embracing the author's latest corrections, notes, etc. Complete in twelve volumes, demi 8vo., with illustrations.

Cloth, gilt backs...............................$12.00.
Library style, marble edges.................. 15.00.
Half Turkey, plain............................ 18.00.
Half Turkey, antique.......................... 24.00.
Half Turkey, antique, fancy edges.......... 25.00.
Full Turkey, antique, brown edges......... 36.00.
Full Turkey, antique, gilt edges............ 40.00.

II. **Royal Octavo Illustrated Edition**, in twelve volumes, splendidly illustrated with over 300 engravings, comprising landscapes, incidents, and portraits of the historical personages, described in the volumes.

Cloth, gilt...................................$18.00.
Sheep, library style........................... 24.00.
Half calf or half Turkey...................... 30.00.

III. **Pictorial Edition.** Twenty-four vols. duodecimo, illustrated with over 300 steel and wood engravings.

Blue and gold..................................$24.00.

IV. **People's Edition.** Complete in six vols. 8vo.

Illustrated cloth .... $8.00.
Sheep... 10.00.

V. **New and Beautifully Illustrated Edition**, published in connection with the Messrs. A. & C. Black, of Edinburgh, in forty-eight volumes, cap 8vo. Printed on a beautiful type, fine paper, and illustrated with over 1500 wood-cuts and steel engravings. $1.25 per vol.

These several editions of the Waverley Novels all possess the advantage of a good readable type, fine paper, and first-rate printing, and are afforded at a reasonable price. The illustrations are taken from the celebrated Abbotsford edition, (now out of print,) and are engraved in a very fine style. It is superfluous to commend these masterly productions of genius to the reading public. They are the model and standard of all subsequent writers of fiction, and for dramatic power they are unapproachable.

Bloomfield's Greek Testament.

The Greek Testament: With English Notes, critical, philological, and exegetical, partly selected and arranged from the best commentators, ancient and modern, but chiefly original. The whole being especially adapted to the use of academical students, candidates for the sacred office, and ministers, though also intended as a manual edition for the use of theological readers in general. By the Rev. S. T. BLOOMFIELD, D.D., F.S.A., Vicar of Bisbrooke, Rutland. Fifth American, from the second London edition. Two vols. 8vo. $6.00.

Book of Days.

The Book of Days: A New, Popular, and Interesting Miscellany. Edited by ROBERT CHAMBERS. This work is published in Parts periodically, and is designed to be completed in two, or at the utmost three, volumes. It will consist of—

I. **Matters connected with the Church Calendar**, including the Popular Festivals, Saints' Days, and other Holidays, with illustrations of Christian antiquities in general.

II. **Phenomena connected with the Seasonal Changes.**

III. **Folk-lore of the United Kingdom**: Namely, Popular Notions and Observances connected with times and seasons.

IV. **Notable Events, Biographies, and Anecdotes** connected with the days of the year.

V. **Articles of Popular Archæology**, of an entertaining character, tending to illustrate the progress of civilization, manners, literature, and ideas in those kingdoms.

VI. **Curious, Fugitive, and Inedited Pieces.**

It is the design of this work, while not discouraging the progressive spirit of the age, to temper it with affectionate feelings towards what is poetical and elevated, honest and of good report; while in no way discountenancing great material interests, to evoke an equal activity in those feelings beyond self on which depend remoter but infinitely greater interests. The publishers wish that these volumes should be a repertory of old fireside ideas in general, as well as a means of improvement.

The work will be printed in a new, elegant, and readable type, and will be illustrated with an abundance of wood engravings.

Bulwer's Works.

The Works of Sir Edward Bulwer Lytton, Bart., D.C.L. Uniform library edition, in forty vols. 12mo., elegantly printed on tinted paper. Cloth, $1.00 per volume; sheep, $1.25; half calf, $1.75.

The Caxton Novels.

The Caxton Family	2 vols.
My Novel	4 vols.
What will he do with it?	3 vols.

Historical Romances.

Devereux	2 vols.
The Last Days of Pompeii	2 vols.
Rienzi	2 vols.
The Siege of Granada	1 vol.
The Last of the Barons	2 vols.
Harold	2 vols.

Romances.

Pilgrims of the Rhine	1 vol.
Eugene Aram	2 vols.
Zanoni	2 vols.

Novels of Life and Manners.

Pelham	2 vols.
The Disowned	2 vols.
Paul Clifford	2 vols.
Godolphin	1 vol.
Ernest Maltravers—FIRST PART	2 vols.
Ernest Maltravers—SECOND PART, (ALICE)	2 vols.
Night and Morning	2 vols.
Lucretia	2 vols.

Several of the volumes have been already published, and the remainder will follow in rapid succession.

☞ Each work furnished separately if desired.

Cooke's U. S. Cavalry Tactics.

Cavalry Tactics; or, Regulations for the Instruction, Formations, and Movements of the Cavalry of the Army of the United States. Prepared under the direction of the War Department, and authorized and adopted by the Secretary of War, November 1, 1861. By PHILIP ST. GEORGE COOKE, Brigadier-General U.S.A. Two vols. 18mo. $1.50.

Vol. I. School of the Trooper, of the Platoon, and of the Squadron.

Vol. II. Evolutions of a Regiment and of the Line.

Plants of the Holy Land.

Plants of the Holy Land, with their Fruits and Flowers. Beautifully illustrated by original drawings, colored from nature. By Rev. HENRY S. OSBORN, author of "Palestine, Past and Present." One vol. 4to. Muslin, embossed, $3.00; muslin, full gilt, $4.00; Turkey, full gilt, $5.50.

This work is intended to comprise notices of every plant mentioned in the Scriptures, with its fruits and flowers. In this respect we believe the work is complete—not one having been omitted.

Prescott's Works.

Conquest of Mexico. History of the Conquest of Mexico, with a preliminary view of the ancient Mexican civilization, and the life of Hernando Cortez. By WM. H. PRESCOTT. Three vols. 8vo. Cloth, $6.75.

Conquest of Peru. History of the Conquest of Peru, with a preliminary view of the civilization of the Incas. By WM. H. PRESCOTT. Two vols. 8vo. Cloth, $4.50.

Ferdinand and Isabella. History of the Reign of Ferdinand and Isabella the Catholic. By WM. H. PRESCOTT. Three vols. 8vo. Cloth, $6.75.

Philip the Second. History of the Reign of Philip the Second, King of Spain. By WM. H. PRESCOTT. Three vols. 8vo. Cloth, $6.75.

Charles the Fifth. History of the Reign of the Emperor Charles the Fifth. By WM. ROBERTSON, D.D. With an account of the Emperor's life after his abdication. By WM. H. PRESCOTT. Three vols. 8vo. Cloth, $6.75.

Prescott's Miscellanies. Biographical and Critical Miscellanies. By WM. H. PRESCOTT. One vol. 8vo. Cloth, $2.25.

Prescott's Complete Works, in 15 vols. 8vo. Muslin, $33.75.

Do.	do.	do.	sheep, $37.50.
Do.	do.	do.	half calf, gilt, marble edges, $50.00.
Do.	do.	do.	half calf, antique, " $55.00.
Do.	do.	do.	full calf, " " $67.50.

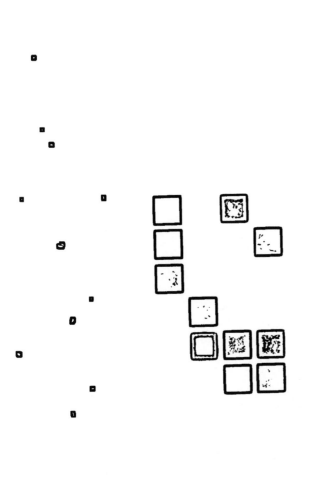

Lightning Source UK Ltd.
Milton Keynes UK
UKHW020645190722
406066UK00005B/547